INTRODUCTION TO THE COMPUTER
The Tool of Business

INTRODUCTION

WILLIAM M. FUORI B.A., M.S., Ph.D., C.D.E

Professor and Chairman
Data Processing Department
Nassau Community College, New York

TO THE COMPUTER

COMPUTER

THE TOOL OF BUSINESS

SECOND EDITION

PRENTICE-HALL, Inc., Englewood Cliffs, New Jersey   07632

Library of Congress Cataloging in Publication Data

Fuori, William M
  Introduction to the computer

    Bibliography: p.
    Includes Index.
    1.–Business—Data processing.   I.–Title.
HF5548.2.F86—1977   658'.05'4   76–46547
ISBN 0-13-480103-2

INTRODUCTION TO THE COMPUTER
The Tool of Business, Second Edition
William M. Fuori

Printed in the United States of America

10 9 8 7 6 5

Prentice-Hall International, Inc. *London*
Prentice-Hall of Australia, Pty. Limited, *Sydney*
Prentice-Hall of Canada, Ltd., *Toronto*
Prentice-Hall of India Private Limited, *New Delhi*
Prentice-Hall of Japan, Inc., *Tokyo*
Prentice-Hall of Southeast Asia, Pte. Ltd., *Singapore*
Whitehall Books Limited, Wellington, *New Zealand*

**To my wife Elizabeth
and my children Elizabeth E. and Michael T.**

CONTENTS

UNIT

I

INTRODUCTION TO DATA PROCESSING AND BUSINESS

1 Automation and Data Processing 4

*A discussion of information processing,
the impact of automation on business, the meaning of data processing,
the uses of computers in business,
and the effect of the computer on society.*

2 A Brief History 36

*A brief history of data processing including the abacus,
Pascal's Machine Arithmetique, Joseph Marie Jacquard,
Charles Babbage, Herman Hollerith, Howard H. Aiken,
John Von Neumann, computer generations and minicomputers*

UNIT

II

PUNCHED-CARD AND COMPUTER SYSTEM FUNDAMENTALS

3 Unit Record Concepts 68

*A discussion of what is meant by a unit record or punched-card system,
operation of the card punch,
and the typical functions and devices associated with this type of system.*

4 Processing and Storage Devices   120

A discussion of the components and functions of the central processing unit together with
an introduction to currently used auxiliary storage devices including tape, disk, drum, magnetic card devices
and an introduction to the virtual storage concept.

5 Input/Output Media and Devices   154

A presentation of the various input/output devices and media associated with computers from punched card devices and media through the more recent and sophisticated devices and media including terminals, film devices, audio devices, and plotters.

6 Computer Number Systems   204

An introduction to the decimal, binary, octal, and hexadecimal number systems, the BCD and EBCDIC coding schemes, and how they relate to computer processing and storage.

UNIT

III

SOFTWARE, PROGRAM PREPARATION, AND PROBLEM-SOLVING CONCEPTS

7 Introduction to Computer Languages and Programming   264

A discussion of machine language, symbolic language, and procedure-oriented languages.
The areas of application together with the advantages and disadvantages of each type of computer language, program debugging, and program documentation will also be discussed.

8 Fundamentals of Flowcharting and Decision Tables   304

A discussion of the preparation necessary for programming, flowcharts and decision tables, and program documentation.

COMMON PROGRAMMING LANGUAGES
USED IN BUSINESS

A SYSTEMS APPROACH

PREFACE

Today's educator, who must prepare a student to enter the automated world of business, faces a most challenging task. He must anticipate the needs of the business community up to five years hence so that his students will be prepared to serve productively and efficiently in tomorrow's business environment.

A major goal of the educator, then, is to determine those new trends that are destined to become an integral part, if not the very foundation, of the business structure in future decades.

Automation and the use of computers in every phase of business is today the driving force for change. Educators at all levels, from the private business school, to the community college, to the university, have recognized the impact of the computer on business and have had the foresight not only to recommend but, in many instances, to require that students planning to enter the business field at any level, and in any capacity, be exposed to the computer as an integral part of their business education. To quote Dr. R. L. Bright, Associate Commissioner for Research of the United States Department of Health, Education, and Welfare, anyone who graduates from a college or university ". . . without being instructed in the use of computers has been severely cheated."

This book is written to serve the beginning or advanced business student. It provides him with a basic understanding of what the computer is, what the computer can do, and how the computer can serve him in his professional endeavors. In addition, this text covers those topics recommended by the American Institute of Certified Public Accountants. This text is recommended for use in a one semester survey course or in an introductory course designed for the business student contemplating an in-depth study of computers or programming languages. In either case, having completed this one semester course, the student will be equipped to communicate his needs and requirements to the data-processing personnel in his organization.

As in the first edition, this edition is organized to facilitate the student's comprehension of the relevance of data processing in business. To accomplish this end, the text has been divided into five units as follows:

Unit 1 introduces the student to the impact of computers on business so that he may clearly understand why he is undertaking such a study, and can determine to what future goals he may apply this knowledge. This unit also traces the development of computers so that the student may study recent trends and innovations in their historical perspective. The topics of computers in society and minicomputers have been added to this unit in this edition.

Unit 2 provides a detailed introduction to the basic components of a typical data-processing system in addition to an introduction to the peripheral equipment surrounding the computer. This edition places far less emphasis on computer number systems than did the first edition. Discussions of the newer and more sophisticated input/output devices, terminal devices, and the concept of virtual storage have been added in the second edition.

Unit 3 discusses program preparation and problem-solving concepts. The student learns what is involved in preparing an application for programming, how to flowchart the logic of the application, and how the flowchart is used in preparing the computer program. It is not uncommon for business people to review flowcharts before an extensive programming effort is begun. They do this to make certain that the programmer has considered, and understood, all aspects of the problem. Changes in the second edition include expanded coverage of the area of executing and debugging a program and an entirely new section on program documentation containing numerous illustrations of the use of standard forms.

Unit 4 exposes the student to two of the most commonly used programming languages in business—COBOL and BASIC. This exposure familiarizes the student with the fundamentals of each language and instructs him on their differences, as well as the advantages and disadvantages of each. The student is then prepared to understand computer programs—in either language—that may be written by a professional programmer to solve his particular problem. COBOL (Common Business Oriented Language) is the most widely used computer language in business and is easily understood because of its Englishlike nature. Since many companies do not have their own on-site computers, they must often resort to time-sharing. BASIC is one of the most common languages used in time-sharing applications and is, therefore, covered in this text. It is easily learned and, thus, quickly applied by both data processing and non-data processing personnel in business. Changes in the second edition include greatly expanded coverage of the BASIC language and appendexes to each chapter which contain complete and detailed reference summaries for the COBOL and BASIC languages.

Unit 5 discusses system analysis and design. The student is introduced to the concepts of feasibility and application studies, system design considerations, information systems, and other similar items with which he may become associated later in his professional career. In addition, representative payroll, accounts receivable and accounts payable systems are discussed in depth and provide the student with a practical knowledge of what is involved in a typical computerized business system so that the student understands how he can most effectively interact with and use such a system in business. In addition, this unit provides the student with insight into types of information that are—and are not—typically processed on a computer. It also serves to tie together all material previously presented in the text.

This book is different from others that appeal to students in business or business-related areas in several ways:

UNIQUENESS

1. Instead of presenting isolated topics in each chapter, this book provides continuity chapter-to-chapter by means of the unit concept discussed above. This chapter-to-chapter continuity causes the student to view the subject as a whole and not as a series of disjointed topics.
2. Changes in the second edition were the result of a detailed survey of professors teaching an introductory data processing course at colleges across the country.
3. The material in this text has already been successfully "field-tested" for several semesters at Nassau Community College. The enthusiastic response of students has convinced the author that the text is interesting, informative, and easy-to-read.
4. The emphasis of this book differs substantially from most introductory data processing texts. It does not concentrate on teach-

ing data processing students how to program computers, but instead emphasizes how business students can make effective use of the computer as an information-processing tool. Nevertheless, the student will be able to write simple but complete computer programs using the BASIC language in either a conversational or batch mode. Throughout the text, material presented is reinforced with illustrative business examples.

5. This text includes topics in asterisked sections and in chapter appendixes. These sections and appendixes make available to the instructor topics of a more complex and "in-depth" nature should they be desired. The instructor may thus gear the level of the course to fit the interest and backgrounds of his students.

6. This text includes a substantial number of exercises at the end of each chapter in addition to numerous self-study exercises interspersed throughout each chapter. These exercises have been expanded over the first edition and are far in excess of the number and scope of such exercises found in other texts of this type.

7. Programmed questions are provided throughout the text to reinforce previously presented material. In this way, the student derives the benefits of programmed instruction as well as the advantages of a lecture presentation.

TEACHER'S MANUAL
A teacher's manual is available to aid in structuring the course to fit the interests and backgrounds of students. Included in this unprecedented 300 page manual per text chapter is:

- A detailed summary which can be utilized by the instructor as a lecture outline.
- Class discussion questions.
- Text correlated illustrations that may be used directly for the preparation of overhead projector foils.
- Complete and detailed answers to all text exercises.
- Suggested examination questions with corresponding answers.

ACKNOWLEDGMENTS

The author wishes to thank the Honeywell Corporation, Radio Corporation of America, and the Univac Division of the Sperry Rand Corporation for graciously granting permission to use the illustrations that helped to make this text more meaningful. In particular the author would like to thank the International Business Machines Corporation for their assistance and for their granting permission to use photos and illustrations provided directly by IBM or contained in their publications.

The author also wishes to thank the following people for technical assistance and constructive criticism during the production of this second edition:

Mr. Joseph Pacilio, Associate Professor of Data Processing, Nassau Community College, Garden City, New York.

Mr. Thomas Taylor, Senior Technical Assistant, Nassau Community College, Stewart Avenue, Garden City, New York.

Mr. John Shaner, Technical Assistant, Nassau Community College, Stewart Avenue, Garden City, New York.

Mr. George Zink, Data Processing Consultant, Jamaica, New York.

Mr. Karl Karlstrom, Assistant Vice President, Computer Science and Applied Mathematics, Prentice-Hall, Inc.

Mr. Leon J. Liguori, Production Editor, Prentice-Hall, Inc.

Mr. Marvin Warshaw, Art Director, Prentice-Hall, Inc.

Mr. Mark. A. Binn, Senior Designer, Prentice-Hall, Inc.

Mr. Ron Ledwith, Marketing Manager, Prentice-Hall, Inc.

But most of all, the author would like to thank his wife, Elizabeth, without whose consideration, patience, understanding, and constant encouragement, this book would not have been possible.

I

INTRODUCTION TO DATA PROCESSING AND BUSINESS

BUSINESS AND INFORMATION PROCESSING

Need for More Efficient
Processing Methods

IMPACT OF AUTOMATION ON BUSINESS

WHAT IS DATA PROCESSING?

Fundamental Data-processing
Operations

Recording
Classifying
Sorting
Calculating
Summarizing
Reporting

USES OF COMPUTERS IN BUSINESS

Characteristics of Problems Suitable
for Computerized Solutions

Justifiable
Definable
Repetitive
Volume Data or Numerous Calculations

COMPUTERS IN SOCIETY

1

AUTOMATION AND DATA PROCESSING

Every business, regardless of its size or purpose, is concerned with processing facts, or data, about its operations in order to provide current accurate information to management. Executive decisions are based on data such as operating expenses, market statistics, inventory levels, and other quantitative factors. The depth, accuracy, and currentness of the factual information at the disposal of management can provide a business with a substantial edge over its competition.

However, like raw talent or raw materials, raw data are of limited use. Only after these data have been examined, compared, classified, analyzed, and summarized do they become usable information and take on real value for management. Over 300 billion pieces of paper filling nearly 100 million file drawers are generated annually by the nation's businesses. Papers piled up over the years

Bookkeeping System — Pencil And Paper

Accounting With Key-Driven Machines

Punched Card Accounting

Data Processing System

FIG. 1-1
Introduction of Automated
Devices into Accounting.

4

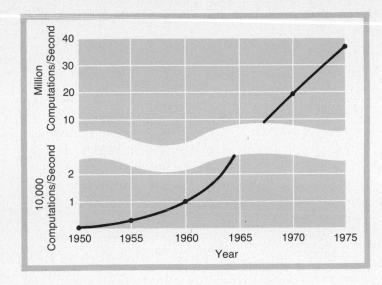

FIG. 1-2

Computer Internal Processing Speeds.

in offices and storerooms throughout the nation equal over 1 trillion (1,000,000,000,000) pieces. A large segment of the working population, comparable in size to the entire United States Army, has as its daily chore the recording, processing, and analyzing of the factual data generated by industrial, professional, and governmental organizations. This army of white-collar workers, consisting of more than 20 million people, does not buy or sell or manufacture or even service goods, but is concerned exclusively with the manual and automated processing of the data relating to these activities in our complex civilization.

Need for More Efficient Processing Methods

With the advent of the industrial revolution, and ever-increasing amounts of data to be processed in shorter and shorter times, business felt the need for faster, cheaper, more efficient methods of processing data.

To fill this need, various types of automated devices were developed and introduced on the business scene. Most recently, and foremost among them, was the introduction of the electronic computer, the fastest and most sophisticated business tool thus far devised by man. Even with their tremendous initial speed advantage, computers have continued to become even faster.

For example, in the early 1950s it cost approximately $1 to process 35,000 instructions, whereas today, little more than two decades later, the same dollar would pay for the processing of more than 1 billion machine instructions.

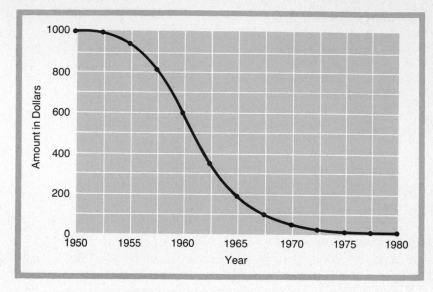

FIG. 1-3

Cost of Processing a Job.

SELF-STUDY EXERCISES 1-1

Each question in the exercises will be followed by a line containing five asterisks, which indicate that the solution will follow. Use a piece of paper to cover the solution when testing yourself.

1. Every business must process _____ relating to the operations of the business.

*****

data

2. Raw _____ are of limited use and must be processed to become usable _____ for management.

*****

data
information

3. The most recent device used to process data is the _____.

*****

electronic computer

4. Computers can process _____ data at _____ cost than ever before.

*****

more

less

The computer revolution is for all practical purposes a second industrial revolution. And, as in the case of the industrial revolution, the computer revolution has opened many new careers for tens of thousands of people making the automated processing of data big business. In 1970, for example, approximately 1 million people were employed in occupations resulting from, and directly related to, the computer. From an origin traceable to the abstractions of a few creative mathematicians, the concepts underlying automatic computers have grown into a billion-dollar industry. In terms of capital investment alone, this represents an increase from 30 million dollars in 1950 to an expected 75 billion dollars by 1980.

There isn't a home or a business that hasn't felt the impact of the electronic computer. Computers are used to calculate gas and electric bills, to control electric equipment during surgical operations, to control the takeoff and landings of rockets and space vehicles, to control intricate chemical processes, to predict enemy troop movements during a time of war, and most important to the business world, computers are used to control the financial and management activities of business.

IMPACT OF AUTOMATION ON BUSINESS

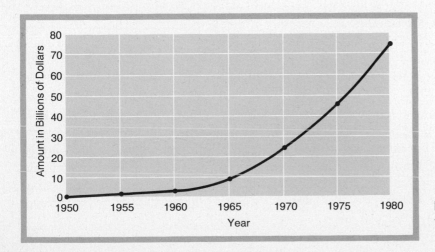

FIG. 1-4

Value of Computing Equipment in Use.

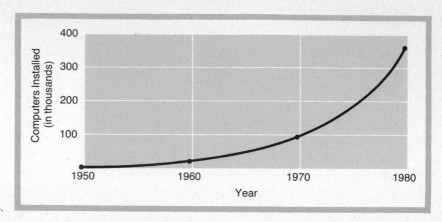

FIG. 1-5
Computers Installed
in the United States.

SELF-STUDY EXERCISES 1-2

1. The computer revolution can be thought of as _____.
   *****

   a second industrial revolution

2. The computer is responsible for the creation of over _____
   jobs.
   *****

   1 million

3. Computers are currently utilized in _____ field.
   *****

   virtually every

WHAT IS DATA PROCESSING? Let us begin our analysis of data processing by answering the question: What does data processing really mean? "Data" is the plural of "datum," which means "fact." *Data processing*, then, is simply the manipulating and using of facts.[1] Accounts kept during the Egyptian civilization 3400 B.C. are examples of data processing. For over a decade, many business concerns have relied almost

[1]Refer to Appendix A for the American National Standards Institute definition of data processing.

exclusively on automated devices such as electrical accounting machines (EAM) and computers to process their data. It is for this reason that the term "data processing" and the concept of processing data by computer or electrical accounting machine have become synonymous.

"Business data processing," on the other hand, is used to distinguish those operations relating to management control of business from other application areas such as those relating to science and industry. This latter form of data processing is called "scientific data processing."

FIG. 1-6
An Automated Airline Reservation System.

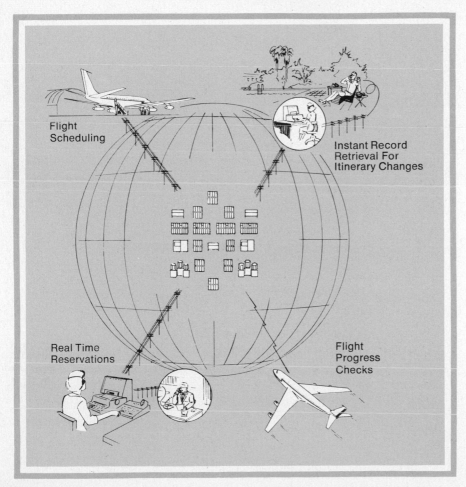

Flight Scheduling

Instant Record Retrieval For Itinerary Changes

Real Time Reservations

Flight Progress Checks

Fundamental Data-processing Operations Regardless of whether the system used to process the data is manual, mechanical, or electronic, certain fundamental operations must be performed. These operations are:

FIG. 1-7

Journal Entry in a Manual Accounting System.

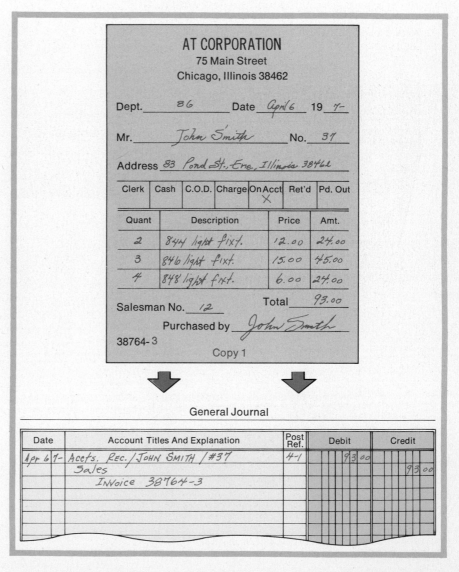

1. Recording
2. Classifying
3. Sorting
4. Calculating
5. Summarizing
6. Reporting

FIG. 1-8

Recording Sales Information on Machine Readable Punched Cards.

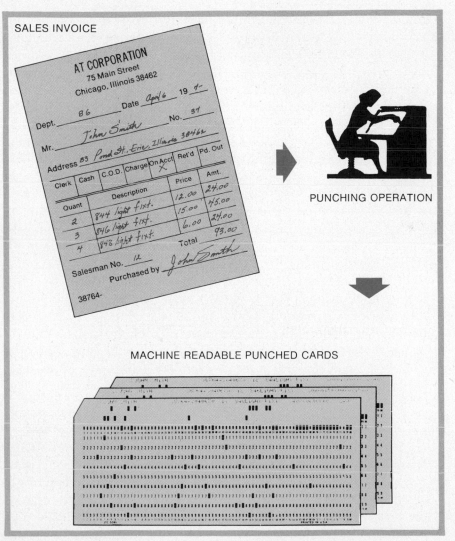

Recording. Recording is the transcribing of data into a permanent form. When one or more items of data have been reproduced into machine readable cards called punched cards, or into a magnetic tape similar to that commonly used with home tape recorders, or into some other permanent form, they have been recorded.

The punching of information relating to a single transaction into a punched card corresponds to a journal entry in manual methods of accounting.

Classifying. Classifying involves the *grouping* of like items or transactions. Classifying is a preliminary step to the accumulating and printing of totals for these like items on a report form. Data are generally classified according to a code in the form of an alphabetic or numeric abbreviation. In charting accounts, for example, one identifies each account as an asset account, a liability account, a proprietorship account, an income account, a cost account, or an expense account. To distinguish these accounts from one another, an identifying code number is usually assigned to each account classification. Each account within a classification is also assigned a number. For example, if we were to consider an asset account, we might assign CASH the number 11. The first digit or first 1 would represent the classification, ASSET. The second digit or second 1 would represent the placement of the account within the classification. Therefore, CASH would be the first account in the ASSET classification.

Classifications also take place in more routine and less sophisticated applications. For example, the store clerk who wrote out the sales invoice for John Smith (Fig. 1-7) was classifying data when he distinguished the items on the sales slip: the name and address of the customer, the quantity sold of each item, the description of each item sold, the unit price of each item, the total selling price for each item, and the total sales amount of the invoice. In the Post Office, for example, mail is classified by ZIP CODE.

Sorting. Sorting is concerned with the *arranging of data into sequence* according to a common characteristic. Generally, data are arranged into either an alphabetic or numeric sequence. Sales invoices, for example, may be sorted into groups according to the date of the sale, the geographic region in which the sale took place, or other common characteristic. In a banking operation,

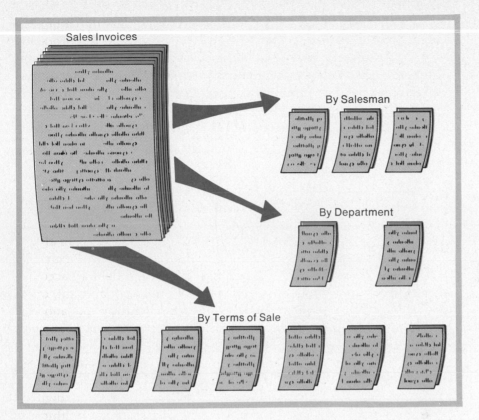

FIG. 1-9

Classifying Sales Invoices.

personal checks are sorted numerically by customer account number.

Before recording invoices in the journal, the accounting clerk must sort the sales invoices into a numerical sequence. In so doing, the accounting clerk can make certain that no invoices are missing and that the journal entries will be in chronological order.

Calculating. Calculating (or computing) is the adding, subtracting, multiplying, or dividing of raw data to produce usable results. In a typical sales situation, the number of units of an item sold is multiplied by the unit price of that item, yielding the total selling price of the item. The total selling prices of all items sold are then added, producing the total sales. And still further, the total sales may be multiplied by a percent, yielding the sales-man's commission.

To produce a charge account statement, one must perform numerous calculations, including determining the interest charges on the past balance; adding this interest charge to the past balance, to produce an updated past balance; adding recent purchases to, and subtracting recent payments from, the updated past balance

FIG. 1-10
Sorting Sales Invoices.

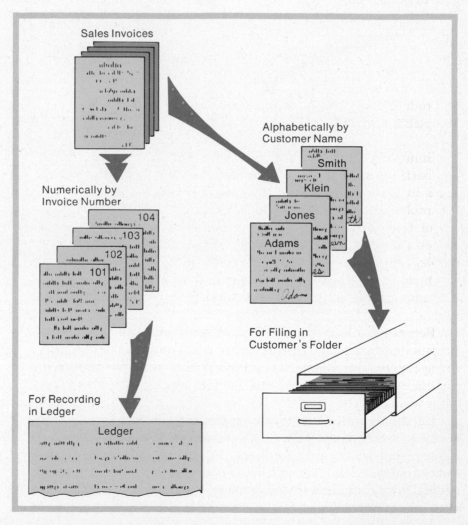

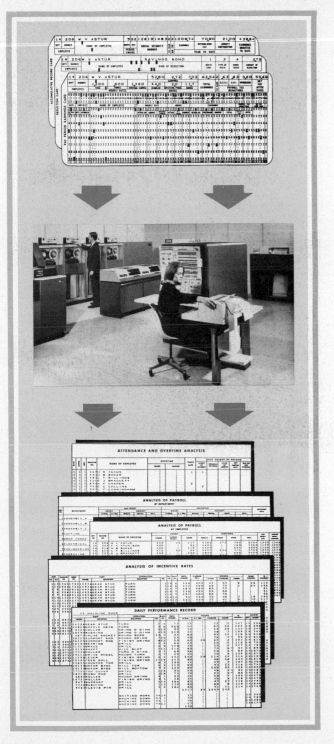

FIG. 1-13
Input, Processing, and Output.

SELF-STUDY EXERCISES 1-3

1. Data processing is defined as _____.

   ****

   the manipulating and using of facts

2. Data-processing applications are broadly classified as _____ or _____ applications.

   *****

   business
   scientific

3. The five fundamental operations required in the processing of data—be the processing manual, mechanical, or electronic—are _____, _____, _____, _____, and _____.

   *****

   recording
   classifying
   sorting
   calculating
   summarizing

4. Recording is defined as _____.

   *****

   the transcribing of data into a permanent form

5. Classifying is defined as _____.

   *****

   the grouping of like items or transactions

6. Sorting is defined as _____.

   *****

   the arrangement of data into a particular sequence according to a common characteristic.

7. Calculating, or computing, is defined as _____.

   *****

the adding, subtracting, multiplying, or dividing of raw data to produce usable results.

8. Summarizing is defined as _____.

*****

the consolidating of data, emphasizing main points and tendencies

9. The three basic functions performed by punched-card machines and electronic computers are _____, _____, and _____.

*****

input
processing
output

10. The input function is one in which _____.

*****

data are recorded on a computer-acceptable medium and transferred to a computer or punched-card device for processing.

11. Processing consists of _____.

*****

logical and arithmetical operations performed on input to produce meaningful results.

12. The output function is one in which _____.

*****

the result of the processing of input in finished or edited form are put out from the computer.

A computer is a very useful tool but certainly not the answer to all man's problems. There are certain types of problems that a computer is better equipped to handle economically and efficiently than others.

USES OF COMPUTERS IN BUSINESS

Characteristics of Problems Suitable for Computerized Solutions

Problems for which a computer is ideally suited generally have the following characteristics:

1. Justifiable
2. Definable
3. Repetitive
4. Volume data or numerous calculations

Justifiable. The first consideration in determining the suitability of an application for a computerized solution must be that the end result—knowledge gained, data or output created, financial saving, or time saved—substantiates the cost of preparing, writing, and executing the computerized solution.

All too often in today's automated world, employing a computer and the saving of time and money are assumed to be synonymous, when in reality these two factors can operate in opposite directions. That is, many menial tasks can be performed more economically by noncomputerized devices.

Definable. The problem must be in a form that can be clearly and explicitly stated, with objectives that can be reached as the result of a finite series of logical and arithmetic steps. In an inventory system, for example, the steps required in order to determine whether or not to reorder a particular stock item consist of both logical and arithmetical considerations. Somewhat simplified they are:

1. Determine the number of items on hand.
2. Compare the number of items on hand with the required minimums.
3. If the above comparison reveals that the number of items on hand is less than the required minimum number on hand, reorder; otherwise delay reordering.

Repetitive. The application or task is one which will be performed over and over again. The generation of a company's weekly payroll, for example, is a repetitive operation in that the same basic computations are required to produce a paycheck for each of a company's thousands of employees. Such repetitive calculations would include the determination of gross pay; federal, state, and local taxes; social security deductions; union dues and other such deductions; and net pay. In addition to amortizing preparation and documentation costs, a computerized solution for a repetitive operation eliminates the boredom factor. This is a recurring problem for human beings who perform tasks that are repetitive and monotonous, but it is a nonexistent factor with respect to computers.

Volume Data or Numerous Calculations. "Volume" is a term that signifies an operation or task that requires large quantities of data to be stored or processed by the computer and/or numerous logical or arithmetic calculations to be performed. In most cases, applications requiring limited calculations on limited amounts of data can be more easily and economically handled by manual or punched-card systems than by a computer system.

Computers, then, are ideally suited to handle such major business functions as payroll, personnel accounting, and inventory, since each of these functions is justifiable, definable, repetitive, and deals with a large volume of data. New applications of computers are continually being discovered. If we were to attempt to produce a list of all the applications for which computers are presently being used, it would be obsolete before it could be completed.

Some general areas that employ electronic computers extensively are:

1. General business—accounts receivable, accounts payable, inventory, personnel accounting, and payroll
2. Banking—account reconciliation, installment-loan accounting, interest calculation, demand deposit accounting, savings, and trust services
3. Education—attendance and grade-card reports, computer-assisted instruction, and research analysis
4. Government—income-tax-return verification, motor-vehicle registration, budget analysis, tax billing, and property rolls

Other areas of application include law and law enforcement, military, sports, transportation, real estate, business forecasting, medicine, and broadcasting, to mention but a few.

It should be apparent at this point that the uses of computers in business are boundless and that present applications are only a sample of things to come.

FIG. 1-14

General Business Reports Produced by Computer.

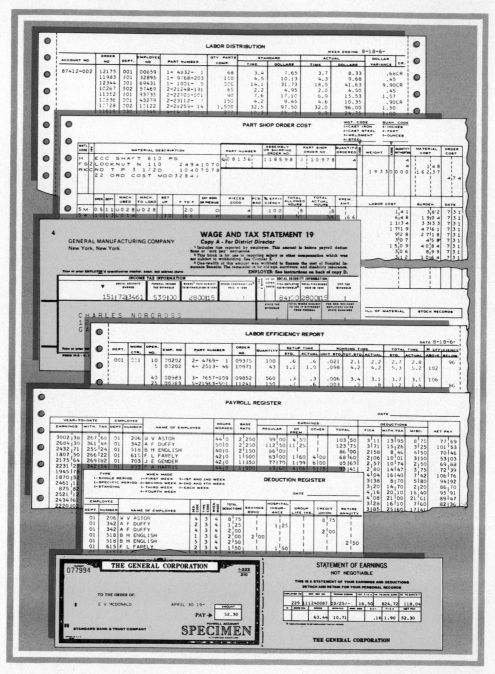

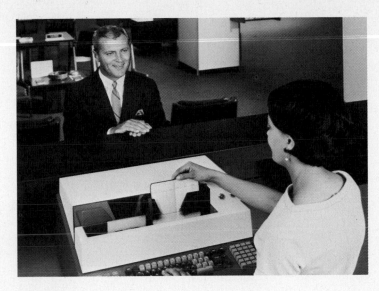

FIG. 1-15
The Computer in Banking.

FIG. 1-16
The Computer in the Construction
Industry.

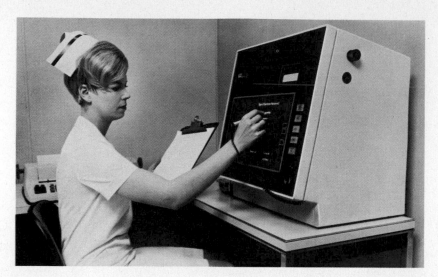

FIG. 1-17

The Computer in the Hospital.

FIG. 1-18

The Computer in Scientific Research.

FIG. 1-19
Computers in Education.

The early applications of computers (1940s) were in the area of
government research and were applied to the solution of scientific
and engineering problems. Approximately ten years later (1950s),
as a result of the increased speeds and capabilities, greatly reduced
costs, and commercial availability, computers were economically
applied to the solution of business problems. Recently, however,
the computer either directly or indirectly has affected the lives of
each and every one of us. It has benefited us by monitoring and
controlling air and water pollution, improving weather forecasting,
facilitating more effective urban planning and more efficient law
enforcement techniques, making possible electronic advances
which have been applied to improving household appliances, providing improved medical techniques for analysis and diagnosis,
and so on. It has, however, also brought about many new problems. The complete dependence on computers can lead to serious
and often insurmountable problems should they malfunction or fail
completely. The advantage of using numbers or codes in computers has led to a high degree of impersonalization where people
are reduced to mere statistics. There is a great deal of concern
on the part of many individuals with respect to their lack of control or knowledge concerning information stored about themselves
and concerning who might have access to this information and

**COMPUTERS IN
SOCIETY**

for what purpose. These are but a few of the problems that have accompanied the unprecedented growth in the number and diversity of computer applications. In light of the many new areas of computer application predicted by experts from all over the world (see Fig. 1-20), it is imperative that we address ourselves to these problems now and formulate clearly defined policies concerning the application of computers and carefully delineate who may use, and for what purposes, the data contained in centralized computer data banks.

Only time will tell whether the use of the computer can be controlled so as to reduce if not eliminate the multitude of problems which have and will continue to arise as new areas of application for the computer are discovered. In any case, one thing is for certain—*computers are here to stay.*

SELF-STUDY EXERCISES 1-4

1. A computer _____ the most efficient method of solving all types of problems.

*****

is not

2. Problems which are ideally suited to a computerized solution generally are _____, _____, _____ and involve _____ _____ or _____ _____.

*****

justifiable
definable
repetitive
volume data
numerous calculations

3. The computerized solution of a particular problem is justifiable if _____.

*****

the end result warrants the cost of the computerized solution

FIG. 1-20

Computer Applications by the Year 2010.

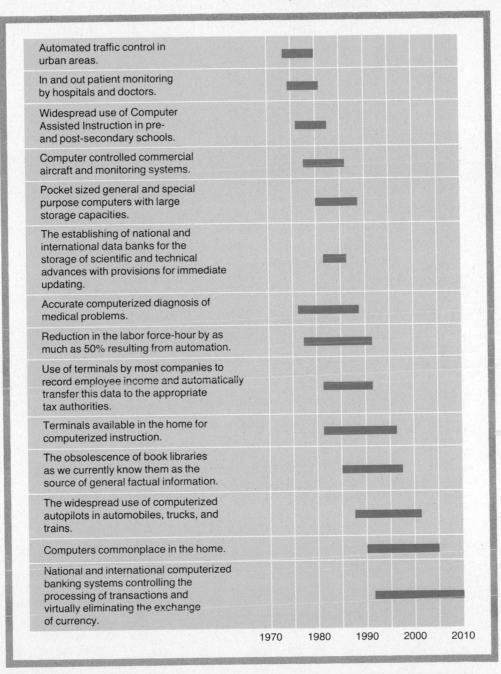

4. A problem is definable if _____.

*****

its objective can be clearly and explicitly stated and can be reached as the result of a finite series of numerical comparisons and arithmetic steps

5. A problem is repetitive if _____.

*****

it involves a task which will be performed over and over again

6. A problem involves volume data or numerous calculations if _____.

*****

the particular application is one which involves the storing or processing of large quantities of data and/or the performing of numerous logical or arithmetical calculations

7. With modern computers capable of processing more _____, _____ and _____ than ever before, the computer has become a billion-dollar industry with a virtually infinite potential.

*****

data
faster
cheaper

8. The advantages of using _____ in computers has led to a high degree of impersonalization where people are reduced to mere statistics.

*****

numbers or codes

EXERCISES

1-1 True-false exercises

1. ____ The need for automatic data processing began just after the industrial revolution.

2. ____ Operations that require handling of large volumes of data are not suited for computer applications.

3. ____ A problem need not be explicitly stated to be suitable for a computerized solution.

4. ____ The first fundamental step in data-processing operations is classifying.

5. ____ The computer revolution has been called a second industrial revolution.

6. ____ In today's automated world, the employing of a computer and the saving of time and money are synonymous.

7. ____ Computers can be economically applied to the solution of all types of problems.

8. ____ The computer has proven to be the answer to all man's problems.

9. ____ Arranging names in alphabetical order is an example of sorting.

10. ____ A problem that is suited for computer application is usually repetitive in nature.

11. ____ Calculating uses arithmetical operations on raw data to produce usable results.

12. ____ Classifying is the arranging of data into a particular sequence.

13. ____ Data processing is a relatively recent study with its beginnings in the early 1900s.

14. ____ The result of the processing of input in finished or edited form is called output.

15. ____ The computer is responsible for more new jobs and careers than any other technological development since the industrial revolution.

16. ____ Very few problems lend themselves to a computer solution.

17. ____ The six fundamental data-processing operations can be combined into three very basic computer functions: input, processing, and output.

18. ____ Repetitive operations require large quantities of data to be stored and processed.

19. ____ A bridge player arranging his hand into suits is an example of classifying.

20. _____ Income tax returns are too varied and complex for the government verification by computers.

21. _____ Today, virtually every home and business has been affected by the electronic computer.

22. _____ Summarizing is an important part of reporting.

23. _____ The use of the ZIP CODE by the Post Office Department is an example of classifying.

24. _____ The cost of processing a job by computer has consistently decreased since its inception.

25. _____ Reporting concerns the timely and effective transmittal of data that have been summarized for management.

26. _____ There are certain fundamental operations which must be performed regardless of the system that is used to process data.

27. _____ Sorting always follows the classifying operation.

28. _____ Every business is concerned with processing facts or data.

29. _____ If the end result warrants the cost of a computerized solution, it is considered to be justifiable.

30. _____ Data processing can be defined as the manipulating and using of facts.

I-2 Multiple-choice exercises

1. _____ A complete list of computer applications would consist of
   (a) a virtually unlimited number of items
   (b) 5000 items
   (c) 7500 items
   (d) 10,000 items
   (e) none of the above

2. _____ General business applications utilizing computers include
   (a) payroll
   (b) inventory
   (c) personnel accounting
   (d) accounts receivable
   (e) all the above

3. _____ Data processing had its beginnings
   (a) 3500 B.C. in Egypt
   (b) during the American Civil War
   (c) just after World War I

(d) just after World War II

(e) none of the above

4. ____ Raw data do not take on any real value for management until they have been

(a) examined and compared

(b) classified and analyzed

(c) summarized

(d) all the above

(e) none of the above

5. ____ The first fundamental operation of data processing is

(a) classifying

(b) accumulation

(c) recording

(d) omnification

(e) sorting

6. ____ Summarizing is defined as the

(a) consolidating of data

(b) reporting of data

(c) grouping of all calculations

(d) all of the above

(e) none of the above

7. ____ Classifying is defined as the

(a) coding of data

(b) grouping of like items or transactions

(c) punching of information into punched cards

(d) all the above

(e) none of the above

8. ____ Calculating includes

(a) addition

(b) subtraction

(c) multiplication and division

(d) all the above

(e) (a) and (b) only

9. ____ Summarizing

(a) emphasizes main points

(b) emphasizes tendencies

(c) specifies results pertaining to particular names or codes

(d) all the above

(e) none of the above

10. ____ A question in determining whether or not a problem is suitable for a computerized solution is

(a) Is the job repetitive?
(b) Is the job justifiable?
(c) Is the job definable?
(d) all the above
(e) none of the above

11. _____ Which of the following is not one of the fundamental data-processing operations?
(a) adding
(b) calculation
(c) sorting
(d) reporting
(e) none of the above

12. _____ Classifying is arranging data in
(a) alphabetical order
(b) Numerical order
(c) groups of similar items
(d) none of the above
(e) (a) and (b)

13. _____ Sorting is arranging the data
(a) before classifying
(b) in numerical order
(c) in alphabetical order
(d) all the above
(e) (b) and (c) only

14. _____ Every business is conerned with the efficient processing of
(a) raw material
(b) information
(c) facts or data
(d) all the above
(e) (b) and (c) only

15. _____ A problem suitable for computer solution should
(a) be definable
(b) be justifiable
(c) be repetitive
(d) all the above
(e) none of the above

16. _____ The fundamental operations, when performed on electronic computers, can be combined into three basic functions:
(a) input, calculation, reporting

(b) processing, printing, output

(c) input, processing, output

(d) all the above

(e) none of the above

Problems   1-3

1. What is the difference between data and information?

2. Discuss the impact of computers and automation upon business.

3. Discuss the fundamental operations associated with the processing of data to produce usable information.

4. Discuss several applications of computers in business that you have read about or with which you have been associated.

5. If you were asked to point out the single most important contribution of the computer to business, what would you answer? Answer fully.

6. Why have business concerns been forced to resort to automatic data processing?

7. The computer revolution has been referred to as a second industrial revolution. Support or refute this contention.

8. What are some of the social problems brought about by the introduction of the computer?

ITEMS FOR DISCUSSION

Data
Information
Data Processing
Scientific Data Processing
Business Data Processing
Recording
Classifying
Sorting
Calculating
Summarizing
Reporting

Input
Processing
Output
Justifiable
Definable
Repetitive
Volume Data or Numerous
    Calculations
Computers and
    Privacy
Computer Data Banks

2

A BRIEF HISTORY

INTRODUCTION The purpose of this chapter is to present to the reader a brief survey of the more important events in the short history of computers so that he may better understand current developments in their proper perspective.

ABACUS The most appropriate place to begin a discussion of the history of data processing is with the abacus, a device that was probably used by the Babylonians as early as 2200 B.C. As the first mechanical calculator, it existed in various forms: knotted strings, a pebble tray, and a frame of beads. The most widely known form is illustrated in Fig. 2-1.

PASCAL'S MACHINE ARITHMÉTIQUE Blaise Pascal, an eminent French philosopher and mathematician, in 1647 devised the world's first adding machine capable of counting, adding, and subtracting. The machine, which he called his Machine Arithmétique, was based on gear-driven counterwheels, similar in operation to the odometer (mileage indicator) in an automobile. Similar gear-driven counterwheels were employed in the development of mechanical calculators for the next 300 years.

FIG. 2-1
The Abacus, Used in the Orient Since the Thirteenth Century.

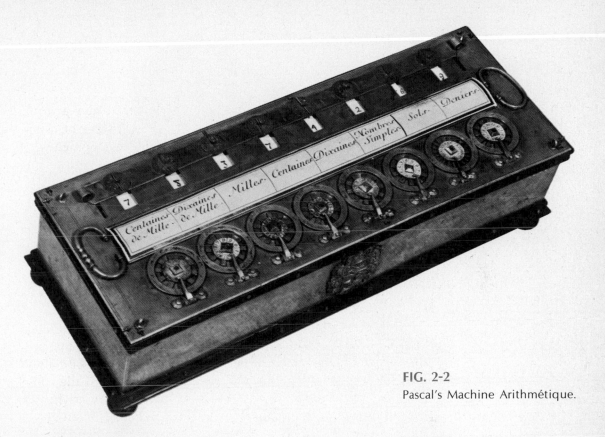

FIG. 2-2
Pascal's Machine Arithmétique.

Figure 2-3 illustrates some of the calculators developed in the late nineteenth century.

In 1801 a Frenchman named Jacquard designed a loom capable of weaving patterns in cloth automatically. He used a continuous belt of metal plates similar to a modern-day tank tread. Each plate contained a series of punched holes, through which needles moved as the belt revolved. This scheme, utilizing a series of holes punched in metal plates to control the specific operations performed by the machine, pointed the way for punched holes in cards to provide data and direct the actions of punched-card machines and computers.

JOSEPH MARIE JACQUARD

Babbage, a rather obscure English mathematician and inventor, believed it possible to build a machine-driven automatic calculator

CHARLES BABBAGE

"MACARONI BOX"
1885   Dorr E. Felt   U.S.A.

Experimental model of the first successful multi-order, key-driven calculating machine. A wooden macaroni box was used, with meat skewers serving as keys, staples for key guides, and rubber bands for springs.

CALCULATOR
1850   Parmelee   U.S.A.

The first keyboard adding machine. Readings are taken from the calibrated vertical shaft which is raised through the top of the case when the keys are depressed. Only one column of digits can be added at one time.

THE FIRST COMPTOMETER
1887   Dorr E. Felt   U.S.A.

This machine was a direct successor to the "Macaroni Box". Two years later the first printing device was added.

THE ADDER
1868   Webb   U.S.A.

A pocket size stylus-operated counter useful for addition only.

BURROUGHS ADDING AND LISTING MACHINE
1890   W. S. Burroughs   U.S.A.

This machine operates on the rocking segment principle and employs a series of pivoted bars with toothed racks at either end, and a device for printing.

ODHNER
1878   W. T. Odhner   Sweden

The principle was basically the same as that of the Baldwin, and was used in many different makes of European manufacture including the Brunsviga.

BALDWIN
1872-75   F. S. Baldwin   U.S.A.

The Baldwin variable-cogs principle was incorporated into numerous other makes. This marked the beginning of the calculating machine industry in the United States.

FIG. 2-3

Highlights in the Story of the Calculator.

FIG. 2-4
Charles Babbage's Difference Engine.

capable of generating special-purpose mathematical tables. In this venture, Babbage obtained the aid of the British government in 1823 and began designing what he called his Difference Engine. But only 12 months later he was forced, for financial reasons, to discontinue the project temporarily. However, by 1830 he had completed the preliminary design of the Difference Engine and had begun its construction. He was never satisfied with this design and was continually improving it. As a result, he never completed construction of a Difference Engine. Construction of the Difference Engine was finally abandoned in 1834 so that he could pursue development of his new idea for a more advanced device which he referred to as the Analytical Engine. The Analytical Engine was intended to be a general-purpose digital computer that would have flexible control over the operations and the sequence of operations that it could perform. Unfortunately, again as a result of financial, engineering, and design problems, this brilliant conception was never made operational. Babbage continued unsuccessfully for the remainder of his life to construct an operational calculator, but, being far ahead of his time, was unsuccessful. A model of a difference engine, based on Babbage's principles, was constructed

FIG. 2-5

Model of the Analytical Engine Constructed from One of Babbage's
Many Designs. (*Copyright Science Museum, London*)

in 1854 by a Swedish printer named George Scheutz and subsequently copied and used by the British government in the calculation and publication of life insurance tables. Several years ago IBM constructed an Analytical Engine according to Babbage's original drawings (see Fig. 2-5). It proved to be capable of performing the basic arithmetic operations and lent itself to some of the more recent programming techniques.

Hollerith is credited with applying punched-card techniques for use in compiling and tabulating the census of 1890. The census data were punched into 3 × 5 in. cards in the form of holes by a hand-operated punch (Fig. 2-6). To process these coded cards, now referred to as punched cards, Hollerith devised a tabulating machine (Fig. 2-7) capable of processing approximately 65 cards per minute.

HERMAN HOLLERITH

The use of the punched card and tabulating machine resulted in such substantial savings in cost and time that Hollerith began to adapt his Census Tabulator to commerical work. To this end, he organized the Tabulating Machine Company, which subsequently merged with other companies to become the International Business Machines Corporation (IBM). An example of the present widely used 80-column punched card with its coded rectangular punches is shown in Fig. 2-8.

The next significant development in this area did not occur until 1937 when a Harvard physicist named Aiken designed, and with the aid of IBM, constructed a computing device capable of perform-

HOWARD H. AIKEN

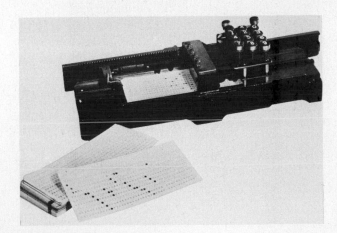

FIG. 2-6
Mechanical Keypunch, Circa 1901.

FIG. 2-7

Herman Hollerith's Punched Card
Tabulating Machine.

ing arithmetic operations on data input using Hollerith punched
cards. This machine which Aiken called his MARK I was applied
to the solution of problems requiring extensive arithmetic operations (see Fig. 2-9). Professor Aiken subsequently constructed three
more models culminating in his MARK IV.

FIG. 2-8

Example of Standard IBM Punched Card with Rectangular Shaped
Coded Holes.

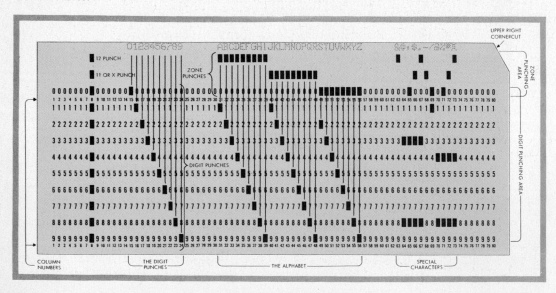

FIG. 2-9
Mark I Computer.

43

JOHN VON
NEUMANN

Von Neumann's contributions to the development of computers can be considered second to none. His contributions ranged from setting forth, in detail, the logical design of the computer, to introducing the concept of instruction modification and to working out the details of the computer's electronic circuitry. Together with Burks and Goldstine, von Neumann developed the revolutionary concepts of the stored program and the application of the binary number system. These concepts are employed today in the most modern and sophisticated computers. Concerning the characteristics of a commercial computer, von Neumann, Burks, and Goldstine wrote a report entitled "Preliminary Discussion of the Logical Design of an Electronic Computing Instrument."

"Inasmuch as the completed device will be a general-purpose computing machine it should contain main organs relating to arithmetic, memory-storage, control and connection with the human operator. It is intended that the machine be fully automatic in character, i.e., independent of the human operator after the computation starts.

"It is evident that the machine must be capable of storing in some manner not only the digital information needed in a given computation . . . but also instructions which govern the actual routine to be performed on the numerical data. . . . [This is the basic idea of the stored program. The paper continues:]

"For an all-purpose machine it must be possible to instruct the device to carry out any computation that can be formulated in numerical terms. Hence there must be some organ capable of storing these program orders. [This is the memory unit.] There must, moreover, be a unit which can understand these instructions and order their execution.

"Conceptually we have discussed above two different forms of memory: storage of numbers and storage of orders. If, however, the orders to the machine are reduced to a numerical code and if the machine can in some fashion distinguish a number from an order, the memory organ can be used to store both numbers and orders." In other words, the machine should be able to store instructions and data in the same memory unit.

"If the memory for orders is merely a storage organ there must exist an organ which can automatically execute the orders stored in memory. We shall call this organ the Control.

"Inasmuch as the device is to be a computing machine, there must be an arithmetic organ in it which can perform certain of the elementary arithmetic operations. There will be, therefore, a unit capable of adding, subtracting, multiplying and dividing. It will be seen that it can also perform additional operations that occur quite frequently.

"The operations that the machine will view as elementary are clearly those which are wired into the machine. To illustrate, the operation of multiplication could be eliminated from the device as an elementary process if one were willing to view it as a properly ordered series of additions. Similar remarks apply to division. In general, the inner economy of the arithmetic unit is determined by a compromise between the desire for speed of operation—a non-elementary operation will generally take a long time to perform since it is constituted of a series of orders given by the control—and the desire for simplicity, or cheapness, of the machine.

"Lastly, there must exist devices, the input and output organ, whereby the human operator, and the machine can communicate with each other. . . . [For example, a punched card reader or punch, a printer, or display device.]

"In a discussion of the arithmetic organs of a computing machine one is naturally led to a consideration of the number system to be adopted. In spite of the long-standing tradition of building digital machines in the decimal system, we must feel strongly in favor of the binary system for our device. [Here is the proposal for the binary system of data representation.] Our fundamental unit of memory is naturally adapted to the binary system. . . . On magnetic wires or tapes and in acoustic delay line memories one is also content to recognize the presence or absence of a pulse or of a pulse train, or of the [algebraic] sign of a pulse . . . if one contemplates using the decimal system, one is forced into the binary coding of the decimal system—each decimal digit being represented by at least a tetrad [four] of binary digits. Thus an accuracy of ten decimal digits requires at least 40 binary digits. In a true binary representation of numbers, however, about 33 digits suffice to achieve a precision of 10^{10}. The use of the binary system is therefore somewhat more economical of equipment than is the decimal. . . . An important part of the machine is not arithmetical, but logical in nature. Now logic, being a yes-no system, is fundamentally binary. Therefore a binary arrangement of the arithmetic organs contributes very significantly towards producing a more homogenous machine, which can be better integrated and is more efficient.

"The one disadvantage of the binary system from the human point of view is the conversion problem. Since, however, it is completely known how to convert numbers from one base to another and since this conversion can be effected solely by the use of the usual arithmetic processes there is no reason why the computer itself cannot carry out this conversion."

SUBSEQUENT DEVELOPMENTS

It wasn't until 1945 that the first true electronic computer appeared, the ENIAC (*E*lectronic *N*umerical *I*ntegrator *A*nd *C*alculator). Designed and built by Eckert and Mauchly, the ENIAC combined a unique method of coding information into a completely electronic computer. It was used mainly in producing tables and was programmed by means of switches and plug-in connections. Several years later, in 1949, at Cambridge University, the first stored-program electronic computer, called the EDSAC (*E*lectronic *D*elay *S*torage *A*utomatic *C*omputer), was completed. A stored-program computer is a computer controlled by internally stored instructions that can synthesize, store, and in some cases alter instructions as though they were data, and that can subsequently execute these instructions.

Until early 1951, computers were not available commercially but were only used in research and by the government. However, in 1951, the Sperry Rand Corporation built the UNIVAC I (*UNIV*ersal *A*utomatic *C*omputer). The UNIVAC I went into operation for the Bureau of Census, thus becoming the first commercially available computer. The first computer installation designed to handle business applications was set up in 1954 at General Electric Park, Louisville, Kentucky. In recognition of these events as the true advent of the computer age, the UNIVAC I is now on display in the Smithsonian Institution in Washington, D.C.

COMPUTER GENERATIONS

In the decade after 1954 over 3000 computers were put into operation, and today over 50,000 computers are in use. Computer developments over the years have included the incorporating of computer storage or memory of substantial size and greatly increased processing speeds. These developments were so significant and numerous that they have been categorized by generations, with each generation being initiated by a significant advance in *computer hardware* or a significant advance in *computer software*.[1]

[1]See Appendix A for a definition of hardware and software.

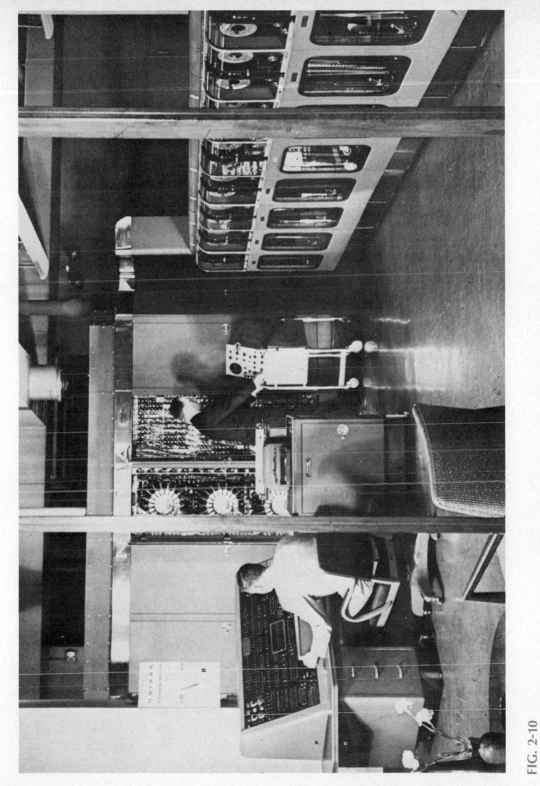

FIG. 2-10

Univac I—First Commercial Computer. (Courtesy of UNIVAC, Division of
Sperry Rand Corp.)

FIG. 2-11
First-generation Components.

**First Generation
(1942–1959)**

The first generation of computers utilized the vacuum tube for the storage of data (Fig. 2-11). The vacuum tube, however, was bulky, caused tremendous heat problems, and was never a completely reliable electronic device; it caused a great number of breakdowns and inefficient operations. Programming was principally done in *machine language.*[2]

**Second
Generation
(1959–1965)**

The second generation of computers saw the replacement of the vacuum tube with the transistor. A transistor can be thought of as a switch, such as a light switch, but with no moving parts (Fig. 2-15). Because of the speed with which the transistor can operate and its small size, computers were able to be made that could perform a single operation in millionths of a second and were capable of storing tens of thousands of characters.

[2]See Appendix A.

FIG. 2-12
First-generation Computer.

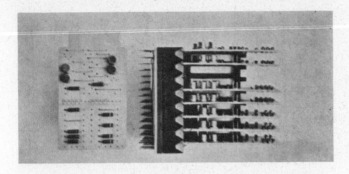

FIG. 2-13
Second-generation Components.

Computer manufacturers began producing business-oriented computers with more efficient storage and faster input and output capabilities. This generation of computers was extremely reliable, compact in size, and virtually free of heat problems.

Programming was done using both machine and *symbolic coding.*[3]

Third-generation computers were characterized by microminiaturized integrated circuits with components so small, in many cases, that they were hardly visible to the naked eye. In addition to the actual components used in their construction, third-generation computers were characterized by increased input/output, storage, and processing capabilities.

**Third Generation
(1965–1970)**

[3]See Appendix A.

FIG. 2-14
Second-generation Computer.

FIG. 2-15
Second- and Third-generation Components.

FIG. 2-16
Third-generation Computer.

Input/output devices were introduced that could communicate with computers over great distances via telephone lines, that could scan a page and input the "observed" information directly into the computer, that could display pictures on a television-like screen, and that could even accept voice input and respond in the same manner.

Storage capabilities were increased to the point where over 3 billion characters could be stored and randomly accessed by a computer in fractions of a second.

In terms of processing speeds, third-generation computers could process instructions in billionths of a second. In addition, computers were able to process several programs[4] concurrently ushering in the era of time-sharing and multiprogramming. Programmers were able to make extensive use of *problem-oriented* and *procedure-oriented languages* in addition to symbolic and machine language.[5]

Fourth Generation (1970-)

The fourth generation has been responsible for, and promises to offer still greater input, output, storage, and processing capabilities. The fourth generation of computers saw the introduction of the monolithic storage devices (see Fig. 2-18), improved and further miniaturized integrated logic circuits (see Fig. 2-19), and the construction of an actual laser memory for the National Aeronautics and Space Administration. Predictions have been made that with laser storage we soon will be able to store over 50 billion characters in the space occupied by a postage stamp. Concerning the potential of the laser, John M. Carrol in *The Story of the Laser* wrote, "The beam of the laser has the ability to carry all the conversation going on at one time on the planet Earth." More important are the advancements that have occurred with respect to the software or programs available with these computers. Great strides have been and are being made in the areas of high-level user-oriented programming languages, multiprogramming and multiprocessing techniques, data communications, and operating systems to name but a few. These terms and concepts will be discussed in detail later in the text. As a result of these changes, access to substantial computer power is now economically feasible for the small business previously only justifiable by the very large business concerns.

[4]Program—a preplanned series of instructions designed to solve a given problem.
[5]See Appendix A.

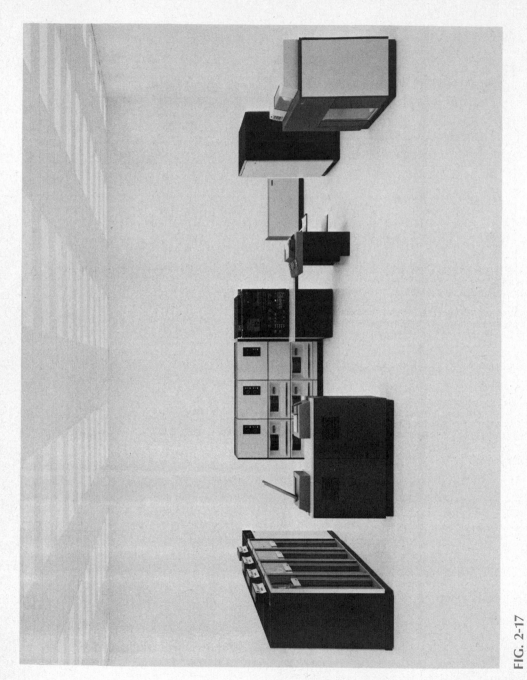

FIG. 2-17
IBM 370 Model 135, Early Fourth Generation Computer System.

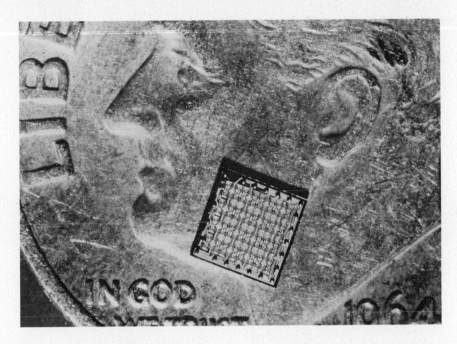

FIG. 2-18
Fourth-generation
Monolithic Storage
Circuit Containing
664 Individual
Components Shown
on the Head of
a Dime.

In 1974 IBM introduced the concept of *virtual storage* into their
370 series of computers (see Fig. 2-20). Machines previously limited to a maximum internal storage capability of approximately
1 million characters now possessed a virtual storage capability in
billions and trillions of characters.

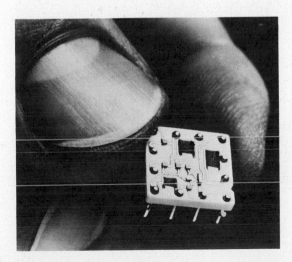

FIG. 2-19
Integrated Logic Circuit Further Miniaturized.

FIG. 2-20
IBM 370/168 Virtual Storage Computer System.

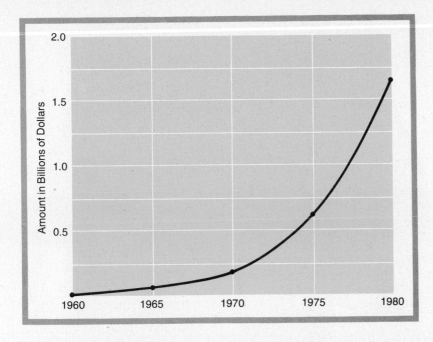

FIG. 2-21

Value of Minicomputers in Use.

Minicomputers. In addition to increasing the capabilities of large-scale computer systems, significant advances were made in the area of minicomputers. Minicomputers perform the basic arithmetic and logic functions and support some of the programming languages used with larger computer systems but are physically smaller, less expensive, and are generally limited in their storage capability. These smaller or minicomputer systems are ideally suited for processing tasks not requiring access to large volumes of stored data. As a result of their low cost, ease of operation by noncomputer-oriented personnel, and versatility, minicomputers have gained rapid acceptance from their infancy only a few years ago to today where they represent a capital investment of over a billion dollars (see Fig. 2-21).

In late 1975 IBM shook the minicomputer market with its introduction of the IBM System 5100. This computer system weighs only 50 pounds, is capable of storing up to 64,000 characters in its memory, supports two programming languages, is equipped with a CRT (Cathode Ray Tube) for displaying output and an optional 132 character per line printer, all for a cost of slightly more than $8000. This price tag refers to the purchase price, not the monthly or yearly rental price. By comparison, a large IBM 370 can rent for as high as $100,000 *per month*. Figure 2-22 illustrates the IBM System 5100.

FIG. 2-22
IBM 5100 Portable Computer for
On-site Problem Solving.

SELF-STUDY EXERCISES 2-1

1. The first calculating device developed in approximately 2200 B.C. was the _____?

     *****

     abacus

2. Pascal's _____, developed in approximately 1647, was based on gear-driven counterwheels which were used in mechanical calculators for the next 300 years.

     *****

     Machine Arithmétique

3. _____ designed an automated loom which pointed the way for the punched card.

*****

Joseph Marie Jacquard

4. _____ was an inventor and a designer of computers in the early nineteenth century. His designs include the _____ and the _____, designs which laid the foundation for computers developed in the 1930s and 1940s.

*****

Charles Babbage
Difference Engine
Analytical Engine

5. _____ was responsible for standardizing the punched card and the punched-card code and for developing the machines to process these cards in the computation of the 1890 census.

*****

Herman Hollerith

6. The Tabulating Machine Company organized by Hollerith was merged with other companies to form the company presently known as _____.

*****

International Business Machines Corporation

7. The MARK I was designed by _____ at Harvard in 1937.

*****

Howard H. Aiken

8. John von Neumann was a famous mathematician whose _____.

*****

revolutionary ideas concerning computer design were principally responsible for the design of modern-day computers

9. The ENIAC (Electronic Numerical Integrator And Calculator) was _____ .

*****

the first all-electronic computer

10. The EDSAC (Electronic Delay Storage Automatic Computer) was _____ .

*****

the first stored-program computer

11. The first commercial computer was the _____ , built by the Sperry Rand Corporation.

*****

Univac I

12. The first generation of computers utilized the _____ , the second-generation computer the _____ , and the third-generation computer the _____ .

*****

vacuum tube

transistor

microminiaturized integrated circuit

13. The _____ concept was introduced by IBM into their 370 series of computers in 1974.

*****

virtual storage

14. Minicomputers perform the basic arithmetic and logic functions but are _____ as compared with larger computer systems.

*****

physically smaller, less expensive, and are generally limited in their storage capacity

True–false exercises 2-1

1. _____ UNIVAC I, built by Sperry Rand, was used by the government for the U.S. census.

2. _____ A primitive form of calculating machine can be made from knotted strings.

3. _____ The number system suggested by von Neumann was the decimal or base 10 system.

4. _____ Charles Babbage's Analytical Engine was developed after the great success of his Difference Engine.

5. _____ The total storage capability of third-generation computers is billions of characters.

6. _____ The fourth-generation computers will make processing capabilities economically feasible for the small business that previously were only practical for larger business concerns.

7. _____ Herman Hollerith was the founder of General Electric.

8. _____ EDSAC means Electronic Digital Systemized Automatic Computer.

9. _____ Computers were not commercially available until 1951, when the UNIVAC I was built.

10. _____ The ENIAC's main purpose was to produce tables.

11. _____ The laser is a commonly used storage device in fourth-generation computers.

12. _____ The second-generation computers utilized both symbolic languages and machine languages for their programming.

13. _____ The first electronic computer to use the stored program was the ENIAC.

14. _____ Procedure and problem-oriented languages did not come into being until the fourth generation.

15. _____ "Access time" is the time a user is allowed access to the computer.

16. _____ According to von Neumann, the unit which can execute the orders stored in memory is called the Supervisor.

17. _____ John von Neumann's wide ranging contributions justify his being called "The father of the modern computer."

18. _____ The abacus was first used in the Orient in the fifteenth century.

19. _____ Programming methods were significantly improved in the third generation of computers.

20. _____ Programming for first-generation computers was done mostly in machine language.

21. _____ A form of the abacus is the pebble tray.

22. _____ Microminiaturized circuits distinguish fourth-generation from third-generation computers.

23. _____ When used in computers, transistors were smaller and produced far less heat than vacuum tubes but were less reliable.

24. _____ UNIVAC was developed for the processing of election returns of 1952.

25. _____ The concept of the stored program was developed by Herman Hollerith.

26. _____ The first true electronic computer came into being in the 1930s.

27. _____ The punched card as developed by Herman Hollerith was used in the taking of the census in the early 1900s.

2-2 Multiple-choice exercises

1. _____ The development of the stored program concept is credited to
   (a) Charles Babbage
   (b) Herman Hollerith
   (c) John von Neumann
   (d) Echart and Mauchly
   (e) none of the above

2. _____ UNIVAC I was
   (a) developed by General Electric
   (b) the first commercially available electronic computer
   (c) developed in 1951
   (d) all the above
   (e) (b) and (c) only

3. _____ According to John von Neumann, the number system which makes the most efficient use of the computer is
   (a) binary or base 2
   (b) octal or base 8

(c) decimal or base 10

(d) none of the above

(e) (a) or (b)

4. ____ ENIAC was

(a) developed toward the end of World War II

(b) used in making mathematical tables

(c) the first all-electronic computer

(d) designed and built by Echart and Mauchly

(e) all the above

5. ____ One of the characteristics of third-generation computers is

(a) increased storage capabilities

(b) processing speeds in billionths of a second

(c) time-sharing capabilities

(d) multiprogramming capabilities

(e) all the above

6. ____ First-generation computers are characterized by

(a) vacuum tube operation

(b) machine language programming

(c) bulkiness

(d) high number of breakdowns

(e) all the above

7. ____ Herman Hollerith is

(a) the inventor of the punched card

(b) the inventor of the punched-card tabulating machine

(c) the organizer of Sperry Rand

(d) all the above

(e) (a) and (b) only

8. ____ The first true electronic computer came into being in 1945. It was the

(a) EDSAC

(b) EDVAC

(c) ENIAC

(d) UNIVAC

(e) none of the above

9. ____ The abacus is

(a) an ancient calculating machine still used today

(b) a calculating device, using the base 10 to add

(c) physically, a frame of beads or knotted strings

(d) all the above

(e) (a) and (c) only

10. ____ Second-generation computers
    (a) used transistors instead of vacuum tubes
    (b) were extremely reliable
    (c) were programmed by both machine and symbolic code
    (d) gave way to the third generation about 1965
    (e) all the above

11. ____ Pascal's Machine Arithmétique was similar in operation to
    (a) electronic calculators
    (b) automotive odometer
    (c) the abacus
    (d) all the above
    (e) none of the above

12. ____ Charles Babbage developed
    (a) the Difference Engine
    (b) the Analytical Engine
    (c) the Macaroni Box
    (d) all the above
    (e) (a) and (b) only

2-3   Problems

1. Briefly discuss the concept of operation of the abacus. Why do you think it was not more universally used?

2. Trace the development of the computer from the ancient abacus to modern computers.

3. Describe the circumstance that led to the development of punch-card accounting.

4. What were some of the motivating forces that you believe were responsible for the development of computers?

5. What had Charles Babbage hoped to accomplish with his Analytical Engine? Why didn't he succeed?

6. John von Neumann has been called the "father of computers." Support or refute this claim.

7. Why do you think computer developments were so sparse between 1812 and the early to mid-1900s?

8. Modern-day computers (1940 to present) are categorized by generations. List and discuss these generations and their characteristics.

9. How did von Neumann, Burke, and Goldstine propose to store both instructions and data in the memory of the computer?

10. With respect to question 9, what arithmetic operations did they propose?

11. What number system did they propose, and why?

12. Explain the concept of the "stored program" and explain its impact on the development of computers.

ITEMS FOR DISCUSSION

Abacus
Blaise Pascal
Machine Arithmétique
Joseph Marie Jacquard
Charles Babbage
Difference Engine
Analytical Engine
Herman Hollerith
John von Neumann
Howard H. Aiken
MARK I
ENIAC
EDSAC
UNIVAC I
First-generation Computers
Hardware
Software

Vacuum Tube
Machine Language
Second-generation Computers
Transistor
Symbolic Coding
Third-generation Computers
Microminiaturized Integrated
    Circuits
Time-sharing
Multiprogramming
Problem- or Procedure-oriented
    Languages
Fourth-generation Computers
Laser Storage
Virtual Storage
Minicomputers

II

PUNCHED-CARD AND COMPUTER SYSTEM FUNDAMENTALS

UNIT-RECORD
CONCEPTS

References to unit-record or punched-card equipment have been made in previous chapters as appropriate. The particulars of this type of equipment now deserve some elaboration.

Small business concerns have, for some time, utilized punched-card equipment in solving problems. Among the areas in which these machines are utilized are (1) accounts receivable, (2) accounts payable, (3) personnel accounting, (4) paryoll, and (5) inventory.

Let us begin our discussion of punched-card or unit-record systems by answering the question: What is a unit-record system? A *unit-record system* is a complex of machines designed to create and process unit-records or punched cards. The term "unit record" has come to be associated with the punched card in that for a number of years after the punched card was introduced, a complete record concerning one item or transaction was recorded on one punched card (Fig. 3-1). As is the case with computer applications, punched-card machines perform three basic functions:

1. Input—Data are represented by coded holes punched into cards.
2. Processing—The input data are processed by passing the cards through machines that can read the coded holes and follow a predetermined set of directions.
3. Output—The results of the processing are printed, punched, or reported in some other manner.

Figure 3-2 illustrates how the information from a sales invoice might appear when recorded on punched cards, one punched card for each item on the invoice.

After the punched cards illustrated in Fig. 3-2 have been processed by a unit-record system, numerous output records could be produced. Some possible output reports from unit-record systems are illustrated in Fig. 3-3.

Since unit-record systems rely almost exclusively on the punched card as an input medium, it is appropriate at this time that we discuss the punched card in detail. And, as IBM punched

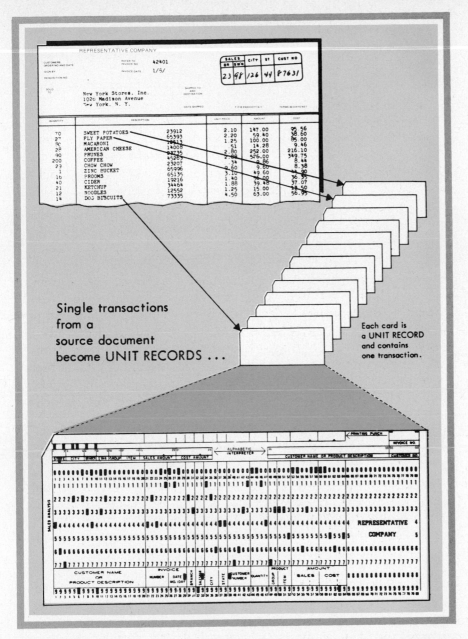

Single transactions
from a
source document
become UNIT RECORDS ...

Each card is
a UNIT RECORD
and contains
one transaction.

FIG. 3-1

The Punched Card as a Unit Record.

cards are by far the most commonly used punched cards, we shall limit our discussion to the 80-column IBM punched card and the IBM System/3 96-column punched card.

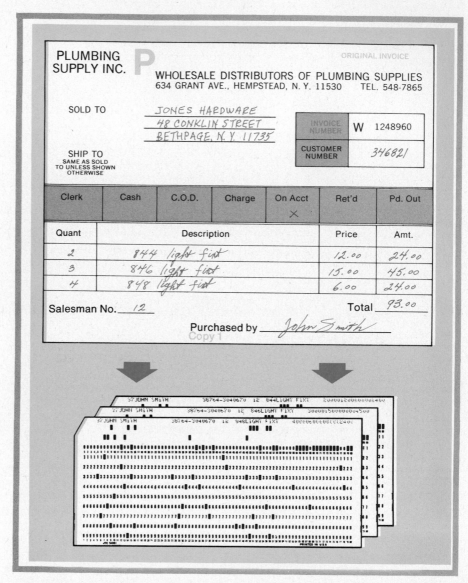

FIG. 3-2

Information from a Sales Invoice Recorded on Punched Cards.

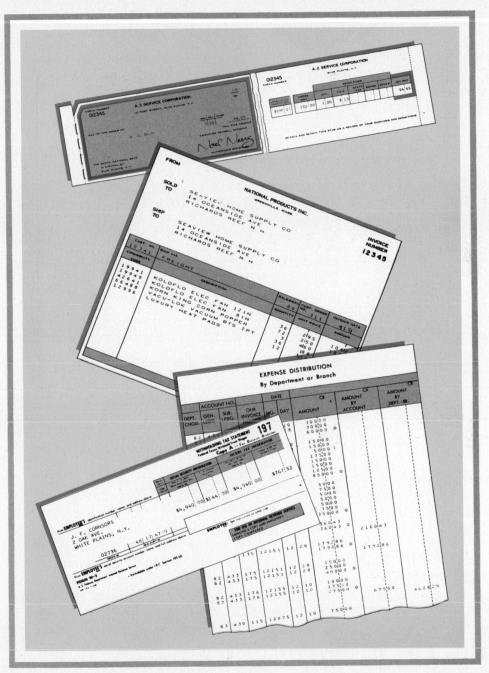

FIG. 3-3

Reports Generated by a Unit-Record System from Punched Card Input.

SELF-STUDY EXERCISES 3-1

1. Punched-card equipment is principally used in the _____ business concern.

*****

small

2. A unit-record system is _____.

*****

a complex of machines designed to create and process unit-record or punched cards

3. Punched-card machines perform the three basic functions of _____, _____, and _____.

*****

input
processing
output

4. Unit-record systems rely almost exclusively on the _____ as an input medium.

*****

punched card

PUNCHED CARD   The development of the punched card and the machines to process the cards was stimulated in the late nineteenth century by the needs of the United States Census Bureau. In 1880 the 10-year census was taken as required by law.

By 1885 the Census Bureau was still struggling to compile the collected facts of the 1880 census into meaningful form. When it became apparent that in the future this compilation would take longer than the 10-year span between each census, the fact became obvious that a more accurate and faster way of performing this task would be required. In response to this need, Herman Hollerith, then a statistician with the Census Bureau, devised a method of recording the census data crosswise on a strip of paper. Hollerith's

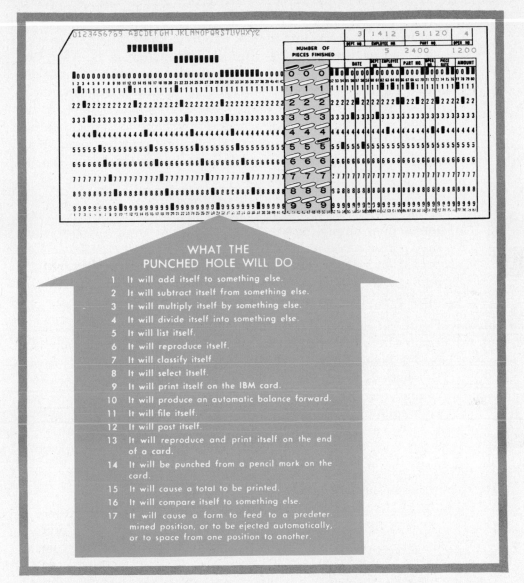

WHAT THE
PUNCHED HOLE WILL DO

1   It will add itself to something else.
2   It will subtract itself from something else.
3   It will multiply itself by something else.
4   It will divide itself into something else.
5   It will list itself.
6   It will reproduce itself.
7   It will classify itself.
8   It will select itself.
9   It will print itself on the IBM card.
10 It will produce an automatic balance forward.
11 It will file itself.
12 It will post itself.
13 It will reproduce and print itself on the end of a card.
14 It will be punched from a pencil mark on the card.
15 It will cause a total to be printed.
16 It will compare itself to something else.
17 It will cause a form to feed to a predetermined position, or to be ejected automatically, or to space from one position to another.

FIG. 3-4
What the Punched Hole Will Do.

method was quite simple. Information was coded on this strip of paper by means of a series of punched holes in a planned pattern, with each hole having a specific meaning. This system of coding information on strips of paper quickly proved to be an efficient and effective method of recording information for future processing. For better durability and ease of handling, these paper strips were soon replaced by three-by-five inch rectangular cards. Each card contained the entire record of an individual or family—a unit record. These cards were the forerunners of today's punched cards, or unit records. In recent years, however, the data required to describe an entire record has increased in volume to the point where it is seldomly possible to contain it on one punched card. And, as the term "unit record" has come to be synonymous with the punched card, a new term was introduced—the logical record. A *logical record* is a collection of items independent of their physical environment. It would be, for example, a complete record of a transaction, family, or other logical entity. A unit record, then, may not be a complete or logical record but will contain data recorded on a single punched card. Machines that deal exclusively with punched-card input, previously referred to as punched-card machines, are now more commonly called unit-record machines.

IBM 80-Column Card   Figure 3-5 shows a present-day IBM 80-column punched card. Upon careful examination of Fig. 3-5 you will notice that the IBM card is divided into 80 vertical spaces or *columns*. A *column number* is assigned to each column beginning on the left of the card with column number 1 and ending on the right-hand side of the card with column number 80. Each of the 80 columns is capable of

FIG. 3-5
IBM General-purpose Punched Card.

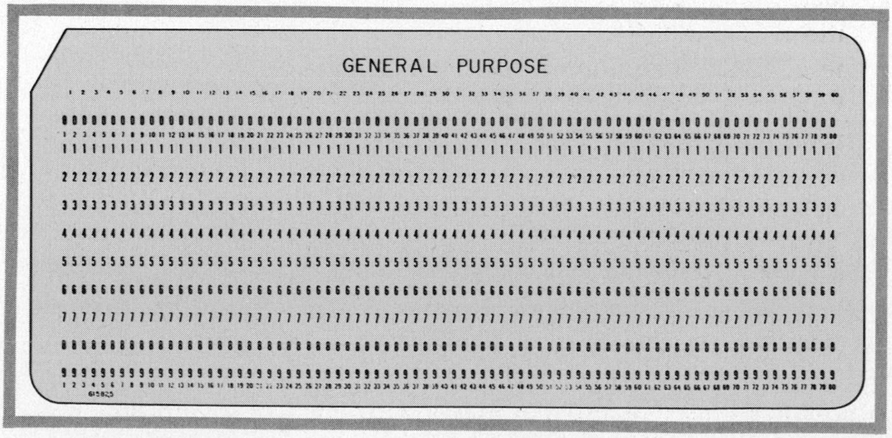

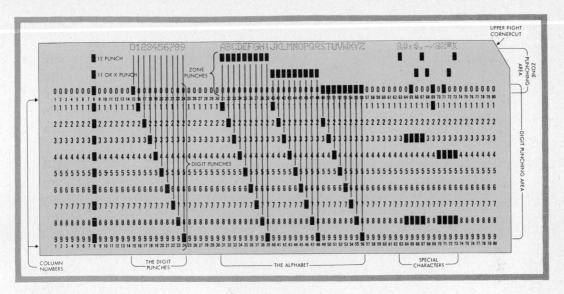

FIG. 3-6

IBM Punched Card Containing Digits, Letters, and Special Characters.

storing one *character*, which can be one letter of the alphabet, one digit, or one special character (period, comma, etc.).

Also note that the IBM card is divided horizontally into 12 spaces or *rows*. The upper three rows constitute the *zone punching area* and are called the 12 row, 11 or X row, and 0 row, while the lower 10 rows constitute the *digit punching area* and are called the 0 row through the 9 row. It should be noted that the zero row serves as both a zone row and a digit row. Numbers, letters, and special characters are recorded on the IBM card in predetermined combinations of punched holes in the zone and digit punching areas. Some of these combinations are illustrated in Fig. 3-6.

One corner is generally cut on an IBM card for ease of alignment of a series of punched cards. Such a group of cards is technically referred to as a card *deck*. Any corner may be cut; the corner cut has no effect on the information punched on the card.

You are probably wondering how one records a number or a name on a card where the number or name consists of more than one character. For example, how would one punch 28 FAST-WOOD DRIVE on a punched card? One would simply punch this address, character by character, including blank spaces, in successive columns. That is, the digit 2, or 2 row, would be punched

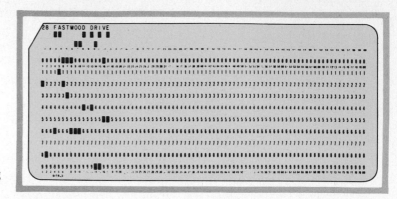

FIG. 3-7

Punched Card Containing
One Item of Data.

in column number 1, the digit 8 would be punched in column number 2, a blank in column number 3, and so forth until an E would be punched in column number 17. Figure 3-7 illustrates how such a card would appear.

The address, 28 FASTWOOD DRIVE, is called a field. According to IBM,[1] a *field* is "a set of one or more bits (binary digits) or characters treated as a unit of information," with a *card field* being defined as "a fixed number of consecutive card columns assigned to a unit of information." In the above example, the street address, 28 FASTWOOD DRIVE, is a field. More specifically, it is an *alphanumeric field,* an alphanumeric field being defined as a field consisting of combinations of letters of the alphabet, digits, and certain special symbols (period, comma, etc.). Several illustrations of alphabetic, numeric, and alphanumeric fields are given in Table 3-1. It should be mentioned at this time that within a field, numeric data are *right-justified* and alphabetic or alphanumeric data are *left-justified.* That is, numeric data are placed as far right as is possible within the field and alphabetic or alphanumeric data are placed as far left as is possible within the field.

To demonstrate your understanding of the field concept, identify the nonblank fields punched in Fig. 3-8 and determine, with the aid of Fig. 3-6, what information is punched in each field.

You should have determined that the card in Fig. 3-8 contains four nonblank fields:

[1]International Business Machines, *Reference Manual: Glossary for Information Processing* (White Plains, N.Y.: International Business Machines, 1963), pp. 2, 6.

TABLE 3-1

Examples of Different Type Fields

ALPHABETIC	NUMERIC	ALPHANUMERIC
HARRY	314	47,200
DEBIT	4172	3 BEST ST
CREDIT	81	DEBIT 2
FASTWOOD	900473	3 APPLES

1. Student number
2. High school
3. Birthday
4. Major department

You should also have determined, after referring to Fig. 3-6, that the following information was contained on the card:

Student number: 13421
High school: WALTER E. HOWARD
Birthday: 102551
Major department: ACCOUNTING

What you have just done is to *interpret* a card. When a card is punched and does not contain printing along the top to indicate the information punched, it must be read or verified by eye. This process is called *interpreting*. Interpreting can be done manually, as

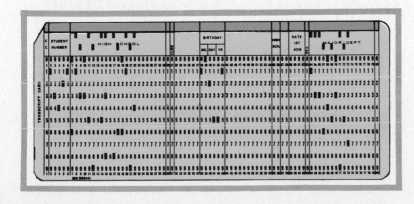

FIG. 3-8
IBM Punched Card
Containing No Printing.

you have just done, or by a special machine known as an Inter-preter, which will be discussed later. It is not necessary, however, to interpret cards that are to be read by computers, since these machines read the punched holes and not the printing on the top of the card. Punched cards may also be produced by a computer via a card punch, an output device of a computer system.

The punched card has the advantages of being inexpensive (about 0.1 cent each), easily prepared and stored, and it can be sorted, reproduced, etc., on readily available and relatively inexpensive unit-record equipment. Their main disadvantages, however, are their limited storage capacity (80 characters), slow processing and transfer speeds, bulkiness, sensitivity to high humidity and poor durability.

IBM 96-Column Card* In the late 1960s IBM introduced its System/3, a computer system designed to provide high-speed processing capabilities for the small computer user. Accompanying the System/3 was a newly designed punch card. This new punched card differs from the 80-column IBM punch card in several ways:

FIG. 3-9

IBM System/3, 96-Column Punched Card.

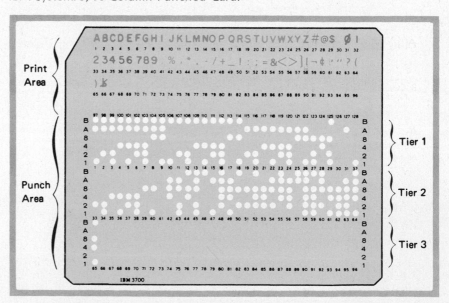

1. It is smaller in size and is squarer in shape (Fig. 3-9).
2. It is subdivided horizontally into three punching areas or *tiers,* each running the length of the card and capable of recording 32 characters of information. Thus one System/3 card can contain up to 96 characters, as opposed to the traditional 80.
3. Punched holes are round, as opposed to rectangular.
4. There are three rows at the top of the card for printing, one for each tier or punching area.
5. The coding system employed is no longer the Hollerith code but a code based on the BCD[2] (*Binary Coded Decimal*) code and requiring only six rows (B row, A row, 8 row, 4 row, 2 row, and 1 row) to represent one character.
6. It is slightly more than half the cost of an 80-column card.

An analogy between the punches on the 80-column card and those on the 96-column System/3 card as they relate to the punching of numeric and alphabetic data is given in Table 3-2. Using this table, one could verify that a Hollerith E (12 punch and a 5 punch) would have a BCD equivalent of a B, A, 4, and 1 punch. The complete System/3 BCD character set is given in Fig. 3-11 and illustrated in Fig. 3-9.

SELF-STUDY EXERCISES 3-2

1. A logical record is _____.

$$*****$$

a collection of items independent of their physical environment

2. A unit record is _____.

$$*****$$

another name for a punched card

3. The standard IBM punched card is divided into _____ columns and _____ rows, with each column being capable of

[2]There are slight variations between the standard BCD code pattern and the BCD code used with the System/3 96-column card. These variations occur in the codes for the digit 0 (zero) and for certain special characters.

TABLE 3-2

Comparison of Hollerith and BCD Punches

80-COLUMN CARD												96-COLUMN SYSTEM/3 CARD					
12	11	0	1	2	3	4	5	6	7	8	9	B	A	8	4	2	1
X												X	X				
	X											X					
		X											X				
			X														X
				X												X	
					X											X	X
						X									X		
							X								X		X
								X							X	X	
									X						X	X	X
										X				X			
											X			X			X

holding one _____ of information.

*****

80

12

character

4. A character can be a _____, a _____, or a _____.

*****

digit

letter (of the alphabet)

special character (period, comma, etc.)

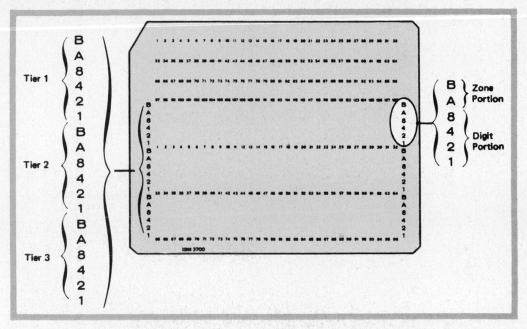

FIG. 3-10

Punch Positions on IBM System/3, 96-Column Card.

5. Characters contained on a punched card are expressed as a combination of punches in the _____ area and the _____ area.

*****

zone punching
digit punching

6. A field can be defined as _____.
*****

a set of one or more bits (binary digits) or characters treated as a unit of information

7. A card field, on the other hand, is defined as _____.
*****

a fixed number of consecutive card columns assigned to a unit of information

Numeric Characters

Punch Positions			0	1	2	3	4	5	6	7	8	9
	Zone	B										
		A	A									
	Digit	8									8	8
		4					4	4	4	4		
		2			2	2			2	2		
		1		1		1		1		1		1

Alphabetic Characters

Punch Positions			A	B	C	D	E	F	G	H	I	J	K	L	M	N	O	P	Q	R	S	T	U	V	W	X	Y	Z
	Zone	B	B	B	B	B	B	B	B	B	B	B	B	B	B	B	B	B	B	B								
		A	A	A	A	A	A	A	A	A	A										A	A	A	A	A	A	A	A
	Digit	8								8	8								8	8							8	8
		4				4	4	4	4						4	4	4	4					4	4	4	4		
		2		2	2			2	2				2	2			2	2			2	2			2	2		
		1	1		1		1		1		1	1		1		1		1		1		1		1		1		1

Special Characters

Punch Positions			}	¢	.	<	(	+	|	!	$	*	)	;	¬	-	/	&	,	%	—	>	?	:	#	@	'	=	"
	Zone	B	B	B	B	B	B	B	B	B	B	B	B	B	B	B													
		A	A	A	A	A	A	A	A								A	A	A	A	A	A	A						
	Digit	8		8	8	8	8	8	8	8	8	8	8	8	8				8	8	8	8	8	8	8	8	8	8	8
		4				4	4	4	4			4	4	4	4					4	4	4	4			4	4	4	4
		2		2	2			2	2	2	2			2	2				2			2	2	2	2			2	2
		1			1		1		1		1		1		1		1		1		1		1		1		1		1

FIG. 3-11

IBM System/3, Punch Card Character Set and Punch Combinations.

8. Fields are classified according to the type of information that they may contain as _____, _____, and _____.

*****

alphabetic (letters)
numeric (digits)
alphanumeric (letters, digits, and certain special characters)

9. 417, 347A3B, and SALARY are _____, _____, and _____ fields, respectively.

*****

numeric

alphanumeric
alphabetic

10. The advantages of using punched cards are _____.
*****

they are inexpensive
they are easily prepared
they are easily stored
they are easily sorted
they are easily reproduced
etc.

11. The disadvantages of using punched cards are _____.
*****

they have a limited storage capacity (80 characters)
they have slow processing speeds
they are bulky
they do not lend themselves to correction
they are sensitive to high humidity

12. The IBM 96-column card was designed for use on IBM's
_____ computer.
*****

System/3

13. The IBM System/3 96-column punched card is _____ than
the 80-column card, uses _____ punched holes, and employs the _____ coding system.
*****

smaller
round
BCD (Binary Coded Decimal)

Let us now discuss those unit-record machines that are commonly found in a unit-record system together with the functions that they perform.

MACHINE FUNCTIONS[3]

Card Punching

Card punching is the method by which source data can be converted into punched cards. The card-punch operator reads the source document and, by depressing keys as done by a typist, converts this source information into punched holes on the card.

The card punch is similar to a typewriter in that it causes a character to be printed on the card when a key is depressed, and unlike the typewriter in that the card punch punches information in the form of rectangular holes, in addition to just printing the character corresponding to the key that has been depressed. At the option of the card-punch operator, machine printing can be suppressed, in which case only punching will occur.

A punched card may also be produced by a computer as a form of output. In this instance, it is interpreted separately, as computers generally do not produce an interpreted punched card.

In addition to punching information from a source document, the card punch can be utilized to duplicate selected information already recorded on a punched card. *Duplicating* can be defined as the automatic punching of repetitive information from a master card into succeeding detail cards. This is normally performed as part of the card-punching function. Instead of depressing keys repetitively for common information, the operator need only punch the common information in the first card and then depress a special DUPlication key to cause the desired information to be punched into the next card. This card then serves as the master for duplicating the information into a third card, if required, etc. (see Fig. 3-13). If information is to be duplicated into a number of cards, the card punch can be programmed to automatically copy the desired information into each succeeding card thus reducing the work per card, ensuring consistency of common data, and increasing the productivity of the operator.

The keyboard of most modern card punches is arranged in a manner similar to an ordinary typewriter differing principally with respect to the location of the numeric keys (see Fig. 3-12).

The Punching Operation

As a card is punched, it moves through four areas of the card punch, namely:

[3]Much of this material has been taken with permission of The International Business Machines Corp. from the copyrighted publication 224-8208, pp. 6, 8, 10, 11, 13, 15, 16, 17, 18, and 21.

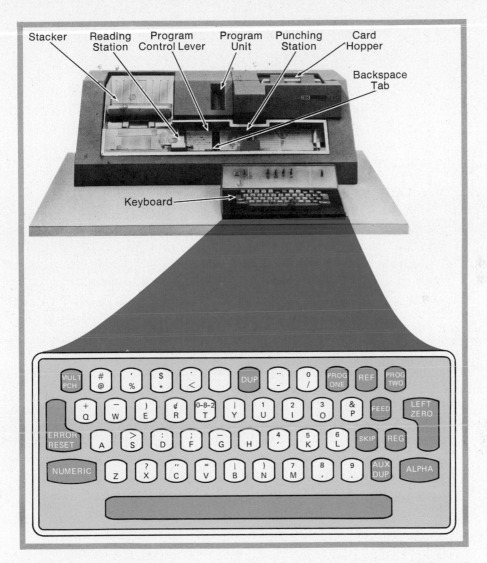

FIG. 3-12

IBM 029 Card Punch and Alphabetic Keyboard.

1. Card hopper
2. Punching station
3. Reading station
4. Card stacker

The keypunching operation is initiated by the operator's depressing the FEED key on the keyboard. This causes a single card

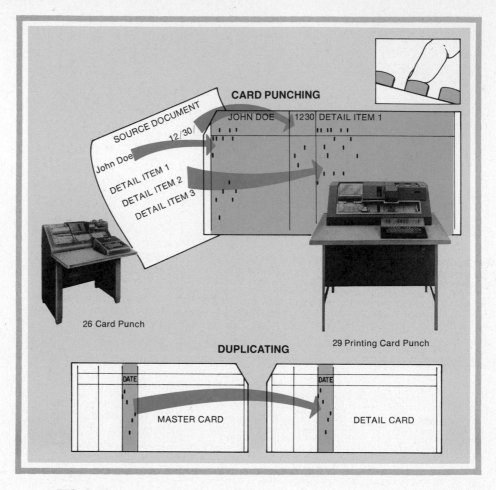

FIG. 3-13

Card Punching and Duplicating.

to be released from the card hopper. The subsequent depressing of the REGister key by the operator causes the card to be advanced until column 1 of the card is positioned at the punching station. If several cards are to be punched, the AUTO FEED switch located above and behind the keyboard should be turned on. In this case, the FEED key is depressed a second time instead of depressing the REG key. This causes the first card fed to be registered and the second card to be fed from the card hopper and not registered. As the result of either procedure, column 1 of the first card is positioned at the punching station.

The punching station contains a set of 12 *dyes* or *blades*, one for each row on the card. As a key is depressed by the operator, the appropriate blades are energized punching the Hollerith code for the keyed character into the card. Figure 3-14 illustrates the punching of the character "D" into a card. After the character has been punched into the column of the card positioned below the blades, the card is automatically advanced to the next card column. The column at which the card is positioned and where punching will occur is shown by a *column indicator* located at the bottom of the program unit (see Fig. 3-15). After the punching of this card has been completed, a second card may be registered at the punching station by one of the two methods described above. This causes

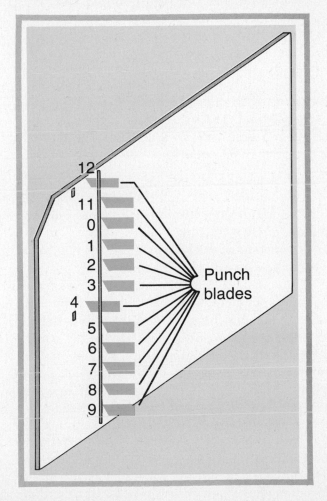

FIG. 3-14

The Letter "D" Punched into a Card.

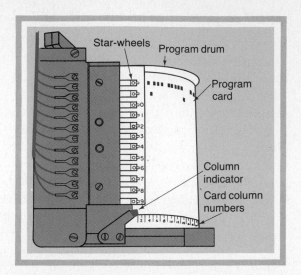

FIG. 3-15
Program Control Unit.

the previously punched card to simultaneously move to and be registered at the reading station. The second card may be punched in the same manner as the first card or some or all of the data punched into the first card may be duplicated into the second card.

Duplicating and Correcting a Card

If a second copy of the first card is desired, the operator need only hold down the DUPlicate key and column by column the data will be read from the first card under the reading station and punched into the second card under the punching blades.

    The keying and duplicating operations may also be combined to facilitate the correction of a keying error in a previously punched card. For example, let us assume that the character X was incorrectly punched in column 18 of a card and that the correct character should have been a Y. After punching of the card containing the error has been completed, a second card is registered at the punching station and the error card is registered at the reading station. To punch the new and correct card, the operator depresses the DUP key until the column indicator points to column 18 at which point the DUP key is released. The Y key is then depressed causing the character Y to be punched into column 18 of the new card. The DUP key is again depressed and held down until the remaining characters from the first card have been duplicated into the second card. The feeding of a new card will cause each card to advance to the next station with the first error card advancing to the card stacker, the correct card advancing to the read station, and the new card advancing to the punch station.

The card punch can also be programmed to perform certain operations automatically. For example, if data were to be punched into columns 10 through 20 of a large number of cards, the card punch could be programmed to automatically skip past columns 1 through 9 and position column 10 of each new card under the punching blades at the punching station. After the manual punching of columns 10 through 20, the card punch would cause the remaining columns of the card to be automatically skipped and the next card read in, registered, and advanced to column 10. In this way, the only manual operations the operator would have to perform would be the punching of the actual data into card columns 10 through 20. The card feeding and skipping operations would be handled automatically.

Programming the Card Punch

In order to program the card punch to automatically perform such operations, the operator must complete the following steps:

1. Punch the appropriate codes into a program card to indicate to the machine which operations to perform, where to start, and where to end. A list of program control card codes is given in Table 3-3.
2. Remove the program drum located above the column indicator, wrap the program control card around the drum, and replace the program control drum.
3. Move the program control lever to the automatic position. Care should be taken to ensure that the lever is *not* in the

---

TABLE 3-3

Program Control Card Codes

Type of Punch	Function
Blank	Indicates the beginning of a numeric field to be punched
11 (−)	Indicates the beginning of a field to be skipped
0	Indicates the beginning of a field to be duplicated
12 (&)	Signifies the remaining positions of the field defined by the blank, 12, 11, or 0 codes
1	Used in combination with the above punches to designate alphabetic fields; otherwise, the card punch will be in numeric mode

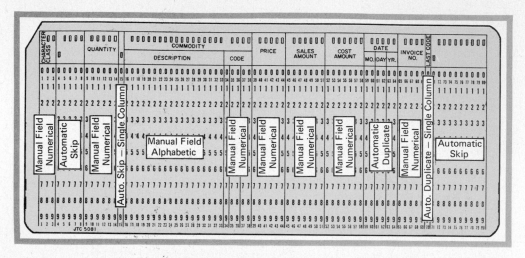

FIG. 3-16
Punched Program Control Card.

automatic position when the drum is inserted or removed. This could result in damage to the card punch.

An example of a punched program control card is shown in Fig. 3-16.

Card Verifying   Card verifying is an efficient and effective means of checking the accuracy of a previous card-punching operation. This operation entails a second operator depressing keys on the verifier while reading the same source data utilized to produce the cards being verified (see Fig. 3-19). These are precisely the same operations as were performed by the first operator, with one major difference. Here, no punching takes place. What happens is that instead of punching holes in a card, the verifier compares the key depressed with the holes previously punched in the card by the first operator. Any difference causes the machine to stop and an error light to come on, indicating that a discrepancy exists. An error key can then be depressed and a second attempt at verification made. If no agreement is reached, a third attempt is made. If still no agreement is reached, the card will advance to the next column after an error notch is placed directly above the column in error. This will allow for easy identification of cards with errors and the column in error. If no errors are detected, a notch will be automatically placed on

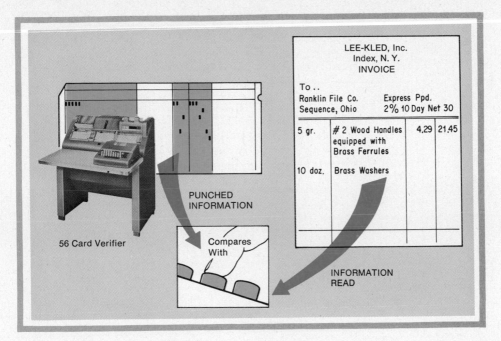

FIG. 3-17
Card Verifying.

the upper right edge of the card to indicate that it has been punched correctly and verified to be correct. Figure 3-18 illustrates how a correctly and incorrectly punched card might appear after having been verified.

Univac and IBM have both produced devices that are capable of keypunching[4] cards and verifying cards in the same machine (see Fig. 3-19). This capability greatly increases space utilization and combined operating speeds. In addition, each of these devices is equipped with a *buffer*, a temporary storage area which holds the keyed characters prior to their actual punching. That is, punching does not actually occur as the operator presses a key. Instead, the character corresponding to the key depressed is stored in the buffer until a given amount of punching has been completed. At this time, the operator can cause the characters stored in the buffer to be punched onto a card. In this way, if an incorrect key has been depressed, it can be corrected in the buffer before it is punched

[4]The terms keypunching and card punching are synonymous.

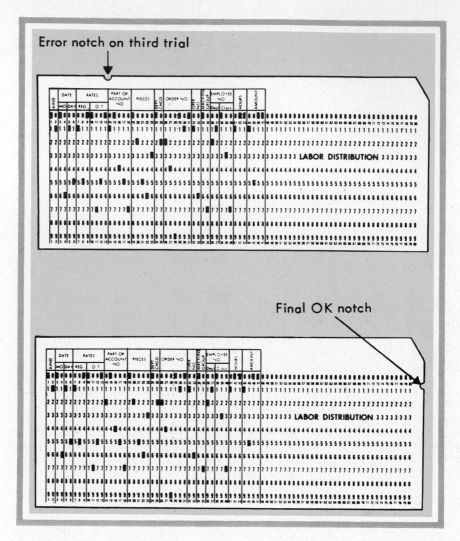

FIG. 3-18
Final OK and Error Notches Punched During Card Verification.

into the card. This eliminates the expense of wasting a card and the time lost in having to prepare a new card.

Other features of these machines include such items as a production statistics feature, which totals the operations performed on a particular machine by the number of characters keyed, the number of records, or the number of errors. It is also possible to obtain an accumulator, which adds up the data in selected fields

FIG. 3-19

IBM 129 Card Data Recorder Capable of Card Punching and Verifying.

so as to allow them to be balanced against predetermined totals and reduce the amount of required verification. An advantage for the novice as well as the professional key-punch operator is the fact that the column about to be punched is now displayed via an indicator light on the keyboard.

Reproducing

Reproducing, like duplicating, is an operation which causes data to be copied from one card to another (see Fig. 3-20). A comparison of these two operations is given below.

REPRODUCING	DUPLICATING
1. Is performed on the reproducer	1. Is performed on the card punch
2. Causes the data on one or more cards to be copied onto an equivalent number of other cards	2. Causes data to be copied from one card to the card immediately following it
3. Is performed row by row	3. Is performed column by column
4. Is performed on large volumes of data	4. Is performed on limited amounts of data
5. Data may be copied on the new cards into the same or different columns than it appeared in the original card	5. Data may only be copied on the new card into the same columns that the data appeared in the original card

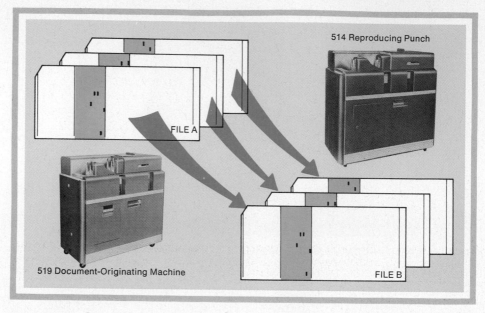

FIG. 3-20
Reproducing.

Reproducers are capable of copying all or part of the data from one card to another. Reproducers are also available with a comparing feature that indicates to the operator of the machine if an error has occurred while copying the data from one card to another and in what column(s) the error(s) occurred.

Gangpunching* Gangpunching, as duplicating and reproducing, involves the punching of data from one card to another. It is different from duplicating and reproducing in that it involves the punching of all or part of the data from a master card into one *or more* detail cards that follow the master card. As with reproducing, the information can be copied into the same or different card columns on the detail cards from the columns the data occupied on the master card.

Two kinds of gangpunching are possible: (1) single master gangpunching and (2) interspersed master gangpunching. Single master gangpunching utilizes a single master card placed in front of a deck of blank or detail cards to provide the data which will be copied onto all subsequent blank or detail cards.

If groups of cards are desired, one group for each of several different master cards, the operation required would be called interspersed master gangpunching. In this method, master cards are interspersed into a deck of blank or detail cards with a master card preceding each group of blank or detail cards. Information read from a master card is then automatically copied onto all succeeding cards until another master card is detected. Data from this second master card are then automatically copied onto the blank or detail cards following it. This process continues until all master cards have been read and the data contained on them copied onto the blank or detail cards following them (see Fig. 3-21).

Gangpunching can be performed separately or in combination with other operations, such as reproducing and summary punching for both alphabetical and numerical information. Summary punching will be described later.

Mark-sensed punching is the automatic punching of a card by means of electrically conductive marks made on a specially marked area on the card with a special pencil (see Fig. 3-22).

Mark-sensed Punching*

FIG. 3-21
Gangpunching.

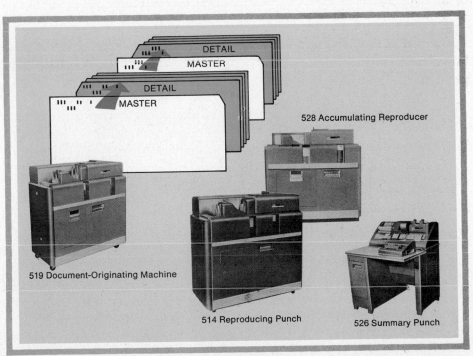

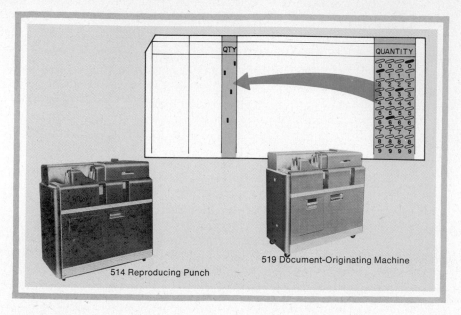

FIG. 3-22
Mark-sensed Punching.

The principal advantage of using the mark-sensed punching is that the original data can be recorded anywhere—in the office, plant or field, by workmen, timekeepers, or field workers—and then these data can be quickly and easily translated directly into punched-hole form.

One disadvantage, however, is that each space required for a sense mark is approximately three times that which would be required to record the same data in punched-hole form. This would then limit the capacity of one card to 27 mark-sense columns instead of the normal 80 punching columns.

Interpreting   Interpreting is a means by which punched cards which do not contain printing at the top can be read, and the information read printed on the top of the card (see Fig. 3-23). Depending upon the particular model of interpreter used, printing will take place on one or two lines near the top of the card or on various lines throughout the body of the card (see Fig. 3-24). Alphabetic or numerical information can be printed by the interpreter. Common data can also be repetitively printed, on a group of detail cards, from punched information on a master card.

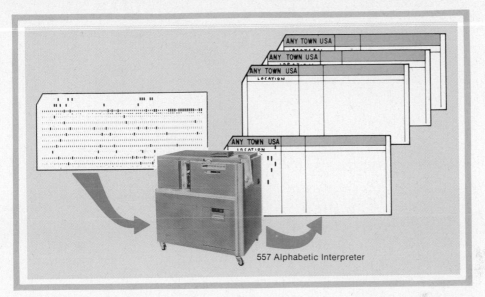

557 Alphabetic Interpreter

FIG. 3-23
Interpreting.

FIG. 3-24
Upper and Lower Line Interpreting.

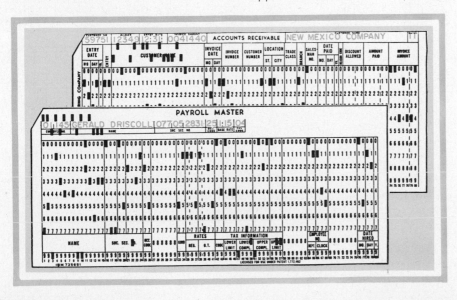

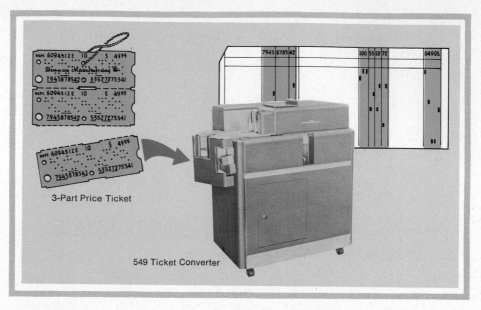

FIG. 3-25
Ticket Converting.

FIG. 3-26
Sorting.

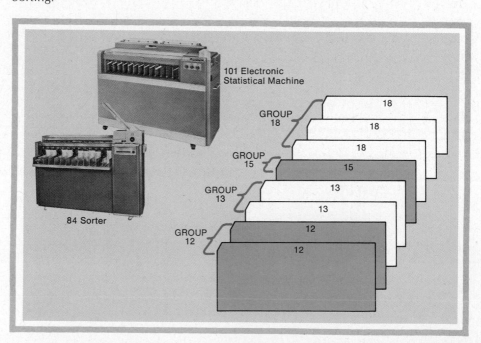

Interpreting is most advantageous when the punched cards are to be used as documents on which additional information is written or marked, or to facilitate the manual filing, sorting, or selecting of cards at a later date.

Ticket converting is the process of changing prepunched ticket stubs (2.7 inches wide by 1 inch deep) into IBM cards (see Fig. 3-25). The ticket is made up of a basic section and one or more stubs that are numerically prepunched and printed with identical information.
Ticket Converting*

When a transaction occurs, one stub is detached from the ticket and put into a receiver, which in turn is placed into a ticket converter. In the ticket converter, the ticket stubs are fed from the receiver, read, and initiate the punching of an IBM card containing corresponding information. The ticket converter is generally used in merchandising operations, where a large volume of transactions involve price tickets.

Sorting is a process by which a deck of cards is arranged in a numerical or alphabetical sequence according to any classification punched into them (see Fig. 3-26).
Sorting*

The sorter provides an automatic means by which cards can be arranged in a predetermined fashion for the preparation of various reports, each originating from the same punched cards but each requiring a different sequence of information. The sorter may also be used to select cards with a specific punch or punches from a group of cards.

Selecting is the process by which punched cards containing coded data concerning some particular quality or characteristic may be selected or pulled out from a deck of cards (see Fig. 3-27). Machines capable of performing this function automatically are the sorter and the collator, depending on the type of selection desired. Some common types of selections are
Selecting*

1. Cards punched with specific digits
2. Certain types of cards for a specific date
3. All cards containing a specific number
4. All cards higher than a specific number
5. All cards lower than a specific number
6. Cards between two specific numbers
7. First card of each group

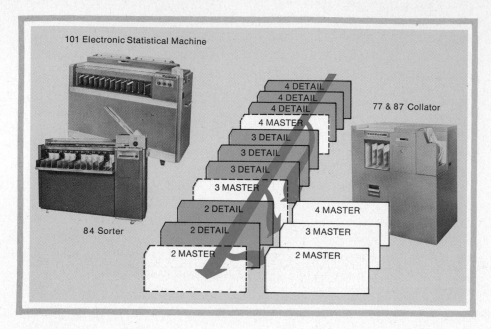

FIG. 3-27
Selecting.

8. Last card of each group
9. Unmatched cards
10. Cards out of sequence

Merging* Merging is the process by which two decks of cards, arranged in some predetermined sequence, are combined to produce one large deck of cards in the same sequence. It is essential, however, that both files be arranged in the same sequence before they are merged. That is, the sequence of the decks of cards to be merged may be in an ascending or descending sequence, but both decks are in the same sequence. This process makes it possible to automatically file a new deck of cards, in sequence, into an existing sequenced file of cards.

Matching* Matching is a procedure by which two decks of cards, arranged in the same sequential order, can be compared with respect to specific data to determine if they are identical. Groups of cards in one file are compared with similar groups in a second file on a card-by-card basis. If one or more cards of a particular group do

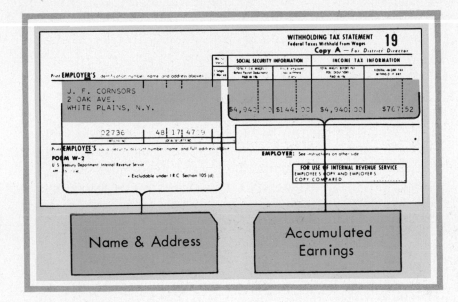

FIG. 3-28
Report Resulting
From a Merging
Operation.

FIG. 3-29
Merging.

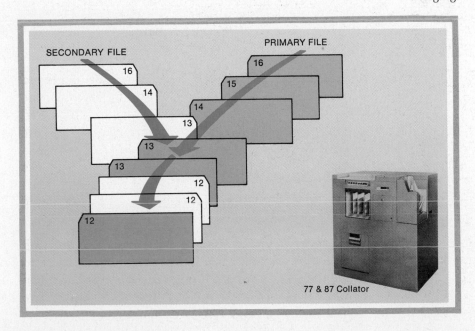

77 & 87 Collator

not match with cards in the other group, they may be selected out or separated from the group and filed separately in a special stacker on the machine (see Fig. 3-30). Matching is often done in connection with a merging operation.

Detail Printing* Detail printing refers to the process by which selected data from each card are printed as the card passes through the machine. Detail printing is utilized in the preparation of reports which show complete detail concerning each transaction (see Fig. 3-31). A typical example would include the printing of a customer invoice for goods or services purchased. In the process of this listing operation, the accounting machine adds, subtracts, cross-adds or cross-subtracts, and prints various combinations of totals.

Group Printing* Group printing or tabulating is a process in which the data obtained from cards input to the accounting machine are accumulated by groups and the totals for given groups printed out on a report. Any descriptive information necessary to identify the totals is also printed on the report.

FIG. 3-30
Matching.

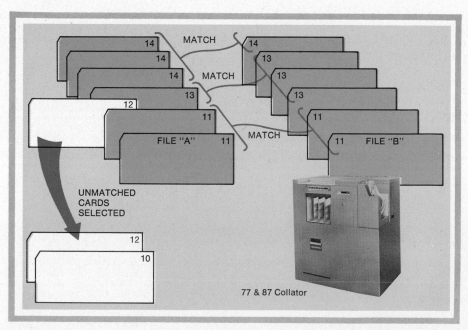

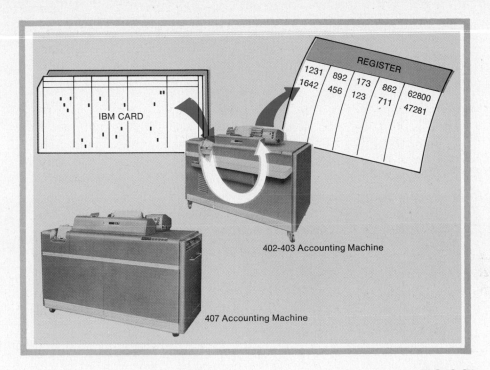

FIG. 3-31
Detail Printing.

Group printing is utilized in preparing all types of reports requiring summarized totals (see Fig. 3-32).

Summary punching is the name used to describe the process in which totals developed by the accounting machine are converted into punched-hole form and recorded on a punched card (see Fig. 3-33). Summary punching is used for two purposes:

Summary Punching*

1. To carry balance figures forward. To facilitate this, it is only necessary to include the previous total-to-date card with the current card(s) and, while a current report is being run, to summary-punch new balance-to-date cards. These cards are saved and in turn used for the next balance-to-date operation, at which time the process will be repeated.

2. To reduce volume and carry summary data. Summary cards reduce peak-load periods because of accumulated card volume and can serve as entries to general ledger accounting.

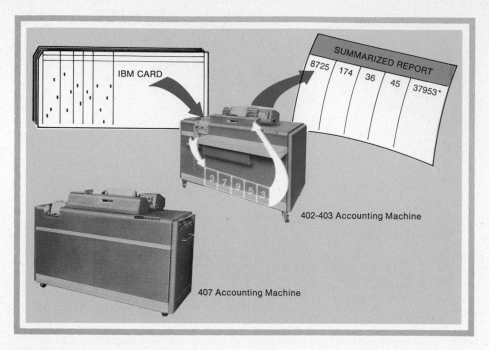

FIG. 3-32
Group Printing.

SELF-STUDY EXERCISES 3-3

1. Functions performed by unit-record equipment which can cause data to be converted from a source medium to punched cards include _____, _____, and _____.

*****

card punching
mark-sensed punching
ticket converting

2. Functions performed by unit-record equipment which can cause data to be copied from one card to another include _____, _____, and _____.

*****

duplicating
reproducing
gangpunching

3. Functions performed by unit-record equipment that involve printing include _____, _____, _____, _____, and _____.

*****

card punching
duplicating
interpreting
detail printing
group printing

4. Functions performed by unit-record equipment relating only to the arrangement of punched cards include _____, _____,

FIG. 3-33
Summary Punching.

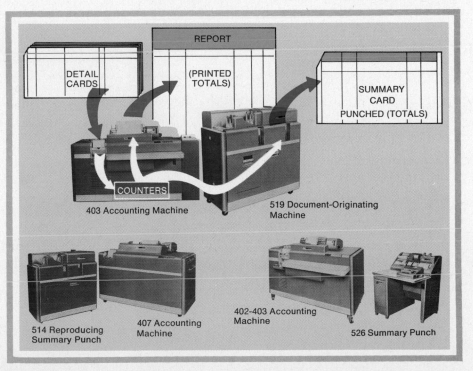

_____, and _____.

*****

sorting
selecting
merging
matching

5. Duplicating differs from reproducing in that _____.

*****

duplicating is performed on a card-punch machine and only involves a limited number of cards, whereas reproducing can
involve a large number of cards and is performed on the
reproducer

6. Gangpunching differs from reproducing in that _____.

*****

gangpunching copies data from a master card to one or more
detail cards, whereas reproducing copies data from one card
to a single other card.

7. Group and detail printing are performed on the _____.

*****

accounting machine

8. Summary punching involves the combined use of the _____
and the _____.

*****

accounting machine
reproducer

9. Summary punching can be described as a process by which
_____.

*****

totals developed on the accounting machine are transferred to
the reproducer for recording onto a punched card.

For years, computer experts have been predicting the demise of unit-record equipment. However, no matter what installation you visit, you will find various types and quantities of unit-record devices. They were right in one respect. There have been changes in recent years concerning the specific equipment in use and the applications to which it is applied. For example, one seldom sees an accounting machine in an installation today. This is simply because the functions performed by this machine can be performed more quickly and economically by a minicomputer or by using a terminal device tied into a large computer system. Minicomputers and terminal devices will be discussed later in the text. Reproducers, sorters, collators, and interpreters are commonly found in data-processing installations. In most cases, however, these machines are only used to perform routine and menial tasks. They are principally used in conjunction with and not in place of a computer system.

In addition to the fact that one will encounter such equipment in the field, the study of unit-record equipment is useful in that many of the concepts discussed in connection with these machines also apply to the computerized processing of data. Only the level of sophistication and the mechanics of their implementation change.

UNIT-RECORD EQUIPMENT AND THE FUTURE

SELF-STUDY EXERCISES 3-4

1. Many of the operations that are performed by unit-record equipment are also capable of being performed on _____.
   *****

   electronic computers

2. The concepts on which unit-record equipment are based are the same as the concepts on which the computer is based only the _____ are different.
   *****

   level of sophistication and the mechanics of their implementation

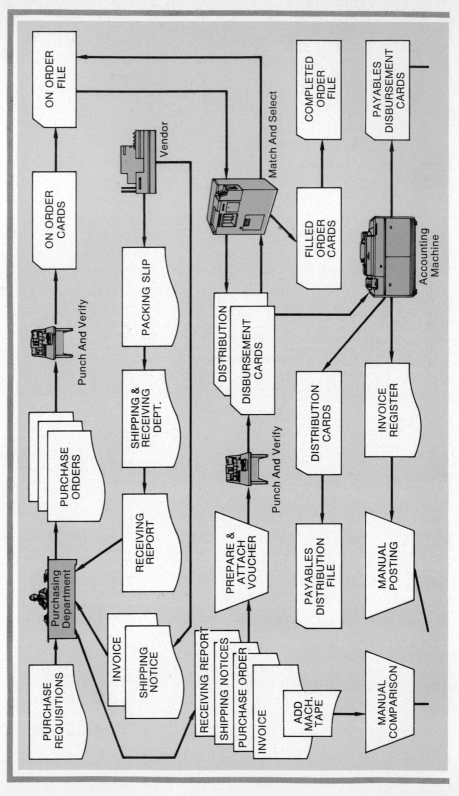

PURCHASE REQUISITIONS

PURCHASE ORDERS

Purchasing Department

ON ORDER CARDS

Punch And Verify

ON ORDER FILE

Vendor

PACKING SLIP

SHIPPING & RECEIVING DEPT.

RECEIVING REPORT

INVOICE

SHIPPING NOTICE

RECEIVING REPORT

SHIPPING NOTICES

PURCHASE ORDER

INVOICE

ADD. MACH. TAPE

MANUAL COMPARISON

PREPARE & ATTACH VOUCHER

Punch And Verify

DISTRIBUTION DISBURSEMENT CARDS

Match And Select

FILLED ORDER CARDS

COMPLETED ORDER FILE

PAYABLES DISBURSEMENT CARDS

DISTRIBUTION CARDS

PAYABLES DISTRIBUTION FILE

INVOICE REGISTER

MANUAL POSTING

Accounting Machine

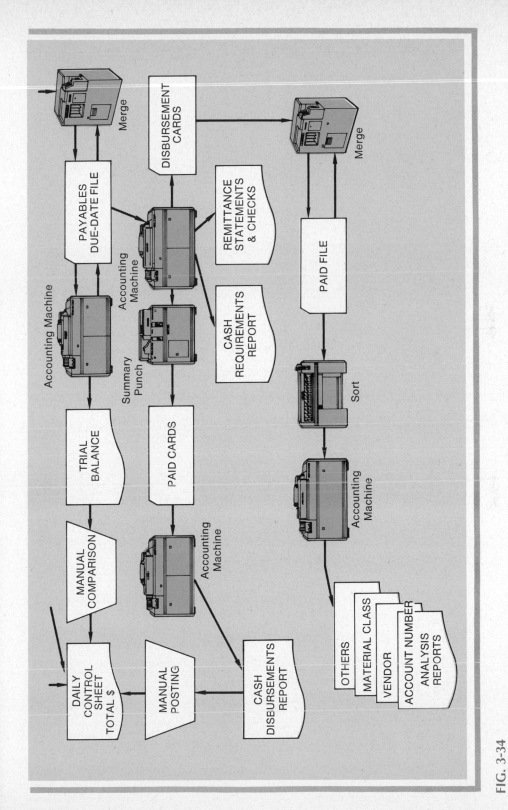

FIG. 3-34

Overall Flow Diagram of a Unit-Record Accounts Payable Procedure.

EXERCISES

3-1 True-false exercises

1. ____ IBM 80-column cards are capable of storing more than one character per column.

2. ____ The interpreter converts punched information into printed information.

3. ____ Punched-card machines are not capable of performing arithmetic operations.

4. ____ A notch placed at the right of the card means that it has been verified.

5. ____ A punched-card system would be appropraite for the inventory of a medium-sized business ($10 million per annum).

6. ____ Round holes are used on the standard IBM punched card.

7. ____ An alphanumeric field contains only numbers and letters.

8. ____ In duplicating, data must be copied into the same columns on the new card as they were on the original.

9. ____ Cards with a sequence 8, 14, 18, 21, 23, 23, 23 could not be matched with cards with a sequence 8, 8, 8, 14, 14, 18, 21, 21, 23.

10. ____ The IBM 96-column card is smaller in size than the 80-column card.

11. ____ The top three rows on a card are zones used for the punching of numeric characters.

12. ____ The three basic functions (input, processing, and output) are the same for punched-card systems as for electronic computers.

13. ____ The cost of ten punched cards is about 0.1 cent.

14. ____ A way to reduce the number of data cards with specific information is through the use of summary cards.

15. ____ The Binary Coded Decimal code consists of a combination of six possible column punches.

16. ____ Duplicating involves both the reading and punching stations of the card-punch machine.

17. ____ Computers generally produce an interpreted punched card as output.

18. _____ Ticket converting may be used to advantage in a large clothing store.

19. _____ A standard 80-column card is used to produce a program control card.

20. _____ Unit-record systems rely on punched cards as the primary input medium.

21. _____ The term "unit record" is derived from the concept of one card representing one transaction.

22. _____ Error notches are cut into the card only after the third trial.

23. _____ Reports requiring summarized totals would involve the group printing process.

24. _____ The collator causes punched information to be listed in reports.

25. _____ The card punch converts the data contained on source documents into punched cards.

26. _____ Cards with a sequence 8, 14, 18, 21, 23 will not merge properly with cards sequenced 22, 19, 16, 10, 7.

27. _____ On the IBM 80-column card, the letter S is represented by two punched holes appearing in the 0 and 1 rows.

28. _____ A sorter can select cards with specific punches.

29. _____ The first punched cards were made of paper.

30. _____ The standard IBM punched card contains 80 columns.

31. _____ A logical record is a collection of items independent of their physical environment.

32. _____ The top-corner cut is used to facilitate ease of handling the punched cards.

33. _____ Mark-sensed punch cards would be suitable for a 30-question multiple-choice class quiz.

34. _____ Reproducing is performed on a card punch.

35. _____ In a merging operation, it is essential that the two decks of cards to be merged be in the same sequential order.

36. _____ Several available machines can both punch and verify.

37. _____ Only one data field may be gangpunched.

38. _____ No punching takes place when verifying.

39. _____ The Hollerith code provides for numbers, letters, and special characters.

40. ____ The basic difference between the IBM 029 and 129 is that the 029 contains a storage facility.

41. ____ The top row of the punched card is the 12 row; the bottom row is the 9 row.

42. ____ Mark-sense punching restricts the number of characters that may be recorded on a standard-sized punched card.

43. ____ Interpreting transfers data from a master card into a group of succeeding detail cards.

44. ____ Data may be selectively taken from cards in a deck and printed on a report. This process is called selective printing.

3-2 Multiple-choice exercises

1. ____ Which of the following is untrue of the IBM System/3 punched cards?
   (a) They have three tiers for punched holes.
   (b) There are 32 punching positions per tier.
   (c) They can print 64 different characters.
   (d) There are three rows on the top of the card for printing.
   (e) None of the above.

2. ____ The amount of data that can be stored on a standard IBM card is restricted by the
   (a) number of cards
   (b) number of rows on the card
   (c) number of column splits
   (d) number of characters
   (e) physical size of card

3. ____ Transferring data from one card to another utilizing the card punch is
   (a) gangpunching
   (b) duplicating
   (c) reproducing
   (d) all the above
   (e) (b) and (c) only

4. ____ The IBM general-purpose punched card does not contain
   (a) column numbers
   (b) row numbers
   (c) corner cut
   (d) zone punching area
   (e) none of the above

5. _____ The characters which contain a 3 punch when punched into an 80-column card are
   (a) C, L, V
   (b) L, J, B
   (c) J, L, C
   (d) T, C, L
   (e) none of the above

6. _____ A card used for a detachable sales slip is a
   (a) stub card
   (b) ticket card
   (c) sales card
   (d) detachable card
   (e) none of the above

7. _____ Which of the following is not related to reproducing?
   (a) It is performed on large volumes of data.
   (b) Data can be copied into different card columns from the original.
   (c) It is performed row by row instead of column by column.
   (d) Data are copied onto the following card.
   (e) None of the above.

8. _____ Unit-record equipment
   (a) is obsolete
   (b) still maintains its position in business
   (c) is principally used to support a computer system
   (d) is increasing in its use in business
   (e) none of the above

9. _____ Data are represented on punched cards by
   (a) magnetic punches
   (b) holes
   (c) printed data
   (d) paper punches
   (e) none of the above

10. _____ The automatic punching of repetitive information from a master card into a group of succeeding detail cards is
    (a) duplicating
    (b) verifying
    (c) reproducing
    (d) interpreting
    (e) none of the above

11. _____ A unit record refers to
    (a) a deck of punched cards

(b) corner cuts
(c) one transaction
(d) one transaction punched into one card
(e) none of the above

12. _____ Cards that represent accumulated results are called
(a) gross total cards
(b) summary cards
(c) total cards
(d) accumulated cards
(e) none of the above

13. _____ The disadvantages of punched cards do not include
(a) bulkiness
(b) slow processing speeds
(c) sensitivity to high humidity
(d) difficulty in sorting
(e) none of the above

14. _____ A field is
(a) a group of columns
(b) a standard unit of measuring columns
(c) one or more adjacent columns
(d) the first grouping on a card
(e) none of the above

15. _____ The zone positions on a standard IBM card include
(a) 12, 4, 0
(b) 11, 0, 1
(c) 12, 1, 0
(d) 13, 4, 0
(e) none of the above

16. _____ Which of the following can be used for either a zone or digit punch in the Hollerith code?
(a) 1
(b) 12
(c) 11
(d) 0
(e) none of the above

17. _____ The standard IBM card contains
(a) 96 columns, 7 rows
(b) 80 columns, 9 rows
(c) 80 columns, 12 rows
(d) 80 columns, 10 rows
(e) 96 columns, 5 rows

18. _____ Cards may be selected from a deck
    (a) which are higher than a specific number
    (b) from between two specific numbers
    (c) if it is the middle card of the group
    (d) all the above
    (e) (a) and (b) only

19. _____ Operations that affect the arranging of a card deck include
    (a) merging, sorting, and selecting
    (b) sorting, selecting, and matching
    (c) selecting, matching, and merging
    (d) matching, merging, and sorting
    (e) matching, merging, sorting, and selecting

20. _____ Which of the below areas does a card pass through as it is punched?
    (a) card stacker
    (b) reading station
    (c) punching station
    (d) card hopper
    (e) all the above

21. _____ Which of the program control card codes below is correct?
    (a) A blank indicates the beginning of a numeric field to be punched.
    (b) An 11 punch indicates the beginning of a field to be skipped.
    (c) A 12 punch indicates the remaining positions of a field defined by a blank, 12, 11, or 0 code.
    (d) A 0 punch indicates the beginning of a field to be duplicated.
    (e) None of the above.

Problems 3-3

1. Discuss the similarities and differences between a typewriter and a keypunch.

2. Describe the Hollerith code used to record data on punched cards.

3. Give the Hollerith and BCD codes for each of the following characters:
   (a) A   (e) 4
   (b) J   (f) 0 (zero)
   (c) L   (g) +
   (d) X

4. What differences exist between the recording of alphabetic data and the recording of numeric data on both the 80-column card and the 96-column card?

5. What is the unit-record concept? How did it arise?

6. Describe the advantages and disadvantages of using punched cards.

7. What functional differences exist between the reading and punching stations of a card punch? In what operation are both stations used?

8. Describe the Program Control Card needed to gangpunch the current date from one card into the same columns (columns 1 through 6) of 50 cards following this card and containing data in columns 7 through 80.

9. List and describe the various pieces of equipment that one would expect to find in a computerized installation.

10. Could a utility company utilize mark-sense cards in its billing of customers? Explain.

11. Explain the difference between single master gangpunching and interspersed master gangpunching.

12. Explain the similarities and differences between reproducing, duplicating, and gangpunching.

13. What is the function of the card verifier? How does it differ in operation and purpose from a card-punch machine?

14. Discuss why it is necessary for punched cards to have restrictions insofar as card sizes and the paper composition used to manufacture the cards are concerned.

ITEMS FOR DISCUSSION

Unit Record
Unit-record Machines
Unit-record System
80-column Card
Character Logical Record
Column
Row
Zone
Zone Punching Area
Digit Punching Area
Deck

Field
Card Field
Numeric Field
Alphanumeric Field
Right-justified
Left-justified
Interpreting
96-column Card
Tier
Binary Coded Decimal
Card Punch

Duplicating

Verifying

Punching a Card

Correcting a Punched Card

Programming Card Punch

Buffer

Reproducing

Gangpunching

Interspersed Master
  Gangpunching

Mark-sensed Punching

Offset Operation

Sorting

Selecting

Merging

Matching

Detail Printing

Collating

Group Printing

Detail Printing

Summary Punching

Current Uses of Unit-record
  Equipment

Future of Unit-record Equipment

CENTRAL PROCESSING UNIT

CONTROL UNIT

ARITHMETIC/LOGIC UNIT

STORAGE UNIT

Concept of Core Storage

Noncore Storage

Virtual Storage Concept

SECONDARY STORAGE

Sequential-access Storage Devices

Magnetic-tape Files

Random-access Storage Devices

Magnetic Drum
Magnetic Disk
Data Cell

PROCESSING AND
STORAGE DEVICES

CENTRAL
PROCESSING
UNIT

Every computer system contains a unit whose primary purpose is to process data. This unit is the control center of the entire computer system. It accepts data from any of the various input devices, processes these data according to the programmer's instructions, and sends the results to the printer or other output device for recording. This unit can, in millionths of a second, add, subtract, multiply, divide, move items of data from one place in its storage area to another, or compare two quantities, to mention but a few of its capabilities. The name of this unit is the *central processing unit*, more commonly referred to as the CPU. The CPU is composed of three functional subunits:

1. Control unit
2. Arithmetic and logic unit
3. Storage unit

CONTROL UNIT

The control unit controls and coordinates the activities of a computer system much as the human brain coordinates and controls the activities of the human body. Table 4-1 illustrates how closely the control functions performed by the human brain relate to equivalent functions performed by the control unit of a computer's central processing unit.

In executing an instruction, the control unit performs the following functions:

1. Determines the instruction to be executed
2. Determines the operation to be performed by the instruction
3. Determines what data, if any, are needed and where they are stored
4. Determines where any results are to be stored
5. Determines where the next instruction is located
6. Causes the instruction to be carried out or executed

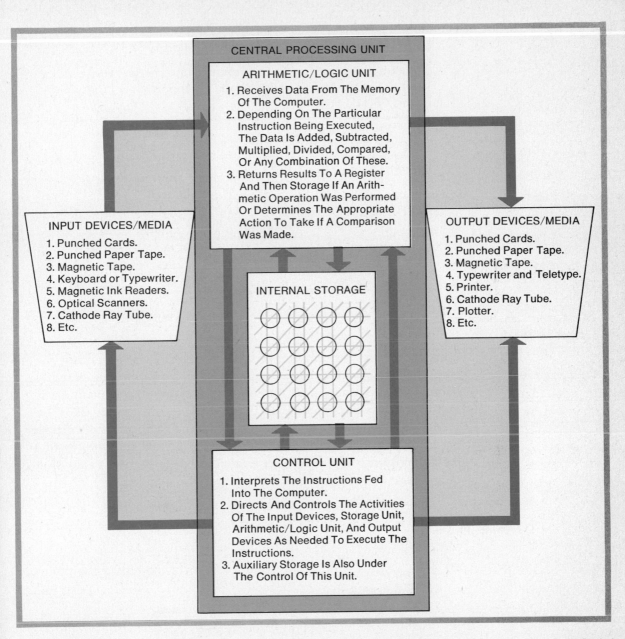

FIG. 4-1

Subunits of Central Processing Unit (CPU).

The arithmetic/logic unit (ALU) performs the three basic functions   **ARITHMETIC/**
of data transfer, arithmetic calculations, and decision making. Data   **LOGIC UNIT**

TABLE 4-1

Similarity Between Control Functions Performed by the Human Brain and Those Performed by the Control Unit of the CPU

HUMAN BRAIN CONTROL FUNCTIONS	CONTROL UNIT CONTROL FUNCTIONS
Five basic senses	Input devices
Storing and retrieving of information from memory	Storing and retrieving of data from the storage unit
Ability to solve analytical problems and make decisions	The operations of the arithmetic/logic unit
Ability to communicate verbally, in writing, etc.	Output devices
Order in which we perform the above operations	Order in which instructions are to be executed

transfer involves the moving of data from one location within the computer to another. Decision making is the ability to speedily compare two quantities or numbers to determine, for example, if one of the numbers is smaller than, equal to, or greater than the second of the numbers and respond by taking an appropriate action based on the result of the comparison. It is also possible to test for the existence of a condition encountered during the processing of a particular application and to alter the sequence of instructions accordingly.

SELF-STUDY EXERCISES 4-1

1. The _____ unit is the control center of the entire computer system.

*****

central processing unit

2. The accepted abbreviation for the term central processing unit is _____.

*****

CPU

3. The three subunits of the central processing unit are the
_____, _____, and _____ units.
**

control
arithmetic/logic
storage

4. The function performed by the control unit is to _____.
**

control and coordinate the activities of the computer system as
the human brain controls and coordinates the activities of the
human body.

5. Specific operations controlled by the control unit include the
following: _____.
**

interpret and direct the order of execution of instructions, control the operations of the peripheral equipment, control the
operations of the other subunits of the CPU (central processing
unit), and control the auxiliary storage devices

6. The three basic functions of the arithmetic/logic unit are
_____, _____, and _____.
**

data transfer
arithmetic calculations
decision making

7. The decision-making capability of the arithmetic/logic unit is
limited to two general types: _____ and _____.
**

comparing two quantities as to size
testing for the existence of a condition

STORAGE UNIT The computer storage unit, or *memory* as it is sometimes called, is as essential to the operations of a computer as your memory is essential to you in the performance of common every-day activities. It must have the capacity to store large quantities of data, any item of which must be capable of being recalled from its location in storage and moved to a location elsewhere in the computer, such as to the arithmetic unit, in millionths or billionths of a second. It is noteworthy that when an item of data is stored in a given location, it replaces the previous contents of that location, but when an item of data is "moved" from one location in storage to another, the item of data is not physically removed from its initial storage location. What does happen is that a copy or image of the data is transferred to where it is needed. This process is analogous to the one which takes place when you request information from your memory. For example, if you wish to write down your telephone number for a friend, you simply transfer an image of the number from your memory to the paper, while the telephone number in your memory remains unaltered. Thus, once an item of data has been stored, it can be used over and over again until no longer needed or until replaced by a new data item.

In addition to storing data, the storage unit of the CPU is also used to store computer instructions. The instructions necessary to direct the computer in the solution of a given problem are fed into the computer via any of a number of input devices and are stored in the computer's memory or storage unit. Once the set of instructions necessary to solve the problem has been stored, the instructions may be recalled in sequence, together with the data they require, and executed. This stored set of instructions is referred to as a *stored program*. We perform a similar process virtually every day. For example, when we go to work or school we recall and execute a sequence of instructions that gets us to our destination. This set of instructions constitutes a stored program, and it is a very complex one at that. For example, before we get on the main highway we must determine whether or not we have sufficient fuel for the round trip. If we have enough fuel, we can consider taking the most direct route. If we do not have sufficient fuel for the round trip, we must determine whether or not there is sufficient fuel for a one-way trip. If we have sufficient fuel for a one-way trip, we must decide whether to stop for fuel on the way to or on the way back from our destination. If we do not have fuel for a one-way trip, we must immediately fuel up. This analysis could

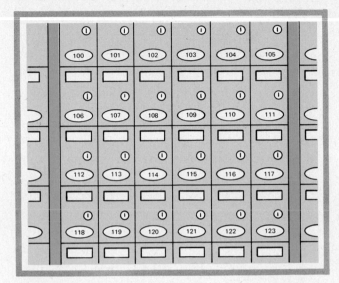

FIG. 4-2
Post Office Mail Boxes.

go on and on to consider such items as how much money we have with us, the best route for the particular day and time, whether or not we have to pick up riders, road conditions and traffic bulletins, where we will park, and so on.

If we were to list the instructions involved in handling all these contingencies, we could fill a notebook. Programs stored in a computer can be equally long if not longer. Thus, an important consideration when selecting a computer system must be whether it has a storage capacity sufficient for the type of problems it will be required to solve.

Computer storage consists of a large number of cells, each with a fixed capacity for storing data, each with a unique location and *address.* The addresses of these cells can be likened to Post Office boxes in that each box has a unique location and address (Fig. 4-2). Each storage cell is capable of holding a specific unit of data and, depending on the sytem, the unit of data may be a fixed number of digits, characters, words, or even an entire record.

Early computer memories utilized vacuum tubes similar to those used in early radio and television sets. Subsequently, these tubes were replaced by tiny iron rings called *ferrite cores* for use in computer memories.

Concept of Core Storage

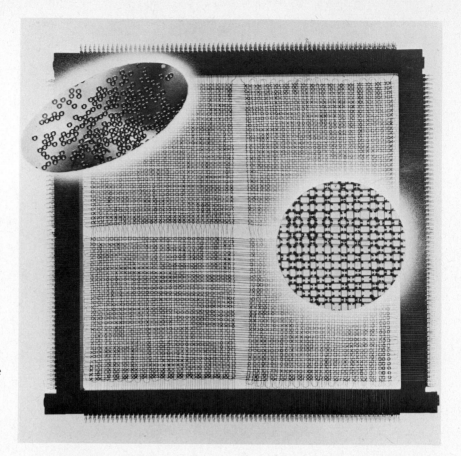

FIG. 4-3

A Series of Ferrite Cores Strung Together for Use in a Computer's Memory.

Core storage consists of thousands of these tiny doughnut-shaped metal rings in which the direction of magnetization indicates a 1 or a 0 (see Fig. 4-4).

Each tiny core measures only a few thousandths of an inch in diameter and is capable of holding one *bi*nary digi*t* or bit of data. Once magnetized to either a 0 or a 1, the core will remain in this state indefinitely, unless deliberately changed (Figs. 4-5 and 4-6). As shown in Fig. 4-7, these cores are threaded at the intersections of a network of wires forming a grid system. With such a grid system, a single core can be uniquely accessed by one vertical and one horizontal wire. For example, only one core in Fig. 4-7 can be identified by G-e. That is, only one core is on both the G-wire and the e-wire.

The reading or writing of information onto a given core requires current on both the horizontal and the vertical wires passing

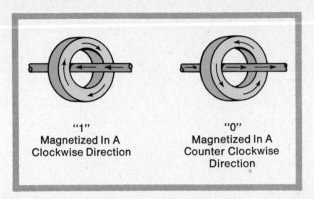

"1"
Magnetized In A
Clockwise Direction

"0"
Magnetized In A
Counter Clockwise
Direction

FIG. 4-4
Magnetic States of a Ferrite Core.

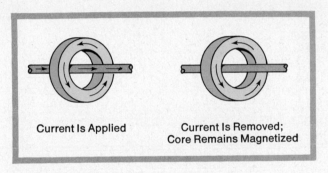

Current Is Applied

Current Is Removed;
Core Remains Magnetized

FIG. 4-5
Magnetizing a Core.

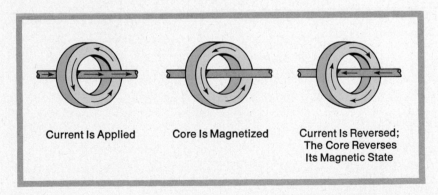

Current Is Applied

Core Is Magnetized

Current Is Reversed;
The Core Reverses
Its Magnetic State

FIG. 4-6
Reversing a Core.

through the core. That is, placing current on the e-wire alone would not be sufficient to affect any core on that wire. But, if current were simultaneously applied to the G-wire, only one core would be affected, as only one core would have current passing through it vertically and horizontally.

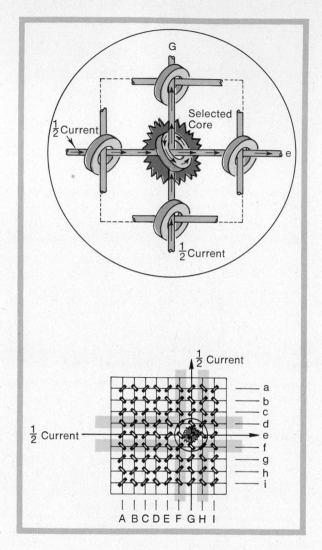

FIG. 4-7

Selecting and Magnetizing a Core.

An additional set of wires are passed through each core so that the state of the core (1 or 0) can be read. This reading process is called *sensing* a core.

Since the core is stationary, and since current travels along these grid wires at the speed of light (186,000 miles/second), the reading or writing of a single core takes place extremely rapidly.

Figure 4-8 illustrates how the character "A" could be represented by a particular combination of 1's and 0's within the core or memory of the computer. From Fig. 4-8 you can see that one

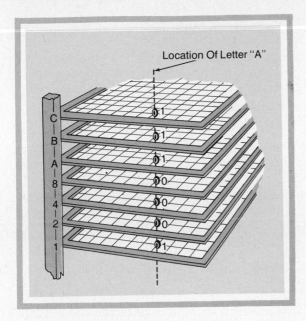

FIG. 4-8
Character "A" Represented in Core Storage.

character consists of one core from each of the seven core planes. Taken together they represent the letter "A." To determine this, the computer must read each of seven distinct cores and determine whether they are set to 0 or 1. Similarly, to store any character in memory, the computer must set each of seven cores, one per core plane or grid, appropriately to a 1 or to a 0. In modern computers, this operation can be completed in billionths of a second.

The IBM 2361 Core Storage Unit contains many sets of core planes.

FIG. 4-9
IBM 2361 Core Storage Unit.

Noncore Storage   A new innovation in computer design in the early 1970s was the integration of the faster MOS (metal-oxide-semiconductor) micro-miniaturized integrated circuit memory with the slightly slower ferrite core memory. Figure 4-10 illustrates two MOS chips mounted on a ceramic base. Each chip has monolithic integrated circuits etched on it to form over 250 memory circuits. This system was first employed in the IBM 370 Series computer.

Many new experimental devices are being considered for future use in computer memories. The most promising of these appears to be a *laser memory,* which employs the polarization of light in the same manner as the magnetic core employs magnetic polarization. It is expected to be less than 1/100 of the current cost of storing data and approximately 10 times as fast as existing average access speeds, with a total *primary storage* (within the CPU) capacity of approximately 1 trillion (1,000,000,000,000) characters.

Virtual Storage   Later models of the System 370 were available with what IBM
Concept   called *virtual storage.* This revolutionary storage technique allowed the user of the computer system to process programs requiring more total storage capacity than was physically present in the storage unit of the CPU. Simply stated, virtual storage is a storage management technique that allows one to view the computer system as one containing many times the storage capacity than is physically contained in the CPU. For example, a program pre-

FIG. 4-10
MOS Miniaturized Integrated Circuit.

viously requiring 100,000 storage locations could now be processed on a virtual storage computer containing many fewer actual storage locations. This is accomplished by breaking the program up into segments of a certain size which are stored outside the CPU. As needed, these segments or groups of instructions are called into the storage area of the CPU and are executed. The remaining segments of the program are stored outside the CPU until needed. When needed, a segment(s) is brought into the CPU replacing a previous segment(s) no longer being used. This process is very similar to that which takes place when we read a book. We begin by reading the first page. When we have finished the first page, we replace it with the next page by turning the page. This process can be continued for as long as we like. If at any time it becomes necessary to refer back or ahead to a particular page, we can access it by simply turning to that page number. Throughout this process we had access to only one page of the book at a time. The factor which most affected our reading rate was the number of times we had to turn to a new page. So it is with virtual storage. The more movement of sections of coding, or *pages* as IBM calls them, that there is in and out of the CPU, the more time-consuming the process will be. The circuitry and control programs provided with virtual storage computer systems are designed to reduce this movement to a minimum.

As a result of this virtual storage capability, the real storage requirements of a program are greatly diminished since it is now necessary to maintain only sections or pages of the program in the CPU at any one time. Thus, where a program might have once required all of a computer's real storage capacity, now it will only require a small portion of the real storage available with a virtual storage computer system. The remainder of the real storage can be used to concurrently process other programs in a similar manner.

SELF-STUDY EXERCISES 4-2

1. The storage unit or _____ has as its main function _____.

*****

memory
the storing of data

2. Once data have been stored, they can be used _____.
   *****

   over and over again until no longer needed and deliberately replaced

3. Each storage cell in the computer is associated with a unique _____.
   *****

   address

4. One ferrite core is capable of storing _____.
   *****

   1 bit (binary digit) of data

5. The state of a core (1 or 0) can only be changed by applying the current to _____.
   *****

   both the horizontal and vertical wires passing through the core

6. Many modern computers have replaced the core type of memory with _____.
   *****

   a system of microminiaturized circuits

7. A new experimental primary storage device is the _____ and is based on the polarization of light.
   *****

   laser memory

SECONDARY   Many data-processing procedures require more storage capacity
STORAGE   than is available in core storage. In these instances, the computer system can be augmented by one or more *auxiliary* or *secondary storage* devices. Data files stored in a secondary storage device are not immediately accessible to the processing unit or to other

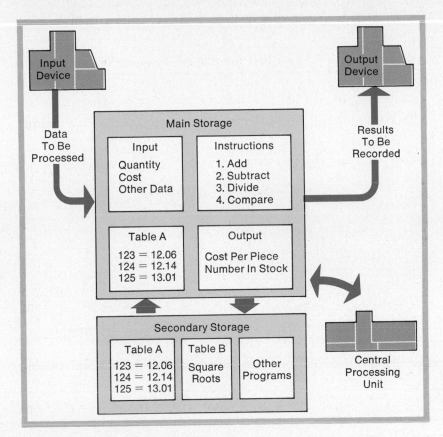

FIG. 4-11

Schematic, Main, and Secondary Storage.

input/output devices and hence must be routed through main storage. As such, the processing of a record of data contained in a secondary storage file first requires that the record be transferred or moved into main core storage, where it can be processed as any other data stored in core storage. Less frequently used data, or items of data whose great volume make their storage in core impractical if not impossible, are reserved for auxiliary storage. Table 4-2 illustrates some of the differences between primary and secondary storage.

Secondary storage files are classified as sequential-access or random-access files, depending on whether data contained in the file must be accessed and/or processed in the sequence in which they occur in the file or whether data can be accessed randomly without regard to sequence.

TABLE 4-2

Comparison of Primary and Secondary Storage

CHARACTER-ISTIC	PRIMARY STORAGE	SECONDARY STORAGE
Location with respect to the CPU	Within CPU	Outside of, but connected to, CPU
Cost*	Most expensive	Less expensive than primary storage
Capacity*	Up to several million characters	Billions of characters
Average access time*	In billionths of a second	In millionths of a second
Data can be processed directly from storage	Yes	No, must first be moved into primary storage
Means of storing information	Magnetic core, thin film, microminiaturized integrated circuit, electrooptical	Magnetic disk, magnetic tape, magnetic drum, data cell, CRAM

*These items will vary with manufacturers and computer systems.

Sequential-access Storage Devices

Sequential-file storage mediums store data in sequential order and can only be read sequentially. Thus, the first record contained in the file must be read before the second record, the second record must be read before the third, etc. That is, if we wished to read the 80th record, for example, we would have to read the 1st through 79th records first.

Magnetic-tape Files. In addition to being a principal input/output medium, magnetic tape is one of the fastest, most inexpensive and most widely used sequential-file storage media. It is so widely used that the term "sequential-access file" is generally understood to mean a file maintained on magnetic tape.

Magnetic tape, such as the tape in a tape recorder, is only in motion when data are being read from it or written onto it. During these operations, the magnetic tape must be moving at a constant speed. Consequently, blank space must be left on the tape before and after each record or *block* (two or more records) of data written. This space or *inter-block gap* (IBG) serves three purposes:

1. While the tape is accelerating from rest to the constant speed at which the tape must be moving before data can be read, no data are lost.
2. While the tape is decelerating from constant speed after having read one record or block of data recorded on the magnetic tape, no data will be lost.
3. It separates physical or tape records from one another.

Tape IBG's range in size from 0.6 to 0.75 inch, a space capable of otherwise storing up to 1200 characters.

Tape records are not limited to any fixed number of bytes, characters, or fields. A tape record can be any size, provided that there is available core storage to store the entire record at the same time as it must be read into primary storage before it can be processed. Figure 4-12 illustrates some of the possible ways in which records can be recorded onto magnetic tape.

Magnetic tape files can be easily protected against accidental erasure of data. The most common means is through the use of a *file protect ring*. This is a plastic ring which fits into a groove in the back of the magnetic tape reel. When installed, the tape can be read and it can be written on. However, when the file protect ring is removed, the tape can no longer be written on but is still capable of being read. The jargon for this is "no ring, no write."

Random-access files facilitate virtually immediate access to specific records within a file without the need to examine previous records. Modern computers can store billions of characters, each of which can be randomly accessed in thousandths of a second. Some of the more commonly used random-access storage devices are the magnetic drum, disk, and data cell (magnetic card).

Random-access Storage Devices

Magnetic Drum. A magnetic drum is a metal cylinder that rotates at a constant speed of about 3500 revolutions per minute. The outer surface of the cylinder is coated with a thin magnetic material. Data recorded on the surface of the drum may be read and utilized an indefinite number of times. However, each time new data are recorded on the surface of the drum, the old data are automatically erased. Information is recorded or retrieved by read/write heads (similar to those on a tape recorder) that are suspended a very slight distance from the surface of the drum. The drum is subdivided into channels and tracks which function in a manner similar to core storage (see Fig. 4-16).

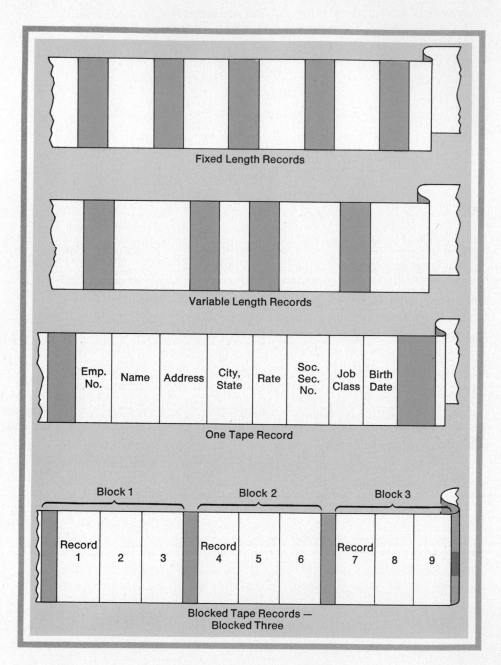

Fixed Length Records

Variable Length Records

| Emp. No. | Name | Address | City, State | Rate | Soc. Sec. No. | Job Class | Birth Date |

One Tape Record

Blocked Tape Records —
Blocked Three

FIG. 4-12
Possible Data Record Arrangements on Magnetic Tape.

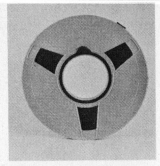

FIG. 4-13
File Protect Ring.

FIG. 4-14
IBM 2301 Drum Storage Device.

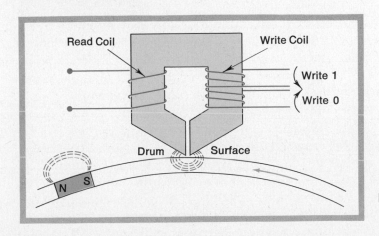

FIG. 4-15
Magnetic Drum Read/Write Head.

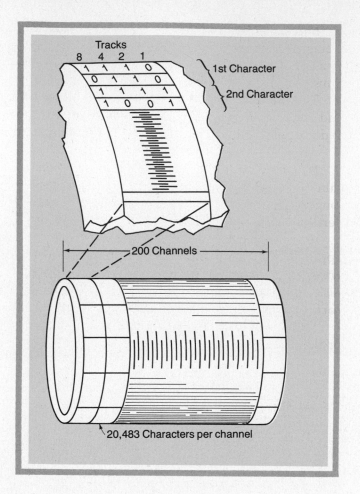

FIG. 4-16

Character Storage on a 2301
Magnetic Drum.

An IBM 2301 drum, for example, can store over 4 million bytes or characters. On the average, it takes approximately 8.6 milliseconds to rotate the drum to the desired position at which point characters can be transferred to or from the CPU and the drum at a rate of 1.2 million characters per second. For example, 1 million characters could be read from or written onto a 2301 drum in approximately 1 second.

The magnetic drum has been utilized as an auxiliary storage device for several years, during which time it has functioned in two general capacities. When it was first introduced it was intended to be used as a high-capacity, intermediate-access storage device. It was used to store data that was repetitively referenced through a computing operation (actuarial tables, interest tables, income-tax tables, etc.) and to augment main storage.

Subsequently, however, it has been utilized as a random-access storage device. In this capacity it was used for program storage and as a temporary storage area for high-activity random-access operations on limited data.

The magnetic drum does not possess the speed of core storage and does not possess the removable feature of the disk pack, but it does offer a versatile capability at a reasonable cost.

Magnetic Disk. Magnetic-disk storage consists of a series of thin magnetically coated disks, similar in appearance to a stack of long-playing phonograph records. These disks are mounted on a vertical shaft, each disk separated from the disks above and below it. As the shaft rotates, it spins the disks at a constant speed of approximately 2400 revolutions per minute. One or more access arms moves into the disk to read or write the data stored on the disk. Each disk consists of a series of concentric paths or tracks each capable of storing data in magnetically coded form.

Disks may be permanently attached to the drive unit (Fig. 4-17) or they may be made up as removable *disk packs* containing six or

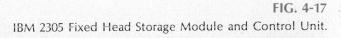

FIG. 4-17
IBM 2305 Fixed Head Storage Module and Control Unit.

FIG. 4-18

IBM 3336 Disk Pack
Consisting of 10 Disks with
a Capacity of 100 Million
Characters.

more disks each (Fig. 4-18). Disk packs, depending upon the particular model, can store as many as 100,000,000 characters. The IBM 3336 Disk Pack pictured in Fig. 4-18, for example, is capable of storing over 100 million characters.

As was the case with magnetic cores, magnetic tape, and magnetic drum storage media, once data have been recorded on a

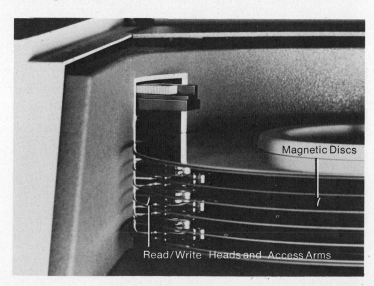

Magnetic Discs

Read/Write Heads and Access Arms

FIG. 4-19

IBM 2311 Disk Storage Drive
Showing a Disk Pack and
Access Arms.

magnetic disk they may be read an indefinite number of times and will remain on the disk until they are written over.

Disk storage devices are capable of reading and writing data sequentially or randomly providing a very flexible storage device. It is, however, slower than the magnetic drum but with a capacity to handle larger volumes of data. Disk packs also provide the capability of easy removal and portability not available with either the core or drum.

Data Cell. A data cell is a device containing removable and interchangeable strips of magnetic film which are capable of storing large volumes of data with direct-access capabilities. A single strip of magnetic film measuring only 2¼ by 13 inches contains 100 tracks for data, with each track capable of storing 2000 bytes— 200,000 bytes of storage in one magnetic strip. With a complement of 20 subcells of 10 strips each, a total capacity of 400,000,000 non-numeric characters or 800,000,000 digits is possible. With a proper controlling device (IBM 2841 Storage Control), up to 8 data cells can be utilized, giving the computer system to a maximum total on-line capacity of 6,400,000,000 characters of storage. Figures such as these can stagger the imagination. However, because access of individual records are so slow, IBM's new 3330 disk storage facility is rapidly replacing the data cell. The 3330 facility can store 800,000,000 characters, access any data item stored in an average

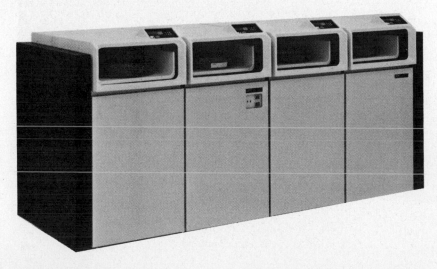

FIG. 4-20

IBM 3340 Disk Drive Unit and Disk Pack. (Storage Capacity 70 Million Characters, Data Transfer Rate 1.25 Million Characters per Second.)

FIG. 4-21
IBM 3330 Disk Storage Facility.

of 30 milliseconds, and transfer characters between it and the CPU at a rate of 800,000 characters per second. Even more staggering than the data cell.

Average access time for a given record is of course longer for the data cell than either the disk or drum simply because of the mechanics involved in accessing a record (Table 4-3). The data cell

FIG. 4-22
IBM 2321 Data Cell Drive Model 1.

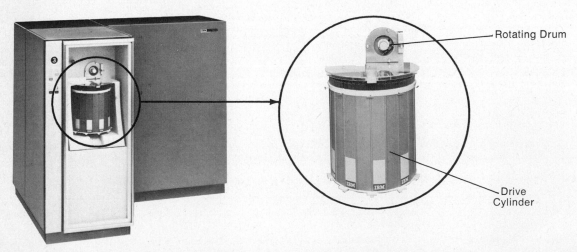

Rotating Drum

Drive
Cylinder

TABLE 4-3

Comparison of Capacity and Access Times of Random-access Devices

DEVICE	STORAGE CAPACITY	RANGE AND AVERAGE ACCESS TIME*
2301 Drum Storage	4.0 million characters	0–17.5 ms; average is 8.6 ms
3330 Disk Storage Facility (8-3336 Packs)	800 million characters	25–135 ms; average is 75 ms
2321 Data Cell Drive	400 million characters	95–600 ms; average is 347 ms

*In milliseconds (ms); 1 ms = 1/1000 second

drive must pluck the appropriate magnetic strip from its subcell and wrap it around a rotating drum located just above the drive cylinder (see Fig. 4-22) before the desired record can be accessed. The CRAM (Card Random Access Memory) unit is a similar device manufactured by the National Cash Register Company (Fig. 4-24). Considering that average access time is still in fractions of a second, its somewhat slower operating speeds are more than compensated for by its virtually limitless storage capacity, sequential- or random-access storage capabilities, easily removable and replacable element, and low cost.

SELF-STUDY EXERCISES 4-3

1. The computer's main memory can be augmented by one or more _____ or _____ devices.

   *****

   auxiliary
   secondary storage

2. All data coming from or going to the processing unit from secondary storage must be _____.

   *****

   routed through main storage

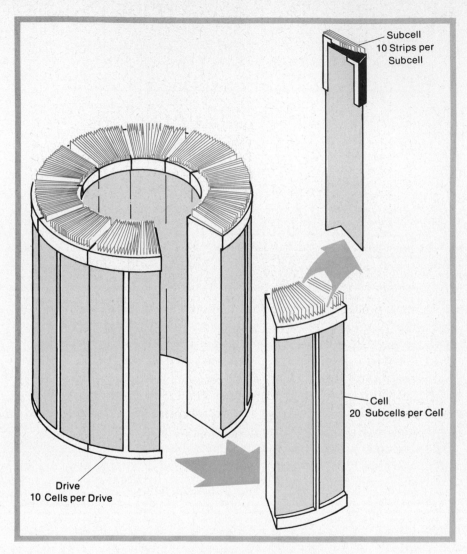

Subcell
10 Strips per
Subcell

Cell
20 Subcells per Cell

Drive
10 Cells per Drive

FIG. 4-23
Data Cell Drive Unit Showing Data Cell and Subcell.

3. Second storage files are classified as either _____ or
_____.

*****

sequential-access
random-access

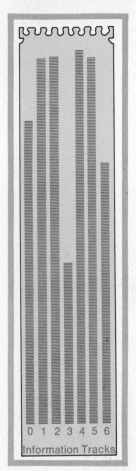

1 Card Has 7 Tracks With 3,100
Characters or 21,700 Characters/Card

1 Cartridge Holds 256 Cards
or 5,555,200 Characters

FIG. 4-24
Arrangement of Data on an NCR
(National Cash Register) Magnetic
Card (CRAM).

4. The principal sequential-access storage medium is _____.

*****

magnetic tape

5. Between every record or block on tape there must always be
an _____, the purpose of which is _____.

*****

inter-block gap (IBG)
to provide tape space to allow the tape to accelerate to or de-
celerate from constant speed

6. Random-access storage devices include _____, _____, and _____.

*****

magnetic drum
magnetic disk
magnetic card

7. The random-access storage device with the fastest access time is the magnetic (*drum, disk, or card*).

*****

drum

8. The random-access storage device with the largest storage capacity is the magnetic (*drum, disk, or card*).

*****

card

9. The most commonly used random-access storage device is the magnetic (*disk, drum, or card*).

*****

disk

10. Magnetic disk units are available with _____ or _____ disks.

*****

fixed
removable

EXERCISES

4-1 True-false exercises

1. _____ Virtual storage is available with all large-scale computer systems.

2. _____ The arithmetic/logic unit can add, subtract, multiply, divide, and compare quantities.

3. ____ In terms of storage capacity, primary storage is generally more restrictive than secondary storage.

4. ____ The size of a tape record cannot exceed the available primary storage capacity.

5. ____ Drum storage provides the most on-line storage capability available today.

6. ____ When data are moved from one storage location to another, the original image of the data remains unchanged.

7. ____ Data stored on magnetic disk may be accessed randomly as well as sequentially.

8. ____ A disadvantage of tape or disk files is that there is a limit as to the number of positions a record may contain.

9. ____ The magnetic drum is the most commonly used random-access storage device.

10. ____ The file protect ring must be removed before installing a tape reel on the tape deck.

11. ____ A distinct advantage of magnetic tape, disk, and drum is that they are reusable.

12. ____ CPU is the accepted acronym for Computer Processing Unit.

13. ____ An inter-block gap is a term used to describe the space between records or blocks in a file.

14. ____ To change the value of a ferrite core, it is only necessary to energize one of the wires passing through the core.

15. ____ Information is retrieved from disk storage via access arms which contain read/write heads.

16. ____ The smallest addressable unit in the computer's memory is a bit.

17. ____ The size of the IBG is related to how fast the tape starts and stops.

18. ____ The three functional subunits of a CPU include a storage unit, control unit, and input/output unit.

19. ____ Magnetic drum storage is faster than other forms of random-access storage media.

20. ____ Primary storage is often referred to as memory.

21. ____ One of the functions of the CPU control unit is to interpret instructions.

22. _____ Inter-block gaps restrict the amount of data that can be stored on magnetic tape.

23. _____ The drum in a magnetic drum storage device is generally removable.

24. _____ Magnetic disk is considered a sequential storage medium.

25. _____ Magnetic tape files are more versatile than magnetic disk files.

26. _____ Magnetic tape is an example of a sequential file storage medium.

27. _____ Each location in storage is associated with an address.

28. _____ A 0 or 1 bit is determined by the direction of magnetization in a ferrite core.

29. _____ Auxiliary storage is necessary only when secondary storage is inadequate for storing data.

4-2 Multiple-choice exercises

1. _____ Virtual storage
   (a) is a storage management tech
   (b) expands the storage capacity   CPU
   (c) expands the storage capacit   e secondary storage devices
   (d) is used exclusively with the
   (e) none of the above

2. _____ A technological development curr   nder consideration for use in future computer memorie
   (a) transistors
   (b) vacuum tubes
   (c) integrated microunits
   (d) laser
   (e) all the above

3. _____ A storage medium which cannot be used for both a direct-access and a sequential application is
   (a) drum
   (b) disk
   (c) tape
   (d) data cell
   (e) all the above

4. _____ Random-access storage devices do not include
   (a) a magnetic drum
   (b) a magnetic disk
   (c) a data cell

(d) magnetic tape
(e) all the above

5. _____ Which of the following units of the CPU directs and controls the activities of input/output devices?
(a) logic unit
(b) control unit
(c) processor unit
(d) arithmetic unit
(e) none of the above

6. _____ The arithmetic/logic unit performs the following operations:
(a) data transfer
(b) arithmetic calculations
(c) decision making
(d) all the above
(e) (b) and (c) only

7. _____ A unit of data can be
(a) a word
(d) a digit
(c) a record
(d) all the above
(e) none of the above

8. _____ Primary storage is _____ than secondary storage.
(a) more expensive
(b) less expensive
(c) capable of storing more information
(d) slower in access time
(e) more expensive and capable of storing more information

9. _____ The access time for retrieving data from primary storage and secondary storage is
(a) the same
(b) primary is faster
(c) secondary is faster
(d) zero
(e) none of the above

10. _____ The _____ of a computer handles decision-making operations.
(a) arithmetic/logic unit
(b) control unit
(c) input/output unit
(d) supervisory unit
(e) none of the above

11. ____ Of the following, which is not generally interchangeable on it's respective device?
    (a) magnetic drum
    (b) magnetic disk
    (c) magnetic card
    (d) data cell
    (e) none of the above

12. ____ One operation which cannot be performed by the arithmetic/logic unit is
    (a) data transfer
    (b) arithmetic calculation
    (c) retrieval of instructions
    (d) decision making
    (e) none of the above

13. ____ Of the following, the device capable of storing the greatest amount of data is the
    (a) magnetic drum
    (b) magnetic disk
    (c) data cell
    (d) ferrite core
    (e) magnetic tape

14. ____ A bit may have _____ possible state(s).
    (a) one
    (b) two
    (c) three
    (d) all the above
    (e) none of the above

4-3 Problems

1. Define the following:
   (a) CPU
   (b) control unit
   (c) core
   (d) secondary storage
   (e) address
   (f) main storage
   (g) arithmetic/logic unit

2. Discuss briefly the features and uses of mass storage devices. How do they relate to and differ from primary storage?

3. What is an inter-block gap? Why is it necessary in tape processing?

4. Describe and contrast primary and secondary storage. Give examples.

5. Describe the concept of core storage.

6. What are some of the advantages of laser storage as compared to other forms of primary storage?

7. Describe and compare sequential-access storage with random-access storage. Indicate what types of jobs would best be suited for each.

8. Compare the various types of storage media with respect to speed, cost, and data accessability.

9. What is the purpose of the file protect ring?

10. What is meant by access time? Why is this an important consideration when selecting a secondary storage device?

11. Why is access time generally given in the form of an average?

12. In large-scale computer systems, several types of secondary storage devices are generally used. Why?

ITEMS FOR DISCUSSION

CPU	Virtual Storage
Control Unit	Sequential Access
Arithmetic/logic Unit	Random Access
Memory	IBG
Storage Unit	File Protect Ring
Primary Storage	Block
Address	Magnetic Tape
Ferrite Core	Magnetic Disk
Stored Program	Magnetic Drum
Bit	Magnetic Card
Monolithic Integrated Circuits	Disk Pack
Auxiliary or Secondary Storage	Data Cell

INTRODUCTION

PUNCHED-CARD INPUT/OUTPUT
Punched-card Readers
Card-punching Devices

PRINTERS
Character-printing Devices
Line-printing Devices

CHARACTER READERS
Magnetic-ink Character Readers
Optical Scanners

TAPE INPUT/OUTPUT
Punched-paper-tape Devices
Magnetic-tape Devices
Key-to-tape Recorders
Magnetic Reel Tape Writers

TERMINALS
Keyboard Devices
Visual Display Devices

OTHER INPUT/OUTPUT DEVICES
Film Devices
Audio Devices
Plotters

**INPUT/OUTPUT
COMMUNICATIONS**
Overlapped Processing*

5

INPUT/OUTPUT
MEDIA AND DEVICES

INTRODUCTION We recall from Chapter 1 that automated operations consist of three basic functions: input, processing, and output. In this chapter we shall discuss input/output media and devices. Computers are available in all sizes, shapes, and colors, and with few exceptions, no matter what type or size of business enterprise you consider, there is available a computer or computer service suitable to handle its data-processing needs efficiently and economically. Furthermore, regardless of type, size, shape, or color, there is one thing about which we can be certain; there must be a means of feeding it data and getting back meaningful and useful information.

Computer applications in business are characterized by their limited computations and by the large volume of data which are input to, and output from, the computer. Handling this volume of data is one of the functions of the input/output devices, or *peripheral devices*, supporting a computer. These devices are responsible for sensing or reading data from the input medium and converting these data into a form that the computer can understand, which we shall call *machine code*. They are also responsible for converting computer output from a machine-coded form into a language and onto an output medium we can read and understand.

As you now most certainly realize, input/output devices perform a significant function and are an indispensable part of a computer complex or computer system. It should also be clear that the faster and more efficiently that we can get the data to the computer, the more efficiently the computer will function and the faster we will obtain our results. Thus, we must examine the various input/output devices so that we will know what devices are available to do what kind of jobs and when to use each. We shall also examine the *media*, or means, used to record data associated with these input/output devices. Specific details such as operating speeds are presented only for purposes of comparison and need only be examined with this purpose in mind. Such specific information is readily available in the specifications available from equipment manufacturers.

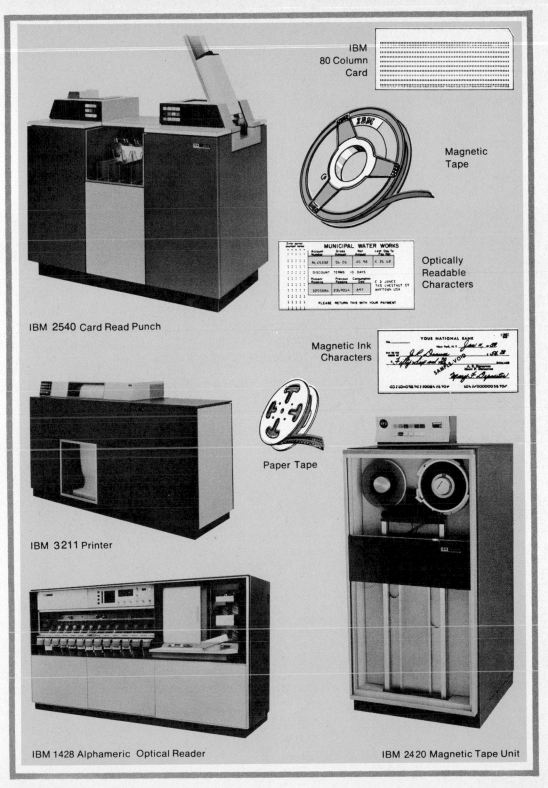

IBM
80 Column
Card

Magnetic
Tape

Optically
Readable
Characters

IBM 2540 Card Read Punch

Magnetic Ink
Characters

Paper Tape

IBM 3211 Printer

IBM 1428 Alphameric Optical Reader

IBM 2420 Magnetic Tape Unit

FIG. 5-1
Input/Output Devices and Media.

SELF-STUDY EXERCISES 5-1

1. Before data can be stored and used by a computer, it must be converted to _____.

*****

machine code

FIG. 5-2
Univac Card Reader.
*(Courtesy of UNIVAC,
Division of Sperry Rand Corp.)*

2. The physical input/output unit is called the _____; the means used to record the data is called the _____.

*****

device

medium

The punched-card reader is the most common of all input devices. This is due, in part, to the fact that the punched-card medium is so inexpensive (about 0.1 cent each) and because the punched card is easily prepared and stored. It can be used with almost any computer system, from the very smallest to the very largest systems in use today. The principal use of the card reader is to transmit the information contained on the punched card directly into the memory or storage unit of the computer. This function can be accomplished at speeds ranging from 200 cards per minute to over 1000 cards per minute.

There are basically two kinds of punched-card readers: the wire-brush type and the photoelectric type. In the wire-brush type, the card is read row by row by a series of 80 wire brushes, one for each card column (Fig. 5-3). A punched hole is detected when a wire brush is pushed through a punched hole in the card and contacts the metal roller just below the card. Most card readers contain two such sets of 80 wire reading brushes. As a card passes

PUNCHED-CARD INPUT/OUTPUT

Punched-card Readers

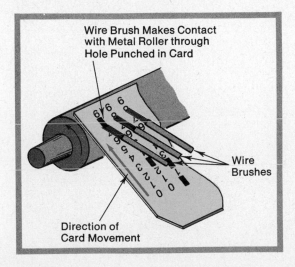

Wire Brush Makes Contact with Metal Roller through Hole Punched in Card

Wire Brushes

Direction of Card Movement

FIG. 5-3
Wire Brush Card Reader.

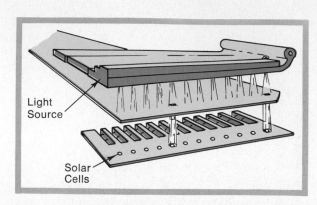

FIG. 5-4

Photoelectric Card Reader.

under the first set of 80 brushes (read-check station), a hole count is taken; that is, the number of punches in the card are determined and held for checking purposes. The card then moves under a second set of 80 brushes (read station), where the punched card is read, the hole count from the read-check station verified, and the data contained on the card are transferred electrically into the computer.

Photoelectric card readers differ from wire-brush card readers in two basic ways. In photoelectric card readers, cards are read column by column, and a light source and light-sensing unit are used to detect the punched holes (Fig. 5-4).

Card-punching Devices
The IBM 2540 Card Read Punch illustrated in Fig. 5-6 is actually two machines in one. The right half of the machine is a card reader

FIG. 5-5

IBM 3505 Card Reader.

FIG. 5-6
IBM 2540 Card Read/Punch Unit.

and the left half of the machine is a card-punch unit. At the direction of the computer or other controlling device, it will punch data onto blank cards which are housed in the *punch hopper.* Punch verification is accomplished in the same manner as was read verification in the wire-brush-type card reader. As a blank card passes under the first station containing 80 punching dies, it is punched row by row. The card then moves to the second station, where it is read by 80 wire brushes to check the accuracy of the punching dies. If an error is detected, the machine stops and an error light comes on; otherwise the card is dropped into a stacker below.

The speed of card-punch devices ranges from punching 50 cards per minute to a maximum of about 500 cards per minute. Card punches are generally not equipped for interpreting the punched output, as this process is too costly. If desired, the punched cards produced by the card punch can be processed through an Interpreter.

The card punch is utilized in many business concerns to produce two-part punched-card bills or invoices, one part of the invoice to be retained by the customer and the second part to be returned to the company, where it will be fed back into the computer together with the customer's payment record for additional processing.

SELF-STUDY EXERCISES 5-2

1. The heavy use of punched-card readers and punches as input/
   output devices can be attributed to _____.

   *****

   the advantages of the punched card as an input medium and
   the fact that the punched-card reader can be used with a computer system of any size

2. The two general types of punched-card readers and punches
   are the _____ type and the _____ type.

   *****

   wire-brush

   photoelectric

3. The principal differences between wire-brush and photoelectric readers or punches are _____.

   *****

Wire brush	Photoelectric
a. All 80 columns are read simultaneously.	a. Card is read column by column.
b. Punched holes are detected by a wire brush contacting a metal roller.	b. Punched holes are detected by light-sensing solar cells which detect light passing through the punched holes.

   FIG. 5-7

   IBM Model 3800 Laser Printer.

   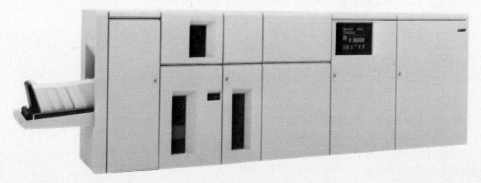

4. Verification of reading and punching operations is _____.

*****

automatic

5. Card punches are generally not equipped for interpreting punched output because _____.

*****

it is too costly

PRINTERS

Of all the output devices used in business, the printer is the most common. It provides the user with a permanent visual record of the data output from the computer. It is one of the few output devices capable of producing business reports and documents. Printers have been developed that are capable of printing from 150 to 2500 lines per minute, with each line consisting of as many as 150 characters. A quick calculation will reveal this to be a maximum printing speed of over 6000 characters per second.

Printers can print on ordinary paper or on specially prepared forms such as invoices, labels, and other special-purpose forms used in the operation of a business (see Figs. 5-8, 5-9, 5-10, 5-11). Printers even fulfill the needs of business for accuracy and speed in printing on card documents such as checks, earnings statements, premium notices, and bills.

Printers can be subdivided into two broad categories: impact and nonimpact, with impact printers being the most common. An impact printer is one in which printing occurs as a result of the impact of a character form striking against an inked ribbon, causing the ribbon to press an image of the character onto paper. This can be done one character at a time or one line at a time.

Character-printing Devices

Typewriters and teletypewriters print one character at a time at maximum speeds of 10 to 70 characters per second, respectively. Another and faster such printer is the wire-matrix printer. It prints characters made up of a pattern of dots formed by the ends of small wires arranged in 5×7 rectangle. By extending certain wires beyond the others, dot patterns can be created which give the appearance of a number, letter, or special character (Fig. 5-13). This character is then pressed against an inked ribbon to print the character. There are 47 usable dot patterns.

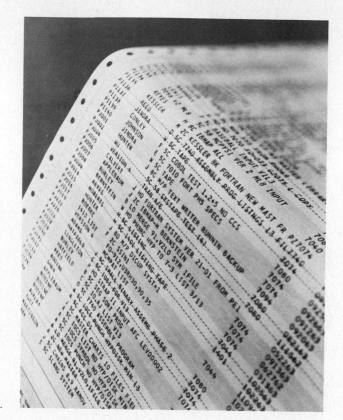

FIG. 5-8
Ordinary Paper Listing.

Line-printing Devices   Impact printers capable of printing a line at a time employ a moving print chain or print wheels (Fig. 5-14). The print-wheel printer consists of a series of print wheels, each containing a full complement of numerals and alphabetic symbols in addition to a set of special characters. At the time of printing, all print wheels are correctly positioned to represent the data to be printed on one line and then impacted simultaneously at a speed of 150 lines per minute.

The print-chain printer is the fastest and most commonly used of all impact printers. As the print chain, containing five 48-character sections, revolves horizontally, each character is printed as it comes into position. Up to 150 characters per line can be printed at speeds of up to 2500 lines per minute.

Nonimpact printers, xerographic, electronic, or laser are the fastest of all printers. The IBM 3800 Laser printer, for example is capable of printing at over 12,000 lines per minute (see Fig. 5-7). Prior to the release of the IBM 3800, printers of this type were not heavily used for several reasons:

1. Special and more expensive paper is required.
2. Printed output is not as sharp or clear as with impact printers.
3. Only one copy can be printed at a time.
4. Output cannot be easily and satisfactorily copied on office copiers.

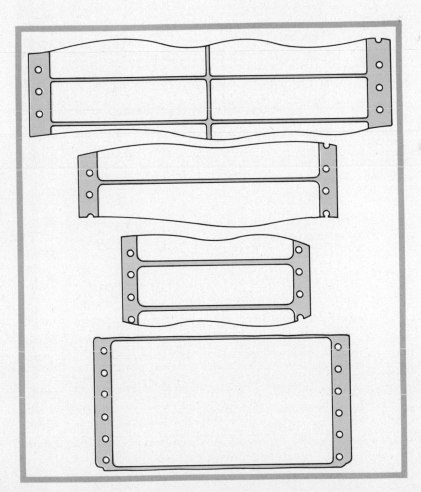

FIG. 5-9
Standard Label Forms.

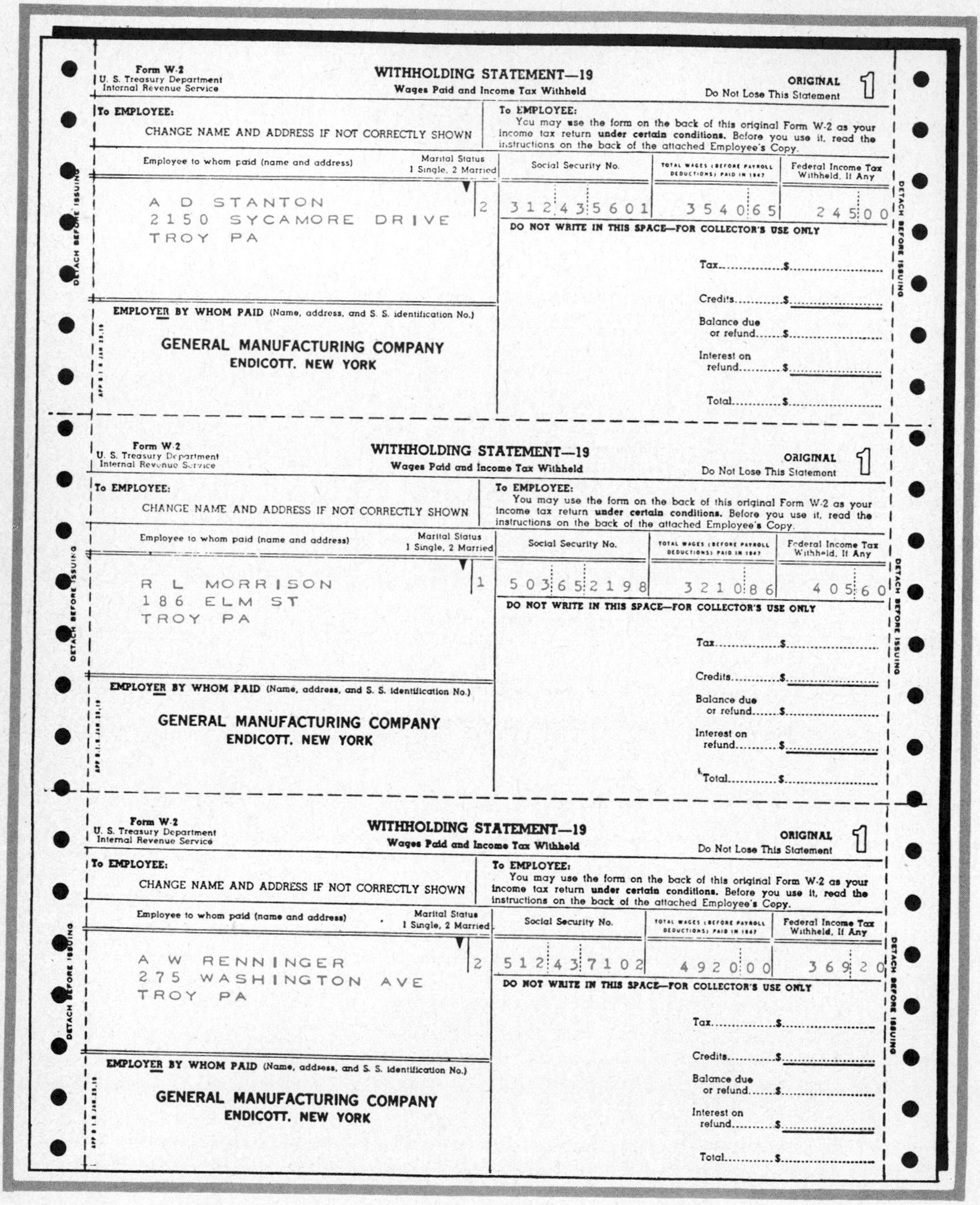

Form W-2
U. S. Treasury Department
Internal Revenue Service

WITHHOLDING STATEMENT—19
Wages Paid and Income Tax Withheld

ORIGINAL 1
Do Not Lose This Statement

To EMPLOYEE:
CHANGE NAME AND ADDRESS IF NOT CORRECTLY SHOWN

To EMPLOYEE:
You may use the form on the back of this original Form W-2 as your income tax return **under certain conditions.** Before you use it, read the instructions on the back of the attached Employee's Copy.

Employee to whom paid (name and address)	Marital Status 1 Single, 2 Married	Social Security No.	TOTAL WAGES (BEFORE PAYROLL DEDUCTIONS) PAID IN 1947	Federal Income Tax Withheld, If Any
A D STANTON 2150 SYCAMORE DRIVE TROY PA	2	312 43 5601	3540 65	245 00

DO NOT WRITE IN THIS SPACE—FOR COLLECTOR'S USE ONLY

Tax..........$..........
Credits..........$..........
Balance due or refund..........$..........
Interest on refund..........$..........
Total..........$..........

EMPLOYER BY WHOM PAID (Name, address, and S. S. identification No.)

GENERAL MANUFACTURING COMPANY
ENDICOTT, NEW YORK

DETACH BEFORE ISSUING

Form W-2
U. S. Treasury Department
Internal Revenue Service

WITHHOLDING STATEMENT—19
Wages Paid and Income Tax Withheld

ORIGINAL 1
Do Not Lose This Statement

To EMPLOYEE:
CHANGE NAME AND ADDRESS IF NOT CORRECTLY SHOWN

To EMPLOYEE:
You may use the form on the back of this original Form W-2 as your income tax return **under certain conditions.** Before you use it, read the instructions on the back of the attached Employee's Copy.

Employee to whom paid (name and address)	Marital Status 1 Single, 2 Married	Social Security No.	TOTAL WAGES (BEFORE PAYROLL DEDUCTIONS) PAID IN 1947	Federal Income Tax Withheld, If Any
R L MORRISON 186 ELM ST TROY PA	1	503 65 2198	3210 86	405 60

DO NOT WRITE IN THIS SPACE—FOR COLLECTOR'S USE ONLY

Tax..........$..........
Credits..........$..........
Balance due or refund..........$..........
Interest on refund..........$..........
Total..........$..........

EMPLOYER BY WHOM PAID (Name, address, and S. S. identification No.)

GENERAL MANUFACTURING COMPANY
ENDICOTT, NEW YORK

DETACH BEFORE ISSUING

Form W-2
U. S. Treasury Department
Internal Revenue Service

WITHHOLDING STATEMENT—19
Wages Paid and Income Tax Withheld

ORIGINAL 1
Do Not Lose This Statement

To EMPLOYEE:
CHANGE NAME AND ADDRESS IF NOT CORRECTLY SHOWN

To EMPLOYEE:
You may use the form on the back of this original Form W-2 as your income tax return **under certain conditions.** Before you use it, read the instructions on the back of the attached Employee's Copy.

Employee to whom paid (name and address)	Marital Status 1 Single, 2 Married	Social Security No.	TOTAL WAGES (BEFORE PAYROLL DEDUCTIONS) PAID IN 1947	Federal Income Tax Withheld, If Any
A W RENNINGER 275 WASHINGTON AVE TROY PA	2	512 43 7102	4920 00	369 20

DO NOT WRITE IN THIS SPACE—FOR COLLECTOR'S USE ONLY

Tax..........$..........
Credits..........$..........
Balance due or refund..........$..........
Interest on refund..........$..........
Total..........$..........

EMPLOYER BY WHOM PAID (Name, address, and S. S. identification No.)

GENERAL MANUFACTURING COMPANY
ENDICOTT, NEW YORK

DETACH BEFORE ISSUING

FIG. 5-10
W-2 Continuous Forms.

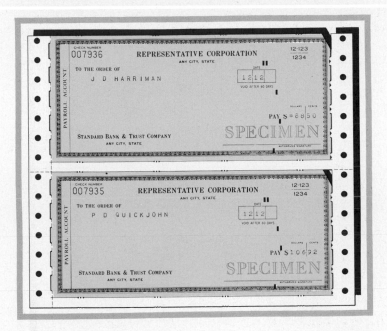

FIG. 5-11
Payroll Check
Continuous Forms.

FIG. 5-12
Character-printing Devices (Teletypewriter
and Printer-
keyboard Typewriter).

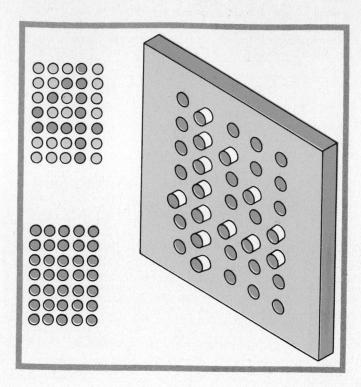

FIG. 5-13

Arrangement of Wire-matrix Dot
Patterns for the Digit 4.

SELF-STUDY EXERCISES 5-3

1. Printers are capable of printing on _____.

    *****

    plain paper, specially prepared paper forms, and on specially
    prepared card documents

2. The two categories of printers are _____ and _____.

    *****

    impact
    nonimpact

3. Impact printers are classified according to _____. The re-
    sulting classifications are _____.

    *****

    the number of characters printed at one time
    character printers and line printers

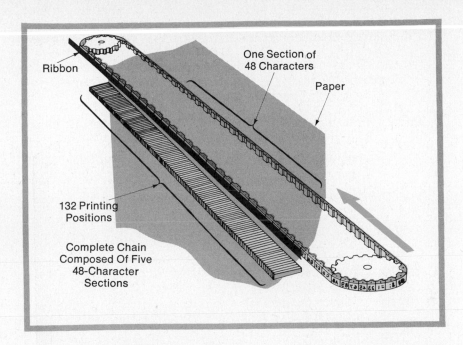

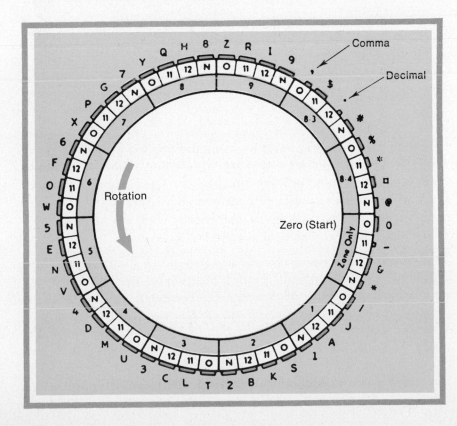

FIG. 5-14
Print Chain and
Print Wheel.

4. Examples of character printers are _____.
*****

typewriters, teletypewriters, and wire-matrix printers

5. Impact line printers contain the character sets on either _____ or _____ with the _____ printer being one of the fastest and most commonly used of all printers.
*****

print wheels
a print chain
print chain

6. The fastest of all possible printers is the _____.
*****

xerographic or electronic nonimpact printer

7. The principal disadvantages of nonimpact printers are _____.
*****

They are more expensive, less clear, capable of printing only single copies, and difficult to copy clearly

CHARACTER READERS

Character readers are capable of accepting printed or written characters from source documents and converting these data into a computer-acceptable code for processing. This process can take place at maximum speeds of approximately 1000 documents per minute. The two basic types of character readers are magnetic-ink character readers and optical scanners.

Magnetic-ink Character Readers

The concept of *magnetic-ink character recognition* (MICR) was first developed by the Stanford Research Institute for use by the world's largest bank, the Bank of America. This system was designed to directly read data prerecorded on checks and deposit slips and then automatically sort the checks and deposit slips by the characters found in these prerecorded data. The data are prerecorded on the checks and deposit slips with a special ferrite-impregnated ink which has a magnetic characteristic. This magnetic character-

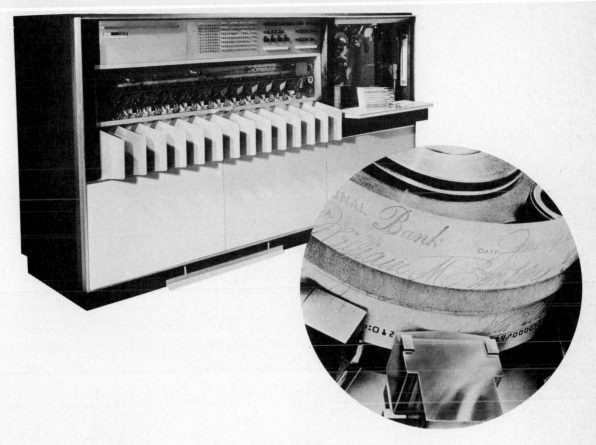

FIG. 5-15

IBM 1419 Magnetic Character Reader and Magnetic Character Reading.

istic can be detected and interpreted by MICR equipment, allowing the input document to be mechanically processed.

In Fig. 5-16 you see a canceled check containing, along the bottom, data relating to the individual bank's assigned number, the customer's account number, and the amount of the check. The amount field is, of course, coded by the bank at the time the check is received for payment.

Optical Scanners

Optical scanners can convert data from a printed source document directly to a machine-recognizable form. Current applications of optical scanning include utility billing, insurance premium notice, and charge sales invoices. Even in their infancy, optical scanners

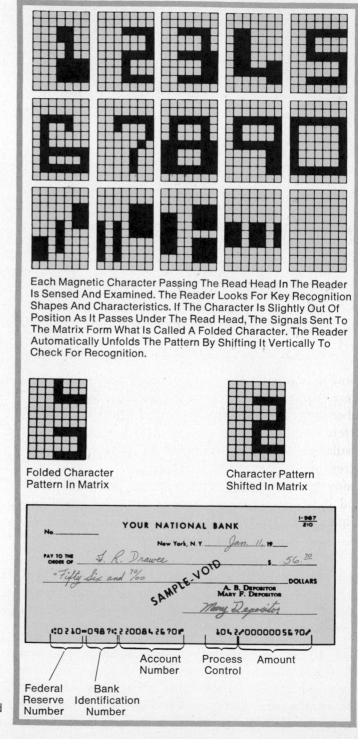

Each Magnetic Character Passing The Read Head In The Reader Is Sensed And Examined. The Reader Looks For Key Recognition Shapes And Characteristics. If The Character Is Slightly Out Of Position As It Passes Under The Read Head, The Signals Sent To The Matrix Form What Is Called A Folded Character. The Reader Automatically Unfolds The Pattern By Shifting It Vertically To Check For Recognition.

Folded Character
Pattern In Matrix

Character Pattern
Shifted In Matrix

Federal
Reserve
Number

Bank
Identification
Number

Account
Number

Process
Control

Amount

FIG. 5-16

Magnetic-ink Characters and a Typical Application.

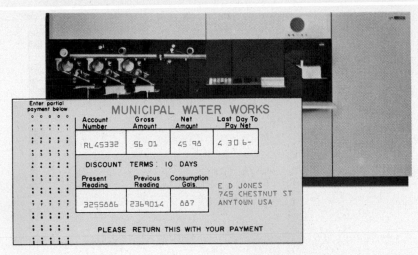

FIG. 5-17

IBM 1287 Optical Scanner.

show promise for greatly reducing, if not ultimately eliminating the need to convert any source document onto punched cards or other input media. Presently such devices are not used to a greater extent because of the poor reliability of character interpretation resulting from source-document typewriter inconsistencies, erasures, etc. Eventually, technological improvements and design innovations should eliminate these problems and permit broad and extensive application of optical character recognition techniques in automated data processing.

SELF-STUDY EXERCISES 5-4

1. Character readers interpret _____ or _____ characters from source documents and _____.

*****

printed

written

convert these data to a machine-readable form

2. The two general types of character readers are _____ and
_____.

*****

magnetic-ink character readers
optical scanners

3. Documents to be read by magnetic-ink readers must be recorded using a special _____.

*****

ferrite-impregnated ink with special magnetic characteristics

4. The main factor responsible for the limited use of optical scanners is _____.

*****

poor reliability

**TAPE
INPUT/OUTPUT**

**Punched-paper-
tape Devices**

Punched-paper-tape readers were among the first input devices
to be used with a computer. Punched-paper-tape readers, like
punched-card readers, are available with wire-brush or photoelectric sensing devices. Modern punched-paper-tape readers operate
at speeds ranging from 200 to 1000 characters per second, with
those utilizing photoelectric reading generally being the fastest.
Information recorded on paper tape can be easily and quickly
transmitted over telephone and telegraph wires at speeds of 150
characters per second. Should it be necessary to transmit data long
distances and where the data are already recorded on another input
medium (for example, punched cards), the data can be converted
by machine from the punched card to punched paper tape and
transmitted over telephone or telegraph wires to produce a duplicate punched paper tape. This punched paper tape is then converted to punched cards or other media. While punched cards
can be transmitted directly, it is often more economical to first convert the data onto punched paper tape and transmit the paper tape.

A paper tape punch can also be used as a computer output
device. In this capacity, the paper tape punch accepts data from the
computer, converts them to a paper tape code, and punches them
onto blank tape. The accuracy of paper tape reading and punching
operations is checked in the same manner as it was for the punched

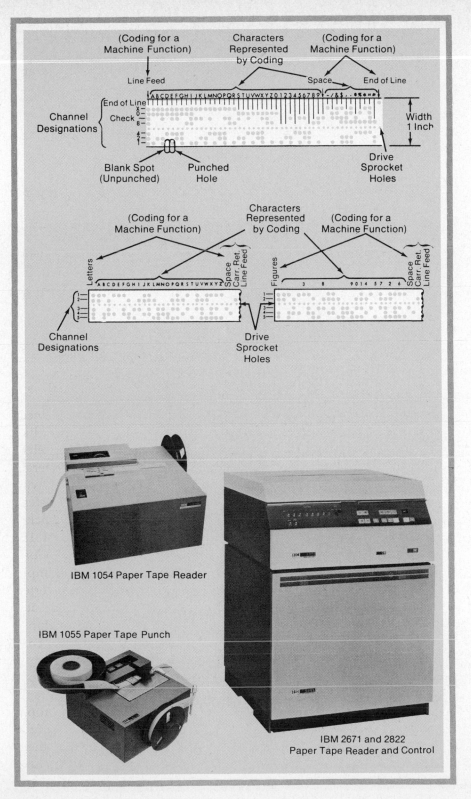

FIG. 5-18

Punched-paper-tape Media and Devices.

173

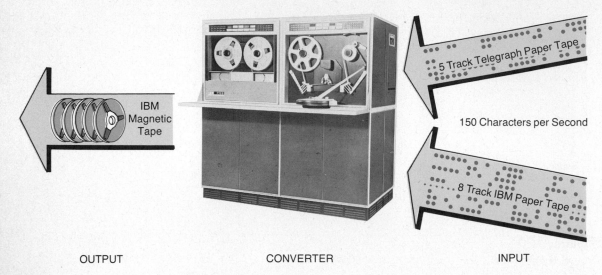

OUTPUT CONVERTER INPUT

FIG. 5-19
Data Conversion—
Paper Tape to
Magnetic Tape.

card. The process of punching paper is, however, a relatively slow process (15 to 150 characters per second) when compared to the recording speeds of other output media. This, coupled with the fact that punched paper tape is easily torn and the fact that it does not lend itself to additions and deletions, are the principal reasons punched paper tape has not become a more widely used output medium. There are, however, industries which do rely on the use of punched paper tape. One such area is the newspaper industry. In this industry, computer-produced punched paper tapes are used to control the operations of paper milling machines, punch presses, etc. It is also utilized by small computer users, as it is relatively inexpensive to use (.25 cents per foot) and is far less bulky than punched cards. In the manufacturing industry, however, many companies utilize punched Mylar tape, a much more durable but more expensive plastic-like material.

Magnetic-tape Devices
Magnetic tape is one of the principal input/output recording media used with computers and is principally used for storing interme- diate results of computations and for compact storing of large amounts of data, in an ordered sequence. This is because of its very high speed, mass storage capability, compact size, and relative low cost of operation. The IBM 2400 series magnetic tape units, for example, are capable of reading or writing in excess of 300,000

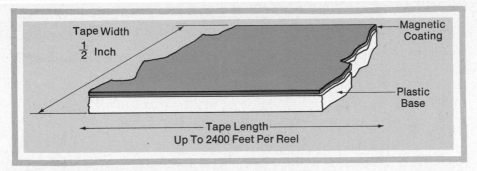

FIG. 5-20
Composition of Magnetic Tape.

characters per second. This is extremely fast when compared to a card reader, which is capable of reading a maximum of approximately 1500 characters per second, or a high-speed impact printer capable of printing a maximum of approximately 6000 characters per second. This, coupled with the fact that as many as 1600 characters can be stored in 1 inch of magnetic tape, has been responsible for the wide use of magnetic tape as an input/output medium.

The magnetic-tape device functions as both an input and output unit and may be operated under the control of the computer (on-line) or independently (off-line) to perform routine functions such as card-to-tape, tape-to-card, and tape-to-printer conversions.

Data are recorded on magnetic tape as magnetized spots called *bits*. Once recorded, data can be retained indefinitely, or recorded data can be automatically erased and the tape reused. The manner in which data are generally recorded on tape is similar in appearance to the way they are recorded on a card. That is, the rows on

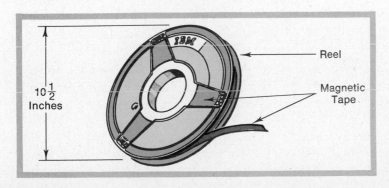

FIG. 5-21
Reel of Magnetic Tape.

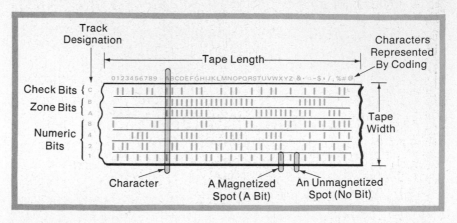

FIG. 5-22

Data Coded on a Section
of 7-Track Magnetic Tape.

a card correspond to the horizontal positions on a tape (tracks), and one character is represented by one vertical column on a card and one vertical column on a magnetic tape (refer to Fig. 5-24). The coding schemes used to represent characters on tape is, however, somewhat different from the punched-card code. It is more closely related to the manner in which data are stored within the computer, thus contributing to the input/output speeds attainable with magnetic tape.

There are also some disadvantages associated with the use of magnetic tape, such as the fact that data must be stored and accessed sequentially, and that data required to update a tape *file*[1] must be sorted into the same sequential order as the tape file before the update can take place. In addition, if the updating of a magnetic tape file involves the addition of new records or accounts or the deletion of old ones, it is usually necessary to completely recopy the tape file.

Key-to-tape Recorders   **Magnetic Reel Tape Writers.** Until the mid 1960s, if data were to be recorded on tape, they were first recorded onto punched cards and then converted from cards, with or without the use of a computer, to magnetic tape. Today, however, with the aid of recently

---

[1]See Appendix A for a definition of a file.

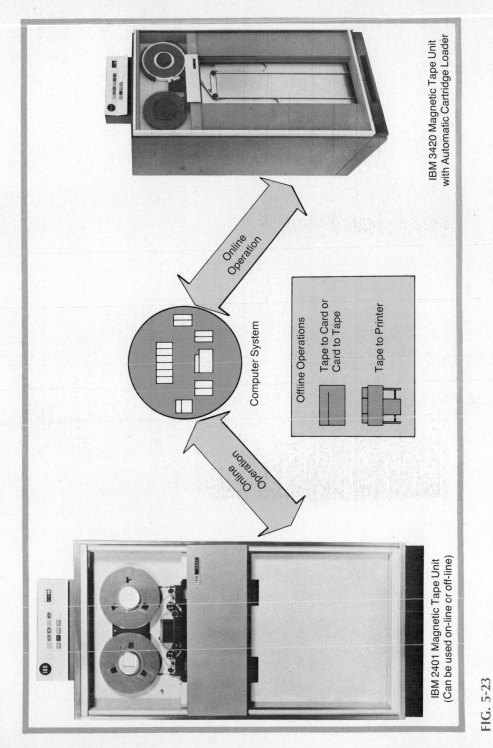

IBM 3420 Magnetic Tape Unit
with Automatic Cartridge Loader

Online Operation

Computer System

Offline Operations

Tape to Card or
Card to Tape

Tape to Printer

Online Operation

IBM 2401 Magnetic Tape Unit
(Can be used on-line or off-line)

FIG. 5-23
IBM Magnetic-tape Units with On-line and Off-line Capabilities.

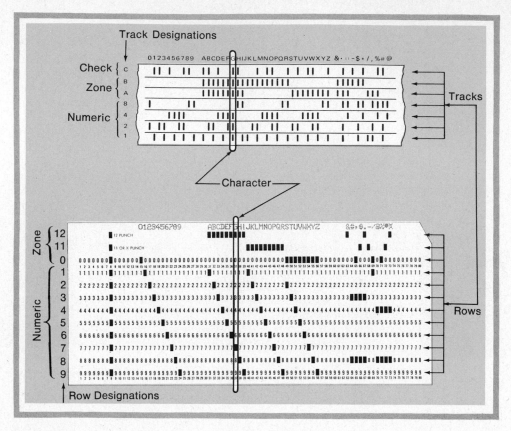

FIG. 5-24

Recording Similarities Between Punched Card
and 7-Track Magnetic Tape.

developed reliable key-to-tape and key-to-disk devices, data can
be recorded directly onto a reel of magnetic tape or magnetic disk
from original source documents or source data.

The NCR 735 Magnetic Tape Encoder, for example, records
directly onto magnetic tape. Keying accuracy is verified by placing
the tape into a magnetic-tape verifier and the original data retyped,
as is done in the case of punched-card verification. Magnetic-tape
encoders and verifiers are generally housed in the same physical
unit. Any errors detected are corrected by simply erasing the mistakes and substituting the correct character(s).

FIG. 5-25
Key-to-tape Recorder.

SELF-STUDY EXERCISES 5-5

1. The two kinds of tape media currently used are _____ and
   _____ .

                    *****

                punched paper tape
                  magnetic tape

2. _____ is an efficient medium for transmission over telephone and telegraph wires.
                    *****

                Punched paper tape

3. Accuracy of paper tape reading and punching is verified in a
   manner similar to the way verification is performed on the
   reading and punching of _____ .
                    *****

                  punched cards

4. The disadvantages of using punched paper tape are _____ .
                    *****

   punching and reading take place at relatively slow speeds, it
   does not facilitate additions and deletions, and it is easily torn

5. _____ is similar to punched paper tape but is much more durable.

*****

Punched Mylar tape

6. _____ is the highest speed and most efficient tape medium.

*****

Magnetic tape

7. Some of the advantages of using magnetic tape are _____.

*****

its mass storage capacity, high speed, compact size, and low cost of operation

8. Data are recorded on magnetic tape as magnetized spots called _____ in a manner similar to that in which data are recorded on _____.

*****

bits (binary digits)
punched cards

9. Some of the disadvantages associated with the use of magnetic tape as an input or output medium are _____.

*****

data must be accessed sequentially, additions and deletions generally require that the entire file be recopied, and data to be used to update a magnetic-tape file must be in the same sequence as the original file

10. Until recently it was only possible to record data on tape by first recording it on cards and then converting it from cards to tape; however, it is now possible to _____.

*****

record data directly onto magnetic tape via key-to-tape recorders

The terminal is one of the more recent and most rapidly growing additions to the family of input/output devices. Terminals are used to facilitate two-way communications with the CPU or with other terminals located from a few feet to thousands of miles apart. Thus, with the aid of a terminal, a user can access a computer physically located a great distance away. Some of the functions that can be performed using terminals include the following:

TERMINALS

1. Message switching—The communication of information input at one terminal to one or more remote terminals. The teletype system used by police departments to communicate with one another represents such a function.

2. Data collecting—Data are input to one or more terminals and stored for subsequent processing. This eliminates the need to record the information on a source document, to keypunch the information from the source document, and to read the punched card into the computer (see Fig. 5-26).

FIG. 5-26
IBM 1092 Programmed Keyboard for Use in Data Collecting.

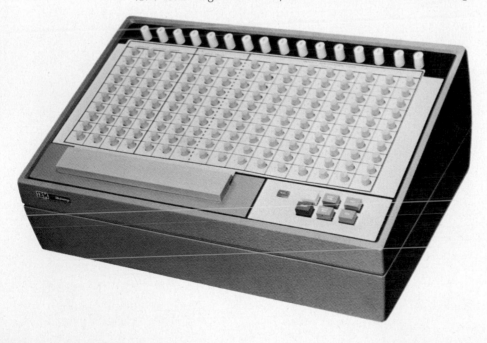

3. Inquiry or transaction processing—Data stored in central data files can be accessed from remote terminals for the purpose of updating these files or to determine the answer to inquiries relating to information stored in these files. The system employed by most airlines to maintain and update flight information is an example of such a function. A terminal used in a hospital information system is shown in Fig. 5-27.

4. Remote job processing—Programs can be input from remote terminals directly to the CPU for processing. After execution, the results can be transmitted back to the terminal or to one or more other terminals for output (see Fig. 5-28).

Keyboard Devices   There are many types of terminals currently on the market with new ones appearing on the scene daily. One of the least expensive and most common type or terminal is of the keyboard variety, similar in operation to a conventional typewriter, but capable of being used to perform any of the above listed functions. Since data must

FIG. 5-27

Patient Records Being Updated Using a CRT Terminal.

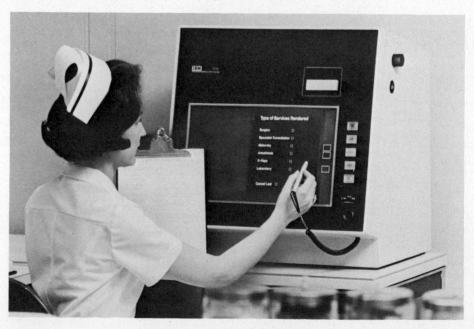

FIG. 5-28
IBM 3780 Remote Job
Processing Terminal.

be keyed into these devices one character at a time, the possibility of error is high and the data transmission rate very low, thus limiting the use of console keyboards to small volume input and inquiries. With proper communication links, inquiry keyboards can be located at great distances from the central processing unit.

It is often desirable to have many keyboard input units with the capability of simultaneously communicating with the processing unit. In an automated banking operation, for example, each teller

FIG. 5-29
Teletype 4210 Magnetic Tape Data Terminal.

may require a separate input unit with file inquiry capabilities. This type of operation can be provided with a relatively small and inexpensive computer. Honeywell, for example, provides their Teller Terminal Series, an on-the-counter, on-line banking system which can be used to process all teller-assigned bank transactions. This system operates in conjunction with the Honeywell 200, a powerful small-scale computer. The Teller Register contains a modular, removable Teller Register Printer designed to print on the journal tape and customer's record simultaneously. A locked supervisor's panel is also available by which the teller supervisors can initialize the Register. Figure 5-30 illustrates such a terminal in use with an IBM computer system.

Visual Display Devices

A visual display terminal might be described as a combination typewriter and television set (Fig. 5-31). By means of the keyboard, a terminal operator can type or key information directly into the computer and receive replies which are pictured on a CRT (cathode-ray tube) display tube. The visual display terminal, therefore, serves as both an input device and an output device.

Transmission speeds to and from the computer and the terminal can be in excess of 2000 characters per second. If the terminal is located at a great distance from the computer, data keyed in at

FIG. 5-30
IBM Teller Register.

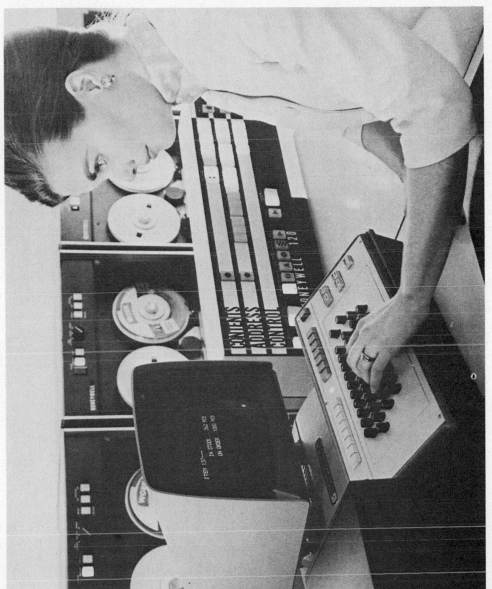

FIG. 5-31

Honeywell Type 303 Display Station.

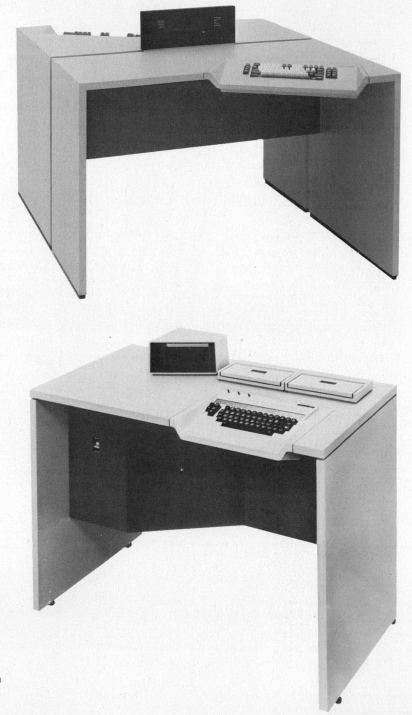

FIG. 5-32

Two of IBM's More Modern
Looking Desk Display
Terminals.

the terminal can be transmitted over telephone lines to the computer at speeds of over 200 characters per second.

Visual display stations such as the Honeywell Type 303 Display Station (Fig. 5-31) are capable of displaying typed information, bar graphs, tables and numerous other forms of visual output. Visual display stations are presently in use in airline reservation offices for the purpose of accepting inquiries about available seats on scheduled airline flights and to display the computer's answer in a matter of seconds; commercial banks to accept inquiries concerning the status of a customer account, possibly displaying the history of that account from several years past up to and including the instant the inquiry is made; and stock-exchange brokerage houses across the country to provide local offices with up-to-the-minute quotations of stock prices useful to customers. This list could go on and on, for as soon as one can jot down an application of a visual display station, another application is created. Figure 5-32 illustrates two of IBM's more modern desk display stations.

The IBM 2250 Display Unit (Fig. 5-33) is capable of displaying tables, graphs, charts, circuit diagrams, and alphanumeric data on a square screen containing over 1,000,000 display points. It is equipped with a *light pen* or penlike device which can be used by the operator to identify a particular point or character displayed on the screen, and can be used alone or in conjunction with a keyboard to add, rearrange, or delete information which is displayed on the screen.

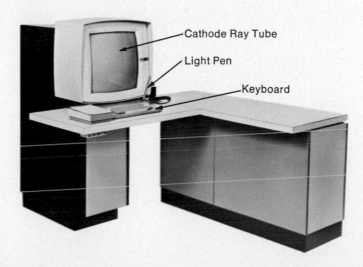

Cathode Ray Tube

Light Pen

Keyboard

FIG. 5-33
IBM 2250 Model 3 Graphical
Display Unit.

OTHER INPUT/OUTPUT DEVICES

Film Devices

Devices such as the IBM 2282 Film Recorder/Scanner (Fig. 5-34) provide the ability to record alphanumeric and graphic computer output directly onto microfilm which can then be internally developed and displayed on a built-in viewing screen 22.8 inches square. It will also accept graphic data input from microfilm.

Audio Devices

In today's automated world it is even possible to obtain voice response to inquiries made from telephone or similar types of terminals. In the IBM 7772 Audio Response Unit, for example, the audio response is composed from a prerecorded vocabulary, selected from the most frequently used words associated with commercial and industrial applications, contained on an external disk file. As an inquiry is received by the 7772, it is sent to the computer for decoding. The computer then decodes and evaluates the inquiry and, from the prerecorded vocabulary on disk, constructs an appropriate digitally coded voice message which is sent back to the Audio Response Unit. The IBM 7772 then converts this message to a vocal reply which is "spoken" to the inquirer.

Plotters

Figure 5-36 illustrates a relatively small and inexpensive device which can be used to create plots accurate to .05 inches from data recorded on magnetic or punched paper tape. This device may also be used to create a magnetic or punched paper tape from a specially prepared plot placed on the device.

Plotters are also available for use in automated drafting with plotting surfaces in excess of 50 square feet and costing as much as a small computer system.

SELF-STUDY EXERCISES 5-6

1. The operation of a console keyboard is similar to _____.
   *****

   a conventional typewriter

2. Console keyboards can be used for _____.
   *****

   program testing, program or data alterations, inquiries, and to enter data directly into processor storage

Rear Projection
Screen

IBM 2282 Film Recorder/Scanner
As Used with IBM 2250 Display Unit Model 2

FIG. 5-34
Film I/O Units.

FIG. 5-35
IBM 7772 Audio Response Unit.

3. The disadvantages of console keyboards are _____.
*****

   high input error rate and low transmission rate

4. Visual display terminals are capable of displaying _____.
*****

   typed information, graphs, tables, etc.

5. CRT (_____) terminals are similar in operation to the ordinary home _____.
*****

   cathode-ray tube
   television tube

6. Film recorders provide the capability of recording alphanumeric and graphic computer output directly onto _____.
*****

   microfilm

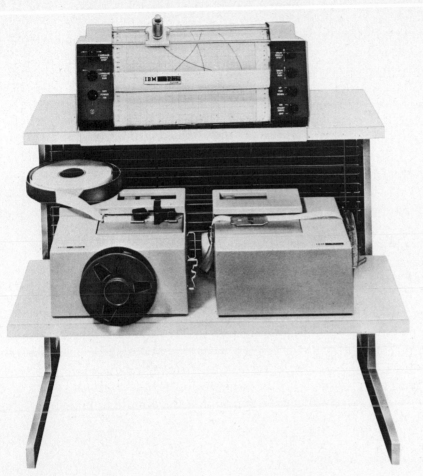

FIG. 5-36
IBM 1627 Plotter Off-line
with Paper Tape Input.

7. Devices which facilitate voice communications with a computer system are called _____.

*****

audio devices

8. When an audio device receives a "spoken" request for information it _____.

*****

decodes and evaluates the inquiry, and from a prerecorded vocabulary on disk, constructs and sends back an appropriate digitally coded voice message

INPUT/OUTPUT COMMUNI- CATIONS There are a number of ways computer manufacturers have attempted to solve the problem of slow input/output devices, which cause the processing unit to have to continually wait, reducing the efficiency of the entire computer system, and the problem of expanding the capabilities of a computer system to handle more and more input/output devices. Their attempts have resulted in the implementation of a concept known as overlapped processing.

Overlapped Processing* All data-processing applications involve the operations of input, processing, and output, with each of these operations requiring a specific amount of time for its completion. The time required to completely solve a problem, then, will be a combination of the times required to complete each of the above operations. The total required time, however, will be heavily dependent on what is meant by a combination of the times required to complete each operation. If, for example, only one of these operations could be performed at a time, the total required time for the completion of the job would be the sum of the times required to complete each input, processing, and output operation (nonoverlapped processing). Figure 5-37 illustrates how this might take place. In this illustration you will notice that only three input-processing-output cycles were possible in the time period represented. In Fig. 5-38, however, in the same time period it was possible to perform more

FIG. 5-37

Nonoverlapped Processing.

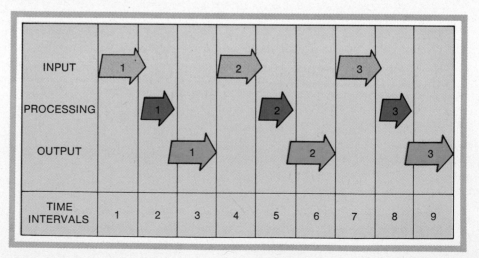

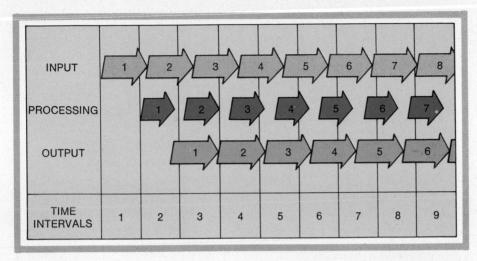

FIG. 5-38
Overlapped Processing.

than seven input-processing-output cycles. This was accomplished by performing more than one operation at a time (overlapped processing). As you can clearly see, overlapped processing is more efficient than nonoverlapped processing. It is for this reason that most computers today employ overlapped processing.

You are probably wondering how it is possible for a computer to do more than one thing at a time. The answer is relatively simple. Attached to the computer are special devices, called *channels,* that control the input/output operations, thereby freeing the processing unit to perform other operations. Thus, at a given time, one channel can be controlling an input operation while a second channel is controlling an output operation and the computer is possibly performing an arithmetic calculation. A computer system may have many channels attached to it, with each channel being responsible for controlling several input or output devices. Figure 5-39 illustrates one of many possible arrangements and uses of channels.

What actually takes place between the input/output device, the channel, and the computer is as follows. Let us assume that we wish to read some data from cards, perform a detailed calculation, and output the results. To begin with, the channel would cause the input device to read one or more cards and store their contents in a temporary storage location, called a *buffer.* This operation can be

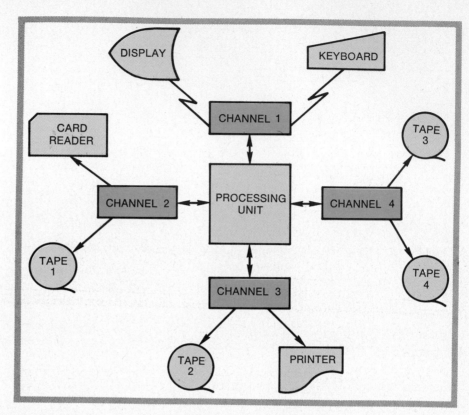

FIG. 5-39

Schematic of Overlapped Processing Computer System Configuration.

performed while the computer is busy with another operation. When these data are needed for processing, they will be called for by, and transferred to, the processing unit at a very rapid rate. While these data are being processed in the processing unit, the channel is causing the buffer to be filled for ready availability. When the processing of the previously read data has been completed, the computer will cause these output data to be rapidly transferred, via another channel, to an output buffer, from which location the channel will control the slower operation of printing, thus freeing the processing unit to accept more data from the input buffer via its channel and begin processing these data. What we have, then, is a condition where the relatively slow operations of reading cards and printing are controlled by the channels, allowing the processing unit to communicate only with the channels at high

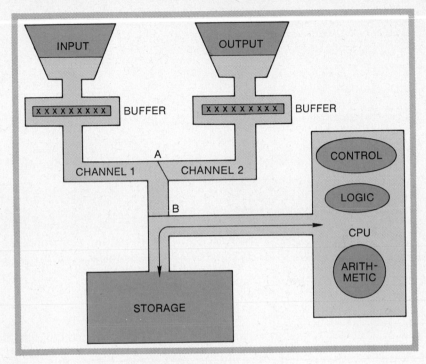

FIG. 5-40

Schematic of Overlapped Processing Computer System Employing Input/Output Buffering.

speeds. In this manner the processing unit is operating as much as possible and is not constantly waiting for the card reader or the printer to become available.

SELF-STUDY EXERCISES 5-7

1. _____ is one of the methods presently employed to solve the problem of slow input/output devices and increase the overall efficiency of a computer system.

*****

Overlapped processing

2. The concept of overlapped processing involves _____.

*****

the performing of more than one operation at a time

3. The special devices which facilitate overlapped processing are called _____.

*****

channels

4. The function of the channel is to _____.

*****

control an input and/or output operation, thereby freeing the processing unit to perform other operations

5. In an overlapped processing operation, data are not read directly from the input medium and stored in the computer's memory but are read and first stored in a temporary location called a _____.

*****

buffer

6. After data have been read and stored in the buffer they can then be _____.

*****

called into the computer at high speeds when they are needed and the processor is available

7. Information to be output in an overlapped-processing system is _____.

*****

transferred to the buffer at high speed and stored until the output device is free and can output the data stored in the buffer

EXERCISES

5-1 True-false exercises

1. _____ Card readers generally have a brush for each row of the card.

2. _____ Input devices convert data into a form that the computer can understand, and output devices convert machine code into a form human beings can understand.

3. _____ A typewriter is an example of a nonimpact printing device.

4. _____ Business applications of the computer require large amounts of data but relatively few computations.

5. _____ Printers are considered the most common output device because they provide for hard copy output.

6. _____ Magnetic-tape devices operate at high speeds yet provide the user with a low-cost medium for storing information.

7. _____ Input/output devices may be described as peripheral equipment.

8. _____ The paper tape is as bulky as the punched card for the same amount of data storage.

9. _____ The most common and fastest type of printer is the nonimpact printer.

10. _____ The CRT terminal provides for both inquiry and response via the keyboard in the case of input data and via the display tube in the case of output data.

11. _____ Channel buffers are storage locations used by the computer to perform minor arithmetic and logic operations.

12. _____ Punched cards are used only by small and medium-sized computer systems.

13. _____ The brushes used for error checking on card reader-punches are called validity brushes.

14. _____ The console keyboard enables high-speed interaction with the central processor.

15. _____ The wire-matrix printer is a nonimpact printing device.

16. _____ Overlapped processing combines the input, processing, and output operations so as to increase the speed with which input is converted to useful output.

17. _____ Channels communicate with both input/output devices and the processing unit.

18. _____ The most commonly used type of terminal has a keyboard similar to that of an ordinary typewriter.

19. _____ Optical scanners convert data from a printed source document directly to a machine-recognizable form.

20. _____ Terminals may be used to access computers thousands of miles away.

21. ____ A disadvantage of printers is their inability to accept different form sizes.

22. ____ Photoelectric card readers read data row by row off the input card.

23. ____ Punched-paper-tape devices were among the first input/output devices to be used with computers.

24. ____ Transmission speeds of the visual display device is dependent on its distance from the computer.

25. ____ Updating a magnetic-tape file does not require that the input files be in the same ordered sequence.

26. ____ Magnetic tapes are economical in that they are a reusable storage medium.

27. ____ One example of a high-speed input/output device is the card reader-punch.

28. ____ A wide variation of paper sizes and types are available for use on computer printers.

29. ____ A key-to-tape recorder may be used to record information directly on magnetic tape.

5-2 Multiple-choice exercises

1. ____ Of the following, the fastest printing device is
   (a) the teletypewriter
   (b) the print-wheel printer
   (c) the print-chain printer
   (d) the nonimpact printer
   (e) the tape-controlled printer

2. ____ The input device used to convert printed source documents into machine code is
   (a) a card reader
   (b) an interpreter
   (c) a teletypewriter
   (d) a console
   (e) an optical scanner

3. ____ The machine that reads paper-tape input and writes the output on magnetic tape is called a
   (a) an input/output or I/O machine
   (b) a tape reader/writer

(c) a converter

(d) a reader and control

(e) none of the above

4. _____ The principal difference between the impact printer and the nonimpact printers is

(a) accuracy

(b) versatility

(c) speed

(d) all the above

(e) (b) and (c)

5. _____ A device that cannot be used for both input and output is a

(a) magnetic-disk unit

(b) magnetic-tape unit

(c) card reader-punch unit

(d) paper-tape reader-punch unit

(e) printer

6. _____ A CRT display device is similar to

(a) a typewriter

(b) a television tube

(c) a telephone

(d) (a) and (b)

(e) all the above

7. _____ Punched-paper-tape devices

(a) are used to control machines

(b) operate at speeds between 200 and 1000 bytes per second

(c) are ideal for transmitting data over telephone lines

(d) all the above

(e) (b) and (c) only

8. _____ The term used to describe the simultaneous operation of input, output, and processing is

(a) overlapped processing

(b) concurrent processing

(c) teleprocessing

(d) channel processing

(e) none of the above

9. _____ Of the following media, which can store the most information in a given amount of space?

(a) paper tape-5 bit

(b) punched cards

(c) paper tape–8 bit

(d) magnetic tape

(e) Mylar punched tape

10. ____ A characteristic of magnetic tape is
    (a) large storage capacity
    (b) low cost
    (c) high speed
    (d) compact size
    (e) all the above

11. ____ The most common form of input device is
    (a) paper tape
    (b) card reader
    (c) magnetic tape
    (d) card punch
    (e) none of the above

12. ____ Optical character readers have seen only limited use because
    (a) they are too slow
    (b) they have poor reliability
    (c) the ink is much too expensive
    (d) they are much too expensive for what they do
    (e) there is no such machine

13. ____ Peripheral devices concern themselves with
    (a) input only
    (b) output only
    (c) both (a) and (b)
    (d) processing only
    (e) (a), (b), and (d)

14. ____ Channels allow data to flow to the central processing unit at
    (a) low speed
    (b) high speed
    (c) average speed
    (d) varying speeds
    (e) none of the above

5-3 Problems

1. Discuss the contribution of input and output devices to the overall performance of a computer system.

2. Compare the similarities and differences of punched paper tape and magnetic tape. Point out the advantages and disadvantages of each.

3. Compare impact and nonimpact printers with respect to their similarities and differences. Point out the advantages and disadvantages of each.

4. What are the two types of card readers? Discuss their differences.

5. Describe the essential hardware elements necessary to facilitate over-lapped processing. Why is overlapped processing advantageous?

6. Discuss any recent input or output devices about which you have heard or read. What do you believe to be their potential?

7. Discuss some of the prime considerations which should be given to the types of input/output devices needed in a computer system.

8. Determine whether each of the devices and/or media listed below are used for input only, output only, input/output, or an off-line device.
   (a) card readers
   (b) card punches
   (c) card reader-punch
   (d) printer
   (e) teletypewriter
   (f) paper-tape reader
   (g) paper-tape punch
   (h) magnetic tape
   (i) console
   (j) optical scanners
   (k) graphical display devices
   (l) magnetic-ink character readers
   (m) paper tape-to-magnetic tape converter
   (n) key-to-tape devices
   (o) film devices
   (p) audio devices

ITEMS FOR DISCUSSION

Peripheral Device
Media
Card Punches
Photoelectric Card Readers
Wire-brush Card Readers
Punched-paper-tape Devices
Magnetic-tape Devices
Mylar Tape
Density
File
Key-to-tape Recorders
Terminals

Impact Printers
Character Printers
Line Printers
MICR
Optical Scanners
Visual Display Devices
Film Devices
Audio Devices
Plotters
Overlapped Processing
Buffer
Channel

COMPUTER
NUMBER SYSTEMS

We have learned that computers deal extensively with numbers and numerical quantities. It is also true that internally computers operate on numbers and numerical quantities which are represented in a form other than in the traditional decimal number system. It is, therefore, appropriate that we continue our study with a brief analysis of number systems.

WHAT IS A NUMBER SYSTEM? Before we can discuss the different number systems used in modern-day computers, we must first answer the question: What is a number system?

Briefly stated, a number system is a method for representing quantities of physical items. The method is a very simple one which is based on and dependent upon a fixed set of weights. To understand this concept, let us consider the hypothetical example of a butcher who sells meat by the pound, employing a simple balance scale. Let us assume that the butcher has available nine weights each of 1 pound, 10 pounds, and 100 pounds. Given the above, how could the butcher weigh out 208 pounds of beef?

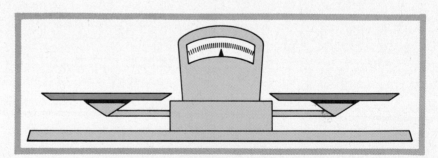

FIG. 6-1
Simple Balance Scale.

First, he could select a combination of available weights which together would equal 208 pounds. This could be accomplished with two 100-lb weights, no 10-lb weights, and eight 1-lb weights:

$$2 \ 100\text{-lb} + 0 \ 10\text{-lb} + 8 \ 1\text{-lb}$$

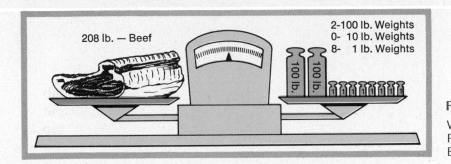

FIG. 6-2

Weighing Out 208
Pounds on a Simple
Balance Scale.

The clerk might then write down the combination as

$$2-0-8$$

for the sake of brevity, realizing that each of these digits represents the quantity of weights used in decreasing order of value. That is, the 2 refers to the number of 100-lb weights, the 0 refers to the number of 10-lb weights, and the 8 refers to the number of 1-lb weights. As the merchant became more familiar with this system, he may even denote the same total as 208, omitting the dashes.

And, we recognize this to be the decimal notation for 208. We also know it to be

$$(2 \times 100) + (0 \times 10) + (8 \times 1)$$

which we shall refer to as the *expanded form* of the number. Therefore, we have the relationship that

$$208 = (2 \times 100) + (0 + 10) + (8 \times 1)$$

In a similar manner, any decimal number could be represented by a combination of weights, related in that the smallest weight is one (1) and successive weights are found by multiplying 10 times the previous weight. That is,

$$\text{or} \quad \begin{matrix} 1, & 10 \times 1, & 10 \times (10 \times 1), & 10 \times (10 \times (10 \times 1)), & \text{etc.} \\ 1, & 10, & 100, & 1000, & \text{etc.} \end{matrix}$$

Since deca means ten, and the weights in this system result from multiplications by 10, this system became known as the base

10 or decimal system. This kind of a system is also termed a *positional* or *place-value number system* in that the actual value of a specific digit in a number is determined by (1) the place that the digit holds in the number and (2) by the value of the digit itself. In the number 30303, for example, there are three 3's, each having a different value since each is associated with a different weight. Writing out the expanded form of this number, we have

$$30303 = (3 \times 10{,}000) + (0 \times 1{,}000) + (3 \times 100)$$
$$+ (0 \times 10) + (3 \times 1)$$

It is now more easily seen that the position of the first 3 gives it a total value of 30,000, while the position of the second 3 gives it a total value of 300, and similarly the position of the third 3 gives it a total value of 3.

We can now more clearly understand our number system and why it is called a positional or place-value number system and why it is given the name decimal number system.

It should also be clear that the decimal number system has two distinctive features: (1) the 10 digits 0, 1, 2, 3, 4, 5, 6, 7, 8, and 9 and (2) weights which are derived from multiplication by 10.

SELF-STUDY EXERCISES 6-1

1. A number system is _____.

*****

a method for representing quantities of physical items

2. A positional or place-value number system is one in which _____.

*****

the value of a given digit within a number is determined by the place the digit holds and by the value of the digit itself

3. The expanded form of the decimal number 4821 is _____.

*****

$$(4 \times 1000) + (8 \times 100) + (2 \times 10) + (1 \times 1)$$

4. The decimal number system has the distinctive features that
_____.

*****

it utilizes the digits 0 through 9 and a set of weights which are
derived from multiplications by 10

Let us now consider a place-value number system with only the
two digits 0 and 1 and with a set of weights which are derived from
multiplications by 2. We shall call this number system the binary
or base 2 number system. The weights would then be explicitly
determined as follows:

**THE BINARY
NUMBER SYSTEM**

. . .	2×16	2×8	2×4	2×2	2×1	1
. . .	32	16	8	4	2	1

Using these weights, the decimal number 13 could be represented as follows:

$$13 = (1 \times 8) + (1 \times 4) + (0 \times 2) + (1 \times 1)$$

You will note that each positional weight is determined by multiplying 2 times the previous one, since the base of this system is
2 (see Table 6-1).

As an additional example, let us consider the binary representation of the decimal number 43. What we need to do, then, is to
select a combination of binary weights which, when added together, equal but do not exceed 43:

BINARY WEIGHTS	DECISION TO ACCEPT OR REJECT	CUMULATIVE TOTAL
128	No	0
64	No	0
32	Yes	32
16	No	32
8	Yes	40
4	No	40
2	Yes	42
1	Yes	43

Summarizing, we have

$$43 = (1 \times 32) + (0 \times 16) + (1 \times 8) + (0 \times 4)$$
$$+ (1 \times 2) + (1 \times 1)$$

Using the place-value notation previously discussed, we have

$$101011 = (1 \times 32) + (0 \times 16) + (1 \times 8) + (0 \times 4)$$
$$+ (1 \times 2) + (1 \times 1)$$

But 101011 could be misinterpreted as meaning one hundred one-thousand eleven. To eliminate this confusion, one inserts a small 2 just after, and slightly below, the rightmost digit of the number to denote that it is a binary or base 2 number. Consistent with this notation, any nondecimal number will contain a small digit to the right of, and just below, the rightmost digit in that number. Decimal numbers are written as usual, without any such digit to indicate the base in which the number is written. The above binary number would then be written

$$101011_2$$

Given a number in this notation, it is a simple matter to determine what its equivalent would be in the decimal or base 10 number system. This is accomplished by assigning to each digit in the binary number its appropriate weight. We begin by assigning the weight of 1 to the rightmost or *low order* bit (binary digit). Each subsequent digit is assigned a weight equal in value to twice or double the weight assigned to the previous digit.

For the binary number 101011_2, this procedure would appear as follows:

Binary digits	1	0	1	0	1	1_2					
Weights	32	16	8	4	2	1					
Decimal value	32	+	0	+	8	+	0	+	2	+	1	=	43

As an added illustration, let us determine the decimal equivalent of the binary number 101011010_2:

TABLE 6-1

Binary Equivalents of Decimal Numbers

DECIMAL VALUE			VALUE IN BINARY NUMBER SYSTEM						
100	10	1	64	32	16	8	4	2	1
		1							1
		2						1	0
		3						1	1
		4					1	0	0
		5					1	0	1
		6					1	1	0
		7					1	1	1
		8				1	0	0	0
		9				1	0	0	1
	1	0				1	0	1	0
	1	1				1	0	1	1
	1	2				1	1	0	0
	1	3				1	1	0	1
	1	4				1	1	1	0
	1	5				1	1	1	1
	1	6			1	0	0	0	0
	1	7			1	0	0	0	1
	1	8			1	0	0	1	0
	1	9			1	0	0	1	1
	2	0			1	0	1	0	0
	2	1			1	0	1	0	1
	2	2			1	0	1	1	0
	2	3			1	0	1	1	1
	2	4			1	1	0	0	0
	2	5			1	1	0	0	1
	2	6			1	1	0	1	0
	2	7			1	1	0	1	1
	2	8			1	1	1	0	0
	2	9			1	1	1	0	1
	3	0			1	1	1	1	0
	3	1			1	1	1	1	1
	3	2		1	0	0	0	0	0
	3	3		1	0	0	0	0	1
	3	4		1	0	0	0	1	0
	3	5		1	0	0	0	1	1
	3	6		1	0	0	1	0	0
	3	7		1	0	0	1	0	1
	3	8		1	0	0	1	1	0
	3	9		1	0	0	1	1	1
	4	0		1	0	1	0	0	0

Binary digits	1	0	1	0	1	1	0	1	0_2
Weights	256	128	64	32	16	8	4	2	1
Decimal value	$256 + 0 + 64 + 0 + 16 + 8 + 0 + 2 + 0 = 346$								

At this point, we realize that we can represent a given quantity of objects using either the decimal or binary number systems just as we can have the same value of money in two different currencies. And, as we would have to understand the French monetary system to do business in France, so must we have a working knowledge of the binary number system to do business with an individual who calculates in binary.

You ask, who calculates in binary? The answer is, no person, but a thing, a computer. Computers, in general, operate in binary, and to understand the working of a computer one must understand the binary number system. As was illustrated above, a number expressed in the binary number system can also be expressed in the decimal system. Similarly, there is a correspondence between the numbers in any one number system and the numbers in any other number system. Therefore, as long as the basic rules of arithmetic are observed, the result of any calculation or series of calculations will lead to equivalent results.

SELF-STUDY EXERCISES 6-2

1. The base 2 number system is called the _____ and employs the digits _____ and weights of _____.
*****
binary number system
0 and 1
1, 2, 4, 8, 16, 32, etc.

2. The expanded form of the binary number 10111 is _____.
*****

$$(1 \times 16) + (0 \times 8) + (1 \times 4) + (1 \times 2) + (1 \times 1)$$

3. To indicate that 1101 is a binary number, one would _____.

*****

place a small 2 just after and slightly below the rightmost digit in the number giving in this case 1101_2

4. The decimal equivalent of the binary number 1101_2 is _____.

*****

Binary digits	1	1	0	1_2
Binary weights	8	4	2	1

Decimal value	8	4	0	1	=	13

5. The binary equivalent of 42 is _____.

*****

Binary weights	32	16	8	4	2	1		
Decision	Yes	No	Yes	No	Yes	No	=	101010_2
Cumulative total	32	32	40	40	42	42		

6. Computers generally operate in the _____ system.

*****

binary

7. Calculations involving _____ numbers in different bases will yield _____ results.

*****

equivalent
equivalent

We know that the result of any calculation is independent of the number system employed, as long as we obey the basic laws of arithmetic. Therefore, a computer should utilize that number system which is most convenient and which can be made to operate most rapidly and efficiently.

WHY NOT BASE 10?

Naturally, the decimal number system is the most convenient for us, since we are most familiar with this system. In the previous illustration, we demonstrated that $101011010_2 = 346$. It would appear that the decimal system is also more efficient, as only three decimal digits were required to represent this quantity in the decimal number system, while nine bits or binary digits were required to represent the same quantity in the binary number system.

Why, then, with these advantages of the decimal system, do computers utilize the binary number system? The answer is a simple one. Designers and engineers can design or develop computers that are faster and much less expensive utilizing the binary number system than if they were to utilize the decimal number system in an otherwise comparable computer. Computer designers have also realized that utilizing the binary system will result in a computer which is significantly more reliable (many fewer components) and significantly smaller.

SELF-STUDY EXERCISES 6-3

1. Computers employ number systems which _____.

*****

can be made to operate most rapidly and efficiently

2. The number system which lends itself to inexpensive implementation and efficient operations is the _____ number system.

*****

binary

OTHER CURRENTLY USED NUMBER SYSTEMS*   In addition to utilizing the binary number system, computers also make use of two other number systems, the base 8 or octal number system and the base 16 or hexadecimal number system. A unique relationship between the binary number system and these two number systems makes them suitable for use in a computer. This relationship will become apparent later.

In the octal system (Table 6-2) there are eight digits, 0, 1, 2, 3, 4,   **Octal**
5, 6, and 7, and a set of weights based on powers of eight. The
octal weights are determined as follows:

· · ·	8×512	8×64	8×8	8×1	1
· · ·	4096	512	64	8	1

Using these weights, the decimal number 15 could be represented as follows:

$$15 = (1 \times 8) + (7 \times 1)$$

In place-value form, this would be

$$15 = 17_8$$

Converting from octal to decimal utilizing the expanded form,
we have

Octal digits	1	7_8		
Weights	8	1		
Decimal value	8	+	7	=	15

Let us consider the more comprehensive problem of determining the decimal equivalent of 1521_8:

Octal digits	1	5	2	1_8	
Weights	512	64	8	1	
Decimal value	512	+ 320	+ 16	+ 1	= 849

As an additional example, let us consider the octal number
532_8:

Octal digits	5	3	2_8	
Weights	64	8	1	
Decimal value	320	+ 24	+ 2	= 346

But we have seen the number 346 before. We have seen this
number to be equivalent to the binary number 101011010_2. We

TABLE 6-2

Octal Equivalents of Decimal Numbers

DECIMAL VALUE			VALUE IN OCTAL			
100	10	1	512	64	8	1
		1				1
		2				2
		3				3
		4				4
		5				5
		6				6
		7				7
		8			1	0
		9			1	1
	1	0			1	2
	1	1			1	3
	1	2			1	4
	1	3			1	5
	1	4			1	6
	1	5			1	7
	1	6			2	0
	1	7			2	1
	1	8			2	2
	1	9			2	3
	2	0			2	4
	2	1			2	5
	2	2			2	6
	2	3			2	7
	2	4			3	0
	2	5			3	1
	2	6			3	2
	2	7			3	3
	2	8			3	4
	2	9			3	5
	3	0			3	6
	3	1			3	7
	3	2			4	0
	3	3			4	1
	3	4			4	2
	3	5			4	3

have, therefore, that

$$346 = 532_8 \quad \text{and} \quad 346 = 101011010_2$$

Examining these two representations for the decimal number 346, we see a very interesting and unique relationship. That is,

$$5 \quad 3 \quad 2_8 \quad \text{(octal equivalent of 346)}$$
$$101 \quad 011 \quad 010_2 \quad \text{(binary equivalent of 346)}$$

Starting from the units or low order side of each number, you will notice that a group of three binary digits is equal in value to one octal digit. That is,

$$010_2 = (0 \times 4) + (1 \times 2) + (0 \times 1) = 2_8$$
$$011_2 = (0 \times 4) + (1 \times 2) + (1 \times 1) = 3_8$$
$$101_2 = (1 \times 4) + (0 \times 2) + (1 \times 1) = 5_8$$

In general, conversions from one system to another are not this simple. The exception in this case is due to the fact that there is a whole power relationship between these bases, that is,

$$2^3 = 2 \times 2 \times 2 = 8$$

Simple and rapid conversions, such as the one illustrated, will exist between numbers when the bases in which the numbers are represented have such a whole power relationship. Moreover, the relationship between the number of digits in one system which corresponds to one digit in the other system will exactly match the relationship between their bases. That is, since three 2's must be multiplied together to produce one 8, three binary digits will be required to equal one octal digit. A complete list of all octal-to-binary digits is given in Table 6-3.

Let us consider several more such conversions.

1. $10110010100_2 = ?$ (octal equivalent)

X10	110	010	100₂	(binary number)
2	6	2	4₈	(octal equivalent)

$$10110010100_2 = 2624_8$$

TABLE 6-3	
Binary-to-Octal Conversions	
BINARY DIGITS	OCTAL DIGIT
000	0
001	1
010	2
011	3
100	4
101	5
110	6
111	7

Note that since the binary number did not split evenly into groups of three bits each, an X or leading zero was assigned to fill in the last or leftmost group. These conversions can be verified with the aid of Table 6-3.

2. $3157_8 = ?$ (binary equivalent)

3	1	5	7_8	(octal number)
011	001	101	111_2	(binary equivalent)

$3157_8 = 11001101111_2$ (eliminating the leading zero)

Hexadecimal   In dealing with the hexadecimal number system, a new problem arises. We know that there should be 16 digits but we are only familiar with the 10 decimal digits 0, 1, 2, 3, 4, 5, 6, 7, 8, and 9. Therefore, we must create 6 additional symbols to represent the 6 additional hexadecimal digits. Traditionally, the symbols chosen and their representations are A, B, C, D, E, and F, where A = 10, B = 11, C = 12, D = 13, E = 14, and F = 15. The 16 basic hexadecimal digits then are 0, 1, 2, 3, 4, 5, 6, 7, 8, 9, A, B, C, D, E, and F.

Let us now consider the hexadecimal number $3B_{16}$. To convert such a number to its decimal equivalent we proceed as we have in the past with binary and octal conversions. That is, we express

TABLE 6-4

Hexadecimal Equivalents of Decimal Numbers

DECIMAL VALUE			HEXADECIMAL VALUE		
100	10	1	256	16	1
		1			1
		2			2
		3			3
		4			4
		5			5
		6			6
		7			7
		8			8
		9			9
	1	0			A
	1	1			B
	1	2			C
	1	3			D
	1	4			E
	1	5			F
	1	6		1	0
	1	7		1	1
	1	8		1	2
	1	9		1	3
	2	0		1	4
	2	1		1	5
	2	2		1	6
	2	3		1	7
	2	4		1	8
	2	5		1	9
	2	6		1	A
	2	7		1	B
	2	8		1	C
	2	9		1	D
	3	0		1	E
	3	1		1	F
	3	2		2	0
	3	3		2	1
	3	4		2	2
	3	5		2	3

$3B_{16}$ in the expanded form utilizing the 16 hexadecimal digits and the hexadecimal weights. The hexadecimal weights are determined as follows:

· · ·	16×256	16×16	16×1	1
· · ·	4096	256	16	1

Employing these weights, we see that the hexadecimal number $3B_{16}$ becomes

$$3B_{16} = (3 \times 16) + (B \times 1)$$

and since $B = 11$, we have

$$3B_{16} = (3 \times 16) + (11 \times 1) = 59$$

Let us consider the slightly more involved problem of determining the decimal equivalent of $15A_{16}$:

Hexadecimal digits	1	5	A_{16}
Weights	256	16	1
Decimal value	256 +	80 +	A = 346 (since A = 10)

TABLE 6-5

Binary-to-Hexadecimal Conversions

BINARY DIGITS	HEXADECIMAL DIGITS
0000	0
0001	1
0010	2
0011	3
0100	4
0101	5
0110	6
0111	7
1000	8
1001	9
1010	A
1011	B
1100	C
1101	D
1110	E
1111	F

Thus,

$$15A_{16} = 346$$

And, since $2^4 = 2 \times 2 \times 2 \times 2 = 16$, we know that there is a relationship between binary and hexadecimal similar to the relationship between binary and octal. Also, since it takes four 2's multiplied together to equal 16, we know that the relationship between binary digits and hexadecimal digits will be 4:1. A complete list of the binary-to-hexadecimal digit conversions is given in Table 6-5. Utilizing this table we can convert the hexadecimal number $15A_{16}$ to its binary equivalent. We see from this table that

$$1_{16} = 0001_2 \quad 5_{16} = 0101_2 \quad A_{16} = 1010_2$$

Combining these and eliminating leading zeros we have

$$15A_{16} = 101011010_2$$

Let us consider two additional examples.
1. $1011010111011001_2 = ?$ (hexadecimal equivalent)

1011	0101	1101	1001	(binary number)
B(11)	5	D(13)	9	(hexadecimal equivalent)

Therefore, $1011010111011001_2 = B5D9_{16}$.

2. $13A4F_{16} = ?$ (binary equivalent)

1	3	A(10)	4	F(15)	(hexadecimal number)
0001	0011	1010	0100	1111	(binary equivalent)

Eliminating leading zeros we have

$$13A4F_{16} = 10011101001001111_2$$

Let us begin our analysis by considering a hypothetical situation. Suppose that we have a child seated at a table with 25 pencils, several pieces of string, and a small box placed on the table in front of him.

CONVERSIONS FROM DECIMAL*

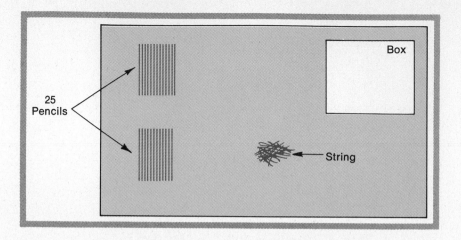

Let us also suppose that we instruct the child to perform a series of simple steps.

> Step 1. Pick up two pencils and tie them together. Repeat this tying process until either all pencils have been tied into bundles of two pencils each, or until only one pencil remains unbundled on the table. If one pencil remains, place it in the box.

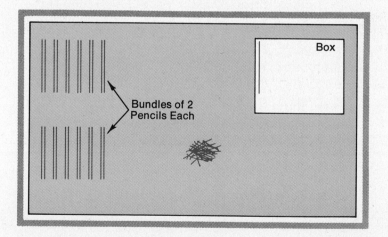

> Step 2. Pick up two bundles and tie them together. Repeat this tying process until either all previous bundles have been tied into larger bundles or until only one small bundle remains. If one small bundle remains, place it in the box.

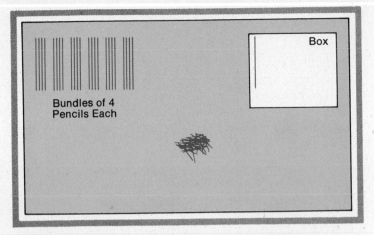

Step 3. Repeat step 2. This would result in

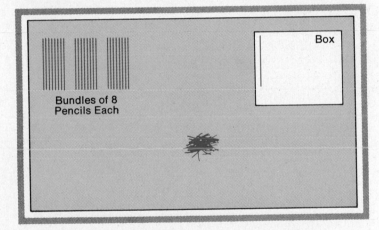

Step 4. Repeat step 2. This would result in

Step 5. Repeat step 2. This would result in

You ask: What does such a process have to do with number systems? To answer this question, let us examine the results of each step in a somewhat less elaborate form.

	PENCILS ON THE TABLE	DISCARDS INTO THE BOX
Initially	25 unbundled pencils	
After step 1	12 bundles, 2 pencils each	1 unbundled pencil
After step 2	6 bundles, 4 pencils each	0 bundles, 2 pencils each
After step 3	3 bundles, 8 pencils each	0 bundles, 4 pencils each
After step 4	1 bundle, 16 pencils	1 bundle, 8 pencils
After step 5	0 bundles, 32 pencils	1 bundle, 16 pencils

Since, at the end of this process, there are no individual pencils or bundles of pencils on the table, it follows that all the original 25 pencils have been discarded into the box. Therefore, if we sum the number of pencils discarded at each step, we should have all the original pencils, or 25 pencils:

$$
\begin{array}{llr}
1 \text{ unbundled pencil} & = & 1 \text{ pencil} \\
0 \text{ bundles, 2 pencils each} & = & 0 \text{ pencils} \\
0 \text{ bundles, 4 pencils each} & = & 0 \text{ pencils} \\
1 \text{ bundle, 8 pencils} & = & 8 \text{ pencils} \\
1 \text{ bundle, 16 pencils} & = & 16 \text{ pencils} \\
\hline
& \textit{Total} = & 25 \text{ pencils}
\end{array}
$$

Or, stated in a slightly different manner,

$$25 = (1 \times 16) + (1 \times 8) + (0 \times 4) + (0 \times 2) + (1 \times 1)$$

But we also recognize this to be the expanded form of the binary number 11001_2.

If we examine the steps leading to this result, we willl see that this bundling process is, in actuality, a division process, or *algorithm*. This process is illustrated below.

$$2\overline{)25}$$

12   remainder 1

$$2\overline{)12}$$

6   remainder 0

$$2\overline{)6}$$

3   remainder 0

$$2\overline{)3}$$

1   remainder 1

$$2\overline{)1}$$

0   remainder 1

Combining steps, we have

$$2\overline{)25}$$
$$2\overline{)12} \quad 1$$
$$2\overline{)\ 6} \quad 0$$
$$2\overline{)\ 3} \quad 0$$
$$2\overline{)\ 1} \quad 1$$
$$0 \quad 1$$

We also see that the remainders from this division process, recorded from the bottom to the top, reveal that

$$25 = 11001_2$$

Similarly, by repeatedly dividing by 8 until a quotient of zero is obtained, and recording the remainders from the bottom to the top, one can determine the base 8 or octal equivalent of 25.

$$8\overline{)25}$$
$$8\overline{)3} \quad 1$$
$$0 \quad 3$$

Therefore, $25 = 31_8$.

Let us consider a more involved problem such as determining the octal equivalent of 2834:

$$8\overline{)2834} \quad \text{remainders}$$
$$8\overline{)354} \quad 2$$
$$8\overline{)44} \quad 2$$
$$8\overline{)5} \quad 4$$
$$0 \quad 5$$

Therefore, $2834 = 5422_8$ since again we read the remainders from the bottom to the top.

Employing the same process, but dividing by 16, we can obtain the hexadecimal equivalent of 28:

$$16\overline{)28} \quad \text{remainders}$$
$$16\overline{)1} \quad 12 = C$$
$$0 \quad 1$$

Therefore, $28 = 1C_{16}$. Let us consider the more involved exercise of determining the hexadecimal equivalent of 37469:

$$16\overline{)37469}$$
$$16\overline{)2341} \quad 13 = D$$
$$16\overline{)146} \quad 5$$
$$16\overline{)9} \quad 2$$
$$0 \quad 9$$

Therefore, $37469 = 925D_{16}$. It is recommended, however, in cases such as this where the division is reasonably extensive, that the division steps be done off to the side using long division. In this way, unnecessary division errors can be avoided.

We have seen that this *remainder system*, or *division algorithm*, applies to problems of converting decimal numbers to equivalent octal and hexadecimal numbers. The division algorithm is also applicable to converting decimal numbers to equivalent numbers in any other number system.

SELF-STUDY EXERCISES 6-4

1. Number systems other than binary used in modern computers are the _____ and _____ number systems.

*****

octal

hexadecimal

2. The octal number system is based on weights which are _____ and employs the digits _____.

*****

multiples of eight

0, 1, 2, 3, 4, 5, 6, and 7

3. In converting a number from octal to its decimal equivalent, one makes use of the _____.

*****

expanded form

4. The expanded form of the octal number 1372_8 is _____.

*****

$$1372_8 = (1 \times 512) + (3 \times 64) + (7 \times 8) + (2 \times 1)$$

5. The decimal equivalent of the octal number 1372_8 is _____.

*****

$$1372_8 = (1 \times 512) + (3 \times 64) + (7 \times 8) + (2 \times 1)$$

$$= \quad 512 \quad + \quad 192 \quad + \quad 56 \quad + \quad 2$$
$$= \quad 762$$

6. Any octal number can be quickly converted to its binary equivalent by equating _____ to each octal digit.

*****

three binary digits

7. The binary equivalent of the octal number 1372_8 is _____.

*****

1	3	7	2_8
001	011	111	010_2

8. The octal equivalent of the binary number 11011101011_2 is _____.

*****

X11	011	101	011_2
3	3	5	3_8

9. The hexadecimal number system is based on weights which are _____ and employs the digits _____.

*****

multiples of 16
0, 1, 2, 3, 4, 5, 6, 7, 8, 9, A, B, C, D, E, and F

10. The hexadecimal digits A, B, C, D, E, and F are equivalent to the decimal numbers _____.

*****

10, 11, 12, 13, 14, and 15, respectively

11. The decimal equivalent of the hexadecimal number $1A3_{16}$ is _____.

*****

$$1A3_{16} = (1 \times 256) + (A \times 16) + (3 \times 1)$$
$$= \quad 256 \quad + (10 \times 16) + \quad 3$$

$$= \quad 256 \quad + \quad 160 \quad + \quad 3$$

$$= \quad 419$$

12. Any hexadecimal number can be quickly converted to its binary equivalent by equating _____ to each hexadecimal digit.

*****

four binary digits

13. The binary equivalent of the hexadecimal number $8C5F_{16}$ is _____.

*****

$$
\begin{array}{cccc}
8 & C & 5 & F_{16} \\
1000 & 1100 & 0101 & 1111_2
\end{array}
$$

14. The hexadecimal equivalent of the binary number 11010010110101_2 is _____.

*****

$$
\begin{array}{cccc}
XX11 & 0100 & 1011 & 0101 \\
3 & 4 & B & 5_{16}
\end{array}
$$

15. The rule for converting a number from decimal to another base is _____.

*****

to repeatedly divide the decimal number by the base to which it is to be converted until a 0 (zero) quotient is obtained, recording the remainders from each successive division. These remainders, recorded from the last to the first, represent the equivalent of the decimal number in the new base.

16. Employing this rule, the binary equivalent of the decimal number 30 is _____.

*****

$$
\begin{array}{ll}
2\overline{)30} & \\
2\overline{)15} & 0 \\
2\overline{)7} & 1
\end{array}
$$

$$2 \overline{)3} \quad 1 \qquad 30 = 11110_2$$

$$2 \overline{)1} \quad 1$$

$$0 \quad 1$$

17. Employing the same procedure, we see that the octal and hexadecimal equivalents of the number 30 are _____ and _____.

*****

$$8 \overline{)30}$$

$$8 \overline{)3} \quad 6 \qquad 30 = 36_8$$

$$0 \quad 3$$

$$16 \overline{)30}$$

$$16 \overline{)1} \qquad 14 = E \qquad 30 = 1E_{16}$$

$$0 \quad 1$$

18. The system for converting from decimal to another base employed above is called the _____.

*****

remainder system or division algorithm

COMPUTER CODING SCHEMES   In the discussion above, we were concerned with determining equivalents of decimal numbers in other bases. In each case, equivalent results were obtained.

BCD   Not all computers, however, utilize these systems. Some utilize a system which is part binary and part decimal, a system called Binary Coded Decimal (BCD). Nondecimal number systems discussed thus far were made up of two parts: the digits we can see and the weights or powers of the base we do not see. In the case of the decimal number 384, we see the digits 3, 8, and 4 but do not see their respective weights of 100, 10, and 1, although we know that they are there. The expanded form of this number, showing both of these parts, would appear as

$$3 \times 100 + 8 \times 10 + 4 \times 1$$

In BCD the number is very similar in structure but different in appearance, the difference in appearance being that only the digits, or coefficients, would be expressed in binary. In the above example, the coefficients were 3, 8, and 4:

$$③ \times 100 + ⑧ \times 10 + ④ \times 1$$

Converting each of these coefficients to an equivalent four-digit binary number, we have

$$3 = 0011_2 \qquad 8 = 1000_2 \qquad 4 = 0100_2$$

Or, we have that the BCD equivalent of the decimal number 384 is

$$0011 \quad 1000 \quad 0100$$

where each group of four binary digits holds the place of one decimal digit. As a practice exercise, let us determine the decimal equivalent of the number 1001 0011 1000 0110 coded in the above fashion. It is a simple matter to ascertain that this number is derived from the decimal number 9386:

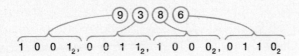

Two advantages of this new system become immediately apparent.

1. This scheme represents a number utilizing only 0's and 1's.
2. The conversions to and from decimal utilizing this scheme can be made with little effort.

To utilize such a system to represent letters and special characters, one need only add 2 bits (*binary digits*) to the existing groups of 4 bits that can represent a decimal digit. We shall call these 2 additional bits B and A, and we shall call the existing 4 numeric bits 8, 4, 2, and 1. Then, any character can be expressed by a unique combination of 6 bits,

$$B \quad A \quad 8 \quad 4 \quad 2 \quad 1$$

The question arises: How can 2 additional bits provide enough additional combinations of bits to allow a unique combination for each of the 26 letters when 4 bits were required simply to represent the 10 digits 0, 1, 2, 3, 4, 5, 6, 7, 8, and 9?

The answer can be found by examining the formula for the number of combinations of N elements, where each element can take on one of two possible values and the value assumed by any one element is independent of the value assumed by any other element. That is, the number of combinations of N elements or binary digits is given by the formula.

$$\text{No. of combinations} = 2^N$$

Therefore, for combinations of from 1 to 8 elements or bits, we would have the number of combinations shown in Table 6-6. From the table we can see that increasing the number of bits from 4 to 6 will cause an increase in the number of combinations from 16 to 64, respectively, an increase of 48 combinations. This is more than enough to allow one unique combination to be assigned to each digit and letter with some left over to be used for special characters such as a period, comma, dollar sign, etc.

In addition to the 6 bits required to represent any character, 1 additional bit is provided by the computer and is called the C bit (parity or check bit). Its only purpose is for internal checking of character validity by the computer. It is possible, although very

TABLE 6-6

Number of Combinations of N Binary Digits

NUMBER OF BITS N	NUMBER OF COMBINATIONS 2^N
1	$2^1 = 2$
2	$2^2 = 4$
3	$2^3 = 8$
4	$2^4 = 16$
5	$2^5 = 32$
6	$2^6 = 64$
7	$2^7 = 128$
8	$2^8 = 256$

unlikely, that the computer could introduce a coding discrepancy while attempting to read, write, or process a character. To prevent such an occurrence going unnoticed, a check or C bit is assigned to each character within the machine in such a way as to make the total number of 1's in the character equal an even or an odd number depending on the machine. For simplicity purposes, we shall limit our discussion to machines in which the total number of 1's in each character is odd. The practice of maintaining an odd number of 1's at all times is called *odd parity*. To further clarify this principle, let us consider the BCD representation of the decimal digit 6:

Bit names	B	A	8	4	2	1
BCD code	0	0	0	1	1	0

You will notice that there are two 1's, or an even number of 1's, in the BCD representation. The computer would, therefore, assign a 1 to the C bit, making the total number of 1's odd, and produce the following BCD representation of the decimal digit 6:

Bit names	C	B	A	8	4	2	1	
BCD code	1	0	0	0	1	1	0	(odd parity)

To see how the maintaining of an odd parity within each character in the computer allows the computer to detect when a single bit has been lost or gained accidently, let us consider two cases.

Case 1. Let us assume that somehow the computer misread the character 6 as follows:

```
C  B  A  8  4  2  1
1  0  0  0  1  0  0    (a 1 bit was lost)
```

This condition would be immediately sensed by the computer's control unit since the parity check, or total number of 1's in this character, is even. And, this is an invalid condition for any legitimate BCD character. The operator would then be signaled by the computer.

Case 2. Let us assume that somehow the computer misread the character 6 as follows:

```
C  B  A  8  4  2  1
1  0  0  0  1  1  1    (a 1 bit was added)
```

As in case 1, this condition would also be easily detected by the computer. The presence of an even-parity character would then be immediately reported to the computer operator.

Therefore, by adding one additional bit, the C bit to the bit configuration of each character, the computer will be able to determine, quickly and easily, whether or not a 1 bit has been gained or lost.

However, if two 1 bits are lost, or two 1 bits are gained, or if one 1 bit is lost and one 1 bit is gained, for example, the computer would be incapable of detecting this situation. The reason for this is simply that the parity would have remained odd. But, computer designers have determined that the likelihood of an error occurring in more than 1 bit of a character at the same time is so small that the additional complex design that would be required to detect such a condition is not practical.

A complete list of the 7-bit BCD codes for representing the 10 decimal digits, the 26 letters of the alphabet, and selected special characters is given in Figure 6-3.

1   0   0   0   1   0   0   (a 1 bit was lost)

1   0   0   0   1   1   1   (a 1 bit was added)

You will notice a similarity between the BCD code and the Hollerith code such that the B and A bits are also called zones and correspond to the Hollerith zones as shown in Table 6-7.

There is also a correspondence between the Hollerith digit punches and the BCD 8, 4, 2, and 1 bits as shown in Table 6-8.

EBCDIC   In recent years, the BCD code was extended to allow for more combinations of bits. This extension of the BCD scheme is called EBCDIC (*Extended Binary Coded Decimal Interchange Code*). Eight bits or one *byte* is required to represent a character in EBCDIC. With respect to digits and letters of the alphabet, the EBCDIC and BCD codes are very similar, differing only in their zone bits as shown in Table 6-9.

This now means that with an 8-bit set in EBCDIC (4 bits for the zone and 4 bits for the digit), there are now 256 possible combinations, or 192 more combinations than were possible with the BCD 6-bit code.

NUMERIC CHARACTERS

CHARACTER	CODE
0	C 8 2
1	1
2	2
3	C 2 1
4	4
5	C 4 1
6	C 4 2
7	4 2 1
8	8
9	C 8 1

ALPHABETIC CHARACTERS

CHARACTER	CODE
A	BA 1
B	BA 2
C	CBA 2 1
D	BA 4
E	CBA 4 1
F	BA 42
G	BA 42 1
H	BA8
I	CBA8 1
‡ (Minus Zero)	B 8 2
J	CB 1
K	CB 2
L	B 2 1
M	CB 4 1
N	B 42
O	CB 42 1
P	CB 8
Q	B 8 1
R	
‡ Record Mark	A8 2
S	C A 2
T	A 2 1
U	C A 4
V	A 4 1
W	A 42
X	C A 42 1
Y	A8
Z	A8 1

SPECIAL CHARACTERS

CHARACTER	CODE
BLANK	C
.	BA8 2 1
□	CBA84
(Left Parenthesis (Special Character)	BA84 1
< Less Than (Special Character)	CBA8421
‡ Group Mark (Note 1)	CBA
&	CB 8 2 1
$	CB 84
*	CB 842
) Right Parenthesis (Special Char.)	B 8421
; Semicolon (Special Character)	B
Δ Delta (Made Change)	C A 1
-	C A8 2 1
,	A84
%	C A84 1
= Word Separator	C A842
' Apostrophe (Special Character)	A8421
" Tape Segment Mark	A
¢ Cent (Special Character Note 2)	C 8 21
#	84 1
@	842
: Colon (Special Character)	
> Greater Than (Special Character)	C 8421
√ Tape Mark	CBA8 2
? (Plus Zero)	

FIG. 6-3
Standard Binary Coded Decimal (BCD) Code.

233

Character	Hollerith card code	EBCDIC Binary	Hexa
0	0	1111 0000	F0
1	1	1111 0001	F1
2	2	1111 0010	F2
3	3	1111 0011	F3
4	4	1111 0100	F4
5	5	1111 0101	F5
6	6	1111 0110	F6
7	7	1111 0111	F7
8	8	1111 1000	F8
9	9	1111 1001	F9
A	12-1	1100 0001	C1
B	12-2	1100 0010	C2
C	12-3	1100 0011	C3
D	12-4	1100 0100	C4
E	12-5	1100 0101	C5
F	12-6	1100 0110	C6
G	12-7	1100 0111	C7
H	12-8	1100 1000	C8
I	12-9	1100 1001	C9
J	11-1	1101 0001	D1
K	11-2	1101 0010	D2
L	11-3	1101 0011	D3
M	11-4	1101 0100	D4
N	11-5	1101 0101	D5
O	11-6	1101 0110	D6
P	11-7	1101 0111	D7
Q	11-8	1101 1000	D8
R	11-9	1101 1001	D9
S	0-2	1110 0010	E2
T	0-3	1110 0011	E3
U	0-4	1110 0100	E4
V	0-5	1110 0101	E5
W	0-6	1110 0110	E6
X	0-7	1110 0111	E7
Y	0-8	1110 1000	E8
Z	0-9	1110 1001	E9

FIG. 6-4

Standard Extended Binary Coded Decimal Interchange Code (EBCDIC) for Selected Characters.

SELF-STUDY EXERCISES 6-5

1. A computer numbering system which is part binary and part decimal is the _____.

*****

BCD (Binary Coded Decimal) system

2. The BCD system is capable of representing any character using _____ binary digits or _____.

*****

7

bits

TABLE 6-7

Table of Zone Equivalences

BINARY CODED DECIMAL	HOLLERITH
11-Zone bits B and A	12 zone
10-Zone bit B only	11 zone
01-Zone bit A only	0 zone
00-Neither zone A nor B	No zone

Note: A numeric zero in BCD has no zone bits "on."

TABLE 6-8

Table of Digit-punch Equivalences

BINARY CODED DECIMAL				HOLLERITH
8	4	2	1	
0	0	0	1	1
0	0	1	0	2
0	0	1	1	3
0	1	0	0	4
0	1	0	1	5
0	1	1	0	6
0	1	1	1	7
1	0	0	0	8
1	0	0	1	9
1	0	1	0	0

TABLE 6-9

Zone-bit Combinations

BCD	EBCDIC
11	1100
10	1101
01	1110
00	1111

3. The names of the 7 BCD bits required to represent any character are _____.

*****

C, B, A, 8, 4, 2, and 1

4. The C bit serves to control the _____ of a BCD character.

*****

parity

5. Given an odd-parity machine and the bits below, the C bit would have to be a _____.

?   1   1   1   0   0   1

C   B   A   8   4   2   1

*****

1 bit, to make the total number of 1 bits an odd number (5)

6. The B and A bits are called the _____ bits and the 8, 4, 2, and 1 bits are called the _____ bits.

*****

zone
numeric

7. The BCD code for the characters A, 3, 0 (zero), and S are _____, _____, _____, and _____, respectively.

*****

0   11   0001

1   00   0011

1   00   1010

1   01   0010

8. EBCDIC, which stands for the _____, is similar to the BCD code except for the fact that _____.

*****

Extended Binary Coded Decimal Interchange Code
the EBCDIC used 4 zone bits instead of the 2 used in BCD

9. The EBCDIC for the characters A, 3, 0 (zero), and S are
_____, _____, _____, and _____, respectively.

*****

1100 0001
1111 0011
1111 0000*
1110 0010

EXERCISES

True–false exercises 6-1

1. ____ In 10000001_2, the first digit on the left represents 2^8 or 256.

2. ____ The names of the BCD bits are A, B, C, 8, 4, 2, and 1, and they occur in that order.

3. ____ The 16 at the lower right of the number 101101001_{16} indicates that it is in the base 16 or hexadecimal number system.

4. ____ The C bit in a BCD character representation is used to help detect lost or gained bits while reading, writing, or processing a character.

5. ____ $64_{10} = 104_6$

6. ____ The BCD system is used on the IBM System/3.

7. ____ The expanded form of the number 31.247_8 is (3×8^2) $+ (1 \times 8^1) + (2 \times 8^0) + (4 \times 8^{-1}) + (7 \times 8^{-2})$.

8. ____ A quick way of converting octal numbers to hexadecimal would be through their mutual conversion to and from binary.

9. ____ $AA_{16} = 100_{10}$.

10. ____ The decimal equivalent of the number 106_8 is 711.

11. ____ 4^2 is equivalent to 8.

12. ____ In the place-value system, the actual value of a specific digit in a number is determined by its position as well as the value of the digit.

13. ____ 1211_2 is a binary number.

*Note: The EBCDIC representation of the digit 0 (zero) differs from the BCD representation of the digit 0 (zero) in both the zone and the numeric portions.

14. _____ In the hexadecimal system, E = 14.

15. _____ Two commonly used coding schemes are BCD and EBCDIC.

16. _____ The binary system utilizes the digits 0 and 1 and a set of weights which are derived from multiples of 2.

17. _____ A convenient way to multiply a binary number by 2 would be simply to add a 0.

18. _____ The EBCDIC system consists of more possible combinations of bits than the BCD system.

19. _____ The expanded form of the number 372 can be written as $(3 \times 100) + (7 \times 10) + (2 \times 1)$.

20. _____ $1010101_2 = 85_{10}$.

21. _____ The decimal system is the base 10 number system.

22. _____ Computers also make use of the octal and hexadecimal number systems.

23. _____ The BCD equivalent of the digit 6 is 000110, excluding the check bit.

24. _____ Maintaining an odd number of 1's in a character is called odd parity.

25. _____ A number system can be defined as a method for representing quantities or physical items.

26. _____ The remainder system is valid for any integer base.

27. _____ Computers deal extensively with numbers and numerical quantities.

28. _____ The binary number system is utilized in most computers.

29. _____ The decimal system uses nine unique digits, 1, 2, 3, 4, 5, 6, 7, 8, and 9.

30. _____ The binary number system is also known as the base 8 number system.

31. _____ The octal equivalent of the binary 101000110_2 is 506_8.

32. _____ The binary equivalent of the decimal number 37 is 100101_2.

33. _____ 36^0 is equivalent to 1.

34. _____ An integer is a whole number.

35. _____ The Hollerith, BCD, and EBCDIC schemes utilize zones when representing alphabetic characters.

36. _____ There are more characters possible using the BCD system than using the EBCDIC system.

37. _____ Every odd number in the binary system ends in 1.

38. _____ The parity system allows the computer an internal check during the reading, writing, or processing of a character.

39. _____ One byte is required to represent 1 EBCDIC character.

Multiple-choice exercises   6-2

1. _____ The decimal system as we know it is based upon
    (a) the digits 0 through 9
    (b) a fixed set of weights
    (c) the place-value concept
    (d) all the above
    (e) none of the above

2. _____ $BBD_{16} =$
    (a) 101110111101_2
    (b) 5675_8
    (c) 1100   0010   1100   1100   0100 in 8-bit code
    (d) all the above
    (e) (a) and (b) only

3. _____ 54 in octal =
    (a) 66
    (b) 76
    (c) 52
    (d) 74
    (e) none of the above

4. _____ The decimal equivalent of 10111_2 is
    (a) 40
    (b) 37
    (c) 23
    (d) 27
    (e) none of the above

5. _____ 489 in BCD =
    (a) 000100   001000   001001
    (b) 0100   1000   1001
    (c) 111101001
    (d) 100101111
    (e) none of the above

6. ____ The weight associated with the digit 0 in the binary number 1011_2 is
   (a) 8
   (b) 4
   (c) 2
   (d) 0
   (e) none of the above

7. ____ The hexadecimal equivalent of 1110110110011_2 is
   (a) 1C37
   (b) E73
   (c) 1DB3
   (d) E3B
   (e) none of the above

8. ____ The hexadecimal number system is based on multiples or powers of
   (a) 2
   (b) 8
   (c) 16
   (d) 60
   (e) none of the above

9. ____ Increasing the number of bits from 4 to 6 increases the number of possible combinations by
   (a) 2
   (b) 4
   (c) 24
   (d) 48
   (e) none of the above

10. ____ A decimal number is converted to hexadecimal by
    (a) dividing successively by 16
    (b) multiplying successively by 16
    (c) dividing successively by 10
    (d) multiplying successively by 10
    (e) none of the above

11. ____ 54 in binary is
    (a) 110110
    (b) 111110
    (c) 101010
    (d) 101000
    (e) none of the above

12. ____ Unlike the decimal number system, the binary number system
    (a) is not a place-value system

(b) cannot be used in calculations
(c) uses only the digits 0 and 1
(d) uses only the digits 0, 1, and 2
(e) none of the above

13. _____ The BCD equivalent of the letter X in an odd-parity machine is
(a) 1010101
(b) 1010111
(c) 0010111
(d) 0010101
(e) none of the above

Problems 6-3

1. Write the expanded form of the following numbers with respect to the indicated base:
(a) 231 (base 10)
(b) 231 (base 8)
(c) 231 (base 4)
(d) 231 (base 16)
(e) 3472 (base 8)

2. Convert the following binary numbers into decimal numbers using the expanded form:
(a) 10110_2
(b) 110110_2
(c) 1000110110_2

3. Convert the following decimal numbers into octal:
(a) 76
(b) 89
(c) 346
(d) 979

4. Consider the "quartal" or base 4 number system.
(a) Would you expect to convert it easily from binary?
(b) Why or why not?
(c) Give an example.
(d) Would this system be useful in a computer application?
(e) Why or why not?

5. Assuming odd parity, convert the following to BCD:
(a) 327
(b) 3759
(c) 937.77
(d) computer number systems

6. Convert the following octal numbers to equivalent decimal numbers:
   (a) 417_8
   (b) 76300_8
   (c) 100110_8

7. Express the following base 10 numbers in hexadecimal:
   (a) 124
   (b) 25359

8. Convert the following numbers from octal to binary, then from binary to hexadecimal:
   (a) 74_8
   (b) 321_8
   (c) 7452_8
   (d) 32453_8

9. Convert the following to EBCDIC:
   (a) 1347
   (b) AX7L

ITEMS FOR DISCUSSION

Number System
Decimal Number System
Expanded Form
Place-value Number System
Weights
Binary Number System
Conversions to Decimal
Octal Number System
Hexadecimal Number System

Binary-octal-hexadecimal
   Conversions
Conversions from Decimal
Division Algorithm
BCD
Parity
EBCDIC
Byte
Bit

APPENDIX

Advanced Computer Arithmetic

To this point we have discussed whole numbers or *integers* expressed in and converted to and from different bases. But we also know that everything cannot be expressed using only integers. For example, one and one-half cannot be expressed as an integer. It can, however, be represented as 1.5, which we shall call a *mixed number*. Mixed numbers also exist in other bases. In order to understand mixed numbers in other bases, we shall first examine their meaning in the decimal number system.

MIXED NUMBERS*

$$31.46 = 3 \times 10 + 1 \times 1 + 4 \times \frac{1}{10} + 6 \times \frac{1}{100}$$

$$= 3 \times 10 + 1 \times 1 + 4 \times \frac{1}{10^1} + 6 \times \frac{1}{10^2}$$

For simplicity of writing, mathematicians have adopted certain notations. They are

$$\frac{1}{10^1} = 10^{-1}$$

$$\frac{1}{10^2} = 10^{-2}$$

or, in general,

$$\frac{1}{x^a} = x^{-a}$$

Simply stated, any number raised to a positive power in the denominator of a fraction can be moved to the numerator of that fraction by simply changing the sign of the power. For example,

(a) $$\frac{1}{3^4} = 3^{-4}$$

(b) $$\frac{7}{9^4} = 7 \times 9^{-4}$$

(c)
$$3 \times \frac{1}{10^3} = 3 \times 10^{-3}$$

One additional mathematical notation worthy of mention at this time is

$$a^0 = 1$$

That is, *any* number raised to the zero power equals 1. For example,

$$10^0 = 1$$
$$2^0 = 1$$
$$16^0 = 1$$
$$8^0 = 1$$

With these notations in mind, the previous example,

$$31.46 = 3 \times 10 + 1 \times 1 + 4 \times \frac{1}{10^1} + 6 \times \frac{1}{10^2}$$

can also be written as

$$31.46 = 3 \times 10^1 + 1 \times 10^0 + 4 \times 10^{-1} + 6 \times 10^{-2}$$

Notice that the exponents associated with each term are related in that the exponent associated with any one term is one less than the exponent associated with the preceding term. For clarity, two additional examples are presented:

$$472.418 = 4 \times 10^2 + 7 \times 10^1 + 2 \times 10^0 + 4 \times 10^{-1}$$
$$+ 1 \times 10^{-2} + 8 \times 10^{-3}$$

$$10.4806 = 1 \times 10^1 + 0 \times 10^0 + 4 \times 10^{-1} + 8 \times 10^{-2}$$
$$+ 0 \times 10^{-3} + 6 \times 10^{-4}$$

Similarly for other bases:

$$101.011_2 = (1 \times 2^2) + (0 \times 2^1) + (1 \times 2^0) + (0 \times 2^{-1})$$
$$+ (1 \times 2^{-2}) + (1 \times 2^{-3})$$

$$37.14_8 = (3 \times 8^1) + (7 \times 8^0) + (1 \times 8^{-1}) + (4 \times 8^{-2})$$

$$C4.87A_{16} = (C \times 16^1) + (4 \times 16^0) + (8 \times 16^{-1})$$
$$+ (7 \times 16^{-2}) + (A \times 16^{-3})$$

Converting a nondecimal mixed number to its decimal equivalent is simply done by employing the expanded form of the number as shown in the following example:

$$101.011_2 = (1 \times 2^2) + (0 \times 2^1) + (1 \times 2^0) + (0 \times 2^{-1})$$
$$+ (1 \times 2^{-2}) + (1 \times 2^{-3})$$

$$= (1 \times 2^2) + (0 \times 2^1) + (1 \times 2^0) + \left(0 \times \frac{1}{2^1}\right)$$
$$+ \left(1 \times \frac{1}{2^2}\right) + \left(1 \times \frac{1}{2^3}\right)$$

$$= (1 \times 4) + (0 \times 2) + (1 \times 1) + \left(0 \times \frac{1}{2}\right)$$
$$+ \left(1 \times \frac{1}{4}\right) + \left(1 \times \frac{1}{8}\right)$$

$$= (4) + (0) + (1) + (0) + (.25) + (.125)$$
$$= 5.375$$

The conversion of the remaining two examples above is left to the reader.

SELF-STUDY EXERCISES

1. A mixed number is _____.

*****

a number which contains both an integer part and a fractional part

2. The expanded form of the mixed number 4.72 is _____.

*****

$$4.72 = (4 \times 1) + \left(7 \times \frac{1}{10}\right) + \left(2 \times \frac{1}{100}\right)$$

3. The mathematical notation for $\frac{1}{100}$ is _____.

*****

$$100^{-1} \text{ or } 10^{-2}$$

4. Using this mathematical notation, the mixed number 4.72 can be expressed in expanded form as _____.

*****

$$4.72 = (4 \times 1) + (7 \times 10^{-1}) + (2 \times 10^{-2})$$

5. Any number raised to the zero power is equal to _____.

*****

1

6. Therefore, we can now rewrite the above expanded form of the number 4.72 using this convention as _____.

*****

$$4.72 = (4 \times 10^0) + (7 \times 10^{-1}) + (2 \times 10^{-2})$$

7. The expanded form of the hexadecimal number $3A.4E_{16}$ using above notations is _____.

*****

$$3A.4E_{16} = (3 \times 16^1) + (A \times 16^0) + (4 \times 16^{-1}) + (E \times 16^{-2})$$

8. The decimal equivalent of the binary mixed number 1011.101_2 is _____.

*****

$$= (1 \times 2^3) + (0 \times 2^2) + (1 \times 2^1) + (1 \times 2^0) + (1 \times 2^{-1}) + (0 \times 2^{-2}) + (1 \times 2^{-3})$$

$$= (1 \times 8) + (0 \times 4) + (1 \times 2) + (1 \times 1) + (1 \times \tfrac{1}{2}) + (0 \times \tfrac{1}{4}) + (1 \times \tfrac{1}{8})$$

$$= \quad 8 \quad + \quad \cdot 0 \quad + \quad 2 \quad + \quad 1 \quad + \quad 0.5 \quad + \quad 0 \quad + \quad 0.125$$

$$= 11.625$$

ARITHMETIC OPERATIONS IN OTHER BASES* An in-depth treatment of arithmetic operations in nondecimal number systems is beyond the scope of this book. Therefore, only basic addition, multiplication, and subtraction will be introduced.

Addition Let us first consider an addition problem in the binary number system:

$$11.11_2$$
$$1.11_2$$
$$1.01_2$$
$$\underline{(+)\ 1.11_2}$$

The basic steps necessary to solve this type of problem are as follows:

Step 1. Add the column in decimal.

Step 2. Convert the column total to binary.

Step 3. Record the rightmost digit of the converted binary total just below the column added, and record any carries, one per column to the left of the column added.

Step 4. Repeat steps 1–3 for the next column to the left of the column just completed.

Applying this procedure to the above exercise, we have

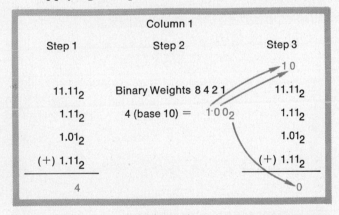

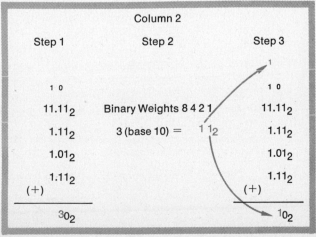

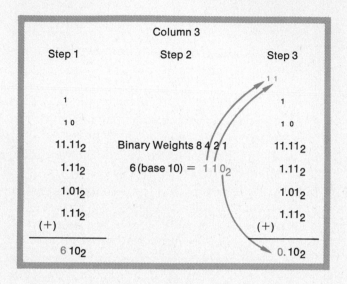

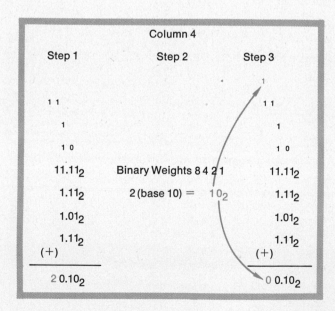

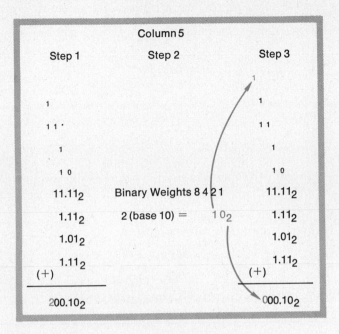

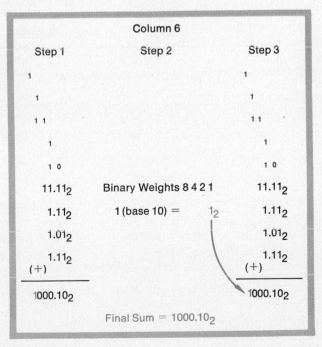

Since column 6 had only one digit, no addition was actually necessary and the digit could simply be brought down.

The same solution, more compactly done, would appear as follows:

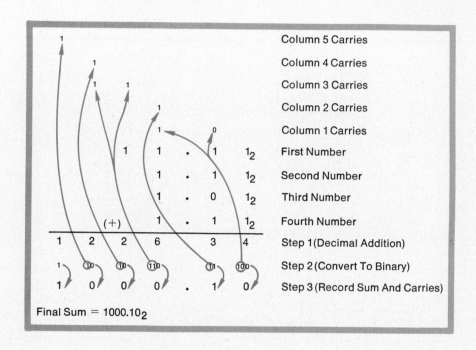

As an additional example, let us consider the following addition:

$$11.11_2$$
$$101.11_2$$
$$111.01_2$$
$$(+)\quad 1.11_2$$

The solution, compactly done, would look as follows:

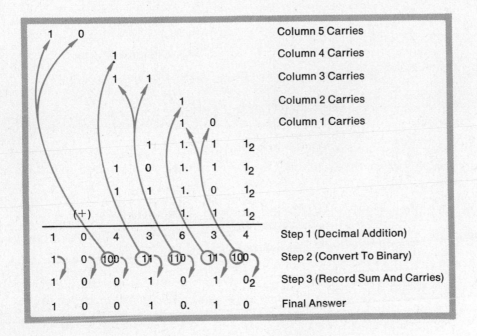

Let us consider the following octal addition:

$$34.72_8$$
$$1.74_8$$
$$(+)25.63_8$$

One should bear in mind that, for an octal addition, the only deviation from the foregoing illustrations is in step 2. In step 2 of an octal addition problem, the decimal total is converted to its octal equivalent instead of to its binary equivalent.

Proceeding then, with this one variation, we have

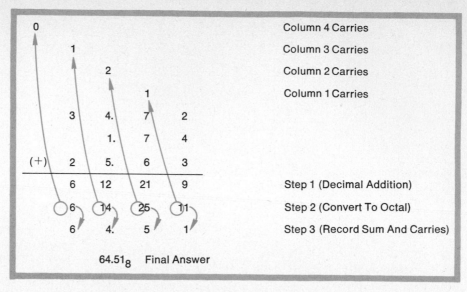

Multiplication The three steps required to perform a multiplication in a number system other than decimal are very similar to those used in addition. They are

> Step 1. Multiply the first column in decimal, adding any carries to the product.
>
> Step 2. Convert the decimal product to an equivalent number in the base being considered.
>
> Step 3. Record the rightmost digit of the converted subtotal in the answer column just below the digit being multiplied and record any carries, one per column to the left of the digit being multiplied.
>
> Step 4. Repeat steps 1–3 for the next digit in the multiplicand (top number).

Column 1

Step 1	Step 2	Step 3
14.47_8	Octal Weights 64 8 1	$\overset{5}{14.47_8}$
$(\times)\ .6_8$	42 (base 10) = 52_8	$(\times)\ .6_8$
42		2_8

Column 2

Step 1	Step 2	Step 3
$\overset{5}{14.47_8}$	Octal Weights 64 8 1	$\overset{3\ 5}{14.47_8}$
$(\times)\ .6_8$	29 (base 10) = 35_8	$(\times)\ .6_8$
$24 + 5 = 29$ 2_8		52_8

Column 3

Step 1
3 5
14.47₈

(×) .6₈
—————
24 + 3 = 27 52₈

Step 2
Octal Weights   64 8 1

27 (base 10) = 33₈

Step 3
33 5
14.47₈

(×) .6₈
—————
3 52₈

Column 4

Step 1
33 5
14.47₈

(×) .6₈
—————
6 + 3 = 9 3 52₈

Step 2
Octal Weights   64 8 1

9 (base 10) =   1 1₈

Step 3
1 33 5
14.47₈

(×) .6₈
—————
1 1 3 52₈

And, as in any number system, the number of decimal places in the product equals the number of decimal places in the multiplier (1 in this case) plus the number of decimal places in the multiplicand (2 in this case). Therefore, in this example, there will be three decimal places in the product, or

$$14.47_8$$
$$(\times)\ \ .6_8$$
$$\overline{11.352_8}$$

More compactly stated, this solution would appear as follows:

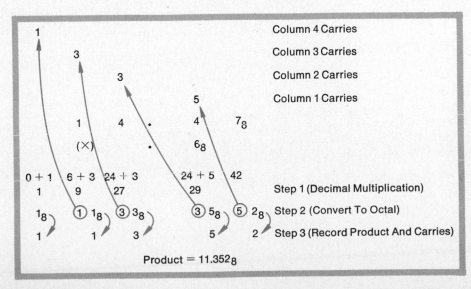

Product = 11.352₈

253

A multiplication with a multiplier of 2 or more digits is accomplished using the same basic steps, but, as in the decimal system, the subproducts are recorded beginning under the digit of the multiplier to which they correspond. For example,

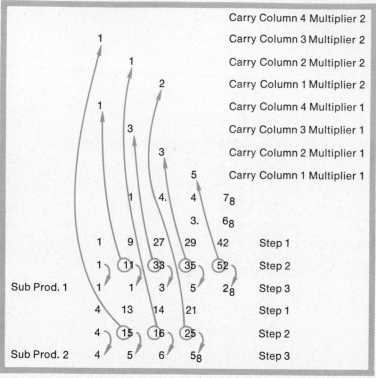

Now, as in a decimal multiplication, the subproducts are now added. One must realize, however, that this must be an addition in octal, since each subproduct is in octal. Adding the subproducts in octal would yield

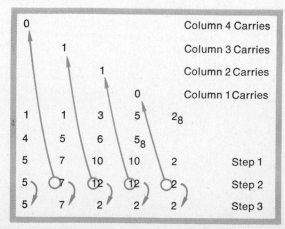

Finally, affixing the decimal point, we have

$$14.47_8$$
$$3.6_8$$
$$57.222_8$$

Subtraction in a nondecimal number system is the same as in a   **Subtraction**
decimal system with one simple difference. *When borrowing from the*
next column, one borrows an amount equal to the base of the system in which
the subtraction is performed, as opposed to the borrowing of 10 in the
decimal system.

For example, let us consider the following octal subtraction:

$$314.52_8$$
$$(-)\ 75.16_8$$

As is the case with subtraction in the decimal system, it must
be performed column by column. Therefore, let us begin with
column 1:

$$2$$
$$(-)6$$

Six from 2 will not go; therefore, as in a base 10 subtraction,
we must borrow from the adjacent digit to the left. However, in an
octal subtraction, we borrow 8 (the octal base), whereas in a decimal subtraction, we borrow 10 (the decimal base). We then have

$$
\begin{array}{r}
4\quad 8+2=10 \\
3\ 0\ 4\ .\ \cancel{5}\ 2_8 \\
(-)\quad 7\ 5\ .\ 1\ 6_8 \\
\hline
4_8
\end{array}
$$

Proceeding to column 2,

$$
\begin{array}{r}
4\quad 10 \\
3\ 0\ 4\ .\ \cancel{5}\ \cancel{2}_8 \\
(-)\quad 7\ 5\ .\ 1\ 6_8 \\
\hline
3\ 4_8
\end{array}
$$

Column 3:

$$
\begin{array}{ccccccc}
 & 2 & 7 & 8+4=12 & & 4 & 10 \\
 & \cancel{3} & \cancel{0} & \cancel{4} & . & \cancel{5} & \cancel{2}_8 \\
(-) & & 7 & 5 & . & 1 & 6_8 \\
\hline
 & & & 7 & . & 3 & 4_8
\end{array}
$$

Notice that column 4 could not be decremented to compensate for lending 8 (the octal base) to column 3. Therefore, the 30 in columns 4 and 5 combined was decremented by 1. And, in octal 30_8 less 1_8 is 27_8 since $27_8 + 1_8 = 30_8$. Column 4:

$$
\begin{array}{ccccccc}
 & 2 & 7 & 12 & & 4 & 10 \\
 & \cancel{3} & \cancel{0} & \cancel{4} & . & \cancel{5} & \cancel{2}_8 \\
(-) & & 7 & 5 & . & 1 & 6_8 \\
\hline
 & & 0 & 7 & . & 3 & 4_8
\end{array}
$$

Column 5:

$$
\begin{array}{ccccccc}
 & 2 & 7 & 12 & & 4 & 10 \\
 & \cancel{3} & \cancel{0} & \cancel{4} & . & \cancel{5} & \cancel{2}_8 \\
(-) & & 7 & 5 & . & 1 & 6_8 \\
\hline
 & 2 & 0 & 7 & . & 3 & 4_8
\end{array}
$$

Let us consider another example, this time a hexadecimal subtraction:

$$
\begin{array}{l}
A3\,4\,B.3\,8_{16} \\
(-)6\,A8\,6.4\,1_{16}
\end{array}
$$

Proceeding, column by column, as before, we have

Column 1

$$
\begin{array}{cccccccc}
 & A & 3 & 4 & B & . & 3 & 8_{16} \\
(-) & 6 & A & 8 & 6 & . & 4 & 1_{16} \\
\hline
 & & & & & & & 7_{16}
\end{array}
$$

Column 2

```
                    A    16 + 3 = 19
          A   3   4   B̶   .   3̶   8₁₆
    (−)   6   A   8   6   .   4   1₁₆
    ─────────────────────────────────
                         15 = F   7₁₆
```

Notice that in hexadecimal, when we borrow, we borrow 16 (the hexadecimal base).

Column 3

```
                    A = 10
          A   3   4   B̶   .   3̶   8₁₆
    (−)   6   A   8   6   .   4   1₁₆
    ─────────────────────────────────
                      4   .   F   7₁₆
```

Column 4

```
          2  16+4=20  A            19
      A   3̶     4̶     B̶   .   3̶    8₁₆
(−)   6   A     8     6   .   4    1₁₆
───────────────────────────────────────
      12 = C    4     .   F    7₁₆
```

Column 5

```
        16+2=18
    9    2̶    20    A          19
    A̶    3̶    4̶     B̶   .   3̶    8₁₆
(−) 6    A    8     6   .   4    1₁₆
──────────────────────────────────────
    8    C    4     .   F    7₁₆
```

Column 6

```
         18
    9    2̶    20    A          19
    A̶    3̶    4̶     B̶   .   3̶    8₁₆
(−) 6    A    8     6   .   4    1₁₆
──────────────────────────────────────
    3    8    C    4    .   F    7₁₆
```

Thus, we have that

	A	3	4	B	.	3	8_{16}	(1)
(−)	6	A	8	6	.	4	1_{16}	(2)

	3	8	C	4	.	F	7_{16}	(3)

The reader may verify the answer by adding, in hexadecimal, line (2) to line (3), obtaining line (1).

SELF-STUDY EXERCISES

1. The sum of the binary numbers below is _____.

$$1.01_2$$
$$(+)\ .11_2$$

*****

$$
\begin{array}{ccc}
1 & 1 & 1 \\
\hline
1. & 0 & 1_2 \\
(+) & . & 1\ \ 1_2 \\
\hline
1\ \ 2 & 2 & 2 \\
\hline
1\ 10 & 10 & 10 \\
\hline
1\ \ 0. & 0 & 0 \\
\end{array}
$$

1 1 1			
1. 0 1_2			
(+) . 1 1_2			
1 2 2 2			Decimal addition
1 10 10 10			Binary equivalent
1 0. 0 0			Sum

2. The sum of the octal numbers below is _____.

$$3.47_8$$
$$(+)1.22_8$$

*****

	Decimal addition / etc.
1	
3.4 7_8	
(+)1.2 2_8	
4 7 9	Decimal addition
4 7 11	Octal equivalent
4.7 1	Sum

3. The product of the octal numbers below is _____.

$$10.36_8$$
$$(\times)\ \ \ 23_8$$

*****

1					Carries from sum of product 1 and product 2
	1				Carries from second multiplication
	1	2			Carries from first multiplication
1	0	3	6_8		
$(\times)$		2	3_8		
3	1	11	18		Decimal product (first multiplication)
3	1	13	22		Equivalent (first multiplication)
3	1	3	2		Product 1 (first multiplication)
2	0	7	12		Decimal product (second multiplication)
2	0	7	14		Equivalent (second multiplication)
2	0	7	4		Product 2 (second multiplication)
2	4	0.	7	2_8	Sum of product 1 and product 2

4. The difference resulting from the subtraction below is _____.

$$312.46_8$$
$$(-)\ \ 60.37_8$$

*****

2	$9 = 8 + 1$	3	$14 = 8 + 6$	
3	1	2	.4	6_8
$(-)$	6	0	.3	7_8
2	3	2	.0	7_8

III

SOFTWARE, PROGRAM PREPARATION, AND PROBLEM-SOLVING CONCEPTS

INTRODUCTION

PREPARATION FOR PROGRAMMING

PROBLEM ANALYSIS

FLOWCHART APPLICATION

CODING AND EXECUTING THE APPLICATION PROGRAM

Types of Instructions

Machine Language (Actual)*

Symbolic Language*

Procedure-oriented Languages*

Executing and Debugging
the Program

Types of Programming Errors

DOCUMENTATION

Organization of Program
Documentation

Title Page
Control Sheet
Narrative Descriptions
Narrative Modifications
Flowcharts and Decision Tables
Input and Output Data Codes
Input and Output formats
Input Test Data and Sample Output
Other Instruction Sheets
and Worksheets

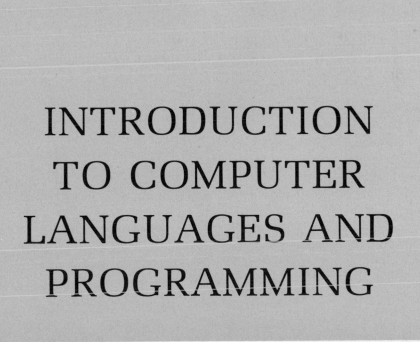

7

INTRODUCTION
TO COMPUTER
LANGUAGES AND
PROGRAMMING

INTRODUCTION It is rarely the case that the accountant, business manager, or other computer user would attempt to prepare his own computer program to solve his problem. More often, he would communicate his problem to the programming department of his company or to an outside consulting firm and ask for a solution. An essential part of this cooperative process is that the accountant or business manager be able to effectively communicate to the programmer the nature and details of his problem in the most understandable and meaningful way. To do this, the accountant or business manager must understand, in general terms, what steps the programmer must go through in order to program a solution to his problem. Armed with a basic understanding of the programmer's needs, the business person can prepare the problem description and solution requirements in a manner which will be most easily understood by, and most meaningful to, the programmer. A mutual understanding, at this point in the development of a computerized solution to the problem, can avoid needless and wasteful changes and revisions in the future.

It is for this reason that we shall describe those facets of the programming function that the business student should clearly understand.

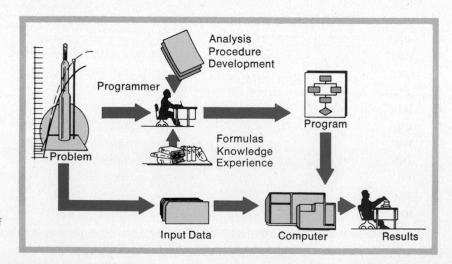

FIG. 7-1
Direct Conversion of Problem to Machine Program.

264

A considerable amount of preparation is necessary before a programmer begins to actually write the computer program. The programmer must direct his attention to many areas and answer many questions about the nature of the problem, its input, and its output. Some of these questions are:

1. What are the desired output data?
2. What are the output media?
3. What input is needed to produce the desired results?
4. What are the input/output formats?

These questions are typical of some of the multitude of questions which must be answered by the problem analyst in preparing an application for a digital computer. The problem analyst must be able to see the problem as a whole as well as its component parts. He must be able to understand the computer's limitations and the computer's advantages. In general, there are four areas that the problem analyst or programmer must consider in the course of developing a computerized solution to a problem:

1. Problem analysis
2. Flowchart application
3. Coding and executing the application program
4. Documentation

The first step in preparing an application for a computer is to precisely define the problem. Once defined, the problem should be carefully analyzed to ascertain whether or not using a computer is the most appropriate and efficient means of solving the problem. Unnecessary and wasteful major changes after the programming of a problem has been started may be avoided only if a detailed problem analysis were to take place prior to the actual preparation of the program. Only after it has been determined that this problem warrants a computerized solution do we proceed to analyze the source data, the logical and practical procedures that will be needed to solve the problem, and the form of the final output. In the case of a simple payroll application, this analysis might reveal that required inputs would include regular hours worked, overtime hours worked, and a tape or disk file to input deductions, exemptions, and other data pertinent to payroll computations. It might also reveal that required outputs would include gross pay, withholding taxes, FICA deductions, accumulated tax-year withholdings and earnings, and, in addition, several detailed reports. Problem analysis is generally carried out conjunctively by the user and programmer or analyst.

FLOWCHART APPLICATION   A flowchart is a method by which the operations and flow of data during the solution of a problem may be shown using symbols and narrative descriptions. The *program flowchart* can be likened to the blueprint of a building. It represents what must be done to produce the desired building. As the designer draws a blueprint prior to beginning construction on a building, so, then, does the programmer draw a flowchart prior to writing a computer program. And, as in the case of the drawing of a blueprint, a flowchart is drawn according to definite rules and utilizing standard flowchart symbols prescribed by the American National Standards Institute.

The flowchart serves three major functions:

1. It allows the user to view the logic of the problem's solution in a pictorial fashion.
2. It serves the programmer by breaking up a large problem into smaller steps which he can individually code or program, without having to be concerned with how this smaller segment of the problem will fit into the total solution.
3. It serves as a means of communication between the management analyst or accountant and the programmer, and as a means of communication from programmer to programmer. The accountant, for example, does not have to be familiar with computer codes if he is able to understand a flowchart. From the flowchart he can easily and quickly determine if the proposed computer solution is logically correct and contains all necessary considerations and limitations. Even if he were capable of reading the programmer's coding, however well written and annotated, it would be very difficult and very dull work. Computers are designed to read code; human beings are more fluent with flowcharts.

When flowcharts were first used, they were crude and often difficult to follow. Every user had his own symbols and style, adding to the difficulty of reading and understanding the logic of the problem's solution. Flowchart writing has, of course, been significantly refined and standardized since that time. A sample program flowchart using IBM's flowcharting worksheet is shown in Fig. 7-2. Flowcharts will be discussed in detail in Chapter 8.

FIG. 7-2

Sample Program Flowchart.

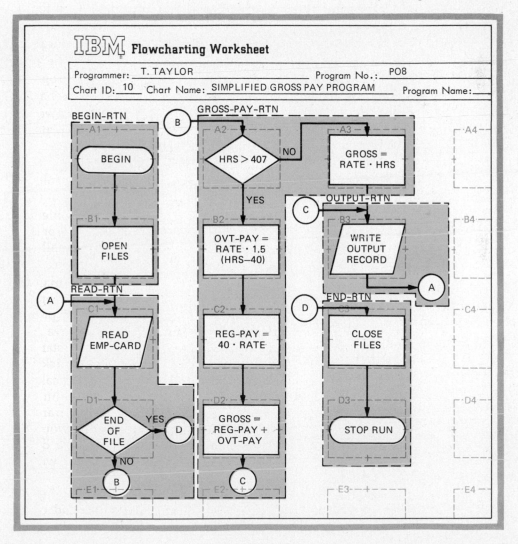

SELF-STUDY EXERCISES 7-1

1. The problem analyst must be able to see the problem _____.
   *****

   as a whole as well as in its component parts

2. The four areas the problem analyst must consider in the course of developing a computerized solution to a problem are _____, _____, _____, and _____.
   *****

   problem analysis
   flowchart application
   coding and execution of application program
   documentation

3. The first step in problem analysis is to determine _____.
   *****

   whether or not the problem warrants a computerized solution

4. Problem analysis is usually carried out by _____.
   *****

   a team consisting of the user and the programmer or analyst

5. The flowchart is _____.
   *****

   a method by which the operations and flow of data during the solution of a problem may be shown using symbols and narrative descriptions

6. The flowchart serves three major functions: _____, _____, and _____.
   *****

   it shows the logic of the problem's solution in pictorial form
   it allows the programmer to concentrate on small portions of the program without trying to visualize the logic of the entire program

it serves as a means of communication between management personnel and the programmer as well as between programmers

After the problem has been analyzed and a detailed program flow-chart has been written, the programmer must now code the program as detailed in the flowchart. Coding simply involves the translation or conversion of each operation in the flowchart into a computer-understandable language. In our study of data processing thus far, we have learned that a computer program consists of a series of instructions that, when successfully carried out or executed, will accomplish the desired result. Let us now discuss the types of instructions that are available to the programmer.

CODING AND EXECUTING THE APPLICATION PROGRAM

Computer instructions consist of five types: (1) input/output, (2) control, (3) arithmetic, (4) logical, and (5) specification.

Types of Instructions

1. Input/output—Instructions of this type direct the computer to move information to and from the computer's memory and an input or output unit.
2. Control—Instructions of this type control the order in which other instructions are performed. That is, they direct the computer concerning what instruction is to be executed next.
3. Arithmetic—These instructions direct the performance of arithmetical computations.
4. Logical—Instructions of this type enable the computer to compare items of data and proceed according to the result of the comparison as well as enabling the computer to deviate from the normal sequence of instructions in accordance with the existence or nonexistence of certain conditions. Logical instructions also include those instructions which direct the computer to move information from one place in the memory of the computer to another.
5. Specification—These instructions are descriptive in purpose, and through them the programmer can inform the computer regarding such items as the types of data items used in the program, the allocation of storage, and so forth.

However, we have not discussed how the programmer can communicate his instructions to the computer. Many types or levels of computer languages are available to aid the programmer in communicating with the computer. Three of the more commonly used types of computer languages are:

1. Machine language (actual)
2. Symbolic language
3. Procedure-oriented language

Machine Language (Actual)* Machine language or actual is a series of numbers, letters of the alphabet, or special characters that are used to represent bit patterns which can be recognized by the computer and cause specific operations to take place. An example of a machine-language instruction to add regular pay to overtime pay, yielding total pay, might appear as follows:

21   300   400   500

In this example, the 21 is a code which means ADD to the computer. The 300 and 400 are addresses or locations at which regular pay and overtime pay are stored. The 500 represents the storage locations for the sum, total pay.

Let us examine more completely what would be happening inside a hypothetical computer before, during, and after the execution of this instruction.

To begin with, let us examine the memory of the computer immediately before the execution of this instruction (see Fig. 7-3). At this point, the instruction being executed is one which is located in storage prior to the ADD instruction under discussion. Since instructions are generally executed in sequential order as they exist in storage, the instruction under consideration will not be executed until the previous instructions have been executed. When the sequence of execution reaches this instruction, it will be taken from storage and executed. The execution of this instruction will consist of taking the contents of memory locations 300 and 400 and moving them to an accumulator. The accumulator then adds these two numbers and the result is returned to storage location 500.

Control is then transferred to the next instruction in storage for execution. At this point, the memory of our hypothetical computer would appear as shown in Fig. 7-4. It is the programmer's task to make certain, via previous instructions, that regular pay and overtime pay are in locations 300 and 400, respectively. The machine has no way of knowing what should be in these locations,

Memory Address	Memory Contents	Content Description
0001	•••	First Instruction
⋮	⋮	⋮
0040	21300400500	ADD Instruction
⋮	⋮	⋮
0210	31	STOP Instruction
⋮	⋮	⋮
0300	3476	The First Number To Be Added
⋮	⋮	⋮
0400	24192	The Second Number To Be Added
⋮	⋮	⋮
0500	•••	Any Number Remaining In This Storage Location From The Previous Operation

FIG. 7-3

Contents of Computer Memory Before Executing ADD Instruction.

and therefore adds their contents regardless of whether these contents are correct or incorrect. The programmer, then, must know what codes correspond to what operations. For example, the code

Memory Address	Memory Contents	Content Description
0001	•••	First Instruction
⋮	⋮	⋮
0040	21300400500	ADD Instruction
⋮	⋮	⋮
0210	31	STOP Instruction
⋮	⋮	⋮
0300	3476	The First Number To Be Added
⋮	⋮	⋮
0400	24192	The Second Number To Be Added
⋮	⋮	⋮
0500	27668	The Sum Of The Numbers Stored In Memory Locations 300 & 400

FIG. 7-4

Contents of Computer Memory After Executing ADD Instruction.

21 means ADD. He must make certain that his instructions are written and executed in the correct order. He must also keep track of what data are stored at what addresses and he must make certain

that the correct information is at this address when it is needed. In short, machine-language programming places a large burden on the person writing the program to keep track of the details involved.

Although machine language is ideal for the computer, programmers find it to be a difficult and tedious one with which to work. Because of this fact, long and detailed programs are rarely written in machine language. Other easier-to-use languages have been devised to make the programmer's task an easier one. However, since the computer is only capable of understanding and executing instructions written in machine language, programs written in other languages will eventually have to be translated into machine language before they can be executed. Translators for other standard languages are generally provided with the computer by the computer manufacturer. Such languages fall into two categories, symbolic languages and procedure-oriented languages.

A symbolic language is one which is very closely related to machine language in that, in general, one symbolic instruction will translate into one machine-language instruction.

Symbolic Language*

The advantage of such a language is in the ease with which the programmer can use the language. A symbolic instruction contains fewer symbols, and these symbols may be letters and special characters, as well as numbers. Let us consider the hypothetical machine-language instruction discussed in the previous section,

21   300   400   500

The symbolic equivalent might appear as

A   RPAY   OPAY   TPAY

When this instruction is translated by a manufacturer-supplied translator, the A will be replaced by 21, the name RPAY replaced by the address 300, the name OPAY replaced by the address 400, and the name TPAY replaced by the address 500.

As you can see, the symbolic instruction would be significantly easier to write than the machine-language equivalent and is certainly easier to read and understand. This last factor is especially important in regard to the ease with which corrections and changes can be made. On the other hand, a certain amount of time is required to convert from symbolic to machine language, but this does

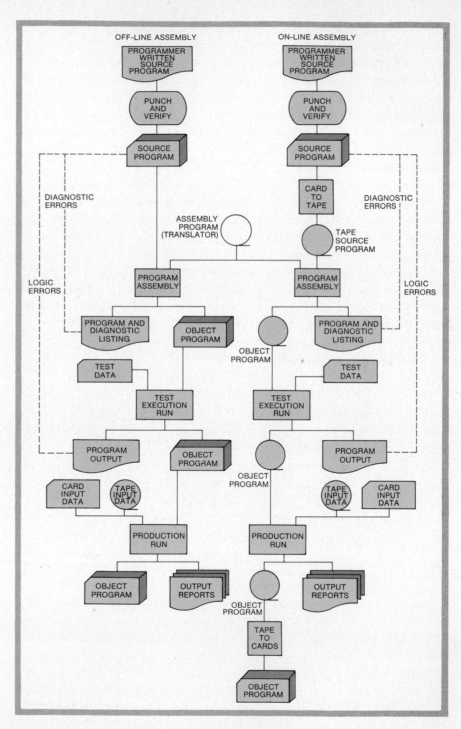

FIG. 7-5
Assembly Process.

not compare to the time saved by the programmer in working with a symbolic language as opposed to working with machine language.

The translation from symbolic to machine language is done by a computer program referred to as an assembly system, or processor. This assembly system keeps track of all memory locations and all names or symbolic tags as associated with memory locations. This translation process also provides the programmer with error diagnostics to assist him in detecting certain types of coding errors.

Summarizing, one could say that when the programming goal is to employ an easy-to-read, easy-to-write, and easy-to-modify language in addition to making the most efficient use of the computer's hardware, a program should be written in the symbolic language.

This, however, leaves two things to be desired: a programming language more similar to that normally used to describe the problem or procedure and a programming language that is virtually machine independent and can be used on various computers. These two desires are, however, properties of the procedure-oriented languages.

Procedure-oriented Languages*

Assembler systems or machine-oriented programming systems require a thorough understanding of the computer system (hardware) to be used in the execution of the program by the programmer. In contrast, procedure-oriented programming systems for all practical purposes remove the necessity, on the part of the programmer, for understanding how the computer system will go about executing his program. The programmer may, instead, concentrate on expressing the procedure or logic of solving his problem. In many cases, it is not even necessary that he know what kind of computer system will be used for the execution of the program. The translation from a procedure-oriented language to machine language is done by a program referred to as a *compiler*. This name was chosen because a procedure-oriented system usually compiles many machine-language instructions from one source-language statement.

There are over 100 procedure-oriented languages currently in existence, the most popular and commonly used of these being FORTRAN (*FOR*mula *TRAN*slator) and COBOL (*CO*mmon *B*usiness *O*riented *L*anguage). The languages of FORTRAN and

COBOL have become so common and heavily used that a variation of, if not the complete FORTRAN and COBOL languages, are available for virtually every medium to large computer manufactured.

Table 7-1 illustrates how the above mentioned assembly-language instruction,

A   RPAY   OPAY   TPAY

might appear in machine language, FORTRAN and COBOL

The advantages of procedure-oriented languages are numerous. Procedure-oriented languages are accompanied by extensive diagnostic routines that often make program checking far simpler than with assembly languages. Procedure-oriented language instructions are written in a manner very similar to that normally used to describe the problem by the scientific- or business-oriented individual (see Figs. 7-6 and 7-7). And, procedure-oriented languages are virtually machine independent. That is, a computer program written for one computer installation can be used on another similar-sized computer system, even one produced by a different manufacturer, with just a few minor changes.

There are, however, several disadvantages associated with the use of procedure-oriented or compiler languages. The first disadvantage is the time lost in translating to machine language. Another disadvantage is that the machine-translated or -compiled program may not make as efficient use of the computer's resources as a program written by an experienced programmer using a symbolic

TABLE 7-1

Comparison of Instructions in Different Computer Languages

COMPUTER LANGUAGE	INSTRUCTION FORMAT
Machine language or actual	21 300 400 500
Symbolic language	AD RPAY OPAY TPAY
FORTRAN	TOTPAY = REGPAY + OVTPAY
COBOL	ADD REGPAY, OVTPAY GIVING TOTPAY

```
00001    001010 IDENTIFICATION DIVISION.
00002    001020 PROGRAM-ID.
00003    001030     PROGRAM-1.
00004    001040 AUTHOR.
00005    001050     WM FUORI.
00006    001060 INSTALLATION.
00007    001070     NASSAU COMMUNITY COLLEGE.
00008    001080 DATE-WRITTEN.
00009    001090     1/15/76.
00010    001100 DATE-COMPILED.
00011    001110     1/18/76.
00012    001120 SECURITY.
00013    001130     NON-CONFIDENTIAL.
00014    002010 ENVIRONMENT DIVISION.
00015    002020 CONFIGURATION SECTION.
00016    002030 SOURCE-COMPUTER.
00017    002040     IBM-370-H155.
00018    002050 OBJECT-COMPUTER.
00019    002060     IBM-370-H155.
00020    003010 DATA DIVISION.
00021    003020 WORKING-STORAGE SECTION.
00022    003030 77  DATA-IN       PICTURE 999V99.
00023    003040 77  DATA-OUT      PICTURE $999.99
00024    004010 PROCEDURE DIVISION.
00025    004020     ACCEPT DATA-IN.
00026    004030     MOVE DATA-IN TO DATA-OUT.
00027    004040     DISPLAY DATA-OUT.
00028    004050     STOP RUN.
```

FIG. 7-6

COBOL Program Source Listing.

or machine-language system. The advantages, as I'm sure you will agree, far outweigh the disadvantages.

As compilers are improved, an on-going process, the advantages of their use will become more numerous, the efficiency greater, and the disadvantages less and less.

After the programmer has determined which level of computer language, and what specific language within this level, is most

FIG. 7-7

Sample of FORTRAN Program Segment

```
C       SAMPLE FORTRAN PROGRAM
        READ (1,10) PRINC, RATE, PERPYR, NOPER
10 FORMAT (F7.2,F4.3,F4.0,I4)
        AMT = PRINC * (1.0 + RATE / PERPYR) ** NOPER
        WRITE (3,20) PRINC, RATE, PERPYR, NOPER, AMT
20 FORMAT (1H1,10X,'PRINCIPAL INVESTED = ',F7.2/
       -          11X,'ANNUAL RATE = ',F4.3/
       -          11X,'COMPOUNDED ',F4.0,' TIMES PER YEAR'/
       -          11X,'COMPOUNDED FOR A TOTAL OF ',I4,' PERIODS'//
       -          8X,'*****************************************'/
       -          8X,'*          AMOUNT = ',F10.2,'          *'/
       -          8X,'*****************************************')
        CALL EXIT
        END
```

appropriate for use in the solution of the problem, he is now prepared to code the solution of the problem. The coding phase can be completed easily and quickly if a sufficiently detailed flowchart has been previously prepared.

Executing and Debugging the Program

Once the problem has been analyzed, flowcharted, and coded, it is ready to be executed, or tested, and debugged. The term *debug* simply means to locate and correct any errors or bugs that have been made in the preparation of the program.

Types of Programming Errors. There are two general types of errors that programmers make—syntax or coding errors and logic errors.

A *syntax* or *coding* error occurs when the programmer fails to follow the rules on how a particular instruction is to be written. For example, if a programmer misspelled the word WRITE in an instruction, the computer would print out a diagnostic message to inform the programmer that a coding error had been made, the statement in which it occurred, and the nature of the error. Figure 7-8 illustrates some of diagnostic messages that appeared in a student program. As a result of the severity of these errors, the computer was unable to completely understand the program and consequently the program was not executed. Compilers available with most large computer systems have reached the level of sophistication that allows them to make corrective assumptions concerning common coding errors. For example, if a programmer

FIG. 7-8

Sample Program Containing Coding Errors.

```
00001    001010 IDENTIFICATION DIVISION.
00002    001020 PROGRAM-ID. PROGRAM1.
00003    002010 ENVIRONMENT DIVISION.
00004    002020 CONFIGURATION SECTION.
00005    002030 SOURCE-COMPUTER. IBM-370-H155.
00006    002040 OBJECT-COMPUTER. IBM-370-H155.
00007    003010 DATA DIVISION.
00008    003030 WORKING-STORAGE SECTION.
00009  **003020 77   DATA-OUT   PIC $999.99.
00010    004010 PROCEDURE DIVISION.
00011    004020 START.
00012    004030     ACCEPT DATA-IN.
00013    004040     MOVE DATA-IN TO DATA-OUT.
00014    004050     DISPLAY DATA-OUT.
00015    004060 STOP RUN.
```

```
CARD   ERROR MESSAGE

11     IKF1100I-W   1 SEQUENCE ERROR IN SOURCE PROGRAM.
11     IKF1087I-W   * START * SHOULD NOT BEGIN A-MARGIN.
11     IKF4050I-E   SYNTAX REQUIRES QISAM-FILE WITH NOMINAL KEY . FOUND END-OF-SENT . STATEMENT
                    DISCARDED.
12     IKF3001I-E   DATA-IN NOT DEFINED. DISCARDED.
13     IKF3001I-E   DATA-IN NOT DEFINED. DISCARDED.
15     IKF1087I-W   * STOP * SHOULD NOT BEGIN A-MARGIN.
```

FIG. 7-9
Computer Diagnostics for Sample Program.

omitted a required comma in an instruction, the compiler would print out an appropriate diagnostic message and proceed with the compilation as if the comma had been present.

Once the programmer has removed all the coding errors, the compiler is able to understand and translate the programmer's instructions. However, when executed, the translated instructions may not be appropriate to solve the problem. Errors resulting from an incorrect sequence of instructions are referred to as *logic* errors. For example, if the programmer added when he should have subtracted, he would have made an error in the program logic—a logic error. There are no fixed rules on how debugging a program containing logic errors should be accomplished because the kinds of bugs that can occur are so varied. Debugging a computer program is like solving a murder mystery. The programmer, as the detective, must exercise all his deductive reasoning powers to determine the culprit. The programmer must collect all clues and try to fit them into a pattern. As the detective reinacts the crime to gain insight into the solution to the crime, the programmer runs or executes the program utilizing carefully prepared sample data. These sample data must be prepared so as to test the results of all possible types of transactions and all possible alternatives that could occur during the actual running of the finished program. This process can uncover an error or bug which might otherwise have gone undetected, and it is certainly better to determine the existence of the error or bug at this point than when the program is in actual use in the field. Once debugged, the program should again be tested using actual data for which a solution is known. In this way, the program can again be tested by the programmer and the results verified by the user, be he an accountant, business manager, or other user. Any discrepancies between the manner in which the user planned to input the data and the manner in which the programmer expected to receive the data will be clearly apparent at this point and can be rectified.

In testing larger or more complex programs, it is usually advisable to test one segment or module of the program at a time. When all segments have been tested, the complete program may then be tested. Segmenting a large program facilitates finding errors, as the more errors that there are in a program, the more difficult they are to find, since one error may obscure clues to other errors.

1. Coding an application involves _____.

        *****

  the translation or conversion of each operation in the flowchart
  into computer-understandable language

2. Computer instruction consists of five types: _____,
   _____, _____, _____, and _____.

        *****

                input/output
                control
                arithmetic
                logical
                specification

3. The purpose of control instructions is to _____.

        *****

  control the order in which other instructions are executed

4. Specification instructions are _____ in purpose.

        *****

                descriptive

5. Machine language or _____ uses a series of _____ that
   are accepted by the computer and cause a specific operation
   to take place.

        *****

                actual
        numbers, letters, or special characters

6. The only language a computer can understand without being
   translated is _____.

        *****

        machine language or actual

7. Symbolic language is most closely related to _____ and has the advantage of being easier to use.

*****

machine language

8. Symbolic-language programs must be _____ before they can be executed.

*****

translated to machine language

9. Procedure-oriented languages allow the programmer to concentrate on _____ and not be concerned with how the computer will solve the problem.

*****

expressing the procedure or logic of the problem

10. The most commonly used procedure-oriented languages are _____ and _____.

*****

COBOL (*CO*mmon *B*usiness *O*riented *L*anguage)
FORTRAN (*FOR*mula *TRAN*slator)

11. Procedure-oriented language translators are equipped with extensive _____ which aid in program checking.

*****

diagnostic routines

12. The two main disadvantages of procedure-oriented languages are _____ and _____.

*****

they must be translated into machine language
resulting machine-language programs do not always make
the most efficient use of the computer's resources

13. Locating and correcting errors made in preparing a program is termed _____.

*****

debugging

The programming process is not complete until the program has **DOCUMENTATION** been written and thoroughly field tested for a substantial period of time. A program is said to be operational when it has been thoroughly tested and completely documented.

It is essential that the programmer adequately document each program. A properly documented program is useful for manage-

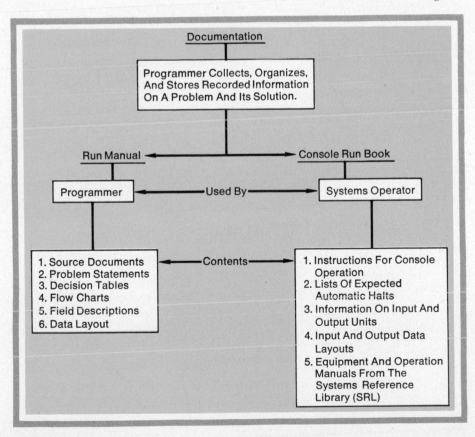

FIG. 7-10

Documentation of a Program.

ment in understanding the application and its solution, aids the public accountant in performing his audit, and serves as a frame of reference for those who would implement or modify the program. It is far easier to modify or update a thoroughly documented program than one which may be absolutely correct and efficient but one which has been shabbily documented.

It is equally essential that each program not be over- or under-documented. Overdocumentation can be needlessly expensive and time-consuming, overwhelming to those who must reference it, and can result in great delays in the implementation of the program. Underdocumentation, however, can also be needlessley expensive and time-consuming because of the confusion and misunderstandings resulting from incomplete or missing information. Therefore, it is essential that a program be *appropriately* documented.

Documentation is not something a programmer considers after a program has been written and debugged but something that is an integral part of the programming process. For example, Fig. 7-11 illustrates two COBOL program segments, both technically correct and both intended to perform the same function. It should be apparent that the programmer of the second version, by appropriately choosing data names, has produced a clearer and better documented program. The additional time and effort expended are easily justified by the added clarity obtained which will ultimately result in time and cost savings.

Organization of Program Documentation[1]

There are numerous forms that can be used in documenting a program. Many forms are shown throughout this chapter, but these forms vary greatly from computer installation to computer installation. Each installation establishes its own documentation standards with respect to the forms used and the information to be placed on each form. Therefore, in this chapter, only those standards are discussed that are required by most existing installations. The programmer generally collects the documentation information into a folder referred to as a procedures or run manual (see Fig. 7-5). Some of the papers that are generally included in this manual are the following:

---

[1]This material is taken with permission from *Introduction to American National Standard COBOL* by William M. Fuori, McGraw-Hill Book Company, 1975.

```
004010    P2.
004020        READ T END GO TO P7.
004030    P3.
004040        IF H > 40 GO TO P5.
004050    P4.
004060        COMPUTE G = R * H.
004070        GO TO P6.
004080    P5.
004090        COMPUTE S = 40 * R.
004100        COMPUTE O = 1.5 * R * (H - 40).
004110        COMPUTE G = S + O.
004120    P6.
```

```
004010    READ-TIME-CARD.
004020        READ TIME-CARD, AT END GO TO END-PROGRAM.
004030    DETERMINE-OVERTIME.
004040        IF HOURS-WORKED > 40, GO TO GROSS-PAY-WITH-OVERTIME.
004050    GROSS-PAY-NO-OVERTIME.
004060        COMPUTE GROSS-PAY = HOURLY-RATE * HOURS-WORKED.
004070        GO TO NET-PAY-ROUTINE.
004080    GROSS-PAY-WITH-OVERTIME.
004090        COMPUTE REGULAR-PAY = 40 * HOURLY-RATE.
004100        COMPUTE OVERTIME-PAY = 1.5 * HOURLY-RATE *
004110            (HOURS-WORKED - 40).
004120        COMPUTE GROSS-PAY = REGULAR-PAY + OVERTIME-PAY.
004130    NET-PAY-ROUTINE.
```

FIG. 7-11

Two COBOL Program Segments.

1. Title page
2. Control sheet
3. Narrative descriptions
4. Narrative modifications
5. Flowcharts and decision tables
6. Input and output data codes
7. Input and output formats
8. Input test data and sample output
9. Other instruction sheets and worksheets

Title Page. The title page of a run manual contains basic information about the program for easy reference. Some of the items generally contained on the title page of a run manual are shown in Fig. 7-12.

Page 1 of 1

TITLE PAGE

PROGRAM NAME	CREATE–EARNINGS–FILE
PROGRAM NUMBER	P003
PROGRAMMER	William M. Fuori, Ext 406
USER	Payroll Department, Ext 493
DATE WRITTEN	January 15, 1975
PROJECT SUPERVISOR	T.M. Taylor, Ext 348
SCHEDULE	Weekly (Wednesday)
ESTIMATED TIME	15 Minutes
CONTROLS	Total of straight and overtime hours with control totals from Payroll Department. Internal & external tape label checks.
SECURITY	None
PURPOSE OF PROGRAM	Generate an Earning File from the Master File and Earnings Cards.

INPUT

    (1) MASTER–FILE
          Reel Label: MASTER–P003
          Data Records: MASTER–REC
          Estimated Volume: 350 records (1 reel)
          Sequence: Numeric by Employee Number
          Tape Labels: Standard volume, header, and trailer
          Record Length: 200 Characters
          Blocking Factors: 5

    (2) PAY–CARD
          Source: Payroll Department
          Data Records: PAY–REC
          Estimated Volume: 350 cards
          Sequence: Numeric by Employee Number
          Forms: 0583 Preprinted Payroll cards

OUTPUT

    (1) CURRENT–EARNINGS
          Reel Label: EARNINGS–P003
          Data Records: CUR–EARN
          Estimated Volume: 350 records (1 reel)
          Sequence: Numeric by Employee Number
          Tape Labels: Standard volume, header, and trailer
          Record Length: 157 Characters
          Blocking Factor: 5

    (2) EXCEPTION–REPORT
          When Issued: Whenever input data exceptions occur
          Form Used: 0585 Preprinted continous forms

DISTRIBUTION	Earnings File to be maintained in Computer Center. Copy 1 of Exception Report (if any) to Payroll Department.
REMARKS	Program provides input to programs P002, P005, P006, and P008.

NCC Form 1887

FIG. 7-12

Sample Run Manual Title Page.

The control sheet is used to indicate to a reader of the run manual that changes have been made in the program since the time it was first documented and implemented. This sheet indicates such items as **Control Sheet**

1. The section of the manual or program that has been changed
2. The name and title of the individual making the change
3. The name and title of the individual who approved the change
4. The date the change became effective
5. The duration of the change

Some of the conditions affecting a program that would require the above entries on the control sheet may include the following:

1. Changes in input or output media
2. Changes in input or output formats
3. Changes in the logic of the program
4. Code or condition changes

Thus, the control sheet not only documents the changes that the program has undergone since its inception but also serves as an indication that the documentation of the program is current.

Narrative Descriptions. Although the purpose of the program is stated on the Title Page, this is not sufficient for documentation purposes. In this section, the program must be discussed in sufficient detail so that the reader can clearly understand what the program does and how it goes about doing it. Many installations refer to this description as a *program abstract*. A typical program abstract for the program described on the sample Title Page is illustrated in Figure 7-13. Note that this abstract describes the input, output, and processing requirements of the program.

In some narrative descriptions it may be necessary to include or refer to specific statements within the program. This situation is rare, however, and should be avoided whenever possible.

Narrative Modifications. This section is intended to contain descriptions of any modifications that the program has undergone, whether or not they involve actual changes in the COBOL program

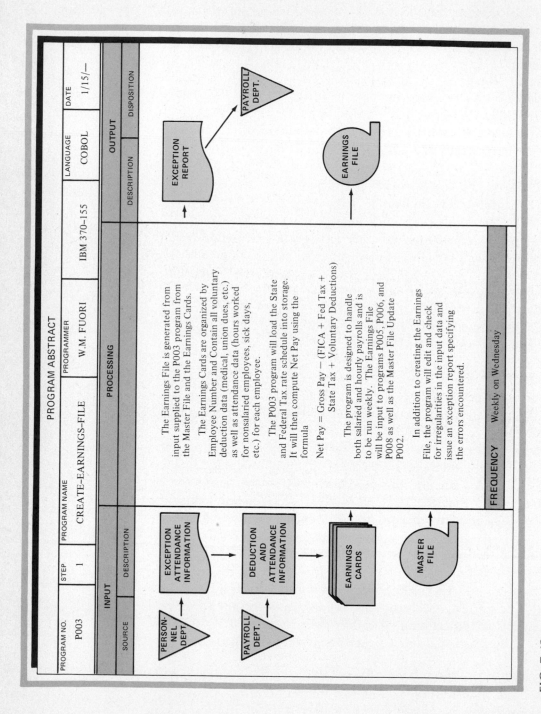

FIG. 7-13
Sample Program Abstract.

288

itself. Entries in this section should be as brief as possible. They should be summaries and not line-by-line analyses.

It is also a good practice to correlate the narrative modifications with the original narrative descriptions to which they refer. This is generally done by placing the number of the narrative modification next to the narrative description that has been modified. When the narrative modification is substantial or sufficiently involved, the narrative description itself should be rewritten.

Flowcharts and Decision Tables. The flowchart is a graphic representation of the nature and order of the operations and decision logic required to solve a problem. It illustrates the sequential order of the steps that must be taken by the computer in processing input data to provide meaningful results. A flowchart is especially useful to someone attempting to follow the logic of a very complex program. When substantial logical analysis is necessary to produce a desired result, a decision table may be used in conjunction with the program flowchart to explain the logical flow of the problem. In most installations, standard flowcharting and decision table worksheets are readily available. One such flowcharting worksheet, shown in Figure 7-2 illustrates a simple program to calculate an employee's gross pay. Note that each flowchart segment corresponding to a paragraph in the COBOL program is enclosed in dotted lines and assigned the same name assigned to the paragraph in the actual program. Thus, a direct relationship is established between the program and the flowchart. To maintain this relationship, the programmer must make certain to update the flowchart whenever the program is modified.

Input and Output Data Codes. A code can be thought of as a system of symbols for representing data. A code provides a substitute, in the form of a set of arbitrary characters, for actual names or numbers.

There are many reasons why data are coded. Among the more important of these reasons are the following:

1. To save space on an input or output medium
2. To give processing and storage advantages
3. To provide file security

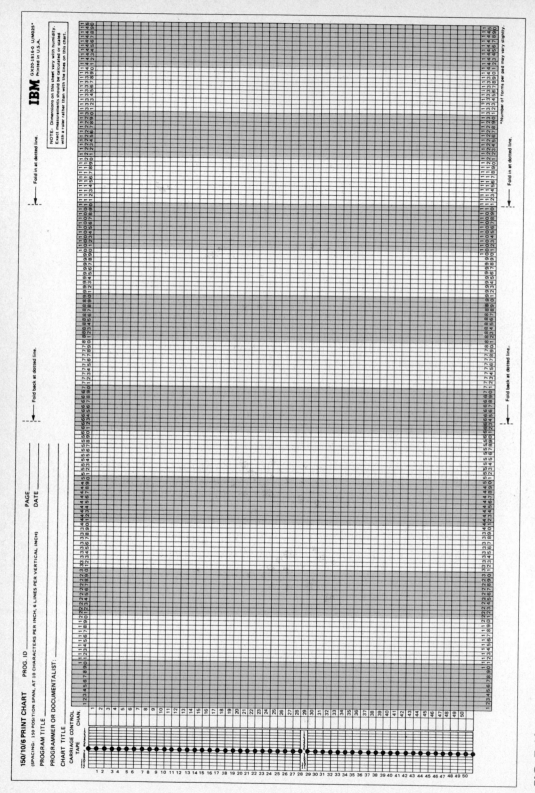

FIG. 7-14
Printer Spacing Chart.

290

4. To increase remote entry speed and accuracy
5. To increase the efficiency of sorting operations
6. To facilitate limited information retrieval

In most cases, however, codes are used simply to save space on an input or output medium or to save internal storage space. Codes such as 1 for male and 2 for female, or the like, have become commonplace in programming. It is important that the programmer set down, with a detailed explanation, every code that is used with any input or output medium, making certain that the place each code is used is indicated.

Input and Output Formats. The COBOL program itself provides a great deal of information regarding the format of input and output records in the DATA DIVISION. This, however, is not sufficient. In many cases, the record descriptions do not describe the contents of each field; they describe only those fields used by the program. The remainder may be assigned the name FILLER and not described at all. However, these fields may be very important to the next program that uses the files.

There are numerous ways in which input and output formats can be shown; they vary greatly from installation to installation. To help standardize the documenting of input and output formats, preprinted standard forms are generally available. One of these forms is used each time an output report is planned: the printer spacing chart (see Fig. 7-14). This chart is generally prepared while the program is being written to aid the programmer in determining the output record layouts, particularly those appearing in the WORKING-STORAGE SECTION of the DATA DIVISION.

Another commonly used preprinted, standardized form is the Multiple-Card Layout Form (see Fig. 7-15). This form provides a better visual image of the card than does a list of card columns and fields. However, it is difficult to use if the record being described contains many small fields; there is very little space in which to describe these fields. However, it is one of the best ways to illustrate multiple-card records. In the case illustrated in Fig. 7-15, for example, a three-card record is illustrated.

Another standard preprinted form that is commonly used when documenting tape and disk layouts is the record layout worksheet

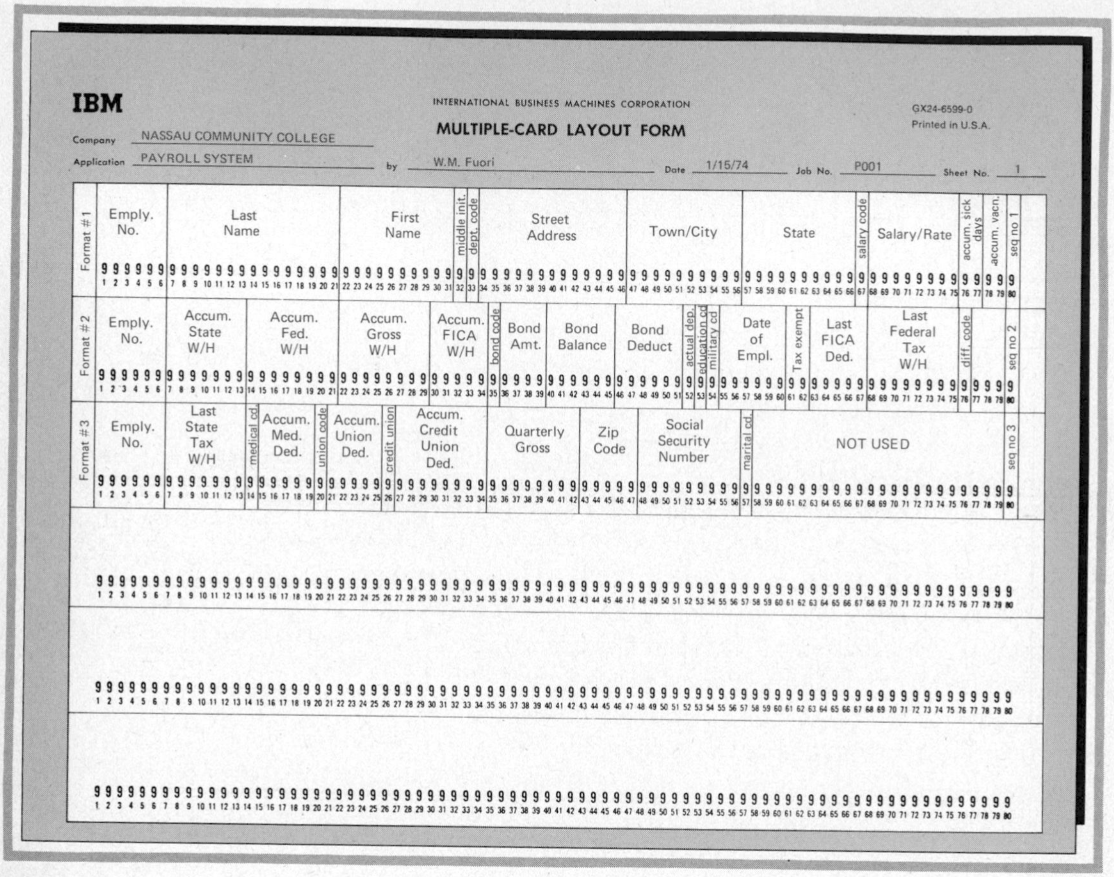
IBM

INTERNATIONAL BUSINESS MACHINES CORPORATION

MULTIPLE-CARD LAYOUT FORM

GX24-6599-0
Printed in U.S.A.

Company NASSAU COMMUNITY COLLEGE

Application PAYROLL SYSTEM by W.M. Fuori Date 1/15/74 Job No. P001 Sheet No. 1

Format #1: Emply. No. | Last Name | First Name | middle init. | dept. code | Street Address | Town/City | State | salary code | Salary/Rate | accum. sick days | accum. vacn. | seq no 1

Format #2: Emply. No. | Accum. State W/H | Accum. Fed. W/H | Accum. Gross W/H | Accum. FICA W/H | bond code | Bond Amt. | Bond Balance | Bond Deduct | actual dep. | education cd | military cd | Date of Empl. | Tax exempt | Last FICA Ded. | Last Federal Tax W/H | diff. code | seq no 2

Format #3: Emply. No. | Last State Tax W/H | medical cd | Accum. Med. Ded. | union code | Accum. Union Ded. | credit union | Accum. Credit Union Ded. | Quarterly Gross | Zip Code | Social Security Number | marital cd. | NOT USED | seq no 3

FIG. 7-15
Multiple Card Layout Form.

illustrated in Fig. 7-16. This form enables the programmer to include such information as the type of characters that are contained within the field and the fields on which the file is sorted.

Input Test Data and Sample Output. Input test data are extremely important. It can be used initially to verify that the program has been adequately checked. Later, if a problem arises, this test can be used again to determine if the program was changed, and if not, whether or not the test data tested the current trouble condition.

ORGANIZATION UNIT		OPERATIONS			INDEX NUMBER	
DISTRIBUTION LIST NO.	SUBJECT OR TITLE	RECORD LAYOUT				
ISSUE DATE					PAGE <u>1</u> OF <u>3</u>	

PROGRAM NUMBER	PROGRAM NAME	MACHINE	PROGRAMMER	STEP		DATE
P001	CREATE-MAST	IBM-370-155	W.M. Fuori	1		1/8/--

RECORD NAME	FILE NAME	FILE NO.	SIZE
MASTER-REC	PAYROLL-MASTER	3147P	1 Reel

FIELD FROM	TO	SIZE	CHAR.	SORT SEQ.	FIELD NAME	REMARKS
1	6	6	N	1	EMPLOYEE-NO	9 (6)
7	21	15	A		LAST-NAME	
22	31	10	A		FIRST-NAME	
32		1	A		MIDDLE-INIT	
33		1	N	2	DEPT-CODE	Code = '1', '2', '3', or '4'
34	46	13	AN		STREET	
47	56	10	A		TOWN-CITY	
57	66	10	A		STATE	
67		1	A		SALARY-CODE	Code = 'S' or 'W'
68	75	8	N		SALARY RATE	9 (6) V99
76	77	2	N		SICK-DAY-ACCUM	99
78	79	2	N		VACN-DAY-ACCUM	99
80	86	7	N		ST-TAX-ACCUM	9 (5) V99
87	94	8	N		FED-TAX-ACCUM	9 (6) V99
95	102	8	N		GROSS-ACCUM	9 (6) V99
103	107	5	N		FICA-ACCUM	999V99

CHAR.
A – ALPHA S – SIGNED NUMERIC
N – NUMERIC AN – ALPHA NUMERIC

SORT SEQ. 1 - MAJOR
2 - INTERMEDIATE
ETC.

APPROVED _____ DATE

_____

NCC

☐ NEW	REPLACES	ISSUED	REPLACES	PAGES
☐ REVISION	INDEX NO.			

FORM NO. MI–165–00 UNIFORM MANUALS AND METHODS

FIG. 7-16
Record Layout Worksheet.

Sample output can be in the form of printed reports, tape dumps, punched cards, or other forms of output that are produced by the program. It is important that a programmer demonstrate a thorough testing of the program with the preprinted forms that will be used in production. Consider the consequences if a program is put into use and prints out several thousand paychecks with all the data in the wrong places. If preprinted forms are not required, the sample output will still serve to verify that report titles are spelled and positioned correctly and that the data are aligned properly with respect to the titles.

Other Instruction Sheets and Worksheets. The preceding documentation is required in most installations. But besides the various forms mentioned so far, there may be others for which the programmer is responsible. These others, which vary with the computer installation, may include such forms as a programming check list, a job request form, an operating instruction sheet, and a run sheet. Using one of these forms or a like form, the programmer must convey specific instructions for running the program. Included would be such information as the following:

1. Input media with identifying data (tape reel number, disk pack number, etc.)
2. Form numbers for special output forms or number of parts of paper to be used
3. Instructions for aligning forms on the printer
4. Hardware devices required
5. Expected processing time
6. Special operator instructions in case the program abnormally terminates
7. Program messages and required operator actions

It must be realized, as was pointed out early in this discussion, that all programs do not receive the same level of documentation. It makes little sense to provide the level of documentation previously discussed for a small, one-shot program. However, even the smallest program must be documented to some extent. The programmer must always bear in mind that until the program has been thoroughly tested and documented, it may not be considered complete or operational.

1. A program is not operational until it has been _____.
   *****

   thoroughly tested and completely documented

2. Programmer documentation requires the preparation of a _____ and _____ containing _____ and _____, respectively.
   *****

   run manual
   console run book
   source documents, problem statements, decision tables, flow-charts, field descriptions, and data layouts
   detailed operations instruction necessary to execute the program

3. Some of the items generally included in a procedures or run manual would include _____.
   *****

   title page, control sheet, narrative descriptions, narrative modifications, flowcharts, and decision tables, input and output data codes, input and output formats, input test data and sample output, and other instruction sheets and worksheets

EXERCISES

True–false exercises   7-1

1. _____ A detailed problem analysis should precede the actual program preparation.

2. _____ The last phase a programmer will complete in programming and application is the documentation of the solution to the problem.

3. _____ Problem analysis generally involves both the programmer and user.

4. _____ Documentation of a program is useful only to the programmer, systems analyst, and operator.

5. _____ Each symbolic instruction will translate into more than one machine instruction.

6. _____ A program written in a procedure-oriented language will be more efficient than a program written in a symbolic language.

7. _____ The logic instructions determine the order in which program instructions are to be executed.

8. _____ Diagnostic routines are not associated with machine language.

9. _____ Flowcharts and decision tables are part of program documentation.

10. _____ Debugging a program involves correcting both coding and logic errors.

11. _____ A compiler is used to translate procedure-oriented languages into machine language.

12. _____ Before a program written in a procedure-oriented language can be executed, it must be translated into machine language.

13. _____ Procedure-oriented languages are the most difficult programming languages to use.

14. _____ Of the three types of computer languages discussed, the symbolic language is the most difficult to program in.

15. _____ A user does not have to be capable of writing computer instruction, but he should be able to read and understand a flowchart.

16. _____ The testing phase of a computer program precedes any documentation of the problem.

17. _____ Coding involves the translation of the flowchart into a computer-acceptable language.

18. _____ A symbolic language generally contains fewer symbols than a machine language.

19. _____ Two examples of procedure-oriented languages are FORTRAN and COBOL.

20. _____ When using procedure-oriented systems, the programmer must fully understand how the computer will go about executing the program.

21. _____ There are five basic types of computer instructions.

22. _____ Procedure-oriented compilers usually generate many machine-language instructions from one source-language statement.

23. ____ Flowcharting symbols have been standardized by the American National Standards Institute.

24. ____ In determining the feasibility of a computerized solution to a given problem, it is generally not necessary to consult with the user.

25. ____ Procedure-oriented languages are virtually machine independent and can be used on various machines with only minor modifications.

26. ____ Computer instructions are generally executed in sequential order.

27. ____ Most commercial computers are equipped with both a COBOL and a FORTRAN compiler.

28. ____ A processor is a computer program that translates symbolic language into machine language.

Multiple-choice exercises 7-2

1. ____ Advantages of procedure-oriented languages include
   (a) diagnostic routines that make checking far easier
   (b) being written in a language easily understood by the user
   (c) being virtually machine independent
   (d) all the above
   (e) (a) and (c) only

2. ____ Debugging does not include
   (a) deductive reasoning
   (b) using sample data
   (c) data with a known solution
   (d) actual data
   (e) none of the above

3. ____ In order to facilitate the execution of a procedure-oriented language, a _____ is provided by the manufacturer for program checking.
   (a) diagnostic routine
   (b) error reconciliation
   (c) compiler
   (d) all the above
   (e) none of the above

4. ____ The second step a programmer must consider in developing a computerized solution is

(a) documentation
(b) flowchart application
(c) problem analysis
(d) coding
(e) none of the above

5. _____ An example of machine-language coding is
(a) 24   0600   0800   1000
(b) ADD A TO B
(c) C = C + B
(d) GO TO I
(e) none of the above

6. _____ Translation from symbolic language to machine language is done by
(a) the programmer
(b) a program called a processor
(c) an assembly system
(d) the systems operator
(e) (b) and (c)

7. _____ Documentation by the programmer does not include
(a) decision tables
(b) flowcharts
(c) data layout
(d) debugging programs
(e) problem statements

8. _____ Flowcharts
(a) break up large problems into a series of detailed steps
(b) allow the user to view the logic of the problems solution
(c) serve to communicate between the programmer and customer
(d) all the above
(e) (a) and (b) only

9. _____ Logical computer instructions
(a) enable the computer to compare data and proceed according to the result
(b) allow the computer to deviate from its normal sequence of instructions
(c) enable the computer to move information from one place to another in its memory
(d) all the above
(e) (a) and (b) only

10. _____ The most commonly used programming languages are
   (a) machine languages
   (b) symbolic languages
   (c) problem-oriented languages
   (d) procedure-oriented langauges
   (e) none of the above

11. _____ Translation from a procedure-oriented langauge to machine language is done by a program called
   (a) a compiler
   (b) an assembler
   (c) a converter
   (d) a translator
   (e) none of the above

12. _____ Which of the following is not a function of an assembler?
   (a) error checking
   (b) keeping track of addresses
   (c) assigning symbolic names to storage locations
   (d) converting source instructions to machine-language instructions
   (e) none of the above

13. _____ Which of the following is not a type of computer instruction?
   (a) implementation
   (b) specification
   (c) control
   (d) logical
   (e) arithmetic

14. _____ Which of the below would be entered on a program control sheet?
   (a) changes in input or output media
   (b) changes in input or output formats
   (c) changes in program logic
   (d) all the above
   (e) none of the above

15. _____ Among the reasons for coding of input and output data are
   (a) to save space on an input or output medium
   (b) to increase remote entry speed and accuracy
   (c) to increase the efficiency of sorting operations
   (d) to facilitate limited information retrieval
   (e) all the above

7-3   Problems

1. What are the steps that a programmer/analyst must consider in developing a computerized solution to a problem? Explain briefly.

2. What is a computer instruction? What does it do?

3. How might a computer distinguish between instructions and stored data.

4. What are the basic types of computer instructions? Explain each briefly.

5. What are the advantages and disadvantages of machine language as compared with symbolic language?

6. Why is it necessary to flowchart a proposed computer application?

7. Compare the advantages and disadvantages of procedure-oriented languages with other types of programming languages.

8. The following is a hypothetical machine language instruction.

   35   600   734   971

   What do each of the numbers indicate?

9. What is meant by "debugging" a program? How is it done?

10. Describe how one would go about testing a large program.

11. What is meant by documenting a program? When does this process begin?

12. What is a computer run manual? What might it contain?

13. How could improper or inadequate documentation hinder program modification?

14. Why is it necessary that the user be consulted for test program results?

15. If a new program operates well with known data, why might it be necessary to test the program with intentionally incorrect data?

ITEMS FOR DISCUSSION

Problem Analysis	Procedure-oriented Language
Program Flowchart	Compilation
Program Documentation	Executing a Program
Coding a Program	Debugging
Instruction Types	Syntax Error

Machine Language
Symbolic Language
Assembly

Logic Error
Program Testing
Run Book

FUNDAMENTALS OF FLOWCHARTING AND DECISION TABLES

INTRODUCTION The flowchart is a means of visually presenting the flow of data through an information processing system, the operations performed within the system, and the sequence in which they are performed. In this chapter, we shall concern ourselves with the program flowchart, which describes what operations (and in what sequence) are required to solve a given program application. The program flowchart can be likened to the blueprint of a building. And, as a designer draws a blueprint before beginning construction on a building, so then does the programmer draw a flowchart prior to writing a computer program. As in the case of the drawing of a blueprint, the flowchart is drawn according to definite rules and utilizing standard flowchart symbols prescribed by the American National Standards Institute, Inc.

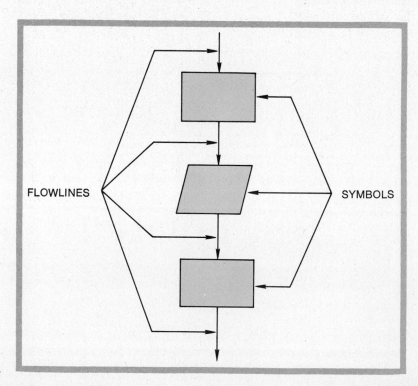

FIG. 8-1
Symbols and Flowlines.

In order to understand a flowchart, we must first understand the two basic parts of the flowchart, the flowchart symbols, and the flowlines connecting these symbols.

When we read a printed page, we read from top to bottom. So, then, do we read a program flowchart in this manner. Since we read a program flowchart from top to bottom, the direction of flow is also from top to bottom.

Thus, a flowchart is a series of symbols, each representing a function in the program, each connected to the next in a vertically downward direction by flowlines. Let us examine a typical flowchart, as illustrated in Fig. 8-2. You will notice that the first and third symbols have the same shape and therefore represent the same function. Within a given function category, we can have several different operations. For example, within the input/output function category are such operations as the reading of a card, the

FLOWCHARTING SYMBOLS, NOTES, AND FLOWLINES

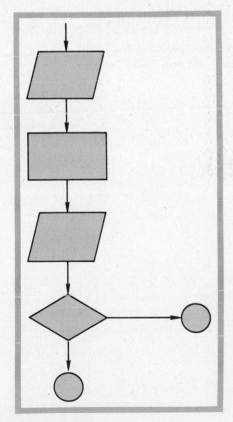

FIG. 8-2

Flowchart Segment Employing Symbols and Flowlines.

punching of a card, and the printing of a line. It is therefore necessary, in a flowchart, to show what specific operation is intended
within a given function category. This is accomplished by means
of a *note* within the flowchart symbol, where the symbol indicates
the function and the note indicates the operation.

In the above example, the symbol indicates an input/
output function, while the note *Read a Card* indicates the specific
operation intended by the programmer.

To aid the programmer in drawing the flowchart symbols there
is a flowcharting template. It is a piece of transparent plastic that
has cutouts of various symbols. Figure 8-3 is an example of such
a template. All of these symbols will not be discussed. At this
time, we shall discuss only the more commonly used *program flowchart symbols.*

FIG. 8-3
Flowcharting Template.

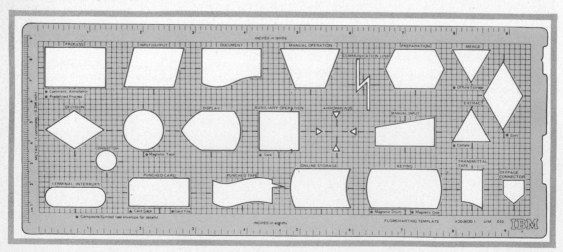

Let us now examine each of these symbols and the functions that they represent in detail. To begin with, we shall consider the input/output symbol:

Input/output Symbol

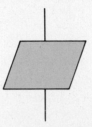

This symbol is used whenever information is to be input to the computer or output from the computer. The note within this symbol will indicate the input or output medium that is to be used.

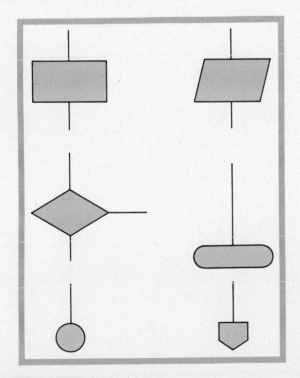

FIG. 8-4
Basic Program Flowchart Symbols.

Processing Symbol Equally, if not more heavily used in a flowchart, is the processing symbol:

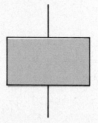

This symbol is used whenever data are to be processed to produce output. *Arithmetic* and *data-transfer* operations can be called processing functions, since they involve the processing of data and since they lead to, if not actually produce, data to be output.

SELF-STUDY EXERCISES 8-1

1. A program flowchart indicates the _____ to be performed at the _____ in which they occur.
   *****

   operations
   sequence

2. The two basic parts of a flowchart are _____ and _____.
   *****

   flowchart symbols
   flowlines

3. Each flowchart symbol represents a unique _____ which is determined by _____.
   *****

   function
   the shape of the symbol

4. To construct a flowchart, one must adhere to prescribed symbols provided by the _____.

*****

American National Standards Institute

5. A program flowchart is read from _____ to _____.

*****

top
bottom

6. Flowcharting symbols are connected together by means of _____.

*****

flowlines

7. Several _____ may be represented by one flowchart symbol.

*****

operations

8. The specific operation intended by a given flowchart symbol can be indicated by _____.

*****

placing a note within the symbol in the flowchart

9. The programmer uses a _____ to aid him in drawing flowchart symbols.

*****

flowcharting template

10. The names of the symbols below are _____ and _____, respectively.

*****

input/output

processing

11. Two types of operations which are represented by a processing symbol are _____ and _____.

*****

arithmetic

data transfer

Decision Symbol The above two symbols, then, cover all the major computer functions but one, the logic function. This function includes those operations which require the making of a decision. Most common among these is the determining of whether two items of data are equal and, if not, which is the larger or smaller. Decisions also involve a determination of whether or not a condition exists. For example, one could request a decision from the computer concerning whether or not the last data card had been read. The symbol representing the logic function is

DECISION SYMBOL

The purpose of any decision is to determine a future course of action. So it is with computers. For any decision there must be alternatives and a definite course of action for each alternative. Decision symbols are of two types:

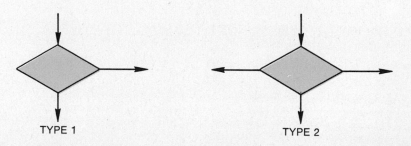

TYPE 1   TYPE 2

Type 1 is used to represent operations in which there are only two possible alternatives for a given decision. To illustrate this type of operation, let us consider a hypothetical situation. Suppose we wish to decide if a quantity, which we shall call QUANT, is equal to a second quantity, which we shall call QUANT2. The possible results are quite simple. Yes, the two quantities are equal or, no, the two quantities are not equal. In a flowchart, this would appear as follows:

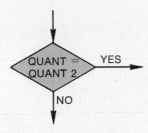

If QUANT is equal to QUANT2, the flow of the program would be into the decision symbol and out to the right along the flowline marked with the word "yes." If QUANT is not equal to QUANT2, the flow of the program would be into the decision symbol and out in a downward direction along the flowline marked with the word "no."

The same decision could be symbolized in a slightly different way:

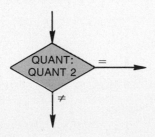

In this representation, the relationship between QUANT and QUANT2 is to be determined. If it is determined that the relationship is one of equality (QUANT = QUANT2), then the direction of flow is to the right:

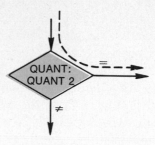

If it is determined that the relationship is one of inequality (QUANT ≠ QUANT2), then the direction of flow is downward:

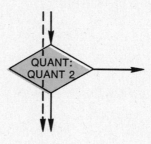

Sometimes, however, we wish to know more than if the two quantities are or are not equal. We may wish to know if they are equal, or if they are not equal, which is larger. In this case, the decision symbol would appear as follows:

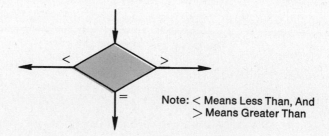

Note: < Means Less Than, And
      > Means Greater Than

Utilizing QUANT and QUANT2, for illustrative purposes, we see that the symbol and note might appear as

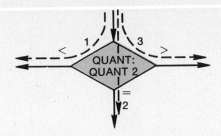

where path 1 will be followed if QUANT < QUANT2, path 2 will be followed if QUANT = QUANT2, and path 3 will be followed if QUANT > QUANT2.

Connectors and the Terminal Symbol

The input/output, processing, and decision symbols are the primary flowchart symbols. Equally essential, although less significant, are the remaining symbols. They are shown in Fig. 8-5. *Connectors* are flowchart symbols that are used to connect remote portions of a flowchart with one another without using long or crossing lines and to avoid making a complex diagram into an unintelligible maze of flowlines and flowchart symbols. A common practice is to place a letter in each connector, the same letter being used at corresponding entrance and exit points. In Fig. 8-6, for example, there are two connectors marked with an "A" and two connectors marked with a "B." In each of these cases, one of the connectors is an *entry connector*, while the other is an exit or *branch connector*. For illustrative purposes, the direction of flow has been indicated by dotted lines.

Quite often, however, the entry and branch connectors are not on the same page of the flowchart. In a case such as this, valuable

FIG. 8-5

Connector and Terminal Symbols.

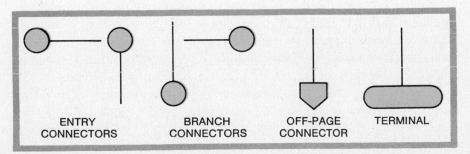

| ENTRY CONNECTORS | BRANCH CONNECTORS | OFF-PAGE CONNECTOR | TERMINAL |

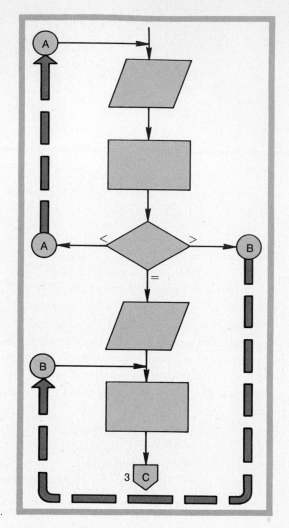

FIG. 8-6

Interconnecting Entry
and Branch Connectors.

time could be wasted while the flowchart reader searches through many pages attempting to locate the other half of the connector. To avoid this situation, *off-page connectors* are used instead of branch and entry connectors to indicate that the corresponding flowchart segments are contained on different pages and to indicate on what page(s) they are contained. In Fig. 8-6, for example, connector "C" is an off-page connector, identified by its unique shape. The number 3 adjacent to the off-page connector symbol indicates that the corresponding entry off-page connector may be found on page 3 of the flowchart.

It should also be pointed out that there may be many branch or off-page connectors associated with one entry connector. That is, there can be many paths from which the entry connector might have come, but there can be *only one* entry connector containing a given letter within it. Let us examine this in Fig. 8-7. In case 1, we

FIG. 8-7

Valid and Invalid Use of Connectors.

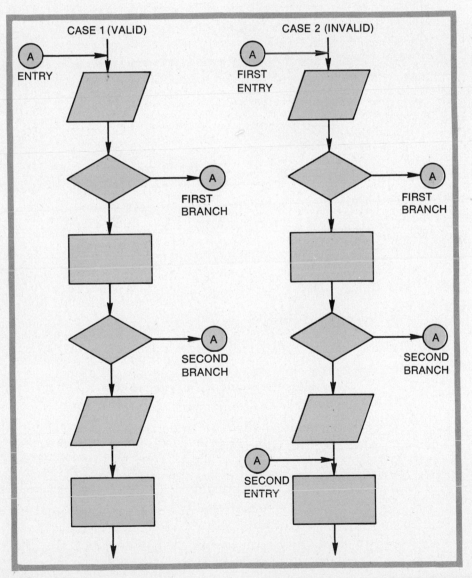

can see that there are two branch connectors labeled with the note "A" and one entry connector "A." This does not lead to a problem, since no matter where the exit occurs, the next step will be to proceed to entry connector "A." In case 2, however, this is not the case. After control is transferred to branch connector "A," there is no way that the appropriate entrance point can be determined. Should one go to the connector labeled FIRST ENTRY or to the connector labeled SECOND ENTRY? There is no conceivable way of determining the answer to this question. It is for this reason that there can be only one entry connector associated with one *or more* branch connectors.

The *terminal* symbol is one used principally to indicate the starting or stopping of instruction execution in a program.

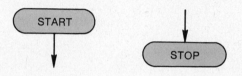

SELF-STUDY EXERCISES 8-2

1. A decision operation is used to _____.

*****

alter the sequence of operations

2. A decision symbol may be used in determining the _____ or _____ of two data items.

*****

equality
inequality

3. _____ are used to indicate the change in the sequence of operations. They include _____ connectors, which specify

where the flow is coming from, and _____ connectors, which specify where the new flow is to begin.

*****

Branch connectors
entry
branch or exit

4. The decision symbol may also be used to determine if the relationship between two data items is _____, _____, or _____.

*****

less than
equal to
greater than

5. _____ are used to join remote portions of a flowchart.
*****

Connectors

6. _____ connectors are used when a flowchart ends on one page and begins again on another page.
*****

Off-page

7. A _____ symbol is used at the beginning and end of a flow-chart.
*****

terminal

Let us consider what would be involved in flowcharting a very simple problem. In this way we may verify and strengthen our understanding of the various flowchart symbols and notes. In this problem we shall assume that we wish to read two cards into a computer, each card containing one number, add the numbers, and print out the answer.

SAMPLE APPLICATION

After analyzing this problem for a brief period, you would probably reason out a plan of attack similar to the following:

1. Start the processing
2. Read the first number
3. Read the second number
4. Add the two numbers
5. Print out the answer
6. Stop the processing

Our next step would be to determine what kind of operation is being called for in each step and the appropriate flowchart symbol to be used. The result of this step is illustrated in Table 8-1.

Once we have the necessary flowchart symbols, we need only connect them with flowlines and insert appropriate notes. This would produce

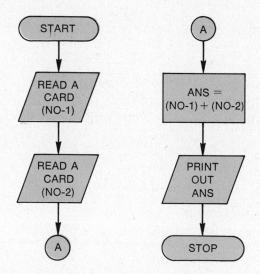

In most cases, however, it is not such a simple matter to determine a complete plan of attack as it was in this case. More often than not, the programmer cannot see a clear path to the solution and begins by attacking the problem one step at a time. For example, let us consider the following hypothetical problem: Read an unknown number of data cards, each data card containing

TABLE 8-1

STEP	TYPE OF OPERATION	SYMBOL
1. Start the processing	Terminal	
2. Read the first number	Input/output	
3. Read the second number	Input/output	
4. Add the two numbers	Processing	
5. Print out the answer	Input/output	
6. Stop the processing	Terminal	

one number. Then determine the average of these numbers and print it out.

As we have previously stated, most flowchart problems must be solved in a series of steps. Therefore, in solving this problem, we shall proceed in small steps, each step refining, clarifying, and adding to the previous steps as a novice programmer might approach the problem. In this way the reader will be able to follow the thinking process that is associated with the solution of this and other more complicated problems. As one develops more and more insight into the process of creating logical and efficient flowcharts, many of the developmental steps can be combined, if not skipped entirely.

Now, let us begin. As we have stated earlier, the terminal symbol is used to indicate the beginning of a flowchart. Therefore, we have

The next step is not such a simple one. To determine it, we must examine our final objective and work backward toward our

TABLE 8-2

QUESTION	ANSWER
What is our objective?	To develop an average of some numbers
What numbers?	Numbers contained on punched cards
How do I determine the average of these numbers?	Add them together and divide the sum by the number of numbers
How do I determine the value of these numbers?	Read them from the cards

present position. This process, in its simplest form, consists of a series of questions and answers. For example, in our case these questions and answers might be those in Table 8-2.

This apparently trivial series of questions and answers had led us to our next step:

READ A CARD

This would now give us the following cumulative flowchart:

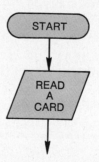

Now we ask ourselves: Why did we read this data card? As we see from Table 8-2, the answer is that we wished to obtain the total of the numbers on the card just read as well as on subsequent cards. For illustrative purposes let us call this total SUM, and the number read NO-READ. We can now begin to develop this total (SUM) by first including the number just read (NO-READ). This can be indicated with the following flowchart symbol and note:

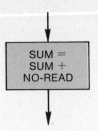

This note may appear somewhat confusing and incorrect, so we shall discuss it in greater depth. Let us begin by discussing the operation implied by the symbol $=$. In a flowchart, the symbol $=$ *does not* mean the same thing that it does in arithmetic. That is, it does not mean "equal." It means "is replaced by." For example,

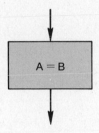

would be read as

A is replaced by B

That is, the data name A now contains the same quantity as is in B. If initially A contained the number 73 and B contained the number 96, after such an operation was performed A would now contain 96 and B would be unchanged or also contain the number 96. Therefore, in the case of our example, we are saying that

SUM is replaced by SUM + NO-READ

But, it appears as though SUM is being replaced by itself plus NO-READ. This conclusion is not completely correct. What is being said is that the value of SUM *after* this step will be the value of SUM *before* this step plus the value of NO-READ.

For example, let us assume that before this operation was performed, SUM contained the number 8 and NO-READ contained the number 7. Then after the operation is performed, SUM will contain the number 15 and NO-READ will contain the number 7. That is,

$$SUM = SUM + NO\text{-}READ$$

$$15 = 8 + 7$$

However, in our example we do not have a previous value for SUM, although we assumed it to be zero. Assuming it to be zero is not sufficient. We must specifically define it initially to be zero. Incorporating this step into our cumulative flowchart will then give us the following:

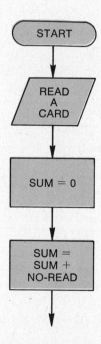

What shall we do next? To answer this we go back to our questions and answers (Table 8-2). Here we see that we wished to obtain a total of the numbers on the data cards. Therefore, we must read the next card and add the number on it to our total. That is, we must first read a card

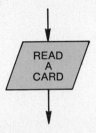

Since we no longer need the number read from the previous card, we can store this new number in the same location NO-READ. When a second number is stored in a location already occupied, the previous contents are destroyed or replaced by the new contents. Therefore, in our case, the data name NO-READ would now contain the number read from the second card.

Proceeding to add this number to our existing subtotal SUM we would have

Our cumulative flowchart would appear as in Fig. 8-8. Notice that the last two symbols and notes are identical to two previously used symbols and notes. The only difference is that the previous symbols were separated by the symbol and note:

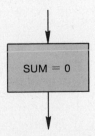

By simply moving this symbol and note up in our flowchart, we now have two identical flowchart sequences, one after the other.

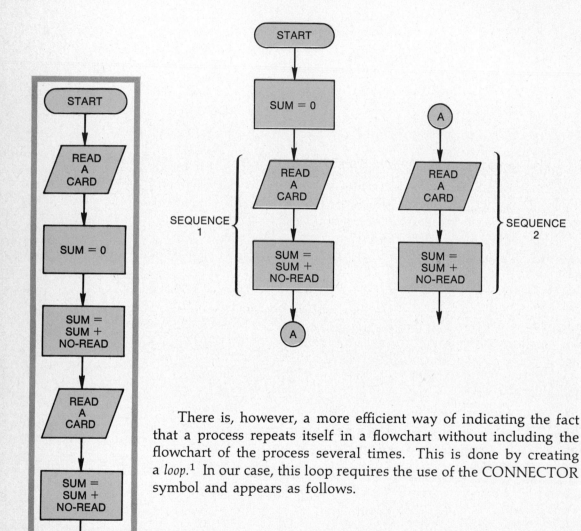

There is, however, a more efficient way of indicating the fact that a process repeats itself in a flowchart without including the flowchart of the process several times. This is done by creating a *loop*.[1] In our case, this loop requires the use of the CONNECTOR symbol and appears as follows.

FIG. 8-8

Cumulative
Flowchart.

[1]An American National Standards definition of a *loop* is: a sequence of instructions that is executed repeatedly until a terminal condition prevails.

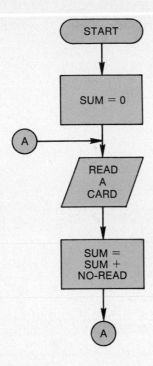

We must now determine a way to exit from this loop at the appropriate time. To do this, we must first determine the circumstances under which we would desire to exit from the loop. Since this loop accomplishes the reading of numbers from cards and the accumulating of these numbers, it would be reasonable to assume that we would desire to exit from this loop *after* the last card has been read and the number contained on it added to SUM. To do this, we must instruct the computer to determine if the last card has been read and, if the last card has been read, to branch out of the loop. If the last card has not been read, another card should be read, that is,

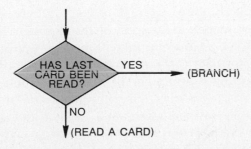

Incorporating this into our flowchart, we have

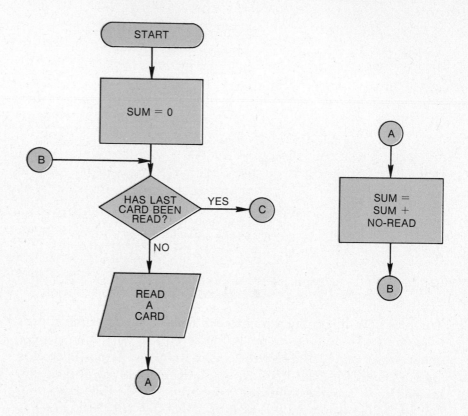

After careful examination of this flowchart, you will see that the only way the loop can be broken is if all cards have been read and accumulated—exactly what we wished to accomplish.

Proceeding, we must determine our next step. Again, we go back to our questions and answers (Table 8-2). Here we see that we wished to determine an average of the numbers input. Since we now have SUM, which is the total of the numbers input, we need only divide SUM by the number of numbers input. Therefore, as the number of data cards was not given, we must determine a means of obtaining the number of numbers input. The simplest way to do this is to instruct the computer to count them as they are read. That is, we must establish a counter and add 1 to it each time a card is read. Let us call this counter N. Then, each time a card is read we can increment, or add 1, to N.

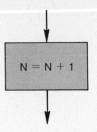

As we found it necessary in the case of SUM to assign an initial value, we also must assign an initial value of zero to N. In the cumulative flowchart, this would appear as follows:

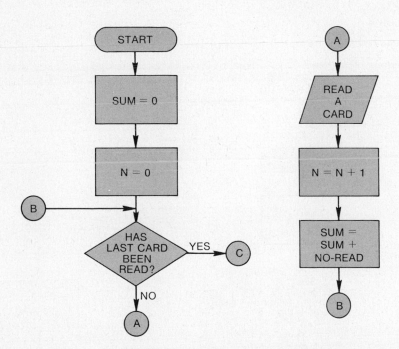

Now that we have the sum of the numbers (SUM) and the number of numbers read (N), we are able to compute the average of the numbers read. We shall call this average AVER. This operation will take place after exiting from the reading loop and would appear as

It is not necessary to assign an initial value to AVER since we are assigning it the value resulting from the division of SUM by N and not relying on or assuming it to have any initial value.

It now remains only for us to print out this result and terminate the program. Incorporating these steps into our cumulative flowchart, we have Fig. 8-9.

FIG. 8-9

Completed Flowchart of Sample Application 1.

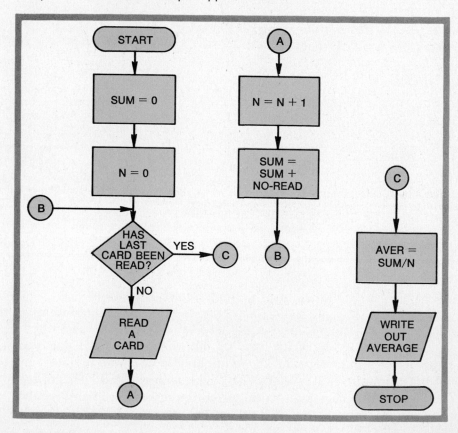

In the course of developing this flowchart we have encountered four major flowcharting techniques: looping, initializing, developing of a sum, and the developing of a counter (see Fig. 8-10). One or more of these techniques will be used in just about every flowchart you will ever write.

The importance of the flowchart as a means of documenting a program and for developing the logic of a program cannot be overemphasized. We shall refer to and utilize the flowchart in subsequent chapters.

SELF-STUDY EXERCISES 8-3

1. The logical sequence of operations required to flowchart a problem can often be discovered using a series of _____.

   *****

   questions and answers

2. In the flowchart note A = A + b, A on the left of the = refers to _____, while A on the right of the = refers to _____.

   *****

   the value of A after the step has been completed
   the value of A before this step

3. When a program repeats the same group of instructions over and over again, the condition is termed _____.

   *****

   looping

4. A loop is terminated by _____ out of the loop.

   *****

   branching

5. In a flowchart, the symbol = means _____.

   *****

   is replaced by

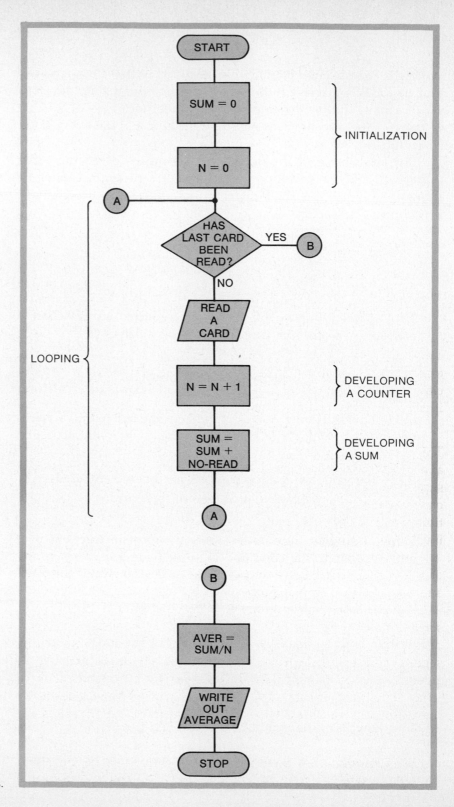

FIG. 8-10

Four Major Flow-charting Techniques.

6. Four major flowcharting techniques include _____,
   _____, _____, and _____.
                          *****

initialization
looping
developing of a sum
developing of a counter

7. The flowchart is one of the best ways of _____ a program
   and _____ necessary to solve the problem.
                          *****

documenting
developing the logic steps

The versatility of flowcharting is illustrated in Fig. 8-11. In this example, the flowchart describes a sequence of operations and decisions to solve a problem. Although it is frivolous, it nevertheless illustrates the versatility of applications of flowcharts.

ADDITIONAL FLOWCHARTING APPLICATIONS

The decision table is a tool of the programmer or systems analyst and can be used either as a subsitute for the flowchart or used to supplement the flowchart. It affords the programmer/analyst a convenient means of recording, in tabular form, the various conditions and possible courses of action when the solution to a problem involves substantial logical decisions.

DECISION TABLES

The decision table separates the conditions from the courses of action and establishes a relationship between specific conditions and appropriate courses of action.

The decision table, as illustrated in Fig. 8-12, physically resembles a rectangle that has been divided into six parts by a series of horizontal and vertical lines. To explain the use of each of these segments in a meaningful way, we shall discuss each segment in a general way and then apply the discussion to the following problem: We wish to construct a decision table which will enumerate the conditions under which a credit sale will be accepted or rejected. The conditions are as follows:

1. If a customer has a charge account with the store and also has a satisfactory credit rating, allow the credit purchase.

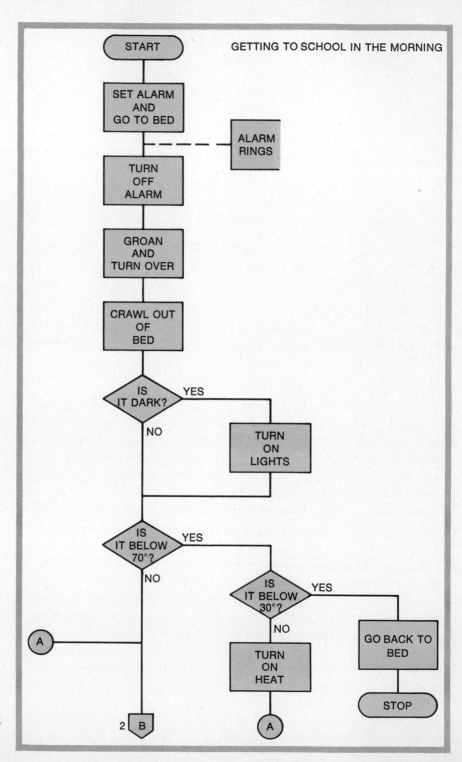

FIG. 8-11

Flowchart for Getting to School in the Morning.

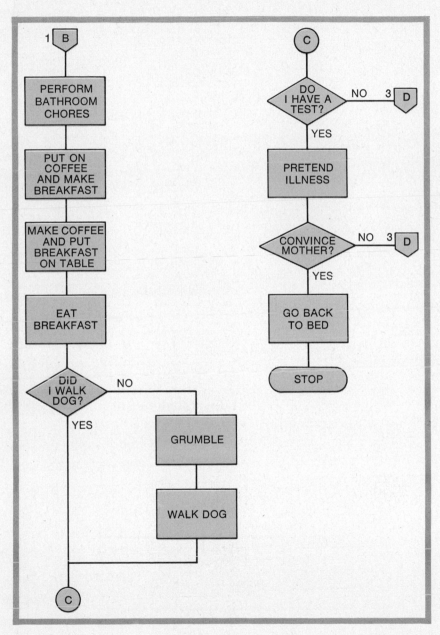

FIG. 8-11
Continued

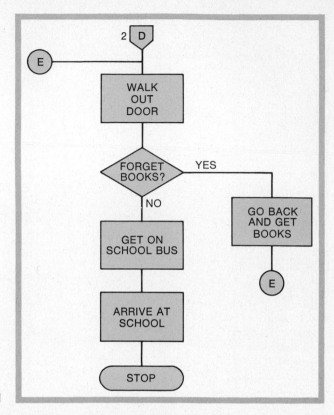

FIG. 8-11
Continued

2. If a customer has a charge account with the store but has an unsatisfactory credit rating, allow credit purchase only if special management approval has been given.

3. Reject the credit purchases in all other cases.

Decision Table Name Or Number	C (Rule Entry)		
A (Condition Stub)	D (Condition Entry)		
B (Action Stub)	E (Action Entry)		

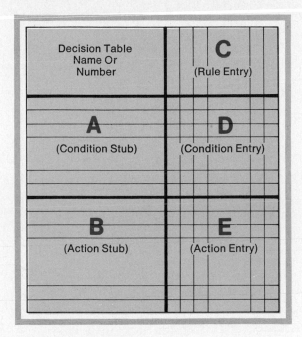

FIG. 8-12

Physical Layout of a Decision Table.

Block A (condition stub) above is to contain the possible conditions that exist in the problem, one condition per row with each condition being answerable with a simple *yes* (Y) or *no* (N) answer. In our sample problem, there are three separate conditions. These conditions are concerned with

1. The existence of a charge account
2. The customer's credit rating
3. Special management approval

Stating these conditions in such a way as to allow them to be answered by a simple yes or no answer and placing them in block A, we have

Decision Table 1	**C**
Customer Has A Charge Account	
Customer Has A **A**ood Credit Rating	**D**
Customer Has Special Management Approval	
B	**E**

Block B contains the possible courses of action. In our sample problem, there are two courses of action: Allow the credit purchase *or* refuse the credit purchase.

Decision Table 1	**C**
Customer Has A Charge Account	
Customer Has A **A**ood Credit Rating	**D**
Customer Has Special Management Approval	
Accept Credit Purchase	
B	**E**
Refuse Credit Purchase	

Blocks C, D, and E are completed together. Each column contains a C, D, and E section and contains a specific combination of conditions (D) and action (E) and a name (C).

In our problem, there are four possible combinations of conditions for which action is to be taken (see Fig. 8-13).

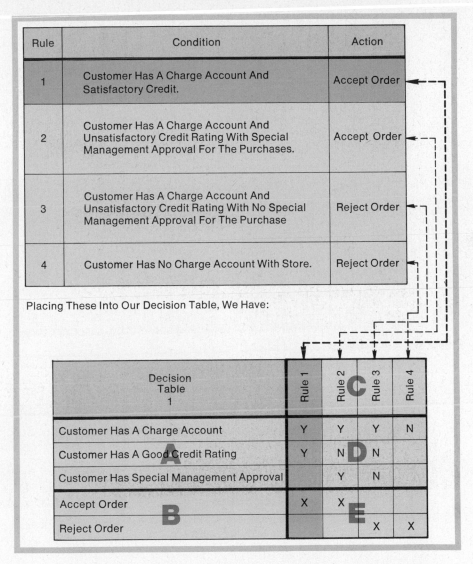

Rule	Condition	Action
1	Customer Has A Charge Account And Satisfactory Credit.	Accept Order
2	Customer Has A Charge Account And Unsatisfactory Credit Rating With Special Management Approval For The Purchases.	Accept Order
3	Customer Has A Charge Account And Unsatisfactory Credit Rating With No Special Management Approval For The Purchase	Reject Order
4	Customer Has No Charge Account With Store.	Reject Order

Placing These Into Our Decision Table, We Have:

Decision Table 1	Rule 1	Rule 2	Rule 3	Rule 4
Customer Has A Charge Account	Y	Y	Y	N
Customer Has A Good Credit Rating	Y	N	N	
Customer Has Special Management Approval		Y	N	
Accept Order	X	X		
Reject Order			X	X

FIG. 8-13

Conditions And Corresponding Actions.

Reading a decision table is simply a matter of reading each rule or action column to determine what combination of conditions suggest what action. For example, let us consider the decision table given below, which illustrates the rules for the multiplication of signed numbers as they relate to the sign of the product.

Decision Table 2	Rule 1	Rule 2	Rule 3	Rule 4
First Number Is Positive	Y	Y	N	N
Second Number Is Positive	Y	N	Y	N
Answer Is Positive	X			X
Answer Is Negative		X	X	

In this decision table one could determine that

Rule 1. (positive first no.) × (positive second no.) = positive answer.

Rule 2. (positive first no.) × (negative second no.) = negative answer.

Rule 3. (negative first no.) × (positive second no.) = negative answer.

Rule 4. (negative first no.) × (negative second no.) = positive answer.

It is also possible to construct a decision table involving conditions where the response can be less than ($<$), equal to ($=$), greater than ($>$), less than or equal to ($\leq$), greater than or equal to ($\geq$), or not equal to ($\neq$) instead of simple "yes" or "no" response. For example, suppose that we wished to determine what letter grade a student should receive for a course, given his numerical average in the course. A possible decision table and program flowchart are given in Fig. 8-14.

SELF-STUDY EXERCISES 8-4

1. A decision table is _____.

*****

a means of recording, in tabular form, the various conditions to be considered in a problem and their associated courses of action

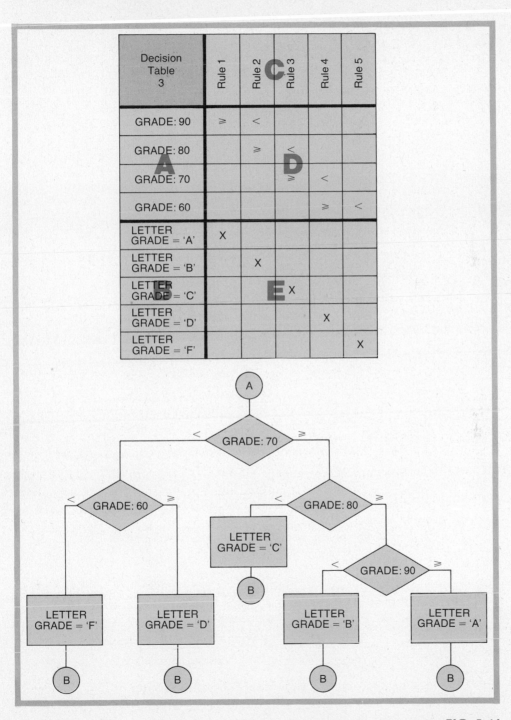

Decision Table 3	Rule 1	Rule 2	Rule 3	Rule 4	Rule 5
GRADE: 90	≥	<			
GRADE: 80		≥	<		
GRADE: 70			≥	<	
GRADE: 60				≥	<
LETTER GRADE = 'A'	X				
LETTER GRADE = 'B'		X			
LETTER GRADE = 'C'			X		
LETTER GRADE = 'D'				X	
LETTER GRADE = 'F'					X

FIG. 8-14

Decision Table and Flowchart for Determining Student's Letter Grade from His Numerical Grade.

X	C
A	D
B	E

2. The six parts of the decision table shown above are _____,
_____, _____, _____, _____, and _____.

*****

> X, name of decision table
> A, condition stub
> B, action stub
> C, rule entry
> D, condition entry
> E, action entry

3. Block A of a decision table above contains _____.

*****

the possible conditions that can exist in the problem

4. Block B of the decision table above contains the _____.

*****

possible courses of action

5. Blocks C, D and E are completed together and they correspond
to _____, _____, and _____, respectively.

*****

the name or rule number
the combinations of conditions
one action for each combination of conditions

6. Apart from the qualitative yes–no responses, a decision table may also contain _____.

*****

quantitative $<$, $=$, $>$ responses

EXERCISES

True–false exercises   8-1

1. _____ The number next to an off-page connector indicates the number of off-page connectors in the program associated with that connector.

2. _____ The symbol $=$ as used in a flowchart is defined as "is equal to."

3. _____ A template aids the programmer/analyst in constructing a flowchart.

4. _____ There are five parts to a decision table.

5. _____ Decision symbols with two alternatives differ in shape from those with three alternatives.

6. _____ Only one entry connector may be used for any number of corresponding branch connectors.

7. _____ The START and STOP symbols are used at the beginning and ending of a program.

8. _____ A decision table separates conditions from courses of action and establishes a relationship between specific conditions and appropriate action.

9. _____ Terminal symbols are used at the beginning and end of a program.

10. _____ A note is used to indicate a specific operation within a function category.

11. _____ The key to developing a successful program is to analyze the problem in depth by setting up and answering a series of pertinent questions.

12. _____ The decision table can be useful in constructing a flowchart.

13. _____ There are three basic types of decisions.

14. _____ The rectangular symbol represents a decision symbol.

15. _____ Flowchart symbols represent general functions.

16. _____ Rules and regulations for flowcharting are prescribed by the National Bureau of Standards.

17. _____ Each function of a program is represented by an appropriate symbol.

18. _____ A program flowchart is similar to a blueprint.

19. _____ Arithmetic and data transfer operations are contained within a rectangular flowchart symbol.

20. _____ The condition entry section of a decision table contains the name of the decision table.

21. _____ A decision operation is required in order to terminate a loop.

22. _____ A loop is a sequence of instructions which is executed repeatedly until an exit condition is met.

23. _____ Flowlines are used to connect symbols.

24. _____ A note in the flowchart symbol indicates a specific operation.

25. _____ The input and output functions are represented by separate and distinct symbols.

26. _____ Flowcharts are generally read from top to bottom.

27. _____ A flowchart is virtually meaningless without note statements.

8-2 Multiple-choice exercises

1. _____ Which of the following symbols is incorrect?

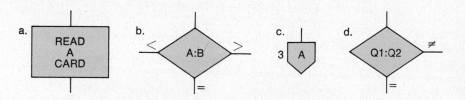

(e) none of the above

2. _____ Which of the following is not true?
(a) a loop requires a decision symbol
(b) a loop is an efficient means of flowcharting
(c) entry and exit connectors must be used to indicate a loop
(d) a conditional branch must be used to terminate a loop
(e) none of the above

3. _____ Of the following, which is not a part of a decision table?
   (a) rule entry
   (b) condition entry
   (c) action entry
   (d) action stub
   (e) rule stub

4. _____ A decision symbol may have _____ relationals.
   (a) two
   (b) four
   (c) three
   (d) (b) and (c)
   (e) (a) and (c)

5. _____ Which of the following is the processing symbol?

a ▭   b ◇   c ▭   d ▱

   (e) none of the above

6. _____ To determine an average of an unknown number of input quantities, the flowchart would most likely contain
   (a) a sum
   (b) a counter
   (c) a decision symbol
   (d) all the above
   (e) (a) and (b) only

7. _____ are used by the programmer to identify specific operations within a function symbol.
   (a) flowlines
   (b) comments
   (c) notes
   (d) off-page connectors
   (e) none of the above

8. _____ Flowcharts include
   (a) symbols
   (b) notes
   (c) flowlines
   (d) all the above
   (e) (a) and (c) only

9. ＿＿ Which of the following is a decision symbol?

10. ＿＿ A branching symbol can be used to ＿＿＿＿＿＿.
    (a) create a loop
    (b) terminate a loop
    (c) make a quantative decision
    (d) all the above
    (e) (a) and (b)

11. ＿＿ A program flowchart is constructed.
    (a) after the problem definition
    (b) before the coding
    (c) as part of documentation
    (d) all the above
    (e) none of the above

12. ＿＿ Major flowcharting techniques do not include
    (a) looping
    (b) initialization
    (c) developing a sum
    (d) developing a counter
    (e) none of the above

13. ＿＿ A decision table
    (a) is never used with a flowchart
    (b) can assist the programmer in constructing a flowchart
    (c) can be used with a flowchart
    (d) (a) and (c) above
    (e) (b) and (c) above

14. ＿＿ There are ＿＿＿＿＿ types of connectors.
    (a) one
    (b) two
    (c) three
    (d) four
    (e) five

Problems 8-3

1. What are the basic flowcharting symbols? What function does each
   represent?

2. Explain and illustrate each of the following:
   (a) initialization
   (b) looping
   (c) developing of a sum
   (d) developing of a counter

3. What are the purpose and uses of a program flowchart?

4. Describe what type of procedure is generally being described in the
   following sequences of symbols.

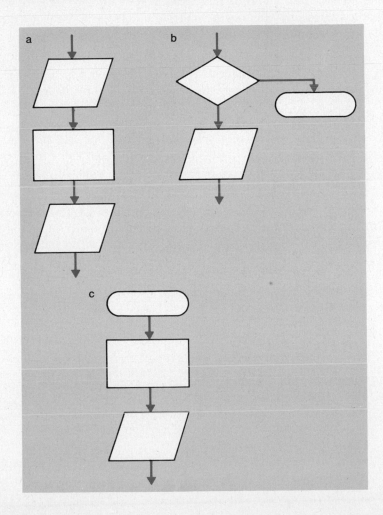

5. What is the purpose of a decision table?

6. Does the decision table replace or complement the program flow-chart? Explain.

7. Name and describe each of the parts of the decision table given below.

(a)	(d)
(b)	(e)
(c)	(f)

8. Draw a program flowchart to solve the following problem: Calculate Gross Pay from input data containing employee name, hours worked, and hourly rate. The formula should include straight time for hours worked through 40 hours and time and a half for hours worked over 40 hours. Print your results.

9. Construct a decision table to determine which of the four quantities A, B, C, and D is the smallest. If two or more of the four quantities are equal, any one of these may be selected as the smallest.

10. Construct a flowchart for the decision table produced in (9) above.

11. Construct a flowchart for a program to determine the amount and denomination of the minimum amount of bills and coins to be given in change for a purchase of D dollars paid for with an X dollar bill (X is not to exceed 10 but may be less than D).

12. Write a flowchart to read in the current date in MM/DD/YY format (MM is the month, DD is the day of the month, and YY is the last two digits in the year) and print out this date in the Julian format YYDDD (YY is the last two digits of the year and DDD is the day of the year. For example, 01/25/77 and 12/31/77 would be 77025 and 77365, respectively, in Julian format). Consideration of leap years is optional.

13. Construct a flowchart to determine the letter grade for each student in a class as follows:
    (a) Read in the student's name and four examination grades.
    (b) Determine the student's numerical average by averaging the student's three highest grades.
    (c) Determine the letter grade appropriate for the numerical average computed in (b) above. Assume $A \geq 90$, $90 > B \geq 80$, $80 > C \geq 70$, $70 > D \geq 60$, $60 > F$.
    (d) Print out the student's name, grades, lowest grade, numerical average, and letter grade.

The numerical average of all students in the class is to be computed when the student name 'END' has been read.

ITEMS FOR DISCUSSION

Flowchart Symbols
Flowlines
Note
Flowchart Template
Processing
Decision
Connectors

Terminal
Developing a Sum
Initialization
Developing a Counter
Looping
Decision Table

IV

COMMON PROGRAMMING LANGUAGES USED IN BUSINESS

9

COBOL

As is the case with any new discovery, the advantages of the discovery are to some extent offset by accompanying limitations and disadvantages. So it was with the introduction of the computer into the business world. Three of the more prominent problems that arose as a result of, and directly attributable to, the introduction of the computer into the business field were

1. The need to develop data-processing systems for existing computers that can also be processed on future larger and more powerful computers with minimal conversion, reprogramming, and retraining costs.
2. Since the data-processing system is so closely linked to the needs of management, the rapidly changing and expanding requirements of management have caused data-processing systems to constantly be revised and augmented. Therefore, documentation of the system in use is required in a form conducive to making such changes and additions with a minimum expenditure of time and money.
3. More and more complicated programs are being required in shorter and shorter times. This condition has caused a need for a computer language with which the average programmer can write a given program in a reasonably short period of time.

To fulfill these and other needs of the business world, development of a computer source language suitable to commercial data processing began. In May 1959, a committee of computer users, computer manufacturers, the federal government, and other interested parties called CODASYL (Conference On DAta SYstems Languages) came in existence. This group produced a report in April 1960 containing the first version of present-day COBOL (COmmon Business Oriented Language). Since that time the language has undergone substantial improvements and revisions. Some of the advantages of the present-day COBOL are

1. COBOL programs are written in precise, easily learned English words and phrases instead of complex codes.

2. COBOL programs make use of ordinary business terminology and therefore can be read by nonprogrammers such
   as accountants, auditors, or business executives with only
   a minimum background in data processing.

3. Retraining and reprogramming costs due to the acquisition
   of new equipment are substantially reduced.

4. COBOL programs written for one computer will run with
   minor modifications on most other computers. This also
   enables a company with more than one computer to reduce
   programming time by using the same programming language (COBOL) for each computer.

5. COBOL facilitates program testing so that, when necessary,
   a program can be tested efficiently and thoroughly by
   someone other than the original programmer.

6. Documentation is simpler and improved. In many cases
   the COBOL program itself provides a substantial portion of
   the necessary documentation.

It is not the intent of this chapter, however, to investigate all
the details of the COBOL language necessary to write a proficient
COBOL program, but instead to introduce the reader to those concepts of the language which are necessary so that he will be able
to examine a COBOL program, understand it, and determine
whether or not it is consistent with the definition and flowchart of
the problem. However, should the reader desire to consider the
COBOL language in greater depth, a reference summary of ANS
COBOL language specifications has been provided following the
exercises at the end of this chapter.

SELF-STUDY EXERCISES 9-1

1. The word "COBOL" is derived from the phrase _____.
   *****

   COmmon Business Oriented Language

2. COBOL is a common language in that _____.
   *****

   it can be used on many makes and models of computers

3. COBOL is business oriented in that _____.

*****

it makes use of ordinary business terminology

4. COBOL is relatively easy to learn because _____.

*****

it uses easily learned English words and phrases

5. Documentation of COBOL programs is simpler than with most other languages since in many cases the program itself _____.

*****

provides a substantial portion of the necessary documentation

OVERVIEW OF THE COBOL LANGUAGE

Like all procedure-oriented languages, the COBOL system consists of a source language together with a translator program to convert or translate the source program into machine language. The machine-language program resulting from the translation process is called the *object program*. Translator programs are generally supplied by the computer manufacturer for use with his computers. As computer users, we need only concern ourselves with the COBOL source language.

The COBOL language provides for four separate and distinct *divisions* within each source program. Each division *must* appear in every program. The divisions must also appear in the order given below, with each of the four divisions serving a unique and special function.

IDENTIFICATION DIVISION

The purpose of the IDENTIFICATION DIVISION is to provide a standard method of identifying the COBOL program to the computer. In this division, the programmer includes such information as the name of the program, his name, the date the program was written, the purpose of the program, and other pertinent information which would be meaningful to anyone analyzing the program.

ENVIRONMENT DIVISION

The ENVIRONMENT DIVISION contains information about the computer which will translate the COBOL program (source-computer), and the computer, if different from the translating computer, which will execute the translated or object program (object computer). This division is concerned with the specifications of the equipment being used and hence is largely computer-dependent.

DATA DIVISION

The DATA DIVISION describes the input and output data to be used by the program. It also describes the constants to be used in the program as well as work areas in storage to be used during the processing of the data.

PROCEDURE DIVISION

The PROCEDURE DIVISION contains instructions in the logical sequence in which they must be executed in order to create the desired end results from the given input or starting data. The instructions in this division are essentially written in meaningful English. To illustrate this, refer to Fig. 9-1, which illustrates a segment of the procedure division from a simple program.

As previously stated, our intention in studying the COBOL language is not so that we should become COBOL programmers, but so that we should be capable of understanding a professionally written, operational COBOL program. It is, therefore, not necessary that we study the COBOL language in the same depth or with the same degree of rigor that is usually found in an introduction to COBOL.

The best way to understand the COBOL language is to carefully examine an actual COBOL source program. We shall begin by examining a very simple program but nevertheless a program which would translate or compile and run successfully on an IBM 360 Model 25 computer. With slight modifications, this program would also run on most other large-scale computers.

SELF-STUDY EXERCISES 9-2

1. COBOL is referred to as a _____-oriented language and utilizes a _____ program to convert a COBOL _____ program into a maching-language or an _____ program.

*****

procedure

translator

source

object

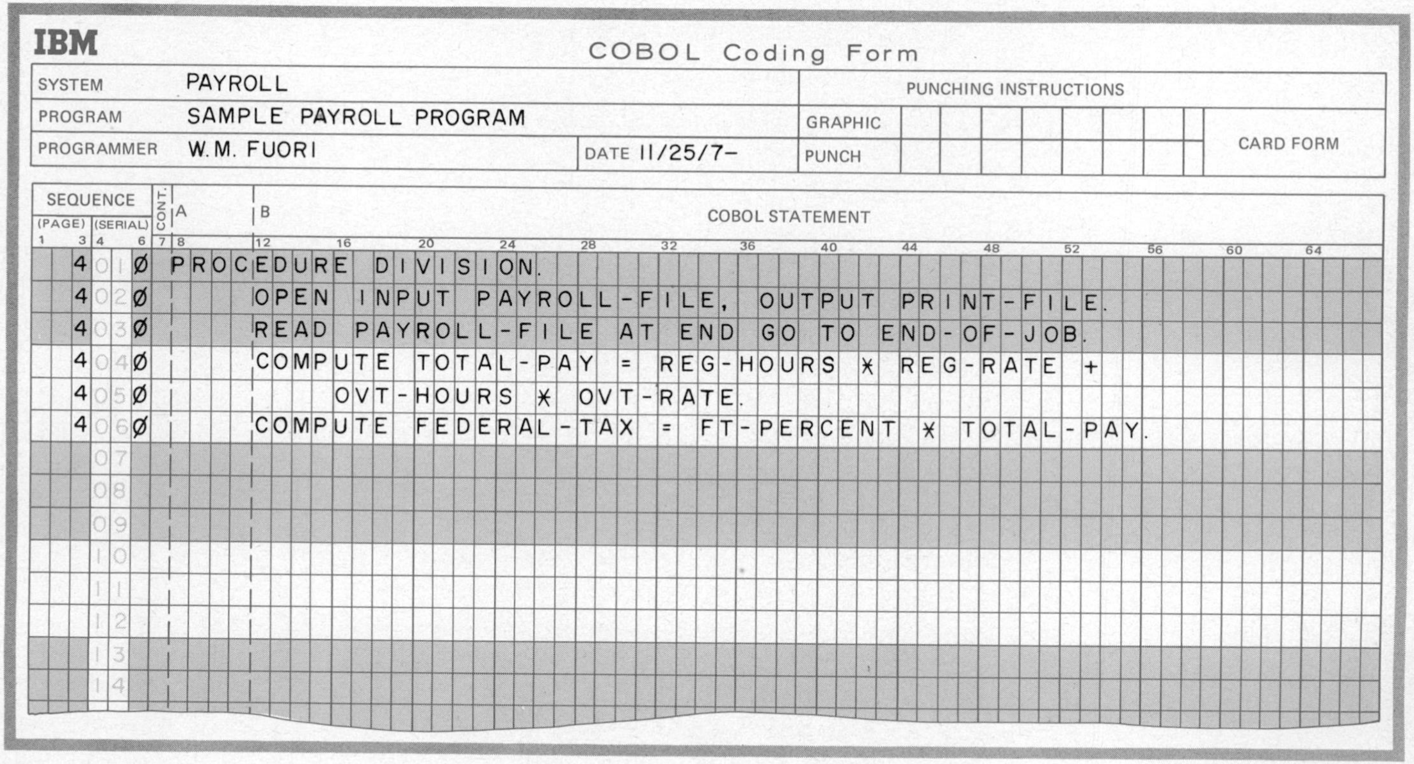

IBM COBOL Coding Form

SYSTEM PAYROLL
PROGRAM: SAMPLE PAYROLL PROGRAM
PROGRAMMER: W. M. FUORI
DATE: 11/25/7–
PUNCHING INSTRUCTIONS — GRAPHIC / PUNCH — CARD FORM

```
SEQUENCE
(PAGE)(SERIAL) CONT. A   B                         COBOL STATEMENT
4 01Ø PROCEDURE DIVISION.
4 02Ø     OPEN INPUT PAYROLL-FILE, OUTPUT PRINT-FILE.
4 03Ø     READ PAYROLL-FILE AT END GO TO END-OF-JOB.
4 04Ø     COMPUTE TOTAL-PAY = REG-HOURS * REG-RATE +
4 05Ø             OVT-HOURS * OVT-RATE.
4 06Ø     COMPUTE FEDERAL-TAX = FT-PERCENT * TOTAL-PAY.
  07
  08
  09
  10
  11
  12
  13
  14
```

FIG. 9-1

Segment of the PROCEDURE DIVISION of a Typical COBOL Program Using a Standard Coding Form.

2. COBOL translator programs are generally supplied by
_____.

*****

the computer manufacturer

3. Before a COBOL source program can be _____ it must be
translated into machine language.

*****

executed

4. Every COBOL program must consist of four _____. They
are the _____, _____, _____, and _____.

*****

divisions
IDENTIFICATION DIVISION
ENVIRONMENT DIVISION
DATA DIVISION
PROCEDURE DIVISION

5. The four divisions appear in every COBOL program in
_____ order.

*****

the same

6. The order in which the divisions must appear is _____.

*****

1. IDENTIFICATION DIVISION
2. ENVIRONMENT DIVISION
3. DATA DIVISION
4. PROCEDURE DIVISION

7. The IDENTIFICATION DIVISION provides _____.

*****

a standard method of identifying the program to the computer

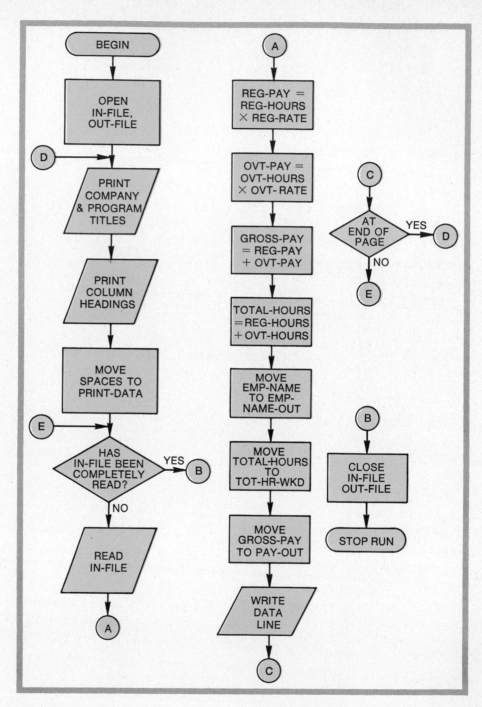

FIG. 9-2
Flowchart of Sample COBOL Application 1.

8. The ENVIRONMENT DIVISION provides _____.
   *****

   information about the equipment used in the program

9. The DATA DIVISION describes _____.
   *****

   the input, output, and work areas of the program

10. The PROCEDURE DIVISION contains _____.
    *****

    the instructions in the logical sequence in which they must
    be executed to attain the desired end results from the given
    starting data

11. COBOL source statements are first written onto a standardized
    _____and then _____.
    *****

                    coding form
           keypunched into punched cards

For any business entity, we can be reasonably certain of one thing—
there will be a payroll to prepare. And with the preparation of a
payroll go the associated reports that accompany it. One such report is an employee earnings statement. It is for this reason that we
have chosen, as our first example, a somewhat simplified version
of this report. For this we shall consider the COBOL program necessary to produce a printout of a company's weekly salary file.

Prepare a program to print a weekly salary listing by employee for
the AT company.

1. The input for this problem will be a card file with the following format:

**SAMPLE COBOL
APPLICATION 1**

CARD COLUMN USED	INFORMATION CONTAINED
1–20	Employee name
21–23	Regular hours worked
24–26	Regular hourly rate
27–29	Overtime hours worked
30–32	Overtime hourly rate
33–80	Not used

2. Employee gross pay is to be calculated according to the following formulas:

REGULAR PAY = (REGULAR HOURS WORKED)
$\qquad$ × (REGULAR HOURLY RATE)
OVERTIME PAY = (OVERTIME HOURS WORKED)
$\qquad$ × (OVERTIME HOURLY RATE)
GROSS PAY = (REGULAR PAY)
$\qquad$ + (OVERTIME PAY)

3. Output is to be printed and should appear as follows:

AT COMPANY—WEEKLY SALARY LISTING		
EMPLOYEE	TOTAL HOURS WORKED	GROSS PAY
XXXXXXXXXXXXXXXXXXXX	XXX	$X,XXX.XX
↓	↓	↓
XXXXXXXXXXXXXXXXXXXX	XXX	$X,XXX.XX

Note: Each X in this illustration represents a digit, letter of the alphabet, or blank in the output report.

Statement of the Problem   The coding in Fig. 9-3 is the sample COBOL application 1 as it would appear written by the programmer William Fury using the COBOL language. The numbers which appear at the left are

```
001000  IDENTIFICATION DIVISION.
001100  PROGRAM-ID.
001200      'SAMPLE'.
001300  AUTHOR.
001400      WILLIAM FURY.
001500  INSTALLATION.
001600      AT COMPANY.
001700  DATE-WRITTEN.
001800      SEPTEMBER 10,1972.
001900  DATE-COMPILED.
002000      SEPTEMBER 12,1972.
002100  SECURITY.
002200      CONFIDENTIAL TO COMPANY.
002300  REMARKS.
002400      PROGRAM TO PREPARE A WEEKLY SALARY LISTING. THE
002500      INPUT IS A CARD FILE CONTAINING EMPLOYEE NAME
002600      HOURS WORKED AND RATES. OUTPUT IS A PRINTED REPORT
002700      BY EMPLOYEE, HOURS WORKED, AND GROSS PAY.
```

FIG. 9-3

Computer Listing of IDENTIFICATION DIVISION
of Sample COBOL Application 1.

simply programmer-assigned sequence numbers. Although these numbers are *not* required in COBOL, they can be an aid if changes or corrections of any kind ever become necessary, and they can be an aid in placing the program (source deck) back in its proper sequence should it ever be dropped or disarranged.

In COBOL, as in all high-level programming languages, certain words or combinations of words have specific meanings to the compiler and may only be used for their intended purposes. In COBOL, these words are referred to as *reserved words.* In Fig. 9-3, for example, each of the words beginning at the left is a reserved word and serves to identify the type of entry following it to the compiler. A complete list of American National Standard COBOL reserved words is given in the Reference Summary following the Exercises at the end of this chapter.

The four divisions of the source program (IDENTIFICATION, ENVIRONMENT, DATA, and PROCEDURE) will now be illustrated and individually discussed.

IDENTIFICATION DIVISION Coding

As you can see, this division serves to identify the program to the computer. The various entries in this division are concise and easily understood. Yet this example can be considered to be as complete an example as you are likely to encounter. This is simply because the above IDENTIFICATION DIVISION contains all possible entries. However, all the entries given above are not required in the IDENTIFICATION DIVISION of a COBOL program. The only required entry in this division is the PROGRAM-ID entry, all others being optional. One should bear in mind, however, that the more entries that the programmer includes in his program, the more complete will be the documentation of the program.

ENVIRONMENT DIVISION Coding

The ENVIRONMENT DIVISION is that part of the COBOL source program that specifies the equipment being used. It names the computer on which the source program is to be compiled and describes the computer on which the object program is to be run. In this division, names can be assigned to particular pieces of equipment. Those aspects of the input or output file that relate directly to the computer's hardware are described also. Since this division deals exclusively with the specifications of the equipment being used, it is largely computer-dependent. This, then, is the division of the COBOL program that would normally require the greatest amount of alteration if a program written for particular SOURCE- and OBJECT-COMPUTER was to be run on a different SOURCE- or OBJECT-COMPUTER. The ENVIRONMENT DIVISION consists of two sections: (1) the CONFIGURATION SECTION and (2) the INPUT-OUTPUT SECTION.

CONFIGURATION SECTION. Here, in line 003300 (IBM 360 E25), the programmer has stated that the source program will be compiled (translated) on an IBM 360 Model 25 computer to produce the machine-language or object program. In line 003500 (IBM 360 E25) the programmer has stated that the object program will also be run or executed on an IBM 360 Model 25 computer. By stating the source and object computers separately, it is possible for the programmer to compile the source program on one computer and process or execute the object program on a different computer.

INPUT-OUTPUT SECTION. This section contains the FILE-CONTROL paragraph. The FILE-CONTROL paragraph specifies the equipment units that are to be used to input and output data during the execution of the object program. In the given example, the programmer has stated that two files are to be utilized in this program. In the source program, these files are called IN-FILE and OUT-FILE. For example, line 003800 (SELECT IN-FILE, ASSIGN

```
003000 ENVIRONMENT DIVISION.
003100 CONFIGURATION SECTION.
003200 SOURCE-COMPUTER.
003300    IBM-360 E25.
003400 OBJECT-COMPUTER.
003500    IBM-360 E25.
003600 INPUT-OUTPUT SECTION.
003700 FILE-CONTROL.
003800    SELECT IN-FILE, ASSIGN TO 'SYSC05', UNIT-RECORD 2540R UNIT.
003900    SELECT OUT-FILE, ASSIGN TO 'SYSOC7', UNIT-RECORD 1403 UNIT.
```

FIG. 9-4

Computer Listing of ENVIRONMENT DIVISION
of Sample COBOL Application 1.

TO 'SYS005', UNIT-RECORD 2540R UNIT) states that the input
file shall be called IN-FILE and shall be input by a UNIT-RECORD
device, namely the IBM 2540 Card Reader. Since the IBM 2540
unit is both a card reader and a card punch, an "R" is placed after
the number 2540 to indicate that only the reader side will be used.
Similarly, line 003900 (SELECT OUT-FILE, ASSIGN TO 'SYS007',
UNIT-RECORD 1403 UNIT) states that the output file shall be
called OUT-FILE and shall be output by a UNIT-RECORD device,
the IBM 1403 printer unit. It is not necessary that the reader know
or understand the meaning of the entries "SYS005" and "SYS007".

Briefly stated, in this section the programmer is assigning
names or labels to the physical pieces of hardware which will be
required for the input and output of all data.

SELF-STUDY EXERCISES 9-3

1. Before attempting to program any application, the programmer
   must have a clear and precise _____, which should contain
   a detailed description of the _____, _____, and _____
   requirements.

                              *****

                    statement of the problem
                            input
                          processing
                            output

2. Program information concerning the date written, installation, and security would be found in the _____.

*****

IDENTIFICATION DIVISION

3. The SOURCE-COMPUTER is the computer that will _____ the program, while the OBJECT-COMPUTER is the computer that will _____ the program.

*****

translate

execute

4. The only required entry in the IDENTIFICATION DIVISION is the _____ entry, but additional entries will provide more complete _____.

*****

PROGRAM-ID

program documentation

5. The FILE-CONTROL paragraph specifies the _____ to be used to input and output data and the names of the input and output _____.

*****

equipment units

files

DATA DIVISION Coding The purpose of the DATA DIVISION is to describe the data that the object program is to read, process, and output. This division is extensively computer-independent, as the data in this division are described in relation to a standard format with no reference to the actual hardware employed.

Initially, the entries in this division may seem very confusing, but with a small amount of background they can be easily understood. Basically, there are two sections in the DATA DIVISION in which data are defined, the FILE SECTION and the WORKING-STORAGE SECTION.

1. FILE SECTION—Data that are defined in the FILE SEC-
   TION of the DATA DIVISION and are stored on an external medium such as on cards, on tape, on disk, and so
   on. Since these data are externally stored, they must be
   brought to the memory of the computer if associated with
   an input file and sent from the memory of the computer if
   associated with an output file. This section of the DATA
   DIVISION serves the primary purpose of describing, in
   detail, these input and output data files.

2. WORKING-STORAGE SECTION—Data that are defined
   in the WORKING-STORAGE SECTION of the DATA
   DIVISION and are not part of input or output, but data
   which are necessary for the processing of input data to
   produce output data. This would include any constants,
   intermediate totals, and work areas which were not defined
   in the FILE SECTION and which affect the processing in
   one manner or another.

FILE SECTION. We have stated that data stored in the FILE
SECTION of the DATA DIVISION describe, in detail, the input
and output data files. In the case of our example, the input file (IN-
FILE) is a card file consisting of a distinct card layout or format;
the output file (OUT-FILE) consists of two different formats, one
from which output titles will be printed and the other from which
the output data will be printed. Each different input or output
format constitutes a different input or output record and is cor-
respondingly identified by the level number 01 placed to the left
of the record name. In the FILE SECTION of our sample program
there are three 01-level items, one input record (EMPLOYEE-
REC) and two output records (TITLE-OUT and PRINT-DATA).
Since the form of each of the input and output records is similar,
we will examine only one of these records in greater detail, the
EMPLOYEE-REC record.

We have seen that the presence of the level number 01 indicates that EMPLOYEE-REC is a record. We can also see that under
the heading FD (FILE DESCRIPTION), this file contains Fixed-
length records (RECORDING MODE IS F), and that each record
is 80 characters in length (RECORD CONTAINS 80 CHARAC-
TERS). We can also see that the file IN-FILE contains the record
EMPLOYEE-REC (DATA RECORD IS EMPLOYEE-REC).

```
005000 DATA DIVISION.
005100 FILE SECTION.
005200 FD  IN-FILE
005300     RECORDING MODE IS F
005400     RECORD CONTAINS 80 CHARACTERS
005500     LABEL RECORD IS OMITTED
005600     DATA RECORD IS EMPLOYEE-REC.
005700 01  EMPLOYEE-REC.
005800     02  EMP-NAME          PICTURE X(20).
005900     02  REG-HOURS         PICTURE 999.
006000     02  REG-RATE          PICTURE 9V99.
006100     02  OVT-HOURS         PICTURE 999.
006200     02  OVT-RATE          PICTURE 9V99.
006300     02  FILLER            PICTURE X(48).
006400 FD  OUT-FILE
006500     RECORDING MODE IS F
006600     RECORD CONTAINS 133 CHARACTERS
006700     LABEL RECORDS ARE OMITTED
006800     DATA RECORDS ARE TITLE-OUT, PRINT-DATA.
006900 01  TITLE-OUT             PICTURE X(133).
007000 01  PRINT-DATA.
007100     02  FILLER            PICTURE X(35).
007200     02  EMP-NAME-OUT      PICTURE X(20).
007300     02  FILLER            PICTURE X(14).
007400     02  TOT-HR-WKD        PICTURE 999.
007500     02  FILLER            PICTURE X(17).
007600     02  PAY-OUT           PICTURE $Z,ZZZ.99.
007700     02  FILLER            PICTURE X(35).
007800 WORKING-STORAGE SECTION.
007900 77  REG-PAY               PICTURE 9999V99 VALUE ZEROES.
008000 77  OVT-PAY               PICTURE 9999V99 VALUE ZEROES.
008100 77  GROSS-PAY             PICTURE 9999V99 VALUE ZEROES.
008200 77  TOTAL-HOURS           PICTURE 999 VALUE ZEROES.
008300 01  TITLE1.
008400     02  FILLER            PICTURE X(47) VALUE SPACES.
008500     02  JOB-TITLE         PICTURE X(40) VALUE 'AT JONES COMPANY - W
008600-         'EEKLY SALARY LISTING'.
008700     02  FILLER            PICTURE X(46) VALUE SPACES.
008800 01  TITLE2.
008900     02  FILLER            PICTURE X(41) VALUE SPACES.
009000     02  EMP-TITLE         PICTURE X(8) VALUE 'EMPLOYEE'.
009100     02  FILLER            PICTURE X(13) VALUE SPACES.
009200     02  THW-TITLE         PICTURE X(18) VALUE 'TOTAL HOURS WORKED'.
009300     02  FILLER            PICTURE X(10) VALUE SPACES.
009400     02  PAY-TITLE         PICTURE X(9) VALUE 'GROSS PAY'.
009500     02  FILLER            PICTURE X(34) VALUE SPACES.
```

FIG. 9-5

Computer Listing of DATA DIVISION of Sample COBOL Application 1.

Succeeding level numbers are used to show the subdivisions of the record. That is, EMPLOYEE-REC has been subdivided into six 02 levels or areas, which have been called

02	EMP-NAME
02	REG-HOURS
02	REG-RATE
02	OVT-HOURS
02	OVT-RATE
02	FILLER

To indicate the size of each of these subdivisions of the EMPLOYEE-REC input record, each level or item has associated with it a PICTURE clause. The purpose of this clause is to describe the number of card columns or print positions assigned to an item and the type of data contained in the item. In the case of our example, the PICTURE clause refers to the number of card columns read since we are dealing with an input card record. Let us consider the following:

02 EMP-NAME   PICTURE X(20).

This data item is a 20-character alphanumeric field, alphanumeric because the code "X" is used, while the (20) indicates a field width of 20 such characters.

In the next 02-level item,

02 REG-HOURS   PICTURE 999.

This data item is assumed to contain three numeric characters, one for each code "9" used in the PICTURE clause.

The third data item introduces a new code, a "V":

02 REG-RATE   PICTURE 9V99.

This data item is a three-character numeric field, one numeric character or digit for each 9 used in the PICTURE clause. For computational purposes, the computer assumes that a decimal point exists between the two digits separated by the V, in this case before the last two numeric characters (although no actual point is punched on the input card).

There is only one other PICTURE clause form that we have not discussed and this is the clause PICTURE $Z,ZZZ.99 appearing in the output record PRINT-DATA. In this clause a "$" will be printed in the first position of the field. The "Z" code is similar to the "9" code in that it represents a digit, but different in that if a leading zero, it will be suppressed from being printed. For more details concerning the PICTURE clause, it is suggested that the reader refer to one of the technical manuals published by the various computer manufacturers.

FILLER is a name that is used to label unused or unreferenced positions in a record. In the case of our example, the input data cards in the EMPLOYEE-REC record contained five fields of usable information. These are EMP-NAME, REG-HOURS, REG-RATE, OVT-HOURS, and OVT-RATE. The remainder of the card was unused by this program. But the computer had been informed in the FD (File Description) that each record would contain 80 characters. Therefore, to make the total number of characters equal 80, the unused columns must be accounted for. As the data contained in these columns will never be used or referenced, all such areas are given the same name, FILLER. To verify that his record description has considered each column on an input card, the programmer should total all of the PICTURE clause dimensions. He should arrive at a total of 80, corresponding to the 80 columns on a card.

For a printed record, the total should be 132 or 133, corresponding to the 132 positions available on the printer; if desired by the programmer, one position is assigned and used to control the advancing of the paper on the printer. This can be likened to the dial or lever on a typewriter, which controls whether the paper advances 1, 2, or 3 lines when the carriage is returned. Later, when we discuss the PROCEDURE DIVISION, you will see specific instructions which will control how many lines the printer will advance. Tape and disk records are not always the same size but can be of varying sizes. But, whatever the size of a tape or disk record, the sum of the lengths of the associated PICTURE clauses should equal the record size.

WORKING-STORAGE SECTION. Thus far, the programmer has not provided for the storage of the results of calculations. For example, no space has been provided in the FILE SECTION for

1. Regular pay (REG-HOURS × REG-RATE)
2. Overtime pay (OVT-HOURS × OVT-RATE)
3. Gross pay (Regular pay + overtime pay)
4. Total hours (REG-HOURS + OVT-HOURS)

Since these items are not specifically described in the input or output files in the FILE SECTION, they must be described in the WORKING-STORAGE SECTION. Individual data items in this section are assigned the level number 77. Notice that these items can be assigned an initial value, in this case zeros (VALUE ZEROS). It is not possible to assign initial values to items described in the FILE SECTION of the DATA DIVISION.

Notice also that the output titles are described in this section. This is simply because of the fact that in this section we can assign initial values, where we could not do so in the FILE SECTION. For example, in the record TITLE1, the item JOB-TITLE was given the initial value AT JONES COMPANY-WEEKLY SALARY LISTING, which is the title we wished to be printed out. The apostrophe (') marks were used to define the extremities of the characters being defined.

Two records have been defined in the WORKING-STORAGE SECTION, TITLE1 and TITLE2, one for each of the title output lines required in the final report.

Now that we have identified the program to the computer (IDENTIFICATION DIVISION), described the equipment being used (ENVIRONMENT DIVISION), and described the input, output, and intermediate storage areas (DATA DIVISION), we are ready to specify the steps the computer is to follow in processing the input data to produce the required output (PROCEDURE DIVISION).

SELF-STUDY EXERCISES 9-4

1. The DATA DIVISION consists of two sections, the _____ SECTION and the _____ SECTION.

*****

FILE
WORKING-STORAGE

2. The primary purpose of the FILE SECTION is to _____.

*****

describe the input and output data files in detail

3. Data defined in the FILE SECTION are stored in _____ on a medium such as _____.

*****

secondary storage

card, tape, disk, drum, data cell, etc.

4. Each file must have a least one _____.

*****

record

5. Each _____ is associated with an 01-level indicator.

*****

record

6. Succeeding level numbers beyond the 01 level are used to show _____.

*****

subdivisions of the record

7. An 02 level would be a subdivision or part of an _____-level item.

*****

01

8. A PICTURE clause is necessary to _____.

*****

describe the length and type of a data field

9. The entry PICTURE 9(5) describes a field which is _____ and _____ long.

*****

numeric

five characters

10. The character V is used as _____.

*****

an implied decimal point

11. When a data field contains both alphabetic and numeric characters an _____ is required in the PICTURE clause entry.

   *****

   X

12. A FILLER is used to _____.

   *****

   label unused or unreferenced positions in a record

13. A storage area for the results of calculations can be found in the _____ SECTION.

   *****

   WORKING-STORAGE

14. Individual data items in the WORKING-STORAGE SECTION are assigned the level number _____.

   *****

   77

15. Initial values $(may, \ may \ not)$ be assigned to 77 level items in WORKING-STORAGE.

   *****

   may

The PROCEDURE DIVISION of a COBOL program specifies the particular steps or instructions that the computer will follow in processing the input data. These instructions are expressed in terms of simple, but meaningful English words, statements, and sentences. This division is essentially computer-independent since it describes what is to be done, and not on what devices it will be done. A detailed flowchart of the logical sequence of steps required to produce the output report from the input data is given in the Statement of the Problem. Note that by using COBOL sentences in the flowchart, the programmer has closely linked the flowchart to the actual coding in the PROCEDURE DIVISION. It should also be noted that thus far there is little or no indication in the flowchart, other than the names used, that any divisons other than the PROCEDURE DIVISION even exist. Since an understanding of

PROCEDURE DIVISION Coding

this division is of prime importance to the business-related user in understanding whether or not the program fulfills its intended purpose, we shall discuss this division in depth in our second sample COBOL program.

In line 009700 of Fig. 9-6 we see the statement OPEN INPUT IN-FILE, OUTPUT OUT-FILE. This statement opens the input and output files for the reading and writing of data as one might open the cover of a textbook before reading it or open a notebook before writing in it. In COBOL, no file can be read or written before it has been opened.

Line 009800 (PRINT-TITLES.) is a *paragraph name* and serves to reference the statements below it. If it is desired to transfer from anywhere in the program to this area, the programmer only need instruct the computer to GO TO PRINT-TITLES), as was done in continuation statement 011150 (AT END-OF-PAGE GO TO PRINT-TITLES). In this paragraph the computer is directed to print out two lines or records. Each of these records is defined in the WORKING-STORAGE SECTION of the DATA DIVISION. These records are then moved to the output record area TITLE-OUT and printed after the paper has been advanced three lines. It is necessary to move the records TITLE1 and TITLE2 to TITLE-OUT before they can be printed since records can only be output

FIG. 9-6

Computer Listing of PROCEDURE DIVISION of Sample COBOL Application 1.

```
CO96CC PROCEDURE DIVISICN.
009700     OPEN INPUT IN-FILE, OUTPUT OUT-FILE.
009800 PRINT-TITLES.
CO99CC     WRITE TITLE-CUT FROM TITLE1 AFTER ADVANCING 3 LINES.
010C00     WRITE TITLE-CUT FROM TITLE2 AFTER ADVANCING 3 LINES.
C101CC START.
C1C20C     MOVE SPACES TC PRINT-DATA.
010300     READ IN-FILE AT END GO TC END-OF-JCB.
010400     MULTIPLY REG-HOURS BY REG-RATE GIVING REG-PAY.
010500     MULTIPLY OVT-HCURS BY CVT-RATE GIVING OVT-PAY.
010600     ACD REG-PAY, OVT-PAY, GIVING GROSS-PAY.
010700     ACD REG-HOURS, OVT-HOURS, GLVING TCTAL-HOURS.
010800     MOVE EMP-NAME TO EMP-NAME-CUT.
010900     MOVE TCTAL-HCURS TC TOT-HR-WKD.
011C00     MOVE GROSS-PAY TO PAY-CUT.
011100     WRITE PRINT-CATA AFTER ADVANCING 1 LINES,
011150     AT END-OF-PAGE GO TO PRINT-TITLES.
011200     GO TC START.
C113CC END-OF-JOB.
011400     CLOSE IN-FILE, OUT-FILE.
011500     STCP RUN.
```

from the FILE SECTION of the DATA DIVISION and not from the WORKING-STORAGE SECTION of the DATA DIVISION.

We can never be certain that storage locations within the memory of the computer are blank unless they are defined in WORKING-STORAGE to be filled with spaces. Therefore, for areas which should be blank, but not specifically defined in WORKING-STORAGE to be blank, the programmer must be certain to clear or fill these areas with blanks before attempting to use them. This is accomplished by moving spaces (blank spaces) into these areas. Such is the purpose of line 010200 (MOVE SPACES TO PRINT-DATA). With this statement, the programmer can cause the clearing of the output areas that are to be used to develop our printed records.

To this point, no data have been input from the card file waiting in the card reader. We have simply printed titles of our report. In line 010300 (READ IN-FILE AT END GO TO END-OF-JOB.) the computer was instructed to read a record (a card). The programmer's purpose in including the latter portion of this statement is to handle the situation that could arise if the computer attempted to read a card and all the cards had already been read. In this case, following the programmer's instructions, the program would skip to the paragraph called END-OF-JOB or the equivalent of line 011300 in the object program. The meaning and purpose of the instructions beginning on line 010400 (MULTIPLY REG-HOURS BY REG-RATE GIVING REG-PAY.) through line 011150 (AT END-OF-PAGE GO TO PRINT-TITLES.) should be quite clear with only a brief examination.

Line 011200 (GO TO START.) instructs the computer to go back to Line 010100 and again execute the paragraph called START.

Line 011300 contains the paragraph name END-OF-JOB, which refers to the next two lines of coding. Within this paragraph line 011400 (CLOSE IN-FILE, OUT-FILE.) closes the input and output files as one might close a book after it has been read or close a notebook when one has completed writing in the notebook. And, as in all processes, there must be a stop or an end to the process. This is accomplished by line 011500 (STOP RUN.). This instruction tells the computer that the job is finished, and to go to the next job.

As you can see, with a little help, the procedure division of a COBOL program can be read and understood with little more difficulty than might be experienced in reading and understanding a good mystery story. It will be left to the reader to verify that this program is consistent with the definition of the problem previously given and with the flowchart of the problem given in Fig. 9-2. It is

```
             AT JONES COMPANY - WEEKLY SALARY LISTING


            EMPLOYEE              TOTAL HOURS WORKED          GROSS PAY
        ALFRED ABARTH                   035              $    131.25
        AL ANDERSEN                     025              $     63.75
        WILLIAM BRONSON                 046              $    130.00
        JOSEPH CONGERO                  045              $    269.25
        FRED JONES                      020              $     55.00
        LOUIS NAPOLI                    040              $    340.00
        BEN NARUCKI                     050              $    231.00
        JACOB SMITH                     052              $    317.00
        JOHN SMITH                      042              $    315.00
        THOMAS TRACO                    025              $     93.75
        FRANCES WILLIAMSON              041              $    136.50
        ROBERT SMITH                    042              $    159.00
        HENRY ROBERTSON                 035              $     87.50
        JOHN WILLIAMSON                 049              $    217.50
        JOE JONES                       047              $    243.00
```

FIG. 9-7

Output from Sample COBOL Application 1.

also suggested that the reader reconstruct the flowchart from the coding in the PROCEDURE DIVISION. Such an analysis will be presented in the discussion of sample COBOL application 2.

SAMPLE COBOL APPLICATION 2

For our second example we shall discuss a COBOL program written to produce a sales report. We shall be given the definition of the problem, the coding of the problem, and from these develop a program flowchart.

Statement of the Problem

Prepare a program to produce a daily sales report.

The input for this problem will be a card file with the following format:

CARD COLUMNS USED	INFORMATION CONTAINED
1–20	Item description
21–25	Invoice number
26–31	Unit price
32–35	Quantity
36–80	Not used

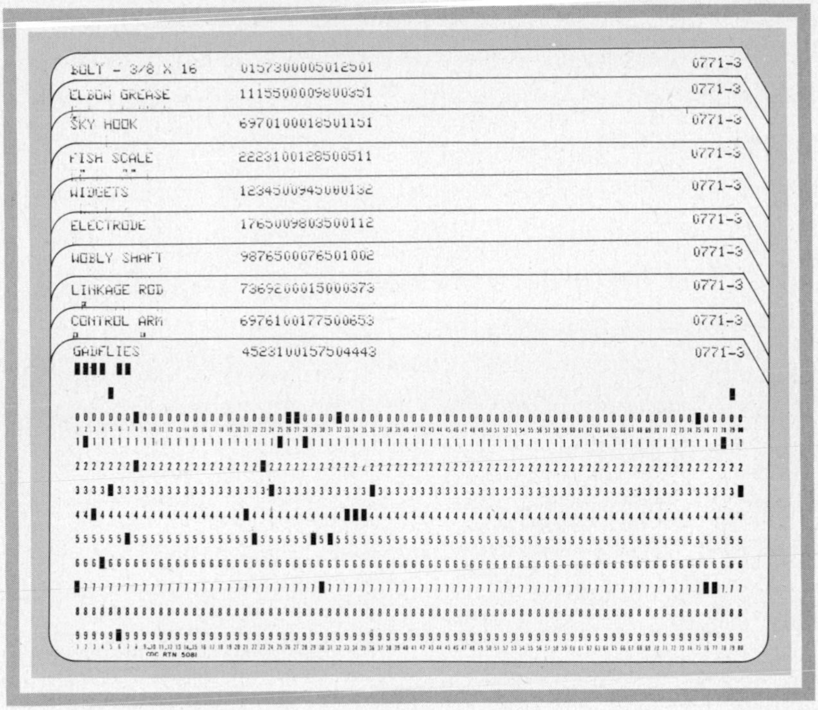

FIG. 9-8

Input Cards Used for Sample COBOL Application 2.

where,

$$\text{Total Item Cost} = (\text{Unit Price}) \times (\text{Quantity})$$

$$\text{Total Cost} = \text{sum of the Total Item Costs}$$

Output is to be printed and should appear as follows:

SALES REPORT				
ITEM DESCRIPTION	INVENTORY NUMBER	UNIT PRICE	QUANTITY	TOTAL
XXXXXXXXXXXXXXXXXXXX	XXXXX	$XXXX.XX	XXXX	$XXXXXXXX.XX
↓	↓	↓	↓	↓
XXXXXXXXXXXXXXXXXXXX	XXXXX	$XXXX.XX	XXXX	$XXXXXXXX.XX
			TOTAL SALES	$XXXXXXXXX.XX

Note; Each X in this illustration represents a digit, letter of the alphabet, or blank in the output report.

```
001010 IDENTIFICATION DIVISION.
001020 PROGRAM-ID. 'PROG2'.
001030 AUTHOR. DR WM FUORI.
001050 ENVIRONMENT DIVISION.
001060 CONFIGURATION SECTION.
001070 SOURCE-COMPUTER. IBM-360 E25.
001080 OBJECT-COMPUTER. IBM-360 E25.
001090 INPUT-OUTPUT SECTION.
001100 FILE-CONTROL.
001110     SELECT IN-FILE ASSIGN TO 'SYSC05' UNIT-RECORD 2540R UNIT.
001120     SELECT OUT-FILE ASSIGN TO 'SYSC07' UNIT-RECORD 1403 UNIT.
001140 DATA DIVISION.
001150 FILE SECTION.
001160 FD  IN-FILE
001170     RECORD CONTAINS 80 CHARACTERS
001180     RECORDING F
001190     LABEL RECORD OMITTED
001200     DATA RECORD IS CARD-IN.
002010 01  CARD-IN.
002020     02 ITEM-DES            PICTURE X(20).
002030     02 INV-NO              PICTURE 9(5).
002040     02 UNIT-PRC            PICTURE 9(4)V99.
002050     02 QUANTITY            PICTURE 9(4).
002060     02 FILLER              PICTURE X(45).
002070 FD  OUT-FILE
002080     RECORD CONTAINS 133  CHARACTERS
002090     RECORDING F
002100     LABEL RECORD OMITTED
002110     DATA RECORD IS PRINTOUT.
002120 01  PRINTOUT              PICTURE X(133).
002130 WORKING-STORAGE SECTION.
002140 77  QUANT1    PICTURE 99999999V99 VALUE ZEROS.
002150 77  FINAL-TOTAL    PICTURE 9999999999V99 VALUE ZEROS.
003010 01  TITLE-1.
003020     02 FILLER              PICTURE X(61) VALUE SPACES.
003030     02 TITLE1              PICTURE X(12) VALUE 'SALES REPORT'.
003040     02 FILLER              PICTURE X(60) VALUE SPACES.
003050 01  TITLE-2.
003060     02 FILLER              PICTURE X(36) VALUE SPACES.
003070     02  TITLE2   PICTURE X(17) VALUE 'ITEM             '.
003080     02  TITLE3              PICTURE X(14) VALUE 'INVENTORY    '.
003090     02  TITLE4              PICTURE X(13) VALUE ' UNIT       '.
003100     02 FILLER              PICTURE X(53) VALUE SPACES.
```

FIG. 9-9

Computer Listing of the Program for Sample COBOL Application 2.

The coding in Fig. 9-9 is for sample COBOL application 2 as it would appear written by the programmer DR WM FUORI using the COBOL language.

Program Flowchart To determine what this program is doing, we must direct our attention to the PROCEDURE DIVISION. It is this division of a COBOL program that contains the logical sequence of instructions designed

```
003110 01  TITLE-3.
003120     02 FILLER                    PICTURE X(33) VALUE SPACES.
003130     02 TITLE5      PICTURE X(20) VALUE 'DESCRIPTION
003140     02 TITLE6      PICTURE X(14) VALUE ' NUMBER
003150     02 TITLE7      PICTURE X(13) VALUE ' PRICE
003160     02 TITLE8      PICTURE X(15) VALUE 'QUANTITY
003170     02 TITLE9      PICTURE X(11) VALUE ' TOTAL
003180     02 FILLER      PICTURE X(27) VALUE SPACES.
003190 01  DETAIL.
003200     02 FILLER      PICTURE X(28) VALUE SPACES.
003210     02 ITEM-C      PICTURE X(20).
003220     02 FILLER      PICTURE X(7) VALUE SPACES.
003230     02 INV-N       PICTURE 9(5).
003240     02 FILLER      PICTURE X(7) VALUE SPACES.
003250     02 UNIT-P      PICTURE $ZZZZ.99.
004010     02 FILLER      PICTURE X(7) VALUE SPACES.
004020     02 QUANT       PICTURE ZZZ9.
004030     02 FILLER      PICTURE X(9) VALUE SPACES.
004040     02 TOTAL       PICTURE $ZZZZZZZZ.99.
004050     02 FILLER      PICTURE X(27) VALUE SPACES.
004060 01  TOTAL-SALES.
004070     02 FILLER      PICTURE X(76) VALUE SPACES.
004080     02 TITLE10     PICTURE X(16) VALUE 'TOTAL SALES
004090     02 TOTAL-S     PICTURE $ZZZZZZZZZZ.99.
004100     02 FILLER      PICTURE X(27) VALUE SPACES.
004120 PROCEDURE DIVISION.
004130     OPEN INPUT IN-FILE, OUTPUT OUT-FILE.
004140 START.
004160     WRITE PRINTOUT FROM TITLE-1 AFTER ADVANCING 0 LINES.
004170     WRITE PRINTOUT FROM TITLE-2 AFTER ADVANCING 3 LINES.
004180     WRITE PRINTOUT FROM TITLE-3 AFTER ADVANCING 1 LINES.
004190 READ1.
004200     READ IN-FILE AT END GO TO WRAP-UP.
004210     MULTIPLY UNIT-PRC BY QUANTITY GIVING QUANTI.
004220     ADD QUANTI TO FINAL-TOTAL.
004230     MOVE ITEM-DES TO ITEM-C.
004240     MOVE INV-NO TO INV-N.
004250     MOVE UNIT-PRC TO UNIT-P.
005010     MOVE QUANTITY TO QUANT.
005020     MOVE QUANTI TO TOTAL.
005030     WRITE PRINTOUT FROM DETAIL AFTER ADVANCING 1 LINES.
005040     GO TO READ1.
005050 WRAP-UP.
005060     MOVE FINAL-TOTAL TO TOTAL-S.
005070     WRITE PRINTOUT FROM TOTAL-SALES AFTER ADVANCING 1 LINES.
005080     CLOSE IN-FILE, OUT-FILE.
005090     STOP RUN.
```

FIG. 9-9
Continued

to solve the problem. From our analysis of the PROCEDURE
DIVISION, we shall construct a flowchart for our second COBOL
sample application.

As is customary when flowcharting an application, the flowchart should begin with a terminal symbol:

SALES REPORT

ITEM DESCRIPTION	INVENTORY NUMBER	UNIT PRICE	QUANTITY	TOTAL
BOLT - 3/8 X 16	01573	$ .50	1250	$ 625.00
ELBOW GREASE	11155	$ .98	35	$ 34.30
SKY HOOK	69701	$ 1.85	115	$ 212.75
FISH SCALE	22231	$ 12.85	51	$ 655.35
WIDGETS	12345	$ 94.50	13	$ 1228.50
ELECTRODE	17650	$ 980.35	11	$ 10783.85
WOBLY SHAFT	98765	$ 7.65	100	$ 765.00
LINKAGE ROD	73692	$ 1.50	37	$ 55.50
CONTROL ARM	69761	$ 17.75	65	$ 1153.75
GADFLIES	45231	$ 15.75	444	$ 6993.00
		TOTAL SALES		$ 22507.00

FIG. 9-10

Output for Sample COBOL Application 2.

Upon examining the PROCEDURE DIVISION of our sample program, we see that the first instruction is a processing operation: the opening of the input file in IN-FILE and the output file OUT-FILE. Adding a processing symbol and an appropriate note within it to our existing terminal symbol we have the following flowchart:

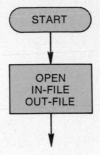

In the next paragraph of the program, we find three consecutive write or output statements which, when flowcharted, give us

In the next paragraph of the program (READ1), we find 10 instructions consisting of several different types. The first instruction (line 004200) is actually two instructions combined into one, an instruction to read a card together with an instruction to branch to the section of the program called WRAP-UP when all data cards in the input file IN-FILE have been read. In the flowchart, this instruction would appear as follows:

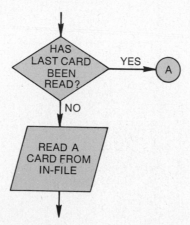

The next seven instructions are simple processing instructions and are symbolized as follows:

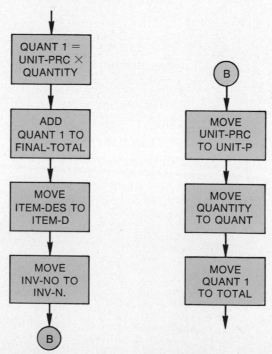

Next in the paragraph READ1 we have an output or write statement followed by a branch instruction back to the beginning of this paragraph. To flowchart these two instructions, we must refer to an instruction previously included in the flowchart (READ IN-FILE AT END GO TO WRAP-UP). This would be accomplished as follows:

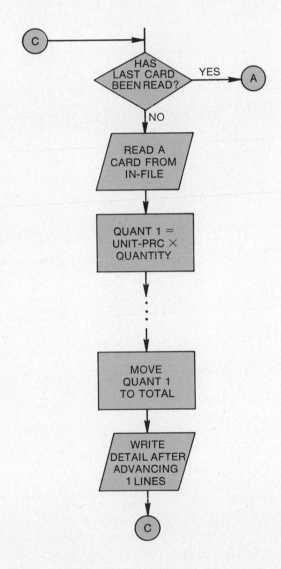

Notice that the last instruction in this paragraph calls for the computer to transfer to READ1, the paragraph label. Yet in the flowchart we transferred, via connector ⓒ , to the first instruction in the paragraph. This is necessary because there is no flowchart-ing symbol reserved for holding paragraph names. If we wish, however, we would indicate the paragraph name as follows:

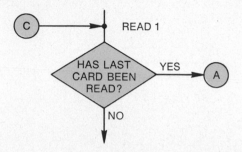

The next paragraph we encounter in the program is called WRAP-UP, a name we have seen before. We have seen it in connection with the first instruction in the READ1 paragraph. You will recall that the flowchart of this instruction (READ IN-FILE AT END GO TO WRAP-UP.) appeared as shown above, where the exit connector

was to connect to the paragraph WRAP-UP. To facilitate this we must begin the paragraph WRAP-UP with the entry connector:

Subsequently in this paragraph we find a processing instruc-tion (MOVE FINAL-TOTAL TO TOTAL-S.), an output statement (WRITE PRINT OUT FROM TOTAL-SALES AFTER ADVANC-ING 1 LINES.), another processing instruction (CLOSE IN-FILE, OUT-FILE), and finally a terminal operation (STOP RUN.). In the flowchart, these instructions would appear as

Figure 9-11 illustrates how this flowchart would appear when all of the parts thus far developed are combined.

It should be emphasized once more that this entire flowchart was constructed from only the procedure division of the program. For an individual who is primarily a computer user and not a computer programmer, this is the most meaningful portion of the COBOL program.

SELF-STUDY EXERCISES 9-5

1. The instructions in the PROCEDURE DIVISION of a COBOL program are expressed in terms of _____.

*****

simple, meaningful English words, statements, and sentences

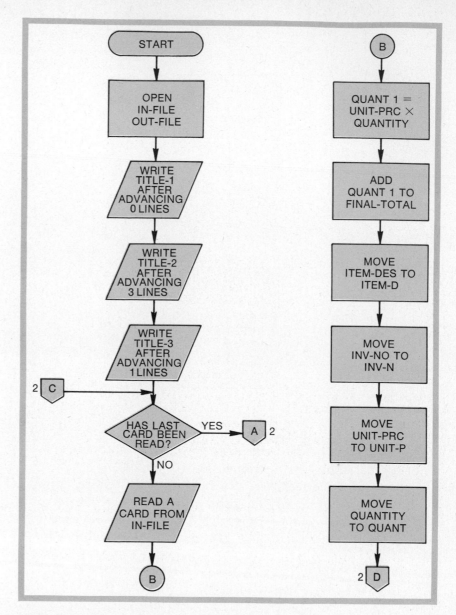

FIG. 9-11

Flowchart for Sample COBOL Application 2.

2. Before data can be read or written the file(s) must be _____ .

*****

opened

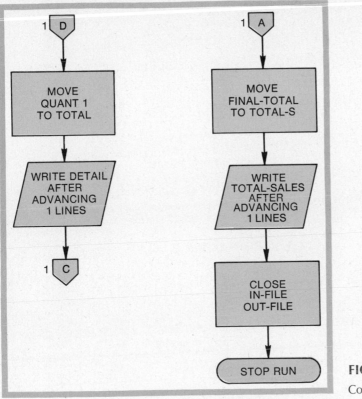

FIG. 9-11

Continued

3. The instruction which brings data into the computer for processing is the _____ instruction.

*****

READ

4. An unconditional branch instruction in COBOL is coded by a _____.

*****

GO TO statement

5. To transmit data from one storage area to another requires a _____ instruction.

*****

MOVE

6. Normally, execution of instructions will proceed sequentially unless a _____ is encountered.

*****

branching condition

7. In the instruction AT END GO TO END-OF-JOB from Sample COBOL Application 1, END-OF-JOB is a _____.

*****

paragraph name

8. A STOP RUN instruction _____.

*****

terminates the program

9. One can, without great difficulty, construct a _____ from the PROCEDURE DIVISION of a COBOL program.

*****

program flowchart

EXERCISES

9-1 True–false exercises

1. ____ All COBOL programs contain four divisions.

2. ____ An advantage of COBOL is that it reduces retraining and re-programming costs normally caused by the acquisition of new equipment.

3. ____ It is not possible for the programmer to compile the source program on one computer and execute the object program on another.

4. ____ A VALUE clause may only be used in the WORKING-STORAGE SECTION of the DATA DIVISION.

5. ____ The number and type of characters contained in each field of input and output records must be specified in a COBOL program.

6. ____ COBOL programming has an advantage over other languages in that it can be easily understood by nonprogramming personnel.

7. _____ The PROCEDURE DIVISION is virtually machine-independent.

8. _____ The IDENTIFICATION DIVISION of a COBOL program contains documentation information.

9. _____ The ENVIRONMENT DIVISION does not contain information about the translating computer.

10. _____ A disadvantage of COBOL is its inability to facilitate easy documentation of problem programs.

11. _____ Numeric data fields must be described by a PICTURE clause.

12. _____ Data on tape, cards, or disks are brought to the memory of the computer. These data files are described in detail in the FILE SECTION of the DATA DIVISION.

13. _____ A file must be opened before it can be processed.

14. _____ COBOL programs are efficient because they are coded in machine language and do not require translation before they are executed.

15. _____ PICTURE X(24) specifies an alphanumeric field with 24 characters.

16. _____ The PROCEDURE DIVISION is divided into the CONFIGURATION SECTION and the INPUT-OUTPUT SECTION.

17. _____ The only required entry in the IDENTIFICATION DIVISION is the PROGRAM-ID entry.

18. _____ Nonnumeric literals are enclosed in quotation marks.

19. _____ The total of the PICTURE clause specifications for a record should equal the number of characters actually contained in the record.

20. _____ The DATA DIVISION describes only the input data to be used by the program.

21. _____ The COBOL system consists of a source language together with a translator for conversion into machine language.

22. _____ The logic contained in a program flowchart would be coded into the PROCEDURE DIVISION.

23. _____ A FILLER entry is used to label unused or unreferenced positions in a data record.

24. _____ An AT END condition occurs on an input file only when the last record has been read.

25. _____ Instructions directing the computer to read input cards would be found in the PROCEDURE DIVISION.

26. _____ Instructions in the PROCEDURE DIVISION are executed sequentially unless a branching condition is encountered.

27. _____ COBOL programs written for one computer are able to be run on similar computers without modification.

28. _____ Of all the divisions in a COBOL program the ENVIRONMENT DIVISION is the most machine-dependent.

29. _____ The name of the programmer and date are not necessary information in the IDENTIFICATION DIVISION.

30. _____ An 02-level indicator is used to specify a record description in the DATA DIVISION.

31. _____ Input and output files must be opened before being read and then they must be closed at the end of the program.

32. _____ A GO TO instruction is an example of a conditional branch.

33. _____ 77 is a level number reserved for the WORKING-STORAGE SECTION.

34. _____ The level number 02 may be assigned to a subdivision of an 01 level data item.

9-2 Multiple-choice exercises

1. _____ When the last record of an input card file has been read
   (a) an AT END condition exists
   (b) control is transferred to the paragraph WRAP-UP
   (c) program execution stops
   (d) the input file closes
   (e) none of the above

2. _____ The IDENTIFICATION DIVISION must contain the
   (a) name of the programmer
   (b) date the program was written
   (c) name of the program
   (d) name of the installation
   (e) all the above

3. _____ To ensure that storage locations contain spaces, they can be filled with spaces. This operation could take place in the
   (a) PROCEDURE DIVISION
   (b) FILE SECTION

(c) WORKING-STORAGE SECTION
(d) CONFIGURATION SECTION
(e) (a) and (c) above

4. ____ The WORKING-STORAGE SECTION can be used to
   (a) describe output headings in detail
   (b) describe constants to be used in the program
   (c) describe work areas not described in the FILE SECTION
   (d) all the above
   (e) (b) and (c) only

5. ____ The ENVIRONMENT DIVISION contains
   (a) CONFIGURATION SECTION
   (b) Identification of the SOURCE-COMPUTER
   (c) Identification of the OBJECT-COMPUTER
   (d) all the above
   (e) none of the above

6. ____ The FILE SECTION
   (a) is part of the ENVIRONMENT DIVISION
   (b) describes all input and output files
   (c) contains a description of each type of record contained on an input file
   (d) all the above
   (e) (b) and (c) only

7. ____ Of the following, which entries would not be found in the DATA DIVISION?
   (a) FD entry
   (b) FILE SECTION
   (c) WORKING-STORAGE SECTION
   (d) FILE CONTROL
   (e) none of the above

8. ____ For an individual who is principally a computer user and not a programmer, which of the following would generally be the most meaningful?
   (a) DATA DIVISION
   (b) INPUT-OUTPUT SECTION
   (c) IDENTIFICATION DIVISION
   (d) PROCEDURE DIVISION
   (e) ENVIRONMENT DIVISION

9. ____ Nonnumeric literals are enclosed in
   (a) brackets
   (b) braces
   (c) parentheses

(d) quotation marks

(e) none of the above

10. ____ Of the following, which would not be found in the PROCE-DURE DIVISION?

(a) an OPEN command

(b) STOP RUN

(c) conditional branch statement

(d) wrap-up paragraph names

(e) none of the above

11. ____ Of the following PICTURE representations, which would be incorrect?

(a) $ZZZ.99

(b) 999V99

(c) 9(4)V99

(d) X(37)

(e) none of the above

9-3 Problems

1. What is the purpose of each of the following?

(a) PICTURE clause

(b) COMPUTE

(c) GO TO

(d) WRITE

(e) MOVE

(f) OPEN

(g) STOP RUN

2. Examine the sample DATA DIVISION shown and answer the associated questions.

```
DATA DIVISION.
FILE SECTION.
FD    SALES-FILE
      RECORDING MODE F
      LABEL RECORDS ARE OMITTED
      RECORD CONTAINS 80 CHARACTERS
      DATA RECORD IS SALES-REGISTER.
01    SALES-REGISTER.
      02   COMPANY-NAME      PICTURE X(30).
      02   ACCOUNT-NO        PICTURE 9(5).
      02   AMOUNT-SOLD       PICTURE 9(6)v99.
      02   DATE.
```

```
        03  MONTH     PICTURE 9(2).
        03  DAY       PICTURE 9(2).
        03  YR        PICTURE 9(2).
    02  FILLER        PICTURE X(31).
```

(a) _____ The name of the file is __.
(b) _____ The name of the record is __.
(c) _____ The data record contains __ characters.
(d) _____ __ positions of the record are set aside for alphanumeric information.
(e) _____ There are __ unused or unreferenced positions in the record.

3. Examine the sample PROCEDURE DIVISION shown and answer the associated questions.

```
PROCEDURE DIVISION.
BEGIN.
        OPEN INPUT SALES-FILE, OUTPUT SALES-LIST.
CALC-RTN.
        READ SALES-FILE AT END GO TO FINISH.
        MOVE ACC-NO TO ACC-NO-OUT.
        MOVE SALESMAN TO SALESMAN-OUT.
        MULTIPLY AMOUNT-OF-SALE BY .06 GIVING
        COMMISSION. IF COMMISSION > 500 MOVE
        500 TO COMMISSION.
        WRITE SALES-REPORT. GO TO START.
FINISH.
        CLOSE SALES-FILE, SALES-LIST.
        STOP RUN.
```

(a) _____ How many times will the OPEN instruction be executed?
(b) _____ An example of a paragraph is __.
(c) _____ Which statement is executed prior to the STOP RUN statement?
(d) _____ Which statement transfers control to CLOSE SALES-FILE, SALES-LIST. statement?
(e) _____ Assuming there are 10 input records, how many output records will be written?
(f) _____ __ is the highest amount a salesman can receive as a commission for an account.

4. Use your own data name to code the DATA DIVISION entries for the following card input record:

```
cc   1-25   employee name (alphabetic)
cc   26-29  not used
```

cc 30–36   year to date earning with dollars and cents
cc 37–39   not used
cc 40–43   hourly wage with dollars and cents
cc 44   not used
cc 45–47   hours worked with one decimal place
cc 48–80   not used

Note: Decimal positions are implied.

5. Construct a program flowchart from the following COBOL PROCE-DURE DIVISION instructions:

```
PROCEDURE DIVISION
BEGIN.
        OPEN INPUT IN-FILE, OUTPUT OUT-FILE.
        MOVE ZEROES TO TOTAL.
CALC-RTN.
        READ IN-FILE AT END GO TO EXIT.
        IF AMOUNT > 100 MULTIPLY AMOUNT
        BY .05 GIVING DISCOUNT ELSE
        MULTIPLY AMOUNT BY .04 GIVING
        DISCOUNT.
        ADD DISCOUNT TO TOTAL.
        SUBTRACT DISCOUNT FROM AMOUNT
        GIVING NET.
        MOVE ACCOUNT-NO TO ACCT-NO-OUT.
        MOVE AMOUNT TO AMOUNT-OUT.
        MOVE NET TO NET-OUT.
        WRITE PRINT-OUT.
        GO TO START.
EXIT.   MOVE TOTAL TO TOTAL-OUT.
        WRITE PRINT-OUT-1.
        DISPLAY 'END OF JOB'.
        CLOSE IN-FILE, OUT-FILE.
        STOP RUN.
```

6. Briefly distinguish between the FILE SECTION and the WORKING-STORAGE SECTION of the DATA DIVISION.

7. Discuss COBOL with respect to its application in business-oriented problems:
   (a) How does it aid documentation?
   (b) How does it relate to nonprogrammer personnel?
   (c) How does it relate to the training of potential programmers and analysts?
   (d) What possible disadvantages might be encountered with the structure of the language?

(e) How does it compare with other computer languages you might be familiar with?

8. Discuss the purpose of each of the COBOL divisions. Which are dependent on the particular machine to be used?

9. Determine how the output would appear after having been edited by the indicated PICTURE.

SENDING		RECEIVING	
Picture	Contents	Picture	Contents
X(5)	344BC	X(5)	
999v99	00726	999.99	
999v99	00726	$99.99	
999v99	00726	$ZZ.99	

ITEMS FOR DISCUSSION

American National Standards
  Institute
COBOL
CODASYL
Division
Object Program
IDENTIFICATION DIVISION
ENVIRONMENT DIVISION
DATA DIVISION
PROCEDURE DIVISION

Reserved Word
CONFIGURATION SECTION
INPUT-OUTPUT SECTION
FILE SECTION
WORKING-STORAGE SECTION
PICTURE Clause
File Description Entry
Paragraph Name
Source Program

APPENDIX

IBM.

AMERICAN NATIONAL STANDARD COBOL Reference Summary

The general format of a COBOL program is illustrated in these format summaries. Included within the general format is the specific format for each valid COBOL statement. All clauses are shown as though they were required by the COBOL source program, although within a given context many are optional. Several formats are included under special headings, which are different from, or additions to, the general format. Under these special headings are included formats peculiar to the following COBOL features: Sort, Report Writer, Table Handling, Segmentation, Source Program Library Facility, Debugging Language, Format Control of the Source Program Listing, Sterling Currency, Teleprocessing, and String Manipulation. Each of these features is explained within a special chapter of the publication — *IBM OS Full American National Standard COBOL*, Order No. GC28-6396-3.

IDENTIFICATION DIVISION—BASIC FORMATS

$\left\{ \begin{array}{l} \underline{\text{IDENTIFICATION}} \ \underline{\text{DIVISION}}. \\ \underline{\text{ID}} \ \underline{\text{DIVISION}}. \end{array} \right\}$

<u>PROGRAM-ID</u>. *program-name*.

<u>AUTHOR</u>. [*comment-entry*] . . .

<u>INSTALLATION</u>. [*comment-entry*] . . .

<u>DATE-WRITTEN</u>. [*comment-entry*] . . .

<u>DATE-COMPILED</u>. [*comment-entry*] . . .

<u>SECURITY</u>. [*comment-entry*] . . .

<u>REMARKS</u>. [*comment-entry*] . . .

ENVIRONMENT DIVISION—BASIC FORMATS

<u>ENVIRONMENT</u> <u>DIVISION</u>.

<u>CONFIGURATION</u> <u>SECTION</u>.

<u>SOURCE-COMPUTER</u>. *computer-name*.

<u>OBJECT-COMPUTER</u> *computer-name* [<u>MEMORY</u> SIZE *integer*

$\left\{ \begin{array}{l} \underline{\text{WORDS}} \\ \underline{\text{CHARACTERS}} \\ \underline{\text{MODULES}} \end{array} \right\}$]

[<u>SEGMENT-LIMIT</u> IS *priority-number*].

<u>SPECIAL-NAMES</u>. [*function-name* IS *mnemonic-name*] . . .

[<u>CURRENCY</u> SIGN <u>IS</u> *literal*]

[<u>DECIMAL-POINT</u> IS <u>COMMA</u>].

<u>INPUT-OUTPUT</u> <u>SECTION</u>.

<u>FILE-CONTROL</u>.

{ <u>SELECT</u> [<u>OPTIONAL</u>] *file-name*

<u>ASSIGN</u> TO [*integer-1*] *system-name-1* [*system-name-2*] . . .

[FOR <u>MULTIPLE</u> $\left\{ \begin{array}{l} \underline{\text{REEL}} \\ \underline{\text{UNIT}} \end{array} \right\}$]

<u>RESERVE</u> $\left\{ \begin{array}{l} \underline{\text{NO}} \\ \textit{integer-1} \end{array} \right\}$ ALTERNATE $\left[\begin{array}{l} \text{AREA} \\ \text{AREAS} \end{array} \right]$

$\left\{ \begin{array}{l} \underline{\text{FILE-LIMIT}} \ \underline{\text{IS}} \\ \underline{\text{FILE-LIMITS}} \ \underline{\text{ARE}} \end{array} \right\} \left\{ \begin{array}{l} \textit{data-name-1} \\ \textit{literal-1} \end{array} \right\} \underline{\text{THRU}} \left\{ \begin{array}{l} \textit{data-name-2} \\ \textit{literal-2} \end{array} \right\}$

$[\left\{ \begin{array}{l} \textit{data-name-3} \\ \textit{literal-3} \end{array} \right\} \underline{\text{THRU}} \left\{ \begin{array}{l} \textit{data-name-4} \\ \textit{literal-4} \end{array} \right\}] . . .$

<u>ACCESS</u> MODE <u>IS</u> $\left\{ \begin{array}{l} \underline{\text{SEQUENTIAL}} \\ \underline{\text{RANDOM}} \end{array} \right\}$

<u>PROCESSING</u> MODE <u>IS</u> <u>SEQUENTIAL</u>

<u>ACTUAL</u> KEY <u>IS</u> *data-name*

NOMINAL KEY IS *data-name*

RECORD KEY IS *data-name*

TRACK-AREA IS $\begin{Bmatrix} \text{\textit{data-name}} \\ \text{\textit{integer}} \end{Bmatrix}$ CHARACTERS

TRACK-LIMIT IS *integer* $\begin{bmatrix} \text{TRACK} \\ \text{TRACKS} \end{bmatrix}$. } . . .

I-O-CONTROL.

RERUN ON *system-name* EVERY *integer* RECORDS OF *file-name*

SAME $\begin{bmatrix} \text{RECORD} \\ \text{SORT} \end{bmatrix}$ AREA FOR *file-name-1* {*file-name-2*} . . .

MULTIPLE FILE TAPE CONTAINS *file-name-1* [POSITION *integer-1*]

[*file-name-2* [POSITION *integer-2*]] . . .

APPLY WRITE-ONLY ON *file-name-1* [*file-name-2*] . . .

APPLY CORE-INDEX ON *file-name-1* [*file-name-2*] . . .

APPLY RECORD-OVERFLOW ON *file-name-1* [*fiile-name-2*] . . .

APPLY REORG-CRITERIA TO *data-name* ON *file-name*

NOTE: Format 2 of the RERUN Clause (for Sort Files) is included with Formats for the SORT feature.

DATA DIVISION—BASIC FORMATS

DATA DIVISION.

FILE SECTION.

FD *file-name*

BLOCK CONTAINS [*integer-1* TO] *integer-2* $\begin{bmatrix} \text{CHARACTERS} \\ \text{RECORDS} \end{bmatrix}$

RECORD CONTAINS [*integer-1* TO] *integer-2* CHARACTERS

RECORDING MODE IS *mode*

LABEL $\begin{Bmatrix} \text{RECORD IS} \\ \text{RECORDS ARE} \end{Bmatrix}$ $\begin{bmatrix} \text{OMITTED} \\ \text{STANDARD} \\ \text{\textit{data-name-1} [\textit{data-name-2}] . . . [TOTALING} \\ \text{AREA IS \textit{data-name-3} TOTALED} \\ \text{AREA IS \textit{data-name-4}]} \end{bmatrix}$

VALUE OF *data-name-1* IS $\begin{Bmatrix} \text{\textit{data-name-2}} \\ \text{\textit{literal-1}} \end{Bmatrix}$

[*data-name-3* IS $\begin{Bmatrix} \text{\textit{data-name-4}} \\ \text{\textit{literal-2}} \end{Bmatrix}$] . . .

DATA $\begin{Bmatrix} \text{RECORD IS} \\ \text{RECORDS ARE} \end{Bmatrix}$ *data-name-1* [*data-name-2*] . . . .

NOTE: Format for the REPORT Clause is included with Formats for the REPORT WRITER feature.

01-49 $\begin{Bmatrix} \text{\textit{data-name-1}} \\ \text{FILLER} \end{Bmatrix}$

REDEFINES *data-name-2*

BLANK WHEN ZERO

$\begin{Bmatrix} \text{JUSTIFIED} \\ \text{JUST} \end{Bmatrix}$ RIGHT

$\begin{Bmatrix} \text{PICTURE} \\ \text{PIC} \end{Bmatrix}$ IS *character string*

[SIGN IS] $\begin{Bmatrix} \text{LEADING} \\ \text{TRAILING} \end{Bmatrix}$ [SEPARATE CHARACTER]   (Version 3)

$\begin{Bmatrix} \text{SYNCHRONIZED} \\ \text{SYNC} \end{Bmatrix}$ $\begin{bmatrix} \text{LEFT} \\ \text{RIGHT} \end{bmatrix}$

[USAGE IS] $\begin{Bmatrix} \text{INDEX} \\ \text{DISPLAY} \\ \begin{Bmatrix} \text{COMPUTATIONAL} \\ \text{COMP} \end{Bmatrix} \\ \begin{Bmatrix} \text{COMPUTATIONAL-1} \\ \text{COMP-1} \end{Bmatrix} \\ \begin{Bmatrix} \text{COMPUTATIONAL-2} \\ \text{COMP-2} \end{Bmatrix} \\ \begin{Bmatrix} \text{COMPUTATIONAL-3} \\ \text{COMP-3} \end{Bmatrix} \\ \text{DISPLAY-ST} \\ \begin{Bmatrix} \text{COMPUTATIONAL-4} \\ \text{COMP-4} \end{Bmatrix} \text{(Version 3)} \end{Bmatrix}$

88 *condition-name* $\begin{Bmatrix} \text{VALUE IS} \\ \text{VALUES ARE} \end{Bmatrix}$ *literal-1* [THRU *literal-2*]

[*literal-3* [THRU *literal-4*]] . . .

66 *data-name-1* RENAMES *data-name-2* [THRU *data-name-3*].

NOTE: Formats for the OCCURS Clause are included with Formats for the TABLE HANDLING feature.

WORKING-STORAGE SECTION.

77 *data-name-1*

01-49 $\begin{Bmatrix} \text{\textit{data-name-1}} \\ \text{FILLER} \end{Bmatrix}$

REDEFINES *data-name-2*

BLANK WHEN ZERO

$\begin{Bmatrix} \text{JUSTIFIED} \\ \text{JUST} \end{Bmatrix}$ RIGHT

$\begin{Bmatrix} \text{PICTURE} \\ \text{PIC} \end{Bmatrix}$ IS *character string*

[SIGN IS] $\begin{Bmatrix} \text{LEADING} \\ \text{TRAILING} \end{Bmatrix}$ [SEPARATE CHARACTER]   (Version 3)

$\begin{Bmatrix} \text{SYNCHRONIZED} \\ \text{SYNC} \end{Bmatrix}$ $\begin{bmatrix} \text{LEFT} \\ \text{RIGHT} \end{bmatrix}$

[USAGE IS] $\begin{Bmatrix} \text{INDEX} \\ \text{DISPLAY} \\ \begin{Bmatrix} \text{COMPUTATIONAL} \\ \text{COMP} \end{Bmatrix} \\ \begin{Bmatrix} \text{COMPUTATIONAL-1} \\ \text{COMP-1} \end{Bmatrix} \\ \begin{Bmatrix} \text{COMPUTATIONAL-2} \\ \text{COMP-2} \end{Bmatrix} \\ \begin{Bmatrix} \text{COMPUTATIONAL-3} \\ \text{COMP-3} \end{Bmatrix} \\ \text{DISPLAY-ST} \\ \begin{Bmatrix} \text{COMPUTATIONAL-4} \\ \text{COMP-4} \end{Bmatrix} \text{(Version3)} \end{Bmatrix}$

VALUE IS *literal*.

88 *condition-name* $\begin{Bmatrix} \text{VALUE IS} \\ \text{VALUES ARE} \end{Bmatrix}$ *literal-1* [THRU *literal-2*]

[*literal-3* [THRU *literal-4*]] . . .

66 *data-name-1* RENAMES *data-name-2* [THRU *data-name-3*].

NOTE: Formats for the OCCURS Clause are included with Formats for the TABLE HANDLING feature.

LINKAGE SECTION.

77 *data-name-1*

01-49 $\begin{Bmatrix} \text{\textit{data-name-1}} \\ \text{FILLER} \end{Bmatrix}$

REDEFINES *data-name-2*

BLANK WHEN ZERO

$\begin{Bmatrix} \text{JUSTIFIED} \\ \text{JUST} \end{Bmatrix}$ RIGHT

$\begin{Bmatrix} \text{PICTURE} \\ \text{PIC} \end{Bmatrix}$ IS *character string*

[SIGN IS] $\begin{Bmatrix} \text{LEADING} \\ \text{TRAILING} \end{Bmatrix}$ [SEPARATE CHARACTER]   (Version 3)

$\begin{Bmatrix} \text{SYNCHRONIZED} \\ \text{SYNC} \end{Bmatrix}$ $\begin{bmatrix} \text{LEFT} \\ \text{RIGHT} \end{bmatrix}$

[USAGE IS] $\begin{Bmatrix} \text{INDEX} \\ \text{DISPLAY} \\ \begin{Bmatrix} \text{COMPUTATIONAL} \\ \text{COMP} \end{Bmatrix} \\ \begin{Bmatrix} \text{COMPUTATIONAL-1} \\ \text{COMP-1} \end{Bmatrix} \\ \begin{Bmatrix} \text{COMPUTATIONAL-2} \\ \text{COMP-2} \end{Bmatrix} \\ \begin{Bmatrix} \text{COMPUTATIONAL-3} \\ \text{COMP-3} \end{Bmatrix} \\ \text{DISPLAY-ST} \\ \begin{Bmatrix} \text{COMPUTATIONAL-4} \\ \text{COMP-4} \end{Bmatrix} \text{(Version 3)} \end{Bmatrix}$

88 condition-name $\begin{Bmatrix} \underline{VALUE} \text{ IS} \\ \underline{VALUES} \text{ ARE} \end{Bmatrix}$ literal-1 [THRU literal-2]

    [literal-3 [THRU literal-4]] . . .

66 data-name-1 RENAMES data-name-2 [THRU data-name-3].

NOTE: Formats for the OCCURS Clause are included with Formats for the TABLE HANDLING feature.

PROCEDURE DIVISION—BASIC FORMATS

$\begin{Bmatrix} \text{PROCEDURE DIVISION.} \\ \text{PROCEDURE DIVISION USING identifier-1 [identifier-2] . . .} \end{Bmatrix}$.

ACCEPT Statement

ACCEPT identifier [FROM $\begin{Bmatrix} \text{SYSIN} \\ \text{CONSOLE} \\ \text{mnemonic-name} \end{Bmatrix}$]

ADD Statement

FORMAT 1

ADD $\begin{Bmatrix} \text{identifier-1} \\ \text{literal-1} \end{Bmatrix} \begin{Bmatrix} \text{identifier-2} \\ \text{literal-2} \end{Bmatrix}$ . . . TO identifier-m [ROUNDED]

    [identifier-n [ROUNDED]] . . . [ON SIZE ERROR imperative-statement]

FORMAT 2

ADD $\begin{Bmatrix} \text{identifier-1} \\ \text{literal-1} \end{Bmatrix} \begin{Bmatrix} \text{identifier-2} \\ \text{literal-2} \end{Bmatrix} \begin{Bmatrix} \text{identifier-3} \\ \text{literal-3} \end{Bmatrix}$ . . . GIVING

    identifier-m [ROUNDED] [ON SIZE ERROR
    imperative-statement]

FORMAT 3

ADD $\begin{Bmatrix} \text{CORRESPONDING} \\ \text{CORR} \end{Bmatrix}$ identifier-1 TO identifier-2 [ROUNDED]

    [ON SIZE ERROR imperative-statement]

ALTER Statement

ALTER procedure-name-1 TO [PROCEED TO] procedure-name-2

    [procedure-name-3 TO [PROCEED TO] procedure-name-4] .

CALL Statement

CALL literal-1 [USING identifier-1 [identifier-2] . . .]

CLOSE Statement

FORMAT 1

CLOSE file-name-1 $\begin{Bmatrix} \text{REEL} \\ \text{UNIT} \end{Bmatrix}$ [WITH $\begin{Bmatrix} \text{NO REWIND} \\ \text{LOCK} \end{Bmatrix}$]

    [file-name-2 $\begin{Bmatrix} \text{REEL} \\ \text{UNIT} \end{Bmatrix}$ [WITH $\begin{Bmatrix} \text{NO REWIND} \\ \text{LOCK} \end{Bmatrix}$]] . . .

FORMAT 2

CLOSE file-name-1 [WITH $\begin{Bmatrix} \text{NO REWIND} \\ \text{LOCK} \\ \text{DISP} \end{Bmatrix}$]

    [file-name-2 [WITH $\begin{Bmatrix} \text{NO REWIND} \\ \text{LOCK} \\ \text{DISP} \end{Bmatrix}$]] . . .

FORMAT 3

CLOSE file-name-1 $\begin{Bmatrix} \text{REEL} \\ \text{UNIT} \end{Bmatrix}$ [WITH $\begin{Bmatrix} \text{NO REWIND} \\ \text{LOCK} \\ \text{POSITIONING} \end{Bmatrix}$]

    [file-name-2 $\begin{Bmatrix} \text{REEL} \\ \text{UNIT} \end{Bmatrix}$ [WITH $\begin{Bmatrix} \text{NO REWIND} \\ \text{LOCK} \\ \text{POSITIONING} \end{Bmatrix}$]] . . .

COMPUTE Statement

COMPUTE identifier-1 [ROUNDED] = $\begin{Bmatrix} \text{arithmetic-expression} \\ \text{identifier-2} \\ \text{literal-1} \end{Bmatrix}$

    [ON SIZE ERROR imperative-statement]

DECLARATIVE Section

PROCEDURE DIVISION.

DECLARATIVES.

{section-name SECTION. USE sentence.

{paragraph-name. {sentence} . . .} . . . } . . .

END DECLARATIVES.

DISPLAY Statement

DISPLAY $\begin{Bmatrix} \text{identifier-1} \\ \text{literal-1} \end{Bmatrix} \begin{bmatrix} \text{identifier-2} \\ \text{literal-2} \end{bmatrix}$ . . . [UPON $\begin{Bmatrix} \text{CONSOLE} \\ \text{SYSPUNCH} \\ \text{SYSOUT} \\ \text{mnemonic-name} \end{Bmatrix}$]

DIVIDE Statement

FORMAT 1

DIVIDE $\begin{Bmatrix} \text{identifier-1} \\ \text{literal-1} \end{Bmatrix}$ INTO identifier-2 [ROUNDED]

    [ON SIZE ERROR imperative-statement]

FORMAT 2

DIVIDE $\begin{Bmatrix} \text{identifier-1} \\ \text{literal-1} \end{Bmatrix} \begin{Bmatrix} \text{INTO} \\ \text{BY} \end{Bmatrix} \begin{Bmatrix} \text{identifier-2} \\ \text{literal-2} \end{Bmatrix}$ GIVING identifier-3

    [ROUNDED] [REMAINDER identifier-4]

    [ON SIZE ERROR imperative-statement]

ENTER Statement

ENTER language-name [routine-name]

ENTRY Statement

ENTRY literal-1 [USING identifier-1 [identifier-2] . . .]

EXAMINE Statement

FORMAT 1

EXAMINE identifier TALLYING $\begin{Bmatrix} \text{UNTIL FIRST} \\ \text{ALL} \\ \text{LEADING} \end{Bmatrix}$ literal-1

    [REPLACING BY literal-2]

FORMAT 2

EXAMINE identifier REPLACING $\begin{Bmatrix} \text{ALL} \\ \text{LEADING} \\ \text{FIRST} \\ \text{UNTIL FIRST} \end{Bmatrix}$ literal-1 BY literal-2

EXIT Statement

paragraph-name. EXIT [PROGRAM].

GOBACK Statement

GOBACK.

GO TO Statement

FORMAT 1

GO TO procedure-name-1

FORMAT 2

GO TO procedure-name-1 [procedure-name-2] . . .

    DEPENDING ON identifier

FORMAT 3

GO TO.

IF Statement

IF condition THEN $\begin{Bmatrix} \text{NEXT SENTENCE} \\ \text{statement-1} \end{Bmatrix}$

    $\begin{Bmatrix} \text{OTHERWISE} \\ \text{ELSE} \end{Bmatrix} \begin{Bmatrix} \text{NEXT SENTENCE} \\ \text{statement-2} \end{Bmatrix}$

MOVE Statement

FORMAT 1

MOVE $\begin{Bmatrix} \text{identifier-1} \\ \text{literal-1} \end{Bmatrix}$ TO identifier-2 [identifier-3] . . .

FORMAT 2

MOVE $\begin{Bmatrix} \text{CORRESPONDING} \\ \text{CORR} \end{Bmatrix}$ identifier-1 TO identifier-2

MULTIPLY Statement
FORMAT 1

MULTIPLY $\left\{ \begin{array}{l} identifier\text{-}1 \\ literal\text{-}1 \end{array} \right\}$ BY identifier-2 [ROUNDED]

    [ON SIZE ERROR imperative statement]

FORMAT 2

MULTIPLY $\left\{ \begin{array}{l} identifier\text{-}1 \\ literal\text{-}1 \end{array} \right\}$ BY $\left\{ \begin{array}{l} identifier\text{-}2 \\ literal\text{-}2 \end{array} \right\}$ GIVING identifier-3

    [ROUNDED] [ON SIZE ERROR imperative-statement]

NOTE Statement

NOTE character string

OPEN Statement
FORMAT 1

OPEN [INPUT { file-name $\left[\begin{array}{l} \underline{REVERSED} \\ WITH\ \underline{NO}\ \underline{REWIND} \end{array} \right]$ } . . .]

    [OUTPUT { file-name [WITH NO REWIND]} . . .]

    [I-O { file-name} . . .]

FORMAT 2

OPEN [INPUT { file-name $\left[\begin{array}{l} \underline{REVERSED} \\ WITH\ \underline{NO}\ \underline{REWIND} \end{array} \right]$ $\left[\begin{array}{l} \underline{LEAVE} \\ \underline{REREAD} \\ \underline{DISP} \end{array} \right]$ } . . .]

    [OUTPUT { file-name [WITH NO REWIND] $\left[\begin{array}{l} \underline{LEAVE} \\ \underline{REREAD} \\ \underline{DISP} \end{array} \right]$ } . . .]

    [I-O { file-name} . . .]

PERFORM Statement
FORMAT 1

PERFORM procedure-name-1 [THRU procedure-name-2]

FORMAT 2

PERFORM procedure-name-1 [THRU procedure-name-2] $\left\{ \begin{array}{l} identifier\text{-}1 \\ integer\text{-}1 \end{array} \right\}$ TIMES

FORMAT 3

PERFORM procedure-name-1 [THRU procedure-name-2] UNTIL condition-1

FORMAT 4

PERFORM procedure-name-1 [THRU procedure-name-2]

VARYING $\left\{ \begin{array}{l} index\text{-}name\text{-}1 \\ identifier\text{-}1 \end{array} \right\}$ FROM $\left\{ \begin{array}{l} index\text{-}name\text{-}2 \\ literal\text{-}2 \\ identifier\text{-}2 \end{array} \right\}$ BY $\left\{ \begin{array}{l} literal\text{-}3 \\ identifier\text{-}3 \end{array} \right\}$

    UNTIL condition-1

[AFTER $\left\{ \begin{array}{l} index\text{-}name\text{-}4 \\ identifier\text{-}4 \end{array} \right\}$ FROM $\left\{ \begin{array}{l} index\text{-}name\text{-}5 \\ literal\text{-}5 \\ identifier\text{-}5 \end{array} \right\}$ BY $\left\{ \begin{array}{l} literal\text{-}6 \\ identifier\text{-}6 \end{array} \right\}$

    UNTIL condition-2

[AFTER $\left\{ \begin{array}{l} index\text{-}name\text{-}7 \\ indentifier\text{-}7 \end{array} \right\}$ FROM $\left\{ \begin{array}{l} index\text{-}name\text{-}8 \\ literal\text{-}8 \\ identifier\text{-}8 \end{array} \right\}$ BY $\left\{ \begin{array}{l} literal\text{-}9 \\ identifier\text{-}9 \end{array} \right\}$

    UNTIL condition-3]]

READ Statement

READ file-name RECORD [INTO identifier]

    $\left\{ \begin{array}{l} AT\ \underline{END} \\ \underline{INVALID}\ KEY \end{array} \right\}$ imperative-statement

REWRITE Statement

REWRITE record-name [FROM identifier]

    [INVALID KEY imperative-statement]

SEEK Statement

SEEK file-name RECORD

START Statement
FORMAT 1

START file-name [INVALID KEY imperative-statement]

FORMAT 2

START file-name

    USING KEY data-name $\left\{ \begin{array}{l} \underline{EQUAL}\ \underline{TO} \\ = \end{array} \right\}$ identifier

    [INVALID KEY imperative-statement]

STOP Statement

STOP $\left\{ \begin{array}{l} \underline{RUN} \\ literal \end{array} \right\}$

SUBTRACT Statement
FORMAT 1

SUBTRACT $\left[\begin{array}{l} identifier\text{-}1 \\ literal\text{-}1 \end{array} \right]$ $\left[\begin{array}{l} identifier\text{-}2 \\ literal\text{-}2 \end{array} \right]$ . . .

    FROM identifier-m [ROUNDED]

    [identifier-n [ROUNDED]] . . .

    [ON SIZE ERROR imperative-statement]

FORMAT 2

SUBTRACT $\left[\begin{array}{l} identifier\text{-}1 \\ literal\text{-}1 \end{array} \right]$ $\left[\begin{array}{l} identifier\text{-}2 \\ literal\text{-}2 \end{array} \right]$ . . .

    FROM $\left\{ \begin{array}{l} identifier\text{-}m \\ literal\text{-}m \end{array} \right\}$ GIVING identifier-n

    [ROUNDED] [ON SIZE ERROR imperative-statement]

FORMAT 3

SUBTRACT $\left\{ \begin{array}{l} \underline{CORRESPONDING} \\ \underline{CORR} \end{array} \right\}$ identifier-1 FROM identifier-2

    [ROUNDED] [ON SIZE ERROR imperative-statement]

TRANSFORM Statement

TRANSFORM identifier-3 CHARACTERS FROM $\left\{ \begin{array}{l} figurative\text{-}constant\text{-}1 \\ nonnumeric\text{-}literal\text{-}1 \\ identifier\text{-}1 \end{array} \right\}$

    TO $\left\{ \begin{array}{l} figurative\text{-}constant\text{-}2 \\ nonnumeric\text{-}literal\text{-}2 \\ identifier\text{-}2 \end{array} \right\}$

USE Sentence
FORMAT 1
   Option 1:

USE $\left\{ \begin{array}{l} \underline{BEFORE} \\ \underline{AFTER} \end{array} \right\}$ STANDARD [BEGINNING] $\left[\begin{array}{l} \underline{REEL} \\ \underline{FILE} \\ \underline{UNIT} \end{array} \right]$

    LABEL PROCEDURE ON $\left\{ \begin{array}{l} \{file\text{-}name\}\ . . . \\ \underline{OUTPUT} \\ \underline{INPUT} \\ \underline{I\text{-}O} \end{array} \right\}$

   Option 2:

USE $\left\{ \begin{array}{l} \underline{BEFORE} \\ \underline{AFTER} \end{array} \right\}$ STANDARD [ENDING] $\left[\begin{array}{l} \underline{REEL} \\ \underline{FILE} \\ \underline{UNIT} \end{array} \right]$

    LABEL PROCEDURE ON $\left\{ \begin{array}{l} \{file\text{-}name\}\ . . . \\ \underline{OUTPUT} \\ \underline{INPUT} \\ \underline{I\text{-}O} \end{array} \right\}$

FORMAT 2
USE AFTER STANDARD ERROR PROCEDURE

    ON $\left\{ \begin{array}{l} \{file\text{-}name\text{-}1\}\ [file\text{-}name\text{-}2]\ . . . \\ [\underline{GIVING}\ data\text{-}name\text{-}1,\ data\text{-}name\text{-}2] \\ \underline{INPUT} \\ \underline{OUTPUT} \\ \underline{I\text{-}O} \end{array} \right\}$

NOTE: Format 3 of the USE Sentence is included in Formats for the REPORT WRITER feature.

WRITE Statement
FORMAT 1

WRITE record-name [FROM identifier-1] [$\left\{ \begin{array}{l} \underline{BEFORE} \\ \underline{AFTER} \end{array} \right\}$ ADVANCING

$$\begin{Bmatrix} \textit{identifier-2 LINES} \\ \textit{integer LINES} \\ \textit{mnemonic-name} \end{Bmatrix}$$

[AT $\begin{Bmatrix} \underline{\text{END-OF-PAGE}} \\ \underline{\text{EOP}} \end{Bmatrix}$ *imperative-statement*]

FORMAT 2

$\underline{\text{WRITE}}$ *record-name* [$\underline{\text{FROM}}$ *identifier-1*]

$\quad$ $\underline{\text{AFTER}}$ $\underline{\text{POSITIONING}}$ $\begin{Bmatrix} \textit{identifier-2} \\ \textit{integer} \end{Bmatrix}$ LINES

$\quad$ [AT $\begin{Bmatrix} \underline{\text{END-OF-PAGE}} \\ \underline{\text{EOP}} \end{Bmatrix}$ *imperative-statement*]

FORMAT 3

$\underline{\text{WRITE}}$ *record-name* [$\underline{\text{FROM}}$ *identifier-1*] $\underline{\text{INVALID}}$ KEY *imperative-statement*

SORT—BASIC FORMATS

Environment Division Sort Formats
FILE-CONTROL PARAGRAPH—SELECT SENTENCE
SELECT Sentence (for GIVING option only)

$\quad$ $\underline{\text{SELECT}}$ *file-name*

$\quad\quad$ $\underline{\text{ASSIGN}}$ TO [*integer-1*] *system-name-1* [*system-name-2*] . . .

$\quad\quad\quad$ $\underline{\text{OR}}$ *system-name-3* [FOR $\underline{\text{MULTIPLE}}$ $\begin{Bmatrix} \underline{\text{REEL}} \\ \underline{\text{UNIT}} \end{Bmatrix}$]

$\quad\quad\quad\quad$ [$\underline{\text{RESERVE}}$ $\begin{Bmatrix} \textit{integer-2} \\ \underline{\text{NO}} \end{Bmatrix}$ ALTERNATE $\begin{bmatrix} \text{AREA} \\ \text{AREAS} \end{bmatrix}$].

SELECT Sentence (for Sort Work Files)

$\quad$ $\underline{\text{SELECT}}$ *sort-file-name*

$\quad\quad$ $\underline{\text{ASSIGN}}$ TO [*integer*] *system-name-1* [*system-name-2*] . . .

I-O-CONTROL PARAGRAPH
RERUN Clause

$\quad$ $\underline{\text{RERUN}}$ $\underline{\text{ON}}$ *system-name*

SAME RECORD/SORT AREA Clause

$\quad$ $\underline{\text{SAME}}$ $\begin{Bmatrix} \underline{\text{RECORD}} \\ \underline{\text{SORT}} \end{Bmatrix}$ AREA FOR *file-name-1* {*file-name-2*} . . .

Data Division Sort Formats
SORT-FILE DESCRIPTION

$\quad$ $\underline{\text{SD}}$ *sort-file-name*

$\quad\quad$ $\underline{\text{RECORDING}}$ MODE IS *mode*

$\quad\quad$ $\underline{\text{DATA}}$ $\begin{Bmatrix} \underline{\text{RECORD}} \text{ IS} \\ \underline{\text{RECORDS}} \text{ ARE} \end{Bmatrix}$ *data-name-1* [*data-name-2*] . . .

$\quad\quad$ $\underline{\text{RECORD}}$ CONTAINS [*integer-1* $\underline{\text{TO}}$] *integer-2* CHARACTERS.

Procedure Division Sort Formats
RELEASE Statement

$\quad$ $\underline{\text{RELEASE}}$ *sort-record-name* [$\underline{\text{FROM}}$ *identifier*]

RETURN Statement

$\quad$ $\underline{\text{RETURN}}$ *sort-file-name* RECORD [$\underline{\text{INTO}}$ *identifier*]

$\quad\quad$ AT $\underline{\text{END}}$ *imperative-statement*

SORT Statement

$\quad$ $\underline{\text{SORT}}$ *file-name-1* ON $\begin{Bmatrix} \underline{\text{DESCENDING}} \\ \underline{\text{ASCENDING}} \end{Bmatrix}$ KEY {*data-name-1*} . . .

$\quad$ [ON $\begin{Bmatrix} \underline{\text{DESCENDING}} \\ \underline{\text{ASCENDING}} \end{Bmatrix}$ KEY {*data-name-2*} . . .] . . .

$\quad$ [$\underline{\text{INPUT}}$ $\underline{\text{PROCEDURE}}$ IS *section-name-1* [$\underline{\text{THRU}}$ *section-name-2*]]
$\quad$ $\underline{\text{USING}}$ *file-name-2*

$\quad$ [$\underline{\text{OUTPUT}}$ $\underline{\text{PROCEDURE}}$ IS *section-name-3* [$\underline{\text{THRU}}$ *section-name-4*]]
$\quad$ $\underline{\text{GIVING}}$ *file-name-3*

REPORT WRITER—BASIC FORMATS

Data Division Report Writer Formats

NOTE: Formats that appear as Basic Formats within the general description of the Data Division are illustrated there.

FILE SECTION—REPORT Clause

$\quad$ $\begin{Bmatrix} \underline{\text{REPORT}} \text{ IS} \\ \underline{\text{REPORTS}} \text{ ARE} \end{Bmatrix}$ *report-name-1* [*report-name-2*] . . .

REPORT SECTION

$\underline{\text{REPORT}}$ $\underline{\text{SECTION}}$.

$\quad$ $\underline{\text{RD}}$ *report-name*

$\quad\quad$ WITH $\underline{\text{CODE}}$ *mnemonic-name*

$\quad\quad$ $\begin{Bmatrix} \underline{\text{CONTROL}} \text{ IS} \\ \underline{\text{CONTROLS}} \text{ ARE} \end{Bmatrix} \begin{Bmatrix} \underline{\text{FINAL}} \\ \textit{identifier-1} [\textit{identifier-2}] \ldots \\ \underline{\text{FINAL}} \textit{ identifier-1} [\textit{identifier-2}] \ldots \end{Bmatrix}$

$\quad\quad$ $\underline{\text{PAGE}}$ $\begin{bmatrix} \text{LIMIT IS} \\ \text{LIMITS ARE} \end{bmatrix}$ *integer-1* $\begin{Bmatrix} \underline{\text{LINE}} \\ \underline{\text{LINES}} \end{Bmatrix}$

$\quad\quad$ [$\underline{\text{HEADING}}$ *integer-2*]

$\quad\quad$ [$\underline{\text{FIRST}}$ $\underline{\text{DETAIL}}$ *integer-3*]

$\quad\quad$ [$\underline{\text{LAST}}$ $\underline{\text{DETAIL}}$ *integer-4*]

$\quad\quad$ [$\underline{\text{FOOTING}}$ *integer-5*]

REPORT GROUP DESCRIPTION ENTRY

FORMAT 1

$\quad$ 01 [*data-name-1*]

$\quad\quad$ $\underline{\text{LINE}}$ NUMBER IS $\begin{Bmatrix} \textit{integer-1} \\ \underline{\text{PLUS}} \textit{ integer-2} \\ \underline{\text{NEXT}} \underline{\text{PAGE}} \end{Bmatrix}$

$\quad\quad$ $\underline{\text{NEXT}}$ $\underline{\text{GROUP}}$ IS $\begin{Bmatrix} \textit{integer-1} \\ \underline{\text{PLUS}} \textit{ integer-2} \\ \underline{\text{NEXT}} \underline{\text{PAGE}} \end{Bmatrix}$

$\quad\quad$ $\underline{\text{TYPE}}$ IS $\begin{Bmatrix} \underline{\text{REPORT}} \underline{\text{HEADING}} \\ \underline{\text{RH}} \\ \underline{\text{PAGE}} \underline{\text{HEADING}} \\ \underline{\text{PH}} \\ \underline{\text{CONTROL}} \underline{\text{HEADING}} \\ \underline{\text{CH}} \\ \underline{\text{DETAIL}} \\ \underline{\text{DE}} \\ \underline{\text{CONTROL}} \underline{\text{FOOTING}} \\ \underline{\text{CF}} \\ \underline{\text{PAGE}} \underline{\text{FOOTING}} \\ \underline{\text{PF}} \\ \underline{\text{REPORT}} \underline{\text{FOOTING}} \\ \underline{\text{RF}} \end{Bmatrix}$ $\begin{Bmatrix} \textit{identifier-n} \\ \underline{\text{FINAL}} \end{Bmatrix}$ $\begin{Bmatrix} \textit{identifier-n} \\ \underline{\text{FINAL}} \end{Bmatrix}$

$\quad\quad$ USAGE Clause.

FORMAT 2

$\quad$ nn [*data-name-1*]

$\quad\quad$ LINE Clause—See Format 1

$\quad\quad$ USAGE Clause.

FORMAT 3

$\quad$ nn [*data-name-1*]

$\quad\quad$ $\underline{\text{COLUMN}}$ NUMBER IS *integer-1*

$\quad\quad$ $\underline{\text{GROUP}}$ INDICATE

$\quad\quad$ JUSTIFIED Clause

$\quad\quad$ LINE Clause—See Format 1

$\quad\quad$ PICTURE Clause

$\quad\quad$ $\underline{\text{RESET}}$ ON $\begin{Bmatrix} \textit{identifier-1} \\ \underline{\text{FINAL}} \end{Bmatrix}$

$\quad\quad$ BLANK WHEN ZERO Clause

$\quad\quad$ $\underline{\text{SOURCE}}$ IS $\begin{Bmatrix} \underline{\text{TALLY}} \\ \textit{identifier-2} \end{Bmatrix}$

$\quad\quad$ $\underline{\text{SUM}}$ $\begin{Bmatrix} \underline{\text{TALLY}} \\ \textit{identifier-3} \end{Bmatrix} \begin{Bmatrix} \underline{\text{TALLY}} \\ \textit{identifier-4} \end{Bmatrix}$ . . . [$\underline{\text{UPON}}$ *data-name*]

$\quad\quad$ $\underline{\text{VALUE}}$ IS *literal-1*

$\quad\quad$ USAGE Clause.

FORMAT 4

$\quad$ 01 *data-name-1*

$\quad\quad$ BLANK WHEN ZERO Clause

$\quad\quad$ COLUMN Clause—See Format 2

$\quad\quad$ GROUP Clause—See Format 2

$\quad\quad$ JUSTIFIED Clause

LINE Clause—See Format 1
NEXT GROUP Clause—See Format 1
PICTURE Clause
RESET Clause—See Format 2

$\left.\begin{array}{l}\text{SOURCE Clause}\\\text{SUM Clause}\\\text{VALUE Clause}\end{array}\right\}$ See Format 2

TYPE Clause—See Format 1
USAGE Clause.

Procedure Division Report Writer Formats

GENERATE Statement

<u>GENERATE</u> *identifier*

INITIATE Statement

<u>INITIATE</u> *report-name-1* [*report-name-2*] . . .

TERMINATE Statement

<u>TERMINATE</u> *report-name-1* [*report-name-2*] . . .

USE Sentence

<u>USE</u> <u>BEFORE</u> <u>REPORTING</u> *data-name*.

TABLE HANDLING—BASIC FORMATS

Data Division Table Handling Formats

OCCURS Clause

FORMAT 1

<u>OCCURS</u> *integer-2* TIMES

$\left[\left\{\begin{array}{l}\underline{\text{ASCENDING}}\\\underline{\text{DESCENDING}}\end{array}\right\}\text{KEY IS } \textit{data-name-2 } [\textit{data-name-3} \ldots] \ldots\right.$

[<u>INDEXED</u> BY *index-name-1* [*index-name-2*] . . .]

FORMAT 2

<u>OCCURS</u> *integer-1* <u>TO</u> *integer-2* TIMES [<u>DEPENDING</u> ON *data-name-1*]

$\left[\left\{\begin{array}{l}\underline{\text{ASCENDING}}\\\underline{\text{DESCENDING}}\end{array}\right\}\text{KEY IS } \textit{data-name-2 } [\textit{data-name-3}] \ldots\right] \ldots$

[<u>INDEXED</u> BY *index-name-1* [*index-name-2*] . . .]

FORMAT 3

<u>OCCURS</u> *integer-2* TIMES [<u>DEPENDING</u> ON *data-name-1*]

$\left[\left\{\begin{array}{l}\underline{\text{ASCENDING}}\\\underline{\text{DESCENDING}}\end{array}\right\}\text{KEY IS } \textit{data-name-2 } [\textit{data-name-3}] \ldots\right] \ldots$

[<u>INDEXED</u> BY *index-name-1* [*index-name-2*] . . .]

USAGE Clause

[<u>USAGE</u> IS] <u>INDEX</u>

Procedure Division Table Handling Formats

SEARCH Statement

FORMAT 1

<u>SEARCH</u> *identifier-1* $\left[\underline{\text{VARYING}} \left\{\begin{array}{l}\textit{index-name-1}\\\textit{identifier-2}\end{array}\right\}\right]$

[AT <u>END</u> *imperative-statement-1*]

<u>WHEN</u> *condition-1* $\left\{\begin{array}{l}\textit{imperative-statement-2}\\\underline{\text{NEXT}}\ \underline{\text{SENTENCE}}\end{array}\right\}$

$\left[\underline{\text{WHEN}}\ \textit{condition-2} \left\{\begin{array}{l}\textit{imperative-statement-3}\\\underline{\text{NEXT}}\ \underline{\text{SENTENCE}}\end{array}\right\}\right] \ldots$

FORMAT 2

<u>SEARCH</u> <u>ALL</u> *identifier-1* [AT <u>END</u> *imperative-statement-1*]

<u>WHEN</u> *condition-1* $\left\{\begin{array}{l}\textit{imperative-statement-2}\\\underline{\text{NEXT}}\ \underline{\text{SENTENCE}}\end{array}\right\}$

SET Statement

FORMAT 1

<u>SET</u> $\left\{\begin{array}{ll}\textit{index-name-1} & [\textit{index-name-2}]\\\textit{identifier-1} & \textit{identifier-2}\end{array}\right\} \ldots\ \underline{\text{TO}} \left\{\begin{array}{l}\textit{index-name-3}\\\textit{identifier-3}\\\textit{literal-1}\end{array}\right\}$

FORMAT 2

<u>SET</u> *index-name-4* [*index-name-5*] . . . $\left\{\begin{array}{l}\underline{\text{UP}}\ \underline{\text{BY}}\\\underline{\text{DOWN}}\ \underline{\text{BY}}\end{array}\right\} \left\{\begin{array}{l}\textit{identifier-4}\\\textit{literal-2}\end{array}\right\}$

SEGMENTATION—BASIC FORMATS

Environment Division Segmentation Formats

OBJECT-COMPUTER PARAGRAPH

SEGMENT-LIMIT Clause

<u>SEGMENT-LIMIT</u> IS *priority-number*

Procedure Division Segmentation Formats

Priority Numbers

section-name <u>SECTION</u> [*priority-number*].

SOURCE PROGRAM LIBRARY FACILITY

COPY Statement

<u>COPY</u> *library-name* [<u>SUPPRESS</u>]

[<u>REPLACING</u> *word-1* <u>BY</u> $\left\{\begin{array}{l}\textit{word-2}\\\textit{literal-1}\\\textit{identifier-1}\end{array}\right\}$

word-3 <u>BY</u> $\left\{\begin{array}{l}\textit{word-4}\\\textit{literal-2}\\\textit{identifier-2}\end{array}\right\}$] . . .] .

Extended Source Program Library Facility

BASIS Card

<u>BASIS</u>   *library-name*

INSERT Card

<u>INSERT</u>   *sequence-number-field*

DELETE Card

<u>DELETE</u>   *sequence-number-field*

DEBUGGING LANGUAGE—BASIC FORMATS

Procedure Division Debugging Formats

EXHIBIT Statement

<u>EXHIBIT</u> $\left\{\begin{array}{l}\underline{\text{NAMED}}\\\underline{\text{CHANGED}}\ \underline{\text{NAMED}}\\\underline{\text{CHANGED}}\end{array}\right\} \begin{array}{l}\textit{identifier-1}\\\textit{nonnumeric-literal-1}\end{array}$

$\left\{\begin{array}{l}\textit{identifier-2}\\\textit{nonnumeric-literal-2}\end{array}\right\} \ldots$

ON (Count-Conditional) Statement

<u>ON</u> *integer-1* [<u>AND</u> <u>EVERY</u> *integer-2*] [<u>UNTIL</u> *integer-3*]

$\left\{\begin{array}{l}\textit{imperative-statement} \ldots\\\underline{\text{NEXT}}\ \underline{\text{SENTENCE}}\end{array}\right\} \left\{\begin{array}{l}\underline{\text{ELSE}}\\\underline{\text{OTHERWISE}}\end{array}\right\}$

$\left\{\begin{array}{l}\textit{statement} \ldots\\\underline{\text{NEXT}}\ \underline{\text{SENTENCE}}\end{array}\right\}$

TRACE Statement

$\left\{\begin{array}{l}\underline{\text{READY}}\\\underline{\text{RESET}}\end{array}\right\} \underline{\text{TRACE}}$

Compile-Time Debugging Packet

DEBUG Card

<u>DEBUG</u>   *location*

FORMAT CONTROL—BASIC FORMATS

EJECT Statement

1   Area B

                   <u>EJECT</u>

SKIP1, SKIP2, SKIP3 Statements

1   Area B

$\left\{\begin{array}{l}\underline{\text{SKIP1}}\\\underline{\text{SKIP2}}\\\underline{\text{SKIP3}}\end{array}\right\}$

STERLING CURRENCY—BASIC FORMATS

Data Division Sterling Formats

Nonreport PICTURE Clause

$$\left\{ \begin{matrix} \underline{PICTURE} \\ \underline{PIC} \end{matrix} \right\} \text{ IS } 9 \ [(n)] \ D \ [8] \ 8D \left\{ \begin{matrix} 6[6] \\ 7[7] \end{matrix} \right\} [[V] \ 9 \ [(n)]]$$

[USAGE IS] DISPLAY-ST

Report PICTURE Clause

$$\left\{ \begin{matrix} \underline{PICTURE} \\ \underline{PIC} \end{matrix} \right\} \text{ IS }$$

[*pound-report-string*] [*pound-separator-string*] *delimiter* *shilling-report-string*
[*shilling-separator-string*] *delimiter* *pence-report-string* [*pence-separator-string*]
[*sign-string*] [USAGE IS] DISPLAY-ST

PROGRAM PRODUCT INFORMATION—VERSION 4

TELEPROCESSING—BASIC FORMATS

Data Division Teleprocessing Formats

CD Entry

FORMAT 1

CD *cd-name* FOR INPUT

[[[SYMBOLIC QUEUE   IS *data-name-1*]
[SYMBOLIC SUB-QUEUE-1   IS *data-name-2*]
[SYMBOLIC SUB-QUEUE-2   IS *data-name-3*]
[SYMBOLIC SUB-QUEUE-3   IS *data-name-4*]
[MESSAGE DATE   IS *data-name-5*]
[MESSAGE TIME   IS *data-name-6*]
[SYMBOLIC SOURCE   IS *data-name-7*]
[TEXT LENGTH   IS *data-name-8*]
[END KEY   IS *data-name-9*]
[STATUS KEY   IS *data-name-10*]
[QUEUE DEPTH   IS *data-name-11*]]
[*data-name-1 data-name-2 . . . data-name-11*]].

FORMAT 2

CD *cd-name* FOR OUTPUT

[DESTINATION COUNT   IS *data-name-1*]
[TEXT LENGTH   IS *data-name-2*]
[STATUS KEY   IS *data-name-3*]
[ERROR KEY   IS *data-name-4*]
[SYMBOLIC DESTINATION   IS *data-name-5*].

Procedure Division Teleprocessing Formats

Message Condition

[NOT] MESSAGE FOR *cd-name*

RECEIVE Statement

RECEIVE *cd-name* $\left\{ \begin{matrix} \underline{MESSAGE} \\ \underline{SEGMENT} \end{matrix} \right\}$ INTO *identifier-1*

[NO DATA *imperative-statement*]

SEND Statement

FORMAT 1

SEND *cd-name* FROM *identifier-1*

FORMAT 2

SEND *cd-name* [FROM *identifier-1*]

$$\left\{ \begin{matrix} \text{WITH } identifier\text{-}2 \\ \text{WITH } \underline{ESI} \\ \text{WITH } \underline{EMI} \\ \text{WITH } \underline{ETI} \end{matrix} \right\}$$

STRING MANIPULATION—BASIC FORMATS

STRING Statement

STRING $\left\{ \begin{matrix} identifier\text{-}1 \\ literal\text{-}1 \end{matrix} \right\}$ $\left[\begin{matrix} identifier\text{-}2 \\ literal\text{-}2 \end{matrix} \right]$ . . . DELIMITED BY $\left\{ \begin{matrix} identifier\text{-}3 \\ literal\text{-}3 \\ \underline{SIZE} \end{matrix} \right\}$

$\left[\begin{matrix} identifier\text{-}4 \\ literal\text{-}4 \end{matrix} \right] \left[\begin{matrix} identifier\text{-}5 \\ literal\text{-}5 \end{matrix} \right]$ . . . DELIMITED BY $\left. \begin{matrix} identifier\text{-}6 \\ literal\text{-}6 \\ \text{SIZE} \end{matrix} \right]$ . . .

INTO *identifier-7* [WITH POINTER *identifier-8*]

[ON OVERFLOW *imperative-statement*]

UNSTRING Statement

UNSTRING *identifier-1*

[DELIMITED BY [ALL] $\left\{ \begin{matrix} identifier\text{-}2 \\ literal\text{-}2 \end{matrix} \right\}$ [OR [ALL] $\left\{ \begin{matrix} identifier\text{-}3 \\ literal\text{-}3 \end{matrix} \right\}$] . . .]

INTO *identifier-4* [DELIMITER IN *identifier-5*]

[COUNT IN *identifier-6*]

[*identifier-7* [DELIMITER IN *identifier-8*]

[COUNT IN *identifier-9*]] . . .

[WITH POINTER *identifier-10*]

[TALLYING IN *identifier-11*]

[ON OVERFLOW *imperative-statement*]

 **AMERICAN NATIONAL STANDARD COBOL Reserved Words**

No word in the following list should appear as a programmer-defined name. The keys that appear before some of the words, and their meanings, are:

(xa)   before a word means that the word is an IBM extension to American National Standard COBOL.

(xac) before a word means that the word is an IBM extension to both American National Standard COBOL and CODASYL COBOL.

(ca)   before a word means that the word is a CODASYL COBOL reserved word not incorporated in American National Standard COBOL or in IBM American National Standard COBOL.

(sp)   before a word means that the word is an IBM function-name established in support of the SPECIAL-NAMES function.

(spn) before a word means that the word is used by an IBM American National Standard COBOL compiler, but not this compiler.

(asn) before a word means that the word is defined by American National Standard COBOL, but is not used by this compiler.

	ACCEPT	(xa)	CALL	(ca)	CONSTANT		DATE-COMPILED
	ACCESS	(xa)	CANCEL		CONTAINS		DATE-WRITTEN
	ACTUAL	(xac)	CBL		CONTROL	(xa)	DAY
	ADD	(xa)	CD		CONTROLS		DE
(asn)	ADDRESS		CF		COPY	(xac)	DEBUG
	ADVANCING		CH	(xac)	CORE-INDEX	(ca)	DEBUG-CONTENTS
	AFTER	(xac)	CHANGED		CORR	(ca)	DEBUG-ITEM
	ALL	(xa)	CHARACTER		CORRESPONDING	(ca)	DEBUG-LINE
	ALPHABETIC		CHARACTERS	(xa)	COUNT	(ca)	DEBUG-SUB-1
(ca)	ALPHANUMERIC	(asn)	CLOCK-UNITS	(sp)	CSP	(ca)	DEBUG-SUB-2
(ca)	ALPHANUMERIC-EDITED		CLOSE		CURRENCY	(ca)	DEBUG-SUB-3
	ALTER	(asn)	COBOL	(xac)	CURRENT-DATE	(ca)	DEBUG-NAME
	ALTERNATE		CODE	(spn)	CYL-INDEX	(ca)	DEBUGGING
	AND		COLUMN	(spn)	CYL-OVERFLOW		DECIMAL-POINT
(xa)	APPLY	(spn)	COM-REG	(sp)	C01		DECLARATIVES
	ARE		COMMA	(sp)	C02	(xac)	DELETE
	AREA		COMP	(sp)	C03	(xa)	DELIMITED
	AREAS	(xa)	COMP-1	(sp)	C04	(xa)	DELIMITER
	ASCENDING	(xa)	COMP-2	(sp)	C05		DEPENDING
	ASSIGN	(xa)	COMP-3	(sp)	C06	(xa)	DEPTH
	AT	(xa)	COMP-4	(sp)	C07		DESCENDING
	AUTHOR		COMPUTATIONAL	(sp)	C08	(xa)	DESTINATION
		(xa)	COMPUTATIONAL-1	(sp)	C09		DETAIL
(xac)	BASIS	(xa)	COMPUTATIONAL-2	(sp)	C10	(ca)	DISABLE
	BEFORE	(xa)	COMPUTATIONAL-3	(sp)	C11	(xac)	DISP
	BEGINNING	(xa)	COMPUTATIONAL-4	(sp)	C12		DISPLAY
	BLANK		COMPUTE			(xac)	DISPLAY-ST
	BLOCK		CONFIGURATION		DATA	(ca)	DISPLAY-n
	BY	(sp)	CONSOLE	(xa)	DATE		DIVIDE

	DIVISION		LABEL
	DOWN	(xac)	LABEL-RETURN
(xac)	EJECT		LAST
	ELSE		LEADING
(xa)	EMI	(xac)	LEAVE
(ca)	ENABLE		LEFT
	END	(xa)	LENGTH
	END-OF-PAGE		LESS
(xa)	ENDING	(ca)	LIBRARY
	ENTER		LIMIT
(xac)	ENTRY		LIMITS
	ENVIRONMENT	(ca)	LINAGE
(xa)	EOP	(ca)	LINAGE-COUNTER
	EQUAL		LINE
(ca)	EQUALS		LINE-COUNTER
	ERROR		LINES
(xa)	ESI	(xa)	LINKAGE
(xa)	ETI		LOCK
	EVERY		LOW-VALUE
	EXAMINE		LOW-VALUES
(ca)	EXCEEDS	(ca)	LOWER-BOUND
(xac)	EXHIBIT	(ca)	LOWER-BOUNDS
	EXIT		
(spn)	EXTENDED-SEARCH	(spn)	MASTER-INDEX
			MEMORY
	FD	(ca)	MERGE
	FILE	(xa)	MESSAGE
	FILE-CONTROL		MODE
	FILE-LIMIT		MODULES
	FILE-LIMITS	(xac)	MORE-LABELS
	FILLER		MOVE
	FINAL		MULTIPLE
	FIRST		MULTIPLY
	FOOTING		
	FOR	(xac)	NAMED
	FROM		NEGATIVE
			NEXT
	GENERATE		NO
	GIVING	(xac)	NOMINAL
	GO		NOT
(xac)	GOBACK		NOTE
	GREATER	(spn)	NSTD-REELS
	GROUP		NUMBER
			NUMERIC
	HEADING	(ca)	NUMERIC-EDITED
	HIGH-VALUE		
	HIGH-VALUES		OBJECT-COMPUTER
(ca)	HOLD	(ca)	OBJECT-PROGRAM
			OCCURS
	I-O		OF
	I-O-CONTROL		OFF
(xac)	ID	(ca)	OH
	IDENTIFICATION		OMITTED
	IF		ON
	IN		OPEN
	INDEX		OPTIONAL
(ca)	INDEX-n		OR
	INDEXED	(xac)	OTHERWISE
	INDICATE		OUTPUT
(ca)	INITIAL	(ca)	OV
	INITIATE	(xa)	OVERFLOW
	INPUT		
	INPUT-OUTPUT		PAGE
(xac)	INSERT		PAGE-COUNTER
(ca)	INSPECT		PERFORM
	INSTALLATION		PF
	INTO		PH
	INVALID		PIC
	IS		PICTURE
			PLUS
	JUST	(xa)	POINTER
	JUSTIFIED		POSITION
		(xac)	POSITIONING
	KEY		POSITIVE
(ca)	KEYS	(ca)	PREPARED

(xac)	PRINT-SWITCH	(xac)	SKIP3
(ca)	PRINTING		SORT
(ca)	PRIORITY	(xac)	SORT-CORE-SIZE
	PROCEDURE	(xac)	SORT-FILE-SIZE
(ca)	PROCEDURES	(ca)	SORT-MERGE
	PROCEED	(xac)	SORT-MESSAGE
	PROCESS	(xac)	SORT-MODE-SIZE
(ca)	PROCESS	(xac)	SORT-RETURN
	PROCESSING		SOURCE
(xa)	PROGRAM		SOURCE-COMPUTER
	PROGRAM-ID		SPACE
			SPACES
(xa)	QUEUE		SPECIAL-NAMES
	QUOTE		STANDARD
	QUOTES	(xac)	START
			STATUS
	RANDOM		STOP
(ca)	RANGE	(xa)	STRING
	RD	(xa)	SUB-QUEUE-1
	READ	(xa)	SUB-QUEUE-2
(xac)	READY	(xa)	SUB-QUEUE-3
(xa)	RECEIVE		SUBTRACT
	RECORD		SUM
(xac)	RECORD-OVERFLOW	(ca)	SUPERVISOR
(xa)	RECORDING	(xa)	SUPPRESS
	RECORDS	(ca)	SUSPEND
	REDEFINES	(xa)	SYMBOLIC
	REEL		SYNC
(ca)	REFERENCES		SYNCHRONIZED
	RELEASE	(sp)	SYSIN
(xac)	RELOAD	(spn)	SYSIPT
	REMAINDER	(spn)	SYSLST
	REMARKS	(sp)	SYSOUT
	RENAMES	(spn)	SYSPCH
(xac)	REORG-CRITERIA	(sp)	SYSPUNCH
	REPLACING	(sp)	S01
	REPORT	(sp)	S02
	REPORTING		
	REPORTS	(xa)	TABLE
(xac)	REREAD		TALLY
	RERUN		TALLYING
	RESERVE		TAPE
	RESET	(ca)	TERMINAL
	RETURN		TERMINATE
(xac)	RETURN-CODE	(xa)	TEXT
	REVERSED		THAN
	REWIND	(xac)	THEN
(xac)	REWRITE		THROUGH
	RF		THRU
	RH	(xa)	TIME
	RIGHT	(xac)	TIME-OF-DAY
	ROUNDED		TIMES
	RUN		TO
		(xac)	TOTALED
(ca)	SA	(xac)	TOTALING
	SAME	(xac)	TRACE
	SD	(xac)	TRACK
	SEARCH	(xac)	TRACK-AREA
	SECTION	(xac)	TRACK-LIMIT
	SECURITY	(xac)	TRACKS
	SEEK	(xa)	TRAILING
(xa)	SEGMENT	(xac)	TRANSFORM
	SEGMENT-LIMIT		TYPE
	SELECT		
(ca)	SELECTED	(ca)	UNEQUAL
(xa)	SEND		UNIT
	SENTENCE	(xa)	UNSTRING
(xa)	SEPARATE		UNTIL
	SEQUENTIAL		UP
(xac)	SERVICE		UPON
	SET	(ca)	UPPER-BOUND
	SIGN	(ca)	UPPER-BOUNDS
	SIZE	(spn)	UPSI-0
(xac)	SKIP1	(spn)	UPSI-1
(xac)	SKIP2	(spn)	UPSI-2

(spn)	UPSI-3	USE	WHEN	(xac)	WRITE-ONLY
(spn)	UPSI-4	USING	WITH	(spn)	WRITE-VERIFY
(spn)	UPSI-5		WORDS		
(spn)	UPSI-6	VALUE	WORKING-STORAGE		ZERO
(spn)	UPSI-7	VALUES	WRITE		ZEROES
	USAGE	VARYING			ZEROS

Structure of <u>system-name</u>

class[-device]-organization-name

> class—a two-character field representing device class.
> Allowable combinations are:

> > DA   mass storage
> > UT   utility
> > UR   unit record

> device—a four- to six-digit field that represents device number.
> Allowable numbers for each device class are:

> > DA   2311, 2321, 2314
> > UT   2400, 2311, 2314, 2321
> > UR   1442R, 1442P, 1403, 1404 (continuous forms only),
> >   1443, 2501, 2520R, 2520P, 2540R, 2540P

Program Product Information (Version 3)

> For Version 3 only, the following additional system devices
> are allowable:

Mass Storage (DA)	2305-1, 2305-2, 2319, 3330
Utility (UT)	2305-1, 2305-2, 2319, 3330
Unit Record (UR)	3211

> organization—a one-character field that specifies file organization.
> Allowable characters are:

> > S   for standard sequential files
> > D   for direct files
> > W   for direct files when the REWRITE statement is used
> > R   for relative files
> > I   for indexed files
> > C   for ASCII files

> name—a one- to eight-character field that specifies the external-
> name by which the file is known to the system.

Program Product Information (Version 4)

> The Version 4 Compiler treats the <u>device</u> field as comments.

10

INTRODUCTION
TO BASIC

Today almost every business concern provides its key personnel with access to a computer. The computer may be large or small and it may be used exclusively by the business, or computer time may be purchased from a service organization; in any case, a computer is accessible. More and more, this access is being provided via conveniently located terminal devices.

In many cases, these terminals are an integral part of a computer system facilitating two-way data communications between the accountant, manager, or other key personnel and the computer, in addition to providing a fast and effective means by which the system can communicate urgent messages to management, such as informing management of the occurrence of any unusual or unexpected circumstances the instant they are detected. Such systems attempt to provide management with information it must have to function efficiently and effectively. But, whether such a complex system is available or not, the accountant or business manager will still encounter numerous small and isolated problems in the course or performing his duties to which the computer can be applied but for which, for one reason or another, no provision has been made for their solution. In such cases, the accountant or business manager could choose one of several possible alternatives. He could choose to solve it manually, or he could request the data-processing department to solve the problem. Either of these solutions could be time-consuming and expensive. On the other hand, should the accountant or business manager have a working knowledge of a modern programming language, he can use this knowledge to develop a simple program to solve the problem, thus eliminating any delay or need to first communicate the problem to a programmer. It should be noted, however, that for other than small or isolated problems, the data-processing department should be consulted. Even in this case, a knowledge of a programming language by the business person will make communications with the programmer that much easier.

An appropriate programming language for use by the business person in solving small and isolated problems is the language BASIC. BASIC (*Beginner's All-purpose Symbolic Instruction Code*) is an easily learned and easily used computer language. It was originally developed at Dartmouth College under the direction of J. G. Kemeny and Thomas E. Kurtz for use on-line with a time-sharing computer, that is, a computer system in which a user can communicate a program to the computer via a console or terminal similar in appearance to a typewriter, with results being returned almost instantaneously. This form of BASIC is generally referred to as *interactive BASIC*.

INTERACTIVE BASIC

The ease with which BASIC can be learned and utilized by the novice and programmer alike is responsible for its wide and rapid acceptance into the computer field. As a result, W. F. Sharpe, of the University of Washington, Seattle, developed and programmed a BASIC compiler called UWBIC (*University of Washington BASIC Interpretive Compiler*), which facilitates the use of BASIC on smaller computers in a batch mode. That is, the user can prepare his program and data on punched cards and submit these cards to the computer center to be processed when computer time becomes available. This form of BASIC is generally referred to as *batch BASIC*.

BATCH BASIC

In this chapter we shall study interactive BASIC, with the intent of being able to write an operational program to be used on a time-sharing computer system. We shall also discuss the minor differences between the interactive BASIC and batch BASIC. A summary of the interactive BASIC language specifications supported by IBM is provided following the Exercises at the end of this chapter should the reader desire to investigate BASIC beyond the extent presented in this chapter.

SELF-STUDY EXERCISES 10-1

1. An appropriate computer language for solving small business-oriented problems is _____.

*****

BASIC

2. BASIC stands for _____.

*****

Beginner's All-purpose Symbolic Instruction Code

3. The two forms of BASIC currently available are _____ and _____.

*****

interactive BASIC
batch BASIC

DIALING UP THE COMPUTER　In a time-sharing computer system, many users share the use of a computer, each having his own input/output terminal from which he can communicate his programs and data to the computer and to which the computer can communicate results. Communication between terminals and the computer usually takes place over telephone lines with the computer servicing possibly 40 or 50 terminals simultaneously.

For a given user to communicate a BASIC program to such a computer he must first determine if the computer is available to handle the job. Using a telephone located on the terminal, the user dials a predetermined number which places him in contact with the computer. If all communication lines to the computer are in use, a "busy" signal will be heard and the user can wait a few minutes and try again or if available, dial up another computer. If a free channel is available, the connection is made and typed communications can take place between the user and the computer through the terminal. A typical conversation might be as follows:

USER:　LOGON (user presses RETURN key)
COMPUTER:　USER NUMBER—
USER:　XXXXXX (user types in his six-character identification
number next to the USER NUMBER—and
presses the RETURN key)
COMPUTER:　SYSTEM—
USER:　BASIC (user types word BASIC next to SYSTEM—to
indicate a BASIC program and then presses
RETURN key)
COMPUTER:　NEW OR OLD—

```
USER:    NEW (user types word NEW next to NEW OR OLD—
              if a new program is to be input for processing
              and then presses RETURN key)
         OLD (user types word OLD next to NEW OR OLD—
              if a previously written program is to be retrieved
              from the location in which the computer has
              stored it and presses RETURN key)
COMPUTER:  NEW PROGRAM NAME—or
           OLD PROGRAM NAME—
USER:    XXXXXX (user types in new or old program name
                 next to previous computer response and
                 presses RETURN key)
COMPUTER:  READY
```

By typing in the world LIST, the entire OLD program will be listed, or by typing in the world LISTn, where n is a one- to five-digit number, only the lines from n on will be listed. The listing process can be stopped at any time by depressing the STOP key. When the program is ready to be processed the word RUN is typed.

If a new program is to be entered, it is typed in at this point line by line, with the typing of each line followed by the pressing of the RETURN key. If errors are present, diagnostics will be returned, indicating that corrections must be made. When the entire program has been keyed in, the user types the word RUN and processing of the program begins. If no errors are present, the results will be returned. If the results are correct, the user can type the word SAVE and the program will be saved for future use. By typing in the word BYE or GOODBYE, the user breaks off the communication line to the computer. If a line is to be corrected, it can be done simply by retyping another line with the same line number as the incorrect line and pressing the RETURN key. All statements or lines must begin with a line number. A complete line can be deleted by typing in only the line number and pressing the RETURN key.

Many other words or commands are available for communication with the computer; for information concerning them, it is suggested that the reader consult the reference manuals appropriate for the system being used.

We shall now investigate the fundamental item in any BASIC program—the statement.

SELF-STUDY EXERCISES 10-2

1. The first step in communicating a BASIC program to a computer is to _____.

*****

dial up the computer and determine if it is available to handle the job

2. All BASIC statements must begin with a _____.

*****

line number

3. A complete list of communication commands can be obtained from _____.

*****

the system reference manuals for the computer system being used

BASIC STATEMENTS

A BASIC program is comprised of a series of instructions or statements. These statements are written in "free form"; that is, they begin anywhere on a line and, with one exception, are unaffected by spaces. The one exception will be discussed later.

Format

Line Numbers[1]

Each BASIC statement must have a line number between 1 and 99999. Statements may be input in any order, as the BASIC compiler automatically sequences them by line number. It is advisable to leave spaces when assigning line numbers so that additions can be made without having to reassign the line numbers. A common scheme is to assign to statements line numbers which are multiples of 10 (i.e., 10, 20, 30, etc.). In this way the numbers are in sequence yet still allow up to nine additional statements to be inserted between existing statements without violating the sequence.

Remarks

In writing a program it is often desirable to annotate it for easier reading. Annotations or remarks are ignored by the computer and

[1]Line numbers are required in batch BASIC on only those statements which will be referenced by other instructions within the program. See pages 448–449 for other differences between interactive BASIC and batch BASIC.

can be used freely as long as the program does not exceed approximately 300 statements. Adding remarks to longer programs (more than 300 statements) will only increase the length of the program and jeopardize its chance of running on smaller computer systems. A remark statement must have a statement number followed by the command REM or REMARK, after which the remark itself appears.

A BASIC constant is a number such as 14, 34.3, -17, and -13.8. **Constants** Constants are divided into two broad types:

1. Integer constants—whole numbers not containing a decimal point (e.g., 46, -16, 3842, -101101)
2. Real constants—numbers containing a decimal point (e.g., $-46.$, 3.418, -16.42, 8.00)

Real constants may also be expressed in another form, referred to as the *exponential form.* In exponential form, the number 3840000. could, for example, appear as

$$38.4E5$$
$$.384E7$$
$$384.E4$$

Each of these can be determined to be equal to the original number 3840000. once we understand the meaning of the "E" within each of the above representations.

The letter E, in the exponential form of a number, simply serves as a placeholder between the actual digits of the number and what we shall refer to as the *shift count.* The shift count, or number following the letter E in a number expressed in exponential form, refers to the number of places that the decimal point must be shifted from where it is presently located to where it would normally appear in nonexponential form.

For example, in the number 38.4E5, the shift count or number following the letter E is a 5. This means that to locate the decimal point in its proper position it must be shifted five places to the right (to the right because the number 5 is positive), giving us

$$38.4E5 = 3 \quad 8 \underset{1 \quad 2 \quad 3 \quad 4 \quad 5}{\underbrace{4 \quad 0 \quad 0 \quad 0 \quad 0}} .$$

Similarly, for the other two numbers given above in exponential form, we have

$$.384E7 = 3\underbrace{\ 8\ \ 4\ \ 0\ \ 0\ \ 0\ \ 0}_{1\ \ 2\ \ 3\ \ 4\ \ 5\ \ 6\ \ 7}.$$

and

$$384.E4 = 3\ \ 8\ \ 4\ \underbrace{\ 0\ \ 0\ \ 0\ \ 0}_{1\ \ 2\ \ 3\ \ 4}.$$

For a number containing a negative shift count, one simply moves the decimal point to the left of where it occurs in the number in exponential form a number of places equal to the shift count. For example, for the number 54.36E-6 we would have

$$54.36E\text{-}6 = .\underbrace{\ 0\ \ 0\ \ 0\ \ 0\ \ 5\ \ 4}_{-6\ \ -5\ \ -4\ \ -3\ \ -2\ \ -1}\ 3\ \ 6$$

Variables and Variable Names

A variable is a quantity that can take on different values at different times during the execution of a BASIC program. A variable name is assigned to each variable to distinguish it from other variables in the program. The variable name can be thought of as a label placed on a mailbox, inside which, at any given time, is an item of data. The data item placed in the mailbox can vary from time to time but is identified and referenced by the name placed on the front of the mailbox.

BASIC variables are of two types: simple variables and string variables. *Simple variables,* generally referred to as *variables,* contain numbers and may be used in computations. A BASIC variable name can be a letter of the alphabet or a letter of the alphabet followed by a digit (e.g., A3, B, R, T6).

String variables are used to store alphanumeric quantities which *are not going to be used in any form of computation.* A string variable name is denoted by a letter followed by a $, for example A$, R$, T$. A string variable can take on the value of a *string,* or group of numbers, letters, or special characters enclosed in quotation marks.[2]

[2]In the BASIC supported by IBM, either of the characters ' or " are understood to be a quotation mark.

Almost all systems can store 15-character strings, counting all blanks, but not quotation marks; many systems can handle considerably longer ones. In IBM BASIC, for example, a character string associated with a string variable may consist of up to 18 characters.

Some examples of the values a string variable (A$) can assume are given below:

$$A\$ = \text{``SELL''}$$
$$A\$ = \text{``S,4''}$$
$$A\$ = \text{``THE ANSWER''}$$

If a quotation mark is to be included as part of the string, it must be distinguished from the quotation marks enclosing the string. This is accomplished by inserting two quotation marks side by side in the position where the quotation mark is desired in the string. For example, if the string ANSWER IS "NO". is to be stored, "ANSWER IS ""NO""." would be input.

In the course of this chapter you will be introduced to many BASIC statements. Each statement must be written in accordance with specific rules. These rules stipulate what words or symbols must be present in the statement and in what relative positions. They also stipulate where and what information is to be provided by the programmer and whether or not this information is required or optional. The task of understanding and remembering the rules associated with each BASIC statement can be a time-consuming endeavor. To simplify this task, each BASIC statement will be presented in a general form. This form is based on the following conventions:

General Form

1. All required parts of the BASIC statement will be underlined.
2. All words which must appear exactly as presented will be capitalized.
3. Whenever used, the symbol = will be required.
4. Optional parts will be included in braces, { }.
5. Information relative to the problem at hand and to be provided by the programmer will be included in parentheses, ( ).

6. The ellipsis . . . indicates that the immediate preceding unit may occur once, or more than once in succession.

For example, let us consider the general form of a particular BASIC statement:

(*line number*) *INPUT* (*list of variables*)

Using our list of conventions, we can determine certain facts about this statement with only a simple inspection.

(*line number*)   A particular line number *must* be chosen by the programmer and substituted for this entry.

INPUT   INPUT is a required word which *must* appear exactly as presented in the general form.

(*list of variable names*)   A list of specific variable names *must* be chosen by the programmer and substituted for this entry.

After the programmer has exercised his options, the statement may appear as

3840   INPUT   A,B3,C6,R$

SELF-STUDY EXERCISES 10-3

1. BASIC statements are written in _____.
*****

free form

2. When assigning line numbers to program statements, provision should be made for _____.
*****

the addition of program statements without the necessity of having to reassign line numbers

3. Remark statements require _____ and _____.

*****

line numbers
must begin with the required word REM or REMARK

4. Constants are classified as either _____ or _____ constants.

*****

integer
real

5. The number 7.34E-2 is expressed in _____ form and is equal
to the number _____.

*****

exponential
.0734 (.0 7 3 4)
‿‿
-2 -1

6. In the example above, the −2 following the letter E is called
the _____.

*****

shift count

7. A variable is _____.

*****

a quantity that can take on different values at different times
during the execution of a BASIC program

8. Each variable in a program is identified by a unique _____.

*****

variable name

9. A string variable can take on the value of a _____ generally
consisting of up to _____ characters enclosed in quotes,

depending on the computer system employed.

*****

string

18

10. In the general form of a BASIC statement all required parts will be _____; all words which must appear exactly as presented will be _____; whenever used the symbol _____ is required; optional parts are _____; and programmer-supplied information will be _____.

*****

underlined

capitalized

=

included in braces, { }

included in parentheses, ( )

INPUT/OUTPUT AND END STATEMENTS

PRINT Statement

Every computer program must contain instructions which direct the computer to input or output information. It is, therefore, fitting that we should begin our study of the various BASIC statements by studying those statements which direct the computer to perform an input or output operation.

GENERAL FORM

$$(line\ number)\quad \underline{PRINT}\ \begin{cases} (\underline{blanks}) \\ (\underline{literal}) \\ (\underline{list\ of\ variable\ names}) \\ (\underline{expression}) \end{cases} \ldots$$

The braces in this statement indicate that there are options open to the programmer. In this particular statement, there are four options:

1. (*blanks*)—In this option, nothing follows the BASIC required word PRINT. This causes a line of blanks or a blank line to be printed. By properly spacing the data presented in a report, the appearance and readability of the report can be substantially increased.

2. (*literal*)—In this option, the exact characters to be printed are included within quotes and follow the BASIC required word PRINT. For example, the statement

$$75 \quad \text{PRINT "ANS} = 34.5\text{"}$$

would cause ANS = 34.5 to be printed out. Blanks within the quotes are a definite part of the literal and will be printed.[3]

3. (*list of variable names*)—In this option, a list of previously defined variable names follow the BASIC required word PRINT. This causes the printing of the current value of each of the variable names in the list. For example, if A = 6, B = 15, and C = −7, the statement

$$80 \quad \text{PRINT A, B, C}$$

would cause 6, 15, and − 7 to be printed.

4. (*expression*)—In this option, an expression, or variables and/or constants involved in arithmetic operations, follows the BASIC required word PRINT. The expression is first evaluated and then the result of the evaluation is printed out. For example, if A = 7, the statement

$$60 \quad \text{PRINT 2} * \text{A} + 6$$

would cause the number 20 to be printed out as 20 = 2 × 7 + 6. Expressions will be discussed in greater detail later.

In addition, it is also possible to use a combination of these options in the same PRINT statement. For example, if A = 7, B = 9, and C = 14, then the PRINT statement

$$45 \quad \text{PRINT A, B, "ANS} = 8\text{", C}$$

would cause 7, 9, ANS = 8, and 14 to be printed out.

---

[3]Literals may be restricted in the number of characters they may contain depending on the computer system used.

BASIC Rules for Printing Numbers. When attempting to print a number, it is essential that the BASIC user be aware of rules governing the printing of numbers. There are three such rules:

1. A maximum of seven significant digits can be printed for a real or integer number.

2. Numbers less than 0.1 will be printed in exponential form unless the number consists of seven or less significant digits.

3. The printing of nonsignificant zeros will be suppressed.

Printed Line Format. We can now control what is printed by using the appropriate option available with the PRINT statement. We will now discuss where the printing will occur.

In BASIC, the page is subdivided into zones of 15 or 18 spaces each across each line (a typical teletype page is 75 characters wide). IBM computer systems generally support 18 character zones while several other manufacturers support 15 character zones (see Fig. 10-1). Any item in quotes (literal) is printed just as it appears within the quotes whether it can be contained in one zone or whether it spans more than one zone. However, for anything which is not a literal, a comma serves to cause the printer to skip to the next zone. For example, on an IBM computer system supporting four 18-character zones the statement

85 PRINT A, "THIS IS A SAMPLE LITERAL", B

would cause the present value of A to be printed in zone 1 beginning in print position 1. The comma following A in the print statement causes the printer to skip to the second zone and print THIS IS A SAMPLE LITERAL beginning in print position 19 and terminating in print position 42. The comma following the literal causes the printer to skip to the next zone or zone 4 and commence printing of the present value of B in position 55.

If the number of items listed in a PRINT statement is such that their printing cannot be completed on one line, then any items

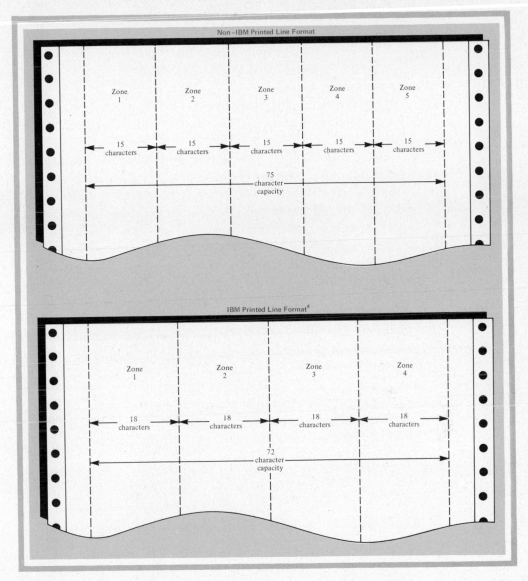

FIG. 10-1
BASIC Printed Line Format.

[4]IBM's interactive BASIC utilizes 18 character zones but will allow for more than 4 zones depending on the capabilities of the printing device employed.

left unprinted on the first line will be printed on subsequent lines. For example, in the PRINT statement,

$$85 \quad \text{PRINT A, B, C, D, E, F}$$

the contents of variables A, B, C, and D will be printed on one line and the contents of variables D, E, and F will be printed on the next line.

Circumstances may arise, however, in which it is desirable to accommodate more than four or five items on a line. This can generally be accomplished by replacing the comma normally used to separate output items in the PRINT statement with a semicolon. This will cause the number of printing areas and the size of each area to be a function of the data being printed and generally result in a line capacity of more than four or five quantities per line. When each number is printed, a space is left before the number for the sign, as the sign is only printed if the number is negative, and up to three spaces will be left after the number, depending on the number of digits to be printed. Table 10-1 illustrates how many spaces will be left, depending on the number of characters to be printed.

For example, if a six-character number were printed, nine spaces would be taken up in the output report—one space for the sign of the number (or a blank if the number is positive), six spaces for the number itself, and two spaces after the number.

TABLE 10-1

Printer Spacing by Number of Digits Printed

NUMBER OF DIGITS TO BE PRINTED	FIELD WIDTH	NUMBER OF SPACES AFTER NUMBER
1	3	1
2, 3, or 4	6	3, 2, or 1
5, 6, or 7	9	3, 2, or 1
8, 9, or 10	12	3, 2, or 1
11, 12, or 13	15	3, 2, or 1
14, 15, 16, or 17	18	4, 3, 2, or 1

It should be noted, however, that if a literal is specified in a PRINT statement and preceded by a semicolon it will be printed immediately after the last character of the previous field. All characters, including any blanks contained within the quotation marks will be printed. On the other hand, if a string variable is preceded by a semicolon in a PRINT statement, the field width will be assumed to be 18 characters *minus any trailing blanks*. For example if A$ = "JOHN   ", the PRINT statement

    50 PRINT A$;" IS YOUR NAME   ";"YES OR NO?"

would cause the following to be printed out:

    JOHN IS YOUR NAME   YES OR NO?

The simple PRINT statement offers the programmer limited control over the format of the printed output. To overcome this limitation, some manufacturers provide two additional options to the PRINT statement—the TAB and the USING option. The TAB option performs the same function in a PRINT statement as depressing the TAB key on a typewriter, that is, it causes the printer to skip a specified number of spaces before printing. The general form of the PRINT with TAB option is

PRINT WITH TAB AND USING OPTIONS[5]

GENERAL FORM

$$(\textit{line number}) \underline{\text{PRINT}} \ \underline{\text{TAB}} \ (\textit{integer}); \begin{Bmatrix} (\textit{literal}) \\ (\textit{list of variable names}) \\ (\textit{expression}) \end{Bmatrix} ; \ \ldots$$

$$(; \underline{\text{TAB}} \ (\textit{integer}); \begin{Bmatrix} (\textit{literal}) \\ (\textit{list of variable names}) \\ (\textit{expression}) \end{Bmatrix} ; \ \ldots) \ \ldots$$

Integer as used above refers to an unsigned integer enclosed in parentheses. *Literal, list of variable names,* and *expression* are as described in the simple PRINT statement. For example, if the value of A were 5, the statement

---

[5]The TAB option of the PRINT statement is not available on IBM computer systems.

60 PRINT TAB(6); "THE VALUE OF A IS"; A

would cause the following to be printed out:

ɓɓɓɓɓTHEɓVALUEɓOFɓAɓISɓ5

where ɓ indicates a blank space. As you can see, the TAB(6) caused the printer to skip the first five printing positions and begin printing in the sixth position. The remainder of the statement produced the same results as with any other PRINT statement.

The PRINT statement with the USING option provides the most sophisticated method of controlling the format of the printed output. When the PRINT statement with the USING option is employed, it must be accompanied by a separate BASIC statement referred to as a *format* statement. This format statement describes the desired output format in detail and may appear anywhere in the program. The same format statement may be used with more than one PRINT USING statement. The general form of the PRINT statement with the USING option is

GENERAL FORM

$$(\underline{line\ number})\ \text{PRINT USING}\ (\underline{line\ number}),\quad \begin{Bmatrix} (\textit{list of variable names}) \\ (\textit{expression}) \end{Bmatrix},\ \cdot$$

The second *line number* entry refers to the line number of the corresponding format statement. The general form of a format statement is

GENERAL FORM

$$(\underline{line\ number}):\quad \begin{Bmatrix} (\underline{label}) \\ (\textit{format-description}) \end{Bmatrix},\ \cdots$$

A *label* as used in a format statement refers to a string of characters *not* containing the # symbol. These characters will be printed out exactly as they appear. This is identical to what can be accomplished with a literal in a simple PRINT statement with the exception that any quotation marks (' or ") appearing in a format statement will be printed out as they appear in the format statement. The *format description* is used to describe the form in which a simple or string variable are to be printed out. The symbols that can be used in a format description and their meaning are as follows:

Symbol[6]	Meaning
#	One character is to be printed. If more than one character is to be printed, one # symbol must be used for each character.
.	A decimal point is to be printed out in the position indicated by the period (.).
!!!!	Four exclamation points indicate that the number is to be printed out in exponential form.

For example, if the variable A is equal to 15.447, the variable B is equal to 96.3, and the value of C$ is "ABCD", the BASIC statements

```
60 PRINT USING 70, A, B, C$
70 :THE VALUE OF A IS $###.##,
   THE VALUE OF B IS .####!!!! AND
   THE VALUE OF C$ IS ####
```

would cause the following to be printed out:

```
THE VALUE OF A IS $ 15.45,
   THE VALUE OF B IS .9630E+02 AND
   THE VALUE OF C$ IS ABCD
```

If, however, the variable A had been equal to 115.451 and C$ had been equal to "ABCDEFG", the above statements would have caused the following to be printed out:

```
THE VALUE OF A IS $******,
   THE VALUE OF B IS .9630E+02 AND
   THE VALUE OF C$ IS ABCD
```

[6]The symbols described here may vary with the computer system used.

That is, when the size of the number to be printed out exceeds the field size that is provided in the format, *'s are printed out to inform the user of this fact. Note, however, that the value of the string variable C$ was printed after being truncated to the specification contained in the format statement. Examples of output produced by the USING option of the PRINT statement for various format specifications are shown below.

FORMAT SPECIFICATION	VALUE	PRINTED OUTPUT
# # #	123	123
# # #	12	b12
# # #	12.3	bb1
# #.# #	123	*****
# #.# #	1.23	b1.23
# #.# #	1.23456	b1.23
# #.# #	.123	b0.12
# #.# #	12.345	12.35
# # #!!!!	123	123E+00
# # #!!!!	12.3	123E−01
# # #!!!!	.1234	123E−03
# #.# #!!!!	123	12.30E+01
# #.# #!!!!	1.23	b1.23E+00
# #.# #!!!!	.1234	12.34E−02
# #.# #!!!!	1234	12.34E+02
# # # #	ABCD	ABCD
# # # #	ABCDE	ABCD
# # # #	ABC	ABCb

Note: In the above illustrations, b represents a blank space.

INPUT Statement

GENERAL FORM

(*line number*)   *INPUT*   (*list of variable names*)

The *list of variable names* is a list of specific programmer-assigned variable names, one variable name for each item of data to be read by the INPUT statement. The order in which the variable names are written must agree with the order in which the corresponding data are to be read, and the variable names must be separated by commas.

When the INPUT statement is executed, it causes the computer to stop executing instructions and wait for the terminal operator to type in the specific data from the terminal. To determine exactly how this works, let us examine the following sequence of instructions:

```
  ⋮
0180    PRINT "TYPE IN HOURS-WORKED AND
            RATE-PER-HOUR"
0190    INPUT H, R
  ⋮
9999    END
RUN
```

After the RUN statement is typed in, the computer would begin executing the program. When execution reached statement number 0180, the computer would cause the following message to be typed out:

TYPE IN HOURS-WORKED AND RATE-PER-HOUR

This would notify the terminal operator that the computer is about to request input data to be typed in and exactly what input data are going to be requested. The next statement to be executed is statement 0190. When the computer executes this statement, it causes three things to happen:

1. A special character, usually a "?," will be printed on the output sheet, notifying the user that the computer is ready to receive the data corresponding to the variables H and R.
2. Execution is terminated until the two data items requested have been typed in and the return key has been depressed. The data items are typed in the order requested and are separated by a comma.
3. The data items input are stored in the locations labeled H and R, respectively, for future use. The computer then proceeds to execute the next instruction.

This statement is principally used when a program is to be used over and over again with various data that the user will determine at the time of execution of the program.

END Statement

GENERAL FORM

(line number) <u>END</u>

The END statement is required in every BASIC program and must be the last statement in the program. This means that the END statement must be assigned the highest line number used in the program. This is due to the fact that interactive BASIC executes statements in sequence according to their line numbers. Since the largest line number possible in BASIC is 99999, assigning this line number to the END statement will make certain the fact that it will be the last statement in the program.

Sample Program 1

In order to clarify and solidify our understanding of the foregoing BASIC concepts, we shall illustrate how these concepts may be used in a relatively small program.

> *Problem Definition:* Write a BASIC program to read in a student's name and three examination grades and print this data out in a report. Assume that the user of the program is unfamiliar with the program and must be provided with instructions concerning when and what to input.

A complete BASIC program for the solution of this problem is shown in Fig. 10-2. Note that in this program the dummy literal " " was used to cause the printer to skip a print zone. For example, in line number 100, " " was used to skip the first print zone and cause STUDENT GRADE LISTING to be printed beginning in the second print zone (print position 19). The same result could have been achieved with a PRINT USING statement.

SELF-STUDY EXERCISES 10-4

1. The general form of the PRINT statement is _____.

*****

(line number) <u>PRINT</u>
$\begin{cases} (blanks) \\ (literal) \\ (list\ of\ variable\ names) \\ (expression) \end{cases}$

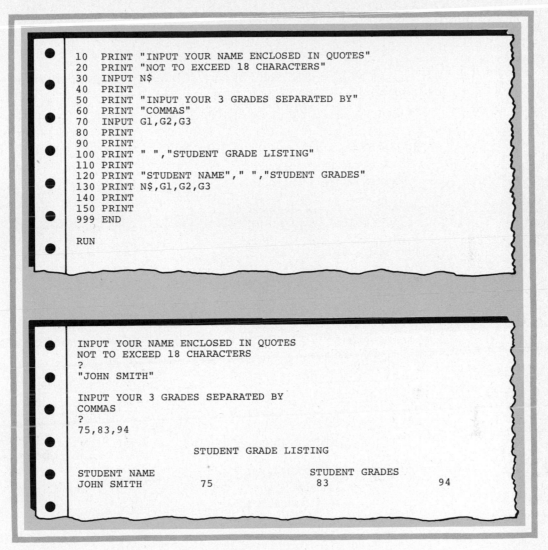

```
10   PRINT "INPUT YOUR NAME ENCLOSED IN QUOTES"
20   PRINT "NOT TO EXCEED 18 CHARACTERS"
30   INPUT N$
40   PRINT
50   PRINT "INPUT YOUR 3 GRADES SEPARATED BY"
60   PRINT "COMMAS"
70   INPUT G1,G2,G3
80   PRINT
90   PRINT
100  PRINT " ","STUDENT GRADE LISTING"
110  PRINT
120  PRINT "STUDENT NAME"," ","STUDENT GRADES"
130  PRINT N$,G1,G2,G3
140  PRINT
150  PRINT
999  END

RUN
```

```
INPUT YOUR NAME ENCLOSED IN QUOTES
NOT TO EXCEED 18 CHARACTERS
?
"JOHN SMITH"

INPUT YOUR 3 GRADES SEPARATED BY
COMMAS
?
75,83,94

                    STUDENT GRADE LISTING

STUDENT NAME                        STUDENT GRADES
JOHN SMITH           75             83             94
```

FIG. 10-2

Sample Program 1, Using a Teletype Input/Output Device.

2. The PRINT statement 50 PRINT would cause _____.

*****

a blank line to be printed

3. The PRINT statement 50 PRINT "I DESERVE AN A IN THIS COURSE" will cause _____.

*****

I DESERVE AN A IN THIS COURSE to be printed out

4. The PRINT statement 50 PRINT A, B, C will cause _____.

*****

the current values of A, B, and C to be printed out in the first 3 zones of the line

5. Given that A = 10, the PRINT statement 50 PRINT 3 * A/2 will cause _____.

*****

15 to be printed out (15 = 3 * 10/2)

6. A maximum of _____ digits can be printed for integer and real numbers.

*****

7

7. Numbers exceeding seven significant digits and smaller than _____ will be printed in exponential form.

*****

0.1

8. When output is from a non-IBM computer system, a BASIC line is divided into five _____ each capable of holding _____ characters to a total of _____ characters per line.

*****

zones

15

75

9. The PRINT statement 50 PRINT A, B, "HARRY" executed on an IBM computer system would cause A to be printed in

_____ beginning in print position _____, B to be printed in _____ beginning in print position _____, and HARRY to be printed in _____ beginning in print position _____.

*****

zone 1

1

zone 2

19

zone 3

37

10. In the above example, if A = 10, the 1 and 0 would be printed in print positions 2 and 3 since print position 1 is reserved for _____.

*****

the sign of the number which will be printed only if the number is negative

11. The PRINT statement 50 PRINT "THE ANSWER IS ABSO-LUTELY", A will cause THE ANSWER IS ABSOLUTELY to be printed in _____ beginning in print position _____ and the value of A to be printed in _____ beginning in print position _____.

*****

zones 1 and 2

1

zone 3

37

12. If the comma separating items in the list of a PRINT statement is replaced with a semicolon, it is possible to _____.

*****

print more data items on one line

13. In the PRINT statement 50 PRINT "JOHN"; "SON", JOHN will be printed beginning in print position _____ and SON

will be printed beginning in print position _____.
*****

1

5

14. The statement INPUT A, B, C would cause _____.
*****

a "?" to be printed out and the execution of program instructions to cease until the data items corresponding to A, B, and C are typed in by the terminal user and the RETURN key is depressed

15. The _____ statement must be the last statement in the program and hence is assigned the _____ line number in the program.
*****

END

highest

16. The statement 80 PRINT TAB(16); "A="; A1 would cause the characters A= to be printed in print positions _____ and the value of A1 to be printed beginning in print position _____.
*****

16 and 17

18 or 19 depending on the algebraic sign of A1

17. The statements 90 PRINT USING 95, A1 and 95 :A=###.## would cause _____ to be printed out if A1 was equal to 17.1.
*****

A=♭17.1♭   (♭ represents a blank)

18. When executed, the END statement causes _____.
*****

the execution of the program to be terminated

One of the great advantages of a computer is its ability to deal quickly and easily with arithmetic computations. As a result, virtually every computer language has symbols which represent the fundamental operations of addition, subtraction, multiplication, division, and exponentiation. These five operations are available in BASIC and are represented by the following symbols:

ARITHMETIC STATEMENTS

Arithmetic Operators

$\uparrow$ (exponentiation)[7]
/ (division)
* (multiplication)
$-$ (subtraction)
$+$ (addition)

The operation of exponentiation refers to the raising of a number to a power. That is, 10 $\uparrow$ 4 would mean that ten is to be raised to the fourth power, mathematically expressed as

$$10^4$$

To determine the value of 10^4, one would simply multiply 10 by itself four times:

$$10^4 = 10 \times 10 \times 10 \times 10 = 10,000$$

An expression is one or more numeric variables or constants combined by arithmetic operators $(+, -, *, /, \uparrow)$. An expression, then, specifies the computations that are to be performed and on what constants or variables in order to obtain the desired result or *value of the expression*. For example, the expression

Expressions

$$A * B + C - 7$$

means that the current value of the variable called "A" is to be multiplied by the current value of the variable called "B." This product is then to be added to the current value of the variable called "C." From this sum, 7 is to be subtracted. If, for example,

---

[7]In batch BASIC, a double asterisk (**) is used instead of an arrow ($\uparrow$) to indicate exponentiation. Refer to pages 448–449 for other differences between interactive BASIC and batch BASIC.

A contained the number 3, B the number 4, and C the number 5, the value of the expression A * B + C − 7 would be

$$A * B + C - 7 = (3 \times 4 + 5 - 7) = 10$$
$$= \text{value of the expression}$$

Other examples of expressions include

1. A3 + 7.4
2. 3 * 6
3. 8 / J
4. R4 − S
5. A ↑ 7
6. 6
7. A
8. 3.46
9. A7

LET Statement

GENERAL FORM

(line number)   *LET*   *(variable)* = *(expression)*

The LET statement is one which causes an expression to be evaluated and the result of the expression to be stored in the computer for future reference. Since the value of the expression evaluated is to be referenced at a future date, some means must be provided to label this quantity so that it can be called back when needed in the future. To accomplish this, a variable name is assigned to the value of the expression at the time it is computed. From this time on and until changed by the programmer, when this assigned variable is used in a computation or other operation, the value of the expression will be recalled from storage and made available. For example, let us assume that A = 3, B = 4, and C = 7. Then the series of statements

$$10010 \quad \text{LET } A7 = A * B - C$$

$$10020 \quad \text{LET } G = A7 * A - 7$$

would, when executed, cause the expression A * B − C to be computed and the value of this expression to be placed in storage and called A7; that is,

$$A7 = A * B - C = 3 * 4 - 7 = 5$$

The next statement would cause the expression $A7 * A - 7$ to be computed and the value of this expression to be placed in storage and called G; that is,

$$G = A7 * A - 7 = 5 * 3 - 7 = 8$$

Therefore, at the completion of the execution of these two statements, the values of the variables concerned would be in storage as follows:

$$A = 3$$
$$B = 4$$
$$C = 7$$
$$A7 = 5$$
$$G = 8$$

It is also possible that no calculation will be involved in a LET statement. As an expression can be a single variable or constant, a legitimate LET statement could be

or

10   LET A4 = 7.2

20   LET A5 = A

In each of these cases, the value of the variable on the left of the equal sign is simply replaced by the value of the constant or variable stated on the right-hand side of the equal sign. For example, if $A = 3$ in the above expressions, the results after their executions would simply be that

$$A4 = 7.2$$

and

$$A5 = 3$$

A second BASIC program is shown in Figure 10-3 to further clarify and solidify our understanding of foregoing concepts. The definition of this problem is as follows: **Sample Program 2**

Problem Definition: Write a BASIC program to read in four numbers, determine the average of these numbers, and print out the numbers and their average with appropriate titles. Assume 5 zones, 15 characters each are available.

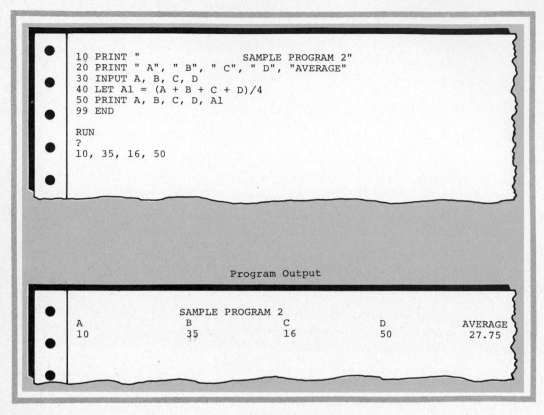

```
10 PRINT "                    SAMPLE PROGRAM 2"
20 PRINT " A", " B", " C", " D", "AVERAGE"
30 INPUT A, B, C, D
40 LET A1 = (A + B + C + D)/4
50 PRINT A, B, C, D, A1
99 END

RUN
?
10, 35, 16, 50
```

Program Output

```
                SAMPLE PROGRAM 2
A               B               C               D           AVERAGE
10              35              16              50          27.75
```

FIG. 10-3
Sample Program 2, Using a Teletype Input/Output Device.

SELF-STUDY EXERCISES 10-5

1. The five operations of _____, _____, _____, _____, and _____ are available in BASIC.

*****

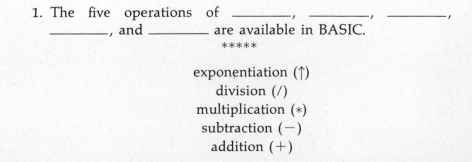

exponentiation (↑)
division (/)
multiplication (*)
subtraction (−)
addition (+)

2. 4 ↑ 3 means that 4 is _____ and is equal to _____.

*****

raised to the 3rd power
$4 \times 4 \times 4 = 64$

3. A * B − 6 is an _____ and if A = 4 and B = 5, then the _____ is 14.

*****

expression
value of the expression

4. Constants and variables are *(valid, invalid)* expressions.

*****

valid

5. The general form of the LET statement is _____.

*****

(line number)   *LET*   *(variable)* = *(expression)*

6. Given that A = 6, B = 3, and C = 9, the statement 340 LET A3 = A * B / C causes _____.

*****

the value of the expression $2 = 6 * 3 / 9$ to be stored in A3

7. In problem 6 the values of A, B, and C after the execution of the LET statement are _____.

*****

6, 3, and 9, respectively

The sequence in which statements are executed is generally in order by statement number. However, situations arise in which it is necessary to deviate from this prescribed sequence. This capability is provided the programmer by a group of statements known as *branch statements.* These statements fall into two general categories:

BRANCH STATEMENTS

1. Unconditional branch statements—statements which cause the normal sequence of execution of instructions to be altered without the consideration of any conditions and without exception
2. Conditional branch statements—statements which cause the normal sequence of instructions to be altered in accordance with some specific condition existing at the time the statement is to be executed

The simplest of all branch statements is the GO TO statement. This statement is an unconditional branch statement and, as such, causes the normal sequence of execution of instructions to be altered without consideration of existing conditions and without exception.

GO TO Statement

GENERAL FORM

(line number)   <u>*GO TO*</u>   *(line number)*

Let us assume that we wish to write a BASIC program to print out the multiples of 3 until the operator stops the process. Such a program could appear as follows:

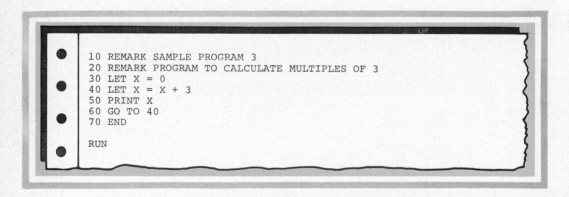

```
10 REMARK SAMPLE PROGRAM 3
20 REMARK PROGRAM TO CALCULATE MULTIPLES OF 3
30 LET X = 0
40 LET X = X + 3
50 PRINT X
60 GO TO 40
70 END

RUN
```

Line 10, 20 These statements serve to identify the program.
Line 30   This statement serves to create a variable called "X" and assigns to it the initial value of 0 (zero).
Line 40   This statement causes a new value to be computed for X, where this new value of X is to be equal to the existing value of X plus 3. Thus, the first time this statement is executed, the new value of X will be 3 since

the old value of X (zero) plus 3 is equal to 3. However, if this statement were to be executed again, this time the new value of X would be 6, or the old value of X (now 3) plus 3. In other words, each time this statement is executed the value stored in X is increased by 3 from its existing value.

Line 50   This statement causes the current value of X to be printed out.

Line 60   This statement causes the program to go back and execute statement number 40 again. Each time this statement is executed, the program will branch to statement number 40 for the next instruction.

Line 70   This statement must be the physically last statement in every BASIC program.

The output of this program would appear as follows:

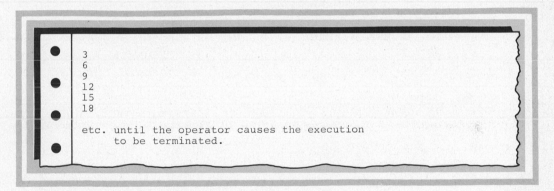

```
3
6
9
12
15
18

etc. until the operator causes the execution
     to be terminated.
```

GENERAL FORM   **IF/THEN Statement**

(line number)   *IF*   *(expression)* *(relation)* *(expression)*

                                         THEN   *(line number)*

This statement is a conditional branch statement and, as such, causes the normal sequence of execution of statements to be altered, depending on the existence of a certain condition at the time of execution of the statement. In this statement, the condition is relational. That is, the condition refers to whether or not a predefined relationship exists between the first and second expressions listed in the IF/THEN statement.

Relational Comparisons. The relation between expressions can be any of the following:

RELATION	MEANING
$<$	Is less than
$< =$	Is less than or equal to
$>$	Is greater than
$> =$	Is greater than or equal to
$=$	Is equal to
$< >$	Is not equal to

Several examples of statements of this type and their meaning are

10 IF A = 7 THEN 30
20   . . .

If the value of the variable A is equal to 7, branch to statement 30, otherwise proceed to statement 20.

10 IF A + B < C + D THEN 50
20   . . .

If the value of the sum A + B is less than the value of the sum C + D, branch to statement 50, otherwise proceed to statement 20.

10 IF A$ = "SELL" THEN 70
20   . . .

If the value of the string variable A$ is SELL, then branch to statement 70, otherwise proceed to statement 20.

10 IF A − B < = C ↑ 2 THEN 50
20   . . .

If the value of the difference A − B is less than or equal to the value of C raised to the second power, branch to statement 50, otherwise proceed to statement 20.

10 IF A$ < B$ THEN 40
20   . . .

If the value of the string variable A$ is less than the value of the string variable B$, branch to statement 40, otherwise proceed to statement 20.

This last example, however, poses a problem. Suppose that the string variable A$ contains an "S" and the string variable B$ contains a "C." Which is smaller, an "S" or a "C"? To resolve this confusion, each character is associated with a particular position in a hierarchy sequence. This sequence can vary with the machine on which the BASIC program is to be run but is generally as follows:

Lowest	Ꝑ (blank)
	special characters
	letters A thru Z
Highest	digits 0 thru 9

If two strings of the same length are compared, the result is based on the relationship between their leading characters, as is the case when two numbers of equal length are compared. That is, MARY is considered larger than JACK since M is larger than J; and JOHN is considered larger than JACK since the J's are the same and the O of JOHN is larger than the A of JACK.

If two strings of different lengths are compared, the shorter string and the corresponding part of the longer string will form the basis for comparison. Should this comparison prove to be equal, the shorter string will be considered to be the lesser; that is, JOHN is considered less than JOHNSON.

Some comparisons are

STRINGS TO BE COMPARED		VARIABLES ACTUALLY COMPARED AND RESULT
AAAAA	7	A < 7
HARRY	JOHN	HARR < JOHN
JOHN	114	JOH < 114
47	36	47 > 36
SMITH	SMITHSONIAN	SMITH < SMITH

Let us now examine a sample program dealing with the IF/THEN statement. Let us assume that we will calculate all multiples of 3, beginning with 3 itself and not exceeding 99, and we wish to print out these multiples. The program might appear as follows:

```
10 REMARK SAMPLE PROGRAM 4
20 REMARK PROGRAM TO PRODUCE MULTIPLES OF 3 TO 99
30 LET X = 0
40 LET X = X + 3
50 PRINT X
60 IF X < 99 THEN 40
99 END
```

You will notice that the basic difference between this program and the previous one is that we now have the capability to control the point at which the program will terminate automatically instead of requiring the operator to depress the STOP or BREAK key when he wishes to terminate the executing of the program. In the above example the program instructs the computer to branch to statement 40 if the multiple of 3 is less than 99, and otherwise to proceed to statement 99 and cause the processing to halt.

Looping. Looping involves the executing of one or more instructions over and over again. In the above sample program, the principle of looping was utilized. In this example statements 40 through 60 were executed over and over again, forming a *loop*. As the program executed these few statements over and over again, it was *looping*.

SELF-STUDY EXERCISES 10-6

1. The two general types of branch statements are _____ and _____ branch statements.

*****

unconditional
conditional

2. The _____ statement is an example of an unconditional branch statement.

*****

GO TO

3. The GO TO statement must contain _____ line numbers.

*****

two

4. The program statement 70 GO TO 90 causes _____.

*****

control to be transferred to statement number 90

5. The _____ statement is a conditional branch statement.

*****

IF/THEN

6. The IF/THEN statement has the general form _____.

*****

(*line number*) <u>IF</u> (*expression*) (*relation*) (*expression*) <u>THEN</u> (*line number*)

7. The relations which can be used with an IF/THEN statement are _____.

*****

less than ($<$), less than or equal to ($<$ $=$), greater than ($>$), greater than or equal to ($>$ $=$), equal to ($=$), and not equal to ($<$ $>$)

8. The sequence of statements:

           50   IF A$<$ $=$ B THEN 90
           60 . . .
           90 . . .

will cause _____.

*****

the program to branch to statement number 90 if A is less than or equal to B; otherwise proceed to statement 60

9. The string JACK is considered _____ the string JACKSON.
    *****

    less than

10. The string MARY is considered _____ the string MARK.
    *****

    greater than

11. A program loop is _____.
    *****

    a series of statements that are executed over and over again

12. A statement that will cause control to be transferred to statement 90 if A doesn't equal B, and cause control to be transferred to statement 120 if A = B is _____.
    *****

    (line number)   IF A < > B THEN 90
        120   . . .
    or
    (line number)   IF A = B THEN 120
        90   . . .

ADDITIONAL STATEMENTS   There are several additional BASIC statements that warrant our examination. These statements are the STOP, FOR/NEXT, READ/DATA, and RESTORE statements

GENERAL FORM

(*line number*)   *STOP*

STOP Statement   The STOP statement can be placed anywhere in the program where it is desired that execution be halted. This statement has the same effect as the statement GO TO n, where n is the line number of the END statement. For example, if the END statement had line number 999, the statements STOP and GO TO 999 would serve identical purposes. The only advantage of using the STOP statement over the GO TO statement in this instance is that the STOP statement immediately tells the computer that execution is to be terminated, while the GO TO 999 statement requires that the computer first locate statement 999 END before it knows that execution is to be terminated.

An example of the STOP statement used in conjunction with two IF/THEN statements is given below and compared with the same program using the GO TO and END statements.

10 REM SAMP. PROG.	10 REM SAMP. PROG.
20 . . .	20 . . .
40 . . .	40 . . .
50 IF A = 5 THEN 70	50 IF A = 5 THEN 70
60 STOP	60 GO TO 999
70 . . .	70 . . .
110 . . .	110 . . .
120 IF B = 9 THEN 140	120 IF B = 9 THEN 140
130 STOP	130 GO TO 999
140 . . .	140 . . .
270 . . .	270 . . .
999 END	999 END

The FOR and NEXT statements are used in the creation of program loops. The FOR statement provides the necessary information for setting up or initializing the loop and the NEXT statement is used by the computer to facilitate a return to the beginning of the loop or an exit from the loop. The general form of the FOR and NEXT statements is

FOR and NEXT Statements

GENERAL FORM

(line number) FOR (variable) = (expression) TO (expression) {STEP (expression)}

(line number) NEXT (variable)

Variable as used here is a computational variable and *not* a string variable. It is the name assigned to the counter or *index* used to control the number of times the loop is executed. The *expression* appearing before the word TO is the initial or starting value that the index will assume; the *expression* following the word TO is the last or termination value of the index; and the *expression* following the word STEP, if used, is the increment by which the index is varied each time the NEXT statement is executed. If the STEP *expression* option is omitted, the increment is assumed to be 1. A program segment containing a loop with and without the FOR and NEXT statements is shown below.

WITHOUT FOR/NEXT	WITH FOR/NEXT
60 LET I = 1	60 FOR I = 1, 10
70 PRINT I, I**2	70 PRINT I, I**2
80 LET I = I + 1	80 NEXT I
90 IF I < = 10 THEN 70	90 . . .
100 . . .	

In each of these program segments, when the loop has been executed 10 times, control will be transferred outside the loop—to statement 100 in the first case and statement 90 in the second case. Following are some points to remember when using the FOR and NEXT statements:

1. Every FOR statement must have a corresponding NEXT statement referencing the same variable.
2. Any number of statements may appear between the FOR statement and its associated NEXT statement.
3. FOR/NEXT loops may be nested within one another so long as the inner loops are completely contained within the outer loop.
4. The index of the loop may not be varied by any statement within the loop.
5. Exiting the loop (through an IF . . . THEN statement) before the termination value of the index has been reached will cause the index to remain at the last value attained before the loop was exited.
6. The results of entering a FOR/NEXT loop at other than the FOR statement are unpredictable.

7. When a FOR/NEXT loop has been exited as a result of the index's reaching the termination value, the value of the index is unpredictable.

GENERAL FORM

(line number)	*READ*	*(list of variable names)*
(line number)	*DATA*	*(list of data constants)*

The READ and DATA statements are used together. The READ statement directs the computer to read certain data, while one or more associated DATA statements provide the data that are to be read. For example, let us assume that we wish to read four numbers into the computer—16, 15, 86, and 85. From the general form we can see that we must provide four items, which comprise two *line numbers*, a *list of variable names*, and a *list of data constants*. Let us assign to the READ statement the line number 30 and to the DATA statement the line number 500 since the DATA statement must appear after the corresponding READ statement, and usually near the end of the program. Since we are intending to read four items of data, we must assign four variable names to the list, one for each item of data. It has been previously stated that a variable name can be a letter of the alphabet, or a letter followed by a single digit, or a letter followed by a $ (string variable). This allows us 312 possible names from which to choose 4. Let us assume that we agree on the names N1, N2, N3, and N4. We now have all the necessary information to construct the READ statement:

30   READ N1, N2, N3, N4

The *list of data constants* required in the DATA statement is a series of constants separated by commas, one constant corresponding to each variable name in the READ list. For the specific data given above, we have

500   DATA 16, 15, 86, 85

GENERAL FORM

(line number)   *RESTORE*

This statement causes the list of data used by the program to be recycled back to the beginning or first item of data. That is, the same data are to be used over again. Let us assume that we wish to have the variable A take on the successive values 1, 2, 1, 2. A program segment showing how this could be done is given below:

```
10    REMARK SAMPLE PROGRAM
20    LET N = 0
30    . . .
40    . . .
50    READ A
60    LET N = N + 1
70    IF N = 4 THEN 999
80    . . .
90    PRINT A
100   IF N = 2 THEN 120
110   GO TO 30
120   RESTORE
130   GO TO 30
140   DATA 1,2
999   END
```

SELF-STUDY EXERCISES 10-7

1. The general form of the STOP statement is _____.
                          *****

        (*line number*)   *STOP*

2. The purpose of the STOP statement is _____.
                          *****

        to halt the execution of the program

3. The general form of the FOR and NEXT statements are _____ and _____.
                          *****

    (*line number*) *FOR* (*variable*) = (*expression*) *TO* (*expression*)
                {*STEP* (*expression*)}
        (*line number*) *NEXT* (*variable*)

4. A FOR/NEXT loop to determine and print out the sum of all even numbers through 100 would be _____.

*****

```
10   LET S = 0
20   FOR N = 2 TO 100 STEP 2
30   LET S = S + N
40   NEXT N
50   PRINT "SUM = "; S
99   END
```

5. If the STEP option of the FOR statement is omitted, a step size of _____ will be assumed.

*****

1

6. In order to read in data, a program must contain a _____ and a _____ statement, or an _____ statement.

*****

READ

DATA

INPUT

7. The general form of the READ statement is _____.

*****

(*line number*)   *READ*   (*list of variable names*)

8. A list of variable names is _____.

*****

a series of programmer-assigned variable names separated by commas with one variable name corresponding to each item of data to be input or output

9. The general form of the DATA statement is _____.

*****

(*line number*)   *DATA*   (*list of data constants*)

10. The combination of statements

<pre>
50   READ A, N3, R$
60   PRINT A, N3, R$
80   DATA 34.6, 76, "THE ANSWER IS NO"
</pre>

will cause _____ to be printed out.

*****

<pre>
34.6   76   THE ANSWER IS NO
</pre>

11. The general form of the RESTORE statement is _____.

*****

(*line number*)　　*RESTORE*

12. The RESTORE statement causes the list of data used by the program to be _____.

*****

recycled to the beginning so that it can be read and used again

A COMPARISON OF INTERACTIVE AND BATCH BASIC

Character Set

TABLE 10-2

Comparison of Interactive and Batch BASIC Character Sets

INTERACTIVE BASIC	BATCH BASIC	USE OR MEANING
↑	**	Exponentiation
"	'	Used to define alphanumeric literal
<	LT	Less than
< =	LE	Less than or equal to
>	GT	Greater than
> =	GE	Greater than or equal to
< >	NE	Not equal to

Line Numbers　Line numbers are required in batch BASIC on only those statements that will be referenced by other statements, while in interactive BASIC line numbers are required on every statement.

In batch BASIC, statements are executed in the order in which they are input regardless of the statement numbers, while in interactive BASIC the statements are executed in order by statement number regardless of the order in which they are input.

Order of Execution of Statements

In batch BASIC, data may be included in DATA statements with or without line numbers, which are placed before the END statement. Batch BASIC will also accept data numbers, and only data numbers, after the END statement in the program and corresponding to the variables listed in one or more READ statements. The amount of data which can appear in a DATA statement before the END statement is generally limited to approximately 1000 numbers, while the data that can appear after the END statement is virtually unlimited.

Data

In interactive BASIC, however, all data corresponding to the variables listed in one or more READ statements must appear before the END statement preceded by the required word DATA and must contain a line number.

In batch BASIC, data corresponding to string and numeric variables listed in INPUT statements must appear after the END statement and in the same format as required in interactive BASIC.

Batch BASIC is equipped with the added statement PRINT ALL not found in interactive BASIC. This statement, when executed, causes the printing of all variables greater than 0.00001 or less than −0.00001, one per line. For example,

PRINT ALL Statement

$$A = 3.479$$
$$A3 = -7.2$$
$$S = 47$$
$$T3 = -97.2$$

Care should be exercised in using this statement because it can often result in a great deal of printing.

Blank cards may be inserted anywhere in a batch BASIC program in order to improve the readability of the program.

Blank Cards

A report concerning the structure of batch BASIC will be of interest to those who wish to investigate the construction of the batch BASIC processor.

UWBIC Technical Report[8]

[8]William F. Sharpe, *University of Washington BASIC Interpretive Compiler—UWBIC.* Technical Report Number 3. Seattle: Graduate School of Business Administration, 1967.

SELF-STUDY EXERCISES 10-8

1. Features common to both interactive and batch BASIC but slightly different in appearance or use are _____.

   *****

   character set, line-number requirements, order of execution of statements, and amount and placement of input data

2. Features available with batch BASIC and not with interactive BASIC are _____.

   *****

   PRINT ALL statement and the ability to insert blank cards or lines in the program for ease of reading

3. Interactive BASIC is designed to be used with a _____ computer system, while batch BASIC is designed to be used with a _____.

   *****

   time-shared
   batch-processing computer system

EXERCISES

10-1   True–false exercises

1. _____ Omitting the string variable, there are 286 other variable names available to the programmer.

2. _____ 314159.E −5 = 3.14159.

3. _____ To create a loop in a BASIC program, a FOR and a NEXT statement must be used.

4. _____ Only commas may be used to separate variables and/or literals in the list of a PRINT statement.

5. _____ All statements or instructions in a batch BASIC program must begin with a line number.

6. _____ There are five options available with a PRINT statement.

7. _____ Shift count refers to the number of places that a decimal point must be shifted.

8. _____ The STOP statement serves the same purpose as a GO TO statement that transfers control to the END statement.

9. _____ A remark is indicated by the command REM or REMARK and is an executable instruction.

10. _____ It is not advisable to skip numbers when assigning line numbers.

11. _____ When a numeric data item is printed out, either a "+" sign or a "−" sign will be printed before the number, depending on the value of the stored number.

12. _____ 475.E5 = 47,500,000.

13. _____ The computer language BASIC was developed at Dartmouth College for use on-line with a time-sharing computer.

14. _____ The IF . . . THEN . . . statement in a BASIC program performs the operation of the decision symbol in flowcharting.

15. _____ A branch statement allows the program to deviate from the sequential order of execution of instructions.

16. _____ BASIC statements are written in a "fixed form."

17. _____ In 6.E5, the shift count is 6.

18. _____ An expression is defined as one or more variables or constants combined with arithmetic operators.

19. _____ A quantity that can take on different values during the execution of a BASIC program is called a variable.

20. _____ Batch BASIC, developed at the University of Washington, facilitates the use of BASIC on smaller computers in batch mode.

21. _____ The number 1,000,000,001 would be printed out as 1.0E + 9 or 1.0E + 09.

22. _____ The typing of the word LIST causes the computer to list the names of all programs on the system.

23. _____ There may be only one NEXT statement for each FOR statement in a BASIC program.

24. _____ When the computer asks "NEW OR OLD", OLD refers to a program which has been previously written and stored and one which may be retrieved from the computer.

25. _____ Constants may appear in three separate forms: integer, real, and exponential form.

26. _____ The value of the expression at the right of the equals sign in a LET statement replaces the previous value of the variable on the left of the equal sign, if any.

27. _____ A string variable would be used in an INPUT statement to store a nonnumeric data item, keyed in during program execution.

28. _____ The END statement is required in every BASIC program and must have the statement number 9999.

29. _____ String variables cannot exceed 15 characters, regardless of the computer system employed.

30. _____ BASIC statements must be written according to specific rules concerning words, symbols, and their relative order.

31. _____ The only difference between integer and real constants is that real constants contain a decimal point.

32. _____ The typing of the word BYE or GOODBYE causes the communication between the terminal and the computer to cease.

33. _____ 3*10E4 < > 3*10↑4.

34. _____ The RESTORE statement will cause the data stored in the program to be recycled starting with the first data listed in the previous DATA statement.

35. _____ On IBM computer systems, the output page is divided into zones of 18 spaces each.

36. _____ The READ and DATA statements must appear on successive lines when used in a BASIC program.

37. _____ A LET statement causes the expression to the right of the = symbol to be evaluated and the result stored as the value of the variable to the left of the = symbol.

38. _____ Many users interacting with the same computer concurrently is called time-sharing.

39. _____ Line numbers must be between 1 and 99999.

40. _____ When the program is to be executed the word START is typed in.

41. _____ 40 READ A, B6, HI$ would be a balid BASIC statement.

42. _____ BASIC is an acronym for Beginners All-purpose Symbolic Instruction Code.

43. ＿＿＿ In interactive BASIC, statements are executed sequentially according to their statement numbers and are independent of the order in which they are input.

44. ＿＿＿ The instruction PRINT A "SPECIFIC GRAVITY =", C would cause the first digit of the variable C to be printed in the 55th print position on an IBM computer system.

45. ＿＿＿ 60 PRINT would cause the printer to skip a line in the print out.

46. ＿＿＿ There are six arithmetic operators in the BASIC language.

47. ＿＿＿ The GO TO statement is an unconditional branch instruction and identical to the COBOL GO TO statement.

48. ＿＿＿ The instruction 70 PRINT "EXAMPLE 12", would cause the computer to print: 70 "EXAMPLE 12".

49. ＿＿＿ $5 \uparrow 3 = 3 \uparrow 5$.

50. ＿＿＿ The options in a PRINT statement may be used in any combination.

51. ＿＿＿ Interactive BASIC was originally developed at Cornell.

52. ＿＿＿ The FINISH statement is the last statement in the program and always has the highest line number.

53. ＿＿＿ A BASIC variable name can be up to six characters long.

54. ＿＿＿ An IF . . . THEN . . . is an example of a conditional branch statement.

55. ＿＿＿ The INPUT statement is used principally in programs where data is available only at the time of the execution of the program.

56. ＿＿＿ By instructing the computer to LIST 25, the computer will print out the first 25 instructions in the program.

57. ＿＿＿ The statement, 60 FOR I = 1 TO K STEP M + N is valid.

Multiple-choice exercises   10-2

1. ＿＿＿ In comparing the value of string variables, which of the following is incorrect?
   (a) SMYTH > SMITH
   (b) SMITH < SMITHSON
   (c) SMITHSON > SMITHS
   (d) all the above
   (e) none of the above

2. ＿＿＿ An option open to the programmer in the PRINT statement is the
   (a) blank
   (b) expression
   (c) literal
   (d) all the above
   (e) none of the above

3. ＿＿＿ Which of the following statements are required in a FOR/NEXT loop?
   (a) a FOR statement
   (b) a NEXT statement
   (c) a counter
   (d) all the above
   (e) (a) and (b) only

4. ＿＿＿ Of the following, which is invalid?
   (a) 80 GO TO 15
   (b) 120 RUN
   (c) LIST
   (d) all the above
   (e) (b) and (c) only

5. ＿＿＿ Which of the following is not a variable?
   (a) A
   (b) A7
   (c) T$
   (d) X
   (e) none of the above

6. ＿＿＿ The special character ↑ symbolizes
   (a) that the advance of the paper will be suppressed after the PRINT statement
   (b) an error in that position on the line above
   (c) exponentiation
   (d) all the above
   (e) none of the above

7. ＿＿＿ Branch to line 60 if X + Y is greater than $3A^2$ would be written in the BASIC as follows:
   (a) 80   IF X + Y < 3A ↑ 2 THEN 60
   (b) 80   IF X + Y < 3A ↑ 2 GO TO 60
   (c) 80   IF X + Y > 3A ↑ 2 THEN 60
   (d) 80   IF X + Y > 3A ↑ 2 GO TO 60
   (e) none of the above

8. _____ A sign (+ or −) is printed before a number only if
   (a) it is requested
   (b) it is placed within quotes in the PRINT statement
   (c) the number is negative
   (d) all the above
   (e) none of the above

9. _____ The statement 010 INPUT A, B in an interactive BASIC program would cause
   (a) two data items to be accepted from the terminal
   (b) two data items to be taken from an associated DATA statement
   (c) two strings to be accepted from the terminal
   (d) (a) or (b)
   (e) (a) or (c)

10. _____ A < B is
   (a) a relation meaning A does not equal B
   (b) a relation meaning A is larger than B
   (c) a relation meaning A is smaller than B
   (d) a comparison of A to B
   (e) none of the above

11. _____ BASIC is a computer language that
   (a) can be processed through a time-sharing terminal
   (b) can be processed only in batch mode
   (c) can be processed only on special computers
   (d) all the above
   (e) none of the above

12. _____ A constant in BASIC can be divided into
   (a) two broad types of numbers and letters
   (b) two broad types of special characters and numbers
   (c) two broad types of integer and real constants
   (d) all the above
   (e) none of the above

13. _____ A possible NEXT statement for the statement 90 FOR I = J TO M STEP N would be
   (a) NEXT M
   (b) NEXT N
   (c) NEXT J
   (d) NEXT I
   (e) none of the above

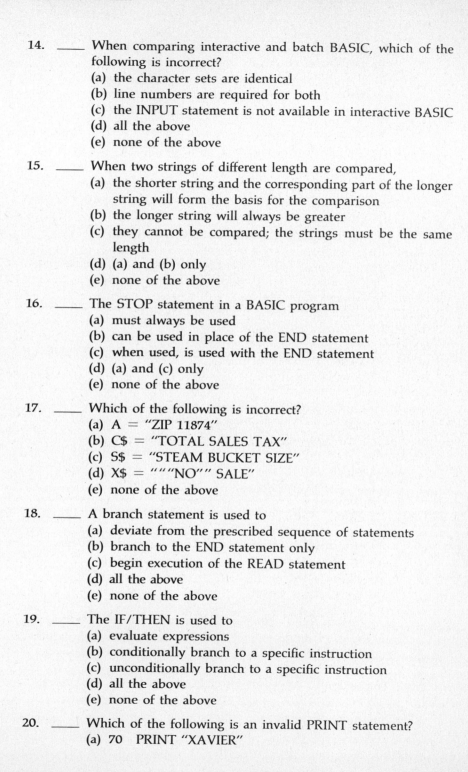

14. _____ When comparing interactive and batch BASIC, which of the following is incorrect?
    (a) the character sets are identical
    (b) line numbers are required for both
    (c) the INPUT statement is not available in interactive BASIC
    (d) all the above
    (e) none of the above

15. _____ When two strings of different length are compared,
    (a) the shorter string and the corresponding part of the longer string will form the basis for the comparison
    (b) the longer string will always be greater
    (c) they cannot be compared; the strings must be the same length
    (d) (a) and (b) only
    (e) none of the above

16. _____ The STOP statement in a BASIC program
    (a) must always be used
    (b) can be used in place of the END statement
    (c) when used, is used with the END statement
    (d) (a) and (c) only
    (e) none of the above

17. _____ Which of the following is incorrect?
    (a) A = "ZIP 11874"
    (b) C$ = "TOTAL SALES TAX"
    (c) S$ = "STEAM BUCKET SIZE"
    (d) X$ = """"NO"" SALE"
    (e) none of the above

18. _____ A branch statement is used to
    (a) deviate from the prescribed sequence of statements
    (b) branch to the END statement only
    (c) begin execution of the READ statement
    (d) all the above
    (e) none of the above

19. _____ The IF/THEN is used to
    (a) evaluate expressions
    (b) conditionally branch to a specific instruction
    (c) unconditionally branch to a specific instruction
    (d) all the above
    (e) none of the above

20. _____ Which of the following is an invalid PRINT statement?
    (a) 70   PRINT "XAVIER"

(b) 71   PRINT
(c) 72   PRINT A, B1, C, D
(d) 73   PRINT (2 * Y/X), A3
(e) none of the above

21. ____ The statements 10 PRINT USING 20, A and 20 :"A =",
###.# would cause _____ to be printed when the value
of A is −89.76.
(a) "A =" −89.8
(b) "A =", −89.8
(c) A =, −89.8
(d) A = −89.8
(e) none of the above

Problems   10-3

1. Determine the errors, if any, in the following expressions:
(a) 3.97
(b) D7
(c) 4C/X + Y
(d) (8.7 + C7)/−5.6
(e) Y1 + Y0
(f) Z25 + X
(g) XY/Z
(h) ((L + M)/(M + N) ↑ (L + M)
(i) A ↑ (X + −Y)
(j) X(Y + Z)
(k) A ↑ .5 * B
(l) A + (X + Y)/Z

2. Determine the errors, if any, in the following input or output statements:
(a) 10   PRINT A, B, C, D
(b) 10   PRINT A, B$, C$, D
(c) 10   PRINT X$, Y, C ↑ 2 + D ↑ 2
(d) 10   PRINT "THE ANSWER IS" Y
(e) 10   PRINT "SAMPLE"; "PROBLEM" "3"
(f) 10   PRINT E; F; G; H$
(g) 10   READ K, L ↑ M + N
(h) 10   READ L; M; N; S
(i) 10   READ X$, "BETTY", Y
(j) 10   READ A, B$, C$, D
(k) 10   READ X, Y
(l) 10   INPUT X; Y
(m) 10   INPUT A, B$, C

(n) 10   INPUT X, "BETTY", Y
(o) 10   INPUT W, X, Y, Z
(p) 10   PRINT TAB(6), A, "X SQUARE = "; X2
(q) 10   PRINT TAB(5); X + Y ** 2
(r) 10   PRINT TAB(I); X; "IS THE ANSWER"
(s) 10   PRINT USING 20, X + Y
     20   :GROSS PAY = $#,###.##
(t) 10   PRINT USING 20, A, B, C$, D
     20   :A = ###., B = ###.#, C$ = ##.#
(u) 10   PRINT USING 20, A, B
     20   :A = #.##!!!!, B = #.##!!!!, C = #.##!!!!
(v) 10   PRINT USING 30, A
     20   :TOTAL NUMBER OF #'S EQUALS ###.#

3. Write BASIC statements to compute the following algebraic statements:

(a) $A = (X + Y)/Z$

(b) $R = \sqrt{H^2 + V^2}$ or $R = (H^2 + V^2)^{1/2}$

(c) $A = 5L + 7M - 6.28$

(d) $X = \dfrac{A^2(3B^2 - 4C^2)}{A - B + C}$

(e) $S = \dfrac{\pi}{4}(4H^2 + C^2)$

4. Write the mathematical equivalents of the following BASIC statements:

(a) LET $A = X \uparrow 2 - 5 * Y * Z$
(b) LET $A = (X \uparrow 2 + B \uparrow 2 + C \uparrow 2) * (1/3)$
(c) LET $X = A * (1 + B/C) \uparrow (C * D)$
(d) LET $L = 3 * C \uparrow 4 * D$
(e) LET $G = H/18 \uparrow .5$
(f) LET $I = B * H \uparrow 3/12$

5. Determine the number of times each of the following loops will be performed:

(a) 10   FOR I = 1 TO 10 STEP 3
         .
         .
         .
     70   NEXT I
(b) 10   LET I = 2
     20   LET J = 15
     30   LET K = 3

```
  40   FOR I = 1 TO J * K STEP K
                    .
                    .
                    .
  90   NEXT I
(c) 10   FOR J = 2 TO 25
                    .
                    .
                    .
  60   NEXT J
(d) 10   FOR J = 1 TO 25 STEP J + 3
                    .
                    .
                    .
  70   NEXT J
```

6. Determine the errors, if any, in the following sequence of instructions:

```
REMARKS   PROBLEM   PROGRAM
010   PRINT "PROBLEM PROGRAM"
020   PRINT A, B
040   READ A, B
060   LET M = (A * B)/4
070   IF M < 4 THEN 100
090   LET N = 0
100   LET N = 1
130   LET P = (M − N) ↑ 2
200   PRINT A, B, N, P
170   END
120   DATA 10, 20
180   RUN
```

7. Write a BASIC program that will compute and print the value of X, where A, B, and C are typed in from the console for the following:
   (a)   X = A + B + C   if A < 0
      and X = A − B − C   if A > = 0
   (b)   X = A(B − C)/(B + C)   if A = 0
      and X = A(B − C) (B + C)   if A < 0 or A > 0

8. Write a BASIC program to calculate the squares and cubes of the numbers from 1 to 25 and print them out in columns with appropriate titles.

9. Write a BASIC program to calculate the amount for P dollars invested at R per cent compounded C times per year for from 1 to N years. P, R, C, and N are to be input at the time the program is executed.

You may assume that P will not exceed 999.99 dollars, R will not exceed 0.050, C will not exceed 12, and N will not exceed 5. The formula to determine amount is

$$A = P(1 + R/C)^{CN}$$

10. Write a BASIC program for the Julian date program flowcharted in Problem 12, Chapter 8.

11. Write a BASIC program for the grade problem flowcharted in Problem 13, Chapter 8.

ITEMS FOR DISCUSSION

Dialing up the Computer	#
BYE	!!!!
LIST	INPUT
RUN	END
RETURN	Arithmetic Operators
General Form	Value of an Expression
Line Number	LET
REMARK	=
Constant	GO TO
Variable	IF/THEN
Value of a Variable	Relational Comparison
PRINT	STOP
Literal	FOR/NEXT Statements
List of Variable Names	READ/DATA Statements
Expression	RESTORE
Zone	Interactive BASIC
;	Batch BASIC
PRINT TAB	PRINT ALL
PRINT USING	

IBM.®

SYSTEM/370
VS BASIC (TSO)
Reference
Summary[1]

Syntax Conventions

- Upper-case characters, digits, and special characters represent information that must appear as shown.

- All characters in italics represent information that is supplied by the user.

- A series of three periods (ellipsis) indicates that a variable number of items may be included in a list.

- Items shown in braces { } represent alternatives of which one is to be chosen. Braces are also used for grouping one or more items where ambiguity might otherwise exist.

- Items shown in brackets [ ] represent options that may be omitted.

- An underscored item represents the assumption made if no alternative is chosen.

- A vertical stroke | indicates that a choice is to be made between the option on the left of the stroke and the option on the right.

- Vertical stacking is sometimes used to represent alternatives.

- For debug subcommands, the variable *line-number-specification* can be a single TSO line number, a range of line numbers specified as *line-number-1:line-number-2*, or a list of line numbers enclosed in parentheses with individual line numbers separated by commas or blanks.

---

[1]This is a digest of the VS BASIC language and the requirements for its use under the TSO system. It assumes you are familiar with the language and system details described in *System/370 VS BASIC Language*, Order No. GC28-8303, and *System/370 VS BASIC TSO Terminal User's Guide*, Order No. SC28-8304, respectively.

System Information

Terminal Operating Procedures

Establishing a Connection

See *System/370 VS BASIC TSO Terminal User's Guide*, Order No. SC28-8304, or *OS/MVT and OS/VS2 TSO Terminals*, Order No. GC28-6762.

Logging On

Type in the LOGON command, followed by your *userid*, and if required, a password, logon procedure name, and account number. Certain terminals permit invisible password entry. See *Terminal User's Guide* for instructions.

Logging Off

From command mode, type in LOGOFF.

Special Characters

Certain characters have different representations on various terminals. For terminals not listed in the following table, see *TSO Terminals* book.

Character	2741 PTTC/EBCD	2741 (# 9812) Correspondence	Teletype Models 33 and 35
|	|	±	!
<	<	[	<
>	>	]	>
↑ or **	**	**	↑ or **
≤	<=	[=	<=
≥	>=	]=	>=
≠	<>	[]	<>

Correction Procedures

Typing Corrections (Any Mode)

Character Deletions: Use BACKSPACE key, or other installation-defined key to delete to point of error; retype correct material

Line Deletions: Use ATTN key or other installation-defined key.

Program Modifications (Edit Mode Only)

Insertions: Type line number, a blank, and text of line.

Replacements: Type line number, a blank, and new text of line.

Deletions: Use DELETE subcommand, or type line number followed by a

Character String Changes: ⓒⓇ Use the CHANGE subcommand.

Renumbering: Use RENUM subcommand.

Modes of Operation

There are three modes of operation that apply to VS BASIC use under TSO.

1. Command Mode (also called ready mode), in which you perform catalog maintenance, system control functions, initiate edit mode, initiate debug mode, execute existing VS BASIC programs. System prompt is READY.
2. Edit Mode, in which you create, store, modify, and execute VS BASIC programs, and initiate debug mode. System prompts are EDIT, E, and click. System prompts in input phase are line numbers and INPUT.
3. Debug Mode, in which you debug programs by examining step-by-step execution. System prompt is TESTVSB.

Commands and Subcommands and Their Formats

The following alphabetical list gives the formats of all commands and subcommands from all three modes. Abbreviations for command names (where they exist) are given in parentheses after the name.

Command/ Subcommand	Format	Mode	Function
ALLOCATE (ALLOC)	ALLOCATE DATASET(*data-set name*) FILE(*file-name*) [VOLUME(*volume-id*)]	command (also edit under VS2 Release 2)	associates a file name from a program with the data set containing the file; required for stream files not following standard file naming conventions and for all record-oriented files.
AT	AT *line-number-specification* [(*subcommand-list*)] [COUNT(*n*)] [NOTIFY | NONOTIFY]	debug	sets a breakpoint within a program; may include a list of debug mode subcommands that are to be performed automatically when the breakpoint is reached.
BOTTOM (B)	BOTTOM	edit	moves the TSO line pointer to the last line in a data set.
CHANGE (C)	CHANGE *line-nbr mrkr string1 mrkr string2 mrkr* [ALL]	edit	changes a string of characters within a line of data set.
DELETE (DEL)	DELETE {*data-set-name* | (*data-set-name-list*)}	command	deletes and uncatalogs a data set previously created.
DELETE (DEL)	DELETE [*line-number* [*line-number-2*]]	edit	deletes a line from a data set.
DOWN	DOWN [*number*]	edit	moves the TSO line pointer down.
EDIT (E)	EDIT *data-set-name* {VSBASIC | DATA} [NEW | OLD] [NUM | NONUM]	command	initiates edit mode; edit mode subcommands are described separately, below.
END	END	edit	terminates edit mode.

Commands and Subcommands and Their Formats (Continued)

Command/ Subcommand	Format	Mode	Function
END	END	debug	terminates debug mode without completing program execution; returns user to mode from which debug mode was initiated.
FREE	FREE DATASET (*data-set-name*) FILE (*file-name*)	command	frees storage space being used by a previously-allocated data set so that further allocations can be performed.
GO/GOTO	GO[TO] [*line-number*]	debug	causes execution of program to resume in normal execution sequence, or from a particular line.
HELP (H)	*For command or subcommand help:* HELP [*command-name*] [<u>ALL</u> | [FUNCTION] [SYNTAX] [OPERANDS[(*operand-list*)]]] *For message help:* HELP VSBASIC OPERANDS (*message-id*) *Alternate Form for Message Help for VS2 Release 2:* HELP VSBASIC MSGID(*message-id*)	command edit debug	provides information on the function, syntax, and operands of any debug mode subcommand; provides explanations of any error messages issued by VS BASIC.
IF	IF (*condition*) {*subcommand* | HALT}	debug	defines a condition to be tested and a single debug mode subcommand to be executed if the condition is true.
INPUT (I)	INPUT [*line-number* [*increment*]]	edit	initiates input phase of edit mode.
Insert/ Replace Delete Functions	*Insertions and Replacements:* *line-number text-of-line* *Deletions:* *line-number* (CR)	edit	facilitates the adding, replacing or deleting of BASIC instructions.
LIST (L)	LIST [*line-number* [*line-number-2*] | *]	edit	lists the contents of a data set, or lists individual lines from the data set.
LIST (L)	LIST {*variable* | (*variable-list*) | *}	debug	lists the value(s) of any program variable(s).
LISTALC (LISTA)	LISTALC	command	lists the names of all data sets that have been allocated.
LISTBRKS	LISTBRKS	debug	lists the currently-set breakpoints within a program along with any WHEN conditions that are defined.
LISTCAT (LISTC)	LISTCAT	command	lists the names of all cataloged data sets in your collection.
LISTFREQ	LISTFREQ [*line-number-specification*] [ZEROFREQ]	debug	lists the frequency of execution of any program statement; lists statements that have not been executed at all.
LOGOFF	LOGOFF	command	terminates a terminal session.
LOGON	LOGON *userid*[/*password*] [PROC(*procedure-name*)] [ACCT(*account-number*)] [<u>MAIL</u> | NOMAIL] [<u>NOTICES</u> | NONOTICES]	command	initiates a terminal session by identifying you to TSO.
NEXT (N)	NEXT	debug	sets a temporary breakpoint at the next program statement in line for execution.
OFF	OFF [*line-number-specification*]	debug	removes a breakpoint set by an AT subcommand.
OFFWN	OFFWN [*condition-id* | (*condition-id-list*)]	debug	turns off monitoring of WHEN conditions; *definitions* of the conditions are unaffected by OFFWN and may be restarted by WHEN subcommand.

Commands and Subcommands and Their Formats (Continued)

Command/Subcommand	Format	Mode	Function
PROFILE (PROF)	PROFILE [CHAR(*character*) | CHAR(BS) | NOCHAR] [LINE(ATTN) | LINE(*character*) | NOLINE] [MSGID | NOMSGID] [INTERCOM | NOINTERCOM] [LIST]	command	allows definition of character-delete and line-delete keys; determines whether user will receive message ids for error messages, and whether user will be able to receive messages sent from other terminals.
QUALIFY (Q)	QUALIFY [*program-unit*]	debug	allows specification of a program unit name so that variables from a program unit (MAIN or user-defined function) other than the currently executing one may be examined, reset, etc.
RENAME (REN)	RENAME *old-name new-name*	command	renames a data set.
RENUM (REN)	RENUM [*starting-number* [*increment* [*location*]]]	edit	renumbers the line numbers of a data set after insertions, deletions, etc.
RUN (R)	RUN *data-set-name* VSBASIC [SPREC | LPREC] [STORE | NOSTORE] [GO | NOGO] [SOURCE | OBJECT] [TEST | NOTEST] [PAUSE | NOPAUSE] [SIZE(*number*)]	command	executes an existing program (see VSBASIC, below).
RUN (R)	RUN [LPREC | SPREC] [STORE | NOSTORE] [GO | NOGO] [TEST | NOTEST] [PAUSE | NOPAUSE] [SIZE(*number*)]	edit	executes the VS BASIC program being edited; addition of TEST option allows initiation of debug mode; additional options allow for storing object code, running with long precision, controlling program chaining, and controlling size of user region.
RUN(R)	RUN [*line-number*]	debug	removes all breakpoints, condition monitoring, etc.; runs the program to completion.
SAVE (S)	SAVE [*data-set-name*]	edit	stores and catalogs a data set.
SET (S)	SET *variable = value*	debug	assigns values to variables.
TOP	TOP	edit	moves the TSO line pointer to the position preceding the first line of a data set.
TRACE (T)	TRACE [STMT | FUNC | OFF]	debug	causes notification of program branching as it occurs; tracing of all program branches, or just of calls to user-defined functions may be traced.
UP	UP [*number*]	edit	moves the TSO line pointer up.
VERIFY	VERIFY [ON | OFF]	edit	causes verification of lines to be printed automatically after any subcommand that moves the line pointer is issued, or after any CHANGE subcommand.
VSBASIC	VSBASIC *data-set-name* [SPREC | LPREC [STORE | NOSTORE] [GO | NOGO] [SOURCE | OBJECT] [TEST | NOTEST] [PAUSE | NOPAUSE] [SIZE (*number*)]	command	executes an existing VS BASIC program; addition of TEST option allows initiation of debug mode; additional options allow for storing object code, running with long precision, controlling program chaining, and controlling size of user region.
WHEN (WN)	WHEN *condition-id* [(*condition*) | *variable*]	debug	defines a condition to be monitored and then starts monitoring it; can be used to turn on monitoring previously turned off with an OFFWN subcommand, in which case no re-definition is required.
WHERE (W)	WHERE [STMT | FUNC | ALL]	debug	informs user where he is stopped in the program; options allow user to trace the calling sequence that led to the current location.

VS BASIC Language Elements

Language Elements

Character Set

Alphabetic character:	A, B, C, . . . , Z, #, @, $
Numeric character:	0, 1, . . . , 9
Alphameric character:	alphabetic character or digit
Special character:	blank $= + - * / \uparrow$) (, . ' " ; :	& ! ?
	$> < \neq \leq \geq$

Operators

Arithmetic Operators

$\uparrow$ or ** exponentiation
* multiplication
/ division
+ addition and unary plus
− subtraction and unary minus

Relational Operators

$=$ equal to
$\neq$ or $<>$ not equal to
$\geq$ or $>=$ greater than or equal to
$\leq$ or $<=$ less than or equal to
$>$ greater than
$<$ less than

Character Operator

| | concatenation

Logical Operators

& and
| or

Data

Arithmetic: Data having a numeric value.
Range: 0 or 10^{-78} through 10^{75} (approx. absolute value)
Precision: 7 significant decimal digits (short)
        15 significant decimal digits (long)
Forms: Integer, Fixed-Point, and Floating-Point

Character: Any string of characters.
Length: At least one and as many as 255 characters.

Variables

Simple Variables (Scalar Variables)

Arithmetic: Named by a single alphabetic character or by an alphabetic character followed by a numeric character. The initial value of all arithmetic variables is 0.

Character: Named by a single alphabetic character followed by the currency symbol ($). The initial value of each character variable is blank characters, the number of which depends on the defined length of the variable; in the absence of such a definition, a length of 18 is assumed.

Array Variables

Arithmetic: Named by a single alphabetic character. The dimension and number of members in an arithmetic array is defined by a DIM statement. In the absence of such a definition, the array will be implicitly defined to have either one or two dimensions (depending on context) and either 10 or 100 members, respectively. All members of an arithmetic array are initially set to 0.

Character: Named by a single alphabetic character followed by the currency symbol ($). The dimensions and number of members of an arithmetic array are defined by a DIM statement. In the absence of such a definition, the array will be implicitly defined to have either one or two dimensions (depending on context) and either 10 or 100 members, respectively. The length of each member of an implicitly-defined character array is 18. All members of a character array are initially set to blanks.

Constants

Arithmetic Constants:

Integer constants:	$[+\ |\ -]$ d . . .
Fixed-point constants:	$[+\ |\ -] \{[d] . . . \{.\} d . . .\} | \{d . . . \{.\} [d] . . .\}$
Floating-point constants:	$\begin{cases} \text{integer-constants} \\ \text{fixed-point-constants} \end{cases} E [+\ |\ -] d[d]$

where *d* is any digit, 0 through 9.

Character Constants:

'c . . .'
"c . . ."

where *c* is any character.

Internal Constants

Constant	Name	Short Form Value	Long Form Value
π	&PI	3.141593	3.14159265358979
Base of natural logs	&E	2.718282	2.71828182845905
Square root of two	&SQR2	1.414214	1.41421356237301
Centimeters per inch	&INCM	2.540000	2.54000000000000
Kilograms per pound	&LBKG	.4535924	.453592370000000
Liters per gallon	&GALI	3.785410	3.78541178400000

Filenames

A filename is a character expression whose value is the name of a record-oriented or stream-oriented file. Under TSO, this value may be from 1- to 8 characters long; the first character must be alphabetic. There may not be any leading or embedded blanks.

Expressions

Any representation of an arithmetic or character value.

Scalar Expressions

Arithmetic: 1. An arithmetic constant.
2. A simple arithmetic variable.
3. A scalar reference to an arithmetic array.
4. An internal constant.
5. An arithmetic-valued function reference.
6. A sequence of the above separated by arithmetic operators and parentheses.

Character: 1. A character constant.
2. A simple character variable.
3. A scalar reference to a character array.
4. A character-valued function reference.
5. A sequence of the above separated by the character operator (| |) and parentheses.

Array Expressions

An array expression may appear only on the right side of the equal sign in an array assignment statement. It can take one of the following forms:

Form	Meaning
a	An array
$a + b$	Sum of two arrays
$a - b$	Difference between two arrays
$a * b$	Matrix product of two arrays
$(e) * a$	Product of a scalar value and an array
IDN	Identity matrix
INV(a)	Inverse of a matrix
TRN(a)	Transpose of a matrix
ASORT(a)	Ascending sort of an array
DSORT(a)	Descending sort of an array

where a and b are array names, and e is a scalar arithmetic expression.

Logical Expressions

A logical expression is either a logical subexpression, or two logical subexpressions joined by a logical operator (& or |).

Logical expressions can appear only in IF statements. The form of a logical expression is as follows:

$subex_1$ [op $subex_2$]

where: $subex$ is a logical subexpression
op is either & or |

Logical Subexpressions

A logical subexpression compares the values of two arithmetic expressions or two character expressions. Its form is as follows:

e_1 rop e_2

where: e_1 and e_2 are scalar expressions of the same data type
rop is a relational operator

VS BASIC Statements and Their Formats

Statement	Format
Array Assignment	MAT $array$ [(r)] = ($scalar$-$expression$) MAT $array_1$ [(r)] = $array_2$ MAT $array_1$ [(r)] = $array_2$ {+ | −} $array_3$ MAT $array_1$ [(r)] = $array_2$ * $array_3$ MAT $array_1$ [(r)] = ($scalar$-$arithmetic$-$expression$) * $array_2$ MAT $array$ [(r)] = IDN MAT $array_1$ [(r)] = INV ($array_2$) MAT $array_1$ [(r)] = TRN ($array_2$) MAT $array_1$ [(r)] = ASORT ($array_2$) MAT $array_1$ [(r)] = DSORT ($array_2$) where: r is a redimension specification
CHAIN	CHAIN $chained$-$program$-$name$ [$,passed$-$value$]
CLOSE	CLOSE [FILE] $filename_1$ [$,filename_2$] . . .
DATA	DATA [$integer_1$*] $constant_1$ [$,[integer_2$*] $constant_2$] . . .
DEF	[DEF] FN $\begin{Bmatrix} a \\ b\$ \end{Bmatrix}$ [($dummy_1$ [$,dummy_2$] . . .)] [= $scalar$-$expression$] ◄— can and must appear only for single-line functions where: a is any alphameric character, specifying the function name and identifying the function as arithmetic. $b\$$ identifies the function as character; b must be an alphameric character.
DELETE FILE	DELETE FILE $filename$, KEY = key [$,$EXIT es [$,$NOKEY s] [$,$IOERR s]] where: es is the number of an EXIT statement. s is the number of any executable statement.

Statement	Format
DIM	DIM $array_1$ [$length_1$] [(row-$size_1$ [$,column$-$size_1$])] [$,array_2$ [$length_2$] [(row-$size_2$ [$,column$-$size_2$])] . . .
END	END [$comment$]
EXIT	EXIT [EOF s] [$,$IOERR s] [$,$DUPKEY s] [$,$NOKEY s] [$,$CONV s] where: s is the statement number of the statement to receive control when an I/O operation results in the condition specified with s.
FNEND	FNEND [$comment$]
FOR	FOR $variable$ = e_1 TO e_2 [STEP e_3] where: $variable$ is a simple arithmetic variable. e_1 is an arithmetic expression
FORM	FORM $\begin{Bmatrix} c_1 \\ [n_1*]d_1 \end{Bmatrix}$ $\begin{bmatrix} ,c_2 \\ ,[n_2*]d_2 \end{bmatrix}$ where: c_i is the X, POS, or SKIP control specification. d_i is a C, NC, PD, S, L, or PIC data form specification. n_i is an unsigned, nonzero, integer constant, or an arithmetic variable whose value is greater than zero.

466

VS BASIC Statements and Their Formats (Continued)

Statement	Format
GET	[MAT] GET *filename*, $v_1[,v_2]$ . . . $\left[\begin{array}{l}\text{,EXIT }es\\ \text{[,EOF }s\text{] [,CONV }s\text{] [,IOERR }s\text{]}\end{array}\right]$ where: $\quad v_i$ is any of the following: $\qquad \bullet$ a scalar variable $\qquad \bullet$ a subscripted array member reference $\qquad \bullet$ the STR pseudo-variable $\qquad \bullet$ an array name optionally preceded by MAT $\qquad \bullet$ an array name with redimensioning and $\qquad$ optionally preceded by MAT $\quad es$ is the number of an EXIT statement. $\quad s$ is the number of any executable statement.
GOSUB	*Simple:* $\quad$ GOSUB *statement-number* *Computed:* $\quad$ GOSUB *number*$_1$ [,*number*$_2$] . . . ON *arith-expression*
GOTO	*Simple:* $\quad$ GOTO *statement-number* *Computed:* $\quad$ GOTO *number*$_1$ [,*number*$_2$] . . . ON *arith-expression*
IF	IF *logical-expression* $\left\{\begin{array}{l}\text{GOTO }number\\ \text{THEN }\{number\mid statement\}\end{array}\right\}$ [ELSE {*number* | *statement*}] where: $\quad$ *statement* may be any of the following statements: array assignment LET RESET CHAIN OPEN RESTORE CLOSE PAUSE RETURN DELETE FILE PRINT REWRITE FILE GET PUT STOP GOSUB READ WRITE FILE GOTO READ FILE INPUT REREAD FILE
Image	$\left\{\begin{array}{l}c_1\\ f_1\\ c_1f_1[c_2f_2]\ .\ .\ .\ [c_n]\\ f_1c_1[f_2c_2]\ .\ .\ .\ [f_n]\end{array}\right\}$ where: $\quad c_i$ is any string of EBCDIC characters without $\qquad$ enclosing quotes. The pound sign (#) cannot $\qquad$ appear in the string. $\quad f_i$ is one of the following specifications: $\quad$ character—one or more # characters $\quad$ I-format —optional sign followed by one or $\qquad\qquad\qquad$ more characters $\quad$ F-format —optional sign followed by $\qquad\qquad\qquad$ combination of # characters and $\qquad\qquad\qquad$ a decimal point $\quad$ E-format—I- or F-format followed by four $\qquad\qquad\qquad$ vertical line characters (||||).

Statement	Format
INPUT	[MAT] INPUT v_1 [,v_2] . . . where: $\quad v_i$ is defined as any of the following: $\qquad \bullet$ a scalar variable $\qquad \bullet$ a subscripted array member reference $\qquad \bullet$ the STR pseudo-variable $\qquad \bullet$ an array name, optionally preceded by MAT $\qquad \bullet$ an array name with redimensioning and $\qquad$ optionally preceded by MAT
LET	[LET] v_1 [,v_2] . . . = *expression* where: $\quad v_i$ is a scalar variable, a subscripted array member $\qquad$ reference, or the STR pseudo-variable.
NEXT	NEXT *variable*
OPEN	OPEN [FILE] *filename*$_1$ $\left\{\begin{array}{l}\text{IN}\\ \text{OUT}\\ \text{ALL[HOLD]}\end{array}\right\}$ $\left[,filename_2 \left\{\begin{array}{l}\text{IN}\\ \text{OUT}\\ \text{ALL[HOLD]}\end{array}\right\}\right]$ . . .
PAUSE	PAUSE [*comment*]
PRINT	[MAT] PRINT [exp_1] [[, | ;] [exp_2]] . . . where: $\quad exp_i$ is a scalar expression or an array name $\qquad$ preceded by the word MAT.
PRINT USING	[MAT] PRINT USING s [,exp_1 [,exp_2] . . .] where: $\quad s$ is the number of the Image or FORM $\qquad$ statement to be used. $\quad exp_i$ is a scalar expression or an array name $\qquad$ preceded by the word MAT.
PUT	[MAT] PUT *filename*, exp_1 [,exp_2] . . . $\left[\begin{array}{l}\text{,EXIT }es\\ \text{[,EOF }s\text{] [,IOERR }s\text{]}\end{array}\right]$ where: $\quad exp_i$ is a scalar expression or array name preceded $\qquad$ by the word MAT. $\quad es$ is the number of an EXIT statement. $\quad s$ is the number of any executable statement.
READ	[MAT] READ v_1 [,v_2] . . . where: $\quad v_i$ is defined as one of the following: $\qquad \bullet$ a scalar variable $\qquad \bullet$ a subscripted array member reference $\qquad \bullet$ the STR pseudo-variable $\qquad \bullet$ an array name, optionally preceded by MAT $\qquad \bullet$ an array name with redimensioning, and $\qquad$ optionally preceded by MAT

VS BASIC Statements and Their Formats (Continued)

Statement	Format

READ	[MAT] READ FILE [USING *sn*] *filename* [,KEY *r exp*],
	
	 $v_1[,v_2]$ . . . $\left[\begin{array}{l}\text{,EXIT } es \\ \text{[,EOF } s\text{] [,IOERR } s\text{] [,NOKEY } s\text{] [,CONV } s\text{]}\end{array}\right]$
	
	 where:
	
	   sn is the number of a FORM statement.
	   r is one of the relational operators =, ≥, or >=
	   exp is a character expression.
	   v_i is one of the following:
	
	     • a scalar variable
	     • a subscripted array member reference
	     • the STR pseudo-variable
	     • an array name, optionally preceded by MAT
	     • an array name with redimensioning, and
	       optionally preceded by MAT
	
	   es is the number of an EXIT statement.
	   s is the number of any executable statement.

REM	REM [*comment*]

REREAD FILE	[MAT] REREAD RILE [USING *sn*] *filename* ,v_1 [,v_2] . . .
	
	 $\left[\begin{array}{l}\text{,EXIT } es \\ \text{,CONV } s\end{array}\right]$
	
	 where:
	
	   sn is the number of a FORM statement.
	   v_i is one of the following:
	
	     • a scalar variable
	     • a subscripted array member reference
	     • the STR pseudo-variable
	     • an array name, optionally preceded by MAT
	     • an array name with redimensioning, and
	       optionally preceded by MAT
	
	   es is the number of an EXIT statement.
	   s is the number of any executable statement.

RESET	RESET [FILE] *filename*$_1$
	
	 $\left[\begin{array}{l}\text{END} \\ \text{KEY } r_1\ exp_1\end{array}\right]$ $\left[,filename_2 \left[\begin{array}{l}\text{END} \\ \text{KEY } r_2\ exp_2\end{array}\right]\right]$ . . .
	
	 where:
	
	   r_i is one of the relational operators =, ≥, or >=
	   exp_i is a character expression

Statement	Format
RESTORE	RESTORE [*comment*]
RETURN	*For Subroutines:* RETURN [*comment*] *For Multi-line Functions:* RETURN *scalar-expression*

REWRITE	[MAT] REWRITE FILE [USING *sn*] *filename* [,KEY *r exp*],
	
	 e_1 [,e_2] . . . $\left[\begin{array}{l}\text{,EXIT } es \\ \text{[,EOF } s\text{] [,IOERR } s\text{] [,NOKEY } s\text{] [,CONV } s\text{]}\end{array}\right]$
	
	 where:
	
	   sn is the number of a FORM statement.
	   r is one of the relational operators =, ≥, or >=
	   exp is a character expression.
	   e_i is a scalar expression or an array name preceded
	      by the word MAT.
	   es is the number of an EXIT statement.
	   s is the number of any executable statement.

STOP	STOP [*comment*]
USE	USE *receiving-character-variable*

WRITE	[MAT] WRITE FILE [USING *sn*] *filename*, e_1 [,e_2] . . .
	
	 $\left[\begin{array}{l}\text{,EXIT } es \\ \text{[,EOF } s\text{] [,IOERR } s\text{] [,DUPKEY } s\text{] [,CONV } s\text{]}\end{array}\right]$
	
	 where:
	
	   sn is the number of a FORM statement.
	   e_i is the scalar expression or array name preceded
	      by the word MAT.
	   es is the number of an EXIT statement.
	   s is the number of any executable statement.

Intrinsic Functions

Function	Meaning
ABS(x)	Absolute value of x
ACS(x)	Arcsine (in radians) of x
ASN(x)	Arcsine (in radians) of x
ATN(x)	Arctangent (in radians) of x
CEN(x)	Centigrade equivalent of x Fahrenheit degrees
CLK	Time of day in 24-hour clock notation
CNT	Number of data items successfully processed by last I/O statement

Function	Meaning
COS(x)	Cosine of x radians
COT(x)	Cotangent of x radians
CPU	Seconds taken by program execution
CSC(x)	Cosecant of x radians
DAT[(x)]	Current Gregorian date or Gregorian equivalent of Julian date x
DEG(x)	Number of degrees in x radians
DET(x)	Determinant of an arithmetic array

Intrinsic Functions (Continued)

Function	Meaning
DOT(x,y)	Dot product of arrays x and y
EXP(x)	Natural exponential of x
FAH(x)	Fahrenheit equivalent of x Centigrade degrees
HCS(x)	Hyperbolic cosine of x radians
HSN(x)	Hyperbolic sine of x radians
HTN(x)	Hyperbolic tangent of x radians
IDX(x,y)	Position of first character of string y within string x
INT(x)	Integral part of x
JDY[(x)]	Current Julian date or Julian equivalent of Gregorian date x
KLN(x)	Length in bytes of embedded key for file x
KPS(x)	Byte position at which embedded key for file x starts
LEN(x)	Length of character string x, minus trailing blanks
LGT(x)	Logarithm of x to the base 10
LOG(x)	Logarithm of x to the base e
LTW(x)	Logarithm of x to the base 2
MAX(x,y [,z . . .])	Maximum value of x,y,z, . . .

Function	Meaning
MIN(x,y [,z . . .])	Minimum value of x, y, z . . .
NUM(x)	Arithmetic value of character string x
PRD(x)	Product of elements in array x
RAD(x)	Number of radians in x degrees
RLN(x)	Length of last record referred to in file x
RND[(x)]	Random number between 0 and 1
SEC(x)	Secant of x radians
SGN(x)	Sign of x (-1, o, or $+1$)
SIN(x)	Sine of x radians
SQR(x)	Square root of x
STR(x,y[,z])	Portion of string x from yth character to end of string or z characters from string x, starting with yth character
SUM(x)	Sum of elements in array x
TAN(x)	Tangent of x radians
TIM	Time of day in seconds since midnight

V

A SYSTEMS
APPROACH

11

SYSTEMS ANALYSIS

The study of "systems" is by no means a new or even recent endeavor. Systems have been in use for thousands of years. The Egyptians employed a form of a bookkeeping system over 5000 years ago for keeping their accounts, while Phoenician astronomers studied systems of stars for the purpose of making predictions. Man has sought, from the beginning of time, to find relationships, to generalize these relationships, and to explain what he can see, hear, touch, smell, and reason.

All man's history has been a continuing enlargement of this theme: Meaningful and durable relationships must be uncovered if we are to expand man's knowledge and successfully administer his affairs. The scientific method of investigation, which necessitates such meaningful and durable relationships for its results, is systems analysis in the broadest sense.

In this chapter, however, we shall only concern ourselves with those systems which are of direct and immediate concern to a business in the processing of information to produce meaningful results for management. That is, systems analysis will refer to the analysis of business systems.

Systems today are essential to the operation of any part of a business. They must be made to function at peak efficiency if a business is to survive. But a system can function only as effectively as users such as the accountant, business manager, and other responsible individuals within the company make it function. To make a system function at maximum capacity demands more of its users than that they have a superficial knowledge of how to use the system.

All too often, managers are told that they only need to know how to access required information, thus making them ignorant of the operations of the system as a whole. In accepting such advice, these managers are, in essence, relinquishing a substantial part of the control of the organization to the system's designers and operators.

It is therefore essential that early in their careers, managers and potential managers be made to clearly understand what a system is, what its objectives are, what kinds of systems there are, what goes into their creation and maintenance, what are their costs and benefits, and how to analyze and evaluate systems. It is to provide such an understanding that this and subsequent chapters are presented.

A business system may be defined as a combination of personnel, equipment, and other facilities operating as a unit according to a set of procedures designed to record and control the actions and activities connected with a business.

WHAT IS A BUSINESS SYSTEM?

Prior to the advent of the computer, a business could survive even though it did not merge and correlate all phases of its activities into a unified whole, but today this is no longer possible. A good system is the key to the efficient operation of each and every part of a business. If a business is to outdistance and outlast its competitors, its operations must be based on carefully planned and operationally current systems.

Modern business systems accept input data, move it methodically through a preplanned series of procedures to a computer, where it is used to create needed reports, to update various records, to make routine decisions automatically, or to provide management with current and meaningful information on which to base its decisions. These systems must be flexible enough to adapt to changes in the structure of the business or the market its serves. They must be able to interact with one another in a productive and meaningful way. The systems which control the prime functions of a business are similar to the systems which, within the human being, work together to keep the body operating efficiently and effectively.

Examples of systems commonly found in business include

1. Accounts payable
2. Personnel accounting
3. Payroll
4. Accounts receivable
5. Inventory

Complex systems such as these certainly were not the result of chance but were developed as the result of careful and detailed investigations. The first of these investigations must be directed toward determining, clearly and precisely, what the objectives of the system study are.

SELF-STUDY EXERCISES 11-1

1. A business system may be defined as _____.

        *****

    a combination of personnel, equipment, and other facilities operating as a unit according to a set of procedures designed to record and control the actions and activities connected with a business

2. The modern business system utilizes computers to _____, _____, _____, and _____.

            *****

                create needed reports
            make decisions automatically
                update various records
    provide management with current and meaningful information on which to base its decisions

3. A system must be flexible enough to adapt to _____.

            *****

    the changes in the structure of the business or in the market it serves

4. Five examples of business systems are _____, _____, _____, _____, and _____.

            *****

                accounts payable
              personnel accounting
                    payroll
                    inventory
              accounts receivable

5. The common overall objective of all systems analysis is
_____.

*****

to increase the effectiveness of the operation or procedure

6. The first step in evaluating a system is to _____.

*****

determine what the specific objectives of the system are

A complete and detailed systems analysis can take many months to
develop and cost thousands of dollars. In light of this, there can be
little doubt that there is a need to establish the objectives of the
system analysis before such substantial energies or monies are
expended. These objectives may be broad, long-range expecta-
tions, or they may be short-range plans. In either case, they will
have one overall objective in common—to increase the effectiveness
and efficiency of an operation or procedure. This objective can be
met by developing new procedures or by improving existing procedures so as to obtain new and better information for management,
to increase the effectiveness of operations, and, where possible, to
reduce operating expenses. However, to make a complete system
analysis these general statements must be converted into definite
steps to be followed. These steps will be discussed in detail later.

Basically, the overall objective of increased effectiveness can
be satisfied in one or more of the following ways:

1. Improved service to the customer or user of the system
2. Improved quantity, quality, depth, and form of information
   provided to management
3. Increased speed and accuracy in the processing of data and
   the preparation of reports
4. Improved coordination between the various operating units
   and associated personnel
5. Improved overall operating efficiency by making possible
   more speedy action on management decisions
6. Eliminating the conflicting or overlapping services
7. Reduced inventory and other working-capital requirements

**OBJECTIVES OF
A SYSTEM
STUDY**

SYSTEMS ANALYSIS AND DESIGN Once the objectives of the system have been determined, the analyst can proceed with his investigation to determine whether the existing system, be it manual, mechanical, punched-card, or computerized, is adequate or whether this system should be modified, up-dated, or replaced. Such an analysis is termed a feasibility study.

Feasibility Study A complete and effective feasibility study would require an overall study of the entire organization. Before initiating such a study, the management of the organization should be apprised of the fact that a sufficiently detailed, well-planned, and executed feasibility study is both expensive and time consuming. Management should also be made aware that such a study can be beneficial to the organization regardless of the study's outcome. For example, should the study reveal that the existing system is sufficient and appropriate for the organization's needs, and therefore should not be changed or replaced, substantial time and money can be saved for the organization in not needlessly attempting to develop a replacement system. Also, management could be assured that, for their purposes, the existing system is the most efficient and competitive possible. The size and complexity of a feasibility study necessitates that it be broken down into several less comprehensive steps. Although these steps may differ in name, they will be similar in content to the following five steps:

1. Initialization
2. Selection of objectives
3. Detailed analysis
4. Resource allocations
5. Conclusions

   Initialization. In this phase of the study, contacts should be made with employees associated with the existing system, from the lowest-level employee through management personnel, in order to develop a clear understanding of the advantages and disadvantages of the existing system as well as to point out any unsolved problems. For future analysis, a study team should be formed, consisting of at least one member from each of these areas. The first task of this team will be to determine the present and future requirements of the system, the extent of available equipment and methods relating to this system, and what expenditures of personnel, time, and money can be anticipated to complete the feasibility study.

Selection of Objectives. In this phase of the study, the system specifications and objectives should be written down in detail, accompanied by a realistic timetable for the completion of the feasibility study. Krauss[1] suggests that the answers to the questions below will help the analyst determine this information.

Management

1. What are the past and future objectives?
2. What is the general attitude?
3. What is the underlying philosophy?
4. What organizational changes are planned?
5. What are the unfulfilled information needs?
6. How receptive is management to new techniques or change?

Procedures

1. What work is performed?
2. In what sequence does the work take place?
3. Who performs the functions?
4. How many people are needed?
5. When is the function performed?
6. What equipment is used?
7. Is the function needed?
8. What inputs and outputs are involved?
9. How much volume is there—average, peak, growth?
10. How much time is required for the functions?
11. How often is the work done?
12. What controls are required?
13. What are the turnaround-time requirements?
14. What "business rules" apply to each function?

Cost

1. How much does the present system cost?
2. How much is spent on forms and supplies?

[1]Leonard I Krauss, *Administering and Controlling theCompany Data Processing Function.* Englewood Cliffs, N.J.: Prentice-Hall, Inc., 1969, pages 51–52.

3. What are the costs for carrying inventory or receivables awaiting collection?
4. What are the personnel costs?
5. What overhead is charged?

Effectiveness

1. Does the current system do what was intended?
2. What are the strong points?
3. What are the disadvantages?
4. What effects would expansion have?
5. Is the current output useful?
6. How much inefficiency and duplication of effort exists?
7. What interdepartment relationships exist?

There are several ways to go about obtaining the answers to these and other questions. Three of the most common fact-gathering techniques which are currently used to obtain information about the present system and future needs are

1. Interviewing
2. Reviewing historical records
3. Sampling and estimating

Interviewing is probably the most productive of the three and usually begins with top management to obtain broad background information; then with middle or first-line management, who provide the details; and, finally, the individual workers are questioned. One must bear in mind that the lowest-graded worker can often point out the imperfections in the existing system and occasionally will even suggest worthwhile remedies. Interviewing techniques will be discussed in greater detail when we discuss developing a system design.

The degree to which historical records can be beneficial is greatly dependent upon the nature and rate of growth of the business. All too often the analyst will discover that the records are too poorly kept or too out of date to serve as predictors with any degree of certainty. In these cases, the records are better put aside and their absence compensated for by a more in-depth analysis of other source data.

It is often helpful to gather sample data from which estimates or projections can be made which will serve to either confirm or cast doubt on conclusions reached by other means. This technique, however, should be used cautiously, as substantial errors are possible if one is not experienced and knowledgable concerning its use.

Detailed Analysis. In this phase, the present and past systems used by the company are examined in comparison to other companies that have instituted such studies. Careful consideration should be given to the relationship between the dollar cost of the systems study and tangible savings and benefits, not only with regard to profits, but with respect to savings in space, time, experience gained, increased competitive potential, and so on.

The relationship between the system under investigation and other independent and interdependent systems within the company should also be determined. In determining this relationship, each of the systems should be analyzed and compared with the remaining systems concerning their functional design as opposed to their organizational arrangements.

Resource Allocations. An account should be taken of all the company's resources, including such items as manpower, money, time, space, etc. For example, a hypothetical list of proposed system costs and benefits is given in Fig. 11-1. Included should be a detailed statement concerning whether or not each of these resources is being efficiently utilized.

Conclusions. A written report incorporating the study team's findings and recommendations should be submitted to management. These recommendations should be supported in detail, making certain to highlight any anticipated benefits in addition to pointing out the degree of uncertainty and risks inherent in the recommendations.

Such a feasibility study could have only two possible outcomes. The first possible outcome is that the present system is superior to any other system thus far proposed or evaluated. In this case the study would be discontinued for the immediately foreseeable future. At such time as new developments should arise, the feasibility study could be reinitiated.

The second possible outcome would be that the present system is not the most effective and efficient system for the company's

```
                                              PROPOSED SYSTEM COSTS

    Hardware
        Basic processor
        Storage and input/output
        Communications
        Facilities
        Equipment maintenance

    Operating Expenses
        Programmers to maintain the system
        Equipment operators
        Keypunch and media preparers
        Data collectors
        Data control and correction
        Electricity, heating, and air conditioning
        Cards, paper, and tapes

    Developmental Costs
        Hiring and training programmers and analysts
        Salaries of programmers and analysts
        Salaries of additional study team or developmental personnel
        Disruption of normal operations
        Retraining of displaced personnel
        Establishment of new files

                                            PROPOSED SYSTEM BENEFITS

    Decreased Operating Costs
        Fewer people
        Less inventory
        Fewer penalties for late delivery or payment
        Reduced spoilage of goods
        Lower transportation or purchasing costs for material
        Fewer shortages to interrupt production
        Better scheduling of production

    Increased Revenues
        Ability to handle more customers with existing facilities
        More customers by faster or more dependable service
        Higher price or more customers from better quality of product
```

FIG. 11-1

Hypothetical List of Proposed
Systems Costs and Benefits.

From Automatic Data-Processing Systems Principles and Procedures, Second Edition by Robert H. Gregory and Richard L. Van Horn. © 1960 and 1963 by Wadsworth Publishing Company, Inc., Belmont, Calif. 94002. Reprinted by permission of the publisher.

needs. In such a case, two possible alternatives could be suggested as a result of the feasibility study: Modify the existing system or develop a new system.

Inexpensive modifications to the existing system are often sufficient for the user's needs. A simple modification such as the standardizing of invoice layouts that had previously varied from one department to another within the company would, for example, lower the cost of the forms, simplify personnel training, and reduce possible errors in using and understanding these forms. Modification of the existing system could also include the replacing of manual methods with mechanical or computerized methods, or the replacement of existing equipment with more sophisticated and more efficient equipment.

Modify the Existing System

To develop a new system is a long and tedious procedure and will be discussed in detail in the next section.

Developing a New System

SELF-STUDY EXERCISES 11-2

1. A _____ is used by the analyst to determine if the existing system is adequate.

*****

feasibility study

2. A complete and effective feasibility study would require _____.

*****

an overall study of the entire organization

3. An integral part of a feasibility study is the selecting of the objective of the system and establishing of _____.

*****

a realistic timetable for the completion of the feasibility study.

4. The five steps generally required in a feasibility study are _____, _____, _____, _____, and _____.

*****

initialization
selection of objectives
detailed analysis
resource allocations
conclusions

5. The _____ step of a feasibility study involves contact with employees in order to understand _____ .

*****

initialization
the relative advantages, disadvantages, and unsolved problems associated with the existing system

6. In collecting data for the feasibility study the analyst may utilize _____ , _____ , and _____ techniques.

*****

interviews
review of historical records
sampling and estimating

7. It is often _____ to update the existing system than to develop a new system.

*****

more expensive and tedious

8. In the detailed analysis phase of the feasibility study, the relationship between the system under investigation and _____ should be determined.

*****

other independent and interdependent systems

DEVELOPING A SYSTEM DESIGN The developing of a system can be reduced to three fundamental stages: the investigation stage, the hypothesis stage, and the implementation stage.

The first phase of any system investigation is to acquire a detailed **Investigation**
understanding of the existing system. A great deal of this information should have been revealed in the feasibility study, but it will
be restated for emphasis.

The investigation stage is a period of intensive data collection
and interviewing. A substantial amount of written material must
be collected in this process and generally takes one or more of the
following forms:

1. Representative input and output data
2. Practical examples of the existing system's malfunctions,
   if any
3. Reports and commentaries indicating previous studies of,
   or attention given to, the same or similar problems

Equally as important as written materials is the interview. Many
items can be determined from an interview that would be almost
impossible to obtain from written documents. However, one must
approach the interview with caution since interviews can easily become confused, redundant, and time-consuming. The interviewer
must make every effort to eliminate any bias that might be injected
as a result of the position and personality of the person being interviewed. He must also be careful to avoid the common pitfalls that
can occur in interviewing. Some of these common errors are

1. Interrupting the story to insert your own ideas and views
2. Allowing the direction of the interview to be diverted onto
   nonproductive paths
3. Allowing blanket statements and broad generalizations to
   obscure the facts
4. Leaving the interview only half understanding an issue
   or problem
5. Allowing oneself to be overpowered by the person being
   interviewed and end up as the interviewed instead of the
   interviewer
6. Allowing oneself to become involved in operational problems, thus distracting your attention from the prime purpose of information gathering
7. Asking leading questions which can be answered with a
   "yes" or "no," as very often this kind of question calls for
   an opinion and not fact

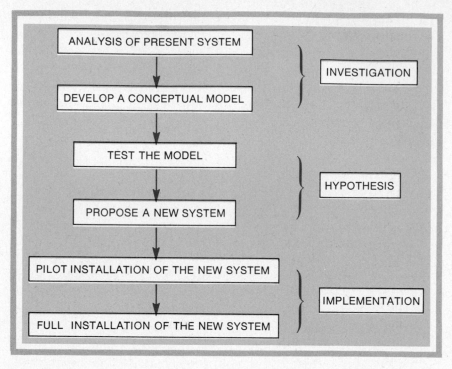

FIG. 11-2
Steps in a System Design.

After all interviews have been completed and their results have been assembled, the conceptual model will begin to take shape. The conceptual model is the analyst's first idea concerning how to attack the problem and concerning the manner in which the system should be redesigned. The analyst should be careful not to attempt to draw conclusions or to attempt to solve the problem during this stage, but to make a concerted effort to simply collect data.

Hypothesis   Upon completion of the analysis of the existing system and the development of a conceptual model (investigation stage), the analyst must test the conceptual model and propose a new system (hypothesis stage).

The conceptual model to be tested can appear in many forms. If it were to appear in a mathematical form, for example, its analysis would be reasonably routine; however, the problem does not usually appear this way. Therefore, there remains only one effective means to evaluate the model. This means is simply to expose the model to its potential users for their analysis and comments. This should be done as early as possible after the completion of the investigation stage. The problem becomes even more difficult in the case of a new system, where the potential users have had little or no previous exposure to this or a previous, but similar, system. In such cases it is desirable to test subsystems of the overall system separately as well as testing the overall operation of the system in any way feasible. It is important to verify that the subsystems are compatable and can function together to produce the desired results. The unstructured or nonmathematical nature of most business systems must be given careful consideration in designing the testing format to be utilized. This should be considered in much the same way as it will be in the design of the system itself.

Implementation

If possible, a pilot implementation study should be performed, as this type of study has the distinct advantage of allowing the system in miniature to operate under battle conditions. This means that any defect can be corrected or any changes made prior to the making of any large-scale commitments. In his analysis of this pilot study, the analyst must realize that it is difficult, if not impossible, to design a completely optimum system. Even if one were able to develop such a system, changes in input or output requirements might necessitate that the analyst settle with a system design which is somewhat less than optimum. The system designer must realize that his role is simply to improve the existing process to the greatest extent *practically* possible in the shortest possible time. Otherwise, a great deal of time can be needlessly expended by the analyst in an attempt to produce the optimum system, not realizing that, in so doing, the completion date of the system is being postponed and the company is losing the benefit of the use of the new system.

Once the pilot study has been made to perform satisfactorily, it can be expanded, step by step, until it covers the full operational scope for which the system was designed.

The system approach that you have just studied closely follows the scientific method. It requires that the system be carefully and methodically analyzed functionally and operationally, and that it consider suitable alternatives. It also dictates that the problem be attacked in an orderly way, first by investigation, then by the establishing of a reliable hypothetical model of the problem, and finally by a careful and thorough testing phase.

SELF-STUDY EXERCISES 11-3

1. The three stages in developing a system design are _____,
_____, and _____.

*****

investigation
hypothesis
implementation

2. The _____ stage is concerned with analyzing the present
system and _____.

*****

investigation
developing a conceptual model

3. The hypothesis stage of the system development includes
_____ and _____.

*****

testing the model
proposing a new system

4. In employing the interview technique, an inteviewer must take
every precaution to eliminate _____.

*****

any bias that might be interjected as a result of the position and
personality of the person being interviewed

5. The ideal form of a conceptual model is _____.

*****

a mathematic model

6. A pilot installation is _____.

*****

a miniaturized version of the planned system designed to test
the system under fire on a small scale

7. The _____ stage of system development is concerned with developing a pilot study.

*****

implementation

8. A system study is based on the _____.

*****

scientific method

EXERCISES

True–false exercises 11-1

1. _____ The conceptual model should be examined by its potential users as early as possible.

2. _____ Historical records are reliable sources of information involving the selection of objectives.

3. _____ Success of a pilot installation guarantees complete success of the full installation.

4. _____ Inventory reduction would not be an objective of a systems study.

5. _____ In an interview it is best to let half-understood problems go so that the interview will not be upset.

6. _____ A business system is designed to record and control activities connected with the running of a business.

7. _____ Notetaking can be distracting and therefore should never be done during an interview.

8. _____ The goal of the systems analyst is to always produce the very best, most complete system possible.

9. _____ The primary aim of a systems study is to increase its efficiency and effectiveness.

10. _____ Regardless of the cost, systems studies should always be made.

11. _____ A detailed understanding of the existing system is a necessary part of any systems investigation.

12. _____ Investigation must include all documented cases of failure in the present system.

13. ____ Minor system modifications are very often sufficient for the user's needs and should always be considered in a feasibility study.

14. ____ Users need only know how to access information from a system.

15. ____ The factor of primary importance in the evaluation of a system is the determining of specific objectives.

16. ____ The only aim of the investigation phase of a systems design is to collect data.

17. ____ Leading questions that call for opinions should not be used in an interview.

18. ____ In the initialization phase of a study, contacts are made with top-level management only.

19. ____ Detailed, well-planned and executed feasibility studies should always be made prior to the design of a system.

20. ____ The initialization phase is the first step in a feasibility study.

21. ____ Systems analysis is a scientific method of investigation that seeks meaningful and durable relationships.

22. ____ Information pertaining to the present system and future needs may be obtained in many ways. The least productive method is through the use of interviews.

23. ____ A complete feasibility study would examine an entire organization.

24. ____ The report of the study team is submitted to management.

25. ____ The testing of the conceptual model and the proposing of a new system is known as the hypothesis stage.

26. ____ It is always allowable to insert your own ideas and opinions during an interview.

27. ____ Modifications of existing systems are always costly.

28. ____ If the outcome of a valid feasibility study is to make no changes in the existing system, the study has been beneficial to management.

11-2   Multiple-choice exercises

1. ____ System costs do not include
   (a) equipment operators
   (b) training of programmers and analysts
   (c) establishment of new files

    (d) disruption of normal operations
    (e) none of the above

2. ____ A request for a systems investigation should include
    (a) price and time
    (b) scope and boundary
    (c) address and location
    (d) scope and cost
    (e) married and single people

3. ____ Systems benefits do not include
    (a) less inventory
    (b) less spoilage
    (c) lower purchasing costs for materials
    (d) increased revenues
    (e) none of the above

4. ____ The feasibility study
    (a) begins with initialization
    (b) is concerned with the objectives of the systems
    (c) involves interviewing all the users of the system
    (d) will consider resource allocations
    (e) all the above

5. ____ A conceptional model is generally evaluated
    (a) mathematically
    (b) by actual use
    (c) by exposure to the potential users for analysis and
        comments
    (d) by computer
    (e) none of the above

6. ____ Systems is concerned with
    (a) administration of personnel
    (b) developing an internal business structure
    (c) methods of translating company policy
    (d) all the above
    (e) none of the above

7. ____ Potential managers should know
    (a) what a system is
    (b) what the system objectives are
    (c) what kinds of systems exist
    (d) how to analyze and evaluate systems
    (e) all the above

8. ____ To effectively modify an existing system, you must
    (a) simplify personnel training
    (b) lower the cost of the existing forms

(c) replace manual methods by more efficient means
(d) all the above
(e) none of the above

9. ____ Pilot studies are
(a) used only to evaluate the abilities of airline pilots
(b) used only for information purposes
(c) used to test the system under nonbattle conditions
(d) all the above
(e) none of the above

10. ____ Which of the following questions should an interviewer avoid asking the manager of a shipping department?
(a) Do you believe the XYZ form is adequate for your use?
(b) Why is the battery information block used on form XYZ?
(c) How many men do you employ in the crating department?
(d) When are the steam buckets wrapped and bagged?
(e) What organizational changes do you plan next year?

11. ____ A systems man must thoroughly familiarize himself with the organization chart because he
(a) must know departmental responsibilities
(b) must know management responsibilities
(c) may suggest changes in the internal structure
(d) all the above
(e) none of the above

12. ____ That part of the system study in which new ideas are proposed is the _____ stage
(a) investigation
(b) hypothesis
(c) implementation
(d) all the above
(e) none of the above

13. ____ Which of the following is *not* a systems function?
(a) administration of personnel
(b) performance measurement
(c) program analysis
(d) work simplification
(e) none of the above

11-3 Problems

1. Name and describe some common business systems about which you have read or have been associated.

2. Describe and justify the importance of each of the five basic steps involved in the feasibility study.

3. As an interviewer, would you accept the following answers in an interview or continue the questioning? Why?
   (a) There is no need for the w-234 form in this department.
   (b) That operation requires 700 straphangers per week.
   (c) We have 14 midget sanders, 27 rod benders, and 3 salami slicers in our manufacturing operation.
   (d) Right now, we hand sort the XYZ form by date and enter the number of items, cost, and color for each article into form XYZ-2. Management is investigating the use of a machine sorter and I understand that we should have one next quarter.

4. Several fact-gathering techniques are used to obtain information about present and future needs. List and discuss three of these techniques.

5. The report of the study team is presented to management. List and evaluate several items that might be in this report.

6. Name and discuss the three basic stages in the development of a system.

7. Why should management be involved in the design and analysis of a system? Explain.

8. How does planning a system differ from planning a program? How is it the same?

ITEMS FOR DISCUSSION

Systems
Busines Systems
Purpose of Systems Study
Feasibility Study
Initialization
Selection of Objectives
Analysis
Resource Allocations

Conclusions
Modifying an Existing System
Developing a New System
Investigation
Hypothesis
Implementation
Pilot Study

INTRODUCTION

FORM DESIGN

PUNCHED-CARD LAYOUT
AND DESIGN

CODING OF INPUT

Block Code

Sequence Code

Faceted Code

DATA FILES

SYSTEM FLOWCHART

SYSTEM TESTING

SYSTEM DOCUMENTATION

12

SYSTEMS
CONSIDERATIONS

INTRODUCTION In this chapter we shall discuss the more important of those items which the manager and potential manager will find helpful in using and understanding his company's systems and with which the systems analyst must concern himself in designing and implementing a system. Specifically, we shall discuss form design, card layout and design, coding of input, data files, system flowcharts, system testing, and system documentation.

FORM DESIGN The analyst is often faced with the task of examining current or designing new forms and form-handling procedures. By periodically examining existing forms, unused and obsolete forms can be uncovered and subsequently modified, combined, simplified, or eliminated. Such decisions should be made in an attempt to satisfy one or more of the following general objectives:

1. The reduction of printing, recording, and distribution costs
2. The reduction or elimination of unnecessary paperwork
3. The combining and simplifying of forms and form-handling procedures

While this analysis is being conducted, verification can be made that all existing forms have been properly classified and indexed by content, type of use, and source and destination of all copies.

Each form should be specifically examined to determine, for example, whether or not it clearly indicates its purpose, commands attention, and allows space for the inclusion of the date. According to Randall and Burgly,[1] a form should also

1. Contain a specific amount and kind of information
2. Make entering the required information easy
3. Make using the data it contains easy
4. Be reproduced as economically as possible

---

[1]Clarence R. Randall and Sally W. Burgly, *Systems and Procedures for Business Data Processing.* Cincinatti: South-Western Publishing Co., 1968, pages 235–236.

5. Be designed to minimize the possibility of error
6. Be related to other forms and to other documents used for the form in question
7. Be designed as concisely and clearly as possible
8. Be related to the characteristics of the machines or the equipment on which it will be used
9. Facilitate the operation for which it is designed

More often, however, the analyst is called on by a department to design a completely new form. Before actual work can be started on the creation of the new form, the analyst must consult the concerned department to determine answers to certain basic questions. Among these one would expect to find the following questions:

1. Will this form replace any existing form(s)?
2. What necessary information will be contained on this form?
3. What source document contains this information?
4. Is this information presently available on existing machine-readable media?
5. How was this information previously gathered and reported?
6. Is it possible to modify an existing form to include the required information?

The analyst, in consultation with appropriate management personnel from the affected department, would then compile and study the answers to the above questions. Based on this analysis, a joint decision would be rendered concerning the necessity and advisability of creating a new form. Should a new form be justified, the analyst could then direct his attention to the matter of the actual design and layout of the new form. It is advisable that the analyst or form designer chosen for this task have a working knowledge of the equipment on which the form is to be used, the considerations and problems involved in the printing of forms, and the cost factors involved in the production of forms.

Forms are generally subdivided into three sections:

1. Introductory
2. Main body
3. Conclusion

INTRODUCTION   *Yes*   *No*

  1. Is the title clearly and concisely stated?   _____ _____

  2. Is the company or agency identified?   _____ _____

  3. Are general instructions reduced to the minimum?   _____ _____

  4. Is the file or reference data properly placed for the type of file to be used?   _____ _____

MAIN BODY

  1. Does the form read left to right?   _____ _____

  2. Are there writing lines?   _____ _____

  3. Are related vertical columns clearly separated?   _____ _____

  4. Can the reading lines be followed without confusion?   _____ _____

  5. Are the writing lines adequate for the load?   _____ _____

  6. Are lines to be filled in by typewriting spaced to conform to typewriter spacing?   _____ _____

  7. Is the vertical alignment on forms to be typewritten such that clerks can use the typewriter tabular-stop device?   _____ _____

  8. Does the form provide larger spaces for handwritten data than typewritten data?   _____ _____

  9. If the form is to take information from or pass information to another form, does it show items in the same order as the other?   _____ _____

10. Does the form have all recurring items printed so that only variables need to be filled in?   _____ _____

11. Have all fact-gathering data been included?   _____ _____

12. Have the data been so arranged that backtracking is unnecessary?   _____ _____

CONCLUSION

  1. Has space been provided for signature, title, and date?   _____ _____

  2. Has space been provided for approval signature, title, and date when required?   _____ _____

  3. Is the identification form number in the proper place for filing, binding, or reordering?   _____ _____

GENERAL

  1. Will the form fit window or other envelopes which may be used?   _____ _____

  2. Is the form the correct size for filing or binding?   _____ _____

  3. Is the form printed on the size and weight of paper that is most economical?   _____ _____

  4. Is a revised form sufficiently different from the older form?   _____ _____

  5. Does the form make use of color as an aid to identification, reference, and prevention of eyestrain?   _____ _____

  6. Does the form make use of combination forms and carbon copies where possible?   _____ _____

  7. Have unnecessary carbon copies been eliminated?   _____ _____

All items checked "Yes" need no further consideration. The items with a "No" require investigation and/or revision.

FIG. 12-1

Form Evaluation Checklist.

From Systems and Procedures for Business Data Processing, Clarence R. Randall and Sally W. Burgly, Cincinatti: South-Western Publishing Co., 1968, pp. 235–236.

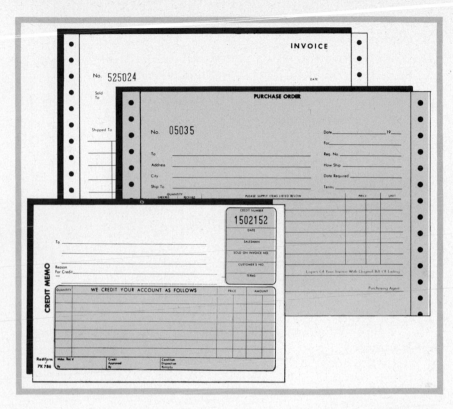

FIG. 12-2
Typical Form Designs.

The introductory material is generally placed at the top of the form and contains information concerning how the form is to be prepared as well as the name and number of the form. The main body of the form should contain the information for which the form was designed, and the conclusion of the form should provide room for the signature and title of authorizing persons, as well as providing room for the date of the authorized signing.

To make certain that no items have been overlooked in the design of the form, the analyst or form designer should have a checklist similar to the one presented in Fig. 12-1.[2] Those items which are checked with a "yes" represent items which have been satisfactorily presented or which do not apply. Those items checked with a "no" represent items which will require further analysis and/or revision.

[2]Clarence R. Randall and Sally W. Burgly, *Systems Procedures for Business Data Processing.* Cincinatti: South-Western Publishing Co., 1968, pages 235–236.

SELF-STUDY EXERCISES 12-1

1. Existing forms should be periodically _____.

   *****

   examined and unused or obsolete ones modified, combined, simplified, or eliminated

2. Objectives to be used when examining forms are _____.

   *****

   cost reduction, eliminating unnecessary paper work, reduction of form handling

3. Forms are generally subdivided into three sections: _____, _____, and _____.

   *****

   introductory
   main body
   conclusion

PUNCHED-CARD LAYOUT AND DESIGN

Punched-card design can be defined as a technique for determining where and in what form data are to be punched into the cards to be processed by a company's data-processing equipment. At first glance this would appear to be a very simple and unimportant task. However, this is not at all the case. The design of a card strongly affects the keypunching and programming operations.

One well-planned and designed card can serve as an input medium for the production of numerous reports. A poorly designed card, however, can increase the possibility of keypunching errors in its preparation, in addition to causing the creation of redundant, repetitive and inefficient programs.

The design of a card begins with the determining of what accounting, management, or statistical reports are to be prepared in part or whole from this card. Once this has been accomplished, the analyst can direct his attention to the actual data that is to be recorded on the card. A series of questions whose answers should reveal the required information concerning these data is as follows:

1. What input data are necessary for the desired report?
2. What source document contains these input data?
3. Are these input data presently available on a punched card already in use?
4. What is the source of additional data needed but not shown on the source document?
5. What information will be punched into the card to identify the source of the data?
6. What are the optimum field sizes for the required input data:
7. Which fields should be interpreted for visual identification and which do not require interpreting?
8. Is the card to be a master, detail, or a summary card?

Figure 12-3 illustrates two of the numerous forms that are available to aid the analyst with the physical design and layout of the

FIG. 12-3

Card Layout Forms.

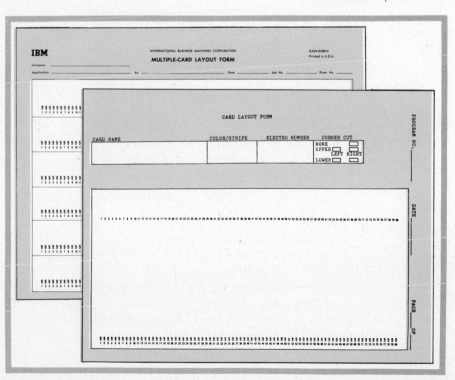

card. With these forms, and the information previously gathered, the analyst can complete the design.

SELF-STUDY EXERCISES 12-2

1. Two considerations that must be given to a card design are _____ and _____.

*****

keypunch
programming

2. _____ are used as an aid to the analyst in the physical design of cards.

*****

Card layout forms

3. Card design begins with the determining of what _____ will be prepared using this card.

*****

reports

CODING OF
INPUT

A code can be described as a system of symbols for representing data. A code provides a substitute name, in the form of a set of arbitrary characters, for the actual names or numbers.

There are several reasons input data are coded. Among the more important of these reasons are

1. *Save space on the input media.* For example, if one were to classify individuals by sex, one would have two categories— male and female. By assigning the code 1 to the category male and the code 0 to the category female, the two categories can be represented by exactly one character, as opposed to the previous possibility of four or six characters. And, the 1–0 coded categories convey exactly the same amount of information as did the original male–female categories.

2. *Processing and storage advantages.* In some computers it is easier and faster to compare and store numeric quantities

than it is alphabetic or alphanumeric quantities. In such machines, nonnumeric input data would be represented by a numeric code.

3. *File security.* By coding information contained in classified files, it affords them some degree of content security.

4. *Remote entry speed and accuracy.* In the case that data are entered via terminals, input data transmission can be speeded up with decreased errors if concise data coding is employed to represent the data with fewer coded characters. Computer output responses will also be faster for the same reason.

5. *Sorting and information retrieval* The coding of input data facilitates the sorting of the data and limited information retrieval.

Determining the actual coding system involves two basic steps. The first step is to determine the classification scheme that is to be used to discriminate between the different types of data. The second step, based on the number of classifications and possible subclassifications, is to determine the type of code that is to be employed. It then only remains to determine specifically what coding scheme will be utilized. Let us now examine each of these steps in greater detail.

A classification scheme is one in which data are systematically divided into classes or groups so that like or similar items are grouped. Depending upon the use of the data, individual group members can be further divided according to their fundamental properties or characteristics. Establishing an efficient and complete classification scheme will often form the basis for sorting and limited information retrieval.

The next step is to determine the type of code to be used. There are three general types:

1. Numeric-a code based on numbers only
2. Alphabetic-a code based on letters only
3. Alphanumeric-a code based on numbers, letters, and possibly some special characters

Block Code

The actual scheme that is chosen will depend greatly on the classification scheme. For example, suppose that we must determine a scheme for coding 63 items classified into four groups, respectively, containing 8, 11, 32, and 12 items each.

A simple two-digit decimal code could be

GROUP	CODE NUMBERS ALLOCATED	UNUSED CODE NUMBERS IN GROUP
1	01–17	9
2	18–37	9
3	38–78	9
4	79–99	9

This scheme is called a *two-digit block code* and nicely fills our immediate need, plus providing room for expansion within each group. In this scheme, the two-digit block codes are arbitrarily assigned depending on the number of items in each group and the total number of items to be represented.

Sequence Code   If, however, the 63 items had been classified into nine groups, respectively, containing 5, 6, 8, 5, 9, 7, 9, 6, and 8 items each, a possible scheme might be

GROUP	CODED NUMBERS ALLOCATED	UNUSED CODE NUMBERS IN GROUP
1	①0 – ①9	5
2	②0 – ②9	4
3	③0 – ③9	2
4	④0 – ④9	5
5	⑤0 – ⑤9	1
6	⑥0 – ⑥9	3
7	⑦0 – ⑦9	1
8	⑧0 – ⑧9	4
9	⑨0 – ⑨9	2
10	unused	10

This type of code is called a *sequence code.* In a sequence code, each digit represents a subclassification of the preceding digit.

For example, the code 84 could mean a recliner chair:

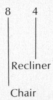

This coding scheme offers some advantages over the block code. To illustrate one such advantage, let us assume that we wish to produce a report indicating the number of chairs of each type currently in our inventory. If a sequence code such as the one described above were employed, it would only be necessary to direct the computer to select out those items whose two-digit code begins with an 8. To accomplish the same thing employing a two-digit block code, at the very least, it would be necessary to provide the computer with the code number of the first chair listed and the code number of the last chair listed and to direct it to select all items with numbers greater than or equal to the first number and less than or equal to the second number. If, however, chairs were not assigned consecutive block numbers, it would have been necessary to input to the computer the block number for each type of chair in the inventory.

Faceted Code

Other coding schemes make use of significantly placed letters and/or digits. Each letter or digit in the code represents a particular characteristic of the item. For example, CT 30 CB could be a code for Chair Type 30 with Chrome legs and a Blue seat. This type of scheme is called a *faceted code* since each component or part of the total code describes a different facet of the item it represents.

As you can see, there are many types of codes that can be used. The job of the analyst in coding input is to determine which code is most advantageous in what particular situation. His decision should attempt to satisfy, as closely as possible, each of the following conditions:

1. Code must be adaptable to automated processing.
2. Code must be as compact as possible.

3. Code must be flexible enough to allow for future additions and changes.

4. Code must allow for easy encoding and decoding.

SELF-STUDY EXERCISES 12-3

1. Analysts often make use of _____ to conserve space on a card layout as well as to reduce keypunching errors.

*****

coded data

2. Some of the more significant reasons why data are coded are
_____.

*****

save space and keypunching errors
more efficient processing and storage
security
faster input speeds from terminals
to facilitate sorting and information retrieval

3. Three codes employed in coding data are _____, _____, and _____.

*****

block code
sequence code
faceted code

DATA FILES   A *file* is a collection of related records treated as a unit. That is, a set of accessible records similar to one another in purpose, form, and content. Files can be broadly classified according to their degree of activity as *dynamic* (very active) or *reference* (relatively inactive) files.

The storage medium used for a particular file is determined by several factors.

1. Activity of the file
2. Access speeds required
3. Manner in which transactions arrive to update file
4. Volume of data in the file
5. Frequency with which records are added to or deleted from the file

If the file is an active one and is to be randomly accessed, for example, a *direct-access* medium would be appropriate.

In such a case, the file would be maintained on either magnetic disk, magnetic drum, or magnetic cards. The fastest of these is the magnetic drum, the least expensive the magnetic card, and the magnetic disk average in cost and speed with a large storage capacity.

If, on the other hand, the data input to update the file will be in sequence and arrive in batches or groups, a *sequential* medium can be used. Punched cards or magnetic tape are commonly used media for sequential files. The magnetic tape is most commonly used since it is faster, cheaper, and less bulky than the punched card for large-volume sequential files.

The manner in which the information is organized on the file is quite technical and generally within the exclusive province of the systems analyst. We shall, therefore, not discuss this further.

SELF-STUDY EXERCISES 12-4

1. A file is defined as _____.

   *****

   a collection of related records treated as a unit.

2. Files are classified according to their degree of activity as _____ or _____ files.

   *****

   dynamic
   reference

3. A very active file can also be called a _____ file.

   *****

   dynamic

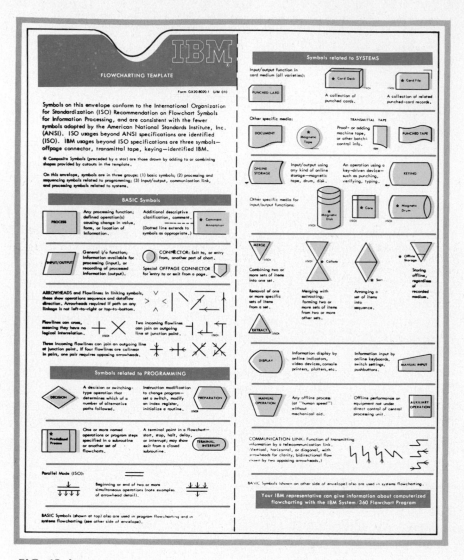

FIG. 12-4

Annotated Flowcharting Template Symbols.

4. The storage medium used for a given file is based on _____,
_____, _____, and _____.

*****

activity of the file

access speeds required

how the file update data will be received

volume of data in file

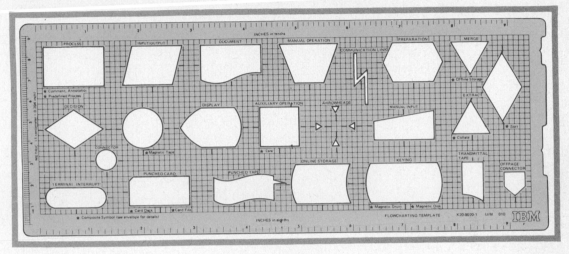

FIG. 12-5

Flowcharting Template.

5. Dynamic files generally use a _____ medium, while reference files use a _____ medium.

*****

direct-access

sequential

We have learned that a flowchart is a means of visually presenting the flow of data through an information-processing system, the operations performed in the system, and the sequence in which these operations are performed. We have discussed in detail how the program flowchart is used to describe the sequence of operations which must be performed to obtain a computerized solution to a particular problem. What we have not discussed, however, is that there is another type of flowchart—the *system flowchart*. And, as we found the program flowchart useful in understanding a computer program, we will find the system flowchart to be even more useful in understanding a computerized system.

A system flowchart pictorially describes the flow of data through all parts of a system. Figures 12-4 and 12-5 illustrate the standard system flowchart symbols together with a description of each symbol.

**SYSTEM
FLOWCHART**

Actual operations to be performed are briefly described with the major emphasis being placed on the media involved and the work stations through which they must pass. As a result, much of a systems flowchart consists of symbols depicting these documents and operations. For this reason, document and operational symbols were designed so that when used in a system flowchart, they are meaningful without comment or text. Therefore, when a note is placed within a flowcharting symbol, the flowchart takes on specific application meaning. For example, the document symbol

represents any kind of paper documents and reports, including source documents and ledgers. On the other hand, the document symbol and note

tell the reader much more. They tell him specifically what document—deduction authorization form—and the area of application—payroll system. Figure 12-6 illustrates a system flowchart describing the creation of a sequential payroll master card file from payroll master source documents. Other system flowcharts are illustrated in Figs. 12-7, 12-8, and 12-9.

SELF-STUDY EXERCISES 12-5

1. A system flowchart visually shows _____, _____, and _____.

*****

the flow of data through the system
the operations performed in the system
the sequence in which the operations are performed

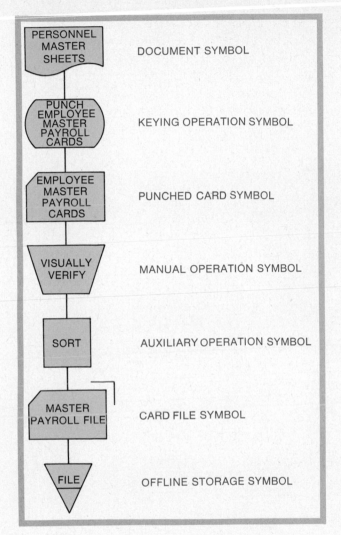

FIG. 12-6
System Flowchart for the Creation
of a Punched-card Master File.

2. Flowcharts consist of two general types: _____ and _____.
*****

program flowcharts
system flowcharts

3. Standard flowcharting symbols are used with _____.
*****

both program and system flowcharts

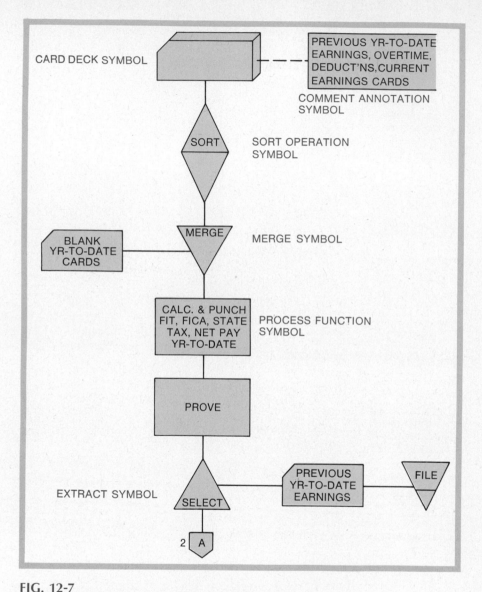

FIG. 12-7

System Flowchart for Check and Statement Run
to Be Processed on Unit-record Equipment.

4. The shape of the system flowchart symbol indicates the _____ to be performed while the _____ within the symbol conveys more specific information about that particular case.

*****

operation

note

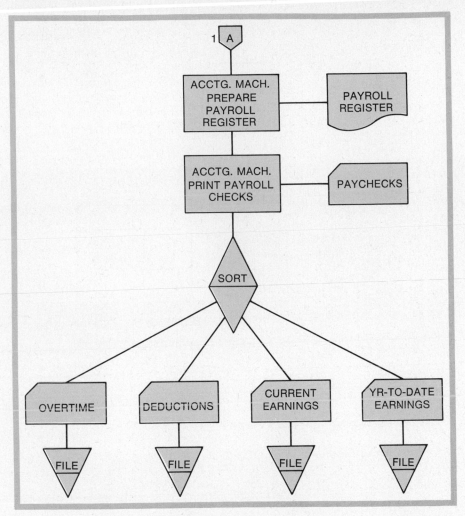

FIG. 12-7
Continued

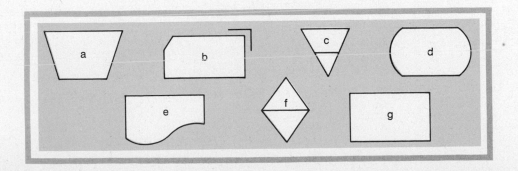

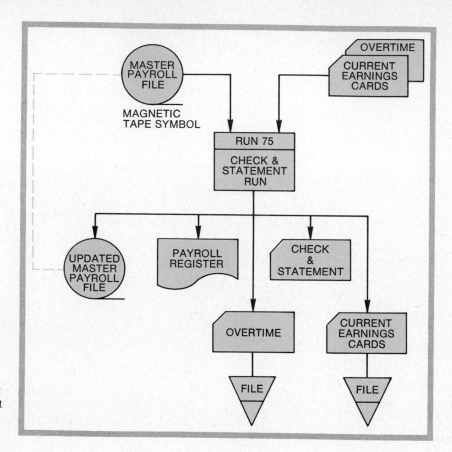

FIG. 12-8

System Flowchart for Check and Statement Run to Be Processed by Computer.

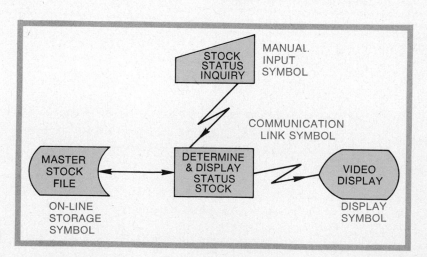

FIG. 12-9

System Flowchart for an On-line Inquiry.

5. The system flowcharting symbols shown on page 513 are used to represent _____, _____, _____, _____, _____, _____, and _____, respectively.

*****

manual operation

card file

off-line storage

keying operation

document

sort

processing function

6. Which of these symbols would be used to indicate a machine-verifying operation?

*****

symbol d

7. Which of these symbols would represent a computer program that is to be keypunched?

*****

symbol e

8. What symbol is used for comments?

*****

———— COMMENT
ANNOTATION
SYMBOL

9. The merge and extract symbols are _____ and _____.

*****

▽   △

MERGE   EXTRACT

10. The symbol and note that would represent a master payroll file is _____.

*****

11. The symbol ⟋⟍ is a _____ symbol.

*****

communications link

SYSTEM TESTING　A system must be thoroughly tested before it is placed into actual operation. The testing process involves analysts, programmers, management, auditors, and individual user departments and generally consists of three phases.

In the first phase, the lead programmer on the project must test each of the program segments separately and in combinations. Program test data and verified output should be included in the final program documentation. When all program testing and documenting has been completed, the lead programmer then forwards a complete set of fully tested and documented programs to the project analyst.

In the second phase of the system test, the analyst checks program flowcharts and decisions tables against original specifications. He will subject the programs to actual data as well as data with planted errors to verify that they will be detected should they arise in actual use. When he has thoroughly examined and reviewed the logic of each subsystem, the flow of information through the system, and the overall system, he will gather together systems test data or actual data and create special test files.

In the third and final phase, the entire system is tested utilizing actual machines and employees. The system is tested down to the most minute detail. Forms are checked, schedules are checked, operating instructions are verified, and the movement of data and results is tested. In cases where there is no existing automated system to test against, individual departments may ask or be asked to check the accuracy of the system's output manually. If a company auditor is available, he should be consulted from time to time throughout this process, as the system may be audited by noncompany data-processing auditors at a future date.

The system is now ready to be put into actual use. This, of course, requires that all files be first created and then tested before the changeover takes place.

Once the system has been implemented, it must be constantly tested and improved if it is to remain efficient and effective. A system can be thought of as a living thing, requiring that it be constantly nurtured and cared for if it is to survive and grow.

SELF-STUDY EXERCISES 12-6

1. Before a system is considered operational it must go through three phases of _____.

*****

testing

2. The first phase of testing a system deals with _____.

*****

testing the computer programs using simulated data to verify the output

3. The second phase for testing a system includes _____.

*****

the checking of program flowcharts and decision tables against original specifications and testing programs using actual data

4. The final phase of testing of a system involves _____.

*****

actual machines and employers who check its performance under operational conditions

SYSTEM DOCUMENTATION

A system cannot be completely effective unless it is adequately documented. It should be documented as it is being created. That is, at various stages or intervals in the system development, status reports should be prepared for those management personnel for whom the system is being designed. Such reports would include flowcharts, decision tables, output or report forms, and other documents thus far developed. Also included would be any problems encountered, suggested solutions, and resulting schedule revisions. In this way management is kept abreast of the system's progress so that where necessary, they can offer criticisms or suggest change while it is still economically and physically possible to make these changes without it being necessary to revise the entire system. These progress reports provide an excellent basis on which to build additional documentation.

Instructions and narrative descriptions must be prepared for every phase and part of the system, including system logic, timings, user instructions, instructions for operations personnel in the data-processing center, and instructions concerning the transmission of data and results. Much of this can be incorporated into a *procedures manual*. This manual stipulates the relationship between personnel in the application areas affected by the system and the data-processing center. It should relate, in detail, exactly what procedures must be employed by the user to operate the system efficiently and effectively.

SELF-STUDY EXERCISES 12-7

1. System documentation is necessary to _____.

     *****

   keep management abreast of current developments and to explain the workings of the system to users and other concerned individuals

2. Documentation reports would include such items as _____.

     *****

   flowcharts, decision tables, output or reports forms, etc.

3. The _____ stipulates the relationship between personnel in the applications areas affected by the system and the data-processing center.

     *****

   procedures manual

True–false exercises 12-1

1. _____ Coding of data can aid information retrieval.

2. _____ Much of the documentation for a system can be incorporated into a procedures manual.

3. _____ Each digit of the number 4731 may represent specific information in a sequence code.

4. _____ Poorly designed cards can lead to redundant, repetitive, and inefficient programs.

5. _____ Field size is not an important consideration in form design.

6. _____ Punched card and magnetic tape are commonly used media for sequential files.

7. _____ Modification of an existing form for use with the new system is generally not documented.

8. _____ Connector symbols used in system flowcharting are the only symbols in common with program flowcharting.

9. _____ Procedures manuals should relate to exactly what procedures must be employed by the user to operate the system efficiently and effectively.

10. _____ It would be poor judgment to assign someone to design a form who did not have a working knowledge of the equipment on which the form will be used.

11. _____ BR72G which stands for Book Rack, 7 shelves by 2 bays, Gray is an example of a faceted code.

12. _____ A thorough forms review should verify the source and destination of all form copies.

13. _____ Card design is a very simple and unimportant task.

14. _____ New forms should not resemble old forms so that there will be no confusion.

15. _____ Generally, a complete three-phase testing of a system involves all the personnel who were involved in its development.

16. _____ A system flowchart is a pictorial description of how data flow through a system.

17. _____ A classification scheme is one which groups data of similar or like items.

18. _____ Forms are generally subdivided into three sections: introductory, main body, and conclusion.

19. _____ Bright red is a good color for a form because it attracts attention.

20. _____ Systems analysts should never have to concern themselves with forms-handling procedures.

21. _____ Only after each subsystem has been thoroughly tested is the entire system tested.

22. _____ In designing forms, consideration need not be given to the spacing and print characteristics of a typewriter or computer printer.

23. _____ A sequence code is used to sequentially order data.

24. _____ A code must allow for future additions or changes.

25. _____ Within the symbols in a system flowchart, the operations are described in detail.

26. _____ A periodic review of all existing business forms is a good business policy.

27. _____ Documentation includes such items as flowcharts, output forms, and decision tables.

28. _____ Other information sources should be checked to make sure that the information needed from the forms is not already available.

29. _____ If a card is designed well, it is possible that it can serve as input for several reports.

30. _____ Systems documentation is prepared primarily for the systems analyst should future updating of the system prove necessary.

31. _____ Any code considered for a form must be adaptable for automated processing and be as compact as possible.

32. _____ Progress reports provide a basis on which to build additional documentation.

33. _____ When designing a form, space should always be provided for the date and the signature of the person filling out the form.

34. _____ When the analyst is called upon to design a completely new form, he must first consult the concerned department to determine the answers to certain basic questions.

35. _____ The form should always be read from left to right.

36. _____ How a form is folded and its final size are important considerations in form design.

37. _____ An example of a random-access device is the magnetic tape unit.

38. _____ The first step in coding data is to determine what type of code is to be employed.

39. _____ File security might be a consideration for coding data.

40. _____ A primary goal in the review of existing business forms is to combine or simplify the forms and their handling procedures.

41. _____ Authorizing signatures should normally be placed at the bottom of the form.

Multiple-choice exercises 12-2

1. _____ System documentation should not include
   (a) progress reports
   (b) decision tables
   (c) report forms
   (d) problems encountered
   (e) none of the above

2. _____ System testing involves
   (a) auditors
   (b) individual users
   (c) analysts
   (d) programmers
   (e) all the above

3. _____ The sequence code and the faceted code are similar in that they both
   (a) are used in the description of textiles
   (b) describe and subclassify the item being coded
   (c) have absolutely nothing to do with the coding of cards
   (d) all the above
   (e) none of the above

4. _____ Conversion of a numeric grading system into an alphabetic grading system is an example of
   (a) alphabetic coding
   (b) block coding
   (c) sequence coding
   (d) faceted coding
   (e) all the above

5. _____ A classification scheme has the purpose of
   (a) systematically dividing data into classes or groups
   (b) systematically dividing data into classes only

(c) systematically dividing data by the color of the card
(d) systematically dividing data into groups only
(e) none of the above

6. _____ A 1-0 code would be applicable on a job application form for
(a) age
(b) weight
(c) eye color
(d) marital status
(e) none of the above

7. _____ A data file is
(a) a type of file used by computer mechanics
(b) a collection of related records treated as a unit
(c) a storage medium in which all data for all programs is placed
(d) all the above
(e) none of the above

8. _____ Information needed in the main body of a form does not generally include
(a) form title
(b) company identification
(c) approval signatures
(d) all the above
(e) none of the above

9. _____ In the final stages of the design and implementation of the system, many reports and narrations are compiled for those management personnel for whom the system was designed. This is called
(a) a system report
(b) system documentation
(c) a system flowcharting report
(d) all the above
(e) none of the above

10. _____ By examining existing forms an analyst may determine that such forms
(a) are obsolete
(b) are in need of modification or simplification
(c) have been eliminated
(d) all the above
(e) none of the above

11. _____ Of the following, which storage method is most likely to be used in the payroll department of a large company?
(a) magnetic tape

(b) magnetic disk
(c) punched card
(d) magnetic card
(e) all the above

12. ____ Which of the following must be considered in the design of a
form by the analyst?
(a) minimize the possibility of error
(b) command attention
(c) be unrelated to other forms
(d) two of the above
(e) none of the above

13. ____ The systems analyst, working in conjunction with _____
would decide whether or not a new form is needed.
(a) top management
(b) middle management
(c) form manufacturers
(d) management of the affected departments
(e) users in the affected departments

14. ____ In the design of punched cards, the analyst must concern himself with
(a) using the largest field sizes possible
(b) size of the card
(c) the information that will be punched into the card to identify the source of the data
(d) all the above
(e) none of the above

15. ____ Which of the following are types of codes that are commonly
used by the analyst?
(a) classification code
(b) program code numbers
(c) analyst code numbers
(d) all the above
(e) none of the above

16. ____ The objectives of form design do not include
(a) reduced overhead
(b) reduced recording
(c) elimination of paperwork
(d) reduction of errors
(e) none of the above

17. ____ Coding of input must satisfy which of the following criteria?
(a) must be adaptable to computer operations

(b) must be as compact as possible
(c) must allow for easy encoding
(d) all the above
(e) none of the above

18. _____ In the coding of input data, which of the following is not a consideration of the analyst?
(a) saving of space on the card
(b) color of the card
(c) use of alphabetic or alphanumeric coding
(d) where the card will be used
(e) all the above

19. _____ When selecting a storage medium, which of the following should be considered?
(a) file activity
(b) amount of data
(c) how data arrive for update
(d) access speeds
(e) all the above

20. _____ Which of the following are not systems flowcharting symbols?
(1) punched card
(2) punched tape
(3) processing
(4) document
(5) keying operation
(6) input/output
    (a) (2) and (3)
    (b) (5) and (2)
    (c) (3) and (6)
    (d) all the above
    (e) none of the above

21. _____ Which of the following personnel might be involved in the testing of the system operation?
(1) analysts
(2) programmers
(3) management personnel
(4) auditors
    (a) one of the above
    (b) two of the above
    (c) three of the above
    (d) all the above
    (e) none of the above

1. List and discuss several of the questions that the designer of a form should have to answer when he has completed his study.

2. List and discuss several reasons for coding input data.

3. Discuss the similarities and differences between the systems flowchart and the program flowchart.

4. Describe what is generally happening in the following program flow-chart segments containing only flowcharting symbols.

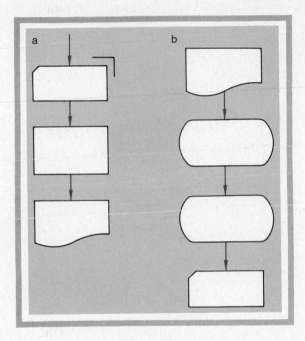

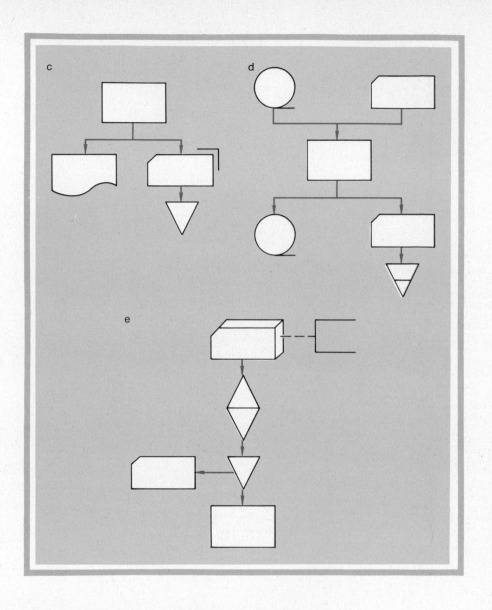

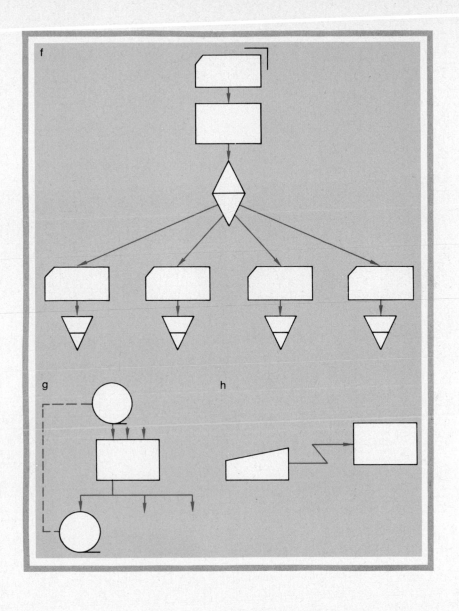

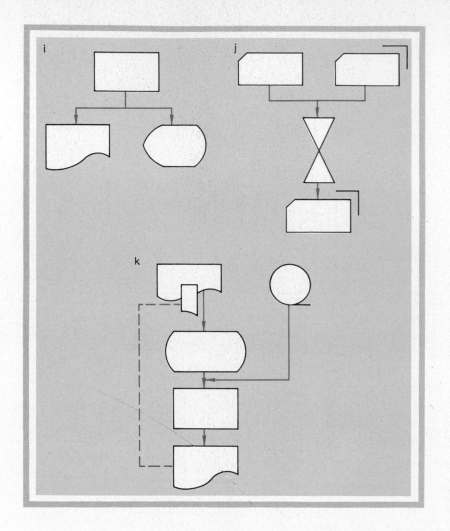

5. Justify the reasoning behind the three-phase testing of a new system.

6. What are some of the reasons for documenting a system?

7. What is a procedures manual? What does it contain?

8. Does system documentation differ from program documentation? Explain.

ITEMS FOR DISCUSSION

Form Design
Punched-card Design
Input Coding
Block Code
Sequence Code
Faceted Code
Sequential File

Direct-access File
Dynamic File
Reference File
System Flowcharting Symbols
System Testing
System Documentation

13

INFORMATION SYSTEMS

Today's business manager cannot possibly assimilate the deluge of facts and figures which confront him daily. Although he is surrounded by data, he often lacks the necessary information which he must have readily available to function effectively. He must be able to quickly and selectively retrieve relevant and essential information. Thus, businesses have turned to information systems in an attempt to provide relevant information to appropriate personnel, in appropriate form, and at the appropriate time.

An information system can be defined as the interacting of man and machine which, under man's control, gathers data and disseminates information. Such a system has as its major objective the providing of information to its user. To accomplish this, data must be evaluated, analyzed, and processed to produce meaningful and useful information on which management can base future decisions. *Unprocessed facts and figures are data, not information.* Information systems have been classified according to various criteria. They have been classified according to system response time, or the elapsed time from data input or inquiry to the output of usable information; according to the number of users or programs which can be serviced simultaneously; and according to the degree of integration of the separate data-processing systems within a company. These are some of the common means that have been used to classify inofrmation systems. Some of these classification schemes overlap, resulting in the fact that particular information systems can be included in one or more classifications. Some of the more common classifications of information systems include

1. Off-line
2. On-line
3. On-line real-time
4. Multiprogramming
5. Multiprocessing

6. Time-sharing
7. Integrated
8. Management

1. An information system can be defined as _____.
*****

   the interacting of man and machine which, under man's control, gathers data and disseminates information

2. Unprocessed facts and figures are _____, not _____.
*****

   data
   information

3. Some of the more common classifications of information systems are _____.
*****

   off-line information system
   on-line information system
   multiprogramming information system
   multiprocessing information system
   time-sharing information system
   integrated information system
   management information system

OFF-LINE INFORMATION SYSTEMS

In Chapter 4 we described an off-line operation as one in which the input/output devices or auxiliary equipment are not under the direct control of the computer. It is the use of off-line operations that characterize an off-line information system. In such a system, input data or transactions are generally collected into groups or batches and sorted into sequence before being submitted to the computer for processing. If these transactions are to be processed against a master file, they are sorted into the same sequence as the master file before processing, and subsequently processed in that order.

The fact that, in an off-line information system, input is batched and sequenced prior to processing has led to the more commonly used names *batch processing* or *sequential processing.*

Batch processing accounts for a large portion of the work performed in today's business installations. This is simply for reasons of economy. Processing a large volume of data through the computer generally results in lower processing costs per record than processing the transactions as they occur. Therefore, transactions are collected until such time as it is most convenient and economically feasible to process them. This means, of course, that there may be a time delay of minutes, hours, or even days between the time the transaction occurs and its eventual processing. For this reason, batch processing is utilized for those applications in which this delay does not reduce the usefulness of the resulting information. In instances where the batched input data is on cards, for example, special off-line conversion devices can be utilized to transcribe the data from cards to a faster and more efficient medium, such as magnetic tape, before it is processed. The results of the processing can then be output from the computer in a machine-readable form, physically removed from the computer to an off-line device, and then converted to the desired output medium.

There are, however, certain inherent disadvantages in batch processing:

1. In certain instances the time required to prepare the batched input could drastically reduce the value of the resulting information.
2. The necessity of arranging input data and master files into sequential order prior to processing is both expensive and time consuming.
3. Other computer users must often wait a substantial period of time for access to the computer if it is involved in a batch run.
4. Inquiries concerning the status of a particular account are time consuming due to the required sequential file organization.
5. Batch systems require very precise scheduling to make the most efficient use of the central processing unit.
6. Master files are only completely up to date immediately after a batch-processing run.

7. Batch processing results in peak-load requirements, result-ing at times in the necessity to operate the system around the clock to produce both special and routine reports. To eliminate such peak-load periods, many organizations have installed oversized systems to handle the peak load at costs far in excess of the overall productivity realized.

SELF-STUDY EXERCISES 13-2

1. An off-line information system is one that is characterized by _____ and _____.

*****

input/output or auxiliary equipment not under direct control of the computer

the collecting of data into groups before being submitted to the computer for processing

2. A name associated with off-line processing is _____ pro-cessing.

*****

batch or sequential

3. Batch processing _(is, is not)_ used in applications where an up-to-date master file is needed at all times.

*****

is not

4. The main advantage of off-line or batch processing is that _____.

*****

it is so economical

5. Some of the disadvantages of off-line or batch processing are _____.

*****

time loss in preparing input batches

necessity to arrange input data and master files into sequence prior to processing

locking out of other users while a batch run is in progress

inquiries are time consuming

necessity for precise scheduling of computer usage on the part of operations personnel

files are not always current peak-load requirements

ON-LINE INFORMATION SYSTEMS

An on-line information system is one in which the terminal or input/output devices are directly tied to and controlled by the central processing unit and where these devices are capable of direct two-way communications with the central processing unit. As one might imagine, such a system would necessitate reasonably fast response times to facilitate effective two-way communications between the user and the central processing unit.

In an on-line system, as data become available they can be input to the system immediately, thus simplifying the precise scheduling procedure required of an off-line or batch system.

In addition, with a capability for processing transactions almost immediately, data files can be kept up to date. This then allows for much easier processing of inquiries and guarantees more accurate inquiry responses than is generally possible with a batch system. The central processing unit, in an on-line system, is in control from the point of origin of the input without human intervention.

There are, however, also disadvantages associated with an on-line system.

1. An on-line system is usually more expensive to operate than a batch system.

2. If data arrive in large quantities, the slow operating speeds of input/output devices as compared to the processing speeds attainable by the central processing unit cause the CPU to be idling, or waiting for data to process, a great deal of the time. This can be both time consuming and expensive.

3. An on-line reporting system occupies the processing system a good deal of the available time, thus limiting its use for processing other applications.

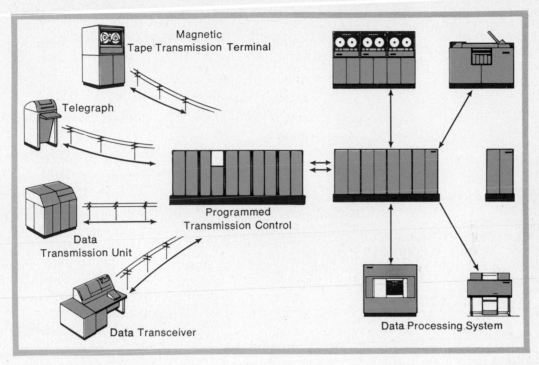

Magnetic
Tape Transmission Terminal

Telegraph

Data
Transmission Unit

Programmed
Transmission Control

Data Transceiver

Data Processing System

FIG. 13-1
On-line Computer System.

SELF-STUDY EXERCISES 13-3

1. An on-line information system is one which is characterized
by _____.

*****

input/output devices which are directly tied to and controlled
by the CPU and which are capable of two-way communications
with the CPU.

2. In an on-line information system transactions can be _____.

*****

input to the system immediately

3. Utilization of an on-line information system will generally result in more up to date _____ than possible with a _____ system.

*****

data files
batch

4. Some of the disadvantages with an on-line information system are _____.

*****

it is usually more expensive than batch processing
it generally cannot handle large quantities of input or output at any one time
it occupies the CPU a great deal of the time, thus limiting its use for processing other applications

ON-LINE REAL-TIME INFORMATION SYSTEMS

An on-line system is not always a real-time system, but a real-time system must consist of equipment with an on-line capability. To be a real-time system, the time delay between the creation of data to be processed and the actual processing of these data must be "insignificant." Whether this time delay is short enough to be insignificant is determined by the needs of the user. That is, if information reaches management in sufficient time and in an appropriated form for management to make required decisions, then we have a real-time situation.

A real-time system with the capability of providing instantaneous access to any and all data would be neither realistic nor economical since much of the data utilized in the operations of a business need only be made accessible to management periodically.

In real-time systems, time delays can range from fractions of a second when necessary to several days where allowable. For example, for a computer system in control of an atomic reactor, a real-time response might be limited to a few millionths of a second, while in looking up a purchase order in a real-time accounts payable system, a response time of 1 or 2 seconds would easily qualify as real time.

As was the case with an on-line information system, an on-line real-time information system must also be capable of effectively handling direct two-way communications between the terminal devices and the central processing unit. The response times associated with an on-line system are, however, generally significantly longer than could be tolerated in an on-line real-time system. Each user must have access to any *required* on-line data stored within the computer system and should be able to alter these data as though the computer was serving him individually and exclusively. Let us consider how an on-line real-time system might be utilized in a typical sales application. In such a system, each sales office would be equipped with terminals capable of communicating inquiries directly to the computer and capable of displaying the computer response. To place an order, the salesman would enter the pertinent information about the proposed order, via a terminal, to the computer. Within a matter of seconds, the system would respond through the terminal with complete information concerning the cost, availability, and status of the item ordered. If the item is in stock, a purchase order would be created and the sales office informed of planned shipping information. Simultaneously the system would update the inventory files and issue a reorder notice for the item if the stock on hand is below the reorder point. If the item is temporarily out of stock or has been discontinued, the sales office would be notified of this fact as well as when a new shipment is expected or what substitute item is currently available. And this entire process could be accomplished in a matter of seconds.

As in the above example, real-time systems provide for the constant and almost instantaneous updating of all files. Real-time systems, such as the one described, consist of five major components:

1. A *computer* to accept, process, and output data in the required format to the user in minimal time
2. The *software* or composite of all routines and programs necessary to operate the system
3. The *terminals* which will accept user input or inquiries and produce or display system output
4. A *communication network* to link the terminals with the computer
5. The *data base* which are large-volume randomly accessible files required for the processing of input or inquiries

Such a system is proving more and more to be essential to provide management with timely, up-to-the-minute information concerning the operations of the business.

The main disadvantage of an on-line real-time system is the tremendous expense associated with such a system. Both the hardware and software costs associated with the system exceed those associated with on-line or batch systems.

Continual improvements in hardware design are providing more efficient random-access storage devices and improved communications equipment at lower costs, thus increasing the reliability and economic feasibility of utilizing on-line real-time processing in more and more areas of application.

SELF-STUDY EXERCISES 13-4

1. In a real-time information system, the time delay between a request for information and the actual delivery of this information is considered "insignificant" if _____.
   *****

   it reaches management in sufficient time and in an appropriate form for use in making required decisions

2. A _____ is the device commonly used to enter inquiries into an on-line real-time information system.
   *****

   terminal

3. The response times associated with an on-line system are generally _____ than associated with an on-line real-time system.
   *****

   significantly longer

4. In an on-line real-time system, each user must have access to any _____ stored within the system as though _____.
   *****

   required on-line data
   the computer was serving him individually and exclusively

5. Real-time systems consist of five major components: _____, _____, _____, _____, and _____.
   *****

computer
software
terminals
communication network
data base

6. The main disadvantage of an on-line real-time information system is _____.

*****

the tremendous associated expense

Often the terms multiprogramming and multiprocessing are confused because of the similar appearance and sound of the two terms. There is, however, a substantial difference between the meaning of these two systems.

A multiprogramming system is one which has the capability of executing two or more programs concurrently utilizing one central processing unit. Hence the name multiprogramming. A multiprogramming system generally consists of one central processing unit and several input/output units. While one program is concerned with an input/output operation, the central processing unit can be performing an arithmetic or logic operation associated with another program. While one program requires a search of a disk file to locate a needed record, for example, requiring conceivably as much as a half-second, a large-scale modern computer could be performing hundreds or thousands of operations on other programs being processed concurrently. This multiprogramming capability makes it possible for the computer to juggle or "swap" several jobs back and forth within its memory and mass data-storage facilities. In so doing, the output or productivity of a computer can, literally, be multiplied by a factor of 5 or 10. The proper operation of a multiprogramming system requires a supervisory program or "supervisor," usually provided by the computer manufacturer with his hardware. One of the prime functions of this program is to determine in what order the programs will be processed as well as performing other essential control functions.

A multiprocessing system, on the other hand, is one which utilizes two or more interconnected central processing units at the same time to solve problems. In this manner, several programs can

MULTIPRO-GRAMMING/ MULTI-PROCESSING INFORMATION SYSTEMS

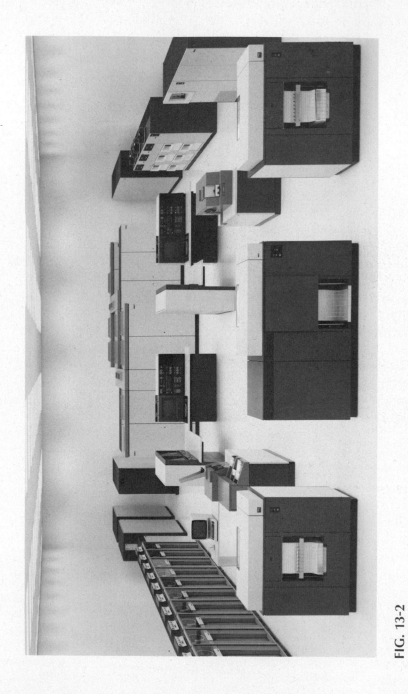

FIG. 13-2
Multiprocessing System Consisting of Two IBM 370 Model 168 Processors.

be processed independently and simultaneously. Each processor has direct access to the system core memory, and each processor can perform computations and request input or output on individual programs stored in the system core memory.

1. A _____ system has the capability of executing two or more programs concurrently utilizing one central processing unit.

*****

multiprogramming

2. A multiprogramming capability makes it possible for the computer to _____ several jobs back and forth within its memory and data storage facilities.

*****

juggle or swap

3. The proper operation of a multiprogramming system requires a _____, usually provided by the computer manufacturer.

*****

supervisory program

4. One of the prime functions of the supervisory program or "supervisor" in a multiprogramming environment is to determine _____.

*****

in what order the programs will be processed

5. A multiprogramming system can facilitate maximum usage of the _____.

*****

central processing unit

6. A _____ system makes use of two or more interconnected central processing units.

*****

multiprocessing

**TIME-SHARING
INFORMATION
SYSTEMS**

An exact definition is difficult, as there are almost as many definitions as there are operational time-sharing systems. There are, however, three basic characteristics which serve both to identify and to explain the meaning of time sharing: multiprogramming, on-line interaction, and real-time response. A time-share information system must have the capability to provide a number of users with simultaneous access to one computer, thus sharing the available computer time. In such a system it is possible to reduce *idle time*—the time that the central processing unit is available for use but is not being used—by having the computer solve more than one problem at a time.

There are two basic modes of time-shared processing:

1. Conversational mode
2. Remote batch-processing mode

To say that a computer system is operating in the conversational mode simply means that real-time man-machine communications are maintained and that the computer system is being used extensively to support and service remote terminals. In this mode, each statement or request input by the user through a terminal is immediately processed and an appropriate reply sent back to the terminal. In this mode, the user may also communicate programs via telephone lines from the terminal to the computer. For this type of application, the language called BASIC was developed. In this mode, the user may also call out previously written programs for the immediate processing of current input data.

Some of the advantages of time-shared processing in a conversational mode are

1. Immediate response to inquiries
2. Easy to learn and use remote terminals
3. Relatively low cost of operation/terminal
4. Availability of the efficient and easily used language BASIC
5. Terminal can be installed virtually anywhere

A time-sharing information system operating in the remote batch-processing mode is also concerned with the shared use of a computer by several users concurrently. Terminals used in this system are quite different from those employed by a conversational time-sharing system, usually consisting of unsophisticated input/output devices such as a card reader and printer and are often connected online to a small computer. This small computer is utilized as a remote terminal. In this manner, relatively inexpensive computers can be utilized to perform the time-consuming input/output operations while feeding a much larger, faster, and more expensive computer. That is, the larger, faster computer can concern itself principally with the processing of data fed to it by the smaller computer terminals.

The major disadvantage of such a system is, however, that telephone lines are not suitable for communicating data from a computer terminal to the central computer necessitating that such computer terminals be within a close proximity and directly wired to the main computer.

A time-sharing information system can be equally beneficial to the large corporation as to the small business. However, when contemplating a time-sharing system, a business must be certain of its operational benefits before expending the 50 to 100 per cent additional dollars that a time-shared information system could cost as compared to the cost of any of the previously mentioned information systems.

In the large corporation, such a system could provide for remote terminals in the office of all decision-making management personnel. From a terminal located hundreds or thousands of miles from the computer, a corporate executive could analyze a previously constructed corporate model concerning possible courses of action in a given situation. In a matter of moments he would receive his response, in the form of displays on a cathode-ray tube (similar in appearance to a commercial television set), or in printed form, containing detailed information concerning available alternatives. Armed with this information, the executive would be able to weigh the consequences of each alternative and select the most desirable course of action.

Equally important, however, is the fact that this entire process could have taken place without interrupting, in any way, the operations of numerous possible other corporate terminal users accessing the same computer and without an awareness on the part of any one user that he is not the only user of the computer.

Today many small business concerns are turning to service bureaus to buy time in a time-shared system. In this way the small user would have storage space made available to him in a centrally stored computer data bank or data base. When operating his terminal he would be totally unaware if he was the only user at that time or if there were 20 or 50 other users using the system at the same time. He would, however, have the computing power of a very large and expensive system available to him at only a fraction

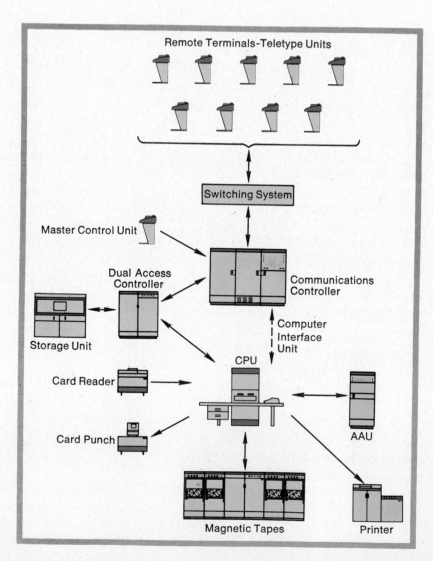

FIG. 13-3

A Typical Time-sharing System Configuration.

of the cost of maintaining the system since he is sharing both the use and expense of the system with the other users.

Time-shared systems, although individually quite different in complexity, cost, and capabilities, possess certain common features:

1. Simultaneous operation—A time-sharing system must be capable of supporting many on-line terminals simultaneously.

2. Rapid response times—A time-sharing system must have response times which do not exceed several seconds. Response time includes the time required to transmit the inquiry from the terminal to the computer, processing time at the computer, the time required to locate and make ready for use any file records or data needed to answer the inquiry, and the time required to transmit the information back to the terminal.

3. Independent operations—A time-sharing system must provide the capability for each terminal to operate independently of every other terminal. System facilities must be capable of being used by any one user or shared with other users.

4. Flexibility—A time-sharing system should be flexible enough to handle, separately and simultaneously, a wide variety of applications ranging from the handling of on-line inquiries to off-line processing.

5. Security controls—A time-sharing system must provide some degree of internal control to protect one user's programs and data from being accessed, used, changed, or destroyed by any unauthorized user.

SELF-STUDY EXERCISES 13-6

1. The three basic characteristics of a time-sharing information system are _____, _____, and _____.

$$*****$$

multiprogramming
on-line interaction
real-time response

2. _____ and _____ are the two basic modes of time-shared processing.

*****

conversational
remote batch processing

3. Time-shared information systems generally employ _____ as a means of communication between remote terminals and the central processing unit.

*****

telephone lines

4. The language _____ was designed for use with time-sharing systems.

*****

BASIC

5. A _____ system often utilizes a small computer as a remote terminal, thus freeing the main computer to concern itself with _____.

*****

remote batch processing
the processing of data fed to it by the smaller computer terminal

6. A major advantage that time-sharing information systems offer to the small business is _____.

*****

the capability of a large-scale computer at a cost which is reasonable to the small user

7. Common features of time-sharing systems are _____.

*****

simultaneous operation of many terminals
rapid response times
independent operation of terminals
flexibility
security controls

An integrated information system is one in which separate but related systems within a business are functionally united through the use of common data. These data are recorded only once, generally at their source of origin, and are utilized directly by the processing systems in existing departments within the business. This minimizes the need to convert these data into different coded forms and minimizes the need to record or copy these data onto different media, thus avoiding duplication of files.

INTEGRATED INFORMATION SYSTEMS

Input recording devices used in an integrated information system include punched paper tape, magnetic tape, and transaction and point-of-sale recorders.

Among the advantages of an integrated information system are

1. All departments within the business having access to the most up-to-date records
2. Reductions in the expense, time, and effort otherwise expended in duplicating input records
3. Increased overall speeds of processing transactions, updating files, and so on
4. Reduction in the amount of manual data handling required

SELF-STUDY EXERCISES 13-7

1. An integrated information system is one in which separate but related systems are functionally united through _____.
    *****

    the use of common data

2. The use of common data minimizes the need to _____, thus avoiding duplication of files.
    *****

    copy or record data onto different media

3. Advantages of integrated information system are _____.
    *****

    common access to up-to-date files
    reductions in cost, time, and effort of duplicating records

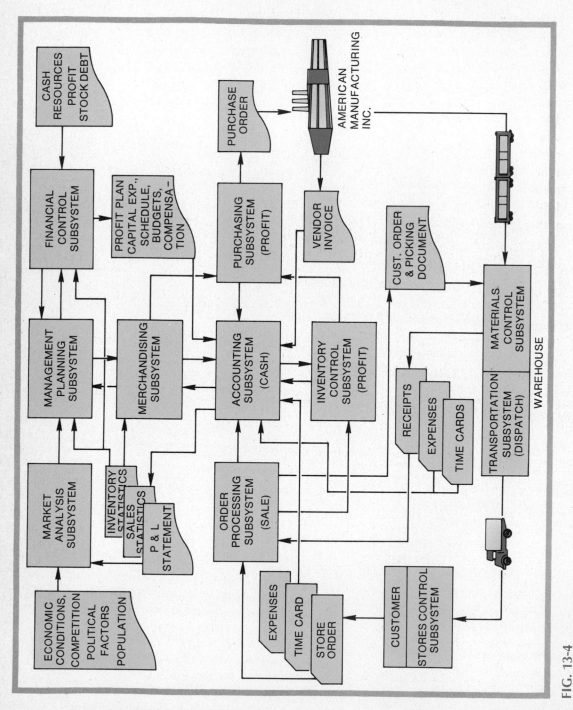

FIG. 13-4

Integrated Information and Control System for the Distribution Industry.

increased overall processing speeds
reduced manual data handling

There is little agreement concerning what a total or management information system (MIS) is supposed to be. It is, however, possible to define a management information system in terms of what it should accomplish. In this context, a management information system can be described as an information system that can provide all levels of management with information essential to the running of the business. This information must be as relevant, timely, accurate, complete, and concise as is economically feasible. More specifically, a management information system should accomplish the following:

MANAGEMENT INFORMATION SYSTEMS

1. A data base which is constantly kept current and accessible. This would necessitate the accurate updating of any and all conceivable files or data banks affected by any transaction occurring anywhere in the company and within an acceptable time span. Transaction data can be input either through an on-site input unit or through a remote data-collection station.
2. Automatic issuance of periodic information and reports in sufficient detail so as to allow management to take appropriate action.
3. Capability of producing special reports on demand.
4. Capability of accepting and answering real-time inquiries for information in greater scope or depth than issued in periodic reports. Such inquiry responses would incorporate any transactions which might have occurred since the last periodic report.
5. An efficient output communication network capable of disseminating management commands and decisions to appropriate output stations.
6. A self-checking feature to indicate a system failure or breakdown.
7. A built-in warning system to immediately inform the appropriate level of management of any out-of-line situations as they occur. This is often called *exception reporting*. In exception reporting, the computer reports only those situations when the actual results obtained differ from the management projected results.

8. Automatic comparison of transaction results with predetermined criteria and the automatic issuance of corresponding action instructions as per predefined policy limits. Such action instructions might include, for example, an instruction to order certain items of stock depleted by a transaction, or an instruction to inform a particular customer that he has exceeded his credit limit.

Today, for most businesses, such a system is a management dream but not a reality. There are very few such systems actually in operation, although more and more are being implemented. By today's standards, this is the ultimate in automated information systems and as costs decrease and the understanding of such a system by management increases, it is not unreasonable to assume that the number of organizations implementing management information systems will increase greatly.

SELF-STUDY EXERCISES 13-8

1. A management information system can be generally described as _____.

*****

an information system that can provide all levels of management with information essential to the running of the business

2. A management information system should maintain a data base which is _____ and _____.

*****

current
accessible

3. Essential requirements of a management information system are _____.

*****

a data base which is always current and accessible
automatic issuance of periodic information and reports
capability of producing special reports on demand

real-time inquiry capability

efficient output communications network

a system self-checking feature

a built-in warning system to inform management of any un-expected occurrences

capability to issue routine instructions based on predefined conditions

4. Exception reporting is _____ .

*****

where the system is designed to report any conditions which oc-cur and are exceptions or out of line from what was anticipated

EXERCISES

True–false exercises   13-1

1. _____ The magnetic-tape storage medium is often used when batched processing.

2. _____ An advantage of off-line or batch processing is that inquiries are not time-consuming.

3. _____ Because of their increased costs, the time-sharing systems are generally limited to large companies.

4. _____ Management information systems generally are used only by top management.

5. _____ Batch processing is simply another name for an off-line infor-mation system.

6. _____ The major advantage of an integrated information system is that it provides for greatly reduced data handling.

7. _____ An off-line information system would be suitable for a medium-sized insurance company.

8. _____ On-line information systems support two-way communication between the user and the CPU.

9. _____ Facts and figures which have not been processed are infor-mation.

10. _____ With the use of a batch system, precise scheduling is no longer needed to use the CPU efficiently.

11. _____ Time-sharing users could possibly pirate information from competitors in the same system unless proper security precautions were taken.

12. _____ Today management information systems are commonly found in use in the field.

13. _____ A large department store which inventories, reorders, adjusts sales commissions, computes tax, etc. from a data bank being updated by sales information is using an integrated information system.

14. _____ The major portion of today's computerized business operations use batch processing information systems.

15. _____ In an off-line information system, input data are collected into groups or batches and sequenced before they are submitted for processing.

16. _____ For many purposes, a time-sharing system could be considered to be operating in real time.

17. _____ Communications in a conversational mode take place only over telephone lines.

18. _____ Computer control of a space mission must operate in a real-time mode.

19. _____ Multiprocessing systems require two or more central processing units with each having direct access to the systems' memory.

20. _____ In an on-line information system, transactions can be input to the system immediately.

21. _____ A major disadvantage of a remote batch time-sharing system is that telephone lines are generally not suitable for communicating data from the terminal to the central computer over great distances at high speed.

22. _____ A globular conglomerate corporation would be the ideal customer for a management information system.

23. _____ Information delays of several days are not uncommon in batch or sequential processing.

24. _____ There is only one basic mode for time-shared systems: conversational mode.

25. _____ Time delays in a real-time system may be as long as several days.

26. _____ A warning system that indicates when actual results differ from projected management results is called exception reporting.

27. _____ Terminals used with a time-sharing system operating in the batch mode require an additional computer near the terminal.

28. _____ A real-time system provides for the constant and almost instantaneous updating of all files.

29. _____ The terminals employed in a time-shared system operating in the remote-batch mode are the same as those employed in a conversational mode.

30. _____ In response to an inquiry for the current price of IBM stock, the price is displayed at the stockbroker's desk in up to 3 seconds. This would not be considered a real-time system.

31. _____ A time-sharing system would be suitable in a large hotel chain for handling reservations originating in many distant cities.

32. _____ A time-sharing information system generally costs 50 to 100 per cent more than any of the other types of information systems.

33. _____ A time-shared information system allows many users to simultaneously access one computer.

34. _____ Programs run on an on-line system occupy the system most of the time, thus limiting its use for processing other applications.

35. _____ In a multiprogramming environment, a computer is able to juggle or swap several jobs back and forth between its memory and secondary storage facility.

36. _____ An airline ticket agency would find the on-line information system useful for booking flights.

37. _____ Conversational mode simply means that the computer is being used extensively to support and service remote terminals.

38. _____ Management information systems are not capable of making minor management decisions.

39. _____ Both management information systems and integrated information systems require an extensive data base.

40. _____ A management information system should be able to supply all levels of management with information essential to the running of the business.

41. _____ Time-sharing and multiprocessing are similar with respect to user access to the system memory.

42. _____ The real-time capability of on-line operations is slightly more expensive than batch processing.

43. _____ A major advantage of on-line processing is that it is more economical than batch processing.

44. _____ Batch processing necessitates immediate input of data, not just when it is economically feasible.

45. _____ The time required to prepare data for batched input can drastically reduce the value of the resulting information.

46. _____ Batch processing facilitates quick access to desired records.

47. _____ The terms multiprogramming and multiprocessing are synonymous.

48. _____ In a multiprogramming information system, the user may execute two or more programs concurrently on one CPU.

49. _____ Many small business concerns are turning to implementing their own systems rather than buying time from service bureaus.

50. _____ The virtually immediate response to inquiries is one advantage of a time-shared information processing system.

51. _____ A multiprogramming system uses only one CPU.

52. _____ Terminals for use with a time-sharing system must be installed near the CPU.

53. _____ Time-shared systems offer certain common features such as simultaneous operation and rapid response time.

54. _____ Multiprogramming efficiency is dependent on the supervisory program.

13-2 Multiple-choice exercises

1. _____ Information systems are classified according to which of the following?
   (a) system response time
   (b) the number of users which can be serviced simultaneously
   (c) the degree of integration of separate data-processing systems within a company
   (d) all the above
   (e) none of the above

2. _____ In a management information system, information must be as
   (a) relevant as possible

(b) accurate as possible

(c) complete as possible

(d) all the above

(e) none of the above

3. ____ The information system best suited for small, active businesses with a large inventory would be

(a) off-line

(b) on-line

(c) on-line real-time

(d) time-sharing

(e) none of the above

4. ____ The ability to swap or juggle several jobs within the mass data-storage facilities and memory is a feature of

(a) multiplexing

(b) multiprogramming

(c) multiprocessing

(d) all the above

(e) none of the above

5. ____ A disadvantage of an on-line information system is

(a) it is more expensive than a batch system

(b) large quantities of data can cause expensive and time-consuming delays

(c) it limits the use of the processing system for processing of other applications

(d) all the above

(e) none of the above

6. ____ Time-sharing can be economically justifiable for

(a) large businesses with several locations across the country

(b) large businesses located in one city only

(c) small businesses with large computer needs

(d) all the above

(e) (a) and (b) only

7. ____ In the conversational mode, each statement or request for input by the user is

(a) held in a buffer until all statements in the program are entered

(b) immediately processed and an appropriate reply sent back to the terminal

(c) held until the user decides to execute it

(d) batching data

(e) none of the above

8. ____ In a multiprogramming system it is possible to reduce idle time by
   (a) shutting off the computer between jobs
   (b) having the computer solve more than one problem concurrently
   (c) there is no way of reducing idle time
   (d) batching data
   (e) none of the above

9. ____ A time-sharing system has major features in common with
   (a) off-line systems
   (b) on-line systems
   (c) multiprocessing systems
   (d) multiprogramming systems
   (e) none of the above

10. ____ An information system requiring immediate responses to inquiries must have
    (a) instantaneous access to the control unit
    (b) real-time capabilities
    (c) continuous access to the CPU
    (d) all the above
    (e) (b) and (c) only

11. ____ Real-time systems consist of _____ major components.
    (a) 1
    (b) 2
    (c) 3
    (d) 4
    (e) 5

12. ____ Off-line real-time systems are
    (a) the least expensive systems available
    (b) not practical
    (c) not possible
    (d) suitable for near instantaneous results
    (e) none of the above

13. ____ A real-time system must consist of
    (a) equipment with an on-line capability
    (b) equipment specifically designed for the applications involved
    (c) equipment with off-line capabilities
    (d) all the above
    (e) none of the above

14. ____ Time-sharing is a more expensive operation than
    (a) on-line
    (b) on-line real-time
    (c) off-line
    (d) all the above
    (e) none of the above

15. ____ A system which has the capability of executing two or more
    programs concurrently utilizing one central processing unit is
    a _____ system.
    (a) multiprocessing
    (b) multiprogramming
    (c) off-line
    (d) two of the above
    (e) none of the above

16. ____ A system in which I/O devices and auxiliary equipment are not
    under the direct control of the computer are classified as
    (a) batched-process systems
    (b) sequential-process systems
    (c) off-line systems
    (d) continuous-process systems
    (e) none of the above

17. ____ A name synonymous with off-line processing is
    (a) batch processing
    (b) random processing
    (c) sequential processing
    (d) (a) and (c)
    (e) none of the above

18. ____ Round-the-clock operation is sometimes necessary during
    peak loads which are prevalent in
    (a) off-line systems
    (b) on-line systems
    (c) time-sharing systems
    (d) all the above
    (e) none of the above

19. ____ Which of the following is not one of the common features of
    time-shared systems?
    (a) multiprocessing capability
    (b) flexibility
    (c) rapid response time
    (d) security controls
    (e) none of the above

20. _____ Time spent by the CPU's waiting to process data
   (a) is called waiting time
   (b) no longer exists with modern computer systems
   (c) is not charged to the user
   (d) is called idle time
   (e) none of the above

21. _____ One advantage to using a time-shared system in the conversational mode is
   (a) the immediate response to inquiries
   (b) the terminals can be installed virtually anywhere
   (c) relatively inexpensive cost of operating terminals
   (d) all the above
   (e) none of the above

22. _____ A requirement of an integrated information system is
   (a) a large, common data base
   (b) separate but related systems
   (c) common type input/output devices
   (d) all the above
   (e) (a) and (b) only

23. _____ One major disadvantage of a time-shared system is that
   (a) the cost of peripheral equipment is very high
   (b) the lack of an efficient programming language
   (c) slow response to inquiries
   (d) all the above
   (e) none of the above

24. _____ BASIC is a computer language developed for
   (a) on-line systems
   (b) on-line real-time systems
   (c) time-sharing systems
   (d) multiprogramming systems
   (e) none of the above

13-3 Problems

1. Discuss several of the more common classifications of information systems.

2. List and discuss the major differences between an off-line information system and an on-line information system

3. What is meant by a real-time system?

4. What are the advantages and disadvantages of a real-time system?

5. Discuss the following statement: "An on-line information system is not always a real-time information system, but a real-time information system must consist of equipment with an on-line capability."

6. Define and discuss the terms "multiprogramming" and "multiprocessing." Indicate their similarities and differences.

7. What are the characteristics of a timed-shared information system?

8. What do you think are the main reasons for the rapid growth of time-sharing information systems?

9. Compare time-sharing in a conversation mode with time-sharing in a remote batch mode.

10. Describe the characteristics of a management information system.

11. Discuss the relationship between an integrated information system and a management information system.

12. Why do you think there are so few currently operational management information systems?

13. Give examples from your own experience of uses for each of the information systems discussed in this chapter.

ITEMS FOR DISCUSSION

Information System
Facts vs Information
Off-line
Batch or Sequential
On-line
On-line Real-time
Software
Terminal
Communications Network

Data Base
Multiprogramming
Multiprocessing
Time-sharing
Conversational Mode
Remote Batch-processing Mode
Integrated Information System
Management Information
System

14

BUSINESS SYSTEMS

When computers were first introduced on the business scene in the early 1950s, they served as a replacement for the tabulating machine and were therefore programmed to perform repetitive and routine calculations. As the advantages and versatility of the computer became more apparent to management, the areas of computer applications were expanded from the performing of simple computations to the handling of business accounting functions, until today the computer has become an integral part of every phase of the operations of a business, a *total-systems concept*. Previously separate and autonomous functions of the business entity, such as payroll and inventory, have been combined into and work harmoniously together as, a total system. One could say that the business organization is one large all-encompassing total system. This large or total system, then, is a composite of many smaller and interrelated systems. Each system is responsible for carrying out a major accounting function within the business enterprise, in addition to working in concert with other systems to function as a total system. This concept is illustrated in Fig. 14-1. Upon examining the individual systems which comprise the total system, you will discover that they represent the major accounting functions required to control the operations of a business no matter how large or small that business might be. In view of the importance of these systems to the overall operations of the business entity, it should be quite clear that a basic knowledge of the purpose and objectives of each system is essential to any individual intending to enter the business world as an accountant, business manager, or in any other position of responsibility. Therefore, in the next section we shall discuss three of these systems: accounts payable, accounts receivable, and payroll.

FUNDAMENTAL ACCOUNTING SYSTEMS

We can see from Fig. 14-1 that the five basic systems within a business entity are

1. Payroll
2. Accounts payable

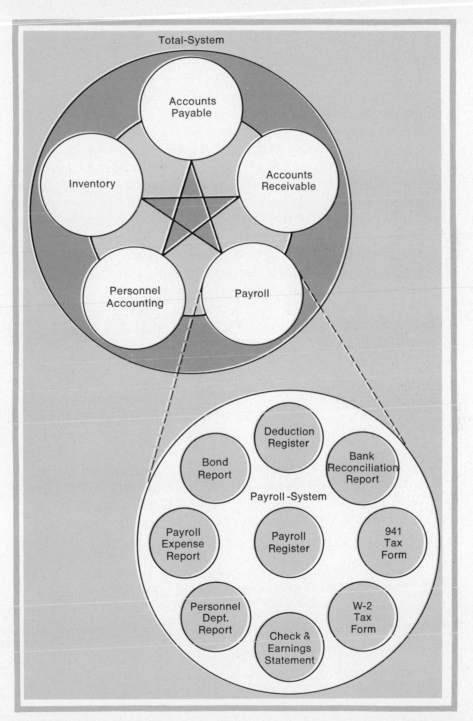

FIG. 14-1

A Total Business System and Its Major Sub-Systems.

3. Accounts receivable

4. Inventory

5. Personnel accounting

We shall now review the output and procedures inherent in an accounts payable, accounts receivable, and a payroll system. The systems which we shall discuss are somewhat simplified, less sophisticated and more card oriented than those presently in use in many business organizations. In using this simplified approach, however, the components and functions commonly found in such systems will be illustrated in a clearer and more easily understood manner. To this end, the detailed documentation that would normally be required as an integral part of the design and programming of these systems has also been omitted. However, to tie together and more clearly illustrate previously discussed concepts and procedures, some of the documentation associated with the development of the Deduction Register in a payroll system has been provided in the Appendix at the end of this chapter. It is suggested that this material be reviewed following the discussion of the Deduction Register presented in this chapter.

SELF-STUDY EXERCISES 14-1

1. The term *total system* as it applies to a business organization is _____.

*****

a composite of many smaller and interrelated systems

2. The individual systems within a total system comprise _____.

*****

the major accounting functions required to control the operations of a business

3. The five basic systems within a total system are _____, _____, _____, _____, and _____.

*****

accounts receivable
accounts payable
payroll
inventory
personnel accounting

Today, organizations of all sizes employ the paycheck as the means **PAYROLL** of remunerating their employees for services rendered. The pro- **SYSTEM** duction of the paycheck and associated reports might seem like a simple task, but in practice it is as involved as any of the other business systems.

Employees have bills to pay and depend on receiving their checks on time and for the correct amount. Considerations must also be made in such a system for special cases such as advanced payment of salaries for employees going on trips or vacations and for corrections of any error which might occur anywhere in the process. In addition, careful consideration should be given to what should be done in the event that the computer should fail before or during the preparation of employee checks. In many companies consideration must also be given to a second or executive payroll run. Since check forms usually contain a statement limiting the amount to which the check can be drawn, special check forms must be used for the larger executive salaries. And, the job of preparing the payroll for an organization becomes increasingly more difficult as the number of persons employed increases.

Therefore, it should be apparent that a payroll system is far from a trivial system, but is a complex one.

The advantages of an automated payroll system are

1. Expensive and time-consuming clerical operations previously required to obtain reports such as the payroll and expense reports can now be drastically reduced, if not eliminated entirely.
2. Present manually produced accounting and analytical reports can now be produced in far greater detail and as a by-product of the payroll preparation.
3. Federal and state reports can now be routinely produced by the computer, eliminating the peak workloads normally associated with their preparation.
4. Departmental payroll expense reports and comparisons of the expended amounts with budget amounts can be

prepared easily and with sufficient dispatch to render them useful.

5. Payroll expense summary reports as well as current period and year-to-date employee earning comparisons can be easily prepared as scheduled, providing management with up-to-the-minute data concerning the company's payroll expenses.

Let us now examine, in detail, the specific objectives of a payroll system and how these objectives can be satisfied.

Objectives   The general objective of a payroll system is to perform certain required accounting functions and to produce associated reports. To accomplish this general objective, the following specific objectives must be reached.

1. Preparation of the payroll audit
2. Preparation of the payroll register
3. Preparation of the check and earnings statement
4. Preparation of the bank reconciliation report
5. Preparation of the deduction registers
6. Preparation of the tax reports
7. Preparation of the management reports

To prepare the reports and maintain the records stated above, one must determine the original documents and files from which required information can be secured. This required information would include such items as

1. Employee name
2. Employee number
3. Employee position, description, and code
4. Social Security number
5. Department/service assigned
6. Authorized deductions and amounts
7. Regular hours worked and rate
8. Overtime hours worked and rate
9. Expense account number charged

Much of this information, if not all, is available from one or more of the following sources:

1. Payroll master file
2. Weekly attendance time cards
3. Earnings file
4. Deduction authorizations
5. Reconciliation file

All pertinent information about each employee is contained on this tape. In many companies the payroll master file is used in their payroll systems and also used in their personnel accounting system, since much of the information contained in this file is required by each of the systems. This file generally contains employee information such as

Payroll Master File

Branch store where employed	Date of Birth
Department	Sex
Employee number	Marital status
Employee name	Actual dependents
Employee home address	Education
Salary code	Military service or status
Base salary	Physical condition code
Scheduled hours	Date employed
City withholding	Special skills codes
State withholding	Dependents declared for tax purposes
Federal withholding	FICA deduction
Accumulated sick days	Accumulated federal withholding
Accumulated vacation days	Accumulated state withholding
Accumulated earnings	Accumulated city withholding
Hourly rate	Disability deduction
Accumulated FICA	Medical deduction
Bond deduction	Credit union deduction
Bond denomination	Union dues deduction
Bond balance	Quarterly gross

Depending upon the company, the payroll master file may be significantly more or less detailed than the one illustrated.

This file is utilized for the preparation of almost every report associated with a payroll system and must therefore be updated weekly if not more often.

Weekly Attendance Time Card

Attendance and time records are the basis of payroll computations in any payroll system. The maintenance of these records is a requirement imposed on a business by the Federal Fair Labor Standards Act.

The source of data for these records is the weekly attendance time card. This card can be the type illustrated in Fig. 14-2 or any of several other types used by business concerns. Regardless of the type of card used, the following basic information will be contained on the card:

1. Employee number
2. Employee name
3. Hours worked

Exception attendance time cards are also prepared for employers who worked other than standard hours or shifts.

Earnings File

This file contains the information about an employee necessary for the printing of his paycheck and statement. It also contains data necessary for the reconciling of outstanding checks. This file is created from the payroll master file and weekly attendance time cards.

Deduction Authorizations

Deduction authorization forms similar to that given in Fig. 14-3 are used by an organization to determine the voluntary deduction an employee desires made. A separate deduction card must be keypunched for each employee-authorized deduction. These deduction cards are then used to update the payroll master file.

Bank Reconciliation File

This file consists of information relative to unreconciled checks. It is processed with the earnings file to reconcile returned checks. Information concerning any unreconciled check for a given pay period is taken from the earnings file for that pay period and is used to update the bank reconciliation file.

Payroll Audit Register

At the end of each week, the employee attendance time cards and exception attendance time cards are input to the computer together with control cards prepunched with departmental budget controls for employee position code counts and hours. Unusual conditions such as missing attendance records or over-budget conditions are

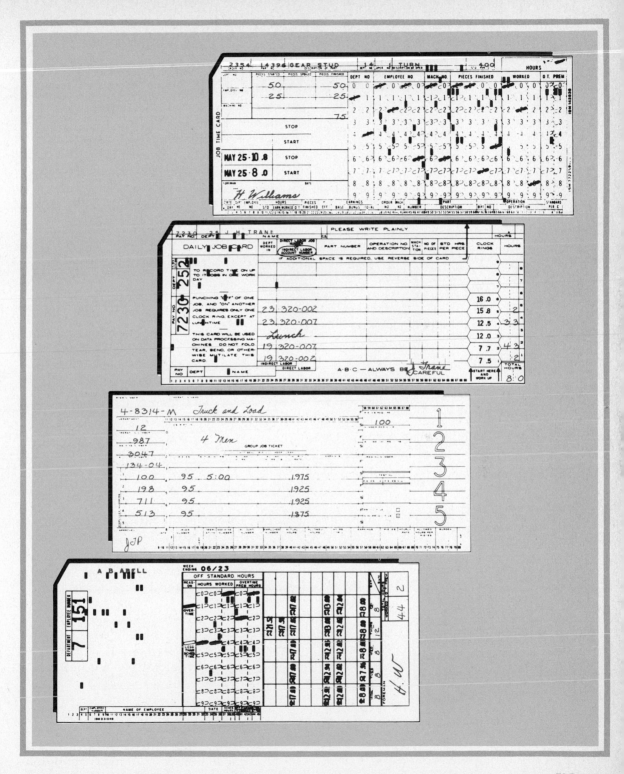

FIG. 14-2
Sample Time Cards.

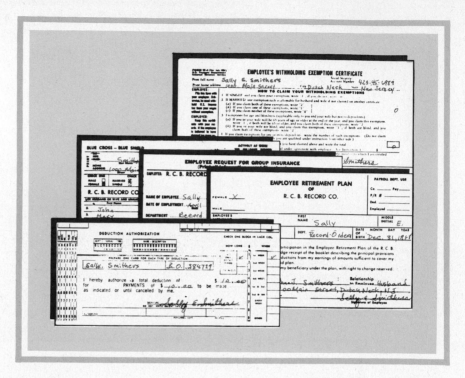

FIG. 14-3
Sample Deduction Authorization Forms.

FIG. 14-4
Payroll Audit Register Showing an Error.

printed out. When management approval is given, the remainder of the payroll procedures can commence.

The payroll register is a report which shows in detail the earnings **Payroll Register** and deductions of all employees. It is produced from the earnings file. Control totals are produced for verification of payroll calculations and payroll account cash requirements.

When the payroll register has been proved, the check and earnings statement can be run.

FIG. 14-5
Flowchart of Payroll Audit Run.

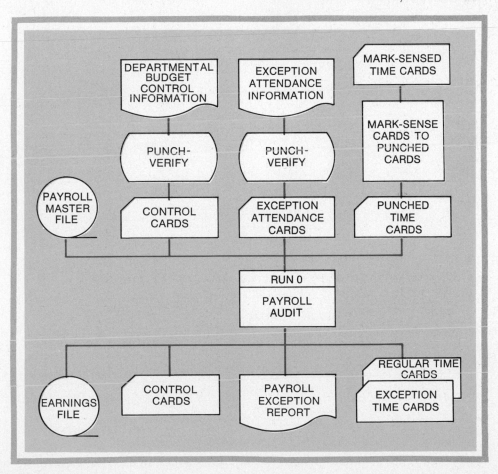

PAYROLL REGISTER

SOCIAL SECURITY NUMBER	T.C.	YEAR TO DATE GROSS EARNINGS	WITHHOLDING TAX	DEPT.	EMPLOYEE	EMPLOYEE NAME	HRLY RATE	HOURS WORKED	OVERTIME PREMIUM	GROSS EARNINGS	FEDERAL	S.U.I.	F.I.C.A.	MISC.	NET PAY
126191438	2	962 13	249 84	1	206	W P ABRAMSON	1 375	44 00	2 00	62 25	1 55	63	3 11	10 17	42 79
126111150	1	115 43	198 73	1	241	F A BATCH	1 500	40 00		60 00		1 60	3 00	3 23	47 07
117153619	2	810 45	175 02	1	253	A S BAKER	1 750	30 00		52 50	1 05	2 62		3 50	45 87
271102140	3	167 42	200 16	1	276	J G FOSTER	1 500	40 00		60 00	4 20	47	3 00	3 50	48 83
126161782	2	406 75	250 44	1	342	F R WILLIAMS	2 000	40 00		80 00	2 10	76	4 00	9 83	57 31
126301575	4	096 86	62 93	1	368	L A BRETT	1 500	40 00		60 00	2 08	63	3 11	8 43	41 75
130152361	3	224 17	319 15	1	379	A F CRASP	1 400	44 00	2 00	64 40	7 12	48	3 22	8 95	43 43
117111887	2	617 31	207 52	1	581	L F SMITH	1 750	40 00	2 00	70 00	5 14	72	3 11	4 17	56 21
126212865	2	581 15	268 22	1	587	S T HAMILTON	1 500	40 00		60 00	6 08	63	3 11	4 17	46 01
126361167	1	619 43	206 53	1	592	F A DAVEN	1 375	44 00	2 00	62 25	4 14	65	7 12	71 95	44 38
126143920	3	344 72	172 36	1	612	S M BILLINGSLY	2 375	40 00		95 00	2 12	95	4 75	11 15	63 03
114280841	4	873 33		1	613	W H FURY	4 000	40 00						91 75	124 53
139202220	4	633 16	342 17	1	1362	D F PATTERSON	4 250	40 00		170 00			8 50	14 85	126 34
124179620	1	203 10	60 16	1	1428	J L GRESHAM	1 500	40 00		60 00	6 08	60	3 00	4 75	45 57
132152612	2	620 40	190 10	1	1542	B A ENGLES	3 375	40 00		135 00		4 07	4 75	12 75	103 95
		342 875 48	62 875 41					4 372 00	48 00	12 842 95	825 42	34 45	542 15	723 18	10 567 75

FIG. 14-6

Typical Payroll Register.

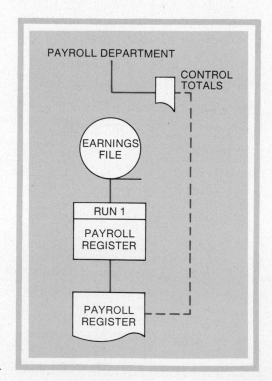

FIG. 14-7

Flowchart of Payroll Register Run.

Checks and earnings statements are produced from the earnings file after the payroll register has been verified. The forms used are preprinted and perforated vertically down the center. One side is the payroll check, the other the earnings statement. As the checks and earnings statements are printed, a reconciliation file is also created and the check numbers are added to the earnings file.

Check and Earnings Statement

As the employee card checks are returned from the bank, they are sorted into check number sequence and matched against the reconciliation file. Outstanding checks are listed on the bank reconciliation report together with the totals of the matched and unmatched checks.

Bank Reconciliation Report

After the earnings file has been used to prepare the check and statement, it is again used to prepare the various deduction registers. One register can be prepared for all types of voluntary deductions, or one register can be prepared for each type of voluntary deduction allowable. These deduction registers may then be used as records to outside individuals or organizations such as banks and insurance associations.

Deduction Registers

FIG. 14-8

Sample Payroll Checks and Earnings Statements.

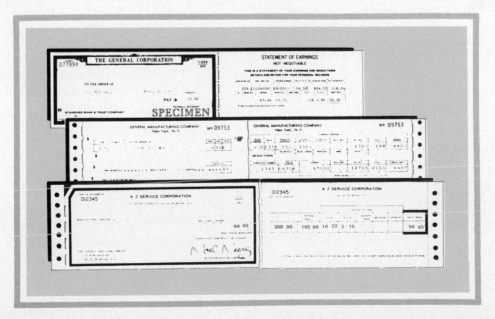

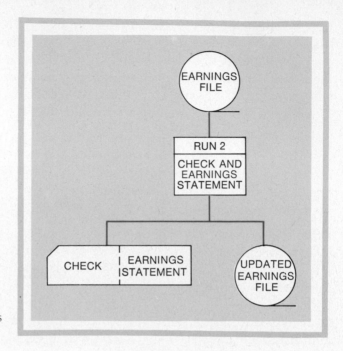

FIG. 14-9
Flowchart for Check and Earnings
Statement Run.

Some of the documentation generated during the design and programming of this subsystem is illustrated in the Appendix at the end of this chapter.

Tax Reports   Tax reports are generated form the payroll master file and contain cumulative totals of taxable earnings, FICA deductions, and federal and state withholding taxes. These are generally prepared annually and include such reports as the federal W2 and 941 forms.

Management Reports   As we mentioned earlier, one of the advantages of a computerized payroll system is that many detailed and timely reports can be prepared for management as a spinoff of the basic payroll runs. Such reports in the hands of management can facilitate a careful and fruitful evaluation of the organization which would otherwise be impossible. Reports which, if desired by management, can be easily provided as the result of an automated payroll system might include

1. Labor cost analysis—This report would contain a cost breakdown per item produced in terms of materials used, man-hours expended, and so forth.

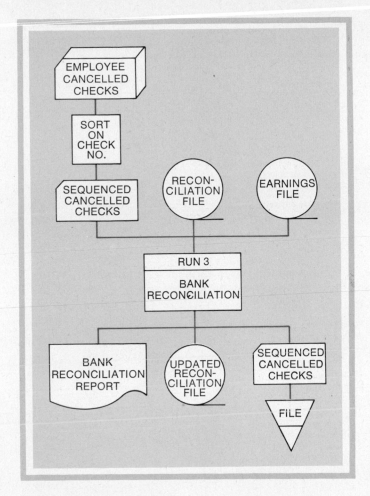

FIG. 14-10

Flowchart
of Bank Reconciliation
Report Run.

2. Employee daily performance record—Such a report might be provided for department heads and would include an analysis of time expended and output produced by employees. Such a report would be useful when considering employees for increases in salary and responsibility.

3. Absentee ratio by department—This report would inform management at a glance if there were any departments with exceptionally good or exceptionally bad attendance records. Appropriate action could then be taken swiftly and effectively.

4. Departmental expense ratio report—This report would inform management of the ratio of supervisory personnel to nonsupervisory personnel. This information could

TYPE 1—SINGLE PERIOD 2—SPECIFIC PERIOD 3—STANDING		WHEN MADE 1—FIRST WEEK 2—SECOND WEEK 3— THIRD WEEK 4— FOURTH WEEK			5—1ST AND 2ND WEEK 6—2ND AND 4TH WEEK 7—EACH WEEK		DEDUCTION REGISTER				

Sample Payroll Deduction Register (FIG. 14-11):

EMPLOYEE			DED. CODE	TYPE CODE	WHEN MADE	TOTAL DEDUCTIONS	SAVINGS BOND	HOSPITAL INSUR-ANCE	GROUP LIFE INS.	CREDIT UNION	RETIRE ANNUITY
DEPT.	NUMBER	NAME OF EMPLOYEE									
01	2 6	A V ASTOR	4	3	4	8 75				8 75	
01	342	A F DUFFY	2	3	4	1 25		1 25			
01	342	A F DUFFY	4	3	4	2 00				2 00	
01	518	B H ENGLISH	1	3	6	2 00	2 00				
01	518	B H ENGLISH	5	3	4	2 50					2 50
01	615	F L FARELY	2	3	4	1 50		1 50			
01	615	F L	3	3	4	2 00			2 00		
01	703					2 50	2 50				

FIG. 14-11

Sample Payroll Deduction Register.

then be matched against the department output record to determine if the department is appropriately staffed or administratively topheavy.

These are only some of the many reports that management might request *and get* quickly and easily as the result of an automated payroll system.

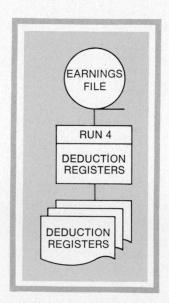

FIG. 14-12

Flowchart of Deduction Register Run.

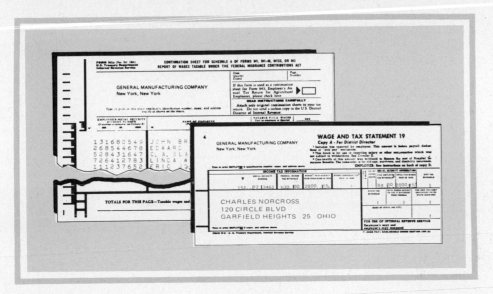

FIG. 14-13
Sample Tax Reports.

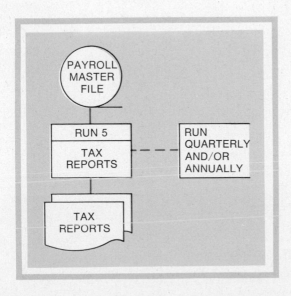

FIG. 14-14
Flowchart of Tax Report Run.

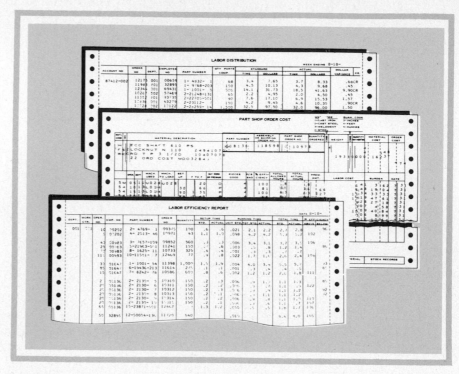

FIG. 14-15

Representative Management Reports.

SELF-STUDY EXERCISES 14-2

1. The principal input for payroll computations is the _____.

      *****

      weekly time card

2. Some of the reports that must be prepared in connection with a payroll system are _____.

      *****

      payroll audit, payroll register, check and earnings statement, bank reconciliation report, deduction registers, tax reports, and management reports

3. The _____ serves to identify any unusual conditions prior to the printing of the payroll register and checks and statements.

*****

payroll audit

4. The payroll register is a report which lists _____.

*****

the earnings and deductions of all employees

5. The _____ is the basic input from which the various tax reports are created.

*****

payroll master file

6. The two most common tax reports are the _____ and the _____.

*****

W2

941

An accounts payable system within a business is basically concerned with the disbursement of company funds and the keeping of associated records. The specific objectives of such a system would include

ACCOUNTS PAYABLE SYSTEM

1. Recording purchase-order requisitions
2. Preparing and recording open purchase-order data for later processing
3. Preparing receiving documents for the receiving department
4. Providing for an automated receiving procedure and back-order processing
5. Updating vendor files as transactions occur
6. Creating vouchers from receipts for items
7. Detecting variations between items ordered and quantities received, issuing appropriate debit memoranda, and updating related records

8. Producing vendor checks, remittances, and disbursement register
9. Vendor performance analysis
10. Producing expense distributions and departmental budget reports

In addition to fulfilling these basic accounting requirements, a well-designed procedure should furnish prompt data to answer potential management questions such as

1. What was the total volume of purchases from each vendor?
2. What cash discounts have been lost, and why?
3. How much of each class of merchandise did each vendor supply?
4. What are the daily cash requirements to meet outstanding payables?
5. How reliable has each vendor been concerning orders received on time and in satisfactory condition?

It is also necessary that the required input data to such a system be determined as well as the source of the original document from which this input data can be obtained. Such sources include records which originate inside the company as well as those records which originate from outside sources. For example, records which originate within the company would include

1. Petty-cash-disbursement vouchers
2. Expense accounts
3. Requisitions, receiving reports, stock issues

Records which originate outside the company would include

1. Vendor invoices
2. Vendor credit memoranda

On such original documents there is certain information that would be essential. This would include

APPROVED REQUISITION	STOCK ISSUES
Department number	Department charged
Item number	Item number
Description	Description
Quantity ordered	Quantity issued
Approved price	Date issued
Vendor number	

An accounts payable system, not unlike any other system, has as a primary purpose, the preparation of required reports and the maintaining of records. To accomplish these ends, it is necessary that the business concerned maintain certain files of information or data. These files are usually maintained on magnetic tape but may also be maintained on another medium such as a magnetic disk. Among the files usually found in an accounts payable system would be

1. Vendor master file
2. Open purchase order file
3. Accounts payable file
4. Paid vendor file
5. Disbursement record file
6. Distribution records file

This file is an up-to-date list of all suppliers or vendors employed by the company. Associated with each vendor listed should be pertinent information such as

Vendor Master File

1. Vendor name
2. Vendor address
3. Vendor telephone number
4. Items description and prices
5. Discount rate and terms
6. Credit limit
7. Delivery instructions

Open Purchase Order File A file containing relative information concerning all issued purchase orders currently unfilled or outstanding. Items are arranged by vendor account number and within vendor account number, by purchase-order number.

Accounts Payable File A file arranged in sequence by vendor account number and by due date within vendor grouping and containing information relative to vendor invoices such as the vendor name and address, gross amount of the invoice, discounts, if any, amount of unsatisfactory merchandise or shortages, and net amount of the invoice.

Paid Vendor File A file of those vendors, by account number, for whom invoices have been paid. This file is updated as invoices are paid and may be utilized to produce such reports as the volume of purchases by vendor.

Disbursement Record File This file consists of those invoices for which checks and statements have been produced and for which petty-cash-disbursement vouchers have been produced. This file is arranged by vendor account number and within an account number, by date. It contains such information as the vendor name and address, amount of payment, invoice number, and purchase order number. This file serves as input for the preparation of the cash disbursement register.

Distribution Records File This file contains all the distribution records created from the invoices or petty-cash-disbursement vouchers received during a given accounting period as well as data relating to shortages or unsatisfactory merchandise received during this period. It is arranged by vendor account number and is used to prepare summary vendor account records and expense statements and analyses.

Let us now examine some of the procedures encountered and the reports generated in connection with, and as a result of, the processing of a purchase requisition in a representative accounts payable system.

Purchase Requisition A purchase requisition will differ in form from company to company, but it should generally contain the following information:

1. The name and description of the items requested
2. The quantity desired
3. The date of the requisition and the date by which the items must be available
4. To what account the items ordered will be charged

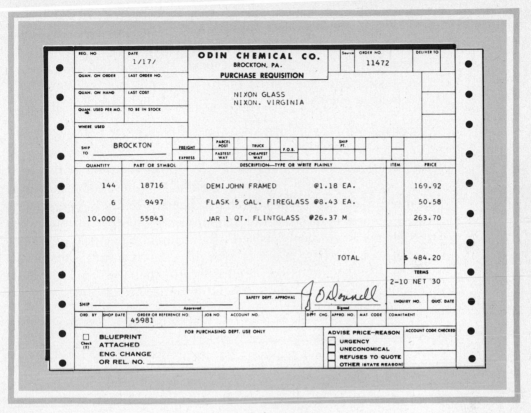

FIG. 14-16
Purchase Requisition.

5. The signature of the individual(s) authorizing the purchase
6. The vendor's name if an item is available from only one vendor
7. The point of delivery to which the items requested are to be directed
8. Space for use by the purchasing department
9. The number of items presently on hand together with the average rate of consumption of these items

After a purchase requisition has been written and approved, it is forwarded to the purchasing department. Here the requisition can be examined concerning:

1. Are the requested items currently in stock?
2. Is the quantity requested in excess of previous requirements and, if so, has the requested quantity been justified?
3. If a particular vendor has been specified, has sufficient justification been given for the excluding of other vendors with a comparable product?

If the purchasing department has questions concerning the current price of the items, or concerning which vendor will offer the best price for the item, or if no appropriate vendor has been previously employed, they may submit a request for a quotation to the vendors under consideration. The information requested on the quotation request should be sufficiently detailed so that when the vendor is ultimately chosen, all information necessary for completing the purchase order is available and at hand. This would imply that the quotation should require that the vendors under consideration supply the following minimal information:

1. Price
2. F.O.B. point
3. Terms of payment
4. Delivery time
5. Any special terms or conditions of purchases

Once the purchasing department has selected a vendor, necessary information such as the vendor's name and address, delivery instructions, etc., should be forwarded to the data-processing center so that the new vendor, or new product line for an old vendor, may be added to the current vendor master file.

The completed purchase requisition is now forwarded to the data-processing center, where the purchase order will be printed.

Purchase Order The purchase order represents the vendor's authority to ship and to charge the buyer for the items specified. It also represents the buyer's commitment to the vendor to pay for the items ordered. The purchase order is the most important of all the purchasing forms. It must be clear and precise to eliminate even the most remote possibility of misunderstanding, which could result in additional correspondence and delay.

After a purchase requisition for the purchase of a particular item or items has been received and approved by the purchasing

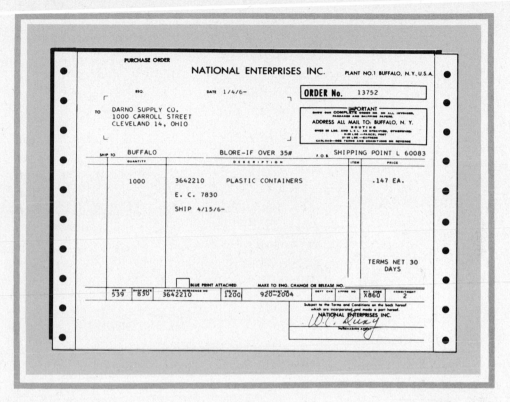

FIG. 14-17
Purchase Order.

department of a company, it is forwarded to the data-processing center for processing with the vendor master file to prepare a purchase order. From the vendor master file is taken such required information as vendor name, vendor address, delivery instructions, and item information not contained on the purchase requisition.

Generally, there should be an original and four copies of the purchase order printed. The original should go to the vendor and the copies should be routed to the accounts payable department, the purchasing department, the department from which the purchase requisition was issued, and the receiving department. Consideration should also be given to the manner in which the vendor is to indicate his acknowledgment and acceptance of the order or to indicate any problems he might have in filling the order.

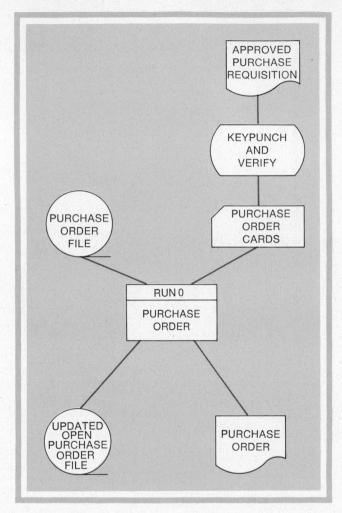

FIG. 14-18

Creation of Purchase Order.

Since the purchase order is being printed by the computer, the information contained on it is also being added to the open purchase order file, which contains all purchase orders previously issued and currently outstanding.

The next major step in an accounts payable system begins when the invoice is received by the purchasing department from the vendor. This invoice serves both to confirm the vendor's commitment to provide the ordered goods and also to authenticate the company's liability.

After the invoice has been received, verified, and audited by the purchasing department, a voucher (invoice authorized for payment) and vendor code number are assigned to the invoice. This

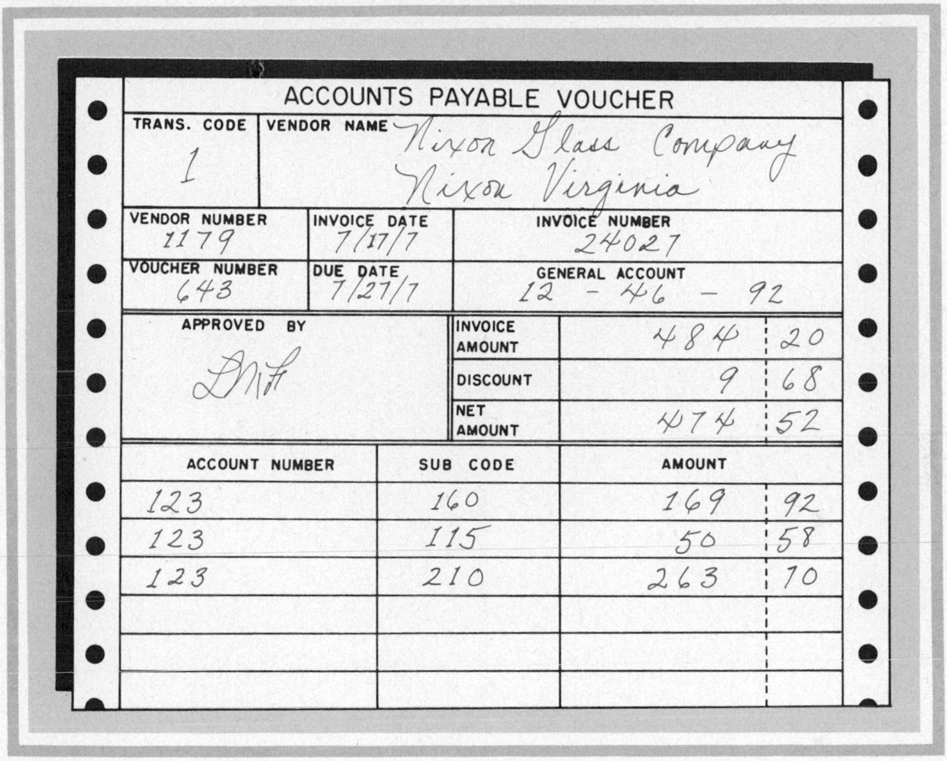

ACCOUNTS PAYABLE VOUCHER

TRANS. CODE	VENDOR NAME		
1	Nixon Glass Company, Nixon Virginia		
VENDOR NUMBER	INVOICE DATE	INVOICE NUMBER	
1179	7/17/7	24027	
VOUCHER NUMBER	DUE DATE	GENERAL ACCOUNT	
643	7/27/7	12 - 46 - 92	
APPROVED BY	INVOICE AMOUNT	484	20
DMH	DISCOUNT	9	68
	NET AMOUNT	474	52

ACCOUNT NUMBER	SUB CODE	AMOUNT	
123	160	169	92
123	115	50	58
123	210	263	70

FIG. 14-19
Accounts Payable Voucher.

information is then forwarded to the data-processing center, where it will be ultimately used to produce the check and remittance statement. Before the check and statement can be produced, however, several other items must be produced.

Distribution Cards

When the invoice or petty-cash-disbursement voucher is received in the data-processing center, it is used as a source document from which distribution cards are punched, one distribution card for each item line on the invoice. Figure 14-20 illustrates several distribution cards which have been produced from a single invoice.

Generally, a distribution card would contain such information as

1. Entry date
2. Invoice date
3. Invoice number

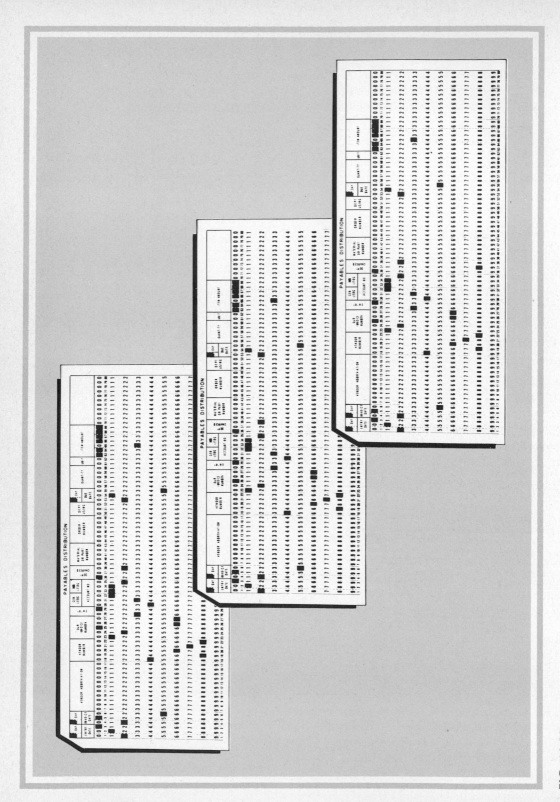

FIG. 14-20
Distribution Cards.

4. Vendor number
5. Vendor invoice number
6. Department charged
7. Invoice or item amount

The disbursement card is also punched from the invoice and is **Disbursement** concerned with the dollar amount of the invoice. Commonly, a **Cards** disbursement card contains such information as

1. Entry date
2. Invoice date
3. Invoice number
4. Vendor number
5. Vendor invoice number
6. Gross amount of invoice
7. Discounts, if any
8. Net amount of invoice

If shortages or unsatisfactory merchandise is noted in a vendor **Credit and Debit** shipment, a debit memorandum is issued and forwarded to the **Memoranda** vendor. There are two plans which may be used concerning the

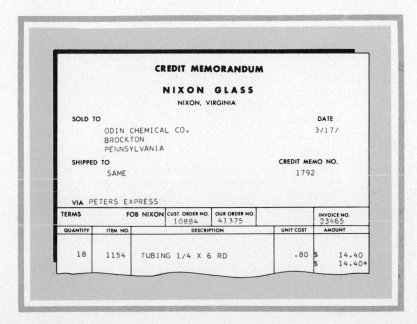

FIG. 14-21
Credit Memorandum.

second copy of this debit memorandum. The first plan is that a copy of the debit memorandum is sent to the data-processing center, where it is keypunched and then added to the open purchase order file. In this case, when the vendor acknowledges the error and reciprocates by issuing a credit memorandum, the creidt memorandum is forwarded to the data-processing center, keypunched, and merged with existing disbursement cards. These cards will be utilized to reduce the net amount of the invoice to which they apply at a time when the disbursement cards are processed.

The second plan differs from the first in that the copy of the debit memorandum is sent to the data-processing center for keypunching at the same time the vendor is notified. After having been keypunched, it is immediately processed and credited. The vendor credit memorandum now only serves as a means of verifying that it is consistent with the previously issued debit memorandum. This latter plan is illustrated in this system.

Invoice Register   All invoices are listed daily, in sequence, on an invoice register. For this purpose, the distribution and disbursement cards, previously punched from the invoices, are utilized. This register serves as a permanent record of all items of indebtedness arranged in

FIG. 14-22

Accounts Payable Daily Invoice Register and Control Tape.

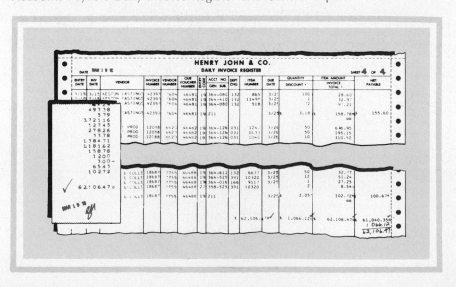

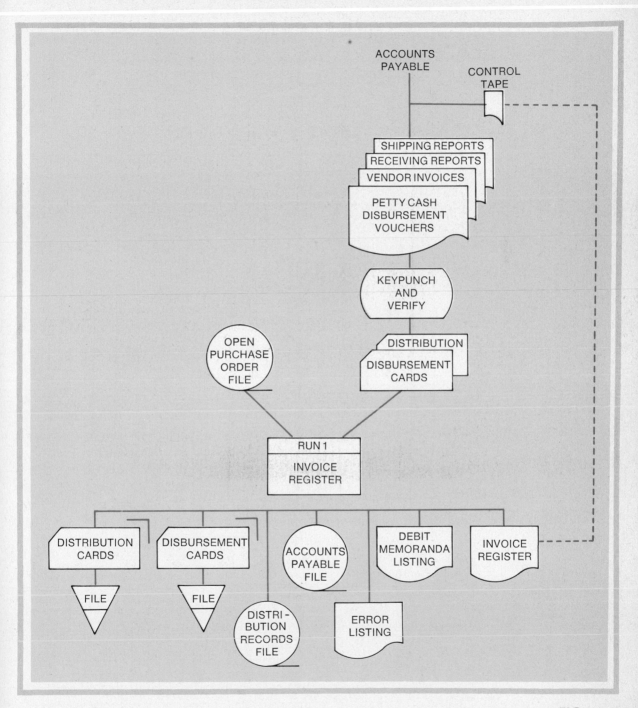

FIG. 14-23
Flowchart of Invoice Register Run.

KRAUSZ MANUFACTURING COMPANY

ACCOUNTS PAYABLE

CASH REQUIREMENTS STATEMENT

DATE APR 1 2 19

ROUT TO *Mr. J.K. Jrowin - Dept 100*

SHEET *1* OF *2*

VENDOR	VENDOR NUMBER	DUE DATE	INVOICE AMOUNT	DISCOUNT	CHECK AMOUNT	
SOLVAY GEN SUP	1016	4/16	$ 773.30	$ 15.47	$ 757.83	
ROCHESTER PR CO	1021	4/16	1,620.18	32.40	1,587.78	
CALABRIA CONT	1049	4/16	143.65	2.87	140.78	
ONONDAGA STL CO	1077	4/16	5,982.82	119.66	5,863.16	
BLACK & NICHOLS	1103	4/16	14.25	.71	13.54	
AUSTERHOLZ INC	1240	4/16	624.77	12.50	612.27	
AUSTERHOLZ INC	1240	4/16	1,833.19	36.66	1,796.53	
CHRISTIE & CO	1366	4/16	745.54		745.54	
WILSON & WILSON	2231	4/16	2,936.12	58.72	2,877.40	
CLAR. HIGGINS	2590	4/16	1,000.00		1,000.00	
HONOUR BROS	3101	4/16	97.36	1.95	95.41	
BASTIANI & SON	3112	4/16	3,580.85	71.62	3,509.23	
DRJ WIRE CO	3164	4/16	256.90	5.14	251.76	
HASTING-WHITE	3258	4/16	1,144.42	22.89	1,121.53	
DARONO ART MET	3427	4/16	32.75	.66	32.09	
DARONO ART MET	3427	4/16	127.52	2.55	124.97	
DARONO ART MET	3427	4/16	96.60	1.93	94.67	

FIG. 14-24

Cash Requirements Statement.

chronological sequence. This report is also useful in that it provides a source for all the information concerning a particular transaction without reference to the original documents. Together with this report, an error and debit memoranda listing is produced. The error listing includes vendor invoices for which there is no corresponding purchase order and the debit memoranda listing serves as a checklist to verify credit memoranda received in the future and as an indication of overall vendor reliability.

The invoice register totals are then balanced against the adding machine total taken by the accounts payable department at the time the invoices were received. This total is then posted to the accounts payable daily control sheet. Another control or check available is that the amount of the distribution cards should equal the amount of the disbursement cards.

Disbursement cards are then recorded on tape and sorted by due date, within vendor grouping, to produce the accounts payable file.

Cash Requirements Report

As the payment of an invoice within the discount date is effectively an increase in revenue for the company, it is essential that enough cash be maintained on hand to take full advantage of these discounts.

Forcasts of obligations in the form of the cash requirements report are easily and quickly prepared from the accounts payable disbursement records maintained by vendor account number and due date on the accounts payable file. Totals for accumulated obligations by due date are automatically printed below detailed transaction listings.

This report can be utilized by the treasurer or other management personnel to verify that the company has availed itself of all possible discounts.

Remittance Statement and Check

The accounts payable records for each due date are processed at the scheduled time and are used to prepare the remittance statement and check. To accomplish this, the accounts payable file is processed with the vendor master file, which contains vendor name and addresses and control totals.

As the checks and statements are being produced, the records which have been paid are added to both the paid vendor file for subsequent vendor analysis and to the cash disbursement record file, which will be used to generate the cash disbursements register, and then deleted from the accounts payable file.

Cash Disbursements Register

The cash disbursements register is prepared from the cash disbursement record file, which was produced from the same run in which the remittance statement and check were printed. The cash

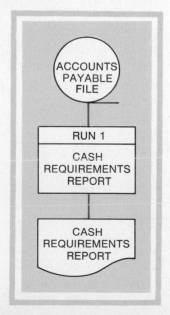

FIG. 14-25

Flowchart of Cash Requirement Run.

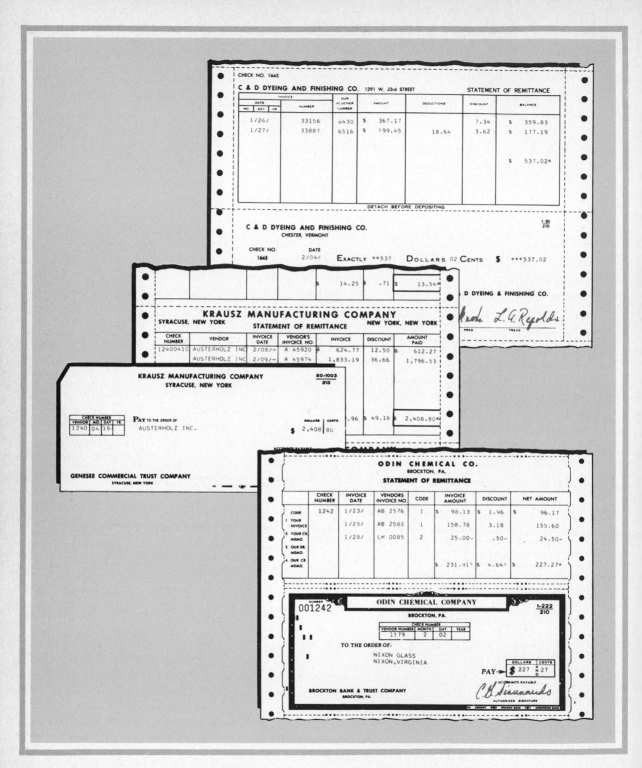

FIG. 14-26
Various Checks and Statements.

596

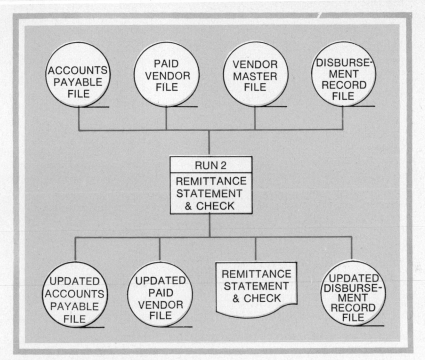

FIG. 14-27

Flowchart of Remittance Statement and Check Run.

KRAUSZ MANUFACTURING CO.

ACCOUNTS PAYABLE

CASH DISBURSEMENTS REGISTER

ROUT TO *Mr. J. P. Patrick*

DATE APR 1 6 19
SHEET *1* OF *2*

VENDOR	CHECK NO.			✓	ACCOUNTS PAYABLE	CREDIT	
	VENDOR NUMBER	MO.	DAY		DEBIT	DISCOUNT	CASH
SOLVAY GEN SUP	1016	04	16		$ 773.30	$ 15.47	$ 757.83
ROCHESTER PR CO	1021	04	16		1,620.18	32.40	1,587.78
CALABRIA CONT	1049	04	16		143.65	2.87	140.78
ONONDAGA STL CO	1077	04	16		5,982.82	119.66	5,863.16
BLACK & NICHOLS	1103	04	16		14.25	.71	13.54
AUSTERHOLZ INC	1240	04	16		2,457.96	49.16	2,408.80
CHRISTIE & CO	1366	04	16		745.54		745.54
WILSON & WILSON	2231	04	16		2,936.12	58.72	2,877.40
CLAR. HIGGINS	2590	04	16		1,000.00		1,000.00
HONOUR BROS	3101	04	16		97.36	1.95	95.41
BASTIANI & SON	3112	04	16		3,580.85	71.62	3,509.23
DRJ WIRE CO	3164	04	16		256.90	5.14	251.76
HASTING-WHITE	3258	04	16		1,144.42	22.89	1,121.53
DARONO ART MET	3427	04	16		256.87	5.14	251.73

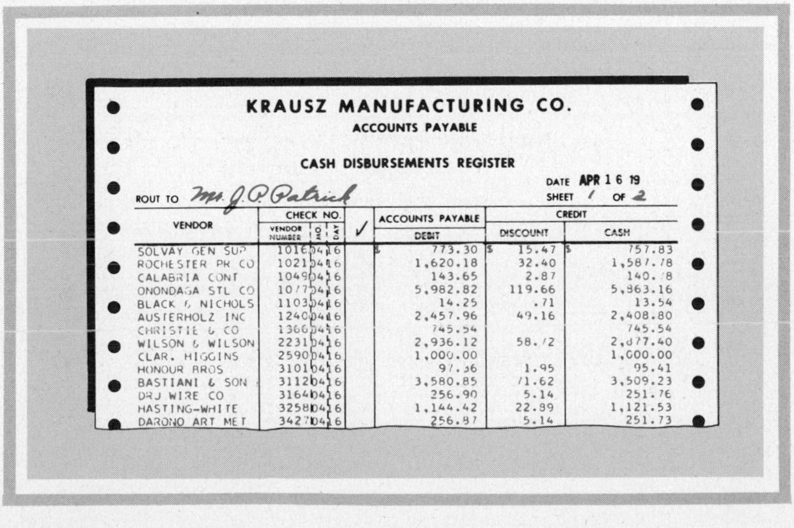

FIG. 14-28

Cash Disbursement Register.

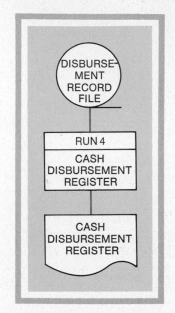

FIG. 14-29

Flowchart of Cash Disbursement
Register Run.

disbursement register is a report showing to whom payments were
made, the amount of the payment, and the invoice and purchase
order numbers.

Accounts Payable
Trial Balance

At the end of the accounting period, all the records in the accounts
payable file are used to prepare a trial balance.

NATIONAL PRODUCTS INC.

TRIAL BALANCE

OPEN ITEMS—ACCOUNTS PAYABLE

CLOSING DATE ⬛⬛ 3 0 1⬛   SHEET _18_ OF _18_

VENDOR	VENDOR NUMBER	INVOICE DATE	DUE DATE	ACCOUNTS PAYABLE	DISCOUNTS	NET PAYABLES	
WALTERS INS	1181	3/24	4/24	382.40		382.40	
WALTERS INS	1181	3/27	4/27	1,647.85		1,647.85	
				\$ 2,030.25	\$	2,030.25	
GREENWICK FUEL	1196	3/22	4/02	126.20	2.52	123.68	
GREENWICK FUEL	1196	3/26	4/05	119.73	2.39	117.34	
GREENWICK FUEL	1196	3/28	4/07	121.45	2.44	119.01	
				\$ 367.38	\$ 7.35	360.03	

FIG. 14-30

Accounts Payable
Trial Balance.

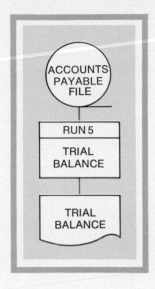

FIG. 14-31
Flowchart
of Accounts Payable
Trial Balance Run.

All unpaid records are first sorted into due date sequence by vendor code. Then the sorted records are listed to produce a trial balance. Totals are compared with the daily control sheet for verification of open liabilities.

Payable Distribution Summary Report

At the end of the accounting period, all the distribution records for the period, arranged by account number on the distribution records file, are used to prepare the distribution summary report. The distribution records file is processed, and summary account records are produced. These summary account records are prepared for ledger entry and are also combined with budget and year-to-date summary records for expense statements and analyses.

Expense Analysis

The current period's expense distribution records are sorted into department number sequence and merged with history and budget records to produce the various expense analyses. Variance, percentage of change, and other measurements are included.

Vendor Analysis

The distribution records in vendor number sequence are itemized to detail specific item purchases from each vendor and the same records summarized by class for vendor analyses of amount, discounts, total purchases, and reliability.

HENRY JOHN & CO.

ACCOUNTS PAYABLE DISTRIBUTION SUMMARY

DATE MAR 30 19   SHEET 3 OF 5

ENTRY CODE	INVOICE DATE	VENDOR ABBREVIATION	INVOICE NUMBER	VENDOR NUMBER	OUR VOUCHER NUMBER	ENT CODE	ACCT. NO. GEN. SUB.	DEPT CHG	ITEM NUMBER	DUE DATE	QUANTITY	INVOICE AMOUNT	GENERAL LEDGER
		MACHINERY					364-080						
3/05	3/03	KESTON CASTINGS	4106'	760-	41/50	19	364-080	132	30236	3/13	6	$ 347.85	
3/12	3/09	KESTIN-WHITE	11333	8420	42916	19	364-080	031	1689	3/19	144	262.19	
3/13	3/12	KESTON CASTINGS	41988	'604	43008	19	364-080	132	51/06	3/22	6	333.60	
3/15	3/13	KRAUSZ MFG CO	24092	3466	43262	19	364-080	100	104008	3/23	1	2,897.45	
3/15	3/13	KRAUSZ MFG CO.	24092	3466	43262	19	364-080	100	20343	3/23	1	1,390.11	
3/19	3/15	KESTON CASTINGS	4239	'604	46401	19	364-08C	132	865	3/25	100	28.60	
3/19	3/15	KESTON CASTINGS	4239?	604	46481	19	364-08C	132	518	3/25	72	97.21	
3/29	3/26	MIDWEST CAST CO	13738	9092	46826	19	364-08C	132	1162	4/09	12	165.95	
3/29	3/26	KRAUSZ MFG CO	25164	3466	46829	19	364-08C	100	18'661	4/0'i	1	944.40	
													$ 6,467.36*
		RAW STORES					364-126						
3/12	3/0'	DRJ WIRE CO	4449;	2910	41801	19	364-126	408	33927	3/1/	1000	180.45	
3/12	3/04	SOUTH LAKE SAND	A1925	464'	42888	19	364-126	100	630	3/19	20000	600.00	
3/12	3/09	CALHOUN & COLLS	1'831	'75'	4289;	19	364-126	100	12882	3/19	72	163.39	
3/12	3/03	ERIEN & HAYNES	55630	9132	4289;	19	364-126	408	6491	3/19	100	491.00	
3/19	3/16	AMER REF PRUD	12084	'620	46523	19	364-126	031	1242	3/26	50	6/5.95	
3/19	3/16	AMER REF PROD	12086	762	46523	19	364-126	031	1633	3/26	50	195.15	
3/19	3/16	AMER REF PROD	12088	'620	46523	19	364-126	031	1040	3/26	10	310.52	
3/19	3/14	BUTLER BF	55592	7731	46402	19	364-126	408	39117	3/24	144	53.05	
3/19	3/13	ERIEN & HAYNES	55898	913;	432'5	19	364-126	408	?459	3/23	15	49.56	
3/21	3/18	OLONSEN SUPLY	924'	7622	46124	19	364-126	100		3/28	144	12.00	
3/21	3/18	SOUTH LAKE SANU	A1994	464	46136	19	364-126	100	630	3/29	20000	600.00	
3/21	3/18	CALHOUN & COLLS	18926	'75'	46139	19	364-126	391	10320	3/28	12	51.24	
3/21	3/15	DRJ WIRE CO	45318	2910	45733	19	364-1'6	408	38618	3/25	5000	764.25	
3/21	3/15	AMER REF PROD	1963'	7620	45687	19	364-126	031	1242	3/25	50		

FIG. 14-32

Accounts Payable Distribution Summary Report.

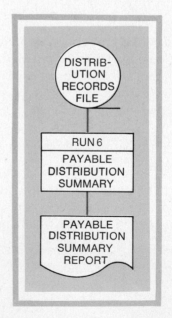

FIG. 14-33

Flowchart of Accounts Payable Distribution Summary Report Run.

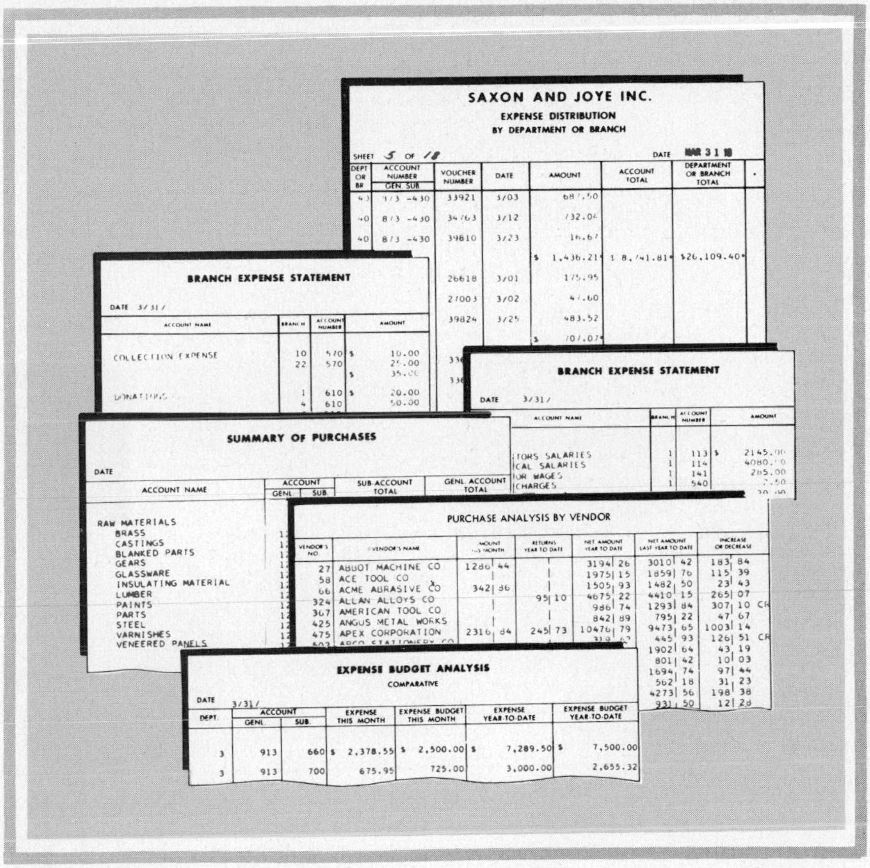

FIG. 14-34

Expense Analysis Reports.

SELF-STUDY EXERCISES 14-3

1. The primary functions of an accounts payable system within a
business organization are the _____ and the _____.

*****

disbursement of funds

maintaining of associated records

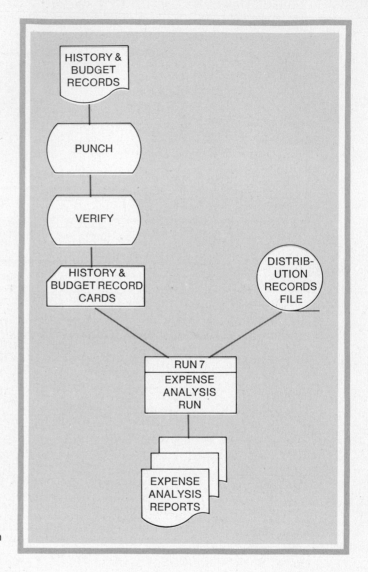

FIG. 14-35
Flowchart for the Generation
of Expense Analysis Reports.

2. Of the numerous files required in an accounts payable system, the _____ is a principal one and contains an up-to-date list of all suppliers or vendors employed by the company.

*****

vendor master file

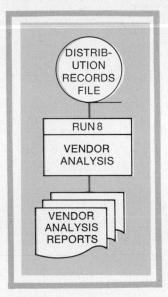

FIG. 14-36
Flowchart of Vendor Analysis Report Run.

3. The accounts payable file contains information that is relative to _____.

*****

vendor invoices, such as vendor name, address, amount owed, and discounts

4. A record of all distribution records is maintained in the _____ file.

*****

distribution records

5. A purchase order represents _____.

*****

the vendor's authority to ship and charge the buyer for those items specified on the purchase order

6. A debit memorandum is sent to the vendor when _____.

*****

shortages or unsatisfactory merchandise is noted in a vendor shipment

7. Upon receiving and verifying the validity of the debit memorandum, the vendor issues a _____.

*****

credit memorandum in the amount of the short or unsatisfactory merchandise

8. An _____ is the source document from which distribution cards are generated in an accounts payable system.

*****

invoice

9. The invoice register is a summary of all _____.

*****

items of indebtedness arranged in chronological sequence

10. The cash requirements report lists _____.

*****

the payments necessary to each vendor so that the company can take full advantage of of all discounts available

11. The vendor analysis report is _____.

*****

an itemized list of specific item purchases from each vendor in addition to summaries by vendor for amounts, discounts, and total purchases

RETAIL ACCOUNTS RECEIVABLE SYSTEM

Introduction

The purpose of an accounts receivable system within a retail business concern is to determine and maintain records concerning the amount of money owed to the business by its customers for merchandise sold or services rendered on a credit basis. These records are the foundation of a company's existence and their creation and maintenance is an extremely important function since almost 90 per cent of the nation's business is done on a credit basis and the estimated income from accounts receivable is a prime source of revenue for any business. In addition to accounting for all receivable transactions, an accounts receivable system must provide facilities for the collection of money owed, for minimizing losses from bad debts, and to maintain customer good will. Profit losses from inadequate and unsatisfactory billing, collection, and customer account analysis procedures cannot be compensated for by economies and cost reductions in other areas of the business. A business must also realize that the foundation of an effective credit operation is mutual confidence, confidence on the part of the business that the customer can and will pay for merchandise purchased or services received, and confidence on the part of the customer that he will be accurately billed, that he will be given fair treatment, and that if he is not pleased with merchandise or services received, he will be given satisfaction.

To begin our analysis of accounts receivable systems, we shall consider the recording of transactions.

The value of an accounts receivable system is heavily dependent on the degree of completeness with which individual transactions are recorded and processed. Charges for goods sold and services rendered, payments, credit and debit memos, and journal entries must all be recorded in sequence by date of occurrence before being charged or credited to appropriate customer accounts. This can be accomplished by one or two possible methods:

Methods of Processing Transactions

1. Open-item
2. Balance-forward

The open-item method is one in which cash receipts are credited against individual invoices. That is, if a payment made to an account is less than the total of all unpaid invoices, it is credited against these invoices beginning with the oldest, and a credit memo issued for any remaining amounts not sufficient to cover an additional invoice. Paid invoices are then deleted from the particular customer account, leaving only unpaid invoices in the account file. The open-item method is commonly utilized by manufacturers, wholesalers, and jobbers who sell to other businesses (mercantile credit).

The balance-forward method, utilized by companies dealing directly with consumers (individual credit), is one in which cash receipts are credited against the customer's total outstanding balance. That is, if a payment is made to an account, it is deducted from the total outstanding balance, leaving a new outstanding balance.

We shall, for purposes of this discussion, assume that the business concern operates under the balance-forward method.

To maintain an efficient and effective accounts receivable system, it will be necessary to maintain files of information or data. Among the files found in an accounts receivable system would be a master and a control file.

Master File Once credit has been established, the customer information is entered on the master file. These customer master records contain data that are generally not subject to change. Included will be the customer number, name, mailing address, job address if any, zip code, and telephone number. A code representing the account's credit rating is also included and only updated after careful consideration is made. Along with the credit rating is a credit limit. This field contains the maximum amount that a customer may owe at any one time. This credit limit should be realistically based on the customer's ability to pay.

Control File A file of information by customer account number containing data subject to change and not contained on the master file. This file is generated at the same time as the accounts receivable transaction register and usually contains such information as

1. Customer number
2. Invoice number
3. Statement date
4. Invoice amount
5. Amount paid
6. Date paid
7. Returns and allowances
8. Customer unpaid balance
9. Days overdue

This file, containing the account outstanding balances, can be processed with the customer invoices and adjustments to determine current account balances, required payments, and so on.

Let us now examine some of the procedures encountered and the reports generated in connection with, and as a result of, the establishing of a charge account and with the processing of a charged purchase as it applies to a typical accounts receivable system.

New Account File A file containing information on accounts created within a predetermined period of time. This file would generally contain information by customer account number similar to that contained on the master file.

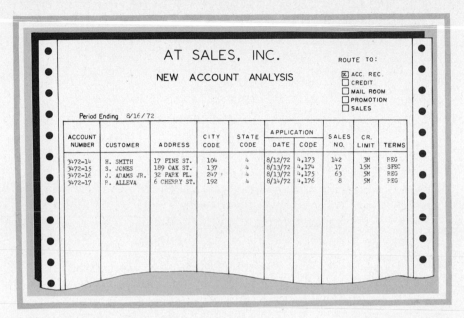

FIG. 14-37

New Account Analysis Report.

The time for a business to apply its greatest effort in attempting to avoid future difficulties with customers who will buy on credit is before these individuals are approved for credit and assigned a credit limit. All sources must be carefully examined to determine whether or not the applicant is a good credit risk. Some sources which can be employed in an effort to obtain credit information are

Establishing a Charge Account

1. General mercantile credit agencies
2. Information secured from banks
3. Data obtained from the customer himself

Each applicant must, however, very clearly be made to understand the credit policies of the business so that there can be no future doubt concerning these policies. Among the credit policies found in most businesses are

1. All credit applicants are carefully and thoroughly investigated and realistic credit limits set.
2. A prompt and systematic follow-up is made to each and every past-due account.

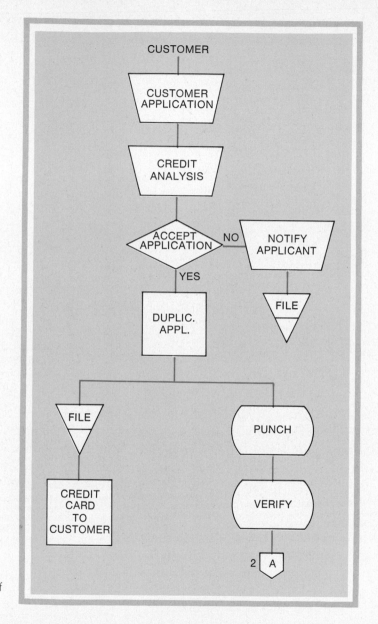

FIG. 14-38
Flowchart for the Creation of
a New Account.

3. When an account becomes delinquent beyond a predetermined period, credit privileges are stopped until payments have been restored on a regular basis.

4. Every effort is made to make satisfactory payment arrangements with a delinquent customer before legal action is threatened or resorted to.

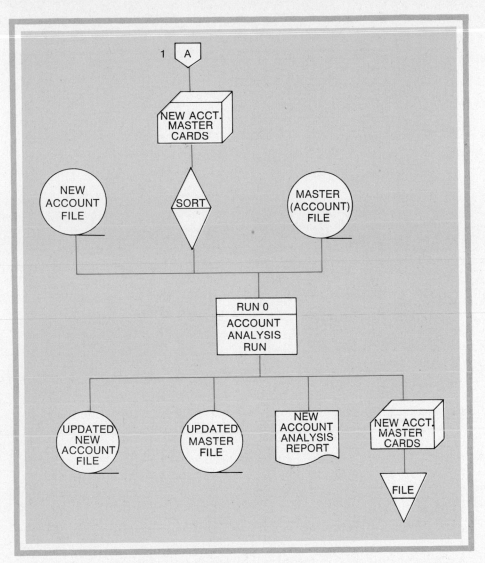

FIG. 14-38
Continued

5. Terms are fair and clearly stated on the credit application and on every customer's invoice.

Once an applicant has been carefully screened, accepted for credit, and assigned a credit limit, he is then added to the master file and, in the case of some companies, added to a new account file. This new account file is utilized to produce periodic listings of new

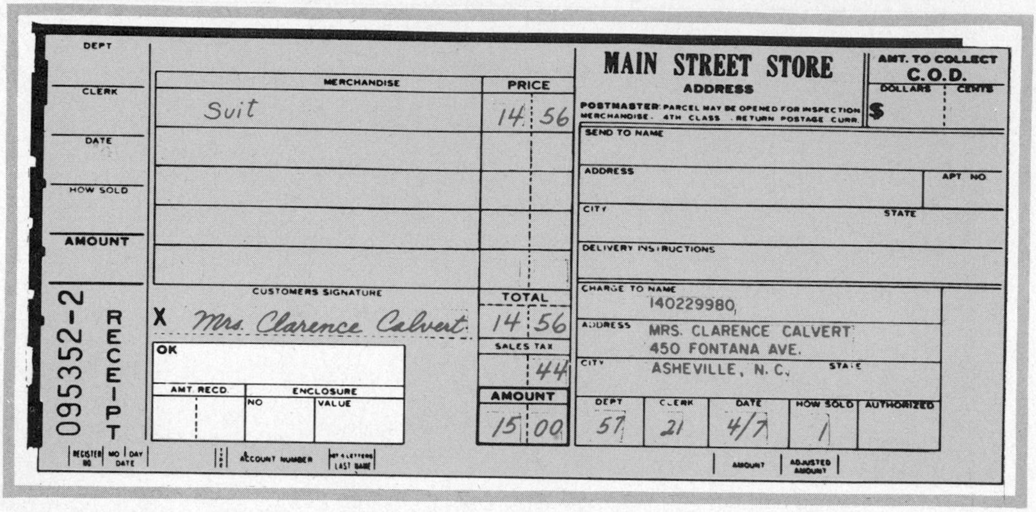

FIG. 14-39

Punched-card Sales Check.

accounts. Such a listing could be forwarded to the sales department for the possible revision or addition of the territorial assignments of salesmen, to the sales promotion department for future mailings of advertisements, and to the public relations department for the sending of letters of acceptance and congratulations.

Recording Transactions for Computer Processing

The next consideration in an accounts receivable system is to develop a means of making entries to an account and for producing corresponding management and customer reports for items purchased on credit.

To do this we must begin with the means used by the business to record the purchase. In general, a business employs one of two possible means of recording purchases: the punched-card sales check or the sales slip.

The punched-card sales check is used in the same manner as a sales slip for the recording of a sale; however, it is handled quite differently subsequently. After a substantial number of transactions have been recorded on punched-card sales checks, or at the end of the day, the cards are then forwarded to the data-processing center where, with the aid of optical character-sensing devices, they may be read. These data are then cross-checked with register totals and input directly into the automated accounts receivable system.

ACCOUNTS RECEIVABLE REGISTER

ACCT NO.	ACCOUNT NAME	TRAN ABBR	DATING MO DAY	INVOICE NUMBER	INV. DATE MO DAY YR	MDSE TRMS	ACCOUNTS RECEIVABLE	SHIPPING	MERCHANDISE AMOUNT	SLM
1188	J. R. SMITH	INV		3051	4 18 –	2	86 40		86 40	16
1209	H. T. SIMMONS	INV		3025	4 18 –	2	403 10		403 10	41
1212	S. R. FLORES	INV		3046	4 18 –	2	345 05		345 05	43
1220	S. A. STEIN	INV		3017	4 18 –	2	70 06		70 06	16
1272	M. KARP	INV		3022	4 18 –	2	131 86		131 86	40
1280	S. M. FRANKEL	INV		3029	4 18 –	N	48 52	3 02	45 50	17
1281	E. E. FREEMAN	INV		3049	4 18 –	2	73 46		73 46	38
1284	P. FORSTER	INV		3042	4 18 –	2	146 79		146 79	42
1286	S. T. GIBNEY	INV		3027	4 18 –	2	9 83		9 83	13
1289	G. L. HAYES	INV		3024	4 18 –	N	43 60	2 95	40 65	43
1292	B. DROBNY	INV		3044	4 18 –	2	126 45	6 50	119 95	19
1293	G. R. TANNER	INV		3037	4 18 –	2	16 80		16 80	24
1300	S. LITTON	INV		3019	4 18 –	2	42 74		42 74	9
1302	J. BRIDGES	INV		3034			104 60		104 60	42
1303	R. J. STONE	INV							164 86	42
1307	C. T. HARRIS					2				
1311	J. R. SLOAN		477	4 18 –	N		14 86			

```
            TRANSACTION TOTALS        $ 14,386.97   $ 182.47  $ 14,204.50
            TOTAL CASH RECEIPTS          6,472.14
            TOTAL VOUCHERS                 347.52
            TOTAL                     $ 21,206.63
```

FIG. 14-40

Accounts Receivable Transaction Register.

If a business utilizes sales slips, the additional step of keypunching the information on the sales slip onto a punched card or invoice card becomes necessary. Punched onto an invoice card would be the essential facts concerning a single invoice, for example,

1. Customer number
2. Sales slip or invoice number
3. Date of sale
4. Invoice amount
5. Shipping charges (if any)
6. Department number
7. Amount paid (if any)

Whether the invoice cards are filled out directly by the sales clerk or keypunched from the sales slip, they must eventually be forwarded to the data-processing center for processing. In the data-processing center they will be read, sorted by customer account number, and processed with the journal entry cards and the cash

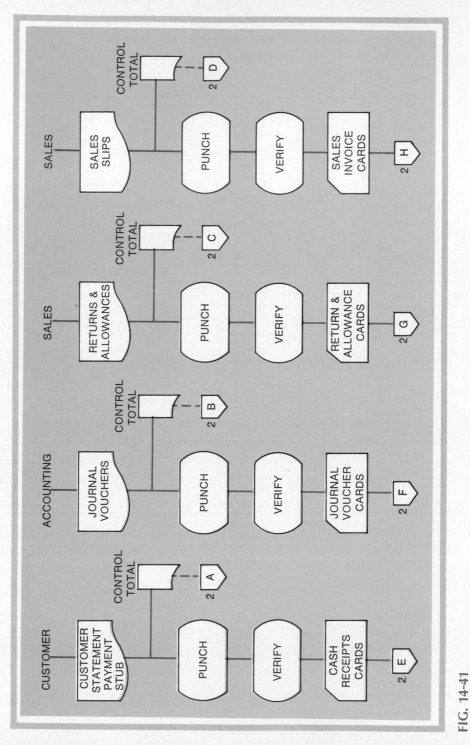

FIG. 14-41

Flowchart of Accounts Receivable Transaction Register Run.

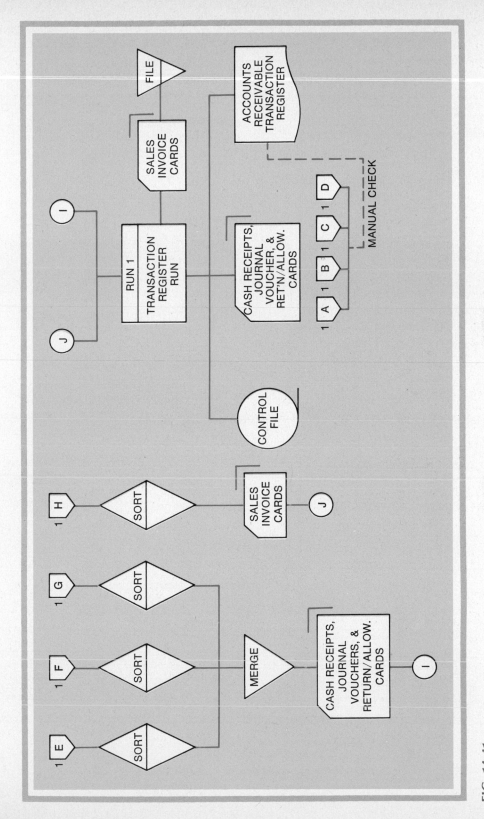

FIG. 14-41
Continued

receipts cards to produce the accounts receivable transaction register and the accounts receivable control tape.

Accounts Receivable Transaction Register   The transaction register is a listing of entries to accounts receivable. These entries include sales invoices, cash receipts, and daily journal entries. Among the specific items listed, one would expect to find

1. Account number
2. Account name
3. Purchase or credit date
4. Shipping charges
5. Invoice number
6. Invoice amount

This register is then used in conjunction with the journal and cash receipts control totals to verify all entries.

As the transaction register is being generated, the accounts receivable control file is also being generated. As mentioned earlier, this file is used together with the master file for customer invoicing.

Other reports and records required of an effective accounts receivable system would include

1. Cash receipts register
2. Trial balance
3. Aged trial balance
4. Customer statements
5. Delinquency notices

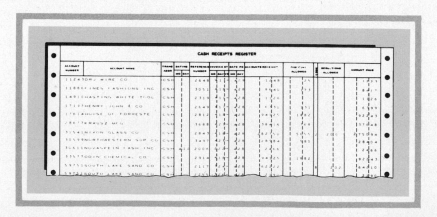

FIG. 14-42
Cash Receipts Register.

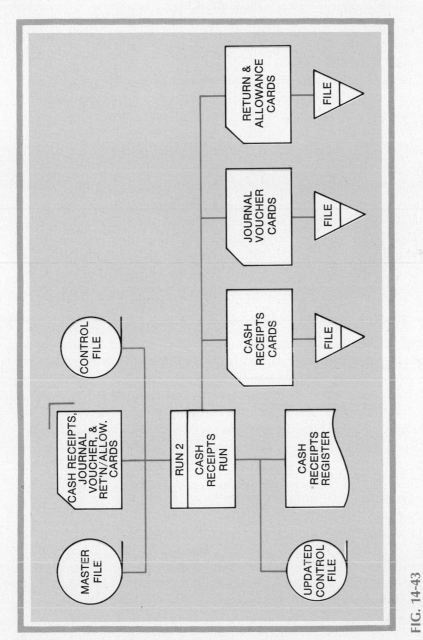

FIG. 14-43

Flowchart of Cash Receipts Register Run.

Cash Receipts Register   Once the transaction register has been balanced using the journal entry summaries and cash receipt summaries, the cash receipts register is prepared. This register is a permanent record of accounts receivable cash entries and also provides a means of reference which becomes the basis of auditing cash entries to the accounts receivable file.

The first step in preparing this report involves the receipt and recording of a customer payment. There are two commonly used means to accomplish this. One method is to provide a detachable portion on the customer statement returnable with partial or full payment of the statement. The other method is to provide a self-addressed envelope for return payment. In the latter case, it may be necessary to cross-reference the customer name to identify the payment by customer number. The paid installments are then added to the cash receipts control totals and punched onto cash receipts cards, which are subsequently sorted into account number sequence.

From the controller, or other responsible individual within the accounting department, journal vouchers are submitted to the data-processing center, where they are punched onto journal voucher cards and sorted into account number sequence (Fig. 14-44).

From the sales office, sales return and allowance slips are forwarded to data processing, where they, too, will be keypunched. They will be punched onto return and allowance cards and then sorted into account number sequence.

Since each of these groups of cards is in numerical sequence by account number, they can now be merged into one composite card file in account number sequence. This composite deck is then processed with the master and control files to produce the following:

1. Updated control tape
2. Cash receipts summary cards
3. Journal entry summary cards
4. Cash receipts register

The cash receipts register totals can then be verified with the adding machine control totals received from the accounting and sales offices together with the summary cards output with the cash receipts register.

Customer Statements   Customer statements are printed for all customers with open balances at the end of the customer's billing cycle. These statements, in triplicate, are produced from the master file and control file. The

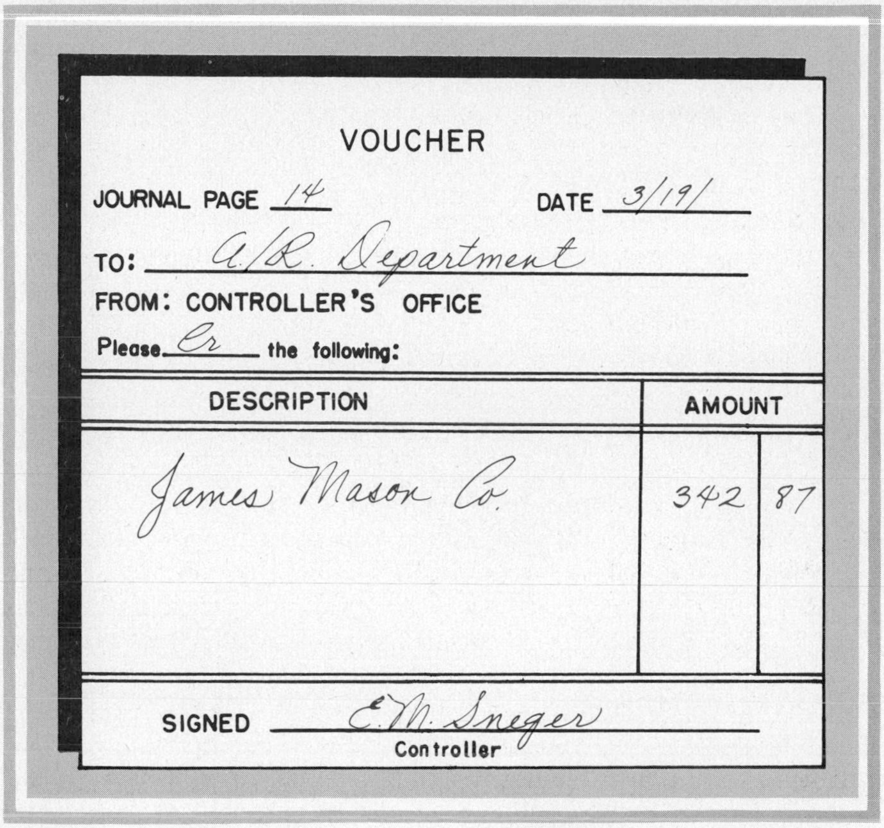

VOUCHER

JOURNAL PAGE *14*   DATE *3/19/*

TO: *A/R. Department*

FROM: CONTROLLER'S OFFICE

Please *Cr* the following:

DESCRIPTION	AMOUNT	
James Mason Co.	342	87

SIGNED *E.M. Sneger*
Controller

FIG. 14-44
Controller's Office Voucher.

first copy of the statement is sent to the customer, the second copy to the credit department, and the third copy filed for reference. At the same time the statement is being printed, the customer is producing an open balance file, which contains data on all customers having outstanding balances.

This report is generally a quarterly or an annual listing of all open items and it serves to prove or verify that the accounts receivable ledger balances with the control sheet issued by the controller or accounting department. **Trial Balance**

To accomplish this, the totals obtained from the transaction register, control file, and the accounts receivable summary card are compared. If in agreement, the accuracy of all accounts receivable has been assured, and if a discrepancy is noted, the transaction

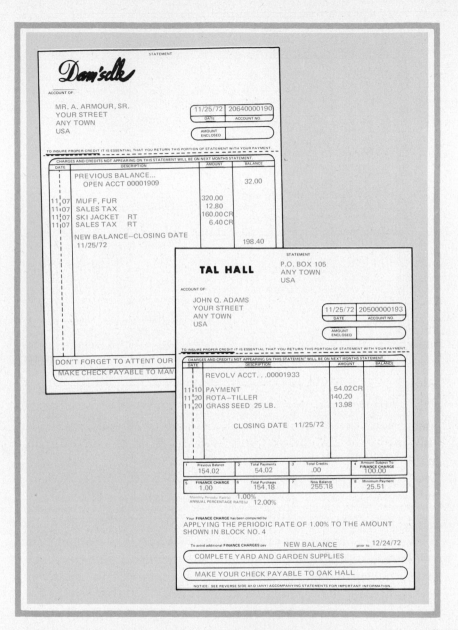

FIG. 14-45

Typical Customer
Statements.

register can be compared with the cash receipts register for verification. Any errors detected at this point can be traced by determining the particular register on which the error was detected. From this register the sales slip number can be determined, the

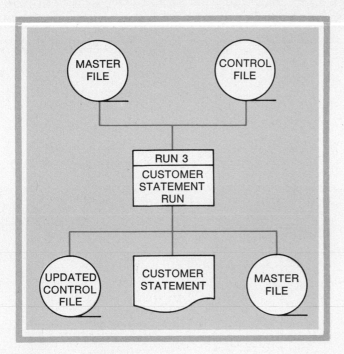

FIG. 14-46
Flowchart of Customer Statement Run.

sales slip retrieved, and the error pinpointed. Should the error be traced to accounting, a review of their operation would be necessary.

This report is very similar in content to the trial balance. It differs only in that the aged trial balance is generally run monthly and that it lists the open items by age, for example by items billed between 30 and 60 days, by items billed between 60 and 90 days, and by items billed in excess of 90 days from the billing date.

Aged Trial Balance

TRIAL BALANCE

CUST. NUMBER	CUSTOMER NAME	PREVIOUS BALANCE	PAYMENT	NEW BALANCE	OVERDUE AMOUNTS				COMMENTS
					1 WEEK	2 WEEKS	3 WEEKS	4 WEEKS	
24	ANCON DRUGS	143 50	143 50	116 10					
29	APPLIED MEDICINES	57 26	57 26	57 26					
74	BANCROFT PHARMACY	127 30		326 20	127 30				
135	COLLINS SODA SHOP	321 15	321 15	231 12					
191	EVANS PHARMACY	173 14	173 14	210 10					
215	FORESAIL DRUGS	215 30	215 30	116 22					
300	HOFSTAD DRUG CO.	219 20		350 16	75 14	87 30	51 76		
384	JONES DRUGS	242 50		108 15	242 50				
406	LAWSONS PHARMACY	86 25	86 25	97 42					
863	YANCY MEDICINES	196 20		286 40	94 20	62 48	39 52		
874	YATES DRUGS	93 58	93 58	110 30					
922	ZERCON DRUG CO.	141 85		386 20	141 85				

FIG. 14-47
Accounts Receivable Trial Balance.

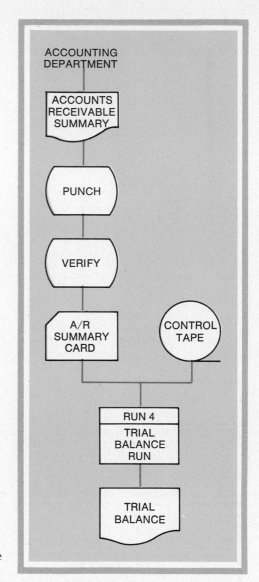

FIG. 14-48

Flowchart of Accounts Receivable
Trial Balance.

It is created by merging the master file and unpaid balance file. Extracted from these files is the information required to create the aged trial balance. This would include such items as

1. Customer name
2. Account number

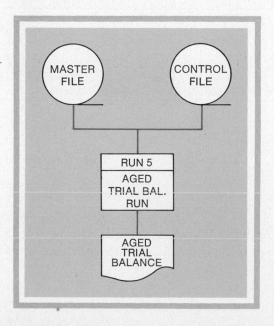

ACCOUNT NUMBER	ACCOUNT NAME	SLSM	CREDIT LIMIT	CREDIT AVAIL.	TOTAL	CURRENT	30-60 DAYS	60-90 DAYS	OVER 90 DAYS	TELEPHONE NUMBER
			ACCOUNTS RECEIVABLE AGED TRIAL BALANCE							
1188	J. R. SMITH	16	1,000.00	138.61	1861.39	17.30		844.09		212LU5-8400
1209	H. T. SIMMONS	41	1,500.00	148.62	1351.38	351.38				212422-5391
1210	R. A. CUMMINGS	32	2,000.00	1,203.86	1796.14	93.00%	125.43		763.71	212565-8490
1211	A. A. FRANZISSI	27	1,500.00	423.50	76.50	38.25				212GR3-5371
1272	M. KARP	16	1,500.00	63.27	436.73	40.59	396.14			212787-1133
1274	R. A. ALLEVA	12	500.00	254.79	245.21	245.21				201322-1243
1277	M. P. CASEY	44	500.00	1296.30%	796.30	306.10	301.80	102.60	85.80	212SP7-9400
1280	S. M. FRANKEL	17	1,000.00	208.48	791.52	132.50	96.32	153.20	409.50	212AX7-2389
1281	E. E. FREEMAN	38	5,000.00	1,018.63	3,981.37	3,656.80	324.57			201BI3-2200
1291	S. L. BARTON	36	1,000.00	659.20	340.80	67.39	169.79	68.42	35.20	212494-6000
1304	H. M. BARBIN	19	500.00	342.35%	842.35		421.03		421.32	203595-6900
1311	J. P. SLOAN	17	200.00	32.82	167.18		68.53	98.65	203.21	212264-5193
1319	M. L. ALLAN	42	1,500.00	139.46	1360.54	12.03	145.30			201721-3800
1332	A. M. BAXTER	38	1,200.00	96.75	103.25		103.25			212MU9-9301
1346	S. R. BIGFORD	35	1,000.00	252.69	747.31	325.63		421.68		516543-3589
1362	J. T. BAINES	17	5,000.00	2,374.20						516742-0700
1377	A. M. BERNSTEIN	16								
	G. P. GERSTAN									

FIG. 14-49

Accounts Receivable Aged Trial Balance.

FIG. 14-50

Flowchart of Aged Trial Balance Run.

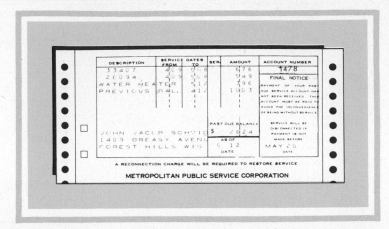

FIG. 14-51

Delinquent Account Notice.

3. Total outstanding balance
4. Current balance
5. Aged balances

Delinquent Account Listing　Column totals are accumulated and recorded on the last line of the report and can be used to cross-check the trial balance and the total overdue account.

It is a known fact that the older an outstanding balance becomes, the more difficult it becomes to collect. It is, therefore, essential that management be notified of any delinquent accounts as

DELINQUENT ACCOUNTS						
CUSTOMER NUMBER	CUSTOMER NAME	TELEPHONE NUMBER	LAST PAYMT DATE			CURRENT BALANCE
			MO	DAY	YR	
1188	J. R. SMITH	212LU5-8400	12	15	71	861 39
1209	H. T. SIMMONS	212422-5391	9	10	71	351 38
1210	R. A. CUMMINGS	212565-8490	12	12	71	796 14
1211	A. A. FRANZISSI	212GR3-5371	10	21	71	76 50
1272	M. KARP	212787-1133	12	10	71	436 73
1274	R. A. ALLEVA	201322-1243	11	14	71	245 21
1277	M. R. CASEY	212SP7-9400	6	15	71	796 30
1280	S. M. FRANKEL	212AX7-2389	9	15	71	791 52
1291	S. L. BARTON	212FL3-7400	10	18	71	340 80
1311	J. R. SLOAN	203595-6900	11	23	71	167 18
1319	M. L. ALLAN	212264-5193	12	20	71	360 54
1332	A. M. BAXTER	201721-3800	8	16	71	1103 25
1346	S. R. BIGFORD	212MU9-9301	10	18	71	1747 31
1362	J. T. BAINES	51654-3589	6	15	71	21685 00
1377	G. P. GERSTAN	212565-4792	8	23	71	85 14
1390	J. H. PAGE	82-3778	11	16	71	1476 28
			28	71		47 96

FIG. 14-52

Delinquent Account Listing.

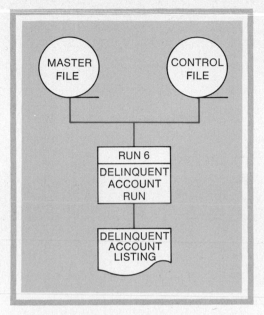

FIG. 14-53
Flowchart of Delinquent Account Run.

soon as possible so that the appropriate follow-up procedure may be initiated. The delinquent account listing serves to provide such a means of identifying delinquent accounts to the credit department.

The master file and open balance file are input to this report, and from them the number of days each account is overdue is computed. Any account overdue in excess of 30 days is listed as a delinquent account (Fig. 14-52). One copy of this report is sent to the credit department for determination of whether or not it should be forwarded to a collection agency for further action and the second copy is filed.

SELF-STUDY EXERCISES 14-4

1. The purpose of an accounts receivable system is to _____.
   *****

   determine and maintain records concerning the amount of money owed to a business for merchandise sold or services rendered on a credit basis

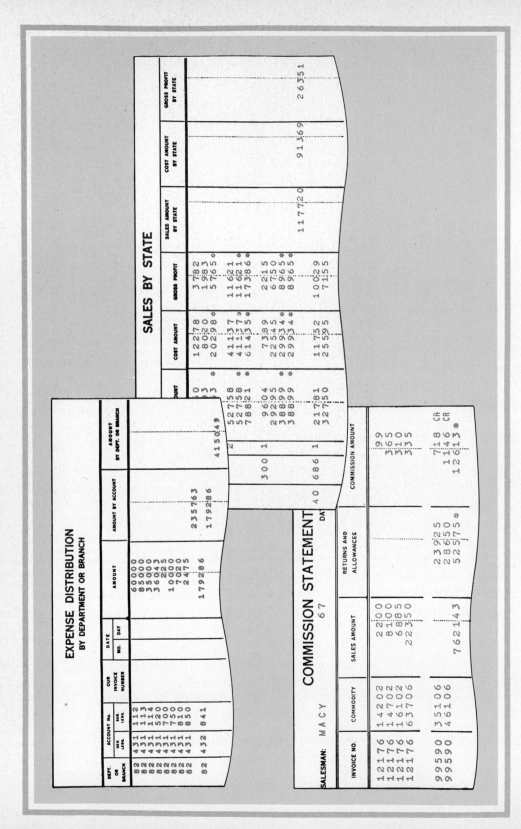

FIG. 14-54
Several of the Many Possible Special Management Reports.

2. The two methods used to maintain and update customer accounts in an accounts receivable system are the _____ and _____ methods.

*****

open-item

balance-forward

3. Businesses dealing with merchantile credit utilize the _____ method, while businesses dealing with individual credit utilize the _____ .

*****

open-item

balance-forward

4. The two files maintained in an accounts receivable system are a _____ file and a _____ file.

*****

master

control

5. The master file contains customer information that is generally _____ .

*****

not subject to change

6. Great care must be taken when _____ new applicants as well as in assigning a _____ to the new account.

*****

screening

credit limit

7. A _____ is commonly used in automated systems for recording sales.

*****

punched-card sales check

8. The accounts receivable transaction register is a _____ and is used in conjunction with journal and cash receipt control totals to _____ .

*****

listing of all entries to accounts receivable
verify all entries

9. Once the accounts receivable transaction register has been _____ , the _____ register is prepared.

*****

balanced
cash receipts

10. The cash receipts register is a permanent record of all _____ and provides a reference for _____ .

*****

cash entries
auditing cash entries to A/R

11. The trial balance is used to verify _____ .

*****

that the accounts receivable ledger balances with the control sheet issued by the accounting department

12. The output produced by an accounts receivable system includes _____ .

*****

transaction register, cash receipts register, customer statements, trial balance, aged trial balance, delinquent account listing, and various management reports

EXERCISES

14-1 True–false exercises

1. ____ The term "total system" as it pertains to a business is made up of many smaller subsystems.

2. ____ Subsystems of a total system usually deal with the primary accounting functions of a business.

3. ____ Approximately 50 percent of the nation's business is conducted on a credit basis.

4. ____ With the open-item method of recording transactions, payments made to an account are deducted from the total amount owed.

5. ____ The master file in an accounts receivable system contains information on customers who have established credit.

6. ____ In an A/R system, at the end of a day's transactions, sales slips are converted to punched-card data which are then read and cross-checked against cash register totals.

7. ____ The date should always be recorded on invoice cards and sales slips.

8. ____ Accounts receivable transactions are normally sorted into account number sequence.

9. ____ A list of all entries to accounts receivable is called a control file.

10. ____ The earnings file is needed as input for preparation of the deduction registers.

11. ____ The W2 is a required earnings statement issued by the company on a semiannual basis.

12. ____ The accounts payable file is updated when running the remittance statement and check.

13. ____ The accounts payable file is sorted into due date sequence by vendor code for the trial balance.

14. ____ An increase of 8 percent in this period's expenses over last period's expenses would be noted in the expense analysis report.

15. ____ The vendor analysis report summarizes the performance quality of individual vendors.

16. ____ Most retail transactions are done on a credit basis.

17. ____ The transaction register is a permanent record of accounts receivable entries and a means of reference which becomes the basis of auditing cash entries.

18. ____ A vendor master file contains specific information on all vendors dealing with the company.

19. ____ Credit limit is a data item which is normally recorded and updated in the vendor master file.

20. _____ Vendor names are not normally entered on a purchase requisition if the requested item is available from more than one vendor.

21. _____ Data from purchase requisitions are transferred directly to distribution cards.

22. _____ Time cards may take the form of mark-sensed punch cards.

23. _____ Details concerning earnings and deductions, gross pay, and tax withheld for all employees are shown in the payroll audit register.

24. _____ There is no significant difference between disbursement and distribution cards.

25. _____ Vendor verification is always needed when shortages or unsatisfactory merchandise are noted.

26. _____ A permanent record of all items of indebtedness arranged in chronological order is called an invoice register.

27. _____ Information needed to produce the cash requirements report is acquired from the accounts payable file.

28. _____ The open purchase order file contains data concerning all issued purchase orders currently unfilled or outstanding.

29. _____ The purchase order represents the vendor's authority to ship and charge to the buyer for the items listed.

30. _____ The cash requirements report indicates the cash on hand necessary to ensure that the company can avail itself of all possible discounts.

31. _____ An aged trial balance is run more often than a trial balance and lists open items by age.

32. _____ Accounts overdue 30 days or more are delinquent and can be determined from the data contained on the master and control files.

33. _____ Accounts payable systems are mainly concerned with the disbursement of company funds.

34. _____ The accounts payable department generally has no responsibility for the receiving procedure and back-order processing.

35. _____ The earnings file of a payroll system is created from the payroll master file and weekly attendance time cards.

36. _____ The payroll register is a report which lists all exceptions found during the payroll audit.

37. _____ The open-item method of crediting is used by companies dealing directly with customers.

38. _____ One function of an accounts payable system is to provide the daily cash requirements to meet outstanding payables.

39. _____ Two examples of records which would originate outside the company when dealing with payables are vendor invoices and expense accounts.

Multiple-choice exercises   14-2

1. _____ Of the following accounts receivable transactions, which is not recorded chronologically?
    (a) charges for goods and services
    (b) credit memo
    (c) debit memo
    (d) journal entries
    (e) none of the above

2. _____ Information punched onto invoice cards in accounts receivable should include
    (a) sales slip number
    (b) invoice amount
    (c) customer number
    (d) all the above
    (e) none of the above

3. _____ Income recorded in the cash receipts register includes
    (a) cash receipts
    (b) sales allowance slips
    (c) journal vouchers
    (d) all the above
    (e) (a) and (b) only

4. _____ Accounts receivable ledger balances and accounts receivable summary cards are compared against each other for verification in the
    (a) cash receipts run
    (b) trial balance
    (c) customer statement
    (d) all the above
    (e) none of the above

5. _____ Of the following, which is not an objective of an accounts payable system?

(a) recording purchase order requisitions
(b) updating vendor files as transactions occur
(c) creating vouchers from receipt for items
(d) vendor performance report
(e) none of the above

6. _____ The data base for accounts payable does not include
(a) open purchase orders
(b) petty-cash-disbursement vouchers
(c) vendor invoices
(d) distribution records
(e) none of the above

7. _____ Purchase order copies do not go to the
(a) accounts payable department
(b) vendor
(c) issuing department
(d) receiving (shipping) department
(e) none of the above

8. _____ Approved purchase requisitions and information from the _____ are used to produce purchase orders.
(a) control file
(b) vendor master file
(c) distribution cards
(d) all the above
(e) none of the above

9. _____ The remittance statement and check are produced from the
(a) accounts payable file
(b) vendor master file
(c) cash disbursement and record file
(d) all the above
(e) (a) and (b) only

10. _____ General objectives of a payroll system would not include preparation of the
(a) tax table
(b) bank reconciliation report
(c) checks
(d) deduction register
(e) none of the above

11. _____ The data base for a payroll system does not include
(a) authorized deductions and amounts
(b) Social Security number

    (c) Employee job description

    (d) Time cards

    (e) none of the above

12. ____Payroll Files should be updated

    (a) quarterly

    (b) monthly

    (c) weekly

    (d) daily

    (e) at the beginning of each pay period

13. ____ Time cards do not contain information on

    (a) overtime hours

    (b) regular time hours

    (c) days worked

    (d) employee pay rate

    (e) none of the above

14. ____ Payroll audit run inputs do not contain information on

    (a) vacations

    (b) departmental budget controls

    (c) tax deductions

    (d) none of the above

    (e) (a) and (b) only

15. ____ Deductions generally listed on a payroll deduction register include

    (a) hospital insurance

    (b) income tax

    (c) FICA

    (d) all the above

    (c) (b) and (c) only

Fill-in exercises (payroll)   14-3

1. Two mandatory tax reports are _____.

2. The earnings file is used to _____.

3. Three specific objectives of a payroll system are _____.

4. _____ records are the initial source of data for payroll computations.

5. The _____ is a report which shows in detail the earnings and deductions of all employees.

14-4 Fill-in exercises (accounts payable)

1. The accounts payable file provides information relative to _____.

2. The _____ is a listing and permanent record for all items of indebtedness in chronological sequence.

3. The cash disbursement register shows _____.

4. The _____ file contains an up-to-date listing of all suppliers or vendors employed by the company.

5. Three specific objectives of an accounts payable system are _____.

14-5 Fill-in exercises (accounts receivable)

1. Three sources that are generally used in determining a credit rating are _____.

2. The transaction register is used to _____.

3. _____and _____ cards are used to update the control tape.

4. The file which contains information that is subject to change is the _____.

5. _____ and _____ are used as input sources to generate the trial balance report.

6. The two common ways of recording sales are _____.

7. The five basic systems found in a typical business are _____.

8. The _____ is a report which lists all open items and serves to prove or verify that the accounts receivable ledger and control sheet balance.

9. Four common facts contained on most sales slips are _____.

10. The _____register is a permanent record of accounts receivable cash entries.

14-6 Problems

1. From the knowledge that you have gained from this and preceding chapters, discuss what type of equipment would be needed to implement one of the illustrated business systems for a medium-sized company.

2. Discuss how the addition of specialized equipment such as terminals would facilitate the centralization of data processing for a national corporation's needs.

3. Discuss which of the systems presented in this chapter, if any, would lend itself efficiently to a tape system, a disk system, or a card system.

4. What source documents are used in each of the business systems described in the chapter?

5. Discuss the relationship that might exist between the accounts receivable department and the credit department in a department store.

6. Discuss the various management reports that would be produced from each of the systems presented.

7. In what respects would an accounts receivable system differ from a manufacturing company to a retail company?

8. What specific operations are required in a payroll system in order to obtain an employee's gross pay and tax deductions?

9. Salesmen operating on a commission basis receive a specific percentage of their sales. What information would be required and where would it be input in an accounts receivable system to produce a file of total sales by salesmen for use in the payroll system?

10. Where and how would the file produced in (9) above be incorporated into the payroll system?

ITEMS FOR DISCUSSION

Total System Concept
Payroll System
Files in a Payroll System
Payroll Audit Register
Payroll Register
Check and Earnings Statement
Bank Reconciliation Report
Deduction Registers
Tax Reports
Management Reports
Accounts Payable System
Files in an A/P System
Purchase Requisition
Purchase Order
Invoice Register
Credit and Debit Memoranda
Cash Requirements Report
Remittance Statement and Check

Cash Disbursements Register
A/P Trial Balance
Payable Distribution Summary
    Report
Expense Analysis
Vendor Analysis
Retail Accounts Receivable
    System
Files in an A/R System
Open-item Method
Balance-forward Method
Recording Transactions
A/R Transaction Register
Cash Receipts Register
Customer Statement
Trial Balance
Aged Trial Balance
Delinquent Account Listing

SAMPLE ITEMS USED IN SYSTEM DOCUMENTATION

DESCRIPTION   The Deduction-Register Report (P004) generates a listing of all employee's earnings, withholdings, and itemized deductions for the pay period. In addition, it provides a summary report of the entire payroll; itemizing all the voluntary deductions.

Input to the program is the Current Earnings File. The date that the report is run must also be input to the program by the operator prior to processing the Earnings File.

Output from the program will be forwarded to the Payroll Department for audit and control considerations. Normally, this report is run after each payroll has been completed.

Page 1 of 1

TITLE PAGE

SYSTEM	PAYROLL
PROGRAM NAME	DEDUCTION-REGISTER
PROGRAM NUMBER	P004
PROGRAMMER	T. M. Taylor, Ext. 384
USER	Payroll Department, Ext. 493
DATE WRITTEN	June 18, 1976
PROJECT SUPERVISOR	William M. Fuori, Ext. 406
SCHEDULE	Weekly (Thursday)
ESTIMATED TIME	15 Minutes
CONTROLS	Visual comparison with previous pay period totals. Internal and external tape label checks.
SECURITY	Proprietary to Payroll dept. & designated recipients
PURPOSE	Generate Deduction Register & Summary from Earnings File

INPUT (1) EARNINGS-FILE
Reel Label: EARNINGS-P000E
Data Records: EARNINGS-REC
Estimated Volume: 350 records (1 reel)
Sequence: Numeric by Employee Number
Tape Labels: Standard volume, header, and trailer
Record Length: 127 Characters
Blocking Factor: 5

OUTPUT (1) DEDUCTION-REGISTER
Form Used: General purpose 6 lines/inch, 4 ply paper
Estimated Volume: 15 pages
Post Processing Requirements: Burst & collate
Carriage Control Tape: P004

DISTRIBUTION (2) SUMMARY
Form Used: General purpose 6 lines/inch, 4 ply paper
Estimated Volume: 1 page
Post Processing Requirements: None
Carriage Control Tape: P004
Original and 3 copies to Payroll Dept. Copy 3 returned
to Data Processing following review and validation.

REMARKS None

NCC Form 1888

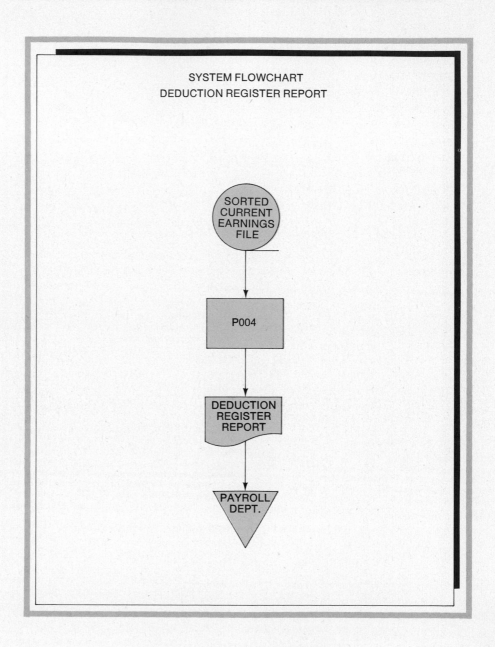

SYSTEM FLOWCHART
DEDUCTION REGISTER REPORT

SORTED
CURRENT
EARNINGS
FILE

P004

DEDUCTION
REGISTER
REPORT

PAYROLL
DEPT.

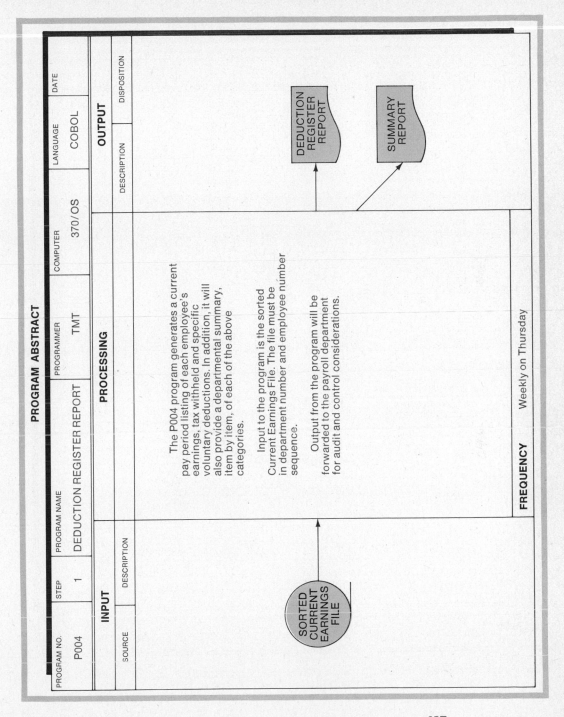

PROGRAM ABSTRACT

PROGRAM NO.	STEP	PROGRAM NAME	PROGRAMMER	COMPUTER	LANGUAGE	DATE
P004	1	DEDUCTION REGISTER REPORT	TMT	370/OS	COBOL	

INPUT

SOURCE	DESCRIPTION

SORTED CURRENT EARNINGS FILE

PROCESSING

The P004 program generates a current pay period listing of each employee's earnings, tax withheld and specific voluntary deductions. In addition, it will also provide a departmental summary, item by item, of each of the above categories.

Input to the program is the sorted Current Earnings File. The file must be in department number and employee number sequence.

Output from the program will be forwarded to the payroll department for audit and control considerations.

OUTPUT

DESCRIPTION	DISPOSITION

DEDUCTION REGISTER REPORT

SUMMARY REPORT

FREQUENCY   Weekly on Thursday

637

PROJECT: Payroll			APPLICATION: Payroll System				

PROJECT: **Payroll**   APPLICATION: **Payroll System**

FILE NAME: **Earnings–File**   FILE NO: **1134–76**

OTHER NAME(S):   RUN NAME: **PAY-DED**   RUN NO:

OUTPUT FROM: **Check and Earnings Statement**   INPUT TO: **P003, P004**

ACTIVITY % OF RECORDS: **100**   LAYOUT NO: FORM NO:

MEDIA: AVG. VOL.   NUMBER   PER   PERIOD   MAX. VOL.   SAME PERIOD

TIME DUE IN/OUT: PROJECTED VOL. (5 YRS.):

DISTRIBUTION: NO. OF COPIES   USE

CONTENTS   TOTAL NO. OF CHAR: AVG. **127**   MAX.

FIELD NO.	FIELD NAME	SORT SEQ.	NO. OF CHAR. AVG.	NO. OF CHAR. MAX.	A/N	PROCESSING
1	Employee No.	1	6			999999
2	Employee Name		20		A	
3	Dept. No.	2	1		N	
4	Social Security No.		9		N	999999999
5	Check No.		5		N	99999
6	Hours Worked		5		N	999v99
7	Rate Per Hour		4		N	99v99
8	Gross Pay		8		N	999999v99
9	Net Pay		8		N	999999v99
0	Med. Deduction		5		N	999v99
1	Union Dues Deduction		5		N	999v99
2	Credit Union Deduction		5		N	999v99
3	FICA Deduction		5		N	999v99
4	State Tax W/H		5		N	999v99
5	Federal Tax W/H		6		N	9999v99
6	Sick Days Taken		2		N	99
7	Vacation Days Taken		2		N	99
8	Year/Date FICA		5		N	999v99
9	Year/Date State Tax		6		N	9999v99
0	Year/Date Fedl. Tax		7		N	99999v99
1	Year/Date Gross Earnings		8		N	999999v99

DATE: **5/12/76**   ANALYST: **TMT**   SOURCE: PAGE __1__ OF __2__

(SP-1)   TEAM LDR: DATE:

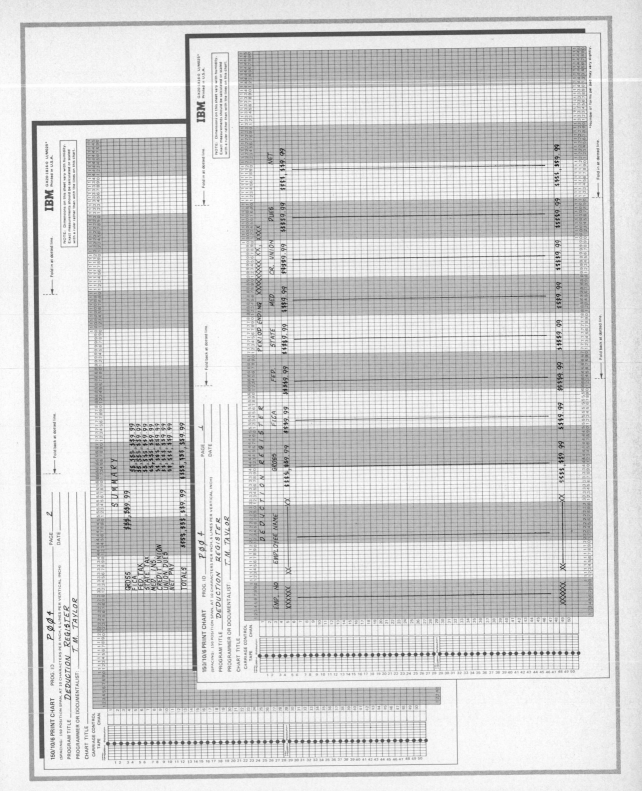

PROGRAMMER ___T. M. TAYLOR___ PROGRAM NAME ___P004___ PROJECT ___PAYROLL___ DATE ___

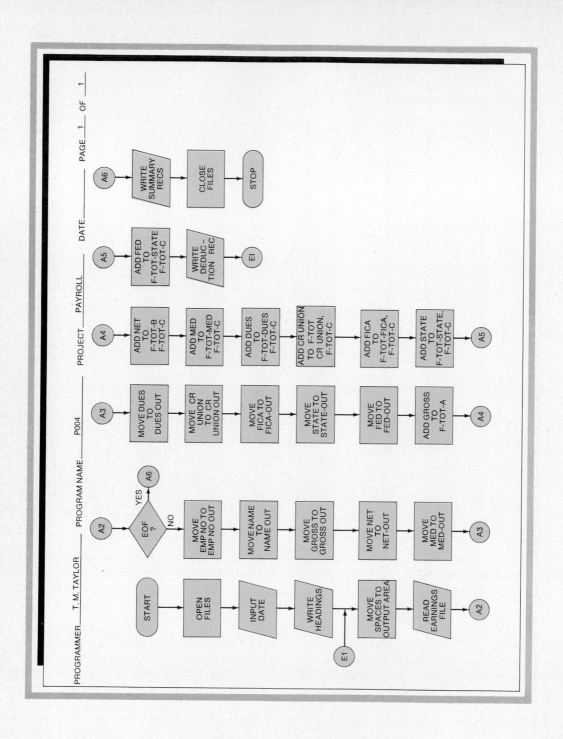

Flowchart:

START → OPEN FILES → INPUT DATE → WRITE HEADINGS → MOVE SPACES TO OUTPUT AREA → READ EARNINGS FILE → A2

E1 → WRITE HEADINGS

A2 → EOF ?
- YES → A6
- NO → MOVE EMP NO TO EMP NO OUT → MOVE NAME TO NAME OUT → MOVE GROSS TO GROSS OUT → MOVE NET TO NET-OUT → MOVE MED TO MED-OUT → A3

A3 → MOVE DUES TO DUES OUT → MOVE CR UNION TO CR UNION OUT → MOVE FICA TO FICA-OUT → MOVE STATE TO STATE-OUT → MOVE FED TO FED-OUT → ADD GROSS TO F-TOT-A → A4

A4 → ADD NET TO F-TOT-B F-TOT-C → ADD MED TO F-TOT-MED F-TOT-C → ADD DUES TO F-TOT-DUES F-TOT-C → ADD CR UNION TO F-TOT CR UNION, F-TOT-C → ADD FICA TO F-TOT-FICA, F-TOT-C → ADD STATE TO F-TOT-STATE, F-TOT-C → A5

A5 → ADD FED TO F-TOT-STATE F-TOT-C → WRITE DEDUCTION REC → EI

A6 → WRITE SUMMARY RECS → CLOSE FILES → STOP

640

PROGRAM LISTING

```
101000RALPH JOHNSON    4126385991
0053R46R
102000PETER PHILIPS    2138648290    0800000450000360000029561002000025000000001872006180034990000262080088520045990
0504000
103000JAMES KERR       1144873895    0810002500000203750001786600200000000001059000056001374000014817000784001923360
0285250
104000ESTER KESSLER    3193721843    0800003600002880000025518000200000000001497000054001531000002095800075600214340
0403200
105000JOHN LOPEZ       11253R4203    000000000005769200004364100200000000029990219200R66000000419860305980121240D
0R07692
106000SHIRLEY MOORE    2126378592    080000060000840000003439100200000250000002496018650079R0000349440261100123172D
0672000
107000MATHEW LANE      4134812641    000000000001923080013429200000000000000001R256039780000004056012558405566400
2692308
108000MARK ADAMS       11R7381859    0R000075000060000004842600200000250000000029920R8320000040560032088012364R0
0844000
109000ADA PERRY        2142873890    0800002600002080000011340020000000000000010B100271100211400001513400379400295960
0291200
110000JOHN PERRONE     3126033008    0R0000344400275200002344400020000000000014310030300214200020034000242002998R0
0385280
111000ETHEL SILVER     2127048592    0R0000344400275200002344400020000000000014310030300214200020034000242007299880
0385280
112000JOHN STEWART     1134521859    0800002500002000000167820020000000000004000243001735000021040137243255673752
1120135
113000WILLIAM SIEGAL   4166385242    000000000009615400074633000000000005122016399000004056008170802295770
1366154
114000SALLY BENDER     2174395388    0R00004500003600000626404002000250000001872011670061070000261380163480085498D
0504000
115000STEPHEN AFILLO   3192623854    0800009550007640000562300020002500000000410601561400004056005784840218596D
1069600
116000RONNEY AXLER     4177618550    00000000001153850008271400000000000079360247350000040560111104346290D
161538R5
117000ROBERT RACH      2170700111    0800005000004000000325390020002500000020R00079200041390003012001108800579460
0560000
118000MAE BADER        3182398742    0R500045000039375000326110020000250000000027990156400068990000393810218960966130
0551250
119000MAUREEN WEST     4142385910    000000000005384600042384020000000000000010400044500253900007300006330003055160
0753R46
120000COLINS REID      1144543877    0R00002500002000000157760020000000000004310062700385R00002003400877800530120
0280000
121000JOSEPH MOLONEY   2149738941    0R0000344400275200002140040020000000000014310006270038580026940000154280053900377160
03R5280
122000PHILIP OLSEN     2167R241R7    0R00002650002120000168190020000000000001102003850026940000136600643300004056001904009006200
0296800
123000NORMAN MONACO    115282238R    080000075000060000000515750020000250000000002496088700046280000349440124180006479200
0840000
124000THOMAS MOHERN    1134185996    0R000060000040000003978900200000000000002496088700046280000349440124180006479200
0672000
125000THOMAS GONER     3134185996    0R00002500002000000153610020000000000000010400044500029540000104560006230004135600
02R0000
ABNORMAL EOJ EXIT
```

DEDUCTION REGISTER   PERIOD ENDING   PAGE NO 001

EMP. NO	EMPLOYEE NAME	GROSS	FICA	FED.	STATE	MED.	CR. UNION	DUES	NET
101000	RALPH JOHNSON	$384.62	$20.00	$59.25	$10.73	$2.00	$0.00	$0.00	$292.64
102000	PETER PHILLIPS	$360.00	$18.72	$34.99	$6.18	$2.00	$0.00	$2.50	$295.61
103000	JAMES KERR	$203.75	$10.59	$13.74	$0.56	$2.00	$0.00	$0.00	$176.86
104000	ESTER KESSLER	$288.00	$14.97	$15.31	$0.54	$2.00	$0.00	$0.00	$255.18
105000	JOHN LOPEZ	$576.92	$29.99	$86.60	$21.92	$2.00	$0.00	$0.00	$436.41
106000	SHIRLEY MOORE	$480.00	$24.96	$87.98	$18.65	$2.00	$0.00	$2.50	$343.91
107000	MATHEW LANE	$1,923.08	$0.00	$397.60	$182.56	$0.00	$0.00	$0.00	$1,342.92
108000	MARK ADAMS	$600.00	$0.00	$88.32	$22.92	$2.00	$0.00	$2.50	$484.26
109000	ADA PERRY	$200.00	$10.81	$21.14	$2.71	$2.00	$0.00	$0.00	$171.34
110000	JOHN PERRONE	$275.20	$14.31	$21.42	$3.03	$2.00	$0.00	$0.00	$234.44
111000	ETHEL SILVER	$275.20	$14.31	$21.42	$3.03	$2.00	$0.00	$0.00	$234.44
112000	JOHN								$167.82
113000	WILL								
114000	SALL								
115000	STEP								
116000	RODN								
117000	ROBE								
118000	MAE								
119000	MAIR								
120000	COLI								
121000	JOSE								
122000	PHIL								
123000	NORM								
124000	THOM								
125000	THOM								

S U M M A R Y

GROSS $12,313.57

FICA	$328.13
FED. TAX	$1,871.50
STATE TAX	$530.00
MED. INS.	$44.00
CREDIT UNION	$0.00
UNION DUES	$20.00
NET PAY	$9,519.94
TOTALS $12,313.57	$12,313.57

GLOSSARY OF DATA-PROCESSING TERMS

A

*absolute coding

Coding that uses machine instructions with absolute addresses. Synonymous with specific coding.

†acceleration time

The elapsed time between the interpretation of tape read or write instructions and the transfer to or from tape and internal storage.

*access arm

a part of a disk storage unit that is used to hold one or more reading and writing heads.

*access time

(1) The time interval between the instant at which data are called for from a storage device and the instant delivery begins.
(2) The time interval between the instant at which data are requested to be stored and the instant at which storage is started.

*accounting machine

(1) A keyboard actuated machine that prepares accounting records.
(2) A machine that reads data from external storage media, such as cards or tapes, and automatically produces accounting records or tabulations, usually on continuous forms.

*Definitions preceded by an asterisk are reproduced with permission from American National Standards *Vocabulary For Information Processing*, X3.12–1970, copyright 1970 by the American National Standards Institute, copies of which may be purchased from the American National Standards Institute at 1430 Broadway, New York, N.Y. 10018.

*accuracy

The degree of freedom from error, that is, the degree of conformity to truth or to a rule. Accuracy is contrasted with precision. For example, four-place numerals are less precise than six-place numerals, nevertheless a properly computed four-place numeral might be more accurate than an improperly computed six-place numeral.

*acoustic delay line

A delay line whose operation is based on the time of propagation of sound waves in a given medium. Synonymous with sonic delay line.

†acronym

A word formed from the first letter or letters of the words in a name, term, or phrase, for example, SAGE from semi-automatic ground environment, and ALGOL from algorithmic language.

*adder

(1) A device whose output is a representation of the sum of the quantities represented by its inputs.
(2) See *half-adder*.

*address

(1) An identification, as represented by a name, *label*, or number, for a *register*, location in *storage*, or any other *data* source or destination such as the location of a station in a communication network.
(2) Loosely, any part of an *instruction* that specifies the location of an *operand* for the instruction.

†IBM definition.

*address format
  (1) The arrangement of the *address parts* of an *instruction*. The expression "plus-one" is frequently used to indicate that one of the addresses specifies the location of the next insturction to be executed, such as one-plus-one, two-plus-one, three-plus-one, four-plus-one.
  (2) The arrangement of the parts of a *single address*, such as those required for identifying *channel, module, track,* etc. in a disc system.

†addressing
  The means whereby the originator or control station selects the unit to which it is going to send a message.

*address register
  A register in which an address is stored.

†add time
  The time required for one addition, not including the time required to get and return the quantities from storage.

*algorithm
  (‡SC1) A prescribed set of well-defined rules or *processes* for the solution of a problem in a finite number of *steps*, e.g., a full statement of an arithmetic procedure for evaluating sin x to a stated *precision*. Contrast with *heuristic*.

†allocate
  To grant a resource to, or reserve it for, a job or task.

*alphabetic code
  (SC1) A code whose code set consists only of letters and associated special characters.

*alphameric
  Same as *alphanumeric*.

‡SC1 identifies definitions that have been discussed, and agreed upon at meetings of the International Organization For Standardization Technical Committee 97/Subcommittee 1.

*alphanumeric
  Pertaining to a character set that contains letters, digits, and usually other characters such as punctuation marks. Synonymous with *alphameric*.

*alphanumeric character set
  A *character set* that contains *letters, digits,* and usually other *characters*.

*alphanumeric code
  (SC1) A *code* whose *code set* consists of *letters, digits,* and associated *special characters*.

*analog
  (1) (SC1) Pertaining to representation by means of continuously variable physical quantities.
  (2) Contrast with *digital*.
  (3) See *network analog*.

*analog computer
  (1) (SC1) A computer in which analog representation of data is mainly used.
  (2) A computer that operates on analog data by performing physical processes on these data. Contrast with *digital* computer.

*AND
  A logic operator having the property that if P is a statement, Q is a statement, R is a statement. . . . , then the AND of P, Q, R . . . is true if all statements are true, false if any statement is false. P and Q is often represented by P·Q, PQ, P ∧ Q. Synonymous with logical multiply.

arithmetic operation
  Any of the fundamental operations of arithmetic, for example, the binary operations of additon, subtraction, multiplication, and division, and the unary operations of negation and absolute value.

*arithmetic unit
  The unit of a computing system that contains the circuits that perform arithmetic *operations*.

*arm
  See *access arm*.

*array

An arrangement of elements in one or more dimensions.

*artificial intelligence

The capability of a device to perform functions that are normally associated with human intelligence, such as reasoning, learning, and self-improvement. Related to *machine learning*.

artificial language

A *language* based on a set of prescribed rules that are established prior to its usage.

*ASCII (American National Standard Code for Information Interchange, X3.4–1968)

The standard *code*, using a coded *character set* consisting of 7-bit coded characters (8 bits including *parity check*), used for information interchange among *data processing systems*, communications systems, and associated equipment. Synonymous with USASCII.

*assemble

To prepare a *machine language program* from a symbolic language program by substituting *absolute operation codes* for symbolic operation codes and *absolute* or relocatable addresses for *symbolic addresses*.

*assembler

A computer program that assembles.

*asynchronous computer

(SC1) A computer in which each event or the performance of each operation starts as a result of a signal generated by the completion of the previous event or operation, or by the availability of the parts of the computer required for the next event or operation. Contrast with *synchronous computer*.

*automatic

(SC1) Pertaining to a process or device that, under specified conditions, functions without intervention by a human operator.

*automatic computer

A *computer* that can perform a sequence of *operations* without intervention by a human *operator*.

*automation

(1) (SC1) The implementation of processes by *automatic* means.

(2) The theory, art, or technique of making a process more *automatic*.

(3) The investigation, design, development, and application of methods of rendering processes *automatic*, self-moving, or self-controlling.

(4) (SC1) The conversion of a procedure, a process, or equipment to *automatic* operation.

*auxiliary operation

An *offline operation* performed by equipment not under control of the *central processing unit*.

auxiliary storage

See *secondary storage*.

B

*background processing

The *automatic* execution of lower priority *computer programs* when higher priority programs are not using the system resources. Contrast with *foreground processing*.

*base

(1) A reference value.

(2) A number that is multiplied by itself as many times as indicated by an exponent.

(3) Same as *radix*.

(4) See *floating-point base*.

*batch processing

(1) Pertaining to the technique of executing a set of computer programs such that each is completed before the next program of the set is started.

(2) Pertaining to the sequential input of computer programs or data.

(3) Loosely, the execution of computer programs serially.

*BCD

Binary-coded decimal notation.

*binary

(1) Pertaining to a characteristic or property involving a selection, choice, or condition in which there are two possibilities.

(2) Pertaining to the *number representation system* with a *radix* of two.

(3) See *Chinese binary, column binary, row binary.*

*binary cell

A *storage cell* of one *binary digit* capacity, e.g., a single bit *register*.

*binary code

A *code* that makes use of exactly two distinct characters, usually 0 and 1.

*binary-coded decimal notation

Positional notation in which the individual *decimal digits* expressing a *number* in *decimal notation* are each represented by a *binary numeral*, e.g., the number twenty-three is represented by 0010 0011 in the 8-4-2-1 type of binary-coded decimal notation and by 10111 in *binary notation.* Abbreviated BCD.

*binary digit

(1) In *binary notation,* either of the characters, 0 or 1.

(2) See equivalent binary digits. Abbreviated *bit.*

*binary element

A constituent element of data that may take either of two values or states.

binary notation

Fixed radix notation where the radix is two. For example, in binary notation the numeral 111 represents the number 1×2 squared plus 1×2 to the first plus 1×2 to the zero power, that is, seven.

*binary number

Loosely, a binary numeral.

*binary numeral

A binary representation of a number, e.g., "101" is a binary numeral and a "V" is the equivalent Roman numeral.

†binary to decimal conversion

Conversion of a binary number to the equivalent decimal number, that is, a base two number to a base ten number.

*bit

(1) A binary digit.

(2) Same as *Shannon.*

(3) See check bit, information bits, parity bit, sign bit.

black box

A generic term used to describe an unspecified device which performs a special function or in which known inputs produce known outputs in a fixed relationship.

*blank

A part of a *medium* in which no *characters* are recorded.

*block

(1) A set of things, such as *words, characters,* or *digits* handled as a unit.

(2) A collection of contiguous *records* recorded as a unit. Blocks are separated by *block gaps* and each block may contain one or more records.

(3) A group of bits, or n-ary digits, *transmitted* as a unit. An encoding procedure is generally applied to the group of bits or n-ary digits for error-control purposes.

(4) A group of contiguous characters recorded as a unit.

(5) See *input block.*

*block diagram

A diagram of a *system,* instrument, or *computer* in which the principal parts are represented by suitably associated geometrical figures to show both the basic functions and the functional relationships among the parts. Contrast with *flowchart.*

*block gap

An area on a data medium used to indicate the end of a *block* or *record.*

blocking

Combining two or more records into one block.

*block length

A measure of the size of a *block,* usually specified in units such as *records, words, computer words,* or *characters.*

*boolean

(1) Pertaining to the *process* used in the algebra formulated by George Boole.
(2) Pertaining to the operations of *formal logic.*

*boolean operator

A logic operator each of whose *operands* and whose result have one of two values.

*bootstrap

A technique or device designed to bring itself into a desired state by means of its own action, e.g., a machine *routine* whose first few instructions are sufficient to bring the rest of itself into the computer from an input device.

*branch

(1) A set of instructions that are executed between two successive decision instructions.
(2) To select a branch as in (1).
(3) A direct path joining two nodes of a network or graph.
(4) Loosely, a conditional jump.

buffer

A *routine* or *storage* used to compensate for a difference in rate of flow of *data,* or time of occurrence of events, when transmitting data from one device to another.

*bug

A *mistake* or *malfunction.*

*burst

(1) To separate continuous-form paper into discrete sheets.

(2) In data transmission, a sequence of *signals* counted as one unit in accordance with some specific criterion or measure.

*business data processing

(1) (SC1) Use of automatic data processing in accounting or management.
(2) Data processing for business purposes, e.g., recording and summarizing the financial transactions of a business.
(3) Synonymous with administrative data processing.

*byte

A sequence of adjacent binary digits operated upon as a unit and usually shorter than a computer word.

C

*calculator

(1) (SC1) A *data processor* especially suitable for performing arithmetical *operations* which requires frequent intervention by a human *operator.*
(2) Generally and historically, a device for carrying out logic and arithmetic digital operations of any kind.

†card code

The combinations of punched holes which represent characters (letters, digits, etc.) in a punched card.

*card column

A single line of *punch positions* parallel to the short edge of a 3¼ by 7⅜ inch *punched card.*

*card deck

Same as *deck.*

*card row

A single line of *punch positions* parallel to the long edge of a 3¼ by 7⅜ inch *punched card.*

†card-to-tape

Pertaining to equipment which transfers information directly from punched cards to punched or magnetic tape.

*cathode ray storage

An *electrostatic storage* device that utilizes a cathode ray beam for access to the *data*.

cathode ray tube display

(1) A device that presents data in visual form by means of controlled electron beams. (Abbreviated "CRT display".)

(2) The data display produced by the device as in (1).

*central processing unit

(SC1) A unit of a *computer* that includes the circuits controlling the interpretation and execution of *instructions*. Synonymous with *main frame*. Abbreviated CPU.

*chain printer

A printer in which the type slugs are carried by the links of a revolving chain.

*channel

(1) A path along which *signals* can be sent, e.g., *data* channel, *output* channel.

(2) The portion of a *storage medium* that is accessible to a given reading or writing station, e.g., *track, bank.*

(3) In communication, a means of one way transmission. Several channels may share common equipment. For example, in frequency multiplexing carrier systems, each channel uses a particular frequency band that is reserved for it. Contrast with *circuit.*

(4) See *input channel, output channel.*

*character

A *letter, digit,* or other *symbol* that is used as part of the organization, control, or representation of *data.* A character is often in the form of a spatial arrangement of adjacent or connected strokes.

*character printer

A device that prints a single *character* at a time. Contrast with *line printer.*

*character recognition

The identification of graphic, phonic, or other *characters* by *automatic* means. See *magnetic ink character recognition, optical character recognition.*

*character set

A set of unique representations called characters, e.g., the 26 letters of the English alphabet, O and I of the Boolean alphabet, the set of signals in the Morse code alphabet, the 128 characters of the ASCII alphabet.

character string

A linear sequence of characters.

*check bit

A *binary check digit*, e.g., a *parity bit.*

Chinese binary

See *column binary.*

*circuit

In communications, a means of two-way communication between two points, comprising associated "go" and "return" channels.

*clock

(1) A device that generates periodic *signals* used for synchronization.

(2) A device that measures and indicates time.

(3) A *register* whose content changes at regular intervals in such a way as to measure time.

*closed subroutine

A *subroutine* that can be stored at one place and can be linked to one or more calling *routines.* Contrast with *open subroutine.*

*COBOL

(COmmon Business Oriented Language) A *business data processing* language.

*code

(SC1) A set of unambiguous rules specifying the way in which *data* may be represented, for example, the set of correspondences in the standard code for information interchange.

*collating sequence
An ordering assigned to a set of items, such that any two sets in that assigned order can be collated.

*column
(1) A vertical arrangement of characters or other expressions.
(2) Loosely, a digit place.

column binary
Pertaining to the binary representation of data on punched cards in which adjacent positions in a column correspond to adjacent bits of data. (Synonymous with *Chinese binary.*)

*common field
A field that can be accessed by two or more independent routines.

communication
Transmission of intelligence between points of origin and reception without alteration of sequence or structure of the information content.

*communication link
The physical means of connecting one location to another for the purpose of transmitting and receiving data.

*compile
To prepare a machine language program from a computer program wirtten in another programming language by making use of the overall logic structure of the program, or generating more than one machine instruction for each symbolic statement, or both, as well as performing the function of an assembler.

*compiler
A program that compiles.

*complement
A *number* that can be derived from a specific number by subtracting it from a second specified number. For example,

in *radix notation,* the second specified number may be a given power of the *radix* or one less than a given power of the radix. The negative of a number is often represented by its complement.

*computer
(1) (SC1) A *data processor* that can perform substantial computation, including numerous arithmetic or logic operations, without intervention by a human *operator* during the *run.*
(2) A device capable of solving problems by accepting data, performing described operations on the data, and supplying the results of these operations. Various types of computers are calculators, digital computers, and analog computers.

*computer code
A *machine code* for a specific *computer.*

*computer instruction
A *machine instruction* for a specific *computer.*

*computer program
A series of *instructions* or *statements*, in a form acceptable to a *computer*, prepared in order to achieve a certain result.

computer statement
The CPU and associated peripheral equipment which function as a unit.

*computer word
A sequence of *bits* or *characters* treated as a unit and capable of being *stored* in one *computer location.* Synonymous with *machine word.*

*concurrent
Pertaining to the occurrence of two or more *events* or activities within the same specified interval of time. Contrast with *consecutive, sequential, simultaneous.*

*connector
(1) (SC1) On a *flowchart,* the means of representing the convergence of more than one *flowline* into one, or the divergence of one flowline into more than one. It may also represent a break

in a single flowline for continuation in another area.

(2) A means of representing on a *flowchart* a break in a line of flow.

*consecutive

Pertaining to the occurrence of two *sequential* events without the intervention of any other such event. Contrast with *concurrent, sequential, simultaneous.*

*console

That part of a *computer* used for communication between the *operator* or *maintenance* engineer and the computer.

†constant

A fixed or invariable value or data item. See *figurative constant.*

*control panel

A part of a computer console that contains manual controls.

control total

A sum resulting from the addition of a specified field from each record in a group of records, used for checking machine, program, and data reliability.

control unit

In a digital computer, those parts that effect the retrieval of instructions in proper sequence, the interpretation of each instruction, and the application of the proper signals to the arithmetic unit and other parts in accordance with this interpretation.

conversational mode

Communication between a terminal and the computer in which each entry from the terminal elicits a response from the computer and vice versa.

*core

See *magnetic core, multiple aperture core.*

CPS

"Characters per second" or "cycles per second", depending on context.

*CPU

Central Processing Unit.

*CRT display

Cathode Ray Tube display.

*cryotron

A device that makes use of the effects of low temperatures on conductive materials such that small magnetic field changes can control large current changes.

*cybernetics

(SC1) That branch of learning which brings together theories and studies on communication and control in living organisms and machines.

*cycle

(1) An interval of space or time in which one *set* of *events* or phenomena is completed.

(2) Any set of *operations* that is repeated regularly in the same *sequence*. The operations may be subject to variations on each repetition.

D

*data

(1) (SC1) A representation of facts, concepts, or *instructions* in a formalized manner suitable for communication, interpretation, or processing by humans or automatic means.

(2) Any representations such as *characters* or *analog* quantities to which meaning is or might be assigned.

(3) See *input data, numeric data, output data.*

*data bank

A comprehensive collection of *libraries* of data. For example, one line of an invoice may form an *item*, a complete invoice may form a *record*, a complete *set* of such records may form a *file*, the collection of inventory control files may form a *library*, and the libraries used by an organization are known as its data bank.

data base

See *data bank.*

data item

The name for an individual member of a set of data denoted by a data element. For example, the data item "Tuesday" is a member of the set denoted by the data element "weekday".

*data medium

(1) (SC1) The material in or on which a specific physical variable may represent *data*.

(2) (SC1) The physical quantity which may be varied to represent *data*.

data name

An identifier that names unambiguously an item of data.

*data processing

(SC1) The execution of a systematic sequence of *operations* performed upon *data*. Synonymous with information processing.

†data processing system

A network of machine components capable of accepting information, processing it according to a plan, and producing the desired results.

*data processor

(SC1) A device capable of performing *data processing*, including desk *calculators*, *punched card machines*, and *computers*. Synonymous with *processor(1)*.

data set

(1) The major unit of data storage and retrieval in the operating system, consisting of a collection of data in one of several prescribed arrangements and described by control information to which the system has access.

(2) A device which performs the modulation/demodulation and control functions necessary to provide compatability between business machines and communications facilities.

*debug

To detect, locate, and remove *mistakes* from a *routine* or *malfunctions* from a *computer*. Synonymous with *troubleshoot*.

*decimal

(1) Pertaining to a characteristic or property involving a selection, choice, or condition in which there are ten possibilities.

(2) Pertaining to the *number representation system* with a *radix* of ten.

(3) See *binary-coded decimal notation*.

*decimal digit

In *decimal notation*, one of the *characters* 0 thru 9.

*decimal notation

A *fixed radix notation* where the *radix* is ten. For example, in decimal notation, the *numeral 576.2 represents the number* 5 × 10 squared plus 7 × 10 to the first power plus 6 × 10 to the zero power plus 2 × 10 to the minus 1 power.

*decision

A determination of future action.

*decision table

A *table* of all contingencies that are to be considered in the description of a problem, together with the actions to be taken. Decision tables are sometimes used in place of *flowcharts* for problem description and documentation.

*deck

(1) A collection of *punched cards*. Synonymous with *card deck*.

(2) See *tape deck*.

*decode

To apply a set of unambiguous rules specifying the way in which *data* may be restored to a previous representation, i.e., to reverse some previous *encoding*.

*delay

The amount of time by which an event is retarded.

*destructive read

A read process that also erases the data from the source.

*detail file

Same as *transaction file*.

*digit

A *symbol* that represents one of the non-negative integers smaller than the radix. For example, in *decimal notation,* a digit is one of the *characters* from 0 to 9. Synonymous with numeric character.

*digital

(1) (SC1) Pertaining to *data* in the form of *digits.*

(2) Contrast with *analog.*

*digital computer

(1) (SC1) A *computer* in which *discrete* representation of *data* is mainly used.

(2) A *computer* that operates on *discrete data* by performing arithmetic and logic processes on these data. Contrast with *analog computer.*

*direct access

(1) Pertaining to the process of obtaining *data* from, or placing data into, *storage* where the time required for such access is independent of the *location* of the data most recently obtained or placed in storage.

(2) Pertaining to a *storage* device in which the *access time* is effectively independent of the location of the *data.*

(3) Synonymous with random access(1).

*disc

Alternate spelling for disk. See *magnetic disc.*

*disk

Alternate spelling for disc. See *magnetic disc.*

*display

(1) A visual presentation of data.

(2) See *cathode ray tube display.*

†DOS

Disk operating system.

*double precision

Pertaining to the use of two computer words to represent a number.

†double punch

More than one numeric punch in any one column of an IBM card.

†downtime

The time interval during which a device is *malfunctioning.*

*drum

See *magnetic drum*

*dump

(1) To copy the contents of all or part of a *storage,* usually from an internal storage into an external storage.

(2) A process as in (1).

(3) The *data* resulting from the process as in (1).

†duplexed system

A system with two distinct and separate sets of facilities, each of which is capable of assuming the system function while the other assumes a standby status. Usually both sets are identical in nature.

*duplicate

To *copy* so that the result remains in the same physical form as the source, e.g., to make a new *punched card* with the same pattern of holes as an original punched card. Contrast with *copy.*

*dynamic storage

A device *storing data* in a manner that permits the data to move or vary with time such that the sepcified data are not always available for recovery. *Magnetic drum* and *disc* storage are nonvolatile dynamic storage. An *acoustic delay line* is a volatile dynamic storage.

*dynamic storage allocation

A *storage allocation* technique in which the location of *computer programs* and *data* is determined by criteria applied at the moment of need.

E

*EAM

Electrical Accounting Machine.

*edit

To modify the form or *format* of *data,* e.g., to insert or delete *characters* such as page numbers or decimal points.

*EDP

Electronic Data Processing.

*eleven-punch

A punch in the second *row* from the top, on a *Hollerith punched card.* Synonymous with x-punch.

*emulate

To imitate one *system* with another such that the imitating system accepts the same *data,* executes the same *programs,* and achieves the same results as the imitated system. Contrast with *simulate.*

encode

To convert data to a coded form.

*ENQ

The *enquiry character.*

*enquiry character

A *communication control character* intended for use as a request for a response from a remote station. The response may include station identification and, if required, the type of equipment in service and station status. Abbreviated *ENG.*

*error message

An indication that an *error* has been detected.

*error range

The difference between the highest and lowest *error* values.

*exclusive OR

A logic operator having the property that if P is a statement and Q is a statement, then P exclusive OR Q is true if either but not both statements are true, false if both are true or both are false. P exclusive OR Q is often represented by $P \oplus Q$, $P \not\vee Q$.

†execute

To carry out an instruction or perform a routine.

†expression

A source-language combination of one or more operations.

†extent

The physical locations on input-output devices occupied by, or reserved for, a particular data set.

†external storage

A storage device outside the computer which can store information in a form acceptable to the computer, for example, cards and tapes.

F

feasibility study

(1) One of the initial steps in a systems study to determine whether the existing system, be it manual, mechanical, punched card, or computerized, is adequate or whether it should be modified, up-dated, or replaced.

(2) Usually the initial procedures and criteria for determination of suitability, capability, and compatibility of computer systems to various firms or organizations. A preliminary systems analysis of potential cost savings and increased problem solving capability as a result of the procurement of the first or a different computer.

*feedback loop

The components and processes involved in correcting or controlling a system by using part of the output as input.

*ferrite

An iron compound frequently used in the construction of magnetic cores.

*field

(1) In a *record,* a specified area used for a particular category of *data,* e.g., a group of card columns used to represent a wage rate, a set of *bit* locations in a *computer word* used to express the *address* of the *operand.*

wage rate, a set of *bit* locations in a *computer word* used to express the *address* of the *operand*.

(2) See *common field*.

*figurative constant

A preassigned, fixed, *character string* with a preassigned, fixed, *data name* in a particular *programming language*.

*file

A collection of related *records* treated as a unit. For example, on line of an invoice may form an *item*, a complete invoice may form a *record*, the complete set of such records may form a file, the collection of inventory control files may form a *library*, and the libraries used by an organization are known as its *data bank*.

*file layout

The arrangement and structure of *data* in a *file*, including the *sequence* and size of its components. By extension, a file layout might be the description thereof.

*file maintenance

The activity of keeping a *file* up to date by adding, changing, or deleting *data*.

†first generation computer

A computer utilizing vacuum tube components.

fixed-length record

Pertaining to a file in which all records are constrained to be of equal, predetermined length. (Contrast with *variable-length record*.)

*fixed storage

Storage whose contents are not alterable by *computer instructions*, e.g., *magnetic core* storage with a lockout feature, photographic disc. Synonymous with *nonerasable storage*, *permanent storage*, *read-only storage*.

floating-point base

In floating-point representation, the fixed positive integer that is the understood base of the power. (Synonymous with "floating-point radix".)

floating-point radix

Same as *floating-point base*.

*floating-point representation

A *number representation system* in which each *number*, as represented by a pair of *numerals*, equals one of those numerals times a power of an implicit fixed positive integer *base* where the power is equal to the implicit base raised to the *exponent* represented by the other numeral.

Common Notation	A Floating Point Representation
0.0001234 or $(0.1234) \times (10^{-3})$	1234 -03

*flowchart

(SC1) A graphical representation for the definition, analysis, or solution of a problem, in which *symbols* are used to represent *operations, data*, flow, equipment, etc. Contrast with *block diagram*.

*flowchart symbol

(SC1) A *symbol* used to represent *operations, data*, flow, or equipment on a *flowchart*.

*flowline

(SC1) on a flowchart, a line representing a connecting path between flowchart symbols, e.g., a line to indicate a transfer of data or control.

*foreground processing

The automatic execution of the computer programs that have been designed to preempt the use of the computing facilities. Usually a real time program. Contrast with background processing.

*format

(1) The arrangement of data.

(2) See *address format*.

FORTRAN

(FORmula TRANslating system) A language primarily used to express computer programs by arithmetic formulas.

G

†gang-punch
To punch all or part of the information from one punched card into succeeding cards.

*general purpose computer
(SC1) A *computer* that is designed to handle a wide variety of problems.

H

*half-adder
A combinational logic element having two outputs, S and C, and two inputs, A and B, such that the outputs are related to the inputs according to the following table.

input		output	
A	B	C	S
0	0	0	0
0	1	0	1
1	0	0	1
1	1	1	0

S denotes "Sum Without Carry," C denotes "Carry." Two half-adders may be used for performing binary addition.

*half-word
A contiguous sequence of *bits* or *characters* which comprises half a *computer word* and is capable of being addressed as a unit.

*hardware
(SC1) Physical equipment, as opposed to the *computer program* or method of use, e.g., mechanical, magnetic, electrical, or electronic devices. Contrast with *software*.

*header card
A card that contains *information* related to the *data* in cards that follow.

*heuristic
Pertaining to exploratory methods of problem solving in which solutions are discovered by evaluation of the progress made toward the final result. Contrast with *algorithm*.

*hexadecimal
Same as *sexadecimal*.

*Hollerith
Pertaining to a particular type of *code* or *punched card* utilizing 12 *rows* per *column* and usually 80 columns per card.

*hybrid computer
(SC1) A *computer* for *data processing* using both *analog* representation and *discrete* representation of *data*.

I

*inclusive OR
Same as OR.

*identity unit
An n-*input* unit that yields a specified *output signal* only when all n-input signals are alike.

*idle time
That part of *available time* during which the *hardware* is not being used. Contrast with *operating time*.

*inconnector
In *flowcharting*, a connector that indicates a continuation of a broken *flowline*. Contrast with *outconnector*.

*index
(1) An ordered reference list of the contents of a *file* or *document* together with *keys* or reference notations for identification or location of those contents.
(2) To prepare a list as in (1).
(3) A *symbol* or a *numeral* used to identify a particular quantity in an *array* of similar quantities. For example, the terms of an array represented by X_1, X_2, . . . , X_{100} have the indexes 1, 2, . . . , 100 respectively.
(4) To move a machine part to a predetermined position, or by a predetermined amount, on a *quantized* scale.
(5) See *index register*.

*index register
A *register* whose content may be added to or subtracted from the *operand address* prior to or during the execution of a *computer instruction.* Synonymous with b box.

*information
(SC1) The meaning that a human assigns to data by means of the known conventions used in their representation.

*information bits
In telecommunications, those bits which are generated by the data source and which are not used for error control by the data transmission system.

*information retrieval
(SC1) The methods and procedures for recovering specific information from stored data.

information system
The interacting of man and machine which, under man's control gathers data and disseminates information.

*information theory
The branch of learning concerned with the likelihood of accurate transmission or communication of messages subject to transmission failure, distortion, and noise.

inline processing
The processing of data in random order, not subject to preliminary editing or sorting.

*input
(1) Pertaining to a device, process, or *channel* involved in the insertion of *data* or states, or to the data or states involved.
(2) One, or a sequence of, *input states.*
(3) Same as *input device.*
(4) Same as *input channel.*
(5) Same as *input process.*
(6) Same as *input data.*
(7) See *manual input, real time input.*

*input area
An area of *storage* reserved for *input.* Synonymous with input block.

*input block
Same as *input area.*

*input channel
A *channel* for impressing a state on a device or *logic element.* Synonymous with input(4).

*input data
Data to be processed. Synonymous with input(6).

*input device
The device or collective set of devices used for conveying *data* into another device. Synonymous with input(3).

*input/output
Pertaining to either *input* or *output,* or both.

*input process
(1) The process of receiving *data* by a device.
(2) The process of transmitting data from *peripheral equipment,* or external *storage,* to internal storage.
(3) Synonymous with input(5).

instruction
A *statement* that specifies an *operation* and the values or locations of its *operands.* In this context, the term "instruction" is preferable to the terms "command" or "order" which are sometimes used synonymously. "Command" should be reserved for electronic signals, and "order" should be reserved for sequence, interpolation, and related usage.

*instruction register
A register that stores an instruction for execution.

*interface
A shared boundary. An interface might be a *hardware* component to link two devices or it might be a portion of *storage* or *registers accessed* by two or more *computer programs.*

*internal storage
Addressable *storage* directly controlled by the *central processing unit* of a *digital computer.*

*interpreter
> (1) A *computer program* that *translates* and executes each *source language* statement before translating and executing the next one.
>
> (2) A device that prints on a *punched card* the *data* already punched in the card.

*inter-record gap
> (See *record gap*.)

I/O
> An abbreviation for input/output.

J

*job
> A specified group of tasks prescribed as a unit of work for a *computer*. By extension, a job usually includes all necessary *computer programs, linkages, files,* and *instructions* to the *operating system*.

*job control statement
> A *statement* in a *job* that is used in identifying the job or describing its requirements to the *operating system*.

K

*K
> (1) A abbreviation for the prefix kilo, i.e., 1000 in decimal notation.
>
> (2) Loosely, when referring to storage capacity, two to the tenth power, 1024 in decimal notation.

*key
> (1) One or more characters within an item of data that are used to identify it or control its use.
>
> (2) See *actual key, search key*.

*keypunch
> A keyboard actuated device that punches holes in a card to represent data.

L

*label
> One or more *characters* used to identify a *statement* or an *item* of *data* in a *computer program*.

*language
> A set of representations, conventions, and rules used to convey information.

*latency
> The time between the completion of the interpretation of an *address* and the start of the actual transfer from the addressed *location*. Latency includes the *delay* associated with access to *storage devices* such as *magnetic drums* and *delay lines*.

*library
> (1) A collection of organized *information* used for study and reference.
>
> (2) A collection of related *files*. For example, one line of an invoice may form an *item*, a complete invoice may form a file, the collection of inventory control files may form a library, and the libraries used by an organization are known as its *data bank*.
>
> (3) See *program library*.

line printer
> A device that prints all characters of a line as a unit. Contrast with *character printer*.

literal
> A symbol or quantity in a source program that is iteself data, rather than a reference to data.

*load
> In programming, to enter data into storage or working registers.

*load-and-go
> An operating technique in which there are no stops between the loading and execution phases of a program and which may include assembling or compiling.

*logical file
> A collection of one or more *logical records*.

*logical record

A collection of *items* independent of their physical environment. Portions of the same logical *record* may be located in different physical records.

*loop

(1) A *sequence* of *instructions* that is executed repeatedly until a terminal condition prevails.

(2) See *feedback loop, magnetic hysteresis loop.*

M

machine-code

An operation code that a machine can recognize and execute.

†machine-independent

Pertaining to procedures or programs created without regard for the actual devices which will be used to process them.

*machine instruction

An instruction that a machine can recognize and execute.

*machine language

A language that is used directly by a machine.

*machine learning

(SC1) The ability of a device to improve its performance based on its past performance. Related to artificial intelligence.

*magnetic card

A card with a magnetic surface on which *data* can be *stored* by selective magnetization of portions of the flat surface.

*magnetic core

A configuration of magnetic material that is, or is intended to be, placed in a spatial relationshiop to current-carrying conductors and whose magnetic properties are essential to its use. It may be used to concentrate an induced magnetic field as in a transformer induction coil, or armature, to retain a magnetic polarization for the purpose of *storing* data, or for its nonlinear properties as in a *logic element.* It may be made of such material as iron, iron oxide, or ferrite and in such shapes as wires, tapes, toroids, rods, or thin film.

*magnetic disc

A flat circular plate with a magnetic surface on which *data* can be *stored* by selective magnetization of portions of the flat surface.

*magnetic drum

A right circular cylinder with a magnetic surface on which *data* can be *stored* by selective magnetization of portions of the curved surface.

*magnetic ink

An ink that contains particles of a magnetic substance whose presence can be detected by magnetic sensors.

*magnetic ink character recognition

The machine recognition of characters printed with magnetic ink. Contrast with optical character recognition. Abbreviated MICR.

*magnetic storage

A storage device that utilizes the magnetic properties of materials to store data, e.g., magnetic cores, tapes, and films.

*magnetic tape

(1) A tape with a magnetic surface on which *data* can be *stored* by selective polarization of portions of the surface.

(2) A tape of magnetic material used as the constituent in some forms of *magnetic cores.*

*magnetic thin film

A layer of magnetic material, usually less than one micron thick, often used for logic or storage elements.

*main frame

(SC1) Same as *central processing unit.*

*main storage

The general-purpose *storage* of a *computer*. Usually, main storage can be *accessed* directly by the operating *registers*. Contrast with *auxiliary storage*.

†major total

The result when a summation is terminated by the most significant change of group.

*management information system

(1) (SC1) Management performed with the aid of *automatic data processing*. Abbreviated *MIS*.

(2) An *information system* designed to aid in the performance of management *functions*.

*manual input

(1) The entry of *data* by hand into a device.

(2) The data entered as in (1).

†mark-sense

To mark a position on a punched card with an electrically conductive pencil, for later conversion to machine punching.

*mark sensing

The electrical sensing of manually recorded conductive marks on a nonconductive surface.

†mass storage (online)

The storage of a large amount of data which is also readily accessible to the central processing unit of a computer.

*mass storage device

A device having a large storage capacity, e.g., magnetic disc, magnetic drum.

*master file

A file that is either relatively permanent or that is treated as an authority in a particular job.

*match

To check for identity between two or more items of data.

*mathematical model

A mathematical representation of a process, device, or concept.

*medium

The material, or configuration thereof, on which data are recorded, e.g., paper tape, cards, magnetic tape. Synonymous with *data medium*.

*merge

To combine *items* from two or more similarly ordered sets into one set that is arranged in the same order. Contrast with *collate*.

*MICR

Magnetic Ink Character Recognition.

†microsecond

One-millionth of a second.

†millisecond

One-thousandth of a second.

†minor total

The result when a summation is terminated by the least significant change of group.

*mnemonic symbol

A *symbol* chosen to assist the human memory, e.g., an abbreviation such as "mpy" for "multiply."

*monadic operation

An operation on one operand, e.g., negation. Synonymous with *unary operation*.

†monolithic integrated circuit

A class of integrated circuits wherein the substrate is an active material, such as the semiconductor silicon.

*monitor

Software or hardware that observes, supervises, controls, or verifies the operations of a system.

*multiple aperture core

A *magnetic core* with two or more holes through which wires may be passed and around which magnetic flux may exist. Multiple aperture cores may be used for *nondestructive reading*.

*multiplex

To *interleave* or simultaneously *transmit* two or more messages on a single *channel*.

*multiprocessing

(1) Pertaining to the simultaneous execution of two or more *computer programs* or *sequences* of *instructions* by a *computer* or *computer netowrk*.

(2) Loosely, *parallel processing*.

*multiprocessor

A *computer* employing two or more processing units under integrated control.

*multiprogramming

Pertaining to the *concurrent* execution of two or more *programs* by a *computer*.

N

nanosecond

One-billionth of a second.

*network analog

The expression and solution of mathematical relationships between variables using a circuit or circuits to represent these variables.

*nines complement

The *radix-minus-one* complement in *decimal notation*.

†nominal (rated) speed

Maximum speed or data rate of a device or facility which makes no allowance for necessary delaying functions, such as checking, tabbling, etc.

*nondestructive read

A *read* process that does not *erase* the *data* in the source. Abbreviated NDR.

*number

(1) A mathematical entity that may indicate quantity or amount of units.

(2) Loosely, a *numeral*.

*number representation system

An agreed set of *symbols* and rules for *number representation*. Synonymous with numeral system, numeration system.

*number system

Loosely, a *number representation system*.

*numeration system

Same as *number representation system*.

*numerical analysis

The study of methods of obtaining useful quantitative solutions to problems that have been expressed mathematically, including the study of the errors and bounds on errors in obtaining such solutions.

*numerical control

(SC1) Automatic control of a process performed by a device that makes use of all or part of numerical data generally introduced as the operation is in process.

*numeric character

Same as *digit*.

*numeric code

(SC1) A code whose code set consists only of digits and associated special characters.

numeric data

Data represented by numeric characters and some special characters.

*numeric data code

A code consisting only of numerals and special characters.

O

*object code

Output from a *compiler* or *assembler* which is itself executable *machine code* or is suitable for processing to produce executable machine code.

*object language

Same as *target language*.

*object program

A fully *compiled* or *assembled program* that is ready to be *loaded* into the *computer*. Synonymous with target program. Contrast with *source program*.

*OCR

Optical character recognition.

*octal

(1) Pertaining to a characteristic or property involving a selection, choice or condition in which there are eight possibilities.

(2) Pertaining to the *number representation system* with a *radix* of eight.

*offline

Pertaining to equipment or devices not under control of the *central processing unit.*

*offline storage

Storage not under control of the *central processing unit.*

†on-demand system

A system from which information or service is available at time of request.

†one-for-one

A phrase often associated with an assembly routine where one source language instruction is converted to one machine language instruction.

*ones complement

The *radix-minus-one complement* in *binary notation.*

*online

(1) Pertaining to equipment or devices under control of the *central processing unit.*

(2) Pertaining to user's ability to interact with a *computer.*

*openended

Pertaining to a process or system that can be augmented.

*open subroutine

A subroutine that is inserted into a routine at each place it is used. Synonymous with direct insert subroutine. Contrast with closed subroutine.

*operand

That which is operated upon. An operand is usually identified by an address part of an instruction.

*operating system

(SC1) *Software* which controls the execution of *computer programs* and which may provide scheduling *debugging,* input/output control, accounting, *compilation storage* assignment, *data* management, and related services.

*operating time

That part of available time during which the hardware is operating and assumed to be yielding correct results. It includes development time, production time, and makeup time.

*operation

(1) A defined action, namely, the act of obtaining a result from one or more operands in accordance with a rule that completely specifies the result for any permissible combination of operands.

(2) The set of such acts specified by such a rule, or the rule itself.

(3) The act specified by a single *computer instruction.*

(4) A *program* step undertaken or executed by a *computer,* e.g., addition, multiplication, *extraction,* comparison, *shift, transfer.* The operation is usually specified by the *operator* part of an instruction.

(5) The event of specific action performed by a *logic element.*

*operation code

A *code* that represents specific operations. Synonymous with *instruction code.*

*optical character recognition

The machine identification of printed *characters* through use of light-sensitive devices. Contrast with *magnetic ink character recognition.* Abbreviated *OCR.*

*optical scanner

(1) A device that scans optically and usually generates an analog or digital signal.

(2) A device that optically scans printed or written data and generates their digital representations.

*OR

(1) A logic *operator* having the property that if P is a statement, Q is a statement, R is a statement, . . . then the OR of P, Q, R, . . . , is true if at least one statement is true, false if all statements are false. P OR Q is often represented by $P + Q, P \vee Q$. Synonymous with inclusive OR, boolean add, logical add. Contrast with *exclusive OR*.

(2) The abbreviation for *Operations Research*.

(3) See *exclusive OR, inclusive OR*.

OS

Operating system, q.v.

*outconnector

In *flowcharting*, a *connector* that indicates a point at which a *flowline* is broken for continuation at another point. Contrast with *inconnector*.

*output

(1) (SC1) Pertaining to a device, *process*, or *channel* involved in an *output process*, or to the data or states involved.

(2) One, or a sequence of, *output states*.

(3) Same as *output device*.

(4) Same as *output channel*.

(5) Same as *output process*.

(6) Same as *output data*.

(7) See *real time output*.

*output area

An area of *storage* reserved for *output*.

*output channel

A *channel* for conveying *data* from a device or *logic element*. Synonymous with output(4).

*output process

(SC1) The *process* of delivering *data* by a system, subsystem, or device. Synonymous with output(5).

*overflow

(1) That portion of the result of an *operation* that exceeds the capacity of the intended unit of *storage*.

(2) Pertaining to the generation of overflow as in (1).

(3) Contrast with *underflow*.

†overlap

To do something at the same time that something else is being done; for example, to perform input/output operations while instructions are being executed by the central porcessing unit.

*overlay

The technique of repeatedly using the same blocks of internal *storage* during different stages of a *program*. When one *routine* is no longer needed in storage, another routine can replace all or part of it.

P

*parallel

(1) Pertaining to the *concurrent* or *simultaneous* occurrence of two or more related activities in multiple devices or *channels*.

(2) Pertaining to the simultaneity of two or more *processes*.

(3) Pertaining to the simultaneous processing of the individual parts of a whole, such as the *bits* of a *character* and the characters of a *word*, using separate facilities for the various parts.

(4) Contrast with *serial*.

*parallel operation

Pertaining to the *concurrent* or *simultaneous* execution of two or more *operations* in devices such as multiple arithmetic or logic units. Contrast with *serial operation*.

*parallel processing

Pertaining to the *concurrent* or *simultaneous* execution of two or more *processes* in multiple devices such as *channels* or processing units. Contrast with *multiprocessing, serial processing*.

*parallel transmission

In *telecommunications*, the *simultaneous transmission* of a certain number of *signal* elements constituting the same telegraph or *data* signal. For example, use of a *code* according to which each signal is characterized by a combination of three out of twelve frequencies simultaneously transmitted over the *channel*. Contrast with *serial transmission*.

*parity bit

A *check bit* appended to an *array* of *binary digits* to make the sum of all the binary digits, including the check bit, always odd or always even.

*parity check

A *check* that tests whether the number of ones (or zeros) in an *array* of *binary digits* is odd or even. Synonymous with *odd-even check*.

*patch

(1) To modify a *routine* in a rough or expedient way.

(2) A temporary electrical connection.

*pattern recognition

The identification of shapes, forms, or configurations by *automatic* means.

*peripheral equipment

(SC1) In a data processing system, any unit of equipment, distinct from the central processing unit, which may provide the system with outside communications.

†physical record

A record from the standpoint of the manner or form in which it is stored, retrieved, and moved—that is, one that is defined in terms of physical qualities.

†PL/I

Programming Language/I, a high level programming language.

†point-to-point transmission

Transmission of data directly between two points without the use of any intermediate terminal or computer.

*plugboard

A perforated board into which plugs are manually inserted to control the operation of equipment. Synonymous with *control panel*(2).

*positional notation

(SC1) A *numeration system* in which a *number* is represented by means of an ordered *set* of *digits,* such that the value contributed by each digit depends upon its position as well as upon its value. Synonymous with *positional representation*.

*predefined process

A process that is identified only by name and that is defined elsewhere.

*preventive maintenance

Maintenance specifically intended to prevent *faults* from occurring during subsequent *operation*. Contrast with *corrective maintenance*. Corrective maintenance and preventive maintenance are both performed during *maintenance time*.

†primary storage

The main internal storage.

*printer

See *chain printer, character printer, line printer*.

*printing

See *line printing*.

*problem description

(1) (SC1) In *information processing,* a statement of a problem. The statement may also include a description of the method of solution, the procedures and *algorithms,* etc.

(2) A statement of a problem. The statement may also include a description of the method of solution, the solution itself, the transformations of *data* and the relationship of procedures, data, constraints, and environment.

*problem oriented language

A *programming language* designed for the convenient expression of a given class of problems.

*procedure oriented language
    A programming language designed for the convenient expression of procedures used in the solution of a wide class of problems.

*process
    A systematic *sequence* of *operations* to produce a specified result. See *input process, output process, predefined process.*

*processor
    (1) In *hardware,* a *data processor.*
    (2) In *software,* a *computer program* that includes the *compiling, assembling, translating,* and related functions for a specific *programming language, COBOL* processor, *FORTRAN* processor.
    (3) See *data processor, multiprocessor.*

*program
    (1) (SC1) A series of actions proposed in order to achieve a certain result.
    (2) Loosely, a *routine.*
    (3) To design, write, and test a program as in (1).
    (4) Loosely, to write a *routine.*
    (5) See *computer program, object program, source program, target program.*

*program library
    A collection of available computer programs and routines.

*programmer
    (SC1) A person mainly involved in designing, writing and testing *computer programs.*

*programming
    (SC1) The design, the writing, and testing of a *program.*

*programming language
    A *language* used to prepare *computer* programs.

*punch
    A perforation, as in a *punched card* or paper tape.

*punched card
    (1) A card *punched* with a pattern of holes to represent *data.*
    (2) A card as in (1) before being *punched.*

*punched tape
    A tape on which a pattern of holes or cuts is used to represent *data.*

Q

queue
    (Noun). A waiting line formed by items in a system waiting for service; for example, customers at a bank teller window or messages to be transmitted in a message switching system. (verb). To arrange in, or form, a queue.

*queued access method
    Any access method that automatically synchronizes the *transfer* of *data* between the *program* using the access method and *input/output* devices, thereby eliminating delays for input/output *operation.*

R

*radix
    (SC1) In *positional representation,* that integer, if it exists, by which the *significance* of the *digit place* must be multiplied to give the significance of the next higher digit place. For example, in *decimal notation,* the radix of each place is ten; in a *biquinary code,* the radix of the fives place is two. Synonymous with *base*(3).

*radix complement
    (SC1) A *complement* obtained by subtracting each *digit* from one less than its *radix,* then adding one to the least *significant digit,* executing all *carries* required, e.g., *tens complement* in *decimal notation, twos complement* in *binary notation.* Synonymous with *true complement.*

*radix-minus-one complement
A *complement* obtained by subtracting each *digit* from one less than the *radix*, e.g., *nines complement* in *decimal notation, ones complement* in *binary notation.* Synonymous with diminished radix complement.

*random access
(1) Same as *direct access.*
(2) In COBOL, an *access mode* in which specific *logical records* are obtained from or placed into a *mass storage file* in a nonsequential manner.

random access device
A device in which the access time is effectively independent of the location of the data. (Synonymous with "direct access device.")

*range
(1) The *set* of values that a quantity or *function* may assume.
(2) The difference between the highest and lowest value that a quantity or *function* may assume.
(3) See *error range.*

random access device
A device in which the access time is effectively independent of the location of the data. (Synonymous with "direct access device.")

*read
(1) To acquire or interpret data from a storage device, a data medium, or any other source.
(2) See *destructive read, nondestructive read.*

*real time
(1) Pertaining to the actual time during which a physical *process* transpires.
(2) Pertaining to the performance of a computation during the actual time that the related physical *process* transpires, in order that the results of the computation can be used in guiding the physical process.

*real time input
Input data inserted into a *system* at the time of generation by another system.

*real time output
Output data removed from a *system* at time of need by another system.

*record
(1) A collection of related *items* of *data,* treated as a unit, for example, one line of an invoice may form a record; a complete set of such records may form a *file.*
(2) See *logical record, variable-length record.*

*record gap
An area on a *data medium* used to indicate the end of a *block* or *record.* Synonymous with inter-record gap.

*recording density
The number of *bits* in a single linear *track* measured per unit of length of the recording *medium.*

*record layout
The arrangement and structure of *data* in a *record,* including the *sequence* and size of its components. By extension, a record layout might be the description thereof.

†reel
A mounting for a roll of tape.

*register
A device capable of storing a specified amount of data, such as one *word.*

*relocate
In *computer programming,* to *move* a *routine* from one portion of *storage* to another and to adjust the necessary *address* references so that the routine, in its new *location,* can be executed.

*remote access
Pertaining to communication with a *data processing* facility by one or more stations that are distant from that facility.

†report generation
> A technique for producing complete machine reports from information which describes the input file and the format and content of the output report.

†reproduce
> To prepare a duplicate of stored information, especially for punched cards, punched paper tape, or magnetic tape.

†reproducer
> A device which will duplicate, in one card, all or part of the information contained in another card.

†rewind
> To return a magnetic or paper tape to its beginning.

*roll-in
> To restore in *main storage, data* which had previously been *transferred* from main storage to *auxiliary storage.*

*roll-out
> To record the contents of *main storage* in *auxiliary storage.*

*rounding error
> An *error* due to *roundoff.* Contrast with *truncation error.*

*roundoff
> To delete the least *significant digit* or digits of a *numeral,* and to adjust the part retained in accordance with some rule.

*routine
> (SC1) An ordered set of *instructions* that may have some general or frequent use.

row binary
> Pertaining to the binary representation of data on cards in which adjacent positions in a row correspond to adjacent bits of data; for example, each row in an 80-column card may be used to represent 80 consecutive bits of two 40-bit words.

RPG
> Report program generator.

*run
> A single, continuous performance of a *computer program* or *routine.*

S

*single factor
> A *number* used as a multiplier, so chosen that it will cause a set of quantities to fall within a given *range* of values. To scale the *values* 856, 432, -95, and -182 between -1 and $+1$, a scale factor of $\frac{1}{1000}$ would be suitable.

*scheduled maintenance
> Maintenance carried out in accordance with an established plan.

secondary storage
> A storage device in addition to the main storage of a computer; e.g., magnetic tape, disk, drum, or card. Secondary storage usually holds much larger amounts of data with slower access times than primary storage.

second generation computer
> A computer utilizing solid state components.

seek
> To position the access mechanism of a direct access device at a specified location.

selector
> A device for directing electrical input pulses onto one of two output lines, depending upon the presence or absence of a predetermined accompanying control pulse.

†sequencing
> Ordering in a series or according to rank or time.

*sequential
> Pertaining to the occurrence of *events* in time *sequence,* with little or no simultaneity or overlap of events. Contrast with *concurrent, consecutive, simultaneous.*

*sequential computer

A *computer* in which *events* occur in time *sequence*, with little or no simultaneity or overlap of events.

*sequential control

A mode of *computer operation* in which *instructions* are executed in an implicitly defined *sequence* until a different sequence is explicitly initiated by a *jump instruction.*

*sequential operation

Pertaining to the performance of *operations* one after the other.

*serial

(1) Pertaining to the *sequential* or *consecutive* occurrence of two or more related activities in a single device or *channel.*

(2) Pertaining to the *sequencing* of two or more *processes.*

(3) Pertaining to the *sequential processing* of the individual parts of a whole, such as the *bits* of a *character* or the characters of a *word,* using the same facilities for successive parts.

(4) Contrast with *parallel.*

*serial access

(1) Pertaining to the *sequential* or *consecutive* *transmission* of *data* to or from *storage.*

(2) Pertaining to the *process* of obtaining *data* from or placing *data* into *storage,* where the *access time* is dependent upon the *location* of the data most recently obtained or placed in storage. Contrast with *direct access.*

*serial computer

(1) A computer having a single arithmetic and logic unit.

(2) A computer some specified characteristic of which is serial, e.g., a computer that manipulates all bits of a word serially. Contrast with *parallel computer.*

*serial processing

Pertaining to the sequential or consecutive execution of two or more processes in a single device such as a channel or processing unit. Contrast with *parallel processing.*

†serial transfer

A transfer of data in which elements are transferred in succession over a single line.

*serial transmission

In *telecommunications, transmission* at successive intervals of *signal* elements constituting the same telegraph or *data* signal. The *sequential* elements may be transmitted with or without interruption, provided that they are not transmitted *simultaneously.* For example, telegraph transmission by a time divided *channel.* Contrast with *parallel transmission.*

*service routine

A *routine* in general support of the *operation* of a *computer,* e.g., an *input-output, diagnostic, tracing,* or *monitoring routine.* Synonymous with *utility routine.*

*sexadecimal

(1) Pertaining to a characteristic or property involving a selection, choice, or condition in which there are sixteen possibilities.

(2) Pertaining to the *numeration system* with a *radix* of sixteen.

(3) Synonymous with *hexadecimal.*

*Shannon

A unit of measurement of quantity of information equal to that contained in a *message* represented by one or the other of two equally probable, exclusive, and exhaustive states.

*sharing

See *time sharing.*

*sign bit

A *binary digit* occupying the *sign position.*

*significance

(SC1) In *positional representation,* the factor, dependent on the *digit place,* by which a *digit* is multiplied to obtain its additive contribution in the representation of a *number.* Synonymous with *weight.*

*significant digit
A *digit* that is needed for a certain purpose, particularly one that must be kept to preserve a specific *accuracy* or *precision.*

*sign position
A *position,* normally located at one end of a *numeral,* that contains an indication of the algebraic sign of the *number.*

simplex mode
Operation of a communication channel in one direction only, with no capability for reversing.

*simulate
(1) (SC1) To represent certain features of the behavior of a physical or abstract *system* by the behavior of another system.
(2) To represent the functioning of a device, *system,* or *computer program* by another, e.g., to represent the functioning of one *computer* by another, to represent the behavior of a physical system by the execution of a computer program, to represent a biological system by a *mathematical model.*
(3) Contrast with *emulate.*

*simultaneous
Pertaining to the occurrence of two or more *events* at the same instant of time. Contrast with *concurrent, consecutive, sequential.*

†simultaneous transmission
Transmission of control characters or data in one direction while information is being received in the other direction.

*single-address
Pertaining to an *instruction format* containing one *address part.* Synonymous with *one-address.*

software
A set of programs, procedures, rules and possibly associated documentation concerned with the operation of a data processing system. For example, compilers, library routines, manuals, circuit diagrams.

*solid state component
A component whose *operation* depends on the control of electric or magnetic phenomena in solids, e.g., a transistor, crystal diode, *ferrite* core.

*sort
(1) To segregate items into groups according to some definite rules.
(2) Same as *order.*

*sorter
A person, device, or *computer routine* that *sorts.*

*source language
The *language* from which a *statement* is translated.

*source program
A *computer program* written in a *source language.* Contrast with *object program.*

*SP
The *space character.*

*space
(1) A site intended for the *storage* of *data,* e.g., a site on a printed page or a *location* in a *storage medium.*
(2) A basis *unit* of area, usually the size of a single *character.*
(3) One or more *space characters.*
(4) To advance the *reading* or *display position* according to a prescribed *format,* e.g., to advance the printing or display position horizontally to the right or vertically down. Contrast with *backspace.*

*special character
A *graphic character* that is neither a *letter,* nor a *digit,* nor a *space character.*

*special purpose computer
(SC1) A *computer* that is designed to handle a restricted class of problems.

*spot punch
A device for *punching* one hole at a time.

*statement
  (1) In *computer programming*, a meaningful expression or generalized *instruction* in a *source language*.
  (2) See *job control statement*.

*static storage
  Storage other than *dynamic storage*.

†station
  One of the input or output points of a communications system; for example, the telephone set in the telephone system or the point where the business machine interfaces the channel on a leased private line.

*storage
  (1) Pertaining to a device into which data can be entered, in which they can be held, and from which they can be retrieved at a later time.
  (2) Loosely, any device that can store data.
  (3) Synonymous with "memory."

*storage allocation
  (1) The assignment of *blocks* of *data* to specified blocks of *storage*.
  (2) See *dynamic storage allocation*.

*storage capacity
  The amount of *data* that can be contained in a *storage device*.

*storage cell
  An elementary *unit* of *storage*, e.g., a *binary cell*, a *decimal* cell.

*storage device
  A device into which *data* can be inserted, in which they can be retained, and from which they can be retrieved.

*storage protection
  An arrangement for preventing access to *storage* for either *reading*, or *writing*, or both. Synonymous with memory protection.

*stored program computer
  (SC1) A *computer* controlled by internally stored *instructions* that can synthesize, *store*, and in some cases alter instructions as

though they were *data* and that can subsequently execute these instructions.

*string
  A linear sequence of entities such as characters or physical elements.

†summary punch
  (Noun). A card-punching machine which can be connected to an accounting machine to punch totals or balance cards. (verb). To punch summary information in cards.

†supervisor
  A routine or routines executed in response to a requirement for altering or interrupting the flow of operation through the central processing unit, or for performance of input/output operations, and, therefore, the medium through which the use of resources is coordinated and the flow of operations through the central processing unit is maintained. Hence, a control routine that is executed in supervisor state.

*symbolic address
  An *address* expressed in *symbols* convenient to the *computer programmer*.

*symbolic coding
  Coding that uses *machine instructions* with *symbolic addresses*.

*synchronization pulses
  Pulses introduced by *transmitting* equipment into the receiving equipment to keep the two equipments operating in step.

*synchronous computer
  (SC1) A *computer* in which each *event*, or the performance of any basic *operation*, is constrained to start on, and usually to keep in step with, *signals* from a *clock*. Contrast with *asynchronous computer*.

*syntax
  (1) The structure of expressions in a *language*.
  (2) The rules governing the structure of a *language*.

*system
(1) (SC1) An assembly of methods, *procedures,* or techniques united by regulated interaction for form an organized whole.
(2) (SC1) An organized collection of men, *machines,* and methods required to accomplish a *set* of specific *functions.*

T

*tape deck
Same as tape unit.

*tape to card
Pertaining to equipment or methods that transmit data from either magnetic tape or punched tape to punched cards.

*tape unit
A device containing a *tape drive,* together with *reading* and *writing heads* and associated controls. Synonymous with tape deck, tape station.

*target language
The *language* to which a *statement* is *translated.* Synonymous with object language.

*target program
Same as *object program.*

*telecommunications
Pertaining to the *transmission* of *signals* over long distances, such as by telegraph, radio, or television.

†teleprocessing
A form of information handling in which a data processing system utilizes communication facilities. (Originally an IBM trademark.)

†teletype
Trademark of Teletype Corporation, usually referring to a series of different types of teleprinter equipment such as tape punches, reperforators, page printers, etc., utilized for communications systems.

†teletypewriter
Generic term referring to the basic equipment made by Teletype Corporation and to teleprinter equipment.

*temporary storage
In *programming, storage locations* reserved for intermediate results. Synonymous with working storage.

*tens complement
The *radix complement* in *decimal notation.*

*terminal
A point in a *system* or communication network at which *data* can either enter or leave.

†third generation computer
A computer utilizing SLT components.

*three-address
Pertaining to an *instruction format* containing three *address parts.*

†throughput
A measure of system efficiency; the rate at which work can be handled by a system.

†tie line
A private-line communications channel of the type provided by communications common carriers for linking two or more points together.

tie truck
A telephone line or channel directly connecting two branch exchanges.

time sharing
Participation in available computer time by multiple users, via terminals. Characteristically, the response time is such that the computer seems dedicated to each user.

TOS
Tape Operating System.

trailor record
A record which follows one or more records and contains data related to those records.

*transaction file

A *file* containing relatively transient *data* to be processed in combination with a *master file*. For example, in a payroll applicaton, a transaction file indicating hours worked might be processed with a master file containing employee name and rate of pay. Synonymous with detail file.

†transistor

A small solid-state, semiconducting device, ordinarily using germanium, that performs nearly all the functions of an electronic tube, especially amplification.

†translator

(1) A device that converts information from one system of representation into equipment information in another system of representation. In telephone equipment, it is the device that converts dialed digits into call-routing information.

(2) A routine for changing information from one representation or language to another.

*true complement

Same as *radix complement*.

*truncate

To terminate a computational process in accordance with some rule, e.g., to end the evaluation of a power series at a specified term.

*truncation error

An *error* due to truncation. Contrast with *rounding error*.

†turnaround time

(1) The elapsed time between submission of a job to a computer center and the return of results.

(2) The actual time required to reverse the direction of transmission from send to receive or vice versa when using a half-duplex circuit. For most communications facilities, there will be time required by line propagation and line effects, modem timing, and

machine reaction. A typical time is 200 milliseconds on a half-duplex telephone connection.

*twelve-punch

A *punch* in the top row of a *Hollerith punch card*. Synonymous with *y-punch*.

*twos complement

The *radix complement in binary notation*.

†typebar

A linear type element containing all printable symbols.

*type font

Type of a given size and style, e.g., 10-point Bodoni Modern.

U

*unary operation

Same as *monadic operation*.

*underflow

Pertaining to the condition that arises when a machine computation yields a nonzero result smaller than the smallest nonzero quantity that the intended *unit* of *storage* is capable of storing. Contrast with *overflow*.

*unit

(1) A device having a special *function*.

(2) A basic element.

(3) See *arithmetic unit, central processing unit, control unit, identity unit, tape unit*.

†unit record

Historically, a card containing one complete record. Currently, the punched card.

†update

To modify a master file with current information according to a specified procedure.

*USASCII

Same as *ASCII*.

†user

Anyone utilizing the services of a computing system.

*utility routine
Same as *service routine.*

V

*variable
A quantity that can assume any of a given *set* of values.

*variable-length record
Pertaining to a *file* in which the *records* are not uniform in length.

†verifier
A device similar to a card punch used to check the inscribing of data by rekeying.

*verify
(1) To determine whether a transcription of *data* or other *operation* has been accomplished accurately.
(2) To *check* the results of *keypunching.*

†voice-grade channel
A channel suitable for transmission of speech, digital or analog data, or facsimile, generally with a frequency range of about 300 to 3000 cycles per second.

†volume
The portion of a single unit of storage media which is accessible to a single read/write mechanism.

W

†wait condition
As applied to tasks, the condition of a task such that it is dependent on an event or events in order to enter the ready condition.

*word
A character string or a bit string considered as an entity.

*word length
A measure of the size of a word, usually specified in units such as characters or binary digits.

*working storage
Same as *temporary storage.*

*write
To record *data* in a *storage device* or a data *medium.* The recording need not be permanent, such as the writing on a *cathode ray tube display device.*

X

*x-punch
Same as *eleven-punch.*

Y

*y-punch
Same as *twelve-punch.*

Z

*zero suppression
The elimination of nonsignificant zeros in a *numeral.*

*zone punch
A *punch* in the eleven, twelve, or zero row of a *punched card.*

SELECTED BIBLIOGRAPHY

APPENDIX B

Arnold, Robert R., Harold Hill, and Aylmer Nichols, *Modern Data Processing.* New York: John Wiley & Sons, Inc., 1972.

Awad, Elias M., *Automatic Data Processing.* Englewood-Cliffs, N.J.: Prentice-Hall, Inc., 1973.

————, *Business Data Processing.* Englewood-Cliffs, N.J.: Prentice-Hall, Inc., 1971.

Berkowitz, Nathan, and Robertson Munro, Jr., *Automatic Data Processing and Management.* Encino, Calif.: Dickenson Publishing Company, Inc., 1969.

Birkle, John, and Ronald Yearsley, *Computer Applications in Management.* Princeton, N.J.: Brandon/Systems Press, Inc., 1970.

Blumenthal, Sherman, *Management Information System: A Framework for Planning and Development.* Englewood Cliffs, N.J.: Prentice Hall, Inc., 1969.

Brightman, Richard, Bernard Lusken, and Theodore Tilton, *Data Processing for Decision Making.* New York: The Macmillan Company, 1971.

Chandor, Anthony, John Graham, and Robin Williamson, *Practical Systems Analysis.* New York: Putnam Publishing Co., 1970.

Clark, Frank J., *Information Processing.* Pacific Palisades, Calif.: Goodyear Publishing Co., Inc., 1970.

Crawford, F. R., *Introduction to Data Processing.* Englewood Cliffs, N.J.: Prentice-Hall, Inc., 1973.

Davis, Gordon B., *Computer Data Processing.* New York: McGraw Hill Book Company, 1973.

————, *Introduction to Electronic Computers.* New York: McGraw-Hill Book Company, 1971.

Diebold, John, *Man and the Computer.* New York: Praeger Publishers, Inc., 1969.

Dippel, Gene, and William C. House, *Information Systems.* Glenview, Ill.: Scott, Foresman and Company, 1969.

Elliott, C. Orville, and Roger H. Hermanson, *Introduction to Data Processing.* Homewood, Ill.: Richard D. Irwin, Inc., 1970.

————, and Robert S. Wasley, *Business Information Processing Systems.* Homewood, Ill.: Richard D. Irwin, Inc., 1971.

Farina, Mario, *Computers, A Self-Teaching Introduction.* Englewood Cliffs, N.J.: Prentice-Hall, Inc., 1969.

Feingold, Carl, *Fundamentals of Punched Card Data Processing.* Dubuque, Iowa: William C. Brown Company, Publishers, 1973.

————, *Introduction to Data Processing.* Dubuque, Iowa: William C. Brown Company, Publishers, 1975.

Fink, Stuart S., and Barbara J. Burian, *Business Data Processing,* New York: Appleton-Century-Crofts, 1974.

Fuori, William M., *Introduction to American National Standard COBOL.* New York: McGraw-Hill Book Company, 1973.

————, Anthony D'Arco, and Lawrence Orilia, *Introduction to Computer Operations.* New York: McGraw-Hill Book Company, 1973.

Gray, Mox, and Keith London, *Documentation Standards.* Princeton, N.J.: Brandon/Systems Press, Inc., 1969.

Gregory, Robert H., and Richard L. Van Horn, *Automatic Data Processing Systems.* Belmont, Calif.: Wadsworth Publishing Company, Inc., 1963.

Gruenberger, Fred, *Critical Factors in Data Management.* Englewood Cliffs, N.J.: Prentice-Hall, Inc., 1969.

————, *Fourth Generation Computers.* Englewood Cliffs, N.J.: Prentice-Hall, Inc., 1970.

Gupta, Roger, *Electronic Information Processing.* New York: The Macmillan Company, 1971.

Heyel, Carl, *Computers, Office Machines, and the New Information Technology.* London: Collier-Macmillan Limited, 1969.

Hughes, Marion L., et. al., *Decision Tables.* Wayne, Pa.: MDI Publications, 1968.

Joslin, Edward O., *Management and Computer Systems.* Washington, D.C.: College Readings, Inc., 1970.

Katner, Jerome, *Management Guide to Computer System Selection and Use.* Englewood Cliffs, N.J.: Prentice-Hall, Inc., 1967.

Krauss, Leonard, *Administering and Controlling the Company Data Processing Function.* Englewood Cliffs, N.J.: Prentice-Hall, Inc., 1969.

Langenbach, Robert G., *Introduction to Automated Data Processing.* Englewood Cliffs, N.J.: Prentice-Hall, Inc., 1968.

Lazzaro, Victor, *Systems and Procedures.* Englewood Cliffs, N.J.: Prentice-Hall, Inc., 1968.

Lesson, Marjorie, *Basic Concepts in Data Processing.* Dubuque, Iowa: Wm. C. Brown Company Publishers, 1975.

Li, David H., *Accounting/Computers/Management Information Systems.* New York: McGraw-Hill Book Company, 1968.

Martin, James, *Design of Real-Time Computer Systems.* Englewood Cliffs, N.J.: Prentice-Hall, Inc., 1967.

Massey, David, *EDP Feasibility Analysis.* Braintree, Mass.: D. H. Mark Publishing Co., 1968.

————, *Management Information Systems.* Braintree, Mass,: D. H. Mark Publishing Co., 1969.

McMillan, Claude, and R. F. Gonzalez, *Systems Analysis: A Computer Approach to Decision Models.* Homewood, Ill.: Richard D. Irwin, Inc., 1965.

Meadow, Charles T., *The Analysis of Information Systems.* New York: John Wiley & Sons, Inc., 1970.

Murach, Mike, *Principles of Busienss Data Processing.* Chicago: Science Research Associates, Inc., 1970.

Myers, Charles, *The Impact of Computers on Management.* Cambridge, Mass.: The MIT Press, 1967.

Orilia, Lawrence, et. al., *Business Data Processing Systems.* New York: John Wiley & Sons, Inc., 1972.

Price, Wilson T., *Introduction to Data Processing.* San Francisco: Rinehart Press, 1972.

Sanders, Donald H., *Computers in Business, An Introduction.* New York: McGraw-Hill Book Company, 1975.

Sherman, Phillip, *Techniques in Computer Programming.* Englewood Cliffs, N.J.: Prentice-Hall, Inc., 1970.

Silver, Gerald A., and John B. Silvers, *Data Processing for Business.* New York: Harcourt Brace Jovanovich, Inc., 1973.

Sippl, Charles J., *Computer Dictionary.* Indianapolis: Howard W. Sams & Co., Inc., Publishers, 1966.

Solomon, Irving I., *Management Uses of the Computer.* New York: The New American Library, Inc., 1968.

Stern, Robert, and Nancy B. Stern, *Principles of Data Processing.* New York: John Wiley & Sons, Inc., 1973.

Traviss, Irene, *The Computer Impact.* Englewood Cliffs, N.J.: Prentice-Hall, Inc., 1970.

USA Standard Flowchart Symbols and Their Usage in Information Processing. New York: United States of American Standards Institute, 1968.

Wanous, S. J., E. E. Wanous, and A. E. Hughes, *Introduction to Automated Data Processing.* Cincinnati: South-Western Publishing Co., 1968.

Weiss, Eric A., *Computer Usage Fundamentals.* New York: McGraw-Hill Book Company, 1969.

ANSWERS
TO SELECTED EXERCISES

CHAPTER 1

True/False Exercise

1. T	9. T	17. T	25. T
3. F	11. T	19. T	27. T
5. T	13. F	21. T	29. T
7. F	15. T	23. T	

Multiple Choice Exercise

1. A	5. C	9. D	13. E
3. A	7. B	11. A	15. D

CHAPTER 2

True/False Exercise

1. T	9. T	17. T	25. F
3. F	11. F	19. T	27. T
5. T	13. F	21. T	
7. F	15. F	23. F	

Multiple Choice Exercise

1. C	5. E	9. D	11. B
3. A	7. E		

CHAPTER 3

True/False Exercise

1. F	13. F	25. T	35. T
3. F	15. T	27. F	37. F
5. F	17. F	29. T	39. T
7. T	19. T	31. T	41. T
9. F	21. T	33. T	43. F
11. F	23. T		

Multiple Choice Exercise

1.	E	7.	E	13.	E	19.	E
3.	B	9.	B	15.	E	21.	E
5.	D	11.	D	17.	C		

CHAPTER 4

True/False Exercise

1.	F	9.	F	17.	T	25.	F
3.	T	11.	T	19.	T	27.	T
5.	F	13.	T	21.	T	29.	F
7.	T	15.	T	23.	F		

Multiple Choice Exercise

1.	A	5.	B	9.	B	13.	C
3.	C	7.	D	11.	A		

CHAPTER 5

True/False Exercise

1.	F	9.	F	17.	T	25.	F
3.	F	11.	F	19.	T	27.	F
5.	T	13.	T	21.	F	29.	T
7.	T	15.	F	23.	T		

Multiple Choice Exercise

1.	D	5.	E	9.	D	13.	C
3.	C	7.	D	11.	B		

CHAPTER 6

True/False Exercise

1.	F	11.	F	21.	T	31.	T
3.	T	13.	F	23.	T	33.	F
5.	F	15.	T	25.	T	35.	T
7.	F	17.	T	27.	T	37.	T
9.	F	19.	T	29.	F	39.	T

Multiple Choice Exercise

1. D	5. A	9. D	13. B
3. A	7. C	11. A	

CHAPTER 7

True/False Exercise

1. T	9. T	17. T	25. T
3. T	11. T	19. T	27. T
5. F	13. F	21. T	
7. T	15. T	23. T	

Multiple Choice Exercise

1. D	5. A	9. E	13. A
3. A	7. D	11. A	15. E

CHAPTER 8

True/False Exercise

1. F	9. T	17. T	25. F
3. T	11. T	19. T	27. F
5. F	13. F	21. T	
7. F	15. T	23. T	

Multiple Choice Exercise

1. A	5. A	9. D	13. B
3. E	7. C	11. D	

CHAPTER 9

True/False Exercise

1. T	11. T	21. T	31. T
3. F	13. T	23. T	33. T
5. T	15. T	25. T	
7. T	17. T	27. F	
9. F	19. T	29. T	

Multiple Choice Exercise

1. A	5. D	9. D	11. E
3. E	7. D		

CHAPTER 10

True/False Exercise

1.	T	17.	F	33.	T	49.	F
3.	F	19.	T	35.	T	51.	F
5.	F	21.	T	37.	T	53.	F
7.	T	23.	F	39.	T	55.	T
9.	F	25.	F	41.	F	57.	T
11.	F	27.	T	43.	T		
13.	T	29.	F	45.	T		
15.	T	31.	T	47.	T		

Multiple Choice Exercise

1.	E	7.	E	13.	D	19.	B
3.	E	9.	A	15.	A	21.	B
5.	E	11.	A	17.	A		

CHAPTER 11

True/False Exercise

1.	T	9.	T	17.	T	25.	T
3.	F	11.	T	19.	F	27.	F
5.	F	13.	T	21.	T	29.	F
7.	F	15.	T	23.	T		

Multiple Choice Exercise

1.	E	5.	C	9.	E	13.	E
3.	E	7.	E	11.	D		

CHAPTER 12

True/False Exercise

1.	T	13.	F	25.	T	37.	F
3.	T	15.	T	27.	T	39.	T
5.	F	17.	T	29.	T	41.	T
7.	F	19.	F	31.	T		
9.	T	21.	T	33.	T		
11.	T	23.	F	35.	T		

Multiple Choice Exercise

1. E	7. B	13. D	19. E
3. B	9. B	15. A	21. D
5. A	11. A	17. D	

CHAPTER 13

True/False Exercise

1. T	15. T	29. F	43. F
3. F	17. F	31. T	45. T
5. T	19. T	33. T	47. F
7. T	21. T	35. T	49. F
9. T	23. T	37. T	51. T
11. T	25. T	39. T	53. T
13. T	27. F	41. T	

Multiple Choice Exercise

1. A	7. B	13. A	19. A
3. C	9. B	15. B	21. D
5. D	11. E	17. D	23. E

CHAPTER 14

True/False Exercise

1. T	11. F	21. F	31. T
3. F	13. T	23. F	33. T
5. T	15. T	25. F	35. T
7. T	17. F	27. T	37. F
9. F	19. F	29. T	39. F

Multiple Choice Exercise

1. E	5. E	9. E	13. D
3. D	7. E	11. D	15. A

Fill-In Exercise

Payroll

1. W2, 941

3. preparation of payroll audit, preparation of check and earnings statement, bank reconciliation report

5. payroll register

Accounts payable

1. information dealing with the vendor, gross amount of the invoice, discount, and net amount

3. to whom payments were made

5. recording purchase order requisition, updating vendor files, producing vendor checks

Accounts receivable

1. banks, credit agencies, and the customer

3. voucher, sales

5. accounts receivable summary cards, control tape

7. payroll, accounts payable, accounts receivable, inventory, and personnel accounting

9. slip number, customer number, date, amount

Page numbers printed in italics refer to the illustration or table contained on the page.